HOW DID LUBITSCH DO IT?

HOW DID
LUBITSCH
DO IT?

JOSEPH McBRIDE

COLUMBIA UNIVERSITY PRESS / NEW YORK

....

Grateful acknowledgment is made to Nicola Lubitsch for quotations from
Ernst Lubitsch's July 10, 1947, letter to Herman G. Weinberg, which was
published in *Films in Review* (August–September 1951) and reproduced in
Film Culture (Summer 1962), and to the Friedrich-Wilhelm-Murnau-
Stiftung for permission to use F. W. Murnau's photograph of Ernst Lubitsch.

....

Columbia University Press
Publishers Since 1893
New York   Chichester, West Sussex
cup.columbia.edu
Copyright © 2018 Joseph McBride
All rights reserved

Library of Congress Cataloging-in-Publication Data
Names: McBride, Joseph, 1947–
Title: How did Lubitsch do it? / Joseph McBride.
Description: New York : Columbia University Press, [2018] | Includes bibliographical
    references and index.
Identifiers: LCCN 2017044420| ISBN 9780231186445 (cloth : alk. paper) |
    ISBN 9780231546645 (e-book)
Subjects: LCSH: Lubitsch, Ernst, 1892–1947—Criticism and interpretation.
Classification: LCC PN1998.3.L83 M37 2018 | DDC 791.4302/33092—dc23
LC record available at https://lccn.loc.gov/2017044420

Cover design: Lisa Hamm
Cover image: Lubitsch's 1932 masterpiece, *Trouble in Paradise*,
Kay Francis and Miriam Hopkins. (Paramount/Photofest)

Frontispiece: A portrait of Lubitsch by fellow director F. W. Murnau, taken
in Hollywood, ca. 1930. *(Courtesy of the Friedrich-Wilhelm-Murnau-Stiftung/
Fotoarchiv, Deutsche Kinemathek—Museum für Film und Fernsehen.)*

For Ann Weiser Cornell

"My love parade . . . in you arrayed . . ."

CONTENTS

HOW DID LUBITSCH DO IT?

INTRODUCTION

"How Did Lubitsch Do It?"

"*ow would Lubitsch do it?*" read the sign on the wall of Billy Wilder's modest working writer's office on Little Santa Monica Boulevard in Beverly Hills. Saul Steinberg, the *New Yorker* cartoonist, designed the sign expressly for Wilder. The lettering was elegant old-fashioned cursive, slanted to the right and shaded at its left edge with baroque curlicue. The rectangular gilt frame, with its suggestion of faded elegance, had a modernist shape of roughly Panavision proportions, like the splendid later films Wilder directed while emulating his mentor, including works of varied public reception such as *The Apartment*, *Avanti!*, and *The Private Life of Sherlock Holmes*. Lighting a cigar—in another homage to Lubitsch, who was rarely found without his Upmann—Wilder told an interviewer in 1989, "I made that sign. That way I never allow myself to write one sentence that I would be ashamed to show to my great friend, Ernst Lubitsch."

The director of supremely stylish classics including *Trouble in Paradise*, *Ninotchka*, and *The Shop Around the Corner*, Lubitsch was revered in his day by such other leading filmmakers as Orson Welles, Jean Renoir, Max

Ophüls, Howard Hawks, Alfred Hitchcock, and Preston Sturges. In the words of one of his actors, David Niven, Lubitsch was "the masters' master." Renoir, another great European émigré director, went so far as to say of Lubitsch, "He invented the modern Hollywood." Welles declared in 1964 that Lubitsch "is a giant. . . . Lubitsch's talent and originality are stupefying." Yet today Lubitsch is no longer the familiar name to moviegoers that he once was. What happened?

Lubitsch (1892–1947), a native of Berlin, was imported from Germany to Hollywood by Mary Pickford in 1922. In Germany he had become known as "the D. W. Griffith of Europe" because of his flair for making large-scale historical spectacles but with a refreshingly modern approach to sexuality, including *Carmen* (*Gypsy Blood*), *Madame DuBarry* (*Passion*), *Anna Boleyn* (*Deception*), and *Das Weib des Pharao* (*The Wife of Pharaoh*). But before creating those spectacles, Lubitsch had first made his name with raucous comedies of increasing sophistication and stylization, such as *Ich möchte kein Mann sein* (*I Don't Want to Be a Man*), *Die Austernprinzessin* (*The Oyster Princess*), and *Die Puppe* (*The Doll*). Not long after his arrival in Hollywood, Lubitsch somewhat surprisingly abandoned the spectacle genre. He made the workmanlike *Rosita* (1923) with Pickford in that vein but then mostly left the genre for Cecil B. DeMille and others to mine with lesser skill. Instead, with astonishing swiftness in the silent era, Lubitsch set the tone for obliquely suggestive filmmaking in Hollywood with his subtle and influential 1924 dramatic comedy *The Marriage Circle*.

Lubitsch became Hollywood's most acute commentator on sexual mores, countering American puritanical hypocrisy with European sophistication, and making his adopted countrymen enjoy it. His audacity became more elaborate and subtly stylized in his romantic comedies of the early sound years; sound enabled him to add new layers of depth in exploring the differences between what people say and what they mean. Lubitsch virtually created the romantic comedy genre in both Germany and the United States and brought it to perfection with his cleverly risqué yet touchingly tender masterpiece of and about the Depression era, *Trouble in Paradise* (1932). His other masterworks in that genre include *Lady Windermere's Fan*, *Design for Living*, *The Shop Around the Corner*, and *Heaven Can Wait*. If those were not enough to ensure his cinematic immortality, Lubitsch's bawdy pre-Code musicals such as *The Love Parade*, *Monte Carlo*, *The Smiling Lieutenant*, and *The Merry*

Widow helped invent the musical genre as an integrated form for comical and dramatic exploration of character rather than as a mere framework for disconnected songs and dances.

Lubitsch's work seems timeless because it is so deeply a projection of his imagination, a Platonic ideal of a world that vanished around the time he started making his films; his on-screen version is a more gracious, more elegant world than any that had actually existed. The fact that it was also a world from which Lubitsch himself would have been mostly excluded adds a level of ironic poignancy to his work that helps make it so complex. Lubitsch kept alive some of the more appealing traditions of the old, vanished milieu, viewing imperial pomp with satirical amusement and doing so from the distant geographical outpost of Hollywood studios even while his native land was descending into chaos. An essentially rootless man outside his empire of the studio lot, Lubitsch found his bearings—of necessity, but also by preference—in the artifice of motion pictures. Through his eyes, we can live vicariously in that artificial, largely imaginary world he created and which he made so much more alluring than the messy world outside the movie palaces of his time or the video screens of our day.

THE LUBITSCH TOUCH

The name Ernst Lubitsch stood for the epitome of sophisticated humor and romance in what we now regard as the Golden Age of Hollywood. As fellow producer/director Mervyn LeRoy said when presenting him with an honorary Oscar on March 13, 1947, seven months before Lubitsch's death, "He had an adult mind and a hatred of saying things the obvious way. Because of these qualities and a God-given genius, he advanced the technique of screen comedy as no one else has ever done." His approach to style and theme was widely celebrated as "the Lubitsch Touch," a virtually indefinable yet almost tangible concept embodying an ever-fresh, delightful, tantalizing, slyly witty blend of style and substance. It combines a characteristic joie de vivre in the actors with an elegant visual design that conveys its meanings largely through sophisticated innuendo.

But the phrase was something of a marketing cliché, like calling Hitchcock "the Master of Suspense," and Lubitsch himself was apt to joke about it. When people would ask him what it meant, he would say with a grin, "I would like to know myself. You find out and tell me, maybe?" And he said, "I cannot give you a definitive answer because, fortunately, I'm not conscious of it. If I ever become conscious of it—Heaven prevent—I might lose it."

There *is* such a thing as the Lubitsch Touch; you recognize it when you see it. He is able to convey complex meanings and innuendos with dazzlingly economical strokes of camerawork and editing. He puckishly claimed, "I want no misunderstanding about the 'Lubitsch touches.' A child can understand them." While it actually takes an adult, or an unusually mature child, to understand his touches, he did make his oblique form of expression extraordinarily clear.

How, in fact, did Lubitsch do it? Many of his touches and other means of circumventing censorship were quite elaborate. But let's start with one simple, precise example of how he got away with his subversive style from a scene that goes by in passing and is not talked about, unlike the more famous Lubitsch Touches. This one can be seen and heard in his groundbreaking early sound musical *The Love Parade* (1929). When Queen Louise (Jeanette MacDonald) is having her first date with her Parisian military attaché, Count Alfred Renard (Maurice Chevalier), she confronts him about his "disgraceful" conduct with numerous women in Paris. She demands, "Aren't you ashamed of yourself?" He shakes his head but then says, "Yes, Your Majesty," and laughs broadly. She joins him in the laughter but quickly checks herself, saying, "I don't think it's funny."

The Hays Office may have been satisfied with the literally moralistic dialogue, yet Lubitsch manages to ironically undercut that exchange with Chevalier's cheeky body language and the couple's shared laughter, a mischievous exposure of the transparent hypocrisy within the storyline. Lubitsch jokingly nudges the audience with the film's utter insincerity in conforming to any conventional norms of propriety. As James Harvey notes in his 1987 book, *Romantic Comedy in Hollywood: From Lubitsch to Sturges*, "Like nearly all the working filmmakers in the Hollywood of the time, he played the game," but Lubitsch was special because he "made movies *about* playing the game."

The Lubitsch Touch is about laughter, but it is also about character and the endlessly inventive and fresh ways the director found to tell stories. That he avoided storytelling clichés in favor of cleverly oblique methods of revealing character was a large part of what Welles called Lubitsch's "talent and originality." Lubitsch's method was an intricate blend of unexpected vantage points, character interactions, and surprising uses of the camera and soundtrack. Part of his rare directorial skill was his respect for the audience's intelligence; he lets us participate in filling in his ellipses. Wilder defined the Lubitsch Touch as "a different way of thinking. Lubitsch is difficult to copy. He is a director who is not afraid that people won't understand him, unlike those who say, Two plus two makes four, and one plus three also makes four, and one plus one plus one plus one also makes four. But Lubitsch says, Two plus two—that's it. The public has to add it up." And if you let the audience add it up themselves, Lubitsch added, "They'll love you forever."

In his famous 1968 essay "Lubitsch Was a Prince," French director and critic François Truffaut wrote,

> The essential consideration here is never to treat the subject *directly*. So, if we are kept outside the closed doors of the bedroom when everything is happening inside, stay at the office when everything is going on in the living room, remain in the salon when the action's on the stairway, or in the telephone booth when it's happening in the wine cellar, it's because Lubitsch has racked his brain during six weeks of writing so that the spectators can work out the plot along with him as they watch the film. . . . [Lubitsch] has already examined all the previous solutions as to offer one that's never been used before—an unthinkable, bizarre, exquisite and disorienting solution. There are outbursts of laughter as we discover the "Lubitsch solution"—our laughter is uncontrollable.

To achieve such marvels of storytelling, Truffaut added, Lubitsch "worked like a dog, bled himself white, died twenty years too early."

SOME CROWNING TOUCHES

The subtle and economical suggestiveness of the Lubitsch Touch is exemplified by such memorable moments as the following, all conceived with screenwriter and playwright Samson Raphaelson, who wrote nine of Lubitsch's films:

• Under the credits in *The Merry Widow* (1934), the screen is filled with a map of Europe and Russia. The camera starts searching for the location of the story, the tiny mythical kingdom of Marshovia at the edge of the

Austro-Hungarian Empire. The camera goes out of focus, and a magnifying glass helpfully appears on-screen to make Marshovia visible.

• The opening scene of *Trouble in Paradise* (1932) offers the most unromantic image imaginable: a garbage pail next to a door in a back alley, with a mangy dog prowling around it. A beefy garbage man enters, picks up the can, and dumps it into a gondola. Now we see the elegant architecture and twinkling lights of the Venice Grand Canal, the most romantic of settings. Lubitsch puckishly cuts to a closer shot of the garbage gondola as the man empties the can and begins singing "'O sole mio" (the popular Neapolitan song whose title translates, ironically, as "O My Sunshine"). The garbage man paddles the gondola down the canal, seen again in the kind of glamorous long shot that usually opens a Hollywood romantic comedy.

• Chevalier and Claudette Colbert exchange double entendres in song over breakfast following their (unseen) first night of lovemaking in *The Smiling Lieutenant* (1931). Wilder commented on this delicious Lubitsch Touch: "Ah, but regard how they are sucking their coffee and how they are biting their toast: this leaves no doubt in anybody's mind that other appetites have been satisfied. In those days, the butter was on the toast and not the ass, but there was more eroticism in one such breakfast scene than in all of *Last Tango in Paris*."

• A handsome young count, Chevalier, is standing guard outside the royal bedroom in *The Merry Widow*. After the portly old king (George Barbier) exits, Chevalier puts his sword into its belt and goes in to see the saucy young queen (Una Merkel). The king, realizing he's forgotten his sword belt, returns to the bedchamber. He comes out buckling the belt but finds it is too small to fit around his stomach. His dim mind begins to turn its wheels. He goes back upstairs into the bedchamber to confront the man who is cuckolding him.

But the Lubitsch Touch is not only comic. Andrew Sarris, one of the most perceptive of Lubitsch's critics, wrote in his book *The American Cinema: Directors and Directions, 1929–1968*, "A poignant sadness infiltrates the director's gayest moments, and it is this counterpoint between sadness and gaiety that represents the Lubitsch touch, and not the leering humor of closed doors."

"WHAT ONE SHOULD DO . . ."

Beyond the inspired stylistic shorthand of the Touch, the trademark of Lubitsch's work is an amused indulgence toward the kinds of human behavior, mostly sexual in nature, that are usually condemned on American screens. Lubitsch achieved this freedom of expression in sly ways that allowed him to circumvent the rigid censorship of his day. His use of double entendre, innuendo, ellipses, and other forms of visual shorthand—most famously his extensive and metaphorical variations on both opening and closing doors, a device adapted from his origins in the theater—enabled him to deal with the most elaborately urbane sexual couplings and more. His films not only cast a keenly analytical eye on the problems between couples but also explore unconventional relationships between the sexes and other challenges to traditional gender expectations. He deals audaciously with the complex relationships among love triangles or threesomes, such as in *Design for Living*, his and Ben Hecht's 1933 adaptation of the unorthodox romantic play by Noël Coward about a bohemian ménage à trois.

Lubitsch managed to celebrate such continental and un-American virtues as the joys of adultery and serial philandering while depicting marriage in a far more realistic and nuanced vein than Hollywood was accustomed to doing in a time when even married couples had to sleep in separate beds onscreen. As far back as 1918 in Germany, he made *I Don't Want to Be a Man*, a startlingly modern and transgressive comedy about cross-dressing with an ironic twist that challenges even our most enlightened contemporary assumptions about gender roles.

And yet, with all his tolerance for what is usually considered human misconduct or aberration, Lubitsch's work is essentially moral in its approach, in the highest sense of that often-misconstrued concept as it is defined by Coward's Amanda in *Private Lives*: "Morals. What one should do and what one shouldn't." Paradoxically, while subverting traditional moralism, Lubitsch made morality plays about sexuality and romance, concentrating on ethical issues such as infidelity and commitment and the fostering of equality and mutual respect. At their heart, Lubitsch's films explore how men should treat women and how women should treat men. With infinite variety and the most subtly nuanced gradations of wit and emotion, they offer a benign but sharply observed code of humanistic behavior that challenges social convention. Many of his films (such as his musicals with Chevalier, Mac-Donald, and other female stars) deal critically with what we now term sexist behavior, exposing the hypocrisies of the double standard, although some also problematically endorse the double standard.

One of the censors complained that they knew what Lubitsch was saying, but they couldn't figure out *how* he was saying it, so they usually had to leave his scenes uncut. In any case, much of the meaning of his films appears between the lines and between the shots. Although his background in theater is evident in his style in which he transforms stage devices for his own purposes as a filmmaker, Lubitsch's was an essentially cinematic form of storytelling, using the medium brilliantly and uniquely to convey meanings that would elude any other art form and any other director. James Harvey provides a key to this unmistakably personal style when he observes that Lubitsch's circumvention of censorship was integral to his method but not its sole raison d'être. Harvey notes that a principal reason Lubitsch was so highly regarded by other directors in his time was that he was so clever in getting "his dirty jokes" past the censors. That made Lubitsch "a model and an ideal" for other filmmakers, "for it wasn't just mockery and dirty jokes that he got away with: it was intelligence itself, in a system that tended to empower stupidity." And in discussing *Trouble in Paradise*, Harvey observes that Lubitsch and screenwriter Samson Raphaelson constantly "find some new and surprising way of narrating a scene or telling a joke or even just conveying information. It's as if they had set out to test the expressive limits of indirection—to make those closed Lubitsch doors achieve a kind of maximum eloquence. As a result, more than ever before in a Lubitsch film, our own responses become the subject of the film."

The many upheavals in American society and filmmaking since Lubitsch's day have served as the death knell for the old-style glamour, sophistication, and wit that his films once epitomized. Under the influence of financial and demographic pressures and a general coarsening and dumbing-down of the culture, Hollywood filmmaking has become increasingly crude and violent. Films are aimed at lowest-common-denominator audiences who patronize movies about giant robots smashing into each other (the brain-dead *Transformers* series) and alleged romantic comedies featuring jokes involving vomiting and defecation (*Bridesmaids*), and the screen is dominated by superhero fantasies aimed primarily at the adolescent male sensibility. The collapse of the old system of film censorship in 1968 freed the screen from some of the repressive restraints that Lubitsch worked around and largely outwitted, but it has not led to a greater maturity in American filmmaking; the Motion Picture Association of America ratings system has been one factor in making most modern Hollywood films so juvenile. The increased frankness and raunchiness that the ratings system allows have coarsened the romantic comedy genre, and the musical genre, the most stylized exemplar of Golden Age filmmaking, has almost entirely vanished except for an occasional self-conscious throwback such as *La La Land*.

Along the way, despite his former eminence, Lubitsch's name has largely been forgotten by all but die-hard film buffs, and the style of filmmaking he created is honored largely in the breach, not in the observance. While some of his films—especially the astringent yet heartwarming romantic comedy *The Shop Around the Corner* and the astonishingly daring and emotionally powerful black comedy *To Be or Not to Be*—remain favorites of many film fans, only the most dedicated film aficionados tend to be familiar with more than a handful of Lubitsch's movies. Too often while writing this critical study of the Master, I would mention the name of Ernst Lubitsch only to get a blank stare in return. That lack of reaction—the same response I used to get decades ago when I began writing about John Ford, who now is suitably honored—is disheartening to a film historian who loves Lubitsch. But it serves as a prod to help restore to him the attention he deserves. And as fellow film scholar James Naremore observed to me, a major challenge in writing about Lubitsch is that his work is so "ineffable." I hope this book will serve to begin removing some of those barriers to appreciating Lubitsch.

OLD AND NEW HOMELANDS

Comedy directors, especially those who capture the zeitgeist successfully, have a tendency to be shunted aside when the cultural mood shifts, and Lubitsch's reputation suffered in later years for that reason. But in his heyday, he was the foremost emissary to American cinema from a European culture that flourished artistically in his formative years, a culture that helped nurture his talents in the midst of political and economic upheaval before, during, and after what was then known as the Great War. It is important to understand his roots in that culture in order to understand Lubitsch, whose artistry was an outgrowth of its upheavals and ferment. Although Lubitsch was a native of Berlin, he was a Russian citizen in his youth, the son of an émigré tailor who had fled to Berlin to escape czarist persecution. Because German law at the time regarded a son as a citizen of his father's native land, Lubitsch avoided being called for military service in the war. He was naturalized as a German citizen after the war but was stripped of his citizenship by the Nazis in 1935. For all his eminence in his profession and in his adopted country of the United States, Lubitsch always felt, to some extent, that he was living out the Jewish destiny of being a perennial outsider. He also had a sense of repeated cultural dislocations, which manifest in his work in many ways.

Lubitsch seemed prescient in turning his back on Germany long before Hitler took over. In a time of economic turmoil that would eventually lead to the growth of Nazism, he left for Hollywood. He made only two trips home after emigrating to America, and he never returned after Hitler rose to power in 1933. Unlike Wilder, a Polish citizen who had worked as a reporter in Vienna and Berlin before becoming a refugee from Hitler, Lubitsch did not go back home to document postwar Berlin. He died in 1947, the year Wilder was shooting *A Foreign Affair*, a black comedy daringly set in the ruins of Berlin. But even if the Master had lived longer, it is doubtful, given his antipathy toward his native land, that he would ever have gone back to make another film. After the Nazi takeover, according to his daughter, Nicola, Lubitsch refused to let his family speak German in the house. Wilder's jaundiced view of Europe, even before the war, was influenced by the social circumstances that would lead to his forced departure, and his even harsher later work reflects the impact of the Holocaust in many ways, both overt and covert. Wilder lost his mother, grandmother, stepfather, and other relatives to the Nazis. Although Lubitsch's parents died long before the Nazis seized power, he, too, lost relatives in the Holocaust. Hollywood, in a real sense, became a new homeland for them and for many other colleagues who left Europe.

When Wilder died early in the twenty-first century, Philip French wrote that he "was the last surviving member of that great generation of filmmakers who brought their acerbic wit, social sophistication, and visual flair to Hollywood after being driven out of Germany by the Nazis." There were some eight hundred other German-speaking artists in Hollywood, most of them refugees from Hitler, but a few, spearheaded by Lubitsch, had left their tempestuous homeland voluntarily in search of a better life in Hollywood. That generation also included Max Ophüls, Fritz Lang, Douglas Sirk, Otto Preminger, Fred Zinnemann, William Dieterle, and Robert Siodmak. These directors were among the remarkable wave of refugees from the Nazis and other émigrés who found refuge in the United States, which included many prominent actors, writers, artists, musicians, scientists, and academics. Americans may not have always felt entirely comfortable with the challenges these exiles brought to our cultural prejudices, but their influence on our society was immense. As Peter Gay writes in his 1968 book *Weimar Culture: The Outsider as Insider*, "The exiles Hitler made were the greatest collection of transplanted intellect, talent, and scholarship the world has ever seen." They were part of what has sardonically been described as "Hitler's Gift" to American culture, broadening our outlook in every way, including by making the movies more sophisticated.

Lubitsch was, in effect, twice an outsider, both as a Russian Jew in Berlin and then as an exile in Hollywood. This helps explain his detached comic perspective and his uncanny ability to size up and satirize all variety of social situations. He created an imaginary new homeland in Hollywood that was safer and better than the one outside the soundstage. Lubitsch told fellow director Garson Kanin, "I've been to Paris, France, and I've been to Paris, Paramount. I think I prefer Paris, Paramount." That fictive place in California, where Lubitsch made some of his most memorable films at various studios, was part of the artificial but vital world that these dispossessed artists helped invent in their own image and in bittersweet tribute to their bygone culture. The films of émigrés such as Lubitsch made a major contribution to what film historian Neal Gabler calls "an empire of their own," one largely created by Jewish filmmakers.

The heritage they brought with them included a sensibility formed by violent social transformation. Since the 1871 unification of Germany in the age of Bismarck, the Wilhelmine Empire had grown into an increasingly powerful military, industrial, and political force. In Lubitsch's youth before the war, imperial Berlin had been Europe's third-largest city, the thriving center of banking and commerce. Berlin had also been a major center of science, high culture, and higher learning, at least for those with the right connections. The city's population grew from about 1.6 million people at the time of Lubitsch's birth in 1892 to more than two million by the time he left in 1922. While less than 4 percent of Berliners were Jews at the turn of the century, the city's Jewish population would grow from 92,000 to 180,000 by 1925.

With its expansionist military ambitions and massive armaments buildup, in 1914 Germany provoked the Great War, later called World War I, in which it was allied in the Central Powers with the Austro-Hungarian Empire, the more loosely structured amalgam of regions whose seat was the cosmopolitan city of Vienna. The war ended in catastrophe for the Central Powers and in the exile of Kaiser Wilhelm II in 1918. Prewar Vienna, under the rule of Emperor Franz Josef I, had been regarded as more cultured than Berlin, thanks in large part to its spectacular musical and theatrical heritage. Lubitsch set some of his best films in Vienna or in mythical kingdoms reflecting its values, which he affectionately satirizes. The Viennese tended to feel snobbish toward Berliners, considering them coarse; Wilder felt that Austria was even more flagrantly anti-Semitic than Germany in the years before Hitler's rise to power. Kaiser Wilhelm's authoritarian rule, supported by the aristocracy and business elements, had liberalized some social elements of German national life to provide a safety valve against revolt, but it sternly resisted modernization in other areas of daily life. Respect for authority was strictly enforced; the social class structure, in families and schools as well as in the business class, the working class, and high society, was rigidly stratified. By the early 1900s, as Peter Gay writes, Germany was "a country where Jews had only recently been granted political and legal equality but were still largely excluded from most polite society."

LUBITSCH'S APPRENTICESHIP

Like many other *Ostjuden* (Eastern Jews), Ernst's father, Simcha (later Simon) Lubitsch, left Russia with the mistaken optimism that Berlin would provide Jews with a better existence. Ernst's mother, the former Anna Lindenstaedt, a native of Germany who ran the family's women's clothing shop with her husband, died in 1914, and Simon died in 1927 after Ernst had left for the United States. The family were assimilated Jews and not especially observant. As a Russian citizen, young Ernst escaped having to serve in the meat grinder of the Great War—and thus managed to remain aloof from the rampant jingoism in Germany during those years—and instead was able to pursue an apprenticeship in the theater with the great director Max Reinhardt, beginning in August 1911 when Lubitsch was nineteen.

As a budding artist and a member of Berlin's restive youth culture during those early years of the century, Lubitsch formed his creative personality largely as an expression of rebellion, though not of the kind that carried banners in the streets. His was a more personal form of revolt against the authoritarian nature of German education and the expectation of his middle-class family that he would grow up to join in their clothing trade. He was not interested in that mundane activity, and he seems to have been much more conscious of his outsider status than his more assimilated parents were. As his films from the beginning of his career make abundantly clear, his rebellion took the form of rejection and mockery of bourgeois sexual and familial values, an attitude that permeates his work and serves as the basis for much of his originality and appeal. Lubitsch entered the nascent film industry in 1913 and soon flourished as a film comedian and director. Paychecks from his day-and-night work in both theater and films enabled him to help support his struggling family, whose tailoring business was no longer sufficient to keep them alive during the war. Ernst's film career began with broad farces in which he played Jewish go-getter character types. Those seemed more innocently amusing at the time than they appear after the Holocaust; the films remain a subject of critical controversy today.

Like many others who grow up as outsiders and enter show business as a refuge from conventionality, Lubitsch turned naturally to comedy as a means of expression and a form of protective coloration, mocking himself before others could do it in the great tradition of Jewish humor. While avoiding entrapment in the world of business, he gravitated to Berlin's fertile artistic scene to pursue his eccentric, nonconformist ambition for a livelier life. Lubitsch's early films demonstrate how unimpressed he was with the pomposity and exclusionary nature of German high society and the dullness of business professions. The theater in Berlin had already become a beacon of change, mounting plays by Scandinavians Henrik Ibsen and August Strindberg and Austrian Arthur Schnitzler that shattered social taboos and shone a harsh light on sexual hypocrisy.

Lubitsch's most important influence was his apprenticeship with Reinhardt, who ran the Deutsches Theater in Berlin, the adjacent Kammerspiel-haus for more intimate plays, and the Volksbühne, a center of naturalistic and experimental theater in Lubitsch's neighborhood. Lubitsch had the immense good fortune to be working for the man who was widely regarded as the leading European theatrical director of that era, and he remained with Reinhardt until May 1918, several years after he had entered the film business. With an engaging, comically supple, but homely face and squat physique, Lubitsch was not leading-man material. He was always a minor member of the Reinhardt stock company, playing secondary parts, often servants or buffoons, but he amassed a wide range of experience in many kinds of plays. He also had the opportunity to work backstage in various capacities while observing Reinhardt at work.

The period before the Great War has often been romanticized, not least by Lubitsch himself, as a kind of Golden Age. Lubitsch's portrayal of Germany, Austria, and various mythical kingdoms in his films is marked by a paradoxical blend of satire of imperial pretensions and awe and admiration for the grandeur and luxury from which he, ironically, would have been excluded. Historian Barbara Tuchman points out that the prewar era "did not seem so golden when [people] were in the midst of it. Their memories and their nostalgia have conditioned our view of the pre-war era[,] but I can offer the reader a rule based on adequate research: all statements of how lovely it was in that era made by persons contemporary with it will be found to have been made after 1914" (which is the year Lubitsch began directing). It is worth recalling that in the nineteenth and early twentieth centuries, nostalgia was regarded as a form of neurosis, an affliction rather than the warm and fuzzy sentimental vision of the past that we tend to regard it as today. Nostalgia was seen as a maladjustment to reality, a troubled inability to adjust to the life around you. Lubitsch's films are suffused with the richness and complexity of such nostalgia. Beneath their glittering surfaces lurk feelings of anxiety about exclusion and belonging. This is no doubt a source of his doorway motif, even if he probably more consciously derived it from the prevalence of doors in the theatrical mise-en-scène from which his talent emerged. His often-farcical, sometimes-bittersweet nostalgia was his way of coping by transforming the restrictive reality around him into a more appealing artistic vision, his own private world.

The leading German composer in Lubitsch's youth, Richard Strauss, wrote grandiose music that captured and helped advance the martial spirit of the kaiser's regime, and it was not surprising that Strauss would go on to become a prominent supporter of Hitler. Strauss's 1887 "Symphonic Fantasy," *Aus Italien* (*From Italy*), has a movement that he described as "fantastic pictures of vanished splendor; feelings of melancholy and splendor in the midst of the sunny present," which is all to be played allegro molto con brio. That tone and description can apply to much of Lubitsch's work as well. They capture a peculiar blend of contradictory qualities that can be found in both his German and American films—most of which also are set in Europe—whether they take place before or after the war. His films keep alive the illusory nature of the old European traditions even while ridiculing them from a more modernist viewpoint and, after he emigrated to Hollywood, from the ironic perspective of an exile.

In Lubitsch, the comic side—the allegro that his style expresses molto con brio—tends to be dominant, at least on the surface, and this is part of his way of gently cauterizing the melancholia that was an equally important part of his nature. Perhaps his restless nature and phenomenal work ethic were further outgrowths of that need to avoid the kind of boredom that can cause gloomy introspection. "As a director Lubitsch is a dervish," an American journalist visiting the set of *The Wife of Pharaoh* observed. "He can whirl through more work in a day than most directors can get past in a week. . . . Lubitsch cannot work slowly. He must work while his enthusiasm is ablaze." This relentless drive continued until close to the end of his life. A Twentieth Century-Fox biography of Lubitsch in the 1940s reported, "When he thinks, he likes to pace. 'I cannot work in a small room,' he says. 'My office does not have to be elegant, but it has to be big. If I feel shut in, I get no ideas.' Every night after work he walks the three-and-a-half miles to his home in Beverly Hills. When he is making a picture, he paces his bedroom for a half-hour before going to bed, thinking about the next day's scenes."

Lubitsch's primary method of relaxation throughout his life was playing the piano, both on the set and at his home, and his films use music with great gusto. But while he appreciated Richard Strauss's talents, he would have scoffed at the overblown aspects of the composer's work. Lubitsch made a film, now lost, that was evidently something of a parody of Strauss's *Der Rosenkavalier* (*The Knight of the Rose*), the celebrated comic opera dealing with romantic intrigue in the aristocracy; Lubitsch's bumptious-sounding 1918 version was *Der Rodelkavalier* (*The Toboggan Cavalier*), one of numerous comedies that he shot in rustic settings, a reflection of his fondness for mountain-climbing vacations. In the 1930s Lubitsch entertained the idea of making a Hollywood film of *Der Rosenkavalier*, which he must have seen in 1911 when Reinhardt staged the opera in Berlin. Lubitsch wanted to cast Jeanette MacDonald and Emil Jannings but could not obtain the film rights and was troubled to learn of Strauss's Nazi connections.

Lubitsch's personality was more in tune with the gay but wistful, exuberantly emotional waltzes of the Strauss family and the works of Oscar Straus and Franz Lehár. The director was fond of humming their tunes to amuse himself and orchestrated them in a lively, sumptuously romantic fashion in his films. Viennese operettas sometimes served as source material for his films, including *The Student Prince in Old Heidelberg*, *The Smiling Lieutenant*, and *The Merry Widow*. It may seem deeply paradoxical for a young Jew who came of age during the Great War to spend the rest of his life expressing nostalgia for the authoritarian era into which he was born. But it is not uncommon for anyone to look back at the period just before his maturity as an imagined golden era from which he was excluded by birth and social circumstances, an era that had already collapsed and faded into memory. And Gay points out, "Cultural outsiders like Jews in Central and Eastern Europe, even those who had been partially assimilated into the Western bourgeoisie, paid tribute to their insecure status by clinging to time-tested customs more tenaciously than less vulnerable groups."

When the war was provoked by the militarism that had long dominated German life and was fed by the Nietzschean myth of the Übermensch (the Superman), the darker undercurrents of Berlin society became more pronounced. The grim machinery of death decimated the population and caused terrible hunger, sowing the seeds of revolutionary change. The war's end swept away the old order, seriously challenged the traditional German respect for authority, and was followed by a tidal wave of political chaos and cultural ferment. The Weimar Republic that emerged from the war—shaky in its foundations though it was, riven by violent dissension from left and right causing battles in the streets—was a time of tremendous artistic fervor and revolutionary change in the arts, including painting, theater, architecture, music, and the new modernist art of cinema. Berlin during the tumultuous Weimar period (1919–1933) was the center of all that was fresh, adventurous, avant-garde, and dangerous in postwar Europe. The fast-paced, dizzying street life; vigorously intellectual café society; boldly innovative arts scene; and chaotic political struggle of the late teens and twenties made for a hotbed of intellectuals, artists, journalists, and show people as well as shady characters and con men of all varieties. The explosive, disturbing German expressionist movement, which straddled various art forms, offered the strongest and most indelible creative treatment of the lingering trauma from the war by externalizing the inner turmoil of human beings. Expressionism had a vivid influence on Lubitsch's filmmaking during the early Weimar period even though it took mostly comical form in his work.

Before Germany's defeat and the collapse of the empire, Lubitsch had already begun expanding his range into more sophisticated and stylized comedies and dramas. In the midst of the economic and political turmoil that followed the war, Lubitsch began courting the international market by making large-scale historical spectacles that appealed simultaneously to the period's exoticism and modernism. The direct effects of the trauma of the recent war and the battles in the streets can be seen in the constant social breakdowns, revolutions, and other forms of political unrest and interpersonal conflict that form the backdrop for the spectacles with which Lubitsch made his international name as a director from 1918 to 1922, when he departed for America. Different kinds of social disruption and the riotous quest for new forms of personal freedom can be seen in his German comedies, which ridicule authority and conventional ways of life, celebrate libidinously liberated women and men, and reflect the energy of the times in their flamboyant visual styles and musical rhythms. Even in a "silent" medium, films were always shown with piano, combo, or orchestra accompaniment, and Lubitsch designed his films with that extra dimension in mind, often even incorporating jazzy musical sequences that anticipated the coming of sound.

While busy making comedies and films set in the past, highly political though they were, Lubitsch on a personal level seemed determinedly oblivious to the violence in the streets outside the theaters even if he could not help being psychologically affected. The old order in Germany did not go away easily. The forces of reaction were still strong, and they were regrouping amid the chaos, finally leading to the rise of fascism. Adolf Hitler and his newly formed Nazi Party took advantage of constant changes in government, crippling inflation, and widespread resentment over forced war reparations to the Allied Powers in order to reach members of the disaffected masses who wanted an outlet for their anger and disenchantment. Seeking a scapegoat for those grave social problems, the Nazis turned to the traditional German outlet of largely blaming the Jews. Hitler and his metastasizing gang, who drew support from reactionary business forces, stirred the pot with specious theories of Germany's "crucifixion" and the purported "stab in the back" by Jews and communists. The forces of reaction also often targeted allegedly deleterious cultural influences, and American culture in particular, for what was portrayed as the growing decadence of German society in the postwar era, a time of rampant sexual experimentation and other unsettling social disarray.

Lubitsch had become part of that new culture as a man of the theater, and he captured its zeitgeist strikingly on film. Once the embargo on American films was lifted after the war, he displayed close affinities with the spirit and style of Hollywood filmmaking. In retrospect, it seems almost inevitable that Lubitsch left Germany for America when things went spiraling out of control during the worst economic crisis of the Weimar period, although at the time, his motivation appeared more a matter of personal career advancement. He turned his back on Germany for reasons that partly had to do with his realization that he could have a brighter future in Hollywood, the center of a film industry that led the world in technical advancement and economic might. But his decision to leave was also affected by the economic and social upheavals that followed the war, the privation he and his fellow Berliners suffered during that time, and his assessment of the economic situation of the early 1920s and its negative effects on the German film industry.

For Lubitsch, as for the other artists who sought refuge in Hollywood, exile was a defining experience, one that brought both losses and benefits. Edward W. Said, in his 1984 essay "Reflections on Exile," writes of "the exile's detachment." He states, "The exile knows that in a secular and contingent world, homes are always provisional. Borders and barriers, which enclose us within the safety of familiar territory, can also become prisons, and are often defended beyond reason or necessity. Exiles cross borders, break barriers of thought and experience." Lubitsch became celebrated for precisely that, for breaking barriers and expanding the intellectual horizons of his adopted country and its national cinema.

At a time when few outside avant-garde circles spoke of film as an art form, Lubitsch wrote from Hollywood to a German publication in 1924:

Film is an art, more precisely a popular art; it is open to intellectuals and the masses alike; it results from creative activity; and it can be called successful only when it receives international applause and worldwide recognition. A film is good when the movie theaters in New York are just as sold out as those in Barcelona or Frankfurt. This is the basic principle from which all filmmaking and all advancement of motion pictures must begin. If I may believe the press and the distribution companies, my biggest films succeeded enormously in precisely this sense, and they succeeded without any specific efforts to create an international style; they succeeded because—and I say this without arrogance—I do not make German or American films, but rather Lubitsch films.

Wilder darkly joked that Lubitsch was "one of the talented ones" who were brought to Hollywood rather than one who had to flee Hitler. That characteristic Wilder quip ironically undervalues those who, like him, had narrowly escaped, but it is also a much-deserved nod to Lubitsch as the precursor, the undisputed primus inter pares among that generation of émigré filmmakers. When Hollywood brought him over, it was a coup for the American film industry, a way of combating the rising artistic and commercial threat from Germany. Both in spite of and because of its socioeconomic turmoil, Germany remained a dominant force in twenties filmmaking even after F. W. Murnau and other major filmmakers followed Lubitsch to America. But as film historian Gerd Gemünden writes in his study of German exile filmmakers, "After 1933, Jews like Lubitsch, Edgar G. Ulmer, and Fred Zinnemann were not able to return, even if they had wanted to, turning émigrés de facto into exiles; while they may not have experienced persecution and flight, they were now stateless." Truffaut, who grew up in France during the World War II Nazi occupation, similarly observed to me in the 1970s that directors from totalitarian countries tended to become more successful in Hollywood than those from France and other democratic countries precisely because the directors from Nazi Germany and Soviet bloc countries could not go back and therefore had no choice but to adapt to the American film industry.

Lubitsch was able to find permanent refuge by becoming an American citizen in January 1936, shortly after the Nazis instituted their Nuremberg Laws that classified and disenfranchised Jews and formally restricted their civil liberties. It is a grim measure of Lubitsch's importance that while he was at the height of his eminence in Hollywood, the Nazis used his image to demonize Jews on posters in public places, labeling him "the Archetypal Jew." Lubitsch was also spotlighted in the infamous 1940 anti-Semitic Nazi propaganda film *Der ewige Jude* (*The Eternal Jew*), directed by Fritz Hippler. Calling Judaism "a plague that threatens the health of the Aryan peoples," the narrator says, "A disproportionately great number of Jews attained prominence in Germany. In newspapers and newsreels, their Jewish cronies presented them to the public as German artists. . . . Jews are most dangerous when permitted to meddle in the people's culture, religion, and art, and pronounce their insolent judgment on them. . . . They try to divert mankind's healthy urges down degenerate paths. . . . The Jew Ernst Lubitsch was hailed as a German film producer." Lubitsch is shown relaxedly lighting a cigar in newsreel footage from his final trip to Germany in 1932 and telling the camera with a friendly smile, "I am very pleased to be back in Germany, and especially to be back in my hometown of Berlin." Note that *The Eternal Jew* deliberately ignores Lubitsch's former popularity as a Jewish comedian, an uncomfortable fact for the Nazis. It should come as no surprise that after the calamities that followed the Nazi takeover in the year after Lubitsch's last visit and with the coming of the second World War, he felt compelled in 1942 to use his tools as an artist to respond to that kind of propagandistic venom with his passionate outcry against Nazism, *To Be or Not to Be*.

HIS OWN LANGUAGE

As celebrated as he was in his adopted country during the prime of his career, and as adept as he was at assimilating into a new culture, Lubitsch kept his distinctive German accent and artistic sensibility in Hollywood. He could not entirely escape the role of the outsider both in others' eyes and in his own. Working in a different language and cultural environment, operating under stricter rules of official morality, and having to adapt to the expectations of a predominantly American audience, he managed to flourish while never entirely shedding the mantle of his foreignness.

An exile can never be unaware of the precariousness of his position, and Jewish exiles in the 1930s and '40s were especially aware of it. Nevertheless, Lubitsch embraced American culture and proved remarkably adaptable in his new homeland. "Ernst had, not a German, but an American sense of humor," Jeanette MacDonald felt. "The most American sense of humor I know of." Lubitsch had already shown himself to be simpatico with Hollywood forms of expression while he was working in Germany with one eye toward coming over. With a mixture of shrewd pragmatism and a genuine temperamental affinity for American culture, he had the successful exile's ability to fit in with his new country. But however American he became, Lubitsch never entirely discarded his cultural background in order to be accepted in his new country. He took pride in his European artistic heritage and utilized it as both subject matter and style. His American work was a smooth amalgam of the best of both cultures. In fact, his enthusiasm for American culture blended with his tendency to keep a certain satirical distance from it. That, along with his continental attitudes toward sexuality and other social issues, combined to help make Lubitsch so special in the film business and such a role model for other filmmakers.

One way Lubitsch flourished, despite increasingly strict Hollywood censorship and the American prudery it reflected, was by setting most of his films in the more sophisticated (and hence forgivably "naughty") European environment, which included "Paris, Paramount" and various mythical kingdoms derived from the operetta tradition. That choice of milieu was also a matter of personal preference and artistic temperament. Lubitsch seemed to feel most comfortable re-creating what he knew best, crafting artificially nostalgic images of the world that had formed him before he departed for America at age twenty-eight, a world that, indeed, had already largely disappeared by that time. Such nostalgia for a lost world was characteristic of the exile sensibility that Lubitsch shared with other Germans in Hollywood. And on an even deeper level than even that of subject matter, Lubitsch's sublime originality as a cinematic craftsman was another by-product of his sense of himself as an exile in a city of illusion. The personal cinematic language he developed to express forbidden ideas and feelings was a product of his clever creation of a new self in a foreign land. He worked out a filmic language all his own, which was his way of speaking in code in order to address the audience over the dense heads of the Hollywood censors; ironically, he hid his meanings in plain sight but always with a sly, self-protective deniability.

Exiles in American cinema often adopted a similar strategy of communicating obliquely before, during, and after the world crisis brought about by fascism. By expressing themselves between the lines with wit and innuendo, they were able to clandestinely get around the barriers to self-expression and audience understanding in the highly regulated film industry of their adopted country. Lubitsch was perhaps the most advanced practitioner of that strategy, which, as Gemünden observes, had a strongly political dimension, even while it was employed in genres not often thought of as political:

> We need to think of the political in much broader terms than merely the thematic or ideological content of a given film. . . . In this larger definition of the political, essential exilic strategies such as the shifting and camouflaging of identity, masquerade, impersonation, travesty, cross-dressing, cultural mimicry, and passing come into view as well, devices that are prominent in the comedies of Wilder and Lubitsch and their dark, only seemingly sarcastic, sense of humor. . . . Exile cinema relies heavily on allegory, because [to quote Joel Fineman,] "historically, we can note that allegory seems regularly to surface in critical or polemical atmospheres, when for political or metaphysical reasons there is something that cannot be said."

This kind of secretiveness, paradoxically maintained within a popular medium, was a form of self-protection for exiles as well as a method of achieving success within those strictures. As a way of communicating the unspeakable, it enabled Lubitsch and other filmmakers to comment on subjects that were taboo because of censorship or political limitations, such as Hollywood's general reluctance to deal with the Nazi threat to the Jewish people until after Hitler declared war on the United States in 1941. German critic Frieda Grafe observes, "The audacious artificiality in these [Lubitsch] films is strategy."

Lubitsch not only found many ingenious ways around the censorship of sexual themes in his comedies and musicals, he also defied Hollywood's political taboos when he made *To Be or Not to Be*, the most original and one of the boldest films about Nazism. While that film, in effect, called trepidatious Hollywood's bluff by confronting Nazism directly, it did so through a radical employment of the "exilic strategies" of comedy, disguise, theatricality, and other forms of artifice, including dizzying changes of identity. Lubitsch and other exiles adopted such a coded, often-subversive approach of getting their themes across in order to thrive artistically in another culture that, however welcoming it may have been, could not help but remain somewhat alien. But his European heritage was part of what enabled him to lead his adopted country into more sophisticated artistic territory.

"THE KING OF ALL DIRECTORS"

He went to Hollywood and revolutionized the game.
He's the king of all directors!
Would you like to meet him now?
Mr. Lubitsch! Mr. Lubitsch! Mr. Lubitsch, take a bow!

—"The Super-Special Picture of the Year," sung by The Yacht Club Boys, 1934

Yes, Lubitsch was once close enough to being a household name to be promoted in song. Although there were always some who belittled him, Lubitsch was highly praised in his day for his unparalleled wit and ingenuity. He was regarded as one of the most innovative and influential Hollywood directors. But his exalted reputation among most reviewers and the more discerning segments of the audience did not survive long after his death in 1947. Even if other filmmakers continued to revere him, and though a few have continued to emulate his work more or less successfully, the audience moved on to harsher forms of entertainment. Many of his films simply disappeared even after television began showing features from Hollywood's Golden Age.

Critics who revered Lubitsch became few and far between; all too many of them dismissed him as not weighty enough for in-depth consideration or, worse, simply ignored him. When film schools began to proliferate, Lubitsch's films were seldom important items on the curriculum. Some Lubitsch classics are shown in film schools today—*To Be or Not to Be, The Shop Around the Corner, Ninotchka,* and *Trouble in Paradise*—but he is still less often studied in classrooms, journals, and books than his contemporaries such as Alfred Hitchcock, Orson Welles, Frank Capra, or John Ford. Lubitsch's reputation has been kept alive by a few devoted scholars in Europe and the United States and by people who watch his films on cable television or in archives. Occasional Lubitsch retrospectives have rekindled pockets of interest. He has been the subject of numerous laudatory books, yet he has not received the kind of sustained and voluminous study that some of his peers have been granted.

So what has happened over the years to send the former cinematic king of Berlin and Hollywood into another form of exile? And why is the once-renowned Lubitsch Touch now largely obsolete in the crass world of contemporary American cinema? How much of that problem is due to the inevitability of changing times and how much to a simple lack of knowledge of Lubitsch's work? Until recently, even many of his Hollywood classics were unavailable on DVD or Blu-ray. The majority of his German films are still hard to see in the United States, making it difficult for most film buffs to see his development. Many of his German films are wholly or partly lost, and no more than a few of those that survive have been made available in the United States even after all these years (some rarities have popped up on YouTube as well as on DVD). The situation has improved considerably since the 1990s, but many titles remain virtually inaccessible outside archives and bootleg prints.

I hope the situation will one day be rectified, but for this study, I made trips to Germany and Switzerland to see all Lubitsch's extant films and fragments in the best possible prints. My research expeditions to archives and the opportunity I had to curate a retrospective represented a longtime dream come true; for so many years, I had wished I could see Lubitsch's German films and his rarest American films. I was also given copies of some of his rare films by collectors who pass them around in a sort of worldwide Lubitschean samizdat. Despite these difficulties in seeing his films, the survival rate for Lubitsch's work is relatively good compared to the works of some other directors who began in silent films. Forty-seven of the sixty-nine films he directed are still in existence, although some of the silents are in fragments or have badly needed restoration because of poor preservation, including even some of his American work such as *Rosita* and *Forbidden Paradise* (*Rosita* was recently restored by New York's Museum of Modern Art, which has also been working on *Forbidden Paradise*). One of his most important silent films, *Kiss Me Again*, is lost in its entirety, and only a fragment of several minutes and the trailer exist of his mostly silent 1928 film, *The Patriot*. But in 2010, at the Lubitsch retrospective I curated for the Locarno International Film Festival in Switzerland and the Cinémathèque Française in Paris, we showed the best prints available at the time of all the surviving films.

Although the elaborate retrospective we staged demonstrates that awareness of Lubitsch is higher now in Europe than in the United States, I am told by fellow Lubitsch aficionados in Germany and elsewhere in Europe that they often get that same dreaded blank stare when they mention his name to average moviegoers. It is a shame that it is still so hard for most viewers to follow the progress of this great director's career and artistic development in both countries and to assess his full significance in film history. But enough of his work exists and has surfaced that it is now possible to get a strong sense of his evolution even if Lubitsch's remarkably versatile and wide-ranging German work is generally given short shrift in the literature with a few noteworthy exceptions. His American career has been covered in somewhat more detail, but inadequately for a director of his stature. What has been lacking until this critical study has been a sustained, systematic, fully integrated overview of both Lubitsch's German and American work. Without seeing his career as a single, unified whole, it cannot be fully understood or appreciated.

"THE WITTY PLAYBOY"

The irony of Lubitsch's eclipse is that his work remains remarkably modern and insightful on many levels. His films are far more sophisticated and mature than most anything currently on American screens. Lubitsch's richly cosmopolitan body of work—which he directed at adult sensibilities, never talking down to his audience but respecting their intelligence—puts to shame the largely puerile approach to sexuality in most Hollywood comedies and dramas in recent years. Indeed, a major irony of his career is that he flourished in many ways under the Production Code, which was formally adopted in 1930 but was enforced more strictly after 1934, about halfway through Lubitsch's American career. The censorship strictures of the Hays Office (later known as the Breen Office) forced Lubitsch and other talented makers of sophisticated comedy and drama to tell their stories obliquely. With all their innuendo and suggestiveness, his films are actually racier than the juvenile crudity that substitutes for genuine sensuality in American films today. What Wilder observed in 1975 is even truer now: "Ernst Lubitsch, who could do more with a closed door than most of today's directors can do with an open fly, would have had big problems in this market."

Among the key questions I raise in this book are why this general regression from the high point of cinematic sophistication formerly represented by Lubitsch has occurred and whether the forms of elegant comedy and drama he practiced are truly gone forever. This is not a biography but a critical study, an essayistic investigation into his work and the artistic and cultural influence of a cinematic master. Not only have I always admired Lubitsch as highly as any other filmmaker, but I have also found his contemporary devaluation and marginalization disturbing and dismaying. By examining why Wilder felt the need to continually prod himself by putting the question *"How would Lubitsch do it?"* so prominently on his office wall, I hope to understand more deeply what those words mean for us. Tracing the evolution of Lubitsch's style through his brilliant career of comedic as well as dramatic filmmaking in both his native Germany and his adopted home of Hollywood, I will explore what Jean Renoir meant when he claimed that Lubitsch "invented the modern Hollywood." And in assaying that once-immense influence, I hope to show why his work has been so important to other major directors, why it remains so to those of us who value his artistry, and why his legacy has largely been forgotten today as audiences have moved far away from his brand of wit and sophistication.

The disdain that some reviewers, critics, and film historians have expressed toward Lubitsch over the decades has usually revolved around charges of vulgarity, coarseness, lewdness, sexism, and cynicism. Even in his own time, Lubitsch was often undervalued as well as praised for the wrong reasons. He was often accused of being frivolous, a judgment that endures in some circles. That charge was leveled most acutely against his historical spectacles in Germany by some highly politicized critics of the Left who felt that he overemphasized sex and interpersonal relationships at the expense of the underlying sociopolitical causes of the violent unrest he portrayed. Although the spectacles established his international reputation and led to his summons to Hollywood, they were often found lacking because they were deemed too irreverent toward history even if their mockery was often directed at royalty and the upper classes. The attacks on the "escapism" and alleged frivolity of Lubitsch's spectacles reflect a political bias toward a style of filmmaking that does not focus on the oppression of the masses single-mindedly enough for some tastes. Because Lubitsch's spectacles humanize royalty by showing their sexual foibles (and worse, such as Henry VIII cutting off the head of his queen du jour, Anne Boleyn), they were often condemned by leftists in their time. They were denounced for being overly preoccupied with the libidinal forces in human nature and especially for dwelling on the influence of sex on the political process rather than on the more acceptable theme of historical determinism, that is, they emphasized human passions over socio-political analysis. But the spectacles are hardly apolitical. How could they be? They are about political figures and social upheavals. Their political meanings are complex and capable of varying interpretations. Lubitsch's habitual mockery of royalty might be considered a leftist or populist bent in his work, but since he is a satirist at heart, he is equally scathing about many of the commoners and radicals in those films. That evenhandedness gets him in trouble with some critics, as does his emphasis on personal flaws, especially sexual weaknesses, as determining factors in history.

And no matter how clever or innovative he was in making comedies and musicals, such films were rarely treated with the same degree of respect afforded to dramas. Even some of those who respected Lubitsch's skill as a craftsman felt that his concentration on humor and sexual intrigue and his love of the beautiful surfaces of his films' sets and costumes were limiting factors in his career. As a result, the charge of frivolity would dog him throughout his life. That bias has often colored the reception of even his best comedies, especially if they are overtly political, such as *Ninotchka* and *To Be or Not to Be*. The novelist and screenwriter Graham Greene, when he was writing film criticism in England, damned Lubitsch with faint praise by labeling him "the witty playboy." Lubitsch received three Oscar nominations as best director for *The Patriot, The Love Parade*, and *Heaven Can Wait* (1943). But as Sarris, one of the most perceptive critics of his work, pointed out, "Lubitsch never won a competitive Oscar or a New York Film Critics' award, a symptom, perhaps, of an ultimate lack of respect for the 'mere' stylist and entertainer." He was awarded only an honorary Oscar—and it was almost too late—for "his distinguished contributions to the art of the motion picture."

The prevalence of the phrase "the Lubitsch Touch" in writing about Lubitsch from the 1920s through today can be seen as either a compliment or a subtle devaluation. The "Touch" largely suggests the sexual dimension of Lubitsch's work, which is far from being his entire preoccupation, but he could hardly divorce sexuality from any aspect of human endeavor. That is one reason he seems so modern today while most other directors of his time seem old-fashioned. Nor does his strong emphasis on sexuality mean that the characters in either his comedies or his comedy-dramas are diminished in their ability to affect us emotionally. For Lubitsch, sexuality is always intertwined with human feelings, and the Touch has as much to do with art-fully expressed emotion as it does with bawdy innuendo. And it is important to interpret the Touch in a wider sense as part of a style that subtly deals with so many other aspects of human life and society. Those aspects, includ-ing his films' social criticism and political overtones, are often downplayed in critiques of Lubitsch's work. The focus on sexual innuendo sometimes obscures the power struggles and rapprochement between the sexes on levels beyond that of sexuality.

But in recent years, the political dimensions of Lubitsch's work have become the focus of fresh attention and exploration by some film critics and historians. It is more often acknowledged now that his keenly satirical treat-ment of sexual repression and liberation goes hand-in-hand with his acute sociopolitical commentary on human desire and the consequences of deny-ing that desire. In offering his unorthodox views of sex and morality, Lubitsch had to contend throughout his career with the need to outwit the censors, and he usually managed to do so with conspicuous brilliance. That is one reason he has always been celebrated by those who understand the context in which he operated as well as his ingenuity in subverting much about the traditional morality of his day. In some ways, such as in his accep-tance of the double standard of male sexual behavior despite his satire of it, he was a man of his time with some of the flaws entailed in that. While acknowledging those issues, we have to view his work in its social context, including that of the censorship system under which he labored, as well as assess the continuing value his films have today.

But some of the old biases linger and in more modern forms than those expressed by the more doctrinaire detractors of Lubitsch's day. Even today his Hollywood work, more covertly political in its social satire than his Ger-man films, is viewed with thinly disguised antipathy by some critics and academics who consider his tolerant treatment of philanderers and adulterers to be sexist. Although some of our social viewpoints have advanced, particu-larly regarding sex and gender, there remains a backlash against the kind of liberalism that Lubitsch brought to his work. A new puritanism has infected

American culture in recent decades from both the Right and the Left. Religious fundamentalism and its liberal equivalent, "political correctness"—a term used by both Right and Left for varying polemical reasons, however well-intentioned it may be in some cases—have tended to have puritanically repressive effects on sexual and gender issues in films and elsewhere. Those political strictures have damaged modern American filmmaking, reversing some of the liberalization of Hollywood in the 1960s and '70s, and that inhibiting trend has had its effect on Lubitsch's reputation. Overly doctrinaire strictures on films and filmmakers work against a fuller appreciation of an artist such as Lubitsch, who deals with sex playfully and irreverently, teasing both men and women equally and finding amusement rather than horror in Don Juan figures. Some prudish modern viewers who have problems accepting Lubitsch's views of sex and morality look askance at his irreverent analysis of the power dynamics within couples or (as he likes to portray on-screen and more provocatively) romantic triangles and even threesomes.

"Lubitsch's approach to sexuality was such as to make him of little interest to feminists," E. Ann Kaplan myopically claims in a 1981 essay on the director in *Quarterly Review of Film Studies*. Though she concedes that he was "always praised for his cinematic elegance, his wit and his brilliance at his chosen form," she complains that "Lubitsch's largely aristocratic world is peopled with Czars, Generals, rich playboys and the like, and while he satirizes this world, it is with an affectionate tolerance for the class whose human foibles he reveals." The charge of frivolity keeps recurring. David Thomson writes in his *New Biographical Dictionary of the Cinema*, "Is Lubitsch's touch restricted to the cynical commentary on a comedy of manners? The tragic feeling that Ophuls or Renoir bring to the same form rarely darkens Lubitsch's consciousness." Thomson adds, evidently betraying his limited research, "Only persistent viewing can test the theory that Lubitsch does not have too strong a visual imagination. . . . It seems to me still questionable whether that touch was a matter of cinematic fluency." Lubitsch biographer Scott Eyman oddly seems to not comprehend the special qualities of numerous Lubitsch films: "Played faster, for confusion and duplicity, the story of *Angel* could have been the premise for a fine screwball comedy. . . . While *Design for Living* lacks the clockwork logic of Lubitsch's best work, and nobody would make a claim for it as being among his higher achievements, it's far from the runt of the Lubitsch litter. . . . [*Lady Windermere's Fan* is] well-directed, but it's also nominal silent film material amounting to little more than well-dressed tailor's dummies exchanging significant glances over teacups." Some critics, including the more humorless academics, do worse; they tend to ignore Lubitsch rather than mount direct attacks upon him. Lubitsch films are sometimes shown in university courses, but not as often as those of some other major directors from his time. It seems that some in academia prefer to avoid dealing with the issues Lubitsch raises rather than explore them. Indeed, in not taking Lubitsch seriously enough, they often fail to understand what his satire is actually saying about sexual relationships or the immaturity of sexist figures such as his Maurice Chevalier characters, who tend to receive their comeuppance from strong women along their paths to increased emotional maturation.

Although generally regarded as a comedy director, Lubitsch could blend comedy and drama with seeming effortlessness. He displayed that gift, for instance, in filming Oscar Wilde's classic play *Lady Windermere's Fan* as a silent film that finds greater emotional depths beneath Wilde's brittle epigrams (not one is used as an intertitle). And his romances and musicals were able to pivot with breathtaking gracefulness from farce to feeling. That skill is epitomized when MacDonald's title character in *The Merry Widow*, pretending to be the kind of Parisian prostitute fancied by Chevalier's Count Danilo, expresses her deeper sensibilities by waltzing pensively around him in Lubitsch's most dazzling tracking shot. In *To Be or Not to Be*, Lubitsch executes his own most daring and sustained directorial pirouette from comedy to historical tragedy, which aroused the acute discomfort and disapproval of some of its contemporary observers but draws amazed admiration from audiences today.

The cigar-chomping, slyly grinning Lubitsch could be scathing in his satire, although he usually favored a rapier and not a pistol as his weapon of choice. Though Lubitsch's films help define romanticism in cinema, his is always tinctured with a bittersweet dose of irony. His disciple Billy Wilder was more caustic than Lubitsch and has been both celebrated and flayed for his supposed "cynicism" and "misanthropy," but he had his own broad streak of romanticism, a tendency that, however submerged it was earlier, came out of the closet in his later work, while other filmmakers were reveling in shock, crudity, and brutality. Wilder's longtime writing collaborator I. A. L. Diamond more precisely defined his partner's approach and with it the cultural affinity that Wilder shares with Lubitsch: "It's an old Viennese tradition that comes down from Schnitzler. It is a Middle European attitude, a combination of cynicism and romanticism. The cynicism is sort of disappointed romanticism at heart—someone [critic Andrew Sarris] once described it as whipped cream that's gotten slightly curdled."

Lubitsch's films, with their "Middle European attitude," do show an unusual and generous tolerance for human foibles, stemming from a worldly lack of surprise over such failings. That is one of his major strengths. Especially in such a puritanical country as the United States, both Lubitsch and Wilder are often chastised for their frankly unsentimental attitudes toward human nature, especially where sexual relations between men and women are concerned. Their satirical viewpoints are sometimes reductively labeled as cynicism and treated as if they are detached from human feelings. One perhaps-inadvertent by-product of this problem is a strange lack of warmth and humor in much of the critical writing about Lubitsch. Although some of the books about him are illuminating about his style and themes, they tend to focus more on formal or intellectual aspects of his work than on the basic stuff that makes them play so well with audiences: laughter and emotion.

Lubitsch's reputation today rests largely on his comedies. It is hard to argue that his historical spectacles, for all their considerable merits, have as much lasting importance or artistic originality as the comedies, whether his German comedies, which seem fresher and more original to modern eyes, or his Hollywood classics. For Lubitsch, in both kinds of films, politics is seen through the prism of human behavior rather than the other way around. Critics argue about the value of seeing history through a partly comic vantage point as Lubitsch does; that argument is partly a matter of taste and sensibility. Some of those charges are overwrought and overly doctrinaire, but some are on the mark in analyzing the films' limitations. Lubitsch's German comedies, in their more modest goals of providing zany entertainment, hold up much better today than the historical spectacles, which were seen as more impressive at the time because of their subject matter and scale of production.

From today's perspective, it can be seen that Lubitsch's formative work in Germany in both kinds of filmmaking made him as important a figure in the artistically fertile postwar Weimar cinema as Lang and Murnau even if they generally received more favorable reviews in that period. Those directors, who also went to Hollywood (with less sustained success than Lubitsch), have tended to be more highly regarded by film critics and historians ever since because they consistently worked in a more obviously "serious" and "respectable" vein. However, despite Lang's often-stunning pictorial values, his ponderous style and lack of humor make much of his output heavy going today; Murnau's body of work, just as powerful stylistically, has more variety and flair, more sense of poetry. But neither attempts the kind of witty and incisive social commentary that Lubitsch staked out as his personal domain. The humorous and bawdy aspects of Lubitsch's historical spectacles make them more watchable today than most of the spectacles made by Hollywood filmmakers of the time who were still under the spell of Victorianism.

Dismissing Lubitsch as merely licentious or frivolous in his satire of sexuality and of the human weaknesses of royalty and aristocracy is to miss the point that his work is "only superficially superficial," as Noël Coward said in defense of his own plays. This censorious approach to Lubitsch, among other limitations, ignores the emotional and moral dimensions of his views on social relations. But these questions are complex, not to be dismissed lightly, and they deserve full and searching exploration in these pages.

IS IT A "LOST ART"?

In a 1967 tribute to Lubitsch for the Directors Guild of America magazine, Billy Wilder wrote, "Oh, if we were lucky, we sometimes managed a few feet of film here and there in our work that momentarily sparkled like Lubitsch. *Like* Lubitsch, not *real* Lubitsch.

"His art is lost. That most elegant of screen magicians took his secret with him."

But *is* it lost irrevocably? That is one of the questions this work will explore. It is a question of greater urgency as mainstream American filmmaking sinks into the mire of frenetic hit-'em-over-the-head sensationalism and coarse antihumanism and as it gets farther from the kind of humane, subtle, sophisticated values that Lubitsch's films embody. A greater celebration of his work may not restore him to the centrality he deserves to occupy in our film culture, but perhaps it can repair some of the cultural damage.

A seriocomic romantic exchange in Lubitsch's greatest film, *Trouble in Paradise*, best reveals the profundity beneath his lighthearted surface. In this romantic comedy involving a love triangle, Herbert Marshall's suave jewel thief, Gaston Monescu, is the partner of a pickpocket, Lily (Miriam Hopkins), but he has been conducting a serious flirtation with a wealthy woman, Mariette Colet (Kay Francis), whom they have come to rob. Eventually Gaston falls in love with Mariette, a conflict that makes him doubt his mission and feel guilty over his deception of both women, but when his criminal activities catch up with him, he has to abandon Mariette and escape with Lily. Lubitsch exquisitely balances our sympathies among all three characters; rather than loading the dice toward one woman or the other as movies usually do, he makes it as hard for us to choose between Mariette and Lily as it is for Gaston. Finally, as Gaston is leaving, he ruefully, if presumptuously, asks Madame Colet, "Do you know what you're missing?" Even though she is by now fully aware of his deceit, she closes her eyes and nods, evidently thinking of romantic bliss. Then Lubitsch springs one of his most delicious ironic twists. "No," says Gaston, pulling out a strand of pearls he has stolen from Mariette as a consolation prize for his (regular) mistress. "*That's* what you're missing. Your gift to her." Displaying infinite grace, Mariette tells him, "With the compliments of Colet—and Company." This exquisitely moving scene is a consummate example of Lubitsch's mingling of romance and regret, tenderness and pain. It is an exchange that shows how he could evoke the complex interplay of seriocomic human emotions better than almost any other director.

There is nothing on that level of subtlety or grace in American film today. Much of what passes for American film entertainment today would benefit greatly from a fresh infusion of the sparkling Lubitsch tradition of cinematic wit and intelligence. By examining the gifts that Lubitsch has given to our culture, even if much of his legacy has been lost, misplaced, and forgotten, I hope to show exactly what it is that we are missing in shortsightedly shunting aside his salutary influence. So it is not with despair but with quixotic hope that in this book I find how that missing spirit might not be lost after all and how it might again be felt in our filmmaking, or at least in our film viewing.

1

"HERR ERNST LUBITSCH"

Lubitsch's German period tends to be eclipsed, not without reason, by his more masterly American period. But knowledge of Lubitsch's creative development in his native land during the years just before, during, and immediately following the Great War is indispensable to understanding his overall career path. Despite the fact that many of his early films are lost or exist only in fragments, enough survive to give a good sense of his development as an artist. His German career is extensive and ambitious and features a number of marvelous achievements in different genres. In studying that phase of his work, we can trace his circuitous journey from a maker of rough-hewn knockabout comedies, wildly grotesque farces, and lavish historical spectacles to the more understated and subtle Lubitsch we know from the films of his American period.

Although some of his apprentice work in Germany was crudely executed, both as a director and as an actor, he learned quickly, and by the time he

1.1 The popular comedian Ossi Oswalda as the spoiled American rich girl in *The Oyster Princess*, the 1919 film in which Lubitsch found his style (frame enlargement). *(Projektions-AG Union [PAGU]/Universum Film.)*

1.2 Ossi in Lubitsch's fantastical *The Doll* (1919), with Gerhard Ritterband as the mischievous apprentice of the creator of a sex doll modeled on her (frame enlargement). *(Projektions-AG Union [PAGU]/Universum Film/Photofest.)*

made his audacious cross-dressing satire, *I Don't Want to Be a Man*, in 1918, he had developed into an important filmmaker. That and many of Lubitsch's other German films—especially such varied and ambitious comedies as *The Oyster Princess*, *The Doll*, *Kohlhiesels Töchter* (*Kohlhiesel's Daughters*), and *Die Bergkatze* (*The Wildcat*)—stand the test of time with their delightfully stylized satire and sharp observations of character and milieu. Lubitsch had become a star with the 1914 film *Der Stolz der Firma: Die Geschichte einer Lehrlings* (*The Pride of the Firm: The Story of an Apprentice*), directed by Carl Wilhelm, and followed it in 1916 with a similar comedy that he directed himself, *Schuhpalast Pinkus* (*Shoe Palace Pinkus*), both of which have him playing klutzy but ambitious Jewish shop clerks. While playing a string of buffoonish Jewish characters as well as other kinds of comedic roles for both himself and other directors, he was expanding his directorial horizons with more sophisticated social comedies of Berlin life, broad rustic farces, and zany stylized comic fantasies. Lubitsch also ventured into stark drama with *Kammerspielfilme*—a type of intimate theater on film—in *Rausch* (*Intoxication*) and *Die Flamme* (*Montmartre*). *Rausch* (1919, a lost film) starred Asta Nielsen and was adapted from Strindberg's 1899 play *Brott och brott* (*There Are Crimes and Crimes*) about a playwright whose life is disrupted by drink and sexual temptations. *Die Flamme*, a 1923 period tragedy with Pola Negri as a Parisian demimondaine, marked the end of his German career and exists only in part today.

Lubitsch made his name internationally not with his increasingly inventive comedies or those modestly scaled dramas, however, but with the historical spectacles he made during the first years of the Weimar Republic. He took advantage of the cheap costs of labor in early 1920s Germany, when many people were unemployed due to the financial and political turmoil, to create impressive visual spectacles with grandiose sets and literally thousands of extras. Although they don't hold up as well as the comedies, those richly textured spectacles, including *Madame DuBarry*, *Anna Boleyn*, and *The Wife of Pharaoh*, bring a welcome dimension of human frailty to their historical characters.

Export restrictions during the war kept German films from being seen by international audiences, and immediately after the war, their distribution was limited by anti-German prejudice in the United States and elsewhere and by the belief that foreign audiences would find them too localized in their comic appeal. Lubitsch's frank emphasis in his spectacles on the sexual aspects of history, as well as their increasingly grand production values on a scale rivaling D. W. Griffith's epics, helped revolutionize the film industry and led to his being summoned to Hollywood in the Roaring Twenties. Yet his German comedies, though little-seen in the United States even now, are more imaginative than his spectacles in their depictions of social mores, making them remarkably modern in their attitudes today. Paradoxically, they maintain that timelessness while capturing the frenzied topsy-turvy mood of Berlin and other parts of Germany, such as the Bavarian mountain communities, during those years of upheaval that encompassed the privations of a ruinous war and the political unrest that followed. The spectacles, though set in earlier times and other countries, also reflect the zeitgeist in their depictions of violent social unrest and the warped psychology of mobs and tyrants. Even though those films don't confront Germany's contemporary political turmoil directly, Lubitsch's work from that early period of his career stands as a fascinating record of those times of turbulent social change and enables us to trace his ongoing artistic experimentation and development before his departure for America.

The Great War itself is mostly unreferenced in Lubitsch's existing German work, although it does become the subject of his uncharacteristically grim 1932 Hollywood film *The Man I Killed*. But he dealt with the war in the comedy *Fräulein Seifenschaum* (*Miss Soapsuds*), which was the first film that has been definitely established and confirmed (by Lubitsch himself) that he directed. It was filmed in the summer of 1914 and released on June 25, 1915. Somewhat unusually for Lubitsch, that film made direct reference to the current political situation: women have taken over as barbers because the men are off fighting. Lubitsch, playing a young man named Ernst, falls in love with the daughter of a woman barber, a girl nicknamed Miss Soapsuds, while getting the mother in a lather. Unfortunately, the film is lost, so we cannot see how Lubitsch went about drawing comedy from the war at that early stage as he would do with the Nazi occupation of Poland during World War II in *To Be or Not to Be*.

Before *Miss Soapsuds*, Lubitsch had made his film debut as an actor in a 1913 comedy called *Die ideale Gattin* (*The Ideal Wife*). Little is known about it, not even who directed it, but a fragment turned up at the 2000 Berlinale (the Berlin International Film Festival). In it, Lubitsch plays the supporting role of a "matchmaker for fastidious gentlemen." He was billed as "Karl Lubitsch," which is perhaps a reflection of the wariness stage actors initially had about being seen in films. The German Lubitsch scholar Michael Hanisch reports that Lubitsch performs "crudely" in the fragment, rolling his eyes and "grimacing horribly."

Some sources claim that Lubitsch followed *Miss Soapsuds* with a 1914 film called *Meyer als Soldat* (*Meyer as a Soldier*), but intriguing though that sounds as a possible satire of jingoism, no records can be found that it was actually made. Lubitsch believed that comedy could convey the essence of war more meaningfully than the usual gory battle films; he once said he thought the best filmic depiction of World War I was Charles Chaplin's *Shoulder Arms* (1918). Lubitsch tried his hand at an antiwar comedy with *The Wildcat* in 1921 even if it is carefully distanced from reality by its fantastical mountain setting. The film was a flop, and he later blamed its rejection on "German audiences [being] in no mood to accept a picture which satirized militarism and war."

Lubitsch's German comedies, lighthearted though they may be, are no less political than his historical spectacles. The timeless quality of his comedies and the freshness they maintain today stem from their artificiality, their careful distancing from the mundane reality on the streets, and their concentration on human emotions rather than ideology. But their acute social satire is also firmly rooted in the social context of a rapidly changing world. Lubitsch is able to observe that world clearly with his characteristic duality of perspective, that of someone who did not quite belong yet yearned for social acceptance. Andrew Sarris wrote of Lubitsch in *The American Cinema*, "We shall never see his like again because the world he celebrated had died—even before he did—everywhere except in his own memory." Sarris was referring, in part, to Lubitsch's many cinematic evocations of the old Europe, the periods from before and during his youth that he depicts affectionately but also critically. Lubitsch's historical spectacles do not "celebrate" older times, which he tends to depict with a harsher perspective than he uses in his comedies. But the way the spectacles sweep us back in time is due to his ability to vividly reimagine the past through his highly personal lens. These films fulfill the audience's need to escape their unsettled present into a past that is equally unsettled yet nevertheless represented with some longing for the grandiose trappings of those civilizations shown in the process of collapse.

The lighter world Lubitsch celebrates on-screen in his comedies and musicals often encompasses the dying days of the Wilhelmine and Austro-Hungarian Empires. The prewar *Kaiserreich* of Wilhelm II provided an incongruously grand and old-fashioned architectural backdrop, with its stately stone buildings and broad tree-lined boulevards, for his early slapstick comedies filmed in Berlin. Architecturally, as Barbara Tuchman notes, Berlin in that era was "new and not beautiful. It belonged in style to what in America was called the Gilded Age. Its main public buildings, streets and squares, built or rebuilt since 1870 to house suitably the new national grandeur, were heavily pretentious and florid with gilding. . . . Society, owing to the lack of intercourse between its rigidly maintained categories, was stiff and dull." Lubitsch's irreverent comedies in both Germany and Hollywood mock, sometimes gently, sometimes not, the institutions and traditions of the world that some Germans would refer to after the war as *die gute alte Zeit* (the good old days).

Lubitsch's 1929–1934 Hollywood musicals, mostly set in the past or in mythical kingdoms, tend to portray a fantasy of Europe before the fall. More precisely, he goes outside time to depict an imaginary world of vanished Belle Epoque European royalty and luxury. His cinematic operettas employ his characteristic blend of mockery and nostalgia to ambivalently convey the notion of prewar nobility. The reality, of course, was messier and largely ignoble. The world of the prewar empire he had grown up in was an uneasy blend of decadence, rapidly evolving social mores, traditional social structures precipitously nearing collapse, and artistic innovation. It was a time when the social pressures of the new century were building up against the ancien régime and straining the rigidly stratified German class system. Those factors of change were compounded by the rising nationalistic fervor that would contribute to the breakout of war in 1914 and the social unrest and governmental upheavals that followed the 1918 armistice.

In the years leading up to the cataclysm, young people of Lubitsch's generation were becoming even more restless and dissatisfied than youths naturally are. The right-wing historian Michael Stürmer, an admirer of the imperial regime, concedes,

When those customs and traditions that have governed people's lives for centuries die, there is bound to be anxiety and fear of the future. . . . A new, lighter lifestyle was emerging. . . . A wave of alienation swept middle-class youths, who found official Germany, especially in its Prussian variety, both ridiculous and deplorable. A radical chic also emerged, idealistic more than hedonistic, among young men and women who loved themselves and the art world and who felt pity for the strict conventions of their parents. For them decadence was not a menace, but a new, soft and sensitive form of life.

The war accelerated those social changes, and their effects are felt in Lubitsch's work; they helped spur his creativity and keep him artistically in tune with the times. His aesthetic distance from political issues has fooled some of his critics into thinking him apolitical. But the deep questioning of old sociopolitical traditions was bound to have a powerful effect on his life and art. Even if his artificial life in the theater and in film studios in the years before, during, and after the war helped insulate him to some extent from what was happening around him, he could not help being sensitive to the privations, violent social transformations, and jagged rhythms of the era. The effect of this social ferment on his forming personality was all the more pronounced because he was an outsider to that world of German tradition— someone on the other side of the window looking in, a Jewish member of the middle class and a Russian citizen raised in the garment district of Germany's grand capital.

When the war finally broke out, Lubitsch found himself not only a member of a small ethnic minority group but also a citizen of an enemy power, although he and his family do not seem to have suffered for that particular reason. There was plenty of suffering to go around for all civilians in Germany from inflation, food shortages, and disease. Lubitsch had to have been acutely aware of the precariousness of his particular social position in Berlin during wartime. As both an actor and a director, he became known for an irreverence that reflected the ambiguities of that position and flaunted his outsider status even as he was gradually moving up in the cultural world of Berlin. His status was a curious combination of the popular but disreputable (as an actor and director in the new medium of the movies) and the more reputable (as a member, however humble, of the esteemed Reinhardt company).

With Lubitsch's cultural background in mind, it is evident that the ambivalence his films retrospectively display toward the old-world European nobility and moneyed tradition is composed of equal parts wish-fulfillment and emotional detachment. This is true whether the films are set before the war or in mythical kingdoms existing in a sort of artistic universe parallel to the modern reality outside the borders of the film's frame. Lubitsch satirizes the class distinctions of that bygone or mythical world while still depicting its customs and most of its people with affection, a blend that gives his films a rich complexity of tone. Indeed, his surrogate characters, such as the palace functionaries played by Maurice Chevalier, are often caught in class conflicts stemming from their own ambiguous situations vis-à-vis the world of nobility. Lubitsch's complex cinematic nostalgia makes it clear that his artistic fascination with those opulent aristocratic settings stems from both his regretful recognition that he did not belong to such a society and a resentment of his exclusion.

Even in Lubitsch's romantic musical comedies, we can discern a certain manic need to amuse and be amused, a need for acceptance. Lubitsch's continual return to the closed world of nobility that he, as a doubly exiled Jew, could not enter can be seen as the sign of a blocked attempt to keep repeating an act of fealty in the vain hope that the kings and princes, the uniformed nobles, and their grandly gowned women would eventually allow him entrance, that they would welcome this brash upstart as an equal. He knew that such a thing could not happen in reality, but his artificial world was something he could access at will. By conjuring up his mythical-kingdom fantasies and other glamorous European comic idylls, he invites us into a world that he, the banished Jew, actually, if covertly, rules. His cinematic vision in these regions of his richly varied body of work is that of a society that is basically petty but amusing, one he can manipulate and mock or indulge because he is social director of its ridiculous ritualized extravaganzas. The German philosopher Walter Benjamin, who killed himself in 1940 while attempting to escape from the Nazis, believed that we can reshape the past to some extent, that nostalgia can be revolutionary. Works of art, Benjamin proposed, can give new meaning to history, even if they cannot reverse it.

That is a partially triumphal, partially melancholy response to the problem of the dominance of the past. Lubitsch's reshaping and immortalizing of prewar European history exemplifies that dual notion.

His delightfully satirical films about prewar nobility are set in the kinds of Graustarkian domains that are familiar from Viennese stage operettas and light comedies, a theatrical tradition he transposes to the screen with a prodigiously supple visual style, grace, and wit. He triumphantly transforms the world whose edges he inhabited as a youngster into a better place, more truly graceful, if even more absurd. And because the Weimar Republic came into existence before Lubitsch left Germany, he was also able to make representations, however oblique, of that turbulent time of violently clashing ideologies and political parties as well as rapid changes in social mores. Even today, it is hard for historians, novelists, filmmakers, and other social observers to sort out the complexities and contradictions of the Weimar era into any kind of coherent pattern because no overall pattern exists. Eric D. Weitz captures the prevailing feeling of pandemonium in his 2007 book *Weimar Germany: Promise and Tragedy*:

> The Weimar era, with its heady enthusiasms, its artistic experimentation, its flaunting of sexuality and unconventional relations, its vibrant, kinetic energy, was a direct result of the vast disruptions of World War I, the distorted reverberations of its crashing destructiveness. An intense desire to grasp life in all its manifold dimensions, to experience love, sex, beauty, and power, fast cars and airborne flight, theater and dance crazes, arose out of the strong sense of the ephemeral character of life, of lives so quickly snuffed out or forever maimed by bullet wounds and gas attacks.

Berlin's theater scene during Lubitsch's youth was strongly influenced by the modernism of other leading European playwrights whose works were performed in the German capital. Arthur Schnitzler's plays in particular, with their daring and controversial erotic candor, exemplified the spirit of the new era bubbling up under the stern surface of the old-fashioned order. Lubitsch, coming to the movies by way of the theater in the prewar period, could not have helped being influenced by these leading artistic figures, especially Schnitzler, who combined his flouting of prudishness with a melancholic awareness of human foibles. His work includes the originally scandalous 1897 play

Reigen (*La Ronde*), filmed by Max Ophüls in 1950, and his 1925–1926 *Traum-novelle* (*Dream Novella*), filmed by Stanley Kubrick in 1999. Sigmund Freud, the Austrian father of psychoanalysis, expressed a sense of kinship with Schnitzler, and Lubitsch, who developed into such an incisive analyst of human nature, imbibed both men's influence, directly or indirectly, in his formative years. Toward the end of his time in Germany, Lubitsch would announce plans to adapt an unspecified work by Schnitzler.

And well before the war, the Berlin theatrical world was transformed by Max Reinhardt, who began directing there in 1901, and Frank Wedekind, whose revolutionary works were precursors of the dark visions that German playwrights and filmmakers would offer the public in the 1920s. Wede-kind's 1904 play *Die Büchse der Pandora* (*Pandora's Box*)—memorably filmed in 1929 by G. W. Pabst with the American actress Louise Brooks as Lulu, a dancer turned prostitute—became one of the emblematic works of the Weimar era. The Berlin theater's bold delving into morbid, forbidden forms of sexuality during the waning days of the *Kaiserreich* was "pushed to new limits by Wedekind with a kind of frustrated ferocity," Tuchman observes. "It was a form of rebellion against the overwhelming material success of the country, a sense of something wrong beneath the twelve-course din-ners, the pomp of military parades, the beast of 'blood and iron.' Wede-kind and his kind . . . were a trend feeble in comparison with the dominant mood of self-confident power and pugnacity, yet who felt intimations of disaster, of a city ripe for burning, of Neroism in the air." Wedekind directed Lubitsch in one of his plays, *Franziska*, at Reinhardt's Kammerspielhaus in 1913.

In such postwar Lubitsch films as *The Oyster Princess* and *The Wildcat*, as well as in his historical spectacles, the even-more-dizzying upheavals of the Weimar years are reflected in the changing social climates inhabited by his comical or dramatic characters. The characters' world going out of whack around them exerts its influence by throwing their behavior out of joint. What Lubitsch and his regular screenwriter during most of the silent period, Hans Kräly, labeled on-screen as the "grotesque" nature of their comedies is reflected as well in what was then considered a daring blend of comedy and drama in the historical spectacles, which are also set, not coincidentally, in times of violent change. Lubitsch "registered the shock of the old order in the new medium," German critic Frieda Grafe observes. ". . . All his life he continued to depend on times of crisis. It inspired him to his best films. He benefited from instability."

For those who did not live through those times, Berlin lives in large part in the cinematic memories provided by films such as those by Lubitsch and his protégé Billy Wilder. Before fleeing Hitler, Wilder worked in Germany as a screenwriter (as "Billie" Wilder) on such films as *Menschen am Sonntag, ein Film ohne Schauspieler* (*People on Sunday, a Film without Actors*, 1930), *Emil und die Detektive* (*Emil and the Detectives*, 1931), and *Ein blonder Traum* (*A Blonde Dream*, 1932). The function of the cinema as a time machine makes these filmmakers' pre–World War II German works especially precious as records of a world that now seems so distant to us because, not long after being filmed, it would vanish in the tragic course of twentieth-century history. The bittersweet historical irony is that the images of Berlin that Lubitsch and Wilder portrayed on film before they went to America are now among the central locations we vicariously "visit" whenever we want to see and emotionally experience that bygone Berlin. They are key texts in helping us understand the vibrant but dangerously unsettled life in Berlin before the Nazi takeover. These filmmakers' lost homeland was re-created, idiosyncratically, through their artistry in Hollywood. Hollywood, in a real sense, became their home, not the houses and apartments where they lived and died or the American cemeteries where they are buried but the soundstages where they spent much of their careers.

THE "BERLIN STYLE"

Lubitsch became so influential in American filmmaking largely because he brought with him his continental view of life and his critical if amused eye on American puritanism. He adapted to America so well because he deeply understood its foibles and enjoyed playing with them. His American comedies and dramas are unmistakable products of what Jean Renoir called the "Berlin style." That style, carried on in Wilder's work as well, has been defined as a modernistic knowingness, a brash irreverence, a fast-paced cockiness, and a skeptical if not cynical contempt for conventional morality and authority. Despite (or because of) the fact that Lubitsch began his stage and film career when Germany was on the verge of the Great War, his career as an entertainer thrived during that time of hardship and suffering. Although his work in that period may seem strangely disconnected from the reality in the streets and the trenches, it drew from the German populace's need for laughter and escapism and is imbued with a knowing sense of the grotesque. The nation's film industry prospered because foreign films (other than those from Denmark) were banned from German screens for the duration. Once the war ended, Lubitsch's film career continued to gather steam while the country was embroiled in a period of intense political and economic chaos, and by the time he left, Germany was still in a time of turmoil.

Lubitsch made his name as an actor and director in zany comedies, often laced with satirical social comment about German life both urban and rustic. The comedies began as low-budget rough-and-ready affairs with cheaply constructed sets, but they grew increasingly elaborate and ambitious in decor, tending toward fantastic excess. Eventually his commercial success led him to turn more and more to making historical spectacles, although he still interspersed them with comedies. The low wages and high unemployment in postwar Germany enabled him to make his large-scale historical films for relatively modest costs. Their impressive production values and sophisticated perspectives helped them to compete successfully on the world market, rivaling the American spectacles made by D. W. Griffith. Lubitsch's film about the French Revolution, *Madame DuBarry* (1919), is livelier and more incisive about human nature than Griffith's film on the subject, *Orphans of the Storm* (1921). Lubitsch's 1922 German silent *The Wife of Pharaoh*, an Egyptian spectacle made partly with American backing, is more somber than his other historical sagas, but it is more compelling in the sheer grandeur of its sets and cinematography than Cecil B. DeMille's later biblical epics, which are diminished by their rampant bad taste and visual cheesiness, and it should go without saying that the acting is much better in Lubitsch's film as well.

But the economic calamities affecting Germany in the early twenties made it increasingly difficult to produce films, especially big productions. Inflation was rapidly running out of control, affecting every sector of German life. Meanwhile, Lubitsch spoke out in both the American and German media about what he found to be the general technological inferiority of German filmmaking, which was perhaps an oblique reflection of a more sweeping judgment that his depressed homeland was out of step with the times. These were among the principal reasons he wanted to leave Germany to pursue his larger ambitions in America.

After making his first two American films, *Rosita* and *The Marriage Circle*, Lubitsch wrote an article for a Hollywood trade publication, *American Cinematographer*, in December 1923, praising the superior technical quality of American filmmaking, including its lighting equipment. He contended that cameramen in Hollywood were in a stronger position than their German counterparts: "The American cinematographers are in a class by themselves. I do not want to appear ungrateful to my former German co-workers. My photographers over there were just as conscientious and neat in their work as the American cinematographers. But their whole position in the industry is quite different from the one of their colleagues here. . . . The final question [in Hollywood] is always, 'what does the cinematographer say to this?' and his answer settles the matter." Lubitsch explicitly connected what he considered to be the advantages of working in America with the negative effects on Germany of the war and the resulting economic calamity. He wrote that German cinematographers "haven't had the time nor technical equipment to develop their art to so high a degree. The years of the war were an entire loss to German cinematography, and even during the years following the war there was the handicap of money stringency and economic stress."

Lubitsch added, "Fortunately, there is no hostility in the [American] film industry . . . and, if I may judge from my own personal experience, America welcomes us from across the sea with open arms and a rare cordiality, a spirit muchly conducive to the higher development of the cinematographic art." He was not engaging in idle flattery, for he made even more critical comparisons of Hollywood and Germany when he wrote an article to Berlin in April 1924, telling his former colleagues there that "the modern movie" (that is, the film set in the present day) was "the weak point in the German film industry." Perhaps somewhat surprisingly to those back home who were aware of his great success with historical spectacles before he left for America, Lubitsch urged the German industry to "tear itself away, not forever, but for a time from the historical film. . . . The German film industry owes its great success to the costume drama. . . . [But] countless costume dramas have been produced, so that the American public is tired of this genre, not only from the German, but also from the American film industry."

Lubitsch wanted a more stable, first-class working environment of the kind he found in Hollywood, and he was sensitive to the changing boxoffice market he found in his new country. Reflecting his own decisive turn toward stylish modern pictures in Hollywood with *The Marriage Circle*, which had been released earlier in 1924, Lubitsch told his colleagues back home, "The German film company needs more elegance."

TALES OF THINGS TO COME

That change in Lubitsch's approach was an ironic development because the historical spectacles were what had caused Hollywood to import him. And he was so demonstrably eager to go to America that these spectacles can be seen as a public audition. The Lubitsch who drew on his own experiences and observations to satirize German shop life in such films as *Shoe Palace Pinkus* and Berlin's changing sexual mores in *I Don't Want to Be a Man* and who made such rustic farces as *Meyer aus Berlin* (*Meyer from Berlin*, 1919) and *Kohlhiesel's Daughters* (1920) was increasingly attracted to more exotic settings. His immersion in past historical events encompassed a brief but busy four-year period in his German career, from his first tentative foray into the genre in 1918 with his Pola Negri vehicle *Carmen* through 1922 when he made the visually impressive but dramatically deadly *The Wife of Pharaoh*. (The German title, *Das Weib des Pharao*, was inaccurately translated for the American release as *The Loves of Pharaoh*; the pluralization of the pharaoh's "loves" was a cheap gimmick typical of that period in American exhibition.) In between, Lubitsch made his most internationally successful spectacle, the freewheeling comedy-drama *Madame DuBarry*, and the unrelentingly somber *Anna Boleyn* in 1920.

The historical cycle in Lubitsch's work, which coincided with such grave socioeconomic unrest in Germany, could be regarded as an evasion of contemporary reality, as German film historian and sociologist Siegfried Kracauer accused it of being. But period films are always, to some extent, commentaries on the times in which they are made; otherwise they would not be made, because audiences would find it difficult to relate to them. Lubitsch's spectacles are not reductively readable in ideological terms, and they avoid contemporary German settings, dealing instead with revolutionary France,

England during the Tudor dynasty, and Egypt in the time of the pharaohs. The films are nevertheless overtly political in their critical depictions of societies in various stages of revolution and collapse and in the scathing linkages they draw between scandalous personal behavior and political unrest.

The relationship between the past societies Lubitsch depicts and the reality in the streets of Berlin and elsewhere in the Weimar Republic is somewhat oblique, partly because of his personal inclination to avoid overt social-problem films and partly because of his socially influenced need for caution in a time of revolutionary unrest. When Lubitsch deals in his German comedies with what was then contemporary material, the political implications are mostly subterranean but can still be read in the films' stories, settings, and thematic concerns. Setting some of his films in other times and places is simultaneously evasion and subterfuge. The "Berlin style" is evident throughout his sardonic view of society and history.

THE OLD NEIGHBORHOOD

The neighborhood of historic central (Mitte) Berlin where Lubitsch was born and raised, the Scheunenviertel, is not entirely unrecognizable today despite the effects of the Holocaust and postwar modernization. One of the city's major Jewish enclaves in past times, it took its name, meaning "Barn Quarter," because in the eighteenth century it was where horse barns were concentrated to supply a large cattle market. King Frederick William I of Prussia ordered Jews to live in those earthy, unfashionable surroundings. In Lubitsch's time, the Scheunenviertel was not the primary or more fashionable center of Jewish life in Berlin; that was the neighboring district, Spandauer Vorstadt. But by the time Lubitsch was born in the Scheunenviertel on January 29, 1892, his neighborhood was a crowded mecca for many Eastern European and Russian Jews who had fled worse persecutions. As Michael Hanisch writes, "Berlin's Scheunenviertel reflected a little the atmosphere and culture of the Eastern Jewish *shtetels* from which most immigrants came."

Hanisch also states that the Jews of Lubitsch's neighborhood, known as the "Jewish Switzerland," lived harmoniously with a sizable Catholic community, one of the "examples of how the different faiths in very small spaces peacefully got along" before the coming of Nazism. The all-boys school

Lubitsch attended near his home, the Sophien-Gymnasium, had more Christian students than Jews. The Lubitsches were assimilated German Jews who went to the synagogue mostly on High Holy Days. But screenwriter Hans Kräly recalled, "Although not religious in the conventional sense, nevertheless, Lubitsch never undertook an important action in his life, nor started a day's directing, without pausing for half a minute for a short silent prayer. Few people knew of this. He never spoke of it." Charles Van Enger, the cinematographer on five of Lubitsch's American silent films in the 1920s, recalled, "He was a great man and a very religious man. I used to see him stand with his head up against the set . . . and I would say to [Lubitsch's aide, Henry] Blanke, 'What the hell is he doing?,' and he would say, 'He's praying.' A very religious man, a very good man. We used to have a lot of fun together."

Some inhabitants of the Scheunenviertel did face anti-Semitic resentment, and the neighborhood was exaggeratedly described by the police and the tabloid press as a hotbed of vice, other forms of crime, and imported Bolshevism. Hanisch acknowledges, however, that it actually was a somewhat raffish district; it been a red-light district in earlier days, and streetwalkers were often visible in Ernst's youth. Hanisch suggests that Lubitsch's fascination with con men and the demimonde stems from his childhood there. During the political turmoil of the Weimar period, the neighborhood was the scene of many violent incidents, and Ernst recalled having to climb over barbed wire often.

The apartment building where he was born on January 29, 1892, on the second floor at 82A Lothringer Strasse, has been razed. When I visited there in 2014, a Cajun restaurant called Louisiana Kid had taken its place. That seemed fitting for the birthplace of a director who eventually became Americanized even while retaining his strong accent and other marks of his youth in Berlin. The name of the street where he was born was changed to Wilhelm Pieck Strasse (after the first president of the communist German Democratic Republic) and then to Torstrasse (Gate Street); a campaign in Lubitsch's centenary year of 1992 to rename it Ernst Lubitsch Strasse did not succeed. Since the 1990 reunification of Berlin, this colorful neighborhood has become a polyglot hub, popular with younger city dwellers for its stores, restaurants, and reasonably priced apartments. Although the neighborhood was more homogeneous in Ernst's youth, it also had some of the same flavor back then with its mixture of national backgrounds.

Traces of the old neighborhood could still be seen when I visited, between more modern buildings and in its U-Bahn (underground) train station. At the intersection where Lubitsch was born, the station displays haunting historical photos of the bustling streets from the pre-Hitler days, richly atmospheric scenes of men in traditional Jewish garb walking past kosher poultry markets. Within sight of his home at 183 Schönhäuser Allee, which still exists, was the Volksbühne Theater (the People's Theater) at what in his day was called Babelsberg Square or Bülow Square. During the Nazi regime, the square was renamed Horst Wessel Platz after the Nazi activist who was slain in 1930 and wrote the party marching song. The square is now Rosa-Luxemburg-Platz, honoring the communist leader of Polish descent whose assassination by the right-wing Freikorps during the Spartacist revolt, along with the slaying of Karl Liebknecht on January 15, 1919, was among the most calamitous of the many violent events during the Weimar period when Lubitsch was living in Berlin. The neighborhood's leftist history is further indicated by the presence of the headquarters of Karl-Liebknecht-Haus, the former headquarters of the communist Party of Germany and now of the leftist party Die Linke. The Lubitsches were moderately liberal in Ernst's youth, and he always remained a liberal with a strongly antitotalitarian nature; in his films, he mocks royalty and strongly attacks and satirizes both Stalinism and Nazism.

Despite the foreign origins of many residents, such as those visible in the old photos in the U-Bahn, Berlin's Jewish population in Ernst's youth felt more assimilated than Jews had in the flagrantly anti-Semitic Russia from which his father, Simcha Lubitsch, had fled. Simcha, who would change his name to Simon, was born in 1852 in Grodno, then an important city for trade and culture near the borders of Poland and Lithuania; it is now part of western Belarus. In Simon's youth, Grodno had been part of the Pale of Settlement where five million Russian Jews were forced to live. The city was later taken over by Germany and Poland and then the Union of Soviet Socialist Republics (USSR), and most of its Jews were exterminated in the Holocaust. Simon had been a tailor in the czar's army and spent time in Vilnius, then part of Russia but now the capital of Lithuania. He was thought to have fled his homeland to escape army service and pogroms, like many other Ostjuden who eventually came to Berlin. Simon emigrated there in the 1880s. His wife, Anna Lindenstaedt, was born in 1850 near Berlin in Wriezen-on-the-Oder.

The sense of greater belonging felt by Jewish Berliners was a cruel illusion. The Nazis' destruction of their sense of well-being would be felt as a betrayal by the city's Jewish residents who had longer histories in Germany, some of whom tended to feel superior to the Jews from eastern lands. But Jews of any background were still a small minority in Berlin before the Nazis eradicated their traditional communities. During World War II, the Nazis herded the Jewish population in Scheunenviertel into the neighborhood school and synagogue and shot them unless they were congregated for shipment to death camps.

Ernst had three older siblings, Else, Richard, and Margarethe ("Marga"). The growing and prospering family moved half a block in 1896, from where he was born to apartments in a five-story building owned by a cigarette company, where Simon and Anna also had their tailoring workshop. Somehow, the Lubitsch family's apartment building on Schönhauser Allee has survived all this tumultuous history. In 1992 the city put a plaque on the apartment house in a dedication ceremony attended by the director's only child, his American daughter, Nicola, and his sole surviving niece, Evy Bettelheim-Bentley. The plaque, which later had to be replaced because of wear and tear, honors the "actor, producer, and film director" who "lived here from 1896 to 1919" and whose many films include such classics as *The Oyster Princess*, *Ninotchka*, and *To Be or Not to Be*—good titles if one has to choose three films to represent his diverse body of work.

The apartment building, well preserved though somewhat marred by graffiti on its black wooden front doors, has an elegant, shadowy lobby with ornate metallic designs in its windows and blue-and-white floor tiles. At the end of the first-floor hallway is the apartment space where Simon Lubitsch (officially identified as a "master tailor") and Anna employed a staff of eight to make women's coats, suits, and skirts. Behind it is a small outside patio leading to an alleyway where the employees might have taken a break to smoke. Simon and his wife sold their wares at a store next door, the firm of S. Lubitsch, which they had first occupied while living across the street (when I visited, the store was a beauty salon). A 1900 advertisement for the firm of S. Lubitsch described it as "an establishment for the making of coats for women." Nicola Lubitsch said the firm specialized in large women. The humble but prosperous women's clothing shop was the prototype of the stores that Ernst filmed in *Shoe Palace Pinkus* and *The Shop Around the Corner*

(1940) with affection but also with some degree of rebellious ambivalence toward their patriarchal domination.

In Robert Fischer's 2006 documentary *Ernst Lubitsch in Berlin—Von der Schönhauser Allee nach Hollywood* (*Ernst Lubitsch in Berlin: From Schönhauser Allee to Hollywood*), Nicola says that from what she knows of her family history, Simon Lubitsch did not seem to work very hard. He spent most of his time sitting in cafés, reading newspapers upside down, leading people to assume he could not actually read. His German was never particularly fluent. Evy Bettelheim-Bentley recalled that Anna Lubitsch "always pulled the strings from a distance, with everything" and said that Simon "was the one who bought the fabrics. He had extremely good taste. He was a very elegant man. . . . He was tall and good-looking, and he was always dressed very discreetly and elegantly." Evy said that Anna did the designs and patterns for the establishment. She came from a tailoring family herself, and Nicola calls her "the one who worked. She managed the firm. . . . [My grandfather] certainly wasn't slaving away in the tailoring business. He was out having a good time. And he always liked pretty ladies. He's the model for the [foxy grandfather character played by Charles Coburn] in *Heaven Can Wait*, that's totally modeled on my grandfather. . . . All of my father's work has a lot of autobiographical stuff in it."

The keen sense of glamour and elegance in Ernst's films and his careful attention to costumes and the texture of his settings, along with his general attraction to luxury and showmanship, were inherited from his parents' trade. Another of Ernst's most important traits as a filmmaker, his keen sense of organization and efficiency, can also be seen as a carryover from the family-business background. But Ernst was a late bloomer in coming to embrace his family's influence, probably because he met opposition to his personal artistic ambitions from his father and clashed with his siblings, who reportedly regarded their little brother as an interloper. The fact that his parents were relatively along in years (in their forties) when he was born contributed to his sense of distance from the rest of the family. "He was always a small, delicate child," Evy recalled. "He had a wet nurse. Grandmother didn't have time for him. He was the total opposite of the entire family. And as a child, he was somehow very delicate, and perhaps not very healthy. He loved to eat chocolate, which he shouldn't have eaten." Nicola adds, "And he didn't do anything he didn't want to do, ever." Ernst seems to have had the combination of being spoiled and neglected that is often true of the youngest child in a family, who frequently develops into the family clown.

Because of these familial pressures on him as a misfit child, Ernst developed into a rebel against society at an early age. Showing no interest in schooling, despite the long-standing Jewish tradition of reverence for advanced education, he did not go beyond high school and was never regarded as an intellectual or much of a reader by his friends and peers in Hollywood. But his early interest in the theater made him study the works of great playwrights on his own. He displayed little aptitude for the work his father found him as an apprentice clerk at the Stoffgeschäft Gebrüder Hoffmann (the Brothers Hoffmann Fabric Shop) and then as a bookkeeper at the firm of S. Lubitsch. At the Hoffmanns', Ernst was often found shirking his duties while crouching behind bolts of cloth to read Schiller and other playwrights. While working at his father's shop, he lived what he called a "double life" as an aspiring young man of the theater. Ernst's father wanted him to spend his life in the family business, but his early half-hearted attempts at doing so were a debacle since he was such a schlemiel (a Yiddish term for an awkward and unlucky person who screws up everything). Probably, his father thought him a bit meshuga (crazy), like any other child who defies social norms to pursue an artistic obsession. Ernst comically reenacts his misadventures in the clothing trade in the role that brought him stardom in movies, the bumbling provincial window dresser in *The Pride of the Firm*.

The opening finds Lubitsch's Siegmund Lachmann breaking a store window and getting fired from his job in Rawitsch in the Prussian province of Posen (now part of Poland). After contemplating suicide (but only briefly; suicide is always a joke option in Lubitsch's films), Siegmund journeys to Berlin, goes to work in a high-class women's clothing store, starts to look dapper, and eventually prospers through his chutzpah and talent, marrying the boss's daughter and becoming vice president of the firm of J. C. Berg. That is comical cinema, a wish-fulfillment fantasy of triumph, not the mundane reality of Ernst's youthful life. Although *The Pride of the Firm* is engaging and we enjoy seeing Siegmund conquering obstacles to success, it is telling that his transition from provincial bumpkin to suave urban sophisticate is simply omitted (an intertitle tells us, "Years passed by . . ."), making us take that crucial development mostly on faith. *Shoe Palace Pinkus*, the first hit film Lubitsch directed, is more or less a remake of *The Pride of the Firm*. Ernst takes a similar role as Sally Pinkus, who rises from being a lowly clerk in a Berlin shoe store to running a fancy fashion emporium. Sally, one of the names Lubitsch frequently used for his characters in that period when he became known as a Jewish comedian, was a nickname for Solomon and was pronounced "Solly."

The Lubitsch family's dwellings next door to the firm of S. Lubitsch occupied the second and third floors in two spacious apartments. The second-floor space was reserved for the parents, and the third floor for the children. (With Ernst's help, Simon moved the shop to a fancier part of town, 38 Leipziger Strasse, in 1920, several years after his wife's death.) Given the prevalence of doors in Ernst's films and his extensive use of them as punctuation devices for his elliptical gags, it is striking to see that his old family apartments on Schönhauser Allee are filled with doors and doorways of varying shapes, sizes, and functions. Not only does each apartment have tall triple doors for an entranceway, but inside each apartment is a long hallway connecting the various rooms, with separate doorways leading to the living and sleeping spaces and kitchens. There are yet more doors between those rooms, and comfortable nooks in the front windows overlooking the street create more door-like shapes. The doors give the feeling of living in a maze, yet the overall effect of the Lubitsches' comfortably middle-class dwelling is of unostentatious elegance and comfort with an appealing sense of depth and visual variety.

Although Lubitsch's celebrated penchant for relying on an the intricacies of doors as on-screen storytelling devices can perhaps can be traced back to his youth in that dwelling, he probably more consciously derived his fascination with that motif from the mise-en-scène associated with the theater, where he trained extensively and from which his talent emerged. It is too glib to describe Lubitsch simply as "a director of doors," as Mary Pickford complained to Kevin Brownlow in an interview for his 1967 book *The Parade's Gone By . . .* Although that complaint is much quoted, it is an odd one for her to have made, because her *Rosita* is one of the Lubitsch films with the least reliance on door gags. Nevertheless, doors are a prominent element in his general style, and he finds an almost infinite variety of uses for doors as sources of humorous (and sometimes dramatic) innuendo. These gags or touches are often sexual, though not exclusively so. An integral part of how he tells his stories from fresh, oblique, and insinuating angles, Lubitsch's door shots are painterly ways of suggesting what cannot be shown because of censorship, cleverly planting forbidden images in the minds of his viewers, transforming us into secret voyeurs.

It has been suggested that Lubitsch's concentration on doors, on a deeper level, reflects his profound awareness of the role of social exclusion, which he felt as a Jew and an exile who grew up as a Russian citizen in a somewhat alien country that marginalized Jews and eventually did everything it could to ostracize and destroy them. Lubitsch left little written record of his thoughts and feelings on anti-Semitism and ostracism aside from some comments on the controversial *To Be or Not to Be*, but his films are filled with commentaries, visual and otherwise, satirical and dramatic, on various forms of exclusion and assimilation. By the time he was an exile living more securely and prospering in his career in America, he was using door shots extensively in his films to subtly convey those well-remembered and still partly present feelings, often in subtle ways.

Lubitsch lived at Schönhauser Allee until 1919, when he was a successful film director and star of twenty-eight and it was time for him to relocate to a posh apartment of his own. He moved to the west side of Berlin near the Tempelhof Studios, where he usually worked. That apartment at 13 Kufsteiner Strasse also still exists (though with a different address). He occupied it until departing for America on December 2, 1922.

THE SPEAR-CARRIER

The still-active Volksbühne Theater, a large and imposing stone edifice, was built in 1913–1914. Some of Ernst's early work as an actor took place there after it was taken over in 1915 by Max Reinhardt, who had accepted Ernst into his stage company along with a couple dozen other new hires on August 9, 1911, and announced their hiring in a Berlin newspaper. That theater was so close to Ernst's home that his niece Evy would sometimes come to the stage door with a sandwich for him to eat between acts. She recalled that he was often hungry in that period, as most Berliners were during the war, when food was scarce and people had to wait in long lines for rations. But at least Ernst had steady employment, and the ambitious young man soon prospered by working day and night in both the theater and films.

Most of his work onstage during that formative period took place several miles away with Reinhardt, at his main base, the Deutsches Theater on Schumannstrasse, and its adjacent Kammerspielhaus (smaller, intimate, or chamber theater). Reinhardt had come to Berlin from Austria in 1894. He was the director of Berlin's leading theater from 1904 until he fled Hitler in 1933 to return to Austria. After the Anschluss in 1938, Reinhardt escaped to Britain; he wound up in America, where he ran a theater school on Sunset Boulevard. As early as 1910, Reinhardt showed an interest in the still-déclassé new medium of film, although with little success at first, by filming his stage production of the Friedrich Freksa pantomime *Sumurun*, which Lubitsch would also film in 1920. Another of the films Reinhardt directed in Germany, the 1913 feature *Die Insel der Seligen* (*Isle of the Blessed*), is a pretentiously arty and rather incoherent mishmash. His most important work in his second medium came in Hollywood with his sole American film, the innovative 1935 adaptation of William Shakespeare's *A Midsummer Night's Dream*, a lavish blend of stage and cinematic techniques based on his live Hollywood Bowl production of the previous year (Lubitsch himself had appeared in a 1913 Reinhardt production of the play in Berlin and later expressed interest in making a film of that fantastical comedy). Reinhardt died in 1943, but his son Gottfried was an assistant to Lubitsch in Hollywood on the 1933 film *Design for Living* and eventually became a director and producer himself.

Lubitsch had begun acting as a schoolboy in the Sophien-Gymnasium (Sophia High School), a well-regarded classical and liberal arts academy that taught singing and art as well as French, Latin, Hebrew, and English. An indifferent student, he finished high school in 1908 at age sixteen and did not advance any further in his education. But he showed early signs of talent in the school's amateur dramatics group, always playing old men, according to director Lothar Mendes, who attended the same school. Yet well before then, Ernst had decided he wanted to be an actor. In a 1938 autobiographical article he wrote for Paramount Pictures as a press release, Lubitsch explained how he made his way into the arts:

> I think it was music that led me into this moving picture business. In the Berlin home of my father, who ran a clothing store, I began picking out tunes on the piano when I was five. When the family frowned on my

musical ambitions I decided at the age of six to become an actor. This also was frowned upon and my father decreed I must complete my schooling.

By the time I was eight I was filled with a thorough hatred of schools because they tried to mold my way of thinking and compelled me to study subjects that held no interest for me. I do not think I was different from others of like age.

By saving my allowance I got enough money to buy a cello, and my sister, who played the piano, taught me to sing most of the popular tunes of the day. By that time my ambition still was to become an actor but mainly as a comedian; I like to laugh.

When I got out of primary school I was too young to go to college and so my father put me to work in his store. Little did he realize that a generation later Ben Hecht [the screenwriter of *Design for Living*] would be writing of me that "Lubitsch has a rather interesting face with the dark, mocking leer of a creditor!" Perhaps I acquired the leer while clerking for three years. Ah, me!

Like all youths, I imagined myself a great artist. The first week I was at work I enrolled in a night drama school. My confidence in myself was so great that once [in 1910] I plucked up my courage and called upon Victor Arnold, a noted stage comedian of the day. Somehow I conveyed to him my enthusiasm and my desire to emulate him. Arnold agreed to help me acquire the rudiments of the drama, and I studied with him for two years. I do not think I ever succeeded in making him laugh, but since then I have found that it is impossible to make a professional comedian laugh.

At length Arnold took me to the great Max Reinhardt. My short stature, black hair and that dark, mocking leer must have impressed him for he put me to work. I think it was about then that my father quit resisting me; or perhaps it was that he washed his hands of me.

(As he aged in the 1940s, Lubitsch apparently thought better of having bad-mouthed his father with recollections of how he wanted him to enter the family clothing business. "Those stories are pure fantasy," Ernst claimed. "My parents encouraged my theatrical ambitions. They gave me the money to study drama." Who are you going to believe, Lubitsch or Lubitsch?)

The autobiographical overtones of Ernst's early comical appearances on-screen are obvious, as in his Siegmund Lachmann in *The Pride of the Firm* and some of the first films he starred in and directed such as *Shoe Palace Pinkus* and *Der Blusenkönig* (*The Blouse King*), a 1917 film that survives only in a twelve-minute fragment. It is telling that Lubitsch drew on the garment industry milieu for the settings of those irreverent "store comedies" that established his popular reputation. *Shoe Palace Pinkus* not only deals with a ladies' shoe store but also includes some raucous school scenes that display his Sally Pinkus character as a wildly rowdy, disrespectful cutup. His main pleasures are flirting with girls on the way to and from school, tormenting his stuffy teacher, and climbing an athletic bar to spy over a wall on the girls at a school next door (there was a girls' school next to Ernst's as well). When Sally arrives in the classroom (late), he immediately runs up and down on top of the desks, promoting anarchy among his classmates. He is expelled and naïvely shows prospective employers his terrible school record before realizing that it is a hindrance to his future. These satirical glimpses of the hidebound German educational system are indicative of Lubitsch's own contempt for the institution. Ernst's lack of interest in higher education or in settling down in a mundane occupation was a sign not only of his artistic temperament but also of the insubordination toward his German upbringing that would eventually point the young man in the direction of the New World.

He displayed the subversive attitude characteristic not only of a rebellious outsider but also of an adventurous artist for whom book learning never meant as much as practical experience in his chosen craft. The lessons Lubitsch had begun taking from Victor Arnold—after an audition in which he played Shylock—and his work for several years with Reinhardt were his formal training, and he could not have picked better mentors. Lubitsch acknowledged Arnold, a short and stocky Reinhardt actor, as "a great influence on my entire career and my future." Arnold's comic talents, Hanisch believes, helped steer Lubitsch away from his earlier preoccupation with heavy drama, a pull that continued to manifest itself intermittently throughout his career but that he would mostly forsake for comedy after recognizing his true talents and his physical limitations as a performer. "Maybe it's just this great comedian Victor Arnold who pointed Lubitsch to the value of comedy in art," Hanisch speculates. "Perhaps it was Arnold who freed Lubitsch from his complexes and made clear to him that the stage does not need only Adonis figures."

After Arnold introduced him to Reinhardt, Ernst was hired as an apprentice at the Deutsches Theater when he was nineteen. But Arnold's own life rapidly deteriorated. He was said to have been "tormented by fear of war"—what Hanisch calls "the war psychosis," which affected many Germans—as well as by financial problems caused by prewar investments he had made in Russia. One of Arnold's directors, Felix Hollaender, painted a word picture in Arnold's obituary that helps us appreciate both his psychological unbalance and Lubitsch's fascination with the comedian's personality: "His caustic wit spared nothing and no one. He was goodnatured and childlike, shy, suspicious, and superstitious in the heart. Like most great comedians, he was a heavy melancholic and hypochondriac who inwardly was terribly tormented in life. . . . [At the end] two ideas dominated him—one, that he would starve; and two, that he could never learn to play another role. This fear literally strangled him." After going mad in front of Reinhardt and being sent to a sanatorium, Victor Arnold committed suicide by cutting his throat in October 1914.

Lubitsch would continue acting at the Deutsches Theater and in "different [Reinhardt] stock companies" until May 1918 even though he began making films by 1913, not long after he was hired by the great stage director. Theater actors often worked in movies in the silent era, helping supplement their incomes as well as gaining more public notice. "In those days," recalled Lubitsch, "any actor who had the chance did pictures in the daytime and plays at night . . . if he had the stamina. I did." Early in his career, there was a great deal of resentment by Berlin theater managers over the newer medium, but that gradually subsided as the situation became inevitable and the film industry raised its socioeconomic status by buying adaptation rights to literary and stage properties. Reinhardt's own early interest in movies probably played a role in helping steer Lubitsch in that direction.

Arnold, said Lubitsch, "also was responsible for my first success in pictures in getting me the part of the apprentice [Moritz Abramowski] in *Die Firma Heiratet.*" That film, *The Company Marries*, also known as *The Perfect Thirty-Six*, was directed by Carl Wilhelm and released to great success in January 1914, leading Wilhelm to follow it up with *The Pride of the Firm*. Arnold plays Lubitsch's boss in both films. The triumphant premiere of *The Pride of the Firm* on July 30 was followed only a few hours later with Germany's declaration of a state of war. Overnight, as Hanisch wrote, Berlin "was in a fever frenzy. . . . The repeated, random coincidence of Lubitsch's work with social revolutions is striking." That phenomenon seems particularly ironic because of Lubitsch's determinedly apolitical public stance throughout much of his lifetime, although his films do have political overtones, however subtle or covert they often are.

Lubitsch habitually adopted a wry rather than doctrinaire attitude toward life. In his first known interview, in 1916, when asked to talk "seriously about the art of film," he responded with a joke: "Ernst I have enough in my name" (the German adjective for a person who is earnest is *ernst*). But his work is more serious, more political than it seems on superficial inspection; it reflects and comments on social conditions extensively, but mostly with humorous obliqueness and only rarely directly, in keeping with his overall stylistic approach to his craft of storytelling. A central irony of Lubitsch's career is that the Great War itself would be a boon to him as a comic filmmaker since the German public, deprived of films from overseas and badly in need of diversion, avidly supported his knack for popular entertainment. And during the tumultuous Weimar Republic period, the low cost of labor caused by inflation and widespread unemployment would allow him to make his lavish historical spectacles about political subjects on what seem today to be laughably small budgets. But eventually inflation spiraled so out of control that it priced those films out of existence.

Although Lubitsch achieved far more success as a film actor than he ever did as a member of the Deutsches Theater, his years with Reinhardt (1911–1918) were invaluable training for his own directing career. Being part of a major theatrical company that was widely known in Europe while learning backstage crafts, often playing the fool, and empathizing with the smallest of small-part actors not only taught him his métier from a variety of angles but encouraged his empathy for all those, high or low, who shared that profession. Most crucially, Lubitsch had the opportunity to study, at close range and from behind the scenes, the work of a master director at the peak of his craft. As the German film historians Hans Helmut Prinzler and Enno Patalas write in their 1984 book, *Lubitsch*, "Reinhardt is the theatrical exponent of the positive sides of the Wilhelmine; he has taste, wit, imagination, instinct. To his talents add musicality, atmosphere, mood; light, settings, decoration; the use of a revolving stage, the direction of crowds, an aura with actors. These are all the elements he connects, with what is admiringly called

'Theater Magic.'" Reinhardt was renowned for his unrivaled ability to integrate all the elements of settings, lighting, and performance into a unified whole. That was the major source of Reinhardt's groundbreaking influence on other stage directors throughout Europe. He was the total theater director, and he helped elevate the status of that profession, which in the nineteenth century had been mostly the function of the manager of the stage troupe. Reinhardt's conceptions of plays as visual pieces brimming with orchestrated movement and carefully modulated ensembles are reflected in Lubitsch's film work, which evolved rapidly from its relatively crude beginnings to a far more sophisticated style by the end of the 1910s.

Despite whatever humiliation Lubitsch may have felt as a lowly member of the Reinhardt troupe who was rarely allowed to play major parts, just being with Reinhardt was honor aplenty in the eyes of Berlin and the rest of the world. Lubitsch was able to share the stage with such leading actors as Victor Arnold, Paul Wegener, Albert Basserman, Rudolf Schildkraut, Emil Jannings, and even the tall, redheaded young actor Friedrich Wilhelm (F. W.) Murnau, who also would go on to become a great film director in Germany and the United States. Jannings would star in several of Lubitsch's most important films. Wegener, best known for his title role in his own 1920 classic film *Der Golem, wie er in die Welt kam* (*The Golem: How He Came into the World*), plays a major role opposite Jannings in Lubitsch's *The Wife of Pharaoh*. Also in the cast is Basserman, who became a notable Hollywood character actor after leaving Germany in 1939 with his Jewish wife. A frequent Lubitsch leading man in the early years, the matinee idol Harry Liedtke was a compatriot from their time with Reinhardt. Lubitsch was able to appear in a variety of important plays at the Deutsches Theater, contributing, albeit in small ways, to their artistic success and sharing the limelight of their social prominence in the highly competitive cultural life of Berlin. Reinhardt mounted many productions of European theater classics, and part of his renown came from his frequent staging of Shakespeare at the Deutsches Theater.

Among the Shakespeare plays in which Lubitsch performed under Reinhardt's direction were *Hamlet* (as the second gravedigger), *Henry IV Parts I and II* (Peto), *A Midsummer Night's Dream* (Tom Snout), *Much Ado about Nothing* ("Ein Schreiber," a scribe, perhaps the town clerk), *Romeo and Juliet* (Sampson), *Twelfth Night* (Fabian), *The Winter's Tale* (Autolycus), and *The*

Merchant of Venice (as Shylock's clownish servant Launcelot Gobbo). Lubitsch also appeared in such plays as Molière's *The Miser*, Maurice Maeterlinck's *The Blue Bird*, Friedrich Schiller's *The Robbers*, and Johann Wolfgang von Goethe's *Faust* and *The Funfair at Plundersweilern*. For other directors at the theater, Lubitsch appeared in Maxim Gorky's *The Lower Depths* and August Strindberg's *Master Olaf*.

Lubitsch would have had much to owe his mentor even if only for the influence of his years of apprenticeship with Reinhardt on *To Be or Not to Be*, his late masterpiece about the theater and Shakespeare. But all the films Lubitsch directed show his indebtedness to Reinhardt in the subtly integrated incorporation of theatrical elements in his elaborate cinematic style and his delicacy and understanding in working with all variety of actors. Even that consummate ham Joseph Tura, played by Jack Benny, in *To Be or Not to Be* and the lesser members of his troupe can be seen as a lovingly self-aware nod by Lubitsch to his own checkered career as a minor player in Reinhardt's Shakespearean productions. Lubitsch directed two 1920 films that are more purely comedic takeoffs on Shakespeare, the feature *Kohlhiesel's Daughters*, loosely based on *The Taming of the Shrew*, and the short *Romeo und Julia im Schnee* (*Romeo and Juliet in the Snow*). These farces, made in the mountains of Bavaria, are from scripts Lubitsch wrote with Kräly.

During his long theatrical apprenticeship, Lubitsch learned every aspect of stagecraft from Reinhardt. Lubitsch had to gradually learn the difference between how to play comedy on the stage and how to direct it in film. One lesson that especially stuck with him permeates his work as a director who always had an acute sense of how to make films play best for an audience. In 1940 he told Frank S. Nugent of the *New York Times*, "When I was a young man in Max Reinhardt's company in Germany I was Shakespearean straight man to one of the greatest Shakespearean clowns [Arnold]. If so much as one snicker still could be heard in the balcony, I had to keep my mouth shut. 'Ride the laugh!' [Reinhardt] would yell when we came off the stage. 'Say nothing until the house is ready to listen again!' He would kill me every time I forgot." And yet Lubitsch admitted that comedy was more difficult in filmmaking since he had to rely more on his own judgment and sense of timing, and even then it could be a nerve-racking process: "When a comedy is being shot there is only the audience of a director, the crew, the actors standing around. A lousy audience! I have learned there is no worse sign than when everyone on the set is in hysterics. . . . Now maybe you say 'This is very funny; there will be a big laugh,' so you stretch the action a little, to give them time to laugh. And then you preview and no laugh comes. Horrible, my friends, horrible!"

Lubitsch's cocky persona as a film comedian quickly found public favor in what was still regarded as a lower-class medium, but he never played a leading role for Reinhardt. Because of his lack of physical stature and conventional good looks—qualities offset on-screen by his endearing grin, piercingly intelligent features, and darkly expressive eyes—and because of his limited acting talent, or both, he was usually typecast onstage as a servant or fool and was often an understudy. His roles did have some eccentric variety: he was Famulus in a touring company of *Faust*, the Cold and the Poplar in the fantasy *The Blue Bird*, a bandit, a journalist, a lawyer, a money changer, a prompter, a woman, and even a character named Wilder ("a wild man") in *The Shepherdesses*. But mostly, Lubitsch was the all-purpose kind of frustrated spear-carrier and supernumerary that Felix Bressart and Tom Dugan so memorably play in *To Be or Not to Be*.

You can feel Lubitsch's heart and soul and the memory of those years of creative frustration in Bressart's character in *To Be or Not to Be*, Greenberg. Bressart was a German émigré comedian who also appears in *Ninotchka* and *The Shop Around the Corner*. The warmth and humanity of his characters are so centrally emphasized by Lubitsch that they indicate a high degree of identification between director and actor. Their Jewishness, similar senses of humor, and *haimish* (Yiddish for warm and comfortable, homely, folksy) quality help account for Lubitsch's choice of Bressart for his alter ego. And through Greenberg, Lubitsch pays tribute to the kind of humble role he himself played in a 1913 Reinhardt production of *Hamlet*. His was of course not the title part—which Benny hilariously plays within Lubitsch's film—but a gravedigger. Lubitsch could have described himself in the words of T. S. Eliot's "The Love Song of J. Alfred Prufrock":

No! I am not Prince Hamlet, nor was meant to be;
Am an attendant lord, one that will do
To swell a progress, start a scene or two,

. . . .

At times, indeed, almost ridiculous—
Almost, at times, the Fool.

EVOLVING A PERSONAL STYLE

In contrast to his meager progress on the stage, Lubitsch found movie stardom quickly, and he became popular in Berlin vaudeville and cabaret shows through 1918. He even appeared in blackface in the lost 1916 film *Der schwarze Moritz* (*The Black Moritz*), directed by George Jacoby, which was combined with scenes of stage musical comedy in an experimental hybrid performance. In his early screen appearances, Lubitsch usually played buffoonish, outlandish characters, often drawing from the tradition of Jewish ethnic humor. He sometimes tried more restrained roles, but with less popular success. But the most important by-product of his success as an actor was that it helped jump-start his directing career.

We can track the progress of Lubitsch's directorial style, and the stylistic and thematic scope of his German films (released between 1914 and 1923), by looking at how he developed his artistic personality in those early years over what seems a dizzying range of work. The versatility he learned as a member of the Reinhardt company helped him shift from broad farces to daringly stylized "grotesque" comedies and finally to grandly produced historical spectacles. Nor are the lines between these modes of storytelling always distinct in his body of work. Lubitsch sometimes alternated types of films, thereby asserting his directorial versatility, or blended genres in a single film in ways that enhanced audience appeal and made his work seem more fresh and original than its more conventional competition.

Lubitsch's career epitomized German show business's transitional period between stage and cinema during the mid-1910s. He was evolving his own style in his first few years as a filmmaker but only gradually, in fits and starts. He evidently earned the right to direct (with the topical comedy *Miss Soapsuds*) because of his boxoffice success as the star of *The Pride of the Firm*. For several years, he was busy cranking out short films, usually in two or three reels, sometimes acting and directing, sometimes acting for other directors. He cannily capitalized on his breakthrough role in *The Pride of the Firm* by giving audiences more of the same when he directed *Shoe Palace Pinkus*.

Although that semiautobiographical store comedy gives evidence of Lubitsch's nascent directorial talents and can be seen as a very rough sketch for his mature classic *The Shop Around the Corner*, he often remained typecast in what were then called "Jewish milieu pieces" in his first few years as an actor and director. Those films also included *The Blouse King, Der gemischte Frauenchor* (*The Mixed Ladies' Chorus*), and *Der G.m.b.H. Tenor* (*The Tenor, Inc.*). He began venturing out into more varied social settings in 1917 with *Wenn Vier Dasselbe Tun* (*When Four Do the Same*), a sophisticated romantic comedy foreshadowing his more complex later work in Hollywood, and *Das Fidele Gefängnis* (*The Merry Jail*), based on *Das Gefängnis* (*The Prison*) by German playwright Julius Roderich Benedix. This laboriously convoluted romantic comedy about a wife (Kitty Dewall) disguising herself to entrap her philandering husband (Harry Liedtke) was also inspired by Johann Strauss's celebrated opera *Die Fledermaus* (*The Bat*), which drew from *The Prison*. Featuring a hammy turn by the Reinhardt star Emil Jannings as a rowdy old jailer, but enlivened by the antics of the sexy family maid (Agda Nilsson), *The Merry Jail* is a rough-and-ready precursor of Lubitsch's more stylishly rowdy 1926 Hollywood comedy *So This Is Paris*. In October 1918, just before the war ended, Lubitsch expanded his horizons in new directions, in terms of both subject matter and length, with the release of the film that is considered his first feature, *Die Augen der Mummie Mâ* (*The Eyes of the Mummy*), and he followed it two months later with his first spectacle, a version of *Carmen*.

The Eyes of the Mummy, which runs about an hour, is a deliriously silly "Oriental" melodrama taking place in Egypt (on locations filmed outside Berlin). The absurdity of its plotting is made more palatable by the flamboyantly overwrought players he cast in the lead roles: Jannings, a Swiss who had joined the Reinhardt company in 1915 and would go on to major film stardom, and the newly minted Polish film star Pola Negri, a former stage actress and ballerina. Neither the director nor his actors had yet learned to tone down their styles for the screen in order to make their work seem more cinematic than theatrical. *Carmen*, another frenzied melodrama starring Negri, is based on the oft-filmed 1845 Prosper Mérimée novella that inspired the 1875 opera by French composer Georges Bizet. Although Lubitsch's *Carmen* is on a much smaller scale than the historical films he would make in the next few years, taking place in a few cramped but effective studio sets, it helped him test his talents for the period spectacle genre, with a blending (rather clumsily here) of intimate sexual drama and swirling, frenzied crowd scenes that was influenced by Reinhardt. The German film industry and especially Lubitsch's regular producer, Paul Davidson, were hoping to use such spectacles to break through into the international market in the aftermath of the war.

But a different film released in the same month of 1918 as *The Eyes of the Mummy* is the first of Lubitsch's extant works to show more sustained signs of distinction and his budding sophistication as a director. *I Don't Want to Be a Man* is a tour de force for the saucy and boisterous young blonde comedian Ossi Oswalda, who made her film debut with a small role in *Shoe Palace Pinkus* and went on to star in twelve other Lubitsch silents. Ossi (a name bestowed on her by Lubitsch himself; she was born Oswalda Stäglich) became known as "the German Mary Pickford" and reportedly was romantically involved with the director. *I Don't Want to Be a Man* is a startlingly modern cross-dressing tale revolving around an audacious girl who chafes at the restrictions on her gender and goes out on the town formally dressed as a man. Lubitsch and Kräly were ahead of their time in cinema by reflecting the emancipation of women that was taking place around the world in those days because of the suffrage movement, the war, and other revolutionary changes. But they characteristically employed comedy as their medium to make their complex messages entertaining, a major reason the film holds up so well today. This was the first of several splendid feature-length comedies Lubitsch would make before leaving Germany for America, ranging from the rustic farce *Kohlhiesel's Daughters* to the ambitious "grotesque" comedies *The Oyster Princess*, *The Wildcat*, and *The Doll*.

Lubitsch's silent work was affected by cultural and market factors in that tumultuous time in German history, which contributed to his veering from one genre to another. The panoply of early Lubitsch films may therefore make his works seem bewilderingly different in approach from one another and often strikingly dissimilar from the Lubitsch we know best from his Hollywood classics. But his early efforts contain the seeds of his mature style and themes as well as elements he gradually rejected in the process of refining his filmmaking signature.

From the evidence of Lubitsch's first surviving films as a director, he began with relatively crude farces filmed with simple, static framings, broad acting gestures, and rudimentary interior sets. The derivation of these films from the theater is obvious even if some exterior scenes show more flair for composition. Lubitsch's progression in handling the new medium accelerated once he started directing longer films and had more breathing space to let scenes play out more calmly and with detailed acting that allowed for subtler touches. He began to attract a company of colleagues who would remain with him for many films. From *Miss Soapsuds* onward, his films were often designed by Kurt Richter, who brought a distinctively modernist artistic style to his work. And it is not coincidental that Lubitsch's first notable success as a director with *Shoe Palace Pinkus* was the second of what would become many collaborations in silent films with his gifted and versatile screenwriter Hans Kräly following their 1915 short called *Aufs eis Geführt* (*A Trip on the Ice*) (Kräly also played small roles in *The Company Marries* and *Shoe Palace Pinkus*).

Wilhelm's *The Pride of the Firm* is more accomplished directorially than Lubitsch's own variation on that template for the "store comedy" cycle two years later, *Shoe Palace Pinkus*. *The Pride of the Firm*, with its time-honored plot of a callow youth from the country coming to the big city and winning his way to success and social favor, is generally satisfying as a filmic bildungsroman. The social climbing of Lubitsch's Siegmund may be improbable, achieved through aggressive courtship of well-to-do women, including his boss's daughter, but his sheer energy and chutzpah prove difficult for these women and the audience to resist. At the end, we see a charming split-screen image of the bumpkin Siegmund once was and the suave businessman he has become. Although *Shoe Palace Pinkus* copies *The Pride of the Firm* in broad outline, it is more a series of raggedly filmed comic skits than a sustained story, almost a vaudeville show on film. But the even more strongly personal nature of *Shoe Palace Pinkus*, following the episodic path of Lubitsch's Sally from a ludicrously overgrown Berlin schoolboy to a man of the world directing a fashion show, makes it the most Lubitschean of his early farces (the ones he made before concentrating more on directing and venturing into more elaborately cinematic terrain with *The Oyster Princess*, *The Doll*, and *The Wildcat*). As German critic Frieda Grafe points out, the Sally Pinkus character, in his "vast audacity, success addiction, and unrestricted self-esteem," was similar to the characters Groucho Marx later played, and the type would be echoed by Lubitsch in the irrepressibly cocky, often-obnoxious, but still brashly charming ladies' men played by Maurice Chevalier in his musicals.

Shoe Palace Pinkus is emblematic of the strengths and weaknesses of Lubitsch's early ventures as a director in the period when he was still learning to transcend the limits of filmed theater and tell stories that could only be put on film. With no shortage of authorial chutzpah, *Shoe Palace Pinkus* literally advertises itself as a special attraction. The film begins ingeniously with hands opening a brochure advertising the shoe store that Sally will eventually establish. Somewhat surprisingly, the first credits we see are not for the stars or the director but for the writers, Hans Kräly and Erich Schönfelder, with their pictures displayed opposite their names (today's screenwriters should be so fortunate). Lubitsch's director credit follows on the facing page, illustrated simply and teasingly without his face, with only a drawing of women's shoes. Then the lead actors, including finally Lubitsch, are introduced with their portraits, stylized combinations of photos and drawings like those of the writers. The credits even contain a commercial of sorts for the Berlin firm that supplied the shoes and boots used in the movie, with the addresses of its two outlets helpfully displayed. The frank commercialism of this opening display is amusing and refreshingly appropriate to the storyline about a brash young man making his way up in the ranks of the Berlin ladies' shoe trade.

Sally Pinkus is gifted with such unabashed self-confidence that he seems oblivious to any slights or insults he encounters along the way. Anyone trying to make a career in show business (let alone shoe business) needs that kind of cast-iron stomach and the ability Sally has to make his own way, overcoming opposition from family and school and withstanding rejection after rejection without losing his indomitable spirit. Sally's initial ineptitude as an apprentice gradually gives way to a more canny understanding of how to manipulate women's vanity into buying the merchandise: he changes a shoe size to flatter a woman into thinking her feet are smaller than they are. A shameless flirt, Sally charms that customer, a pretty dancer named Melitta Hervé (Else Kenter), into backing a store of his own. When no customers show up, he dons evening gear to attend her concert and takes over the spotlight to plug his upcoming fashion show. The film climaxes with three sustained long takes of a store ramp on which women models promenade for an appreciative audience in "Die Stiefelschau" (The Boot Show) under the direction of Sally Pinkus, now the essence of savoir faire and confidence. After taking bows, he is seen reading a review of the show while smoking a cigar and congratulating himself: "I think I've achieved success."

The parallels with Lubitsch's budding film career are, in retrospect, inescapable and delightful. From unpromising beginnings as a klutzy ne'er-do-well from a bourgeois family, interested only in pursuing any woman who happens to be around, Sally/Lubitsch promotes himself against all odds to become a successful entrepreneur who knows how to put on a convincing show. To crown this cinematic fairy tale with a humorously cynical touch, Sally proposes to split the profits of the shoe palace with Melitta by marrying her, and she happily agrees to the deal. Though a relatively embryonic piece of filmmaking, the brash and buoyant *Shoe Palace Pinkus* announces itself as the opening not only of a promising shoe store but also of a bright new film career.

Even while Lubitsch was becoming a movie star in the 1910s and beginning to establish himself as a director, his persistence in acting for Reinhardt in more modest stage roles is telling. In that time of economic privation, he probably needed all the work he could get. But sticking with that outwardly less rewarding theatrical apprenticeship, which lasted fully seven years, suggests that he was doing so with deliberation for the experience of honing his craft and learning from his mentor about directing. While Lubitsch scorned traditional German educational institutions, he was wise enough to recognize that the Deutsches Theater was his ideal school, his dramatic academy, his master class. As he developed gradually into a skillful director, Lubitsch was beginning to drift away from acting into a concentration on Reinhardt's profession.

Lubitsch probably could not help recognizing that his acting was incurably florid and broad, to judge from his film work and the testimony of his own actors, for whom he famously demonstrated each scene himself. Cameraman Charles Van Enger recalled that when Lubitsch made his 1920s silents in Hollywood, he went even further: "Lubitsch used to go in and direct and he'd act out the scenes the way he wanted the people to do it. So one time when I had the camera I turned the camera very slowly while he was rehearsing, then I would have them print it and the next day after the rushes I would run it for him. And he thought that was so funny and if I didn't do it, he'd raise hell. He'd say, 'Sharley, where's my scenes?' . . . It was no good. We used to throw it away after the rushes." Acting out scenes for the actors is not regarded as a tactful way to direct actors; it runs the risk of offending them. When I told John Ford that Chaplin and Lubitsch used to act out all the parts, he said, "I'd like to see them acting out. It must have been funny." But Lubitsch seemed to avoid causing offense. How that technique worked so well for him has been described by Peter Bogdanovich, with the help of Jack Benny, whose improbable casting in *To Be or Not to Be* brought him a triumph beyond the wildest imagination of anyone but his director. Bogdanovich reported, "Jack Benny told me that Lubitsch would act out in detail exactly how he wanted everything done. I asked how he was. 'Well,' Jack said, 'it was a little *broad*, but you got the *idea*.' The comedian explained that Lubitsch knew Benny would translate the direction into his own manner and that this would make it work." Bogdanovich added, "Everybody in a Lubitsch movie . . . performs in a certain unmistakable style. Despite their individual personalities—and Lubitsch never stifled these— they all are imbued with the director's private view of the world, which made them behave very differently from the way they did in other films."

"To be directed by Lubitsch is one ambition of every actor and actress," a Hollywood studio biography noted in his later years. "He has a reputation for understanding players. Yet he has never studied psychology." Lubitsch, who never tried to pass himself off as an intellectual, was quoted as saying, "If you make a study of psychology, you run the danger of becoming academic, pedantic, anything but entertaining. But to have been an actor, myself—the value of that to me as a director cannot be overestimated."

LUBITSCH AND JEWISH HUMOR

Most of Lubitsch's distinctive comic roles display a winning brashness and mischievousness. His initial awkwardness in *The Pride of the Firm* and *Shoe Palace Pinkus* is endearing, and he makes us root for his déclassé characters to succeed by overcoming their inadequacies in social and business interactions. His characters do so with aplomb, often with guile, sometimes with a shameless lack of scruples. They seem very human in their mixture of traits, positive and negative, strong and weak. The balance tilts toward off-putting (but not entirely unsympathetic) elements of weakness in his last major roles, such as the absurdly brazen would-be philanderer Sally Meyer in *Meyer from Berlin* and the pathologically jealous Yeggar, the hunchback, in the 1920 melodrama *Sumurun* (*One Arabian Night*), Lubitsch's most ambitious and most disturbing screen role. As an actor, Lubitsch does not hesitate to exchange sly glances with the audience or mug strenuously, making his face seem as

elastic as his often-childlike screen personality. Such broadness of performing in early silent films was not unusual since the medium then was more
balletic than naturalistic. You have to accept the broadness to enjoy the films
even while recognizing that Lubitsch's later fame as a director in his mature
work stemmed from quite a different skill, that of drawing subtle nuances
from his actors.

Lubitsch retrospectively explained why he initially gravitated to comedies
as an actor and director in the 1910s, saying, "The dramatic pictures of that
time were so silly, it was much more honest to make comedies." But as he
admitted, there were more deeply personal reasons, for his acting ambitions
had turned from drama to comedy by the time he was eight ("I like to
laugh"). Lubitsch quickly enough realized, if others did not make it suffi-
ciently clear to him, that his homely but lovable mug was not conducive to
stardom in the theater. His father reputedly tried to tell him that early on by
forcibly showing him his face in the large posing mirror in the family tailor
shop: "Look at you! And you want to go into the theater? I would not say
anything if you were a handsome guy! But with that face? You come into my
business. With me you can make money with this lousy face." Such a paren-
tal insult, along with other discouragement that Ernst said he received from
his father, did not deter him but seemed to goad him to succeed. Ernst was
five feet five, somewhat bowlegged, and squat, but his large, warm, expressive facial features—including a mouth that broke easily into a wide dis-
arming grin and, along with his piercing yet sympathetic eyes, gave him a
characteristically mischievous look—proved perfectly suited for comic acting on-screen if not for conventional leading-man roles.

It must be noted that not everyone has found Lubitsch physically appealing. Although matters of taste in such matters are always subjective and
sometimes unfathomably personal, some of the harshly negative comments
on his appearance reveal as much or more about those making the comments as they do about Lubitsch himself. Some of the comments could even
be taken as having anti-Semitic overtones.

Journalist and historian Curt Riess, though an exile from Nazism and an
opponent of the regime, described him retrospectively in 1956: "There is this
short, stout young man burdened with an almost dreadful ugliness. A typical Berliner. With a mouth that is much too big, he is never at a loss for words.
He cracks jokes about everything. Only few people will ever understand that

he only jokes because he is afraid to be hurt. . . . Only his sad dark eyes show what really goes on in his soul." Géza von Cziffra, in a 1987 German book, referred to Lubitsch as "the man with the big nose" and claimed of his relationship with leading man Harry Liedtke, "Ugly Ernst envied handsome Harry for his looks and felt pity for him because of his lack of talent." American observers, on the other hand, were more likely to find Lubitsch physically appealing and eccentrically charming. As do I; his warm smile, friendly eyes, and look of wry intelligence always make me merry. *Photoplay*'s Herbert Howe described Lubitsch in 1922 as "a Napoleonic little gnome, a Dutch comedian [Germans then were sometimes referred to in the United States as Dutch, a corruption of *Deutsch*] who can make the whole world weep, a little man with a big smiling heart. If he isn't a genius he's what a genius ought to be." Paramount in 1938 called Lubitsch simply "the little man with the big cigar." *Los Angeles Times* film reviewer Philip K. Scheuer referred to "his small but kinetic person." When Mervyn LeRoy presented Lubitsch with his honorary Oscar, he described the arrival from Germany of "a dark stranger with a rather stern face, a big black cigar and the merriest pair of eyes under the sun."

Lubitsch's commanding presence made him look more distinguished as he matured. He struck many people as Napoleonic, a little man with a large personality, and he mischievously displays images of Napoleon in *Design for Living* and *The Merry Widow* in ways that make you feel as if the director recognizes his joshing kinship with the diminutive general who became an emperor. Cecil B. DeMille even offered Lubitsch a chance to play Napoleon in his 1938 film *The Buccaneer*, and though Lubitsch was intrigued, he passed on the offer.

Lubitsch tended to treat his physical appearance and personality with a certain defensiveness, only partly laced with humor. He wrote in 1938,

For 20 years I have worked in Hollywood, so by now I should be accustomed to it. Yet I am continually amazed by the film colony's habit of endowing its members with strange personalities, unusual traits and all manner of idiosyncrasies. I have read of myself as a "mad genius." My wife will tell you that I come home at about the same hour each evening, eat dinner, play with the dog and listen to the radio. Although I exercise daily and am little if any overweight, I am often described in print as "roly poly." Much even has been made of the fact that I smoke cigars. As I look back through the forty-odd years of my life, it is difficult to realize I possess all the weird characteristics that have been attributed to me. Maybe I do not possess them at all!

But, as was previously noted, during the Nazi era, Lubitsch was held up by the Third Reich as an example of a Jewish image to despise in public hate posters as well as on-screen in *The Eternal Jew*. In a German book published in 1935, the year the Nazis put in force the Nuremberg Laws severely restricting Jewish life, Oskar Kalbus wrote of Lubitsch, "Today it seems incomprehensible that movie audiences, during the hard war years, cheered an actor who always played with a brashness so alien to us." This last comment reveals how public opinion (at least as seen by that pro-Nazi author) could have been so influenced by ideology in changing perceptions of a screen actor's appearance from haimish to anathema.

Lubitsch happily displayed himself on both stage and screen for more than a decade before moving decisively behind the camera. That eventual decision may have had more to do with a realistic assessment of his relative talents in those areas than with the negativity of some people's views, but it is impossible to assess now the depth of his private feelings toward his appearance. Comic actors often have complex views of their own images, and the roots of their humor often stem from early experiences of feeling ungainly, so it would be surprising if Lubitsch did not have such qualms and if that was not part of why he gravitated to comedy even as a child. It is a truism that many actors enter the profession because of discontent over who they are. But in Lubitsch's case, the fact that he sometimes plays himself in his German films, or at least plays a character called "Herr Ernst Lubitsch," suggests a certain level of comfort and enjoyment and even exhibitionism with his own image. His easy, sly smile and his hearty, boisterous screen persona in most of his acting appearances are hardly signs of a man who finds himself unpleasant to view in the mirror. Whether or not some people have considered him physically appealing or a first-rate comedian, Lubitsch generally presents a delightful image on-screen, cocky but kindly and inviting. His last confirmed acting role is an exception, that of the hunchbacked clown who is pathetically enamored of Pola Negri's dancer in his own film *Sumurun*. Although one should not read too much into a single acting role out of the many he played, that alarmingly overwrought turn into heavy melo-drama could be seen as an expression of a self-loathing that is usually sup-pressed in his comical parts.

Lubitsch began to phase out his acting career as his films became longer and more ambitious and as he began working with actors better than himself, projecting himself through them instead of through his own imperfect acting talents and physique. His penchant for acting out all the parts in his films, which became the subject of much discussion and amusement, was a symptom of this unusual degree of transference. A studio biography noted, "A small man with an incredibly mobile face, he unconsciously registers every expres-sion of his players as they play a scene. Visitors to one of his sets are more apt to watch Lubitsch than the stars of his picture." His own screen appearances after *Sumurun* were fleeting. He reportedly made a cameo appearance in the 1933 independent film *Mr. Broadway*, dancing at the Central Park Casino in a tour of New York nightspots conducted by entertainment columnist Ed Sullivan, but that film is missing. Lubitsch cannot be spotted in the surviv-ing versions of two other offbeat films he was rumored to have appeared in: Rupert Hughes's 1923 comedy-melodrama about Hollywood, *Souls for Sale*, which shows Charles Chaplin and Erich von Stroheim (among others) directing films, and in the 1945 Gregory Ratoff time-traveling comedy *Where Do We Go from Here?* for which Lubitsch was seen in a publicity photograph as one of Christopher Columbus's sailors. But Lubitsch continued to appear in some of the trailers for his Hollywood films, celebrating himself as a vir-tual household name among directors, as Hitchcock later would do with such success. Lubitsch makes a particularly charming appearance in the trailer for his 1940 film *The Shop Around the Corner*, briefly bantering with actor Frank Morgan on the set.

Lubitsch never entirely lost his fondness for acting. As late as 1943, it was announced that he was interested in playing a major role under the direc-tion of Elia Kazan in a Twentieth Century-Fox adaptation of the Franz Werfel/S. N. Behrman play *Jacobowsky und der Oberst* (*Jacobowsky and the Colonel*). Kazan, who was about to launch his film career at the studio, directed the play successfully in New York in 1944. This seriocomic allegory of World War II is set in occupied France in June 1940 and deals with the escape to England of a haughty, obtuse Polish officer and his Sancho Panza–like partner, a middle-aged Polish Jewish refugee named S. L. Jacobowsky who has been spending "all my life in a futile effort to become a citizen of some country." Jacobowsky's resourcefulness and courage in enabling them to escape and rally support from the British ultimately win him the friendship of the previously anti-Semitic aristocrat. Jacobowsky would have been a marvelous role for Lubitsch and a worthy companion piece to *To Be or Not to Be*. The play says of Jacobowsky, "His cheerfulness is an emanation from a harried past; he knows that the worst will probably happen, so that your only chance is to improvise the immediate present. This he is constantly trying to do in every small relation of life. He likes people and he wants them, if it is at all possible, to like him." The *Hollywood Reporter* disclosed, "Lubitsch, according to his own statement, is anxious to do this one movie role . . . and feels the part of the Polish scapegoat is worth donning grease paint for again." But those plans unfortunately fell through when Columbia outbid Fox for the rights to the play; the film was finally made in 1958 as *Me and the Colonel* with Danny Kaye playing Jacobowsky.

Nevertheless, from the time of *Meyer from Berlin* onward, Lubitsch seems to have harbored serious doubts about his acting ability and recognized that his future potential lay elsewhere. Although he concentrated on directing after *Sumurun*, Lubitsch admitted with regret, "If my acting career had run smoother, I might never have become a director." That would have been our loss!

But are Lubitsch's early comic film portrayals at least to some degree anti-Semitic? That debate has continued inconclusively, with some film historians arguing that they deserve such criticism, others denying it, and some (such as the usually incisive Sabine Hake) sidestepping a clear judgment on this important issue. The *Cahiers du Cinéma* critic Jean-Louis Comolli went so far as to write in 1968, "One could say without exaggeration that *The Pride of the Firm* (and without doubt the entire series [of Lubitsch's early comedies about Jewish characters]) is the most anti-Semitic body of work ever to be produced, if . . . Ernst Lubitsch had not been Jewish himself." Comolli's absolution of Lubitsch seems oblivious to the existence of Jewish anti-Semitism, and more to the point, his judgment on these early comedies seems absurdly exaggerated. Lubitsch himself, in his earliest known interview, told Julius Urgifi of *The Cinematograph* in 1916 that he considered it a "quite incredible position" for people to take offense at his brand of Jewish humor, a comment he no doubt would have repeated if he had lived to read Comolli's intemperate attack. Lubitsch added in that interview, "Jewish humor is, where it may appear, sympathetic and artistic." Nevertheless, despite the predominance of human sympathy he evokes for the characters he plays, there can be no denying that Lubitsch's portrayals of brash apprentices and businessmen, sometimes shady and always relentless social climbers, draw in part from troubling Jewish stereotypes of the time.

These characters, usually given clearly Jewish names such as Sally or Solly or Siegmund or Max, sometimes use Yiddish words in the dialogue contained in intertitles. They behave with the exaggerated leering and gloating mannerisms that are often associated with that period's Jewish stereotypes. Their makeup and costuming draw from the same tradition. The characters Lubitsch plays, and some of the other Jewish characters in those early films, are inveterate lechers, another stereotype promoted by anti-Semites. Lubitsch's flirting mannerisms with women on-screen lack any subtlety. They include thrusting his tongue, licking his fingers, and tickling women whether he knows them or not. In *Shoe Palace Pinkus*, after his schoolboy character flirts with the family maid and departs for school, his father engages in the same kind of behavior, and his first boss, Herr Meirsohn, is also a lecher.

So it is not a question of coded Jewish characterizations in his early German films but rather an overt exploitation of European theatrical and cultural tendencies to treat Jews as "amusing" stereotypes. Or, for some viewers, then as well as now, not so amusing, with reactions that vary from embarrassment to hostility. The comments on Lubitsch's physiognomy by some German authors quoted above (even after the war) indicate what seems to be a shocking degree of naked revulsion in some quarters toward Lubitsch as a person, let alone as an actor. But for Lubitsch himself, playing with such stereotypes was a matter of fun, as it undoubtedly was for some fellow Jews in his German audience as well as for many Gentiles.

Although Lubitsch as a screen actor is mostly known today (as much as he is known at all as an actor) for playing Jewish shop boys, the other film roles he played during that period were also comedic. When playing a husband with a straying eye in *Als ich Tot War* (*When I Was Dead*, 1916, the earliest surviving film he directed), Lubitsch pretends he is committing suicide to escape his wife's clutches, then he jealously masquerades as her servant. Lubitsch dons a grotesque wig and sideburns that fool the wife but not the audience (spectators were more tolerant of such silly contrivances in those early days of film comedy). Oddly, Lubitsch much later misremembered why this film was a flop: "Like every comedian, I longed to play a straight leading man, a sort of 'bon vivant' role. . . . This picture was a complete failure as the audiences were unwilling to accept me as a straight leading man." In fact, it may have been the title rather than the performance that misled audiences in 1916. *When I Was Dead* is obviously a comedy through and through and is even billed as such in the opening credits (a "*Lustspiel in 3 Akten*," or a "Comedy in 3 Acts"). Perhaps Lubitsch's memory deceived him because of his relatively subdued playing in the early scenes before he turns to his usual brand of physical farce or because it is an early stab at what would later be called black comedy (Lubitsch would incur further enmity by exploring that edgy mode of storytelling with the far more momentous subject matter of *To Be or Not to Be*).

The range of Lubitsch's silent roles is also indicated by his venturing into the field of comic aristocracy, which would eventually become one of his favorite milieus, by playing the boorish title character in his *Prinz Sami* (*Prince Sami*, 1918) soon after playing Satan in a fairy tale called *Hans Trutz in Schlaraffenland* (*Hans Defiance in Never-Never Land*, 1917). That extravagantly stylized film was directed by fellow Reinhardt actor Paul Wegener, who plays Hans, a farmer who sells his soul to the Devil. The ironic twist is that Hans finds his land of plenty dreadfully tedious and wants to go home. Lubitsch's antic, capering, wild-eyed Devil wears goatish horns and is festooned with grotesque patches of hair on his bare torso. This film seems more a curiosity, a clumsy experiment, than a sustained work of cinematic fantasy. More strikingly, Lubitsch offered a contemporary version of Satan in the title role of *Doktor Satansohn* (*Doctor Satansohn*), a strange 1916 comedy-fantasy in which he appears with graying hair and a wickedly pointed goatee as the suave, mocking head of a health clinic catering to insecure women who want to become younger through magical means.

Doctor Satansohn can be seen as a subversive parody of the obsessive body-culture movement in Germany, which would become a key component of Nazi ideology within a few years. But the storyline of this film, written and directed by Edmond Edel, is less compelling and coherent than Lubitsch's relish in playing his fancily dressed version of the Devil in modern guise. He was discovering the joys of subtlety in acting, as he was with directing in the following year's *When Four Do the Same* in which he gives himself a secondary part. But any Jewish actor appearing in films in Germany during those years and playing a character with major flaws might find himself dubiously accused by some people of anti-Semitism or "Jewish self-hatred." While it is true that most acting roles would tend to lack interest if the characters had no flaws, playing Satan was pushing the envelope. But Lubitsch's suave Dr. Satansohn bears a close resemblance to Laird Cregar's memorable incarnation of Satan in Lubitsch's late masterpiece *Heaven Can Wait*, a sympathetic performance that delights nearly everyone who sees it. Yet seeing Jewish stereotypes in Lubitsch's acting repertoire linked not only to bumptious young men on the make but also to the Devil incarnate, however engagingly in *Doctor Satansohn*, adds fuel to the ideological fire. Perhaps if so many of Lubitsch's early films were not missing, we might have a more balanced palette of roles to analyze with more nuanced conclusions.

THE "ONE-TIME SHOP ASSISTANT"

But let us confront the question squarely: Is Lubitsch culpable for playing stereotypical Jewish characters, however amusing and empathetic they are on some levels? Should he be criticized today for pandering to public tastes among both Gentile and Jewish audiences in a time when anti-Semitism, while not yet as virulent as it would be in the Hitler era, was strong enough in Germany and environs to be recognized as a long-standing blight on European culture? Sabine Hake claims in her 1992 book *Passions and Deceptions: The Early Films of Ernst Lubitsch* that Lubitsch's early comedies also display an anti-Polish bias because some of his characters are portrayed as country bumpkins from Poland or elsewhere who make their way to the more cosmopolitan environs of Berlin. But perhaps that familiar strain of humor, common to many cultures, is more a reflection of Lubitsch's strongly urban nature and his family's rupture from their more rustic homeland in Russia. It stems from the ancient comedy tradition of mocking rubes from the sticks. Although Lubitsch remained religious enough to pray silently while working, he and his family, both early and later, were not known as observant Jews. Their Jewishness was cultural, reflecting the family's Russian background and their resettling in a predominantly Jewish neighborhood of Berlin, more than a matter of strict religious devotion.

Nevertheless, that an acute awareness of class distinctions, from extreme to subtle, would emerge in Lubitsch's film work and eventually serve as one of its finest, most complex attributes reflects his status in Germany. He was a Russian citizen and a Jew living in Germany, trying to assimilate, but recognizing that he could never fully do so in his native land, before he becoming a Jewish exile in the United States in 1922 and an American citizen in 1936. Walther Rathenau, a prominent German Jewish industrialist and patron of the arts who served as foreign minister during the Weimar Republic, observed, "In the youth of every German Jew there comes a moment which he remembers with pain as long as he lives; when he becomes for the first time fully conscious of the fact that he has entered the world as a second-class citizen, and that no amount of ability or merit can free him of this status."

As Eastern Jews (*Ostjuden*), the Lubitsches were strongly identified culturally as Jews, and as such were seen with disfavor by some German Jews (*Westjuden*), such as the prominent film historian Lotte H. Eisner. Eisner fled to France in 1933 and, after being interned by the Germans during the war, settled permanently in the French capital. Even long after the Holocaust, Eisner remarked harshly on Lubitsch's screen persona and the themes of his early films. Following a Lubitsch retrospective at the Berlin International Film Festival in 1967, she described *The Pride of the Firm* and *Shoe Palace Pinkus* as "too Jewish-slapstick" to Herman Weinberg for his book *The Lubitsch Touch*. She did add some grudging praise for two of his German films that do not feature explicitly Jewish characters. *The Oyster Princess*, she admitted, was "better than I thought it would be," and of *Kohlhiesel's Daughters*, she wrote, "This one I liked very much." But Eisner's comment on his avant-garde feature *The Doll* was inexplicable: "Just ordinary." (Eisner's attitude toward *Kohlhiesel's Daughters* had evolved. She had earlier referred to its "vulgarity" and wrote that it and *Romeo and Juliet in the Snow* "make non-German spectators feel violently indisposed.")

Ironically, though Lubitsch is now hailed by many film historians for his consummate elegance, his reputation suffered to an extent from Eisner's vitriolic attacks on his supposed "'Central European' vulgarity." Like many German Jews of her day, she placed a high premium on cultural prestige and assimilation and tended to feel superior to Ostjuden. That attitude also carried over with some German Jews in the United States after Jewish migration there increased. Jacob Rader Marcus, known as the dean of American Jewish historiography, told me in a 1994 interview for my biography of Steven Spielberg that German Jewish immigrants in the United States often "held Eastern Europeans in utter contempt. The German Jews were predominant socially, culturally, and financially. . . . The lines were drawn very sharply until about 1950." As Gerd Gemünden notes in *Continental Strangers: German Exile Cinema 1933–1951*, Eisner's review of Lubitsch's early comedies as "too Jewish-slapstick" is "a verdict that attests not only to the completely different cultural sensibilities between 'Ostjuden' and 'Westjuden' like herself but also carries overtones of feeling threatened that one's own successful assimilation to German bourgeois culture may be undone by the influx of Jewish immigrants from the East."

Long before issuing her 1967 ukases against Lubitsch, Eisner had written about him in language of unadorned class and cultural condescension in her influential 1952 book *The Haunted Screen: Expressionism in the German Cinema and the Influence of Max Reinhardt*, which refers to him as "Lubitsch, one-time shop assistant." Billy Wilder puts the paradox of Lubitsch's humble beginnings in more sympathetic terms: "He had this very sophisticated French humor, but he, himself, was the son of a Russian tailor." The scorn of a major German film historian is revealing of the barriers of social class and culture that Lubitsch had to climb. This is one reason, perhaps, that he felt he had to leave Germany to rebuild his life in the more culturally open climate of California. Eisner refers to the director as "A typical Berliner, who began his career in the cinema with rather coarse farces." Eisner defines "typical" partly by referencing "the Jewish lower middle-class engaged in the ready-made-clothing trade" (unabashedly rubbing Lubitsch's face in the profession of his Russian immigrant father) who "came in with that sense of comic fatalism peculiar to people used to enduring pogroms and persecutions."

Although noting that Lubitsch "was for a long time a member of Max Reinhardt's troupe," Eisner considers Lubitsch "less sensitive to his influence than other German filmmakers" since she denigrates his Reinhardt-influenced spectacles such as *Madame DuBarry*, *Sumurun*, and *Anna Boleyn*. Among the shortcomings she finds in those films are their "escapism," their mise-en-scène that "debases" the Reinhardt stylistic grandeur with "arid regularity behind the groupings," and their preoccupation with sex. Eisner declares that in Lubitsch's attitude toward historical subject matter, he "turned into the proverbial valet for whom no man is a hero." While conceding that this commonness "does give a breath of humanity to his characters," she writes,

> This is why the Americans, who are not given to respecting historical truth (especially other people's), could think that Lubitsch was "the great humanizer of history," and call him the "German Griffith" who with "a realism in no wise fictitious reconstitutes history in all its barbaric grandeur." But a king manicuring his mistress or artlessly pinching a pretty wench is hardly Unadorned Reality, and even less History As It Was Lived. For Lubitsch, one-time shop assistant, History was never to be more than a pretext for telling love stories in sumptuous period costume: silks, velvets, and trimmings delighted his knowing eye.

Eisner goes on to describe the American films of the "one-time shop assistant" with backhanded praise: "Subsequently, in the United States, Lubitsch was to become more refined and to understand that it was time for him to rid himself of a certain 'Central European' vulgarity. He radically modified the frequently oafish effects in his middle-class comedies, hastily adopting an elegant gracefulness in which there always remained a little of the vainglory of the *nouveau-riche*." Even such demanding American literary and political critics as Edmund Wilson (an admirer of *Lady Windermere's Fan* and Lubitsch's "great knack of shooting commonplace incidents from inobvious and revelatory angles") and Dwight Macdonald (who wrote, "*Trouble in Paradise* almost makes one believe in Hollywood again") found Lubitsch's work in Hollywood far more sophisticated than the general run of popular films, which they tended to view with disdain. American film reviewers generally praised Lubitsch highly. But their high regard for his taste and intelligence was not universally shared in his time. Eisner was far from alone among highbrow film historians in both Germany and the United States for expressing contempt toward Lubitsch for his frankness in both his comedies—tellingly misdescribed as "middle-class"—and his historical spectacles in dealing with a subject usually treated with juvenile squeamishness in movies before and after his reign—carnal knowledge.

The puritanical attitude expressed by Eisner and others helped diminish Lubitsch's critical reputation in some circles even while other critics had no trouble appreciating his work. A related flaw in the most belittling attacks on Lubitsch, even today, is a lack of a sense of humor among certain critics and film historians toward films that commit the sin of viewing social issues satirically. Lubitsch's detractors often insult him with something worse than outright contempt—indifference. In some cases, these disparaging attitudes clearly reflect class condescension and an aversion toward popular cinema.

Eisner's disdain for Lubitsch's Jewish humor in his early work in Germany is symptomatic of the unfortunate tendency even among some other liberal German Jewish intellectuals of that time to view Ostjuden as not as worthy of being a fully accepted part of the German nation. When Lubitsch drew from Jewish humor in his early films, with all their nakedly autobiographical overtones, that was probably as much a matter of drawing from the prevailing social climate and acknowledging his status within that culture as it was a reflection of a personal religious or ethnic obsession. An immersion in such a culture could not help having a profound effect on even a relatively assimilated member of Berlin's Jewish minority. Lubitsch's flaunting of his Jewishness in those early films may have been partly a sign of defensive self-mockery, a not infrequent method of self-protection among comedians from minority groups, but it was also a form of ostentatious identification with his outsider status while another part of him was attracted to the majority and yearned to be accepted by it.

Hake offers a commentary on the context in which these comedies appeared. What she writes is thoughtful until she equivocates when it comes to offering any decisive critical judgment:

> Forced to leave behind the old communities, Eastern Jews were confronted with the task of surviving in a non-Jewish world while at the same time maintaining their cultural identity. Lubitsch's store comedies restage this experience of the newly arrived immigrant in the urban spaces of Berlin. Similarly, Sally Pinkus and his accomplices combine character traits of the *shmendrik*, a stupid but shrewd young man, with the aggressive clumsiness of the *schlemihl*, who makes up for his social disadvantages through his knowledge of human foibles and the art of persuasion.

The presence of Jewish humor in the early comedies is closely linked to the awareness of difference. On the level of performance as well as in the choice of roles Lubitsch creates a distance and provides a framework that makes possible the expression of painful experiences. Humor provides a protective shield against social discrimination and a vehicle for dealing with ambivalent feelings about one's social, sexual, and ethnic identity. It allows for the recognition of sorrow and suggests its overcoming through the liberating power of laughter. Thus humor becomes a weapon in breaking down boundaries; it turns the recognition of otherness into a shared experience, rather than a reason for separation and isolation. Nonetheless, Lubitsch's references to Jewish culture remain problematic. . . . By playing with stereotypes, Lubitsch made them available to critical analysis. But by using them, his humor also stayed within the logic of such distinctions.

Enno Patalas, the prominent German Lubitsch scholar, countered Eisner's snobbish attack on Lubitsch more forcefully:

"Too Jewish-slapstick" was film historian Lotte Eisner's verdict on the early Lubitsch. She was herself a Berlin Jew, but from the genteel Tiergarten quarter where they used to call the "rag-trade Jews" of the Scheunen quarter Mäntelmen (coat-men)—to distinguish them from "gentlemen." Simcha Lubitsch, Ernst's father, was a typical Mäntelman. He had supposedly been a tailor for the Tsar's army, before running a workshop for ladies' garments in Berlin.
"Too Jewish" and "too slapstick."
"Too Jewish." Lubitsch was not ashamed of being Jewish—quite the contrary. In a 1916 interview [with Julius Urgifi]—the earliest that survives—he says that "Wherever Jewish humor is seen, it is likable and well-crafted, and it plays such a major role everywhere that it would be absurd to dispense with it in the cinema." Jewish culture is the only culture with a feeling for comedy at its very heart. Jewish humor cuts the ground from beneath the earnestness of life—a way of asserting oneself in a hostile world.

Lubitsch's characters' paths to success in his early populist/small businessman comedies, his store comedies, result from a combination of cleverness, guile, fawning over social superiors, seductiveness (including the shameless use of women), and boundless energy and optimism. Some, but not all, of these traits can be seen as admirable. The drive of these Lubitsch characters to rise from low social circumstances to social prominence and respectability, though always within the limits of German bourgeois society and the world of small business, is a sign that he and his films regard his Sally, Solly, or Max mostly with affection and admiration, despite their imperfections, and that we are invited to enjoy them that way as well. Such affection alone would tend to counter, at least to some degree, a sense of anti-Semitism in viewing the characters. Lubitsch's inherent tendency, displayed throughout his long body of work, to mock his characters' flaws, even as he largely admires the characters themselves, plays out in the silent comedies not so much as a way of disparaging his Jewish figures as it is a sign of their common humanity, an insistence on audience identification with them. That complex blend of affection and mockery permeates Lubitsch's portrayals of virtually all his characters of any ethnic backgrounds, a further indication of his lack of ethnic bias or self-hatred.

In my view, a sense of affection in presenting ethnic characterizations in comedy or drama can outweigh the potentially troubling aspects to such characters. Although ethnic humor may not be fashionable today, I believe it can be a sign of fellow feeling, a way of breaking down social barriers. Surely Lubitsch saw his Jewish characters mostly in that light, from Siegmund Lachmann to Sally Pinkus to his alter ego Felix Bressart's Comrade Buljanoff in *Ninotchka*, Pirovitch in *The Shop Around the Corner*, and Greenberg in *To Be or Not to Be*.

Even the one Jewish character Lubitsch plays on-screen who seems undeniably obnoxious rather than endearing, Sally Meyer in *Meyer from Berlin*, is treated as somewhat amusing but more an object of the film's mockery than someone to be identified with or admired. Meyer is a city dweller who feigns illness so he can try to cheat on his wife by going to the mountains on vacation. His ridiculous mountain-climbing gear makes him a laughingstock both on the street in Berlin and at the resort, and his brash, clumsy attempts to seduce women are so extreme that they are treated simply as jokes by the women involved. Ultimately, even his remarkably tolerant wife seems to laugh it all off but in a tellingly rushed, unconvincing conclusion. While Sally Meyer is funny in a very broad sense, he is something of a dismaying character as well. Unlike the Jewish characters played by Lubitsch in the earlier films, he is not so much a go-getter with understandably tenacious social-climbing traits as he is a self-centered lecher who does not realize how ridiculously ill-behaved and out of place he seems to almost everyone else in the world of the film, whether in the city or the country. Lubitsch no doubt meant Sally Meyer to be seen in farcical terms as a bumptious comical idiot, someone refreshingly oblivious to social niceties or the limitations of class structures. But films change with the perspective of time, and *Meyer from Berlin* provokes an especially complicated response by modern audiences to this more pointed satire of a Jewish character and the appalled responses he receives on-screen from German society at large.

Our view of these early Lubitsch films, even the ones featuring far more benign Jewish characters than Sally Meyer, is colored by our awareness of the anti-Semitism that marred German society during the period when Lubitsch was making films in that country (1914–1922) and even more so by our awareness, in retrospect, of Germany's catastrophic turn to murderous anti-Semitism. Lubitsch had been in America for more than ten years when Hitler began ruling Germany in 1933. The filmmaker watched, appalled from a distance, as the Nazis gradually instigated "legal" anti-Jewish measures, concentration camps, pogroms and other physical persecution, and finally the killing squads and death camps, all the apparatus of the Holocaust, which killed six million Jews and four million members of other groups treated as *Untermenschen* (subhuman) by the Nazi regime. Lubitsch's response in 1941–1942, as America entered the war, was to use the weapons of art—in his devastatingly original (and controversial) black comedy *To Be or Not to Be*—and propaganda—in *Know Your Enemy: Germany*, which he directed in October 1942 at Twentieth Century-Fox for Frank Capra's U.S. Army unit. Written by Bruno Frank, that film was a dramatized account of the rise of German militarism through several generations as personified by a symbolic German named Karl Schmidt. It was scrapped and reshot, with only vestiges of that thematic approach remaining in the 1945 release *Here Is Germany*, a more conventional *Why We Fight*-style documentary compilation on modern German history that was supervised by Gottfried Reinhardt (Max's son). The younger Reinhardt attributed the "endless" delays in making the film to "friction" within the War Department on the subject of postwar policy toward Germany.

After all the calamitous history involving the land of Lubitsch's birth, it is admittedly hard to look back on the more naïve period of the 1910s, when he was entertaining German audiences with comical Jewish stereotypes, and to view them and their reception as entirely innocent. The very popularity of those portrayals with a mass German audience can be seen as problematic from that point of view. But to blame Lubitsch for "the most anti-Semitic body of work ever to be produced," thereby suggesting that he inadvertently helped pave the way for the Holocaust, seems extreme and unfair, even ridiculous. It's hard to condemn a working actor and director who was a member of a small minority group for, in effect, being himself on-screen or playing roles that drew from himself, however exaggerated comedically, as if he were supposed to be someone else entirely. To some degree, a viewer's reaction to these films today is like a Rorschach test of his or her view of some of the cultural meanings that have accrued around the concept of "Jewishness." At worst, perhaps, Lubitsch could be seen as pandering irresponsibly to popular prejudice during a volatile political and cultural period.

Excusing indulgence in comedy of ethnic stereotypes cannot be based simply on whether it was the norm or popular. Questions of creativity and enduring value come into play as well as questions of basic morality. The cultural impact of Lubitsch's early films is a more complex issue than it has usually been regarded as being. When I raised this question with Anton Kaes, the eminent film historian and expert on the Weimar Republic, he defended Lubitsch's early comic roles by comparing them to the mockery of racism by a modern African American comedian such as Chris Rock. Such comedians, as many commentators have observed, help ventilate the noxious aspects of stereotyping and though their mockery help to partially dispel it. Classic ethnic comedians such as Lenny Bruce and Richard Pryor, Redd Foxx and Dick Gregory, Mort Sahl and Mel Brooks, although controversial in their own times for challenging conventional boundaries of comedy, have helped to liberate society from backward assumptions and clear the air of taboos for more enlightened discussions of race and ethnicity.

Lubitsch's comedic Jewish characters could be seen as serving similar functions as the portrayals of later comedians: he exposed the ridiculousness of social stereotyping in a society that still was rigidly hierarchical. His films demonstrate comedically that such Jewish characters, however limited by their social roles, could rise above them to a measure of success, overcoming social barriers and the rigid class structure of their time. It is undoubtedly a complex and unsettling picture that Lubitsch gives us in films such as *The Pride of the Firm* and *Shoe Palace Pinkus*, as well as in *Meyer from Berlin*, but it is a vivid reflection of and commentary on those times before Nazism took over Germany and destroyed any last vestiges of social acceptance for Jews in Lubitsch's native country.

In any case, Lubitsch gradually abandoned the kind of broadly sketched ethnic humor he mined in his early work. After he became more ambitious as a director and outgrew his farcical originals on-screen, he turned to other kinds of comedy, often highly sophisticated and stylized. One result is that his image changed from simply a Jewish comic to a more versatile filmmaker who worked in three or four distinct genres that sometimes blended and overlapped. The overtly Jewish characters tended to disappear from his work after *Meyer from Berlin*, one of his last film acting roles and not coincidentally one of his most grating (his Arabian hunchback in *Sumurun*, his swan song as an actor, is the most extreme of his extant film roles). Perhaps Lubitsch's abandonment of acting also reflected a growing awareness as times changed of the need to broaden his public image and appeal. "Jewish" humor was more subtly interwoven into Lubitsch's subsequent work as a director and came to the surface most memorably in the tragicomic portrayal by Felix Bressart (a Jewish refugee from Nazi Germany and Austria) of Greenberg, the Jewish actor who courageously confronts "Hitler" and the Nazis in *To Be or Not to Be*. Ironically, he does so by passionately reciting a famous speech by Shylock from Shakespeare's *The Merchant of Venice*, a profoundly *anti-anti-Semitic* work that has been falsely accused of being the opposite.

Joel Rosenberg's brilliantly perceptive 1996 essay on *To Be or Not to Be* notes that despite the virtual absence of explicitly Jewish characters in Lubitsch's films between the early silents and his 1942 black comedy about Nazism, there are what could be called "implicit" Jewish characters in some of the intervening films: "They are there, I think, in metaphorical or implicit ways—as faces, as guides or messengers between social realms, as marginal or subversive presences in the plot, even as the Yiddishizing lilt in a turn of phrase uttered by an otherwise impeccably gentile character. I find the Arabian hunchback in *Sumurun* . . . to be one such implicit Jew."

In that melodrama set in ninth century Baghdad, Lubitsch pays tribute to Reinhardt's stage production and even recycles some of its costumes and sets. When Reinhardt had filmed *Sumurun* in 1910, Lubitsch's acting teacher, Victor Arnold, played the hunchback; Hanisch attributes Lubitsch's frustrated career as an actor partly to his awareness that he could never live up to Arnold's example, try as he might, and he tries awfully hard in *Sumurun*. Lubitsch's film performance as the suicidal clown, opposite Negri as a femme fatale and Jenny Hasselqvist as Sumurun (an Arab sheik's favorite harem girl), is wildly overacted, embarrassingly maudlin and self-pitying, and vindictive to a degree that seems almost parodistic. There is some evidence that his excess may have been partly tongue-in-cheek: Yeggar's prolonged rescue from a suicide attempt becomes a slapstick routine, and the many absurd gags about eunuchs and harem girls are increasingly dominant as the film progresses.

The penchant for the grotesque that usually served Lubitsch well as a comic actor, though in some ways problematic from today's perspective, makes his major attempt at "serious" acting in *Sumurun* appear masochistic, the acting-out of a disturbing psychodrama of what may be self-perceived or subconscious feelings of unattractiveness. Or perhaps, as well, of seeing himself as a symbol of archetypal victimhood. Similarly, Jewish American comedian Jerry Lewis's contorted comic mugging is mingled with touches of often-unnerving bathos and even prolonged ventures into seriocomic roles, such as in his uncompleted Holocaust film *The Day the Clown Cried*, which could serve as an alternate title for *Sumurun*. Perhaps the nature of Lubitsch's most ambitious acting role on-screen is related to his well-documented unhappiness in his own love life, as Scott Eyman discusses in his biography *Ernst Lubitsch: Laughter in Paradise* (1993). The irony was even addressed in a Hollywood studio publicity biography: "Especially famous for his direction of women, how does he explain his knowledge of the female of the species? 'After two unsuccessful marriages,' he says with a wry smile, 'that is an embarrassing thing to ask. . . . I like to direct women, yes. Women are important parts of human life. If you want to portray human life, you have to be able to direct women. Otherwise, there will be no human life in your picture.'" Lubitsch's friends thought he tended to choose women who were wrong for him partly because he went after women he perceived as more refined than they actually were. Such a sadly ironic situation, considering how romantic his films are, could be related to Lubitsch's submerging himself so deeply in the role of a wretched clown who is devoted to a woman who despises him and only shows him pity when he tries to kill himself, as his mentor Arnold had succeeded in doing in real life.

In contrast to that strange filmic blending of comic-opera melodrama, the bumptious exuberance of Lubitsch's early, more purely comical Jewish roles seems a positively rebellious form of self-assertion. That more optimistic attitude is generally characteristic of Lubitsch's screen performances, with his tragic clown a glaring exception, even if it may have been a last gasp of self-revelation. It is noteworthy that the often-giddy buoyancy of Lubitsch's early performances in specifically Jewish roles helped account for German audiences' embrace of his characters in the pre-Hitler period, when he won them over as a lovable social climber who prevails in the end through sheer chutzpah and persistence.

2.1 The most popular of Lubitsch's German historical spectacles: Pola Negri at the guillotine as the title character of the French Revolution story *Madame DuBarry* (1919), retitled *Passion* in the United States. *(Projektions–AG Union [PAGU]/Associated First National Pictures/Photofest.)*

2

"WHO IS ERNST LUBITSCH?"

By the time he departed Germany in December 1922, audiences at home might have been hard pressed to give a simple answer to the question "Who is Ernst Lubitsch?" He had rapidly established himself as a maker of broad physical comedies, both urban and rustic, with a strongly populist bent; as a satirist who brought a highly stylized visual look and tone of comedic exaggeration to what were billed as "grotesque" fantasies; as the spinner of exotic "Oriental" cinematic fairy tales; and as the director of impressively large-scale historical spectacles that the chaotic economic conditions in postwar Germany enabled him to film on relatively modest budgets. The Lubitsch who had done all these things in only a decade was a man of a richly diverse personality. Such versatility, while often prized in the film world, can also bewilder audiences and lessen their identification with a filmmaker. Who was that grinning fellow personally introducing himself and his stories on-screen, anyway?

It would not be until he established himself in America with contemporary comedies (usually set in Europe) whose complex, sophisticated characterizations were expressed through a remarkable economy of means that the Lubitsch known for his delicate Touch would emerge in the media, first as a critical observation and soon as a publicity-enhanced brand name for moviegoers. That is the Lubitsch we tend to think of today, especially since his German films are relatively little known. The question of Lubitsch's evolution in both Germany and the United States, his discarding of elements of his multifaceted style to pare it down to his most original qualities, reveals much about the strengths of his creative personality and how he gradually discovered his most enduring artistic identity.

THE CELEBRITY DIRECTOR

Thanks to his stardom as an actor, Lubitsch's wryly smiling face was a familiar image to German filmgoers from early in his career, even before he began directing. As canny self-promoters such as directors Alfred Hitchcock and Spike Lee later would do, Lubitsch ensured that his face remained before the camera. The first image we see in his mordant marital comedy *When I Was Dead* is of Lubitsch poking his face out from behind a curtain. He scratches his head and smiles impishly with faux-modest embarrassment before going back behind the curtain. Then two other leading cast members are introduced in the same fashion. It was not uncommon to introduce the lead actors with close-ups in early German cinema, and the curtain makes it obvious that this presentational device was intended to give the film a theatrical flavoring. Before Lubitsch even started directing, he had been introduced on-screen with close-ups in *The Pride of the Firm* and as a supporting character in a lackluster 1915 rustic farce directed by Max Mack about two escaped convicts, *Robert und Bertram oder: Die lustigen Vagabunden* (*Robert and Bertram, or the Funny Vagabonds*).

The ways Lubitsch is presented to the audience in those two early films are evidence that his theatrical background, however modest, was regarded as an asset by film companies that were struggling to rival the more established, more prestigious medium. In *The Pride of the Firm*, Lubitsch turns his head and smiles at the camera as he is identified as Ernst Lubitsch of the Deutsches Theater. Even spear-carriers from Reinhardt's company were worth heralding to movie audiences. In *Robert and Bertram*, Lubitsch plays a tailor named Max Edelstein wearing a goatee and sideburns and dressed in a long checked coat. But in the opening, he is introduced without the makeup or costume that he wears in the story; he looks out from behind a curtain with his characteristically sly smile. Characters in these films sometimes cast sidelong glances at the audience during the story itself, breaking the fourth wall to draw us into their confidence as actors sometimes do in the theater. At one point in *Robert and Bertram*, Lubitsch turns to the audience and remarks, "I don't think this situation is kosher."

An inveterate charmer from the beginning, a filmmaker whose interplay with his audience was always as important as what appeared on-screen, Lubitsch found it congenial to make eye contact with his audience. He introduces himself with such a close-up in *When Four Do the Same*, the marital comedy he directed in which he appears in a small role. Pairing off two couples, including a father and daughter (Emil Jannings and Ossi Oswalda) who each find a mate, the film seems rather schematic but points forward to the intricacies of Lubitsch's mature work. Showing his own face at the beginning is shameless directorial self-promotion on a precociously high level, long before the auteur theory existed.

Lubitsch went even further in the art of self-introduction in the brilliant prologue of his 1919 fantasy *The Doll*. In that extremely stylized piece of comic expressionism—spoofing the prominent artistic movement with a film that preceded Robert Wiene's epochal *Das Cabinet des Dr. Caligari* (*The Cabinet of Dr. Caligari*) to the screen by almost three months—Lubitsch appears in a witty prologue as the director. He sets up a miniature set that becomes the artificial setting for the first scene of this fairy-tale film with painted scenery. Lubitsch's spotlighting of his own image for the audience in his early works insists on the audience's awareness of him as director, or puppet master even (or especially), in films in which he is not the leading actor. This tendency reveals how early his screen persona solidified. After his first confirmed film role, his supporting part in *The Ideal Wife* in 1913, he played the lead in *The Company Marries* the following year, and already with his next film, *The Pride of the Firm*, he was a star. But near the end of his life, he still smarted over his frustration at having been typecast by playing Siegmund Lachmann in that film. Finding its success a hindrance, he felt he was foundering in less popular short films. But he succumbed to public demand and reverted to that archetype with his own virtual rip-off that he directed two years later, *Shoe Palace Pinkus*, as Sally Pinkus. Ironically, Lubitsch credited that intervening period of his frustration as an actor with turning him more toward being a director. The starring vehicle, which he directed himself, was written by Kräly and Schönfelder (Schönfelder also worked as an actor for Lubitsch and wrote nine other silents for him before Kräly established himself as the director's regular writer; Kräly is credited on a total of twenty-nine Lubitsch silents in both Germany and the United States).

Lubitsch had made enough of an initial impression that advertisements for his films from 1914 onward featured his name and face with considerable prominence. In May 1915 a German show business journal, *Photo-stage*, declared of Lubitsch, "With the popularity of the artist, we might expect his [next] film with keen interest." And that June an advertisement in the same publication announced, "Theater owner! Make sure you get the one-act play series with Ernst Lubitsch, the indestructible film humorist. Any program would be at a loss without such comedies. The hilarity is colossal." *The Cinematographer* declared, "Through Lubitsch, the art of film has become very funny."

Thus, it should not be surprising that the philandering husband he plays in *When I Was Dead* is actually named Herr Ernst Lubitsch. Such strategies to capitalize on his rapidly growing fame were unmistakable signs of his ambition. It would not be long before he began sending signals to Hollywood that he was ready to move beyond his hometown industry and become a truly international director. When he began making his historical spectacles, he set himself up as a direct rival to Hollywood and succeeded in showing that he could transcend national boundaries. *Madame DuBarry* in 1920 became the first German film to break the U.S. ban on films from that former enemy country. And not only that, it became a major boxoffice success in the United States, paving the way for the rest of the German industry to export its work to America. It was no accident that Lubitsch's last two German films, the lavish Egyptian spectacle *The Wife of Pharaoh* and the delicate tragedy *Die Flamme*, were made partly with American funding.

"ONE OF THE TALENTED ONES"

America recognized Lubitsch's special value as a popular entertainer and backed his period of transition as it gradually lured him away from home. Anti-German sentiment lingered in the United States even after *Madame DuBarry* helped break the cultural ice. Xenophobia would cause continued problems for Lubitsch when he made his first visit to New York in 1921 and again when he first went to Hollywood in 1922. But his films' commercial and critical success led the way for German filmmaking to become a dominant force in the world market during that decade. Hollywood began to import more and more German directors and actors, and when Hitler's rise to power forced Jews and others to escape, the steady flow turned into a tidal wave, decimating much of the talent in the German film industry.

Lubitsch made his name as a transplanted American director remarkably quickly after he arrived in Hollywood. Kristin Thompson writes in her book *Herr Lubitsch Goes to Hollywood* that Lubitsch's was a unique case in which the leading director in one country became the leading director in another. Some film historians go even further and claim that by the time he left Germany, Lubitsch was the leading director in all of Europe. Certainly, he was among the most important filmmakers of that era even before he started working in Hollywood. But there is room for debate over whether Lubitsch, in that somewhat embryonic period of his career, was indeed Germany's leading director by the end of 1922. Fritz Lang and F. W. Murnau were not only his peers but in some circles were held in higher regard because their films were more conventionally "serious."

Still, there is no doubt that Lubitsch showed phenomenal adaptability, culturally and in every other way, not only in that period but throughout his career. His ability to change and grow artistically is one of the reasons he endured as a top director for decades, unlike many other major comedy directors whose careers tended to flame out after tapping into the zeitgeist for about ten years. When the zeitgeist would change, Lubitsch would change with it, partly out of commercial expediency, but also because of the breadth and depth of his talent. Even though he was an exile by choice, someone who was called to a new land rather than one who had to escape, he still had to learn a new set of cinematic conventions and a radically different cultural context. That he showed little difficulty doing so is a tribute to his towering genius and the universality of his artistry. But while Lubitsch's American films began to diverge stylistically, with almost dizzying speed, from the kinds of films he had been making in Germany, the roots, themes, and style of his inarguably superior American work can still be traced back to his beginnings in German cinema.

EVOLVING A STYLE

During that transitional period between stage and cinema, for the German film industry in general and for Lubitsch in particular, he was evolving his own style as a filmmaker, but he did so gradually as he worked his way through various genres. That his early films were derived from the theater is obvious, and the acting and staging are often presentational and primitive, although the brio that Lubitsch brings from his stage experience keeps the stories and his performances amusing. Some exterior scenes show more flair for cinematic composition, and Lubitsch's progression in handling the other demands of the new medium was fairly rapid. But though his first notable success as a director, *Shoe Palace Pinkus*, is engaging and fast-moving, its lack of professional smoothness is evident when it is compared with Wilhelm's *Pride of the Firm*.

The first films Lubitsch directed were considered shorts, comedies in two or three reels. His initial feature-length venture in 1918, *The Eyes of the Mummy*, shows his early weaknesses and nascent strengths with its uneasy mixture of hokum and adroit social commentary. The insanely jealous black man played by Emil Jannings (an Othello who serves as his own Iago) pursues Pola Negri's temple dancer, Mara, from Egypt to England, and tears a passion to tatters. But the film comes briefly alive when the Londoners welcome Mara into high society and onto the vaudeville stage after they become fascinated with her exoticism. This satirical demonstration of the power of show business to overcome social boundaries seems to have awakened Lubitsch's keen sense of the nuances of social exclusion and assimilation, at least until the murder plot takes over. The temporary diversion into the world of showbiz allows the film to rise above its otherwise-simpleminded campiness.

Lubitsch's approximately forty-five-minute 1918 film *I Don't Want to Be a Man* (silent-film running times are estimates because they varied according to projection speeds) is far more assured in developing and carrying off a sharp and consistent tone of social satire. The rebellious young woman played by Ossi Oswalda struts her stuff around Berlin in male dress and short hair, and in a nightclub, she meets up with her drunken male guardian, Dr. Kersten (Kurt Götz). At home, Ossi had viewed him with both flirtatiousness and recalcitrance, but now she makes out with the uninhibited fellow, who in his intoxicated state does not realize that she is actually a girl. Lubitsch gets away with this risqué scene because the audience knows otherwise, but the film nevertheless draws suggestively on Berlin's transgressive sexual climate in that era. The cleverest, most counterintuitive twist in this often-daring satire by Kräly and Lubitsch is Ossi's discovery that being a member of the opposite sex is fraught with its own trials, frustrations, and humiliations and that she prefers being a woman after all. It is a cheeky, challenging paradox worthy of Oscar Wilde, whose work Lubitsch would later film. *I Don't Want to Be a Man* delights audiences today with its advanced attitudes toward gender fluidity and is something of a forerunner of Billy Wilder's 1959 cross-dressing farce *Some Like It Hot*.

So within less than four years as a director, Lubitsch was directing comedies of far greater visual sophistication and much more adroit acting by a wide range of performers. He regarded his raucous, at times almost surrealistic 1919 satire *The Oyster Princess* as the film in which he developed his true sense of style; it is a bravura piece of visually inventive and witty directing. That film, starring Oswalda, is something of a takeoff on the popular 1909 German operetta *Die Dollarprinzessin* (*The Dollar Princess*), a satire about an American coal heiress abroad; its title is taken from English slang of the period and conveys a European mockery of what would later be called the "Ugly American" sensibility. Not content with mastering the stylized comedy genre, Lubitsch expanded his versatility with his lavishly produced spectacles. We can track the rapid, if erratic, progress of his directorial style and the stylistic and thematic range of his German films by looking at how he developed his artistic personality within the oddly assorted genres of broad farces, daringly stylized comedies, and grand but often irreverent historical spectacles.

The growth of Lubitsch's professional skills in a relatively short period of time can be seen by comparing the stylistic crudity of *Shoe Palace Pinkus* with the economy and broad yet graceful wit of another farce he directed in 1920. By Lubitsch's own testimony, the most popular of all his German comedies was *Kohlhiesel's Daughters*, his Bavarian farce about the romantic rivalry between a sweet and lovely young woman named Gretel and her angry, ugly sister, Liesel (both roles are played by Henny Porten). This utterly delightful film, still unreleased in the United States after all these years (other than on YouTube), has been remade four times in Germany, including as a 1979 sex film called *Kohlpiesels Töchter* (*Kohlpiesel's Daughters*). The reason the Lubitsch version has never been exported theatrically or on homevideo is evidently that its rustic humor is mistakenly considered too provincial (Lubitsch himself called the film "typical German"), despite its casual derivation from Shakespeare's *The Taming of the Shrew* (a play that Gary Cooper reads for advice on how to deal with Claudette Colbert in Lubitsch's 1938 screwball comedy *Bluebeard's Eighth Wife*). In *Kohlhiesel's Daughters*, Lubitsch's crowd-pleasing talents, his impeccable comic timing, his adroit handling of a diverse cast, and his effective use of natural settings for slapstick comedy (such as a wildly orchestrated sequence of the very butch Liesel riding a sled through the mountains in fast motion) combine to enhance the film's amiable humor. The unpretentiousness and wide popularity of this Bavarian mountain comedy has no doubt perversely contributed to its critical neglect.

Henny Porten, Germany's most popular female star during the silent era, gives a tour-de-force dual performance in the Lubitsch original. She also starred in both parts in the 1930 talkie version of *Kohlhiesel's Daughters*, but her career faltered when, after the Nazi takeover, she refused to divorce her Jewish husband and was forbidden from emigrating. Under Lubitsch's direction, Porten is especially imaginative in her playing of the "shrew," Liesel, a despised barmaid and bouncer in her father's country inn whose understandably rebellious, "unfeminine" nature puts off every man she glares at uncouthly. Her father wants to marry her off before seeking a husband for the more conventional, kindly, almost matronly Gretel. But that old-fashioned fatherly task seems quixotic until Liesel encounters a wanderer, engagingly played against type by the young and not-yet-so-portly Emil Jannings. This unlikely couple find themselves gravitating toward each other after a quarrel over Liesel's cooking turns into a wild furniture-tossing episode (some flies through a Lubitschean doorway) by Jannings's oafish yet lovable peasant, Peter Xaver. While comically demonstrating his control over Liesel, the wreckage turns her on and helps liberate her own ferocious but repressed sexual passions, which stand in stark contrast to Gretel's pleasant but overly placid femininity. Lubitsch had earlier used the destruction of a room by the rebellious American heiress in *The Oyster Princess* to convey a woman's frenetic sexual frustration. A servant tells Ossi's father in that film, "Your daughter is in a fit of raving madness," but he is unperturbed since this outrageous conduct is obviously a regular occurrence.

Lubitsch's playful, unorthodox approach to sexuality in *Kohlhiesel's Daughters*—Peter tells Liesel after he kisses her, "Much better than Gretel"—gives an underpinning of erotic energy to the story's farcical elements. The director's finely shaded work with the two sides of Henny Porten is one of the early demonstrations of his remarkable ability to draw fresh and surprising performances from actresses. The relish with which Porten embodies the anarchic Liesel makes a startling contrast not only to her equally convincing and appealing Gretel but also to the touching dignity the actress displays in the title role of Lubitsch's tragic spectacle *Anna Boleyn* later that same year. No wonder Lubitsch, at the end of his life, ranked *Kohlhiesel's Daughters* with *The Oyster Princess* and *The Doll* as "the three most outstanding comedies I made as a director in Germany."

The Oyster Princess and *The Doll* indeed remain landmark achievements in his career, each a unique and dazzlingly entertaining feat of cinematic style. These zany films, starring the irrepressibly madcap Ossi Oswalda in very different roles (in *The Doll*, she is a doll maker's daughter who masquerades as a mechanical sex toy), show Lubitsch's already-advanced sense of cinematic style, drawing on the surrealist and expressionist movements that were then so influential in Europe. Characteristically, Lubitsch did not make the kind of solemn expressionist works that film historians have long revered, such as *The Cabinet of Dr. Caligari*, Murnau's *Der letzte Mann* (*The Last Laugh*), or Lang's *Metropolis*, but instead sent up the pretensions of that movement with outrageous abandon. Even the sets are hilarious in these two Lubitsch films and in his Pola Negri comedy *The Wildcat*, with their bizarre, dreamlike shapes or, in the case of *The Doll*, the delicate artificiality of their painted flats. The whole world seems out of whack in these cinematic fantasies, as much as in *Caligari*, but you can almost hear Lubitsch chuckling away behind the camera. When he appears in the prologue of *The Doll* in order to assemble the first set from materials in a toy box and insert the characters into the illusory scene, he is smiling slyly, delightfully displaying himself as a cinematic magician. The sets and costumes by Lubitsch's frequent collaborator Kurt Richter are extravagant yet also elegantly childlike constructions, with a grinning Sun peeking through painted clouds in the actors' first scene. Expressionism's primary function of exposing the inner turmoil of characters is used for comic visual effect in these fantasies, which represent a pivotal point of evolution in Lubitsch's artistic development.

Their stylization is so balletic, the rhythms of their blocking so buoyant, their editing so flamboyant that the films often seem like musicals. Indeed, French critic Jean Douchet told me at the Locarno International Film Festival's Lubitsch retrospective in 2010 that he believed Lubitsch actually "invented the musical" genre in 1919 with the uproarious "Foxtrot

Epidemic" sequence in *The Oyster Princess*, one of the wildest sequences in any silent film. The entire company of party guests and servants erupts into a boisterous wedding dance celebration that snakes throughout the Berlin mansion of a visiting American tycoon. The staging and editing combine with the visual rhythms of an on-screen orchestra and its comically gyrating leader to help set the joyous pace. It is worth remembering that silent films were never silent but always had musical accompaniment, and befitting its flamboyant musical nature, *The Oyster Princess* was accompanied by an original score for a twenty-piece orchestra. The elaborate dance sequences in this and other Lubitsch silents play like his 1930s musicals when watched with music added. The extreme broadness of the acting in these three exercises in grotesque filmmaking—by considerably better actors than Lubitsch himself—turns the characters into marionettes in the hands of the director, figuratively so in *The Oyster Princess* and literally in *The Doll*. The strenuously dance-like pantomime of Negri and her fellow players in *The Wildcat* and the film's extravagant sets make that fantasy, like *The Doll*, resemble a live-action cartoon.

Unlike some of Lubitsch's more laborious silent efforts (such as his spectacles and "Oriental" exotica), the three comedy-fantasy tours de force are crowd-pleasers today and are enjoyable for anyone who can relate to silent cinema. In fact, *The Wildcat* is even more accessible now than when it first appeared. Lubitsch blamed its commercial failure on audience distaste because of its mockery of militarism so soon after the Great War, but today that makes the film seem highly modern in its sensibility. Of the three, different as they are, *The Oyster Princess* is the finest because its comic invention is so relentlessly funny. *The Doll*, for all its inventiveness, becomes laborious in spots, and its thematic material is often more disturbing than amusing. *The Wildcat* becomes so lost in admiration of its own visual ingenuity (which includes the use of an astonishing array of masks of differing shapes to alter the frame sizes) that it sometimes forgets to be funny, and Negri lacks the artful economy of gesture that Oswalda brings to her roles in collusion with the director. But as always, Negri is a force of nature, and in *The Wildcat* she is at her most spontaneous for Lubitsch. He said of her in 1933, "There is something of the savage in her. Perhaps primitive would be a better word. Refined, of course, through education and associations, but dangerous when not under leash."

Oswalda's performances for Lubitsch, on the other hand, are marked by a precision of style that accompanies a sense of keen intelligence and wit. Ossi has blonde cuteness and frolicsome charm but lacks the unreal glamour of a traditional film star. Instead she reflects back to her audience what they might like to see in their own mirror: a somewhat chubby girl with a broad grin that guilelessly displays refreshingly imperfect teeth even as she radiates warmth, unrestrained enthusiasm, and innocent erotic vivacity. Her girl-next-door appeal and lack of fancy posturing make her seem a more modern actress than the wildly exotic Negri, who often seems like a parody of how silent actresses are thought to behave on-screen (a quality Lubitsch exploits cleverly for comic effect). Ossi's well-modulated blend of vivacity and moodiness perfectly complements Lubitsch's excited sense of self-discovery in their films together. Her impish blend of naughtiness and innocence, rebelliousness and shyness, in *I Don't Want to Be a Man* gives the film a captivating sense of nuance throughout her character's gender-bending permutations.

In *The Doll*, the tremulous Lancelot (Hermann Thimig), terrified of women and escaping from a coerced marriage, is offered refuge by a band of gluttonous, woman-hating monks (the monks resemble the palace eunuchs in Lubitsch's Arabian fantasy *Sumurun*) who protect him from the opposite sex by suggesting he make use of a sex doll. The doll is the chef d'oeuvre of Ossi's inventor father, Hilarius (played by Victor Janson, who also plays her father, Mr. Quaker, in *The Oyster Princess*). When the doll breaks, Ossi steps in. She plays the mechanical girl with balletic charm and wittily portrays the real girl pretending to be a mechanical doll. Ossi's effortless incarnation of both her roles in *The Doll* gives the viewer a richly textured satirical portrait of how femininity is (literally) constructed in a dual performance that constantly comments on itself without lapsing into self-consciousness. The film's raison d'être, beyond its obvious pleasure in stylistic experimentation, is to satirize misogyny. But as richly comical as Ossi's dual characterizations are in *The Doll*, her tumultuously rambunctious performance in *The Oyster Princess* is her crowning achievement for Lubitsch (at least of the films that survive; several other Oswalda collaborations with the director are lost, including the tantalizingly titled 1919 film *Meine Frau, die Filmschauspielerin* [*My Wife, the Film Actress*]).

In *The Oyster Princess*, as the horribly spoiled daughter of the ridiculously wealthy American tycoon, Ossi, like her father, has a squad of people to attend to her every bodily need and impulse; Mr. Quaker has a retinue of liveried black male servants while Ossi has a swirling gaggle of lovely young maids who bathe and dress her, managing to keep her nudity just out of our sight. Both father and daughter are childish in the extreme, caricatures of selfish Americans abroad that must have delighted the German audience in the aftermath of the war and remain sharp satirical portraits today. The Quakers' heedless indulgence in food and drink also represented a perverse form of audience wish-fulfillment in 1919, a time of general hunger and want in Germany. Just as the luxurious settings and costumes of Lubitsch's Hollywood films (like those of, say, the chic Fred Astaire and Ginger Rogers musicals) would provide vicarious luxury for world audiences during the Great Depression, these outlandish fantasy elements are the kind of consolatory escape the cinema can give us.

The unrestrained energy of *The Oyster Princess* helped exorcise some of the tensions felt on the streets outside the theaters and released some of the outpouring of creative energy Lubitsch was experiencing in this phase of his career. Ossi is fully his equal in that regard. When she demonstrates her need for sexual fulfillment by trashing her room in a reckless orgy of destruction, she declares, "I'm so happy I could smash the whole house to pieces." Ossi's outburst leaves the placid Mr. Quaker compliant with her demand to marry a titled European. He says, "I'll buy you a prince." Lubitsch has fun at the Quakers' expense with the devious machinations of the impoverished husband-designate, the suggestively named Prinz Nucki (suave Harry Liedtke). Nucki's bald, voraciously hungry servant, Josef (Julius Falkenstein), gleefully impersonates the prince to check out the unsuspecting American consumers, who are naïvely impressed by his bogus nobility. One of the eccentric highlights of the film is the impatient servant's increasingly rapid and balletic pacing and skipping around an ornate, mazelike floor pattern as he awaits his audience with Ossi's phlegmatic father and the eagerly expectant young woman (intercut with the racy scenes of Ossi being bathed by her bevy of female servants). This kind of intricate visual flourish would become a signature for Lubitsch. He regarded it as a stylistic breakthrough in his work, "a piece of business which caused a lot of comment at the time. . . . The poor man in order to overcome his impatience and his humiliation after having waited for hours walked along the outlines of the very intricate patterns on the floor. It is very difficult to describe this nuance and I don't know if I succeeded, but it was the first time I turned from comedy to satire."

The dazzling pirouettes of Lubitsch's visual style throughout *The Oyster Princess* are always in the service of pure humor rather than self-conscious artistry, though unforced cinematic artistry is present in abundance. The grotesquerie of the proceedings makes a suitable setting for the film's absurdist mockery of Ossi's lust and her father's equally boundless greed. The film gaily partakes in her infectious spirit, which enables it to end with an outrageous image that only Lubitsch could get away with in any country at any time—a close-up of Mr. Quaker watching his daughter through a keyhole as she snuggles with her husband on her wedding night; he leers into the camera and exclaims, "NOW I'M IMPRESSED!" Though the subtlety of Lubitsch's mature work is flagrantly absent from this youthful film, the joyous rhythms of its blocking and editing show a director reveling in his newfound command of cinematic language.

CINEMATIC INFLUENCES

Lubitsch's maturation as a director from this point was partly a by-product of his own growing skills and sense of invention and was partly inspired by the work of two other filmmakers, Charles Chaplin and Swedish director Mauritz Stiller. Every comic actor in the silent era acted under the shadow of Chaplin. As a screen comedian in the 1910s, Lubitsch was often compared with Chaplin, but despite Lubitsch's endearing brashness, a trait they shared, his acting lacks Chaplin's subtlety and depth. While Lubitsch's on-screen persona is similarly driven by a fierce survival instinct, which is lightly treated in the Chaplin manner but also reflects the imperatives of an immigrant or outsider, Lubitsch's characters are social climbers who are not content, or fated, to remain in their lower-class costumes or surroundings as Chaplin's Tramp would do. Even in his knockabout comedies, Chaplin always had a more resigned and fatalistic vision than Lubitsch, and that helps account for Chaplin's more lasting stature as an actor. In his 1922 interview with *Photoplay* before he left Germany, Lubitsch said, "The best of all—the greatest actor in the world—*le plus grand*, is—Ch'pln. Great tragedy actor—Ch'pln." His interviewer, seeming surprised, asked, "Chaplin a great tragedy actor?" Lubitsch replied, "Ya.—Ch'pln greatest actor of everything."

Although Lubitsch eventually became a master in his own right at blending comedy and drama, in his early phase, he drew less pathos from his comical characters than Chaplin was already able to find in his. Unlike Chaplin's Tramp, the characters Lubitsch plays in his early silent farces are determined optimists who will not accept rejection as they strive for social acceptance. Their eventual success reflects the importance that Lubitsch, the son of an immigrant Russian Jewish tailor, always placed on social mobility. The director's transgressive way of showing people breaking through barriers was one of the hallmarks of his vision. Lubitsch's films as actor and director in that period were rough sketches for his more mature later work dealing with all the complexities of people caught in and between social strata.

When Chaplin wrote and directed his delicate comedy of manners *A Woman of Paris: A Drama of Fate*, released on October 1, 1923, it was a revelation for Lubitsch. By then he was in Hollywood. He saw it in a private screening after making his first American film, *Rosita* (which was released on September 3). Seeing *A Woman of Paris* was one of the decisive factors that helped Lubitsch establish and consolidate his own style although he had been building up to it already in Germany. The predicament of Edna Purviance's sympathetic female "tramp" character in the Chaplin feature, a young woman of modest means who journeys from the provinces only to become the kept woman of Parisian playboy Adolphe Menjou, would decisively demonstrate to Lubitsch the virtues of underplaying what other directors would treat as melodrama, as well as deft ways of finding both laughter and poignancy in sexual innuendo. Lubitsch's comment to the *New York Times* that December reflected what he would take from the picture: "I think that *A Woman of Paris* is a marvelous production. I like it because I feel that an intelligent man speaks to me, and nobody's intelligence is insulted in that picture."

Three years before his epiphany over Chaplin, however, Lubitsch had seen Mauritz Stiller's *Erotikon*, a less celebrated film in its time but one that seems even more modern today in its saucy, unabashed approach to sexuality. Stiller by 1920 had proven himself a master of urbane, sophisticated comedy, although he is best-known now as the man who discovered Greta Garbo and brought her to America before being discarded by MGM and dying at age forty-five in 1928. *Erotikon* is a light romantic comedy about a restless, daringly footloose wife (the delectable Tora Teje) who teaches her clueless husband, an entomology professor, some lessons about love. The husband (Anders de Wahl) is a prototype of the shy, self-absorbed scientists or professors Cary Grant and Gary Cooper would later play in Howard Hawks's comedies. The sexually aggressive wife is an emancipated woman, an elegant erotic adventurer who would be recognizable in the soigné world of the mature Lubitsch. Billy Wilder related to Cameron Crowe that Lubitsch "told me himself, he learned everything from this picture."

Leisurely and elliptical, *Erotikon* uses the space and objects around its characters and deploys their elaborately balletic behavior in the expressive manner that would become identified with Lubitsch by the midtwenties in America. When you watch *Erotikon* today, it seems almost as if Lubitsch could have directed it himself, so knowing and precise are its emotional interchanges, conveyed with glances and fine points of seriocomic nuance, with the kind of suggestive wit for which Lubitsch would become celebrated. *Erotikon* seems to have made its most substantial impact on Lubitsch not for any particular sequence or any isolated touches but for its low-key naturalistic direction and acting, its mature knowingness toward sexuality, and its amused self-conscious approach toward cinematic style. The characters in *Erotikon* even comment on the romantic comedy genre in ways that are unusually self-reflexive for that early period, such as when the wife's lover remarks, "I am tired of this little comedy," or when the husband says, "I do not care for unhappy endings. In that respect I fully agree with the motion picture audience." *Erotikon* has a daringly extended opera sequence that comments obliquely on the drama in a way that points forward to Lubitsch's elaborately clever interweaving of the play *Monsieur Beaucaire* with the related action of his 1930 musical *Monte Carlo*. The metafilm dimension in *Erotikon* fed into Lubitsch's own penchant for engaging the audience in the playfully winking interchanges that are among the most delightful aspects of his work. At the end of *Monte Carlo*, his lead male character similarly expresses a preference for happy endings.

That self-reflexive tendency is abundantly on view in Lubitsch's German films, which often acknowledge the camera's presence in sophisticated ways while communicating, as if sharing a confidence with the viewer, the director's habitually wry attitude toward sexual intrigue. Lubitsch's effortless ability to blend comedy and drama was well established by 1920 in his German films, which work so many permutations on those two modes of expression. But any filmmaker making a major career shift by moving to another country and hoping to adapt to a new set of cultural mores and imperatives would have to rethink his stylistic approach, and Lubitsch's attentiveness to his audience was always acute. It was mostly elements of tone and attitude that he learned from Stiller as he later did from Chaplin. The Stiller influence did not become strongly manifest until Lubitsch left Germany. By the time he saw *Erotikon*, he already had one foot outside his native land, with only *The Wife of Pharaoh* and *Die Flamme* still to come before he left for America and firmly established the Lubitsch Touch.

THE SPECTACLES

In stark contrast to his comic fantasy films in Germany are Lubitsch's historical spectacles, which almost seem as if they were made by another director. They came about through a timely combination of circumstances affecting both the German film industry and Lubitsch himself.

After the war ended, Germany sought to break the embargo on exporting its films around the world. The newly formed combine Universum Film AG, or UFA, following its organization in November 1917, quickly became the dominant force in German film production. The United States and other countries began to cautiously accept German films after the war, primarily because of Lubitsch's artistic stature and the success of his *Madame DuBarry* after its American release (as *Passion*) in December 1920. But UFA and other companies in Germany still had to contend with lingering and widespread hostility. The groundbreaking *Cabinet of Dr. Caligari* (1920) played in New York to great acclaim when it opened there in April 1921, but when it reached Los Angeles the following month, the Hollywood post of the American Legion organized an anti-German protest. That led to rioting at the theater, abetted by the Motion Picture Directors Association and hundreds of sailors from the U.S. Pacific fleet, and the avant-garde film was withdrawn. American audiences and journalists continued to be suspicious of the German cinema for some time; the boxoffice success of *Passion* was something of a fluke partly because it was promoted without a mention of its German origin. The

New York Times advertisement by Broadway's Capitol Theatre highlighted the film's French subject matter and "Famous Continental Star," Pola Negri. But the paper noted in its film column that the opening was "a matter of speculation for the curious. The film has been imported from Germany, directly or indirectly." In April 1921 the *Times* reported with some skepticism that advance publicity on "the German photoplay" *Deception* (*Anna Boleyn*) alleged that "Mr. Lubitsch is a Bohemian." The following month, *Variety* claimed that Lubitsch was Polish.

There were shared, if not identical, economic interests at play in the German and American film industries. While the Germans wanted access to the American market for their pictures, the Americans wanted to co-opt the rising influence of the German film industry, achieve better distribution in the central and eastern European markets, get around German import quotas by making coproductions, and hire top talent from that country. But Germany had to proceed carefully in the tense aftermath of the war, as the backlash against *Caligari* demonstrated. According to research into Lubitsch's transitional period and the state of German filmmaking in that era by Stefan Drössler of the Munich Film Museum, when UFA made its most concerted effort to compete in the world market with large-scale productions rivaling Hollywood's best, the German studio decided to play it safe by avoiding indigenous subject matter, instead making lavish spectacles drawn from other countries' histories. UFA engaged its most highly regarded and most versatile director, Lubitsch, to make historical films set in France and England, *Madame DuBarry* and *Anna Boleyn*. The German film industry even enlisted the support of the country's president, Friedrich Ebert, to help promote these lavish economic and aesthetic efforts. Ebert made a much-publicized appearance on the set of *Anna Boleyn* in September 1920, posing for newsreel footage with costumed stars Porten and Jannings. Ebert also appeared at a reception to honor *The Wife of Pharaoh* on December 1, 1921. That was two days before Lubitsch and his producer Paul Davidson sailed to New York on the steamship *America* to "study American films and producing methods," bringing along a copy of *Pharaoh*, according to the *New York Times*.

During that time of constant unrest and grave uncertainty about Germany's future, the spectacles Lubitsch made in Berlin during his last four years there—three of which feature Jannings as foreign tyrants (Henry VIII in *Anna Boleyn*, France's King Louis XV in *Madame DuBarry*, and the fictitious Egyptian pharaoh Amenes in *The Wife of Pharaoh*)—were crucial in helping Germany gradually establish itself as an aesthetic force in world cinema as well as in smoothing the way for German films to enter the American marketplace. Lubitsch's spectacles and comedies, with their often-frenzied crowd scenes and wild mood swings, helped encapsulate the zeitgeist of the late 1910s and early '20s. As Klaus Kreimeier writes in his history of UFA,

> The throngs that poured into the movie theaters night after night, UFA's opulent premieres, the sometimes elegant, sometimes crudely comic achievements of Ernst Lubitsch—these were all part and parcel of that immense "ebb and flow of Berlin," of the leviathanlike, voracious, everyday life of the city. It was this everyday life that gave Berliners their equanimity and armed them against the impositions of history. In a state of civil war, it protected them against the icy winds of global historical changes, which were giving free rein to passion but promising little security.

The gradual influx of American films into Germany during the early twenties began to influence the Berlin film industry with Hollywood's more advanced lighting techniques (including three-directional lighting for more sculptural effects and night lighting) and the American industry's smoothly "invisible" storytelling conventions, which seemed less theatrical than the German style. Lubitsch's spectacles dazzle with their impressively opulent and detailed sets and costumes, and *The Wife of Pharaoh* especially represented a notable advance in filmic technique with its use of American lighting equipment and the first extensive night scenes in a German film. The Egyptian spectacle is genuinely monumental and beautifully photographed by Lubitsch's master cameraman Theodor Sparkuhl in collaboration with Alfred Hansen. Regarded as lost for many years, the film was partially restored from a Russian version in 1977 to about 60 percent of its original length. It was then reconstructed and restored by the Munich Film Museum and the Bundesarchiv Filmarchiv from Russian, Italian, and German sources for its 2003–2011 version, though it was still missing about one-fifth of the original footage.

Lubitsch had begun exploring the spectacle genre somewhat reluctantly in 1918 with *Carmen* (retitled *Gypsy Blood* for its belated U.S. release in 1921). Although the film was on a much smaller scale than his subsequent epics,

Lubitsch still had to be urged to venture outside his comedic comfort zone by producer Paul Davidson. *Carmen* was made by Davidson's Projektions A. G. Union (PAGU), a subsidiary of UFA. A former exhibitor, Davidson made ten films directed by Lubitsch between 1917 and 1920 (including *I Don't Want to Be a Man* and *Madame DuBarry*). In Drössler's words, they were "the most productive producer-director team in German cinema during the war." Lubitsch and Davidson eventually left UFA to form their own quasi-independent company, the Ernst Lubitsch-Film GmbH, in April 1921. Lubitsch and Davidson soon began working under the umbrella of a newly formed international joint venture called EFA (the Europäische Film-Allianz). Established in May 1921 as a rival to UFA, EFA was a partnership between a number of leading German filmmakers and the American entrepreneurs Ben Blumenthal and Samuel Rachmann, who formed the Hamilton Theatrical Corporation on a fifty-fifty basis with the American company Famous Players-Lasky (FP-L), the parent company of Paramount, run by the Hungarian immigrant Adolph Zukor. The impressive roster of talent that EFA initially put under contract after raiding UFA included Negri, Jannings, Reinhardt, and several of Lubitsch's key behind-the-scenes collaborators, including Sparkuhl, Kräly, and art director Kurt Richter. Lubitsch's growing importance is indicated by the fact that in the advertisement announcing EFA's formation, his name was listed first among its film directors, followed by the prolific adventure film director/producer Joe May and only then by the great Reinhardt.

Shortly after the founding of the international combine, Lubitsch and Davidson visited New York, where the director declared, "To come to America is the dream of every European artist. I have long realized that America represents the very pulse of modern life. And as every artist dreams and paints his dream in his fancy, I had hoped and expected to realize this. But how different it all is—how amazing! Here I have found not only the big things but the little things exceeding all my expectations." Lubitsch sounded more tentative in speaking to a German film journal, which quoted him as saying, "Now I can make bigger productions than ever before and—if I need to—shoot in Germany as well as in America. But despite my American contract, my film style will not change. I will always keep the basic German strengths which I see as the carefully developed, logically constructed screenplay and the German style of acting." Later in America, Lubitsch characterized the essence of German cinema as "the colossal, mass in movement and realism." But by then (1936) he had moved far away from those artistic tendencies.

Lubitsch benefited from EFA's American coproduction financing on his last two German films, *The Wife of Pharaoh* and the contrastingly intimate *Die Flamme*, both of which were designed as showcases for the world appeal and technical expertise of the German film industry and, not incidentally, for Lubitsch's diverse talents as an international filmmaker. His affinity and enthusiasm for the American style of filmmaking had already been abundantly clear when he made *Madame DuBarry* and *Anna Boleyn*, flamboyant historical sagas that took on Hollywood and D. W. Griffith directly and in many ways surpassed their American prototypes. That caused some grumblings in Germany, especially as his colleagues and the press realized that he was angling for a future in Hollywood. Berlin reviewer Alfred Rosenthal wrote that *The Wife of Pharaoh* had "maybe a little bit too much Hollywood style, and therefore we cannot praise it with the same enthusiasm as other works by Lubitsch."

Although Lubitsch personally benefited from the international platform that EFA afforded him, the company soon turned into a financial disaster for Zukor and his German partners. Lubitsch's films and other EFA films helped the German industry begin to achieve the cachet it would possess throughout the 1920s as a leader in film art, but financial disputes within EFA disrupted its operation, and the runaway inflation within Germany in 1922–1923 soon made large-scale spectacles impossible to make. Filmmakers were no longer able to hire thousands of unemployed workers as extras or continue building such lavish sets. Furthermore, deals Zukor made to import many German films to the United States tended to backfire, except in special cases such as *Madame DuBarry* (*Passion*). American audiences reacted with enthusiasm to the filmmaker's continental sophistication about sexuality in that film dealing with the French Revolution, a striking contrast to the Victorianism that had tended to dominate American filmmaking even beyond the war's end. But American audiences still tended to react negatively to other foreign films, both for political reasons and because most pre-1921 German films lagged behind Hollywood standards in technique. *Anna Boleyn* and *The Wife of Pharaoh* were relative boxoffice disappointments in the American market, partly the fault of their ponderousness (retitling them

Deception and *The Loves of Pharaoh* did not help). But by then Lubitsch's reputation had caused considerable excitement in Hollywood, which was sending feelers for him to come and work there.

Lubitsch's trip to the United States with Davidson in December 1921 was prematurely terminated the following month because, the director told the press, he received "strange" anti-German telephone calls and other messages, although EFA's financial uncertainty was also a factor in his retreat. Lubitsch was not yet ready to wrap up his involvement in the German film industry. After returning from the United States, he outdid himself in 1922 and went as far as he could in the spectacle genre with *The Wife of Pharaoh*, one of the two most lavish productions of his career, along with his 1934 MGM musical *The Merry Widow*. *Pharaoh* was made at EFA's technologically advanced new studio near the Berlin Zoo and on land used for the massive exterior sets of the pharaoh's palace and crowd scenes, including impressive battle footage. Lubitsch also filmed *Die Flamme* (a *Kammerspielfilm*) at the EFA studio in 1922, but because of the company's internal problems, it was not released until the following year. He conducted some tentative explorations of film projects to be made in Vienna and Berlin. In addition to his plan to adapt a work of Arthur Schnitzler's in Austria, he wanted to film Oscar Straus's 1907 operetta *Ein Waltzertraum* (*A Waltz Dream*), which eventually became part of the source material for Lubitsch's 1931 American-made musical *The Smiling Lieutenant*. And he planned to film Shakespeare's *The Merry Wives of Windsor* in Germany with Jannings playing Sir John Falstaff.

Those plans were abandoned before Lubitsch was lured to work in America later in 1922. German distribution rights to *Pharaoh* were sold to UFA, but the film significantly had its world premiere not in Germany but in New York in February 1922 (after Lubitsch's abrupt return home). It was advertised as "THE MASTER WORK OF ERNEST [*sic*] LUBITSCH" and as "The Great Million Dollar Spectacle" although its actual cost in U.S. dollars was between $70,000 and $80,000. For comparison, Griffith's epics *The Birth of a Nation* (1915), *Intolerance* (1916), and *Orphans of the Storm* (1921), cost about $100,000, $385,000, and $340,000, respectively. Money went much farther in Germany because of the currency devaluation and rampant unemployment in the early 1920s. But the publicity about thousands of extras being hired for *The Wife of Pharaoh* was accurate. As film historian Jan-Christopher Horak notes,

"German films were indeed extremely cheap because they were being produced with virtually worthless Reichsmarks and could be bought with hard currency dollars."

By December 1922 Lubitsch was on his way back to the United States to direct a film starring Mary Pickford for her own eponymous company, which released its films through United Artists (UA), the partnership she had formed in 1919 with D. W. Griffith, Charles Chaplin, and her husband, Douglas Fairbanks. So, in that sense, the EFA arrangement succeeded handsomely for Lubitsch by winning him his ticket to America and Hollywood, even if it caused him to sever his ties with Germany. That was a development he did not seem to mind even if he initially assured his colleagues he would return. Lubitsch's departure from EFA and Germany also caused him to break with Davidson, who failed to reestablish himself in Germany and committed suicide in 1927.

"UND NOW A BIG HEAD OF POLA"

If it seems odd in retrospect that the man who would become known for his mastery of the romantic comedy and musical genres made his initial international reputation with historical spectacles, it is also paradoxical that he worked successfully in a genre with such highly political subject matter while he seemed personally detached from politics, even to a comical degree. When President Ebert arrived for his visit during the filming of *Anna Boleyn*'s coronation sequence, Lubitsch, busy directing from a platform, reportedly did not recognize the president at first and shouted for him to get out of the way. That incident supports the observation of Lubitsch's niece Evy Bettelheim-Bentley that he was "absolutely apolitical" personally during the violence and political upheavals that took place in Germany while he was making films there.

And yet he was not entirely oblivious to history, although he was primarily interested in how he could adapt the lessons of the streets to his work. He showed a canny, if not cynical, awareness of current events and exploited it to practical effect while whipping mobs of hungry extras into a frenzy for *The Wife of Pharaoh*. "The most important thing in teaching mobs to rage," he told a *New York Times* reporter visiting the set, "is to make everyone understand that acting is more or less a serious matter. One cannot come into a battle with a foolish grin." So "Herr Direktor" shouted from his directing platform to one large crowd of extras, "Here, you. Run as though the Spartacans were turning machine guns on you" (he was referring to the Spartakusbund, or Spartacist League, the leftist revolutionary organization that had led the January 4–15, 1919, uprising that was crushed by Ebert's government). To another group of extras on the set of *The Wife of Pharaoh* in that time of severe food shortages, Lubitsch bellowed, "The price of bread has gone up. Over there is a rich baker's shop. Go, go for him!"

Lubitsch's most noticeable personal reaction to the world around him during the Weimar period (1919 and beyond), his niece said, was to move from his apartment in the raffish Schönhauser Allee to his fancier new digs at 13 Kufsteiner Strasse. That apartment house, where he would live until departing Berlin for America, was in what German film historian Michael Hanisch describes as "a more respectable, bourgeois area in Berlin's Schöneberg," away from the crowded city center near Alexanderplatz. Lubitsch may have regarded Kufsteiner Strasse as a safer location, and it was closer to his places of work, UFA's Tempelhof studios and the EFA studio; he no longer needed to live near the legitimate theaters downtown.

The guests at the preview party for Lubitsch's period Spanish spectacle *Carmen* at UFA on the night of November 8, 1918, were shaken when they heard gunfire from outside shortly after the picture started playing. When the film's star, Pola Negri, anxiously asked Lubitsch whether he had heard the noises, he told her, "Yes, shh! There's nothing anybody can do. Watch the picture." This incident occurred in the midst of the November Revolution. It was the very night before the German Republic was proclaimed at the Reichstag as a "Free Socialist Republic" and Kaiser Wilhelm II abdicated, and it was just three days before Germany signed the armistice ending the world war. Negri recalled that as the screening of *Carmen* continued, "I crouched back in my chair horrified by our complacence, by the fact that we all knew and preferred to pretend nothing was happening. It was so much easier to put on a blindfold than to ask the forbidden questions." After the screening, everybody lingered at the party as the gunfire persisted outside: "And so we drank more wine and laughed gaily and discussed the merits of the picture." It is hard to imagine a more ostrichlike response to such epochal events than "Watch the picture." This was not an isolated incident with Lubitsch. In

1945, when a Hollywood film he produced, *A Royal Scandal*, was previewed, a mild earthquake shook the theater, and about twenty people left in a panic. It was reported, "Ernst was horrified. 'Don't they like the picture?' he whispered to pals excitedly. 'What's the matter with it, that people should leave? This is awful—' He had been so absorbed he hadn't even felt the quake."

And yet, as Hanisch has commented, "*Carmen* was most clearly connected to the events on the streets. . . . But Lubitsch floated, so to speak, above all of that, and he didn't seem to be particularly affected by it. I believe that Lubitsch wasn't specifically interested in reality. In his films, he didn't want to reflect what was going on or things that might have moved him in some way. He instead saw film as something that was above reality." Nevertheless, even such an aesthete as Lubitsch had to be affected, however subconsciously, by the troubles outside the studio. This was especially unavoidable when he began to make his major historical spectacles, as the fierce critical controversy in their time over their blending of the personal and the political would suggest. Their unsettling mélange of conservative and anarchic elements, loosely drawn from actual historical events, could not help but reflect modern conditions in a time of political unrest when there were rapid changes of government and bitter and often-violent clashes between rival parties from the Far Left to the Far Right.

Hanisch's analysis of Lubitsch's artificiality of style as a seeming lack of interest in reality, a form of escape from sociopolitical events, is true only to a certain point. Even if he did not often make overtly topical films, Lubitsch's mostly comic sensibility always reflects on the reality of human interactions and society in acutely insightful and universal ways. But Lubitsch did evolve toward more overt social consciousness to some extent in his American work, especially when his films were set in the present day, such as *Trouble in Paradise* (1932) and *To Be or Not to Be* (1942).

Carmen deals with a Gypsy femme fatale, a cigar maker in nineteenth-century Spain. The film is a somewhat slapdash, extravagantly overacted takeoff on the original 1845 novella by Prosper Mérimée and (unofficially) the 1875 Georges Bizet opera. *Carmen* had already been filmed in the United States three times in 1915, by Raoul Walsh, Cecil B. DeMille, and as a spoof, Charles Chaplin's *A Burlesque on Carmen*. Chaplin plays Don José as Darn Hosiery. Lubitsch's relatively straight melodramatic version, with Harry Liedtke as Don José, provided Negri with a popular follow-up vehicle to her exotic Egyptian role in Lubitsch's *Eyes of the Mummy*.

A new kind of silent star who was not a classical beauty but more earthy, the recently arrived Polish actress and dancer ravished movie audiences with her carnality. She benefited from large expressive eyes framed by a round face and vigorously uninhibited body language, attributes that serve a silent movie actress well. But in *Carmen*, Negri exhibits only minimal talent in her frequent dance routines and as a comedian; her comic flair would gradually develop under Lubitsch's tutelage. Though captivating in a rough-and-ready way, she lacks the level of quick wit, intelligence, and finesse that Ossi Oswalda brings to her Lubitsch roles, traits that make the relatively obscure Ossi seem more appealing to today's viewers. But these two actresses were suited admirably for the different kinds of films Lubitsch was alternating between during the postwar period. The contrast between the genres shows how the director was torn (or experimenting, depending on how you look at it in retrospect) between broad farce aimed modestly at playful amusement and spectacle calculated to impress audiences by titillating and overwhelming them.

Negri had been imported to Berlin in 1917 to appear onstage for Reinhardt in the "Oriental" pantomime *Sumurun*. Her identification with that vehicle helped land her the starring role in Lubitsch's 1920 film version. She had already made films in Poland, and shortly after coming to Berlin, she began appearing in German films, including several before she teamed with Lubitsch. She was typecast as a wildly sexy temptress, the image she maintained until the coming of sound damaged her career and drove her, for a time, back to Europe. She always had a heavy Polish accent, which discouraged Billy Wilder from casting her as Norma Desmond, the former silent star, in his 1950 classic *Sunset Blvd.* When I acted for Orson Welles in *The Other Side of the Wind* for six years in the 1970s, every time he would call for a close-up, he would intone what he said had been Negri's pet phrase for that purpose: "Und now a big head of Pola." That Pola succeeded so well in her vamp persona and is still engaging in her silent Lubitsch films is a tribute to the shameless self-confidence she projects and her strenuous, even voracious sexuality.

But it is Lubitsch's ability to bring out a sly humor in Negri's "smoldering" sex appeal (which in itself seems somewhat comical today) that is the real key to the success of his work with her in eight films. She is most effective when her roles are at least partly tongue-in-cheek, as with her seductress for all classes and seasons in *Madame DuBarry*, entirely facetious as with her feral title character in *The Wildcat*, or most impressively, when she is directed in a much more restrained way in the tragic *Die Flamme* and in Lubitsch's 1924 Hollywood-made comedy set in Russia, *Forbidden Paradise*. It is noteworthy that all Negri's roles for Lubitsch were in period films, which helps make the flamboyant stylization of her persona more acceptable by setting it an exotic context. Lubitsch's use of Negri in varying modes of sexuality laced with humor and melodrama made his films with her popular because they were a refreshing antidote to the screen trend that he said he was especially reacting against, the lavish Italian spectacle, typified by the influential 1914 *Cabiria*, which he felt lacked the witty human touches he brought to his historical tales.

THE SPECTACLES PRO AND CON

Although Lubitsch's spectacles have been attacked by some critics, both in their day and later, for placing too much emphasis on sex and other personal matters and not enough on dialectics, as well as for their "vulgarity," they are characteristic of his "Berlin style" of irony. That approach includes a tolerant detachment toward human failings, which is among his most admirable qualities in its refusal to judge people in conventionally moralistic terms. If Negri's Madame DuBarry is an incorrigible flirt who bounces recklessly from man to man, from commoner to decadent aristocrat to king, losing her head in the process, Lubitsch would not have been among the crowds calling for her decapitation. He would have viewed her flaws, selfish and self-destructive as they are, with a certain tolerance, detachment, and affection. His ironic view of kings as sharing the same "vices" as commoners and a similarly "low" taste in female companionship is part of his characteristic mockery of royalty, his subversive desire to bring it down to the same level as the common run of humanity.

Lubitsch's Hollywood screenwriter Samson Raphaelson recalled, "We just laughed our heads off at kings. Neither Lubitsch nor I ever met any king. We were just having fun." That mocking tendency seems to have won Lubitsch little respect from his more politically doctrinaire critics. And his characteristic ambivalence toward luxury and royal opulence—a tendency shared by most of his characters—has not done him any favors with those humorless critics, despite adding layers of social and dramatic complexity to his historical films.

As for the social climbing of the commoner Jeanne Vaubernier, later Madame DuBarry, Lubitsch understands and empathizes with that impulse to "better" herself in the limited ways her society allows even if that pursuit does not actually work out to her betterment. His historical spectacles are, in one sense, the tragic inverse of his comedies, with his work in both genres depicting the emotional imperatives of people from lower social classes, minorities, and other outsiders to rise above their socially prescribed stations. Whether their weapons are talent, brains, and chutzpah as in the comedies or sex, charm, and chutzpah as in the tragedies, Lubitsch is not one to judge these characters by the strictures of middle-class morality or the hypocritical standards of what passes for upper-class morality, that is, slumming while making everyone look the other way.

Siegfried Kracauer's influential 1947 study of German film, *From Caligari to Hitler: A Psychological History of the German Film*, avoids the kind of condemnation exhibited by Lotte Eisner of what she calls Lubitsch's "Jewish lower middle-class" traits and offers some praise for the director's wit and skillful handling of crowds in the historical spectacles. But Kracauer's postwar study, relentlessly examining pre-1933 German filmmaking for signs of the country's ultimate descent into Nazism, finds much to deplore about Lubitsch's spectacles as evidence of what he calls their "anti-democratic" and "nihilistic" tendencies in a volatile time. His political criticisms of those films echo Eisner's in many respects and similarly dismiss or overlook the actual political satire and often-trenchant critiques of monarchism that Lubitsch brought to his spectacles.

Noting that the opening night of *Madame DuBarry* in Berlin on September 18, 1919, took place while huge crowds were demonstrating in the streets, Kracauer writes, "Instead of tracing all revolutionary events to their economic and ideal causes, it persistently presents them as the outcome of psychological conflicts. . . . *Passion* [the film's American title] does not exploit the [political] passions inherent in the [French] Revolution, but reduces the Revolution to a derivative of private passions." The fact that *Madame DuBarry*'s portrait of the revolution echoed the unrest in Germany was, in this view, not a mark in its favor but rather the contrary. And yet some other critics have plausibly suggested that the displacement of Lubitsch's political commentaries onto previous eras was a transparent device to get away with political satire and other kinds of social criticism that might not have been allowed if his camera had been pointed directly outside the cinema. A sophisticated viewer with a sense of irony not blinded by ideological preoccupations can appreciate the cleverness of Lubitsch's strategy. Accusing him of "a blend of cynicism and melodramatic sentimentality," Kracauer goes on, like Eisner, to belittle Lubitsch's comedies, writing withering words about his German satires of the early 1920s: "Considering the speed with which Lubitsch exchanged murders and tortures for dancing and joking, it is highly probable that his comedies sprang from the same nihilism as his historical dramas. This tendency made it easy for him to drain great events of their seriousness and realize comical potentialities in trifles."

It is hard to argue that Lubitsch's German historical spectacles, for all their considerable merits, have as much artistic originality or lasting importance as the comedies for which he is better known today, whether we are talking about his Hollywood classics or the more obscure German comedies. While the charge that his spectacles are apolitical is absurd, since they are about political figures and social upheavals, their political meanings are complex and capable of varying interpretations.

From a leftist point of view, it can be argued that the film's showing Jeanne's rejected student lover in *Madame DuBarry*, Armand de Foix (Harry Liedtke), only discovering his political passion as a result of their breakup, rather than because of a sense of high ideals, tends to trivialize the social causes of revolution. Lubitsch could have started (as, say, Jean Renoir does in his great 1938 film about the French Revolution, *La Marseillaise*) by placing more dramatic emphasis on the poverty and other socially unjust conditions of eighteenth-century France under the monarchy and then brought Jeanne and Armand into the picture as victims of that system. Their personal behavior and failed relationship could have been depicted more clearly as being socially determined even though, with a little effort, we can see that such is indeed the case in *Madame DuBarry*.

But Lubitsch instead introduces Jeanne having a good time in her humble trade as a milliner and exploiting her job to make contacts with men who can elevate her in social status. In the process, Armand gets shunted aside, and Jannings's King Louis XV ultimately takes his place as her bewitched admirer. Lubitsch devotes much screen time and relish to showing the king slavishly kissing her foot (the foot fetish is carried over, democratically, from the store comedies) and ironically acting more or less as her besotted, degraded servant. *Madame DuBarry* and *La Marseillaise* similarly contain magnificent and somewhat sympathetic depictions of very human French monarchs by an unusually subdued Jannings in the Lubitsch film and Pierre Renoir (the director's brother) as Louis XVI in *La Marseillaise*. The two films take quite different approaches to the history of the French Revolution—Renoir's is an episodic ensemble piece rather than having a single protagonist—but they share qualities of life-embracing humor and a tendency to resist facile caricature of the monarchy as a way of exalting the common people by contrast (although Lise Delamare's Marie Antoinette is one of the few entirely unsympathetic characters in Renoir's body of work).

It could just as well be argued that Lubitsch's method approaches the conditions that brought about the Revolution from a different angle, an oblique angle characteristic of this director. While *Madame DuBarry* can be faulted for focusing too intently on sexual intrigue at the expense of social upheavals and for making those subjects seem too causally related, we eventually do see the poverty, unrest, and chaos in the streets; the earnest plotting of the revolutionaries; and the thoughtlessness, if not callousness, of the royal mistress toward the slaughter of peasants by royal troops acting on her behalf. Lubitsch's reversal of the conventionally didactic sociological explanation for revolution is his crime in the eyes of those who regard individuals as less important than the masses. That viewpoint is even more fashionable today because of the prevailing "bottom-up" theory of history, which was developed to counter the "great man" theory of history, an important change in our way of studying the past and social developments. But it is worth noting that by following the catastrophic misadventures of the lower-class Jeanne and linking her transgressions to the grievances of the people, Lubitsch is also following a bottom-up theory while not neglecting the flaws flowing from the top down at the palace.

In *Madame DuBarry* the French people finally begin to focus on Jeanne's pampered state and obliviousness to their concerns as a casus belli. She is dragged, fighting every step of the way, to the guillotine, and the original version of the film ends with a grotesque close-up of her severed head—"Und now a big head of Pola," indeed. That close-up was cut from the American release version. There is no disputing the intensity of Jeanne's ambition to rise in society or her willingness to make free use of her sexuality with a series of men to do so, including with the king of France. But though Jeanne has some choices, mistreats her young lover Armand, and slights his affections even while making sporadic attempts to use her position to help him, it should not go without noting that as a member of the lower class, she has few if any options to rise in society other than by using her sexuality. While her ambition is not culpable per se, that does not entirely excuse her willful actions, and though her selfishness earns her the just contempt of the people, she hardly deserves having her head lopped off. Lubitsch cannot be seen as simply endorsing her irresponsible behavior or as simply condemning her. He may be amused by Jeanne's libidinousness and ambition and admiring of her boldness in getting her way, but he keeps us always aware of the impetuousness, recklessness, and callousness of her conduct, especially in contrast with the legitimate grievances of the people who do not share her sexually earned privileges.

The spectacles with which Lubitsch followed *Madame DuBarry*, *Anna Boleyn* and *The Wife of Pharaoh*, are overly solemn, heavy-handed films that lack the relatively unpretentious vitality of performing and seriocomic storytelling that makes *Madame DuBarry* his most satisfactory German historical film, his most Lubitschean spectacle. Although *Anna Boleyn* and *Pharaoh* may be more accomplished visually, they are less compelling as cinematic achievements. They did not have the major international impact on both Lubitsch and German cinema in general that *Madame DuBarry* did, probably because they lack some of the human dimensions of that film. In his successful attempt to audition for Hollywood with his subsequent spectacles, Lubitsch fell prey to the temptation to impress by making his films increasingly pretentious.

It could be argued, in answering another complaint of some leftist critics (although not Kracauer), that *Anna Boleyn* is the most historically accurate of the three films, if that matters much. But even that question is problematic since historians differ so much about the actual Anne Boleyn (the film uses the German version of her first name). The second wife of King Henry VIII, she was beheaded on apparently false charges of adultery so Henry could remarry, an act that helped bring about his schism with the Catholic Church. But Anne remains a figure of controversy today. Historians generally regard her as having been innocent of the charges for which she was executed, but there are various schools of thought on whether or not she was culpable in helping displace the previous queen, the aging Catherine of Aragon, who was banished for failing to produce a surviving male heir. One of Anna's "crimes" is that she had a daughter instead of a son; ironically, her daughter became Queen Elizabeth I.

Lubitsch portrays Anna (Henny Porten) as entirely a victim, a shy creature whose demure behavior toward Jannings's king as a lady of the court stimulates him to force her into a marriage she finds abhorrent. The king terrorizes his bride until he decides to put her to death. In a characteristic stylistic touch that is crucial to how the story unfolds, Lubitsch shows how Anna's behavior during a game of lawn tennis, when the king mischievously knocks his ball into some bushes, is misinterpreted by characters who cannot see what is actually happening. The audience can see that Anna's behavior in the bushes is entirely innocent; she rebuffs the king's advances as she will continue doing until forced to marry him. But her lover, Sir Henry Norris (Paul Hartmann), and Queen Catherine (Hedwig Pauly-Winterstein) assume the contrary when Anna and the king are hidden behind the bushes. That misunderstanding, a product of both the king's lecherous nature and of the others' fatal lack of trust in Anna, helps lend to the film's tragic conclusion.

Why Lubitsch and writers Norbert Falk and Hans Kräly chose this relatively one-dimensional approach to the character of Anna Boleyn, making her simply a victim of Henry VIII's lust, is not clear. More complexity in Anna would have rendered it a richer film, though there is a quiet dignity to Porten's performance that is impressive and moving (the film's use of the German "Anna" could be a further gesture of sympathy and identification). It may be that having made *Madame DuBarry*, with its reckless heroine who helps cause her own downfall, Lubitsch did not want to repeat himself by depicting a coquettish, more sexually active Anne Boleyn.

But given how unjustly the historical Anne Boleyn was treated by her royal husband, Lubitsch may have felt an obligation to give her the benefit of the doubt. He pulls no punches historically in depicting Henry as a psychopathic wife murderer. This makes the film a tragic portrait of the misogyny that is treated satirically in *The Doll*. Jannings's portrayal of a colorful but hideous despot—which influenced Charles Laughton's more humorous depiction in the 1934 Alexander Korda classic *The Private Life of Henry VIII*—is powerfully rendered in one of the Swiss actor's most alarming performances. Critics past and present have focused on the negative views of monarchy in *Madame DuBarry* and *Anna Boleyn* as representing the German film industry's efforts at getting back at France and England, two of the Allied powers that had defeated Germany in the Great War. Complaining that the innocent Anne Boleyn of Lubitsch's picture did not resemble what was then widely thought of the actual queen, the *New York Times* wrote in 1921, "Mr. Lubitsch has laid himself open to the serious charge of being a propagandist first and an artist afterward, for, while no one may legitimately complain against him for truthfully picturizing the disreputable periods in the history of any of Germany's late antagonists, he becomes merely a Prussian agent if he falsifies history in any important matter."

That is an unduly harsh charge, but criticisms of Lubitsch's spectacles by some other European critics of the time as thinly disguised revenge fantasies against the defeated Germany's former enemies have some merit. The films can support that argument. Yet the primary motive for the German industry in making these films, at least consciously, was to reap financial reward and broaden its appeal, not to thumb its nose at its old enemies, which by itself would have been a self-defeating goal. And it is hard to expect that a defeated people should politely abstain from such mockery and contempt toward its conquerors. Most audiences at the time did not seem unduly bothered by Lubitsch's portrayals of French and British despots since the films were of sufficient quality (including their careful respect for physical details of the historical settings even if events and characters were altered) that the films seemed to rise above parochial contemporary political concerns.

Unlike in *Madame DuBarry*, in *Anna Boleyn* Lubitsch shows his female protagonist going to her death stoically rather than hysterically (after some quiet anguish behind the scenes) and depicts Anna's execution as much less of a spectacle than it actually was. Instead, she is shown walking in a simple coarse dark gown, looking like a nun, through a tall Lubitschean door and past the camera to the execution block. The large crowd that was present in history is not shown in what appears instead to be an almost private ceremony, reflecting, perhaps unconsciously, official shame at such a monstrous injustice. This artistic choice to alter history reflects Lubitsch's awareness of the considerable qualities of rectitude in Porten's screen image as well as his admiration for Anna as a martyr to psychotic male urges for lust and dominance. Lubitsch's depiction of women is always affectionate but perhaps never less ambiguously than in this case. Film historian Jan-Christopher Horak has speculated that Lubitsch may have gone with the innocent-victim version of the Anne Boleyn story because he may have been so eager to pair Germany's most beloved female star with Jannings in dramatic roles (after their offbeat teaming in his comedy *Kohlhiesel's Daughters*) that he deprived himself of a more complex characterization that would have been more in line with the women's roles in his other films.

Before her marriage, Anna is polite to the king but repeatedly distressed by his open flirting with her, even in front of the queen; she resists him at every turn; she is appalled when he makes clear his intention to marry her; and she is forced into the union against her wishes. She is permitted a brief moment of vanity before the wedding when, resplendent in her gown and surrounded by ladies-in-waiting, she inspects her image in a looking glass and declares, "Lady Jane, today I must be the fairest woman in England!" But she suffers not from her betrayal of Norris but from his betrayal of her. This development stems from one of those emotional misunderstandings that are the source of much of the director's strength, though here played for drama rather than comedy. The game of lawn tennis from which Anna escapes with her honor intact, but which still causes her to be regarded as having behaved improperly, is an example of Lubitsch's characteristic use of shifts in perspective to allow us privileged access to what some of his characters fail to understand. This is the director's way of critiquing the reactions of the onlookers to this pivotal event, and he does so most effectively by using ellipsis to allow us to draw our own conclusion. As Graham Petrie notes, this "pervasive technique" in Lubitsch displays "what might be called 'misreading of visual evidence,' whereby either a character misinterprets what he or she is seeing, or, more rarely, the audience is led to draw mistaken conclusions from ambiguous visual evidence."

A scene after the wedding echoes and underscores Lubitsch's elliptically presented pattern of injustice. While the king is dallying with a maiden in the woods and Anna is trying to find him, Norris makes advances to the newly crowned queen, which she indignantly rejects. Norris's exit from the woods causes another suitor from the court, Mark Smeaton (Ferdinand von Alten), to assume that Anna has behaved improperly. This second misunderstanding eventually brings about the false accusations of infidelity that cause Anna's doom. Her dilemma in a forced marriage has left no room for her to accept Norris's belated desire to win her back even if she had any remaining interest in him after his earlier faithlessness. But after Norris is killed on the king's orders, the false claim of infidelity is used to justify her execution so the king can take a new bride.

The film vastly oversimplifies the causes for the Reformation by attributing it simply to Henry VIII's sexual passion for Anne Boleyn. However, since this is a film centering on her character, Lubitsch's failure to take adequate account of that context is a less incapacitating flaw than it might be otherwise. Though Anna has no ambition beyond being a member of the court, she has beauty, hardly a crime that makes her worthy of execution. The casting of Porten, who looks more matronly than young, goes somewhat against convention (although Porten was about the same age as Anne when she became queen). As Petrie puts it, Porten represented "the embodiment of middle-class German womanhood, dutiful, loyal, and devoted to the needs of her husband and family, and [was] by no means a typical adulteress." Lubitsch's films often condone or even celebrate adultery and other forms of unconventional sexuality. Here, on the other hand, the director's insistence on Anna's blamelessness accounts for the film's uncharacteristic feeling of monotony. Still, as always, the subjects of adultery and betrayal bring out some of Lubitsch's sharpest artistic impulses, if only intermittently. His elliptical ways of showing how Anna is falsely perceived as an adulteress are among the high points in a film depicting a raw exercise of monstrous patriarchal power.

The same kind of female guilelessness is on display in *The Wife of Pharaoh*. Pharaoh Amenes (a glowering but imposing Jannings) is offered the daughter of an Ethiopian king (Paul Wegener, Golem-like and in blackface) as a political gesture to seal a political alliance. But the pharaoh, after initially lusting more for the jewels that the Ethiopian gives him, turns his appetite to the king's slave girl, Theonis (the newcomer Dagny Servaes). In a tediously predictable plot complication, Theonis is in love with Ramphis, the son of the royal master builder played by Lubitsch's handsome and usually charming leading man Harry Liedtke. The film portrays their relationship as entirely innocent of ulterior motives. But it causes the jealous wrath of the pharaoh, who, like Henry VIII, is a selfish tyrant disregarding the wishes or relationships of anyone within his control. Lubitsch makes it entirely clear that Theonis has no other motive in marrying the pharaoh but saving Ramphis;

as a slave with no rights and a moral innocent, she is as much a victim as Anna, and her death with her lover by stoning is depicted as the monstrous injustice it is. The only one of the three spectacles in question with a morally ambiguous, and hence more interesting, principal female character is *Madame DuBarry*.

The Wife of Pharaoh plays like a calling card for Hollywood. It represents a triumph of cinematic style far advanced from the relative crudity of Lubitsch's first spectacle only four years earlier, *Carmen*. Lubitsch's Egyptian extravaganza is a visual feast with its mammoth sets of the pharaoh's palace, a sphinx, an Egyptian village (created by Kurt Richter and Ernst Stern), hordes of extras, and spectacular cinematography by Sparkuhl and Hansen. Even if the dramaturgy of *Pharaoh* seems ponderous and strangely humorless today compared with *Madame DuBarry* and the human qualities of Griffith at his best, Lubitsch's epic not only rivals but equals its Hollywood competition for sheer grandeur. Dave Kehr, reviewing the restoration of *The Wife of Pharaoh*, pointed out in the *New York Times*, "The film's recreation of ancient Egypt on a lot outside of Berlin clearly left an impression on Cecil B. DeMille, at the time Paramount's leading director but still a specialist in comedies and melodramas about contemporary sexual mores. After *Pharaoh*, DeMille folded his style into Lubitsch's for his first version of *The Ten Commandments* (1923), while Lubitsch, in one of film history's tidier paradoxes, turned away from costume pictures to DeMille-style sex comedies on his arrival in Hollywood."

But in *Pharaoh*, as with *The Eyes of the Mummy* and *Sumurun*, there is something about the so-called Oriental subgenre of the period that seems to work against Lubitsch's more natural tendencies toward lightness of touch, the style he would later rediscover in Hollywood. In his Oriental fantasy films, Lubitsch's lifelong fascination with the textures of fabrics and luxurious settings tends to predominate and make the dramatics as florid as the trappings. Perhaps Lubitsch also found the exotic cultures he was attempting to re-create too alien and alluring for his sensibilities. Perhaps he was overwhelmed by the sheer scale of the production of *Pharaoh* and neglected human values in favor of logistics, a problem that often afflicts film directors when they are given large resources. The banality of the Falk/Kräly screenplay makes the characters wooden, the acting overwrought, and the plotting slipshod and soap-operatic.

Stefan Drössler pointed out that Lubitsch's entire career shows that he periodically reverted to more obviously "serious" projects such as this one whenever he had the power to do so even though these projects do not play to his true strengths. Drössler thought Lubitsch may have made such films partly out of frustration in a bid for greater prestige than is usually afforded to makers of comedy. Michael Hanisch's analysis of Lubitsch's life and work suggests additional psychological reasons for his being a frustrated serious actor and director. Although that kind of insecurity about his special talent is regrettable in a great comedy filmmaker, it is understandable in light of prejudices in the industry and among the public. And it could be argued that Lubitsch's ultimate triumph late in his career in pulling off the difficult feat of making a serious historical film about Nazis that is also very funny, *To Be or Not to Be*, is his resolution of that nagging tendency. That startling achievement might not have been possible had he not experimented from time to time with such grim works as *Anna Boleyn*, *The Wife of Pharaoh*, and *Die Flamme* as well as others in America: *Marguerite and Faust*, an unrealized project to adapt Goethe's *Faust* to the screen with Mary Pickford; *The Patriot*; *Eternal Love*; and his 1932 film about World War I, *The Man I Killed* (an antiwar film that Paramount retitled *Broken Lullaby* in a fruitless attempt to stir up some business).

But as with all Lubitsch's historical spectacles, *Pharaoh* has some elements in common with his lighter works, especially his characteristic concentration on the intricacies of sexual intrigue. That the consequences for such carryings-on are often matters of life or death in the spectacles tends to defeat comedy, however, and in this case, the attempt to blend genres makes the film seem clumsy and often silly. The villainous pharaoh's lusting after the slave girl Theonis is predictable and arbitrary, as is her involvement with Ramphis. This conflict between young lovers and a tyrannical ruler largely repeats the similar conflicts in *Madame DuBarry* and *Anna Boleyn*. As such, it began to seem merely formulaic the third time around, and the youthful romance feels tiresome. The role of Theonis had been planned for Pola Negri, and her absence is felt in *Pharaoh*, with the relatively pallid and ordinary Servaes robbing the part of some of the vitality Negri would have provided. Further damaging the romantic subplot is the fact that Liedtke wears more makeup than Servaes and a clownish pageboy wig. Some of that is standard silent-movie makeup, but allowing Liedtke's natural good looks to shine forth would have helped to underscore the sexual contrast he offers to Jannings's pharaoh, an ugly man who suffers from some of the self-pitying, masochistic tendencies that the actor often brought to his roles (climaxing in his degraded Professor "Unrat," or Professor Garbage, in Josef von Sternberg's *The Blue Angel*).

The pharaoh's sense of humiliation in having to force himself on Theonis and then beg for her love, since she only agrees to become his wife to save the man she truly loves, gives the film some dramatic complexity. But the romantic plot seems trivial in contrast with the calamities that ensue because of it—war and the death of the pharaoh. This gross imbalance could be adduced to validate the criticisms of Lubitsch's leftist attackers that he tended to place undue emphasis on sex as the prime motivating factor in human conflict. Nevertheless, *Pharaoh* qualifies that impression somewhat by opening with a ghastly sequence in which the pharaoh's indifferent reaction to workers being crushed to death in building his treasury building causes a massive protest by their wives that is put down by sword-wielding troops. If one follows the methodology of Kracauer in *From Caligari to Hitler*, one could say that Lubitsch, as he readied himself to leave Germany, was offering his native land urgent warnings about incipient despotism with his portrayals of the monstrous cruelties of tyrants. It is fitting that the tyrants are played by Emil Jannings because he became a prominent Nazi supporter after returning to Germany when the talkies arrived.

Following the examples of *Madame DuBarry* and *Anna Boleyn*, *Pharaoh* was released in Germany with a tragic ending. After Theonis and Ramphis are reunited and she chooses him as the new ruler, the old pharaoh unexpectedly returns, and a mob stones the young couple to death. Then there is a poignant scene featuring the old pharaoh, Lear-like, mad and disheveled, toppling over on his throne. But the ending was truncated for the American market to avoid that bleak finale, and it ends with the lovers together; the epilogue was simply eliminated. As William Dean Howells observed to Edith Wharton, "What the American public always wants is a tragedy with a happy ending." The attempt at pandering to the American audience may have backfired in the case of the retitled *The Loves of Pharaoh*, however. *Variety* complained, "Toward the finish there has been drastic cutting, [and] the story is jumpy and confused," and the adulterated version did not do well after its initial run in New York City.

TWO LUBITSCH MANIFESTOS

Lubitsch usually kept above the critical fray in the debate over his approach to historical spectacles, but on one notable occasion, in a 1924 German article he wrote from America, he was combative in his response to such attacks:

> Whoever continues to strive toward the loftiest heights, whoever creates with his works ever clearer and purer expressions of his own artistic nature will find the path to international success and fame; in so doing, he will gain the world's respect not only for himself but also for his country and his people. But this cultural and political side effect must remain just that: a side effect. At the moment at which we subsume the artistic film under politics, we rob ourselves of all artistic opportunities. . . . For this reason, film's internationality is not an economic matter but an artistic one, even if politico-economic stupidities undeniably make the work of artists difficult or nearly impossible at times.

There was another, equally defiant side to Lubitsch: that of the popular entertainer who resisted artistic pretension. In a 1920 German article entitled "We Lack Film Poetry," he asked,

> Must film be art in order to prove its right to exist? The answer is no. It is very nice and also a good goal to wish in one's heart of hearts that film, or at least a part of film production, may one day reach artistic heights. But we cannot and need not demand that of film production generally. . . . Why should we force art on people who split their sides laughing over a smack on the backside? . . . Are the housemaid's morals more shocked if she cries over an abandoned bride in a film instead of at the end of an operetta's second act? Kitsch cannot be eradicated! We have granted it to the theater; let film have it as well. In the theater, it delights thousands; in cinema, millions. That alone is proof of its right to exist.

Lubitsch admitted that film imagery had not achieved the quality of Raphael's paintings and that film drama had not approached the quality of Shakespeare:

But that would be asking too much in these early years of film. If I had to classify the best film productions currently being made, I would call it good applied art.

Now, can film move beyond applied art into the realm of genuine art? I think I can affirm this in good conscience, as well. The actors are ready, as are the directors and designers; the only thing we do not have yet is film poetry [*Filmdichtung*]. . . . Film poetry as I imagine it must not be written in naturalistic or expressionistic sentences, but rather composed in images. What I mean is that the plot must be formed in such a way that each image furthers the story without the insertion of explanatory text. . . . I would think that someone could string together a series of images, each of high artistic value, and thereby create strong dramatic tension. I imagine that in a film like this, even a photographed room, for example, could express deep ideas.

Maybe that is the path to film poetry.

In these two Lubitsch manifestos, drawing from different but not incompatible aspects of his personality as a popular filmmaker who strove for artistry, he not only thumbed his nose at his critics but also pointed forward to his even greater and more influential work to come.

THE WIZARD ESCAPES TO AMERICA

The attacks on the "escapism" and alleged frivolity of Lubitsch's German historical spectacles reflect a political bias, still prevalent in some circles today, toward a style of filmmaking that does not focus single-mindedly enough on the oppression of the masses and on historical determinism. Behind these critics' complaints is a contempt for the talent for popular filmmaking that would endear Lubitsch to Hollywood. No doubt the contrast between some of the German and American reactions to his ambitious work in the 1918–1922 period contributed to his desire to emigrate to a more hospitable environment.

By 1922 Lubitsch was acknowledging that the international filmgoing public's appetite for spectacles was waning. Perhaps *Madame DuBarry* had been something of an exception after all because of its groundbreaking style, its raucous human qualities. The genre's temporary boxoffice decline largely explained why he abandoned spectacles once he landed in America. In Germany as well, the genre would soon become a thing of the past because of the increasingly out-of-control inflation there and its dampening effect on the scale of production. Lubitsch's next and last German film, *Die Flamme*, represents a conscious return to intimate storytelling; the lovingly designed period sets were on a much smaller scale. It also suffered from the kind of butchery that befell *The Wife of Pharaoh* in America. Not released until 1923 due to its distributor's financial problems, *Die Flamme* was written by Kräly from the 1919 play *Die Sterne* (*The Stars*) by Hans Müller, set in nineteenth-century Paris. Pola Negri is touching as a hopelessly stigmatized prostitute, Yvette, who vainly attempts to escape her milieu through her love for a young composer (Hermann Thimig from *The Doll*) but in the end jumps from a window.

The German version is uncompromising and starkly honest. A *Photoplay* writer who visited the set wisecracked, "I don't know exactly how the tragedy will be turned into a happy-ever-after comedy. Perhaps there will be a shot showing Pola falling on to the studio mattress instead of the supposed paving blocks. The American public—the American public with the mind of a twelve-year-old child, you know—it must have life as it ain't." In the 1924 American release version, *Montmartre*, Yvette is saved from suicide just in time. That ending was reluctantly shot by Lubitsch himself to prevent the Americans from concocting their own ending as they had for *The Loves of Pharaoh*, or so he rationalized it while succumbing to a form of economic and cultural self-censorship. *Montmartre* has not survived. Lubitsch discouraged his friends from seeing the American version, which he later complained had been "cut to pieces and did not give the slightest idea of the dramatic value and the impact this picture had in its original version." The attempt to sanitize the film did not work in the United States after all. After the New York opening, *Variety* reported, "*Montmartre* got off to a bad start with poor notices, and Paramount has done little for it since."

All but one reel of *Die Flamme* is lost. Stefan Drössler and the Munich Film Museum put together a fascinating 2006 version of the film using the single extant reel along with stills and material from the original script and scene drawings to help convey the sense of what seems to have been a subtly affecting tragic work. The visual evidence shows a subdued acting style (particularly striking where the usually expansive Negri is concerned) along with the exquisitely evocative Parisian period flavor provided by Lubitsch's regular set designers Ernst Stern and Kurt Richter and costumer Ali Hubert.

"RATTLESNAKES AND COUNTLESS OTHER WILD ANIMALS"

In January 1922, while in New York exploring studio facilities and attending premieres of major American films, including Griffith's *Orphans of the Storm* and Erich von Stroheim's *Foolish Wives*, Lubitsch had remarked, "To come to America is the dream of every European artist." On December 3 of that year, after his last few months in Europe, he boarded an ocean liner, the *President Roosevelt*, in Bremen, Germany, and set off for his adopted country. He arrived in New York on December 12, accompanied by his recent bride, small-part actress and war widow Helena, or Helene ("Leni"), Sonnet Kraus. The twenty-four-year-old native of Metz, France, had married the thirty-year-old director in Berlin on August 23. Leni had two young sons, Heinz and Edmund, who stayed behind with her parents before joining them in America a year later. Also accompanying Ernst and Leni on the ship was his twenty-year-old assistant, Heinz Blanke, who worked with him for a while in Hollywood but went on to become a prominent producer in his own right after changing his name to Henry Blanke. The seemingly indispensable screenwriter Hans Kräly soon followed as part of the Lubitsch entourage. Kräly recalled that Ernst's seventy-year-old father, Simon, was "nearly in tears at the thought of his son going to California to a world full of Indians, mountain lions, rattlesnakes, and countless other wild animals."

After his first two years in Hollywood, Lubitsch wrote,

No one will be surprised to know that I was in doubt as to various phases of my coming to America. Men who were supposed to know all about America gave me long and intricate warnings about the peculiarities of American taste. I was given the impression that the Americans were as different from Europeans as the inhabitants of Mars from Earth-children. They said that the Americans didn't like this; they wouldn't stand for that; they had to have it this way; they couldn't be interested if it was that way. As a final cheering message, they advised me to deny my German parentage and birthright. They suggested that I should call myself a Pole or a Roumanian or an Austrian. Something in my heart would not allow me to follow their advice. I had an honest admiration for America. I wanted the Americans to like me. But I couldn't bring myself to begin my new life here with a lie. I made up my mind that I would not sail under false colors. If they would not accept me as I was, then I would have to go back to Europe.

Lubitsch's first film after being called to Hollywood, Mary Pickford's 1923 *Rosita*, a period comedy-drama set in seventeenth-century Spain, is in the mode of his German spectacles though less grandiose. He said he was giving Hollywood what it wanted in *Rosita* before turning his attention to the kind of intimate films he really wanted to make. His decision to veer to the opposite extreme, to intimate filmmaking with *The Marriage Circle* (1924) and other Hollywood films, had already been evident in his last German film. Making a *Kammerspielfilm* with *Die Flamme* had been an indication of his new way of thinking. A German reviewer, Kurt Pinthus, wrote in the liberal Berlin journal *Das Tage-Buch*, "It is Lubitsch's merit to free himself and us from the disaster he himself provoked: the monumental period film. Here the essence of the film is solely atmospheric, with poetic imagery and visible human touches. This should have been the right direction for Lubitsch— but instead he chose (for the time being) to go to America."

Before leaving Europe, Lubitsch had told the press he wanted to make films in which acting was emphasized; this may have been his defensive way of acknowledging that the acting in *Pharaoh* had come in for considerable criticism. He said he would change his approach from "longwindedness to depth." He vowed that in future he would make "Lubitsch films," which he defined simply as "films different from the rest." While lending weight to the argument that the spectacles seem like the work of someone else, Lubitsch was also pointing forward to the change of artistic direction he would take in America. In his article from Hollywood published in Berlin in April 1924, he shared the commercial and artistic imperatives that had led to that change. He advised the German industry he left behind to bring its cinematography up to the American standard, to develop more female stars ("It is amazing what abundance the American film industry has of female performers"), and to downplay its former reliance on spectacles even though Germany remained "an ideal country" for the production of such pictures.

Writing that letter in the wake of *Rosita*, while he was already busy making more intimate pictures in America, he declared, "Countless costume dramas have been produced, so that the American public is tired of this genre not only from the German, but also from the American film industry. The American public is currently against the costume films. Even for the American producer, the production of a costume film means such a big risk that almost no one wants to take that gamble anymore." The German film industry, Lubitsch declared, needed to follow Hollywood's lead and focus more on "the modern society film. . . . The German film company needs more elegance." Lubitsch would demonstrate that approach with spectacular success in his Hollywood work, soon becoming the leading director of a second country.

Jean Renoir wrote of Lubitsch in 1967,

To maintain the admirable balance of nature, God provides to the defeated nations the gift of Art. It is what happened to Germany after the defeat of 1918. Berlin, before Hitler, was blossoming with talents. In this short Renaissance, the Jews, not only of Germany but also of the surrounding countries, brought to this capital a certain spirit which was probably the best expression of the time. Lubitsch was a great example of this ironic approach to the big problems of life. His films were loaded with a kind of wit which was specifically the essence of the intellectual Berlin in those days. This man was so strong that when he was asked by Hollywood to work there, he not only didn't lose his Berlin style, but he converted the Hollywood industry to his own way of expression.

3.1 Lubitsch and his star and boss Mary Pickford on the set of his first American film, *Rosita*
(1923). *(The Mary Pickford Company/United Artists.)*

3

THE "BERLIN STYLE" IN HOLLYWOOD

On Lubitsch's last trip to Germany, when he "visited the European studios principally for the pleasure of again greeting my old friends there," a party was thrown in his honor on December 14, 1932, by State Secretary Otto Meissner, who later became a Nazi official. Lubitsch told a Jewish journalist at the event, Bella Fromm, why he was no longer working in his native land: "That's finished. I'm going to the United States. Nothing good is going to happen here for a long time. The sun shines every day in Hollywood."

Lubitsch left Germany for the last time on January 6, 1933, sailing on the SS *Europa* from Bremen to New York, retracing the route he had taken upon his emigration in 1922. In the intervening ten years, he had thrown himself wholeheartedly into becoming an American and a Hollywood director, a process that became irrevocable once he saw the rise of Nazism. But as much as he tried and succeeded in adapting to his new country and the Hollywood system, Lubitsch could not entirely eradicate the influence of his background.

Even though he no longer allowed his family to speak German in the house after Adolf Hitler came to power, Lubitsch never lost his heavy German accent, which endeared him to most of his coworkers (though not to Mary Pickford). Lubitsch initially weathered some protests by superpatriots about Hollywood hiring a "Hun" in 1922, so soon after the Great War, and some of that hostility lingered for quite a while. The *Motion Picture Herald* snidely wrote in November 1933, "Herr Ernst Lubitsch, one-time Berlin actor, but for years a Paramount director in Hollywood, has finally gotten around, after some eleven years, to the important business of declaring allegiance to the land of opportunity, blue eagles [a New Deal symbol], high salary checks, and double features." However belated his action might have seemed to some, it is significant that Lubitsch took a decisive step toward becoming an American citizen shortly after the Nazis took power in his native land in 1933. Lubitsch's delayed decision possibly reflected a lingering feeling of connection to Germany that did not vanish entirely until Adolf Hitler became chancellor on January 30 of that year and dictator on March 23.

Lubitsch had filed a Declaration of Intention for American citizenship with the Immigration and Naturalization Service on April 16, 1924, but did not submit a Petition for Naturalization in that decade. He submitted another Declaration of Intention for citizenship in the U.S. District Court in Los Angeles on June 23, 1933. On January 28, 1935, Germany revoked Lubitsch's citizenship, along with those of other Jewish Berliners who had been naturalized as German citizens after World War I. The *New York Times* reported from Berlin that the Berlin police chief had made the announcement and that "this action was taken under Chancellor Hitler's decree empowering the State authorities to take citizenship from persons naturalized between Nov. 9, 1918, and his accession to office." "LUBITSCH TO BE AMERICAN" was the headline of a January 30 *Times* article from the Associated Press, which reported, "Mr. Lubitsch was one of 207 persons affected by an order revoking the nationality of 'Eastern Jews,' persons dangerous to the State and others." Lubitsch's response to the press was that he was "mildly surprised" by Germany's action. He added, "I am preparing myself for American citizenship, and my allegiance from now on goes to the land of my adoption." After filing his Petition for Naturalization on October 14, 1935, Lubitsch became an American citizen on January 24, 1936.

Since Hollywood was largely a town of immigrants, from all over the United States as well as from other countries, for most people, Lubitsch's Germanness became a central component in his exotic appeal soon after his arrival. His work benefited greatly from his continental sensibility, which helped revolutionize Hollywood's way of looking at romantic love, marital intrigue, and comedy. Lubitsch brought a more sophisticated, urbane approach to American movies, helping counteract the ever-present puritanism that dominated the industry before he arrived and that kept trying to reassert itself even as he continued to outwit it with endless resourcefulness. Lubitsch ran rings around the censors throughout his career, though not without great effort and not without having to adapt some aspects of his style to circumvent their edicts, especially after the Production Code became strictly enforced in 1934. If he had to make some compromises with the system along the way, his successes more than compensated for them. He played a form of jiujitsu with the Hays Office by bouncing off any compromises they demanded so that he could implicitly mock the whole system of censorship.

In managing to bring more truly adult behavior to the American screen during his twenty-five years working in Hollywood, Lubitsch showed his colleagues how to do so and to some degree emboldened them. But few other directors were able to equal his level of ingenuity in generally getting around the system of censorship and having his way artistically without a great deal of moralistic backlash. Anticipating the seismic jolt that Lubitsch would bring to Hollywood, *Photoplay* writer Herbert Howe wrote with tongue in cheek after visiting "the Film Wizard of Europe" on the set of *Die Flamme* in Berlin in 1922, "It's a little bit mean of him . . . just when we were progressing so well in our history[,] to drop us back into kindergarten."

Lubitsch came to America with his exalted reputation earned largely through his historical spectacles, those grandly opulent and racy films that managed to rival Hollywood's spectacles in scope while outdoing them with a wider range, greater depth, and more truthful depiction of human behavior. But he was not simply a director of spectacles, as Europe already knew and Hollywood soon learned. The wide range of cinematic skills he had displayed in Germany provided a bounteous foundation for the new developments his style underwent in America. The phases he had already cycled through in Berlin, from low comedy to surrealistic visual satire to opulent, sardonic spectacles, were indelible parts of his artistic development. They would continue to serve him well by keeping those varied talents on tap whenever he needed to vary his style in order to move with the times and changing mores. Howe reported that Lubitsch "wants to do modern stories of American life as a relief from the long series of historical dramas and as proof of his versatility." As it turned out, Lubitsch would do few stories set in modern America, but his films would bring a distinctly modern sensibility to Hollywood regardless of their genre or setting.

After the twenty-nine-year-old Mary Pickford brought him to America to further her own evolution into a more complex and adult screen performer—a process that, contrary to legend, did not begin with *Rosita* but had been ongoing for some time in her career—Lubitsch was expected to work in the spectacle genre that had brought him fame in the United States, where his work as a comedy director in Germany was virtually unknown. (Lubitsch was technically on loan-out to Pickford from Famous Players-Lasky; his contract was held by the Hamilton Theatrical Corporation, which was half-owned by FP-L, whose distribution arm was Paramount. Hamilton had founded EFA, and so Lubitsch temporarily remained within that European coproduction arrangement that had been formed with Hollywood.) After some parrying with Pickford over film ideas—she rejected his pet project *Marguerite and Faust* (Lubitsch had planned to do a comical version of *Faust* in Germany in 1920 with Ossi Oswalda called *Mephistophela*), and he rejected Pickford's historical romance *Dorothy Vernon of Haddon Hall*—he obliged with the historical romance *Rosita*.

That 1923 film sets its love story against a backdrop of royal intrigue and revolutionary turmoil in the streets of eighteenth-century Spain. *Rosita* does not stint on elaborate period sets or crowds of extras, but the concentration on Pickford's lively character, a street singer whose revolutionary ballads ironically lead to her being pursued romantically by the king, and on other key players keeps it from the spectacle-for-its-own-sake feeling that sometimes makes Lubitsch's German historical films seem excessive and aesthetically distanced from human concerns. *Rosita* was, however, a transitional film in many ways, an entrée into Hollywood through the back door of the genre he had already outgrown in Germany. But doing another spectacle would ease his way into American filmmaking with foreign subject matter while showing Hollywood that he could outdo what they did best.

Once Lubitsch was free of Pickford, he abruptly shifted his focus back to comedy. He worked in an even more intimate comedic vein in his subsequent Hollywood silent films than he had been doing for most of his time in Europe. He began making stripped-down comedy-dramas that were anything but ornate as he refined his style to a finer point of subtlety and irony, with more delicately nuanced acting and an eloquent stylistic simplicity that precisely conveys emotional character interaction at a level that no one had reached before in film. Most of Lubitsch's extraordinary silent work was made for Warner Bros., with which he signed a three-year contract for six films on August 7, 1923, shortly before the premiere of *Rosita*. Aside from reserving story approval and financial control for the studio, the contract provided Lubitsch an otherwise remarkable degree of creative freedom: "Warner agrees that . . . there shall be no interference of any kind whatsoever from any source, with Lubitsch, with respect to any matter or thing connected with the production, cutting and final completion of such photoplays."

Warners was an up-and-coming studio then, financially successful but without the lavish resources that Famous Players-Lasky (Paramount) and MGM enjoyed in the midtwenties; Warners was primarily dependent on the canine star Rin Tin Tin for boxoffice reliability, and the German shepherd helped subsidize the art of the German director. Lubitsch correctly gambled that by bringing Warners the prestige it coveted, he could get his way artistically as long as he delivered commercially successful films set in the contemporary world and dealing with thoroughly modern sexual issues to which his audience could easily relate. Even though three of his five films for Warners are set in Europe—his way of ensuring that their daring modes of behavior would seem both tolerable and exotically appealing to American viewers—and though Lubitsch's style was far more sophisticated than the commercial norm (he was sometimes criticized by exhibitors for that reason; he was never a major boxoffice director), his silent films for Warners were widely admired, not least by his peers. These films quickly established him as an unsurpassed master of cinematic expression in an American idiom inflected by continental attitudes.

Working for a studio without the kind of lavish production resources he had enjoyed in his heyday in Berlin (that is, before the inflation that had enabled such grandeur went out of control) was no problem for the newly Americanized Lubitsch. His leaner approach to settings at Warners enabled him to focus his attention more on the minute gestures and subtle facial expressions of his players. They carry out their carefully orchestrated interplay against almost abstractly stylized, even plain visual settings and in less ornate costuming than was common in the modern Hollywood comedies or dramas of that period. But the films have a delicately molded cinematographic style, benefiting from the advanced lighting equipment and use of glass shots to enhance sets that helped Hollywood maintain its dominance in the face of the rivalry from Europe's aesthetically adventurous filmmakers.

Although *The Wife of Pharaoh* had been Lubitsch's most lavish spectacle, his subsequent concentration on the *Kammerspielfilm* style with *Die Flamme*, his last European film, was a more direct precursor of his intimately stylized work in America. It seems likely that Lubitsch was somewhat bored by spectacles by the time he left Germany and thought he had gone about as far as he could in that vein. As his assistant Henry Blanke, who had accompanied him to America, put it, "How many more thousand people can you show?" When Lubitsch saw the handwriting on the wall commercially, he largely took the opposite path in America with his smaller-scale comedy-dramas. And his American films, especially during his silent period, tended to emphasize drama even more than comedy.

The two surviving masterpieces of Lubitsch's silent years in Hollywood, *The Marriage Circle* (1924) and *Lady Windermere's Fan* (1925), are strikingly serious in their satirical preoccupations with issues of adultery, class, and snobbery. That is especially noteworthy in Lubitsch's paradoxically free yet faithful cinematic adaptation of Oscar Wilde's classic play. The film is more overtly concerned with the underlying moral issues that Wilde tends to treat in mocking fashion. Lubitsch's ten American silents cover such a wide range of genres and styles that it is misleading to reduce that period to a clichéd notion of what it means to call a film Lubitschean. Any assessment of his American silent work must also be qualified by the unfortunate fact that one of his most important silents from that period, *Kiss Me Again*, is missing and another, *The Patriot*, is almost entirely lost. Before the Museum of Modern Art undertook its recent restorations of *Rosita* and *Forbidden Paradise*, those films were available for many years only in rarely seen dupes of poor quality made from prints that had fortuitously been preserved in foreign archives, enough to suggest the quality they must have once had but still only dimly representative of it. Only three of his ten American silents are presently available on DVD. It is nothing short of scandalous how poorly treated Lubitsch's American silent period has been.

But at least *The Marriage Circle* and *Lady Windermere's Fan* are available in sparkling DVD copies, allowing today's viewers to appreciate just how masterful he already was in his first years in America and why he meant so much to his peers in his new country (*Eternal Love*, a much-inferior silent, is also available). Lubitsch's reputation as the "masters' master" was not exaggerated even before he added sound to his repertoire, which enabled him to be even more audacious and experimental in his style.

THE "TOUCH" COMES INTO VOGUE

In defining what made Lubitsch's American silent period so artistically fecund and influential, one of the least fruitful approaches is to focus on so-called Lubitsch Touches. The 1920s American films are less dependent on touches than on their distinctively complex emotional mood and elegant visual settings. The director's most lavish exercise of his penchant for stylized touches is not in these films but in his late German comedies, such as the zany, endlessly inventive *Oyster Princess*, *The Doll*, and *The Wildcat*, and in his early-thirties American comedies and musicals. His American silent work, on the other hand, is more subdued. It needs to be appreciated primarily for the stylistic unity of each film, which is not done by singling out isolated moments, no matter how brilliant. And as always in Lubitsch's body of work, the variations from film to film are as telling as their similarities. Lubitsch himself pointed out the superficiality and reductionism of judging his work by its touches, and it is telling that he made that comment in the late silent period, at the very time when the phrase "the Lubitsch Touch" came into vogue.

In a 1968 book with that title, Herman G. Weinberg recounts a 1928 conversation with Lubitsch in a New York screening room. As Lubitsch was watching Soviet director V. I. Pudovkin's *Storm over Asia* with Paramount executives, one of them remarked, "Lubitsch touches!" Lubitsch replied, "And very good Lubitsch touches, too, if I may say so." But at lunch afterward, Weinberg found that Lubitsch had been "amused" by that discussion. The director said, "I've often wondered who started that phrase. One shouldn't single out 'touches.' They're part of a whole. The camera should comment, insinuate, make an epigram or a *bon mot*, as well as tell a story. We're telling stories with pictures so we must try to make the pictures as expressive as we can."

Kristin Thompson's book on Lubitsch has a useful epilogue in which she tries to pin down the origin of the phrase "the Lubitsch Touch," which she describes as "vague and usually not very helpful. Anyone who knows what it means already knows Lubitsch, and for someone who does not know Lubitsch, the phrase explains little." Although admitting she did not do an exhaustive search for its origin, Thompson fruitfully traced the evolution of the phrase in reviews of Lubitsch films during the 1920s. The earliest inkling, predating his coming to America, is from the 1921 *New York Times* review of

Anna Boleyn (*Deception* in the United States), which states, "His work has a Continental touch." That suggests that the phrase "Lubitsch Touch" derives from the critical importance of the continental nature of his style. It was a perception that would become heightened after he began working in America, viewing sexual intrigue through a European prism. But another example of the Touch having been recognized earlier, from his German work, is evident in what the reviewer for *Exceptional Photoplays* wrote of Lubitsch's first American film, *Rosita*: "As for direction, nowhere is the picture stamped with the Lubitsch touch as prominently as usual; still his hand is recognizable for the artistry that has made him world famous."

By 1924, Thompson notes, "such touches are mentioned regularly" in American reviewers' analyses of Lubitsch's distinctive style in *Three Women* and *Forbidden Paradise*. When the *Film Daily* reviewed *Lady Windermere's Fan* the following year, the phrase was already assumed to be a commonplace. As that trade paper put it, "Lubitsch with his masterful touch has turned this somewhat weak material for pictures [!] into a very fine production replete with typical Lubitsch touches." Thompson points out that though the phrase was often associated with comical and risqué moments in Lubitsch's films—those bits or vignettes in which his continental manner was most distinct from the puritanical American approach to sex—some twenties reviewers also used the word "touches" to refer to his more dramatic moments. Charles S. Sewell did so in *Moving Picture World* while calling attention to various aspects of *Three Women*, an uneasy amalgamation of comedy with largely dramatic, even melodramatic elements: "Mr. Lubitsch's direction is marked by the same subtle touches, the same unerring ability to portray human nature, its fine points and its frailties; the same touches of comedy." This perceptive contemporary reviewer helps us see that the totality of Lubitsch's seriocomic style in his American work was already appreciated as distinctive and integral to his viewpoint as opposed to being noticeable primarily in brief flourishes.

CHAPLIN'S TOUCH

It is sometimes claimed that Lubitsch did not become Lubitsch until after he saw Charles Chaplin's *A Woman of Paris* in Hollywood in 1923. That is obviously a considerable exaggeration, since Lubitsch's artistic personality was distinctive well before he came to America, but Lubitsch himself pointed to the critical influence of Chaplin's film on his work as well as to that of Mauritz Stiller's 1920 sex comedy *Erotikon*. Billy Wilder said that when Lubitsch saw *Erotikon*, "That was when Lubitsch became Lubitsch." Evidently the influence of *Erotikon* slowly incubated in Lubitsch's mind (he was still busy in 1920 doing his almost surreally stylized comedies and lavish spectacles in Germany) until he found further impetus for such a low-key, oblique style in *A Woman of Paris*.

These two droll, highly sophisticated films about sexual relationships—unusually mature for their time and groundbreaking in their subtle yet frank recognition of erotic impulses—helped Lubitsch crystallize his thinking about how to hone his own developing style. Yet as Graham Petrie writes, "It should be recognized that Lubitsch already had been proceeding in much the same direction in his German comedies; Chaplin's and Stiller's films may have made clearer to him exactly what it was that he wanted to do, but they did not cause the radical shift from 'epic' to 'intimate' and from 'dramatic' to 'comic' films that too many film historians have assumed." It is perhaps most accurate to say that during a period of transition in Lubitsch's career, these two films perhaps gave him encouragement to concentrate his approach in order to appeal to an international audience without feeling the need to talk down to them (which, by nature, he would never do) but instead to trust in his great ability to use visual suggestion to convey the most complex emotional states.

His German films, sly and risqué, filled with innuendo, already displaying his expertise in using decor, objects, gestures, and behavior to suggest emotional subtleties rather than spelling them out directly, are nevertheless broader than his American silents. So the refinement of his handling of actors and behavior in the immediate wake of *A Woman of Paris* is no coincidence. Lubitsch's theatrical background had encouraged his more boisterous crowd-pleasing tendencies in Germany, a side of his personality that appealed to American audiences when his often-racy historical spectacles were exported after the war. Although the spectacles were accurately perceived by American reviewers and people in the film industry as more sophisticated than their American counterparts, it was precisely Lubitsch's ability to communicate in a similar entertainment idiom that made Hollywood recognize him as a kindred spirit. But while shifting his career to the States, Lubitsch needed to psych out American audiences carefully and see how he could adapt himself to their peculiar demands. That he was remarkably successful in doing so was not a matter of instant acclimation to a new culture but an incremental, though rapid, learning curve.

After working in the United States for four years, Lubitsch reflected on the extent of the cultural divide he had found in moving from Germany to America, which he called a difference in the "moral slant." In a 1927 interview with the *New York Times*, he said,

> Europe has a widely differing code of morality from that in America. . . . For instance, censorship in Europe is much freer than in America in every sex and moral matter, but far more rigid in matters of cruelty or brutality. As an instance, a man striking another repeatedly and drawing blood will be banned on the screen at once. . . . On the other hand, characters in a screen play can be very free in their love affairs. In America we try to keep matters of sex more or less a mystery, while in Europe they are recognized as a natural manifestation.

He added, "The people of Europe are more serious fundamentally than those in America. The result is that Americans go to a theatre solely to be entertained; the European, subconsciously perhaps, expects a little lesson with his entertainment. Hence a shadow story must be complete and logical to achieve success in Europe, while here the story can be perfectly illogical so long as it amuses."

Lubitsch found the way to please both himself and American audiences when he saw *A Woman of Paris* soon after making *Rosita*. Chaplin's tragicomic take on sex and romance gave Lubitsch the final clue to what he had been looking for, clinching his sense of how to deal with contemporary life in an adult way that would please American audiences while still avoiding censorship. It was a tightrope that Lubitsch needed to walk. Some of his path toward a more sophisticated sense of moralism on-screen was his own, developed gradually in his increasingly ambitious and diverse body of work in Germany, and some was revealed for him by Stiller and Chaplin. In discussing their decisive influences on Lubitsch at a critical junction in his career, perhaps it is most precise to observe that *A Woman of Paris* helped free Lubitsch to be more himself in America and to in turn lead others along his path.

Lubitsch must have been struck by the masterful blending of delicacy and naughtiness in the Chaplin film's sexual nuances. It clearly demonstrated to him how even an American film could deal with eroticism and its consequences in a mature manner. Chaplin uses suggestiveness and innuendo not for salacity but to express the complex emotions, including overtones of tragedy, that can be involved in sexual relations. Just as important, there is a moral dimension to Chaplin's tale that resembles Lubitsch's own profound moralism—a level of seriousness toward the consequences of human behavior that has nothing to do with conventional notions of morality but everything to do with how men and women can and should treat each other. That deeper dimension of drama and comedy preoccupies both Chaplin and Lubitsch throughout their work. Lubitsch's frank concentration on sexuality—*"All kinds,"* as Herbert Marshall says in *Trouble in Paradise*—and his complex attitude toward human conduct make his moralism even more unconventional, paradoxical, and pervasive.

Chaplin's film represented a startling departure for the world's most famous comedian. Although he had wrung audiences' hearts with *The Kid* in 1921, *A Woman of Paris* was his ambitious move into a more expansively dramatic realm without the emotional and comedic safety net of playing the Tramp to protect him from possible criticism. In this tale of a woman's corruption by a Paris playboy, Chaplin himself plays only an unrecognizable bit part, ceding the male lead to the ineffably roguish Adolphe Menjou. This daring turn was a mixed success, applauded by most critics but regarded more as a curiosity by audiences, and it proved a one-shot in Chaplin's career, a brilliant film of most enduring importance, perhaps, for its influence on Lubitsch and others. The British director Michael Powell, as a teenager, was "absolutely knocked out, because suddenly the whole medium grew up before my eyes. . . . Suddenly here was a grownup film, with people behaving as they do in life, and scenes treated with an enormous sophistication."

Lubitsch's succinct declaration to the *New York Times* that he liked *A Woman of Paris* because "nobody's intelligence is insulted in the picture" showed how strongly Chaplin's film called out to and reinforced Lubitsch's essential qualities as an artist. When Lubitsch spoke with another interviewer in December 1923, soon after the release of *Rosita* and only a few short months after he had seen *A Woman of Paris*, he revealed more of how Chaplin's film influenced his evolution in America: "We are groping slowly on the screen for some definite form of screen art. Something that will mean to the movies what the technical school of Ibsen meant to the drama—and we are groping slowly. . . . Chaplin's *Woman of Paris* is a great step forward. . . . So often in pictures one is not allowed to think by the director. But—ah!—in *A Woman of Paris* we had a picture that, as you Americans say, left something to the imagination." Leaving something to the imagination was a key part of how Lubitsch respected the audience's intelligence. The lessons he took from Chaplin in that regard came at a crucial turning point for the German director, when he was taking stock of the American marketplace and its various constraints on filmmakers' abilities to deal with adult subject matter. Chaplin's example helped Lubitsch master that commercial system with remarkable speed and develop his ability to outwit it.

One of the most striking qualities of *A Woman of Paris* is its use of ellipsis, a device Lubitsch had already put to good use in Germany but one that would become a central part of his American style. The plot of Chaplin's film turns on a major ellipsis. In the prologue, Edna Purviance's title character, Marie St. Clair, is planning to elope with her lover, Jean Millet (Carl Miller), to escape the stifling moral atmosphere of their small French town. But his father dies suddenly, and Jean does not come to the train station for their rendezvous. In a scene much praised at the time, Chaplin shows Marie standing anxiously at the station, about to embark for Paris; the train itself is not shown, only lights passing before the camera. Believing herself to have been jilted, Marie boards the train, and her life changes radically, as is suggested in a title: "A year later in the magic city of Paris, where fortune is fickle and a woman gambles with life—" Marie makes a grand entrance in a Paris nightclub accompanying the suave lady-killer Adolphe Menjou; she is entirely transformed as his swankily dressed mistress, and we are left to infer what has taken place in the year that we have not seen. This giant ellipsis, so sly and assured, must have mightily tickled Lubitsch's creativity. Chaplin not only flatters the audience with that suggestive technique, he avoids showing the sordid details of Marie's descent into her kept-woman status. Dramatizing it might have caused him problems with the censors even if he was already getting away with a lot by showing her in that situation and then depicting her attachment to the roguish, perpetually smirking Pierre and her pampered life in the apartment in which he has set her up.

By avoiding melodrama, Chaplin keeps the tone light even though he is dealing with a situation that has some serious implications. He is drawing a moral lesson rather pointedly, but his film manages to do so without seeming preachy. A title card at the beginning (unfortunately dropped when the film was revised, partly by Chaplin himself, for a reissue in the 1970s) states, "All of us are seeking good—We sin only in blindness. The ignorant condemn our mistakes—But the wise pity them." That attitude, more generous than usual for Chaplin, may have been part of what so impressed Lubitsch, for it applies to his own tolerant approach to human nature. Lubitsch was deeply impressed by the clear-eyed look at character he discerned in Chaplin's films and defended him against the frequent charge of sentimentality. "Chaplin is not only the greatest actor in motion pictures," Lubitsch said in 1927. "He is one of the greatest artists in the world. A hundred years from today when all our names have been forgotten, Charlie Chaplin will still be remembered."

At the time *A Woman of Paris* was made, Hollywood was trying to "clean up its act" after a series of notorious scandals had provoked all-out attacks on the industry and its portrayals of sexuality. Hollywood films were in jeopardy from local and state censorship boards, and around that time, thirty-six states introduced censorship bills to intensify the pressure; the specter of federal censorship always worried the industry as well. The industry counterattacked in early 1922 by forming the Motion Picture Producers and Distributors of America (MPPDA) to protect its interests and by hiring former U.S. postmaster general Will Hays as the industry "czar." Those efforts would lead in time to severe self-censorship. But Hays's initial efforts at policing the industry were embryonic and not nearly as strict as the Production Code that would be enforced with such rigor when the Hays Office formed the Production Code Administration (PCA), with Joseph I. Breen as its chief, on June 13, 1934. The censor's name became identified with that institution, which was known informally as the Breen Office. It required prior approval of scripts before they could go into production as well as approval of the finished films. Before then, a version of the Code, written by Jesuit priest Daniel Lord in 1930, had required that films be submitted for approval before they could be released. The MPPDA's Studio Relations Committee (SRC) enforcing that early Code was relatively toothless and acquiescent to studio pressures in contrast to the later, draconian PCA, which made many more demands in exchange for awarding Code seals. Nevertheless, by the time Chaplin began shooting *A Woman of Paris* in November 1922, the anxiety within the industry about external censorship efforts and the growing belief that self-policing was the best remedy had already had a somewhat sobering effect on filmmakers.

"It did not take long for filmmakers to predict many of the actions of these boards and take preemptive countermeasures," Richard Koszarski writes in his history of silent films.

> Cecil B. DeMille was the first master of this technique. Debauched orgies seen in films such as *Manslaughter* (1922) and *The Ten Commandments* (1923) were able to justify themselves through the inevitable scenes of retribution that followed. More witty solutions, often considered the creation of Ernst Lubitsch, actually developed quite early. In Charles Maigne's *The Firing Line* (1919), a startled deer signifies an offscreen suicide. The *New York Times* felt that existing censorship inhibitions were the reason for this artful circumlocution, with a far more poetic image the result.

Because of his great success and wealth and his partnership in United Artists, Chaplin functioned with a rare degree of freedom within the Hollywood system. But even his freedom was never absolute, for he too had to take cognizance of possible censorship efforts, particularly with a subject as risqué as that of *A Woman of Paris*. Adolphe Menjou recalled, "Because of the censorship boards in various states . . . Charlie had to indicate [the relationship between Pierre Revel and Marie] in a way that would not be obvious or offensive. He accomplished it in a manner that was, at that time, amazingly subtle." Setting the film in Paris was another device that enabled Chaplin to be freer than usual with the subject of sexuality since American audiences (and the censors) expected Europeans to be looser in their behavior. That thinly veiled subterfuge would be adopted by Lubitsch as well; most of Lubitsch's American films take place in Europe, notably in that semimythical metropolis he liked to call "Paris, Paramount."

Perhaps the most pervasive influence *A Woman of Paris* had on Lubitsch is in the way it treats scandalous material in an offhand, insouciant manner. He learned from its stylized yet still naturalistic acting style, particularly from Menjou's characteristically wry tone. His perpetual amusement over his and Marie's amorality, the way they are able to get away with flouting convention, is strikingly similar to the way Tora Teje mostly grins with gay abandon through her escapades in *Erotikon*. That light tone is emulated in

Lubitsch's subsequent handling of many of his leading performers. Not coincidentally, Menjou became the leading man of Lubitsch's next film, *The Marriage Circle*, a work of art that would prove even more influential than Chaplin's. The nonchalant acting style practiced by Menjou and other Lubitsch actors reflects the director's relaxed attitude toward sexuality and his refusal, like Chaplin's, to condemn his characters for acting outside the bounds of conventional propriety. That attitude is related to another affinity among Lubitsch, *Erotikon*, and *A Woman of Paris*: they approach their emotionally charged subject matter without resorting to sentimentality. Despite all the drama in Chaplin's film, it is approached in an ironically detached manner, as Lubitsch also tended to do with his work in Germany and would continue to do in the United States. Chaplin reciprocated Lubitsch's admiration, writing in his autobiography, "He could do more to show the grace and humor of sex in a nonlustful way than any other director I've ever heard of."

A Woman of Paris includes a number of celebrated directorial touches that clearly pointed the way for Lubitsch to follow in making the deftly efficient and suggestive innuendos that characterize his Hollywood work. One of the most celebrated moments in Chaplin's film is when Pierre, after breezing into Marie's apartment, kissing her, and taking a drink, strolls into her bedroom and casually takes one of his handkerchiefs from the top drawer of her chiffonier. That bit of business, so wittily suggestive of the sexual familiarity between the man and his mistress and expressive of his smug feelings of entitlement (after all, he is paying for everything, including Marie), is the kind of humorous shorthand that Lubitsch would virtually patent, eclipsing Chaplin's example with both proliferation and perfection.

Lubitsch's ability to build on gags, to top them comedically, and to use them to help escalate and complicate the dramatic tension is a key element in his work that is adumbrated by Chaplin's film. The touch in *A Woman of Paris* involving the chiffonier is directly referenced, or parodied, in the opening of *The Marriage Circle*. Menjou's equally smug, self-centered husband, Professor Josef Stock, feels wronged and neglected when he finds a hole in his stocking and his top drawer in the chiffonier inadequately supplied by his slatternly, resentful wife (Marie Prevost). While her drawer below his is amply stocked with hosiery, his drawer contains only a few shirt collars. In a Lubitschean twist that shows how much dramatic mileage he can wring from a seemingly simple gag, Menjou's disenchantment rapidly turns to glee when he realizes that he can use his wife's inattention to his socks as part of the growing catalogue of complaints in the divorce proceedings he is preparing.

Another figure to be reckoned with in discussing the context in which Lubitsch "became Lubitsch" after moving to Hollywood is Cecil B. DeMille, who helped break down the puritanical strictures in Hollywood films before Lubitsch arrived. Viewers who know DeMille largely through his later spectacles, ponderous and burdened with hammy dialogue and acting, would be surprised to encounter his pre-1923 silent incarnation when he was more versatile and stylish and was known for racy comedies of marital and extra-marital relations. But unlike Lubitsch, DeMille was conventionally moralistic in his treatment of sexuality, as the very titles of some of his silent films show (*Don't Change Your Husband*; *Why Change Your Wife*; *For Better, for Worse*). A signature gambit of DeMille's was showing sexual carrying-on only to condemn it, a tendency that became more pronounced as his career became more self-important and grandiose.

Nevertheless, it has been argued, not entirely implausibly, that DeMille's sex comedies must have had some influence on Lubitsch's American work. But while there are some obvious affinities between their silent films in both content and form, there are more differences than similarities. Lubitsch's more refined, elegantly stylized approach contrasts with DeMille's visual vulgarity, his taste for gaudy settings, fancy women's gowns, and overly flamboyant acting. What Lubitsch may have learned from DeMille was how *not* to approach sexual and romantic intrigue or rather how to take similar stories and tell them from more oblique, less obvious perspectives. When you watch Lubitsch's American silents today, their visual simplicity makes them feel more modern, less obviously dated than DeMille's, which are diminished by some of the qualities that appealed to audiences of their time. His tendencies to show off the latest extravagant fashions and decorate sets with bric-a-brac make his films look distractingly busy and even ugly today in contrast to the sleek simplicity of the production design and costuming in the Lubitsch films. With their overall deftness and precision, Lubitsch's American silents focus not on decor but on human emotions within almost-abstract settings, the better to concentrate our attention on facial expressions and feelings.

THE *ROSITA* CONUNDRUM

What happened with Lubitsch's first American film is the strangest episode of his career. At the time, *Rosita*, the film he directed for Mary Pickford, did not seem particularly controversial. The period film was handsomely produced, showed off Pickford in a pleasing and more adult light, received generally good reviews, and made a profit at the boxoffice. But in years to come, *Rosita* would barely escape being destroyed by its star/producer, whose wrath against it and Lubitsch has not entirely been explained, although she left a number of hints about her reasons. She would claim hyperbolically, "It's the worst picture I ever did, it's the worst picture I ever *saw*." Actually, *Rosita* is a good movie but not a great one.

Because Pickford hated the film so much, she ordered the negative and prints destroyed, and until recently, the film was all but lost. Fortunately, *Rosita* has been rescued and restored by the Museum of Modern Art. Its restoration premiered on August 29, 2017, at the Venice Film Festival. That version was based primarily on an original print discovered in the Soviet Union that was "in horrible condition, and it was just too much for the technology of [an earlier] time to handle," said Dave Kehr, curator of the department of film at the museum. After the restoration was completed, Kehr wrote me in July 2017 that Eileen Bowser, former curator of the MoMA film archive, had obtained the only known nitrate print from Gosfilmofond (the Cinematheque of the Russian Federation, then the USSR) in the 1970s. That print, which had Russian intertitles, was copied for preservation in the 1970s before being lost to decomposition except for its last reel. Most of the restored version came from the preservation copy made by MoMA, but the Mary Pickford Foundation supplied another reel of *Rosita*, the fourth reel, that had survived Pickford's auto-da-fé, including a comical scene of her circling a bowl of fruit.

"The film is now as complete as it probably ever will be," Kehr commented. He continued,

> Eileen also got our two prints of *Forbidden Paradise* from the Czech National Film Archive—they are both incomplete, but when they are combined we will have about 90 percent of the film. . . . And both underwent extensive digital restoration, to remove scratches, dirt, rips, etc. Both

films were in such dicey condition that it wasn't considered practical to undertake a major restoration until just a few years ago—but now we are getting results with digital that are unbelievable to me. Neither will ever look like a print from a camera negative but I think you will be astonished by the quality—I certainly was.

Various sources were used to re-create the English intertitles for *Rosita* (sometimes in approximate language), including an early script draft at the Academy of Motion Picture Arts and Sciences, Swedish and German censorship records, the music cue sheet, and a few lines quoted in contemporary reviews. The visual style of those titles was re-created from the fourth reel. The Film Foundation and the Mayer Foundation provided funding for the project, which yielded a 35 mm polyester preservation negative and DCP exhibition copies, and the Film Foundation also funded the restoration of *Forbidden Paradise*, which is still a work in progress.

I have been able to see just a short clip of the *Rosita* restoration by press time on this book, but it is evident that frame-by-frame restoration from a 4K scan of the print brings back some of the original luster of the cinematography by Charles Rosher, Pickford's regular collaborator and one of Hollywood's most distinguished visual stylists. Before this restoration, we had to judge *Rosita* from the available bootleg copies made from the incomplete, poor-quality Russian print.

Even in that ragged state, this comedy-drama about a rebellious Spanish street singer who moves into the castle of the king she is mocking is a graceful piece of entertainment although a number of other directors might have done as well with it. Stately yet not stodgy, *Rosita* has an engagingly vivacious central character, some amusing sexual intrigue, and emotional scenes that alternate between the overwrought and the quietly touching. The multilayered sets of the eighteenth-century city of Seville and the cavernous royal castle by Sven Gade and William Cameron Menzies are as luxurious, intricate, and ingeniously conceived as any in Lubitsch's German work. Rosher's lighting of these magnificent sets, enhanced by the restoration, shows subtle depths and delicate molding. Lubitsch wrote in 1924 that when he came to Hollywood, "I felt as tho [*sic*] someone had supplied me with an entire collection of Aladdin's lamps." He added, "There are many things in the old home in Europe that I love. But America stirs my blood. It fires my imagination. It is so young; so sympathetic; so happy."

Film historian Kevin Brownlow suggests that Pickford's later antipathy toward *Rosita* may have been prompted by her feeling somewhat adrift in the film's lavish decor and upstaged by the direction. Brownlow writes in his 1999 book, *Mary Pickford Rediscovered*, "Lubitsch was a genius, and Mary recognized that. She probably failed to exercise her usual level of control, and she came to regret the result. And yet it is a film that anyone else would have been proud of." Despite Lubitsch's occasional tendencies to become overly enthralled by the grandeur of the scenery and to film in ponderous long shots, the director deftly guides Pickford's energetic and passionate performance to show off her most sophisticated charms. As a result, *Rosita* generally does not suffer from the seriously damaging tendencies displayed in *The Wife of Pharaoh* of having the sets outact the cast or forcing its star to pull out every hammy trick in the book to avoid being eclipsed by the decor. Pickford as an actress commands the sets as much as her spirited Rosita prevails in the face of the most strenuous royal intimidation.

But what of the star's complex relationship with her equally commanding director? If we are to go by Pickford's comments many years after the fact in her 1955 autobiography, *Sunshine and Shadow*, and Brownlow's classic 1967 book on silent cinema, *The Parade's Gone By . . .* , she thoroughly despised everything about Lubitsch, including his accent, his appearance, his eating habits, and his style of directing. She told Brownlow that Lubitsch was "a very uninspired director" and made the equally absurd claim that "Lubitsch was a man's director, he had no sensitivity about women." Pickford's intemperate mockery of his accent and other personal traits, offered in stereotypical terms ("Lubitsch used to eat German-fried potatoes three times a day, and I was dismayed when the grease on his hands left little frescoes all around the room"), could be construed as a display of anti-German or perhaps even anti-Semitic bigotry. In her autobiography, Pickford admits to realizing, "with a burning sense of shame and self-guilt," during the early stages of Hitler's persecution of Jews in the 1930s, that she suffered from anti-Semitic tendencies. She set out to heal herself: "I was so ashamed of myself that I went home that night and got down on my knees. I asked God to forgive me and show me the right path to help these persecuted people."

Pickford's hiring of Lubitsch in 1922 had prompted some anti-German protests by groups such as the American Expeditionary Force (AEF) Veterans, the American Legion, and the Gold Star Mothers, which may have bothered her more than she admitted at the time. She hired him rather defiantly after earlier xenophobic attacks had driven him away on his initial abortive attempt to establish himself in the United States in 1921. As she writes, she found this a difficult situation: "My first taste of ill-luck came when I brought Ernst Lubitsch from Germany to direct me. The power and originality of his work had already spread far and wide. But for many at that time he was still the 'Hun,' and I soon found myself being denounced almost as a traitor for ignoring our own directors in favor of the erstwhile enemy."

Lubitsch's uncertain command of the English language contributed to his problems during shooting and led to some merriment and ridicule at his expense, which had "an ugly, xenophobic edge," as Scott Eyman notes in his 1990 biography, *Mary Pickford: America's Sweetheart.* Mitchell Leisen, who was the costume designer on *Rosita* and later became a director himself, recalled, "The first day he was on the set, they came to tell him his wife was on the telephone. He said, 'You mean I can have copulation with my wife here?'" Pickford recalls with vindictive relish, "Almost the only compensation I derived from *Rosita* was a small amount of comedy relief I enjoyed at Mr. Lubitsch's expense while we were making the picture." She goes on to tell about him directing her wedding scene by saying, "Quiet, please! This is the scenes vehr Miss Pickford goes mit the beckside to ze altar." She writes that "a volley of laughter boomed through the cathedral" before her maid explained to "poor, dear Ernst" what was wrong with his English. "I never saw a man so covered with confusion." Screenwriter Edward Knoblock recalled that Lubitsch sometimes uncharacteristically lost control of his emotions during the shooting, expressing anger that he was Pickford's hired hand. As Eyman writes, once "Ernst lost his temper and tore all the buttons off his clothing, then pounced on Knoblock's papers, throwing them in the air."

"Lubitsch was a nice enough man, but he was stubborn," Pickford complained to Brownlow. "He was very assertive, but then all little men are." Her comments suggest a clash of wills, real or imagined, between the strong-minded actress/producer ("Nobody ever directed me, not even Mr. Griffith," she boasted to Brownlow) and a director who, although foreign and a newcomer to Hollywood, knew very well what he wanted. That trait usually inspired respect among Lubitsch's collaborators, but in this case, it may have seemed threatening to Pickford's cherished autonomy. It could have caused her to regret having hired a director with his own vision of how the film should be, although as a producer, she had previously worked with such other major directors as Cecil B. DeMille and Maurice Tourneur. Brownlow notes in *The Parade's Gone By . . .* , "Although Mary Pickford says she seldom exercised control over directors, her cameraman, Charles Rosher, declares that she did a lot of her own directing. 'The director would often just direct the crowd. She knew everything there was to know about motion pictures.'" Nevertheless, Pickford thought she was ready for something different. Before the shooting of *Rosita*, she had told an interviewer, "I would like to have Ernst Lubitsch, because he seems to understand so thoroughly the meaning of historic reality and atmosphere. It would be so much better, too, for me to engage someone who does not know me too well, and who would consequently assume complete charge over me. Most directors that I have defer too much to my opinion. I wish they wouldn't."

Pickford's overly quoted complaint that she found Lubitsch merely "a director of doors" is especially odd because the witty door gags for which he would become celebrated are virtually absent from *Rosita*. The doors in that film may be grand, but they are mostly just used for the standard function of doors, to let people in and out of rooms. Lubitsch's style is more subdued in *Rosita* than it had been in Germany, less flamboyant and less winkingly suggestive, perhaps reflecting his subordination to Pickford even if he was imported to jazz up her image. In Germany he had not used door gags as often as he would in his later American work, but the salacious joke that ends *The Oyster Princess*—the wealthy father leeringly observing his daughter's wedding night through a keyhole in her bedroom door—was the kind of broad humor that would not be seen in the decorous Pickford film. Since *Rosita* also preceded Lubitsch's viewing of *A Woman of Paris*, it escaped that risqué influence as well. But the use of doors for suggestively elliptical commentary is fully ripened in Lubitsch's next film, *The Marriage Circle*. Pickford's irrelevant repainting of *Rosita* with a reductive caricature of the style Lubitsch employed in other films suggests that her antipathy stemmed from causes other than *Rosita* itself or perhaps more from what the film represented in her retrospective attitude toward her career than from what it actually is.

Those seemingly irrationally negative comments were made in her alcoholic later years when she was largely a recluse, long retired from acting and from running UA's business affairs so astutely. In her dotage, Pickford even had to be talked out of destroying *all* her films by her longtime friend and colleague Lillian Gish, a pioneer in film preservation as well as in film acting. "I never thought my films were important," Pickford confessed to Brownlow.

"I never did anything to save them. . . . I intended to destroy them because, frankly, I didn't want to be compared to the modern trend." Lubitsch, as much as anyone she ever worked with, exemplifies the "modern trend" in pictures; even today he is ahead of the times. *Rosita* was not the only film that evoked bitterness about the past in Pickford, only the most widely reported example. She may have scapegoated Lubitsch because his reputation was so enduring compared to what she saw as her fading significance in film history.

Pickford's disparaging of Lubitsch also flies in the face of contemporary reports that their working relationship was relatively harmonious. Furthermore, they maintained an overtly cordial relationship for some time after *Rosita*, even repeatedly announcing plans to keep working together. Shortly after shooting on *Rosita* was completed, Pickford wrote to her attorney Dennis F. "Cap" O'Brien, "Lubitsch would be a great asset to our company if he could do spectacles. Personally, I still believe he is the greatest director in the world and would be willing to back him if I could afford it." She followed up by telling O'Brien, "I am very pleased with *Rosita* and think it will be well received." It was reported soon afterward that Lubitsch would do one picture for her company over each of the next three years. That was not idle PR talk: Lubitsch's three-year contract with Warners, signed in August 1923, contained a clause allowing him to do a picture a year with Pickford or her company as a loan-out as long as it did not conflict with Warners' plans. That did not come to pass, but Lubitsch remained friendly with Pickford and helped her edit her 1926 film *Sparrows*, a somber tale about her character taking care of a group of orphans in the American South. She wrote him, "Thanks a thousand times for your prompt and generous cooperation in cutting *Sparrows*. . . . I can't tell you how very much I appreciate your kindness." She added, "Douglas [Fairbanks, her husband], you and I should do something fine together—*nicht wahr* [isn't it so]?" Nor do Lubitsch's warm feelings for *Rosita*, expressed as late as 1943, suggest that he felt the lingering sting of an acrimonious involvement with Pickford even if his fondness then was expressed for a reason other than their artistic collaboration: "I have made better, more significant pictures than *Rosita*, but never one that I have loved more. Because with that I associate the finest thing that ever happened to me—the opportunity to come to America, to become a citizen. Besides that good fortune, all else pales."

The fact that the Pickford/Lubitsch collaboration did not result in another film was the result of more mundane problems: United Artists' "refusal to cosign loans or guarantee outside financing" and the financial caution of Pickford's UA partners Fairbanks and Chaplin, according to Eyman's 1993 biography, *Ernst Lubitsch: Laughter in Paradise*. In those dealings, Pickford tried her best to advocate for Lubitsch. "He wants to know if it is possible to get the money," Pickford wrote O'Brien, "as he has several very fine offers out here, but all of them for very long-term contracts. . . . He is like a little boy and always anxious to get things settled." To some extent, Lubitsch may have been passive-aggressive in wiggling out of his working relationship with the powerful star and producer who had brought him to America. His move to Warner Bros. soon thereafter, with highly advantageous financial terms and for a series of films of a far different nature, would suggest that he was just as happy to be independent of the patron who had brought him to Hollywood but who, according to his aide Henry Blanke, had made him feel as if he were working in a "factory system" without the complete control he had in Germany. Perhaps Pickford's interest in standing up for Lubitsch also waned because, as *Variety* reported in February 1924, *Rosita*, after its rapturous reviews, did not do as well at the boxoffice as was initially expected, although it was not a commercial failure.

Lubitsch may well have seen *Rosita* as a transitional phase in his career, a hybrid of his German spectacles and a Hollywood work for hire, however impressively executed. Brownlow's speculation that "the humiliation of submitting to the control of a woman was almost more than he could bear" seems excessive and suggests a misogyny that is unsupported by the facts. When Lubitsch was asked about Pickford by a *Photoplay* interviewer in 1933, he "shifted his cigar and was thoughtful for a moment" before saying, "Mary Pickford is something more than a great actress. She is a great person. My first American picture, *Rosita*, was made with her. That was eleven years ago. My English was very poor then. Her kindness and cooperation made working with her a joy." But there may have been a subtle double edge to Lubitsch's comment in 1938 that Pickford "will always stand as the most practical artist I have ever met. She can dictate policies, handle finances, bargain with supporting players, attend to booking problems, and still keep her mind on acting. It is no wonder that she held her place at the top longer than any personality in motion pictures." Some dissatisfaction with Pickford, however diplomatically expressed, was evident after making *Rosita* when he admitted to interviewer Harry Carr of *Motion Picture Classic*, "In my first picture, I had to make all kinds of concessions to what they told me the American people wanted. I made my first one that way. This [next] one I am going to make to please Lubitsch."

It is doubly a shame that Pickford's peculiar change of heart in later years not only made *Rosita* a film maudit, nearly a lost film, but also obscured its considerable virtues as a boisterous piece of unpretentiously affecting silent-era entertainment. The choice of subject was a compromise by both director and star. Lubitsch had come to America expecting to direct *Marguerite and Faust*, a version of Johann Wolfgang von Goethe's play *Faust* starring Pickford; this choice of classic German material was one reason for the anti-German protests that Pickford faced in hiring Lubitsch. In Goethe's play, Faust's lover is the innocent Gretchen, but in the 1859 Charles Gounod opera *Faust*, based on Michel Carré's Goethe adaptation *Faust et Marguerite*, the character is renamed Marguerite. A fascinating twelve-minute series of 1923 screen tests has survived in which several actors audition for Lubitsch as Mephistopheles, the representative of the Devil who bargains with Faust for his soul; the approaches to the character by the actors (including Lew Cody, Francis McDonald, and Lester Cuneo) are remarkably uniform, demonstrating that Lubitsch characteristically had a clear conception of the role in mind and made them execute it.

"He have sharm and hoomer," Lubitsch was quoted as saying of Mephistopheles in 1923 in "his queer halting English," as reporter Harry Carr called it. Lubitsch had wanted Fairbanks as Mephistopheles: "Douglas Fairbanks would be the greatest Mephisto who ever played the part. He has humor and lightness and vivacity; yet he has dramatic power. He would go thru [*sic*] Faust like a stroke of lightning—flashing, dangerous, vivid, and intense— yet brilliant. Ach lieber Gott, he would be such a vonderful Mephisto. But he would not play Mephisto even if we did *Faust*." The article included a tantalizing photograph of Fairbanks clowning on the studio lot as Mephisto, wearing a feathered hat and a broad devilish grin, arms cocked rakishly, striking a balletic pose as Lubitsch and Pickford watch with delight.

The actors in the screen tests, each wearing a black skullcap and a black cape over a bare chest and gray tights, sneer and laugh diabolically in highly expressionistic and similarly balletic gestures. But despite the way the character is directed to take wicked enjoyment of his evil influence on the unseen Faust, the screen tests are hammy and pretentious; these would-be demons bear a physical resemblance to Lubitsch's tormented hunchbacked clown in his last acting role in *Sumurun*, which was not a promising sign for what would have been his first American project. Lew Cody, who would play a sinister cad for Lubitsch in the 1924 film *Three Women*, distinguishes himself among those tested by performing in the lightest, most mischievous style. And no doubt, Fairbanks would have pulled off the role with winning élan. Pickford was willing to embark on the most self-consciously artistic and ambitious project in her career by doing *Faust*, but her mother, Charlotte Pickford, upon whose judgment she relied, was horrified at the idea of Mary playing a woman who (as Pickford remembered Lubitsch explaining) "has a bebby, and she's not married, so she stringles the bebby." Lubitsch could not hide his disappointment: "They told me that in America plays must have— what do you call it—only Pollyannas. But they liked *Passion*; DuBarry she wasn't a Pollyanna."

Mary had instead expected Lubitsch to direct her in *Dorothy Vernon of Haddon Hall*, based on a 1902 novel by Charles Major set in Elizabethan England and dealing with a young noblewoman who becomes enmeshed with the rivalry between Queen Elizabeth and Mary, Queen of Scots. Lubitsch, no doubt deeply disappointed over the collapse of his cherished *Faust* project, sneeringly rejected *Dorothy Vernon*, remarking, "Der iss too many qveens and not enough qveens!" By that he meant that the character of Dorothy would be eclipsed by the rival monarchs; the project probably also struck him as unpromisingly similar to his lugubrious *Anna Boleyn*. Pickford made *Dorothy Vernon* in 1924 with Hollywood journeyman Marshall Neilan directing, and it was not successful, much to her frustration. Lubitsch's interest in *Faust* may have helped stimulate F. W. Murnau, before he left Germany for Hollywood, to make a grandiosely expressionistic version of the story in 1926, produced for UFA by Erich Pommer and starring Emil Jannings as Mephisto and Gösta Ekmann in the title role.

HOW GOOD IS *ROSITA*?

Pickford and Lubitsch finally settled on *Rosita*, a project the director had brought over from Germany, which was called *Karneval in Toledo* when Norbert Falk and Hans Kräly wrote the script in the spring of 1922. Filmed under the title *The Street Singer*, the story is based on the 1872 opera *Don César de Bazan* by Adolphe d'Ennery and Philippe Dumanoir, which had been adapted into a 1915 U.S. silent film directed by Robert G. Vignola, *Don Caesar de Bazan*. Edward Knoblock receives screenplay credit for the Lubitsch version, with credit for the story going to Kräly and Falk. Knoblock, born in New York to German parents, had written the 1911 play *Kismet* and worked on the screenplays of Fairbanks's *Robin Hood* and *The Three Musketeers*. Neither Pickford nor Lubitsch could have been pleased that the director's former star Pola Negri, who had come to Hollywood three months before him, was competing with *Rosita* by making a film based on the same story called *The Spanish Dancer*. Although Negri claims in her autobiography that this was just "friendly professional rivalry," she had previously been scheduled to appear in Lubitsch's German version, *Karneval in Toledo*. *The Spanish Dancer*, directed by Irish filmmaker Herbert Brenon, was released by Famous Players-Lasky a month after *Rosita* and did well both commercially and critically. But though *The Spanish Dancer* is handsomely produced, it lacks the grandeur of *Rosita*'s settings and, more important, the warmth, "sharm and hoomer" of the Lubitsch film. The competing project no doubt played its part in diminishing *Rosita*'s boxoffice potential. Negri and Lubitsch had clashed on *Die Flamme*, his last German film. Lubitsch's Hollywood cameraman Charles Van Enger reported that in filming that project, "he had two scripts, one for Negri and one for himself. And she would do her part and then he would let her take a couple of days off while he did his piece. And he did the picture the way he wanted it. And he left Germany before she saw the picture and they were very bitter about one another."

Although *Rosita* has overtly political subject matter—the street singer is protesting the king's unfair taxation of the poor—it treats that theme mostly as a springboard for romantic intrigue. As such, it is in the vein of Lubitsch's European spectacles, which tend to treat history as something that is made at night, and in the American commercial pattern for most historical films, which usually treat personal relationships as determining social movements rather than the other way around. *Rosita*'s deployment of political conflict as a backdrop to romantic intrigue also somewhat foreshadows Lubitsch's 1939 romantic comedy *Ninotchka*. But that film, set in modern Paris just before the outbreak of World War II, includes more pointed and serious political satire than *Rosita*, whose setting in a distant, almost mythical kingdom makes it hard to take the street unrest as more than a plot device. Like other Pickford characters, Rosita is what Brownlow calls "an endearing little spitfire."

When the street singer makes common cause with her proletarian audiences who are swept along by her antimonarchial ballad, it is not because she is especially ideological or ambitious to lead a rebellion but because she instinctively reacts against injustice, sharing and expressing their personal experience of impoverishment.

In disguise, the king (Holbrook Blinn, a short, stocky actor who bears a remarkable resemblance to Lubitsch) listens out of curiosity as she sings against him. Habitually lecherous like the monarchs in Lubitsch's German films, he predictably finds himself attracted to the feisty young woman. But Rosita is arrested for defiance of the king, and her dashing love interest, Don Diego (George Walsh), is sent to prison and condemned to death for fighting a duel to protect her. Seeing a way to help her indigent family and influence the king, Rosita goes along with being moved into his palace at the risk of being mistaken for a kept woman. But while her family comically messes up the place, she resists the king's arrogantly clumsy advances and uses her position to try to save Don Diego. This moral rectitude, which came with the territory when Lubitsch agreed to work with Pickford, sets her heroine apart from the corrupted young women played in his German films by the earthier Negri, whose Carmen (also a Spanish street singer) is a notorious wanton and whose Madame DuBarry literally loses her head after recklessly exploiting her sexuality.

A less virtuous and genuinely seductive, if conflicted, heroine in *Rosita* would have made for more complex drama and provided Lubitsch with greater opportunities for what would become his specialty: the intricate interplay of emotional sympathies among characters drawn into compromising romantic situations. The downplaying of that element makes *Rosita* a relatively minor work in his canon. But Lubitsch still manages to provide a level of subtly nuanced comedy-drama in the machinations of the queen (Irene Rich) to keep her husband under her control by enabling Rosita's lover to escape with her. Rich would go on to give a brilliant performance in Lubitsch's 1925 film of Wilde's *Lady Windermere's Fan*. Her queen in *Rosita* wins more of the audience's sympathy than the title character. The older woman, though under no illusions about her royal husband's wandering eye, thinks he has finally gone too far by moving Rosita into the palace. Lubitsch draws irony from her mistaken belief that Rosita is a harlot and evokes both humor and emotion from the queen's artful scheme to preserve her position.

As she manages to outwit her tyrannical husband, Lubitsch conveys the queen's genuine dignity and ultimate sense of compassion toward Don Diego. This is the complex tone that shows Lubitsch at his best.

Although Pickford brought Lubitsch over from Germany partly to help her make a transition to more adult roles—a process that caused her anxiety because she worried about its effect on her popular appeal—the supposition that she may have hoped to make her sweet but spunky screen image more in the line of his saucy European heroines is misleading because it does not have much to do with the style or substance of *Rosita*. Lubitsch did his best to provide her with a handsomely mounted spectacle with lively human elements as he had done with his German historical films, and Pickford plays a strong, independent-minded young woman. Typical of the enthusiasm with which she was received was the notice in the fan magazine *Picture and Picturegoer*: "The Mary of *Rosita* is a new, unsuspected Mary. She has matured. Her work is slower, more restrained, and consequently more vital. Her acting in the later, intensely dramatic scenes . . . haunts you, pricking at your memory for days afterward. . . . *Rosita* was handled by a director whose second name is genius." The *Film Daily* called *Rosita* "just a wonderful love story with a Spanish background." It added, "The one and only Mary returns to her own. Regardless of how she may have slipped in more recent pictures she is back again more wonderful than ever." The reviewer advised exhibitors about how to sell the movie: "Stick to Mary . . . to the limit. . . . Talk of the gorgeous, magnificent production. . . . You can also play up the name of Ernst Lubitsch. . . . It will pay every American director to go and see his work in this."

Despite her greater maturity, Pickford's Rosita is no femme fatale, and her unshakable integrity of character is built into the storyline and into the actress's carefully nurtured screen persona. So the cause of her later antipathy cannot stem primarily from any distaste she had at the time for the film's sexual overtones, which are relatively mild in any case. Still, she seems to have transferred to Lubitsch her bitterness over the public's unwillingness to let her grow up on-screen, and perhaps she let that color her view of the film and consider it a mistake.

She writes in her autobiography, "After *Rosita* and *Dorothy Vernon*, I was quite ready to surrender to public demand and become a child again." The earliest known record of Pickford publicly voicing that sentiment is an article in a September 1925 issue of *Photoplay* titled "The Public Just Won't Let

Mary Pickford Grow Up." It reported, "Mary regarded them as failures, and saw in them her own failure. They missed. Some element was lacking. Did the public want a return to the old form of characterization, or was the fault in her interpretation of the new?" Pickford asked the magazine to solicit letters from her public about what direction her career should take, and they heartily agreed that she should learn what *not* to do from those examples; her next starring role after *Dorothy Vernon* was as a twelve-year-old tomboy in *Little Annie Rooney* (1925). As a further indicator of how perceptions of *Rosita* evolved, *Photoplay* included the film in an October 1933 article entitled "Famous Film Flops" even though it had been a boxoffice success. Pickford's waning stardom and her seemingly insoluble conundrum about her image had caused her to retire from the screen that March at age forty, though she continued to be active in the business affairs of United Artists. By the time Pickford reached old age and felt bitter over her career, her dislike for *Rosita* had escalated into extreme antipathy.

Brownlow speculates in his book on Pickford that her disappointment over allowing herself to be talked out of making *Marguerite and Faust*, which was "to have been the one film in her career made purely for art's sake," may also have colored her retrospective view of *Rosita*: "However good it was, *Rosita* came nowhere near the heights she hoped to achieve with *Faust*. Perhaps she took out her frustration on the film that her advisers (particularly her mother) persuaded her to make, in place of the one she so longed to make." Another possible explanation is suggested by the way Lubitsch tailored the denouement of *Rosita* to his own characteristic way of working. Was Pickford resentful of Lubitsch and the film that they had made for giving Irene Rich a better part than hers? At any rate, for Lubitsch, the fascination of Rich's character and the inspiration it gave him for her later role as a mature woman of affairs in *Lady Windermere's Fan* may have been some artistic compensation for a relatively impersonal job of work, something of an artistic regression after his audaciously tragic final film in Germany, *Die Flamme*. Lubitsch was marking time with *Rosita*, learning about how to function in the Hollywood system and how to try to outwit it, but he was pragmatic about the opportunity and could look on the project with more equanimity than Pickford ever could. *Rosita* provided a suitable American showcase for his talents, which were shortly to turn in a more salutary direction once he moved to Warner Bros. where he could enjoy more creative freedom.

"PURE CINEMA"

The elements of Lubitsch's mature style came together in his second Holly-wood film, *The Marriage Circle* (1924), an intricate roundelay of marital fidel-ity and infidelity that served as the principal model for the romantic comedy genre. Seldom has a film been so influential. This is the film that, as Renoir put it, "invented the modern Hollywood." It represented a quantum jump in sophistication from the clumsy blend of titillation and heavy-handed, preachy moralizing seen in DeMille's marital comedy-dramas and from the Victo-rian idealization in Griffith's romances. Suddenly appearing on American screens was the truth about modern marriage, its messy complications and many compromises, its blend of sincerity and deceitfulness, its seriousness and absurdity, its tacit need to look the other way to survive.

Lubitsch told the *New York Times*, "In this mixup of modern matrimony I have gone straight to life and thrown aside the melodramatic ideas with which life is usually distorted in the movies." That truthfulness, and the maturity involved in the film's complexity of treatment, was the source of its immense influence on the genre and on the careers of other directors. It helped teach them to analyze romance, marriage, and deceit in their films. One such director, Alfred Hitchcock, said of Lubitsch in 1967, "His greatest contribution, to me, to the cinema, was his making of *The Marriage Circle*. Ernst Lubitsch . . . was a man of 'pure Cinema.'"

"Pure Cinema" was Hitchcock's highest term of praise because it was what he always aimed for in his work. Robin Wood's comment on Hitchcock's use of the term shows why that director applied it to Lubitsch: "Much more than editing is involved, and what finally matters is the *kind* and *quality* of the effects achieved, their nature, their value, their complexity, their intensity . . . from shot to shot, gesture to gesture, line to line, expression to expression, reaction to reaction, frame to frame, composition to composition. . . . This kind of perfection can come only from an artist working at the highest pitch of sustained imaginative-emotional involvement." That is an accurate descrip-tion of the precisely refined, perfectly calibrated style of *The Marriage Circle* since so much of it depends on elaborate visual storytelling involving intri-cate patterns of looks, gestures, objects, and choreography within the frame, brought together by montage, the kind that Hitchcock would also use to convey thought on-screen cinematically with similarly total artistic control.

Conveying thought is perhaps the most difficult challenge in filmmaking; a novelist can easily enter into the minds of his or her characters, but a filmmaker has to use other means, especially if he is trying to do so through implication and primarily through visuals. In *The Marriage Circle*, while adapting a 1909 play by Viennese writer Lothar Schmidt, *Nur ein Traum* (*Only a Dream*), Lubitsch and his screenwriter, Paul Bern, use the cinematic medium with a subtlety and depth that still seems astonishing all these years later. Lubitsch is able to suggest more than his characters could actually see or hear. He relied only slightly on intertitles in his American silent films, as reviewers of the time noted, usually with admiration but sometimes with frustration.

Unlike in his lavishly mounted German spectacles or *Rosita*, the decor in *The Marriage Circle* is elegantly spare, almost to the point of abstraction. Although this unusual choice might be explained by the modest assets of Warners, it is more likely that this was an aesthetic choice on Lubitsch's part, influenced by the intimacy of the *Kammerspielfilm* tradition in Germany that he followed in *Die Flamme*. The largely undecorated gray walls and barely furnished rooms in the contemporary Viennese settings of *The Marriage Circle*—along with the relatively plain costumes, far from the tasteless frippery in DeMille's marital comedies—ensure that the scenery does not distract us from the actors' expressions and gestures, which are all-important here and in Lubitsch's other films for Warners. That unusual level of quasi abstraction also guarantees that the objects Lubitsch selects for dramatic emphasis (breakfast food for two, a bouquet of flowers, a drink trolley, a scarf) are not lost in the kind of busy settings typical in DeMille movies but instead stand out with the clear and precise visual emphasis Lubitsch lends them. His Hollywood silent films have a simpler elegance that makes them seem refreshingly modern in contrast with DeMille's stale and cluttered museum pieces.

Lubitsch's direction, his orchestration of the characters and the significant objects they handle, is an intellectual game with the audience. He enables us to follow the complex thought processes and emotional interchanges among his characters, but what happens on-screen is only part of it. The rest is happening in the minds and hearts of the spectators. Montage asks spectators to close the ellipses between shots and complete the pattern in their heads, so it is no coincidence that Lubitsch would use it so eloquently. And his use of montage would help show the young Hitchcock (and the young Yasujiro Ozu in Japan, another great admirer of *The Marriage Circle*) how to follow his example. And the German American director Douglas Sirk found Lubitsch "incredibly modern as a picture director—particularly one film, *The Marriage Circle*, was very important to me in this respect. It had a kind of lasting impact. . . . Lubitsch was able to walk the *very* narrow path between the absurd and the realistic. And this ties up with another point: he also had taste and elegance, which I hope I learned a little of from him."

Jean Renoir, even though he tended to employ long takes more than the kind of highly fragmented montage that Hitchcock favored or the more deliberately paced stitching together of significant moments in Lubitsch's work, once suggested that films should be interactive. In 1966, long before interactive video games came along, Renoir said, "It's impossible to have a work of art without the spectator's participation, without his collaboration. A film must be completed by the audience. . . . Art is a little bridge that you erect. The director of a film, if he has a little talent, sometimes succeeds in creating a little bridge between the screen and the audience, and then we're all together, and we create together, we build the film together. The audience makes this contribution, and this contribution is very important."

Lubitsch, more and more as time went on, structured his films in that interactive manner, as an intellectual and emotional exchange with his audience, usually expressed in a form of play. His films call on the intelligence and wit of the viewer to fill in the gaps that the director could not or would not deign to put blatantly on the screen. *The Marriage Circle* is a vehicle for the director and his surrogates, the actors, to commune with the sensibilities of the audience, to share his delight in human foibles and in the tragicomedy of the human condition. Lubitsch would continue doing so for the rest of his career in America. No one else before or since, even Chaplin, has done so with such sustained rigor, invention, or sympathetic depth of feeling. In the same *New York Times* interview in which he praised *A Woman of Paris*, Lubitsch said that with *The Marriage Circle*, "I experienced a great change in my career, as it is the first time I have made an important modern drama. I have gotten away from spectacles, as there are only five characters in this film. . . . It is a very intimate drama . . . and I never got so close to real life as I have in this picture."

Lubitsch's characterizations of two sets of intertwined married couples in *The Marriage Circle* (and another man who gets involved with both couples) are recognizably adult in a medium known largely for its juvenility. The director's approach to sexuality is knowing and candid, and his refusal to make easy moral judgments is refreshingly tolerant. *The Marriage Circle* captures the widespread questioning of the institution of marriage at the height of the Jazz Age. It also reaffirms the value of marriage when that institution manages to work. Lubitsch shows how that can only occur when both parties learn to live with each other's flaws as well as their virtues. *The Marriage Circle* demonstrates Oscar Wilde's epigram: "The one charm of marriage is that it makes a life of deception absolutely necessary for both parties."

The principal couple, Dr. Franz Braun (Monte Blue) and his wife, Charlotte (Florence Vidor), have what she too trustingly considers to be an ideal marriage until she starts discovering unmistakably disturbing signs of Franz's wandering eye. Despite the evidence of his deceptions, she nevertheless manages to blind herself for quite a while to the fact that he is being aggressively pursued by her own best friend, the unhappily married Mizzi Stock (Marie Prevost). Mizzi's husband, Josef (Adolphe Menjou), regards his wife with icy contempt, yearning to be rid of her. Josef is delighted with Mizzi's increasingly brazen efforts to seduce Franz, who repeatedly tries to resist but keeps becoming compromised, partly through no fault of his own but partly through his own weakness.

The plot turns around Franz's fundamental lack of honesty in dealing with his wife over what initially seems to be a relatively trivial matter. Most of the character complications would not occur if he simply told Charlotte that he met Mizzi just before they were introduced by his wife at their home. In a taxicab they shared on the way over, Mizzi kept making a play for Franz, and even though he tried his best not to respond, his guilty feelings over his attraction to this alluring stranger make him unwilling to admit that he "knows" Charlotte's friend even that slightly. Franz persuades Mizzi to collaborate in the deception, and she is happy to oblige since it suits her scheming purposes. Meanwhile, the demurely attractive Charlotte behaves in a fashion that defines the term "ladylike," and Lubitsch gently kids the unquestioning nature of her devotion yet does not make her fidelity seem ridiculous.

But as Charlotte learns more about Franz's increasingly peculiar behavior, she develops conflicted emotions of her own toward her marriage. At first she is amused to find that Franz's partner in psychiatry, Gustav Mueller (Creighton Hale), is smitten with her and responding ardently to her innocent flirtations. But gradually the realization of the threats to her marriage from both directions strips away Charlotte's naïveté and illusions. A delicious Lubitsch Touch early in the film teasingly defines the difference between Charlotte's naïve trustfulness and Mizzi's subversiveness toward the Brauns' marriage: as Charlotte stands at her piano, earnestly singing Edvard Grieg's "Ich liebe dich" ("I love thee"), the camera tilts down to Mizzi playing the tune, smirking cynically, and looking off at the unseen Franz as Lubitsch slowly fades out, leaving us to imagine his two-pronged discomfort.

Since Lubitsch's films are often subversive toward sexual conventions, it may seem surprising to some of his more cynical viewers that in this major work of his we have a film that clearly takes a stand in defense of marriage. The film's complex point of view raises questions about whether this celebrated work from early in his Hollywood career is truly subversive or conventional or a mixture of the two. Lubitsch's films often celebrate adultery (there is no other word for how he deals with that subject in much of his work), a most "un-American," continental attitude. But at the same time, he was no implacable foe of marriage as he also shows in his late work *Heaven Can Wait* (1943), one of his personal favorites.

In that film, as he commented just before his death in 1947, "I showed the happy marriage in a truer light than it is usually done in moving pictures where a happy marriage is only too often portrayed as a very dull and unexciting by-the-fireplace affair." The long-lasting marriage of Henry and Martha Van Cleve (Don Ameche and Gene Tierney) survives what appears to be the husband's serial adultery (discreetly suggested by Lubitsch). *The Marriage Circle* also portrays the Brauns' marriage as far from ideal but still worth preserving. It does so with full acknowledgment of the precariousness of the institution of marriage and with a recognition of the sexual double standard that often enabled a middle-class marriage to survive in that era. *Heaven Can Wait*, perhaps because it is set in an upper-class family with the looser standards that often accompany wealth, goes much further in depicting the double standard, showing a remarkable degree of tolerance (as well as tolerance by Martha) in excusing Henry's lifelong philandering. *The*

Marriage Circle, on the other hand, portrays the husband as struggling hard to be faithful (unlike Henry) but clearly tempted and succumbing on one occasion. Yet that does not destroy the marriage as might be expected in a Hollywood film of that era. Lubitsch's approach to marriage was always far from orthodox.

A German reviewer of the time, Heinrich Fraenkel, described *The Marriage Circle* as "one of the finest, most tasteful, technically most successful, most entertaining and—most un-American films ever created." Thomas J. Saunders comments in his 1994 book *Hollywood in Berlin: American Cinema and Weimar Germany*, "Not the least of the 'un-American' features of the film was its refusal to be bound by moral prudery. [*Film-Kurier* reviewer] Heinz Michaelis surmised that a director of Lubitsch's artistic authority was required 'to lead American film comedy out of constraints of Sunday school into the realm of superior comic genius,' confirming once again that German influence had proven determinative." Examining the influence of American cinema on Lubitsch and the mixed German attitudes toward his American work, Saunders traces the German response to Lubitsch as a discourse, often critical, on how much of his continental nature he did or did not manage to preserve after being brought to America because of the international success he had achieved partly as "by inclination arguably the most 'American' of German directors." Although the European flavor of *The Marriage Circle* and subsequent Lubitsch films was largely applauded back home, Lubitsch also came under criticism in Germany for allegedly adapting *too* well to American culture and thereby, from that viewpoint, betraying his German roots. Less nationalistic observers might see it differently: Lubitsch managed to combine the best of both cinematic cultures in his own distinctive approach.

Weinberg astutely observes in *The Lubitsch Touch* that Lubitsch made fun of sex in America even more than he had in Europe precisely because he "decided to make American audiences laugh at something they took so seriously. . . . America was obsessed with sex—the stringent censorship here proved it. . . . Very well: Lubitsch would make sex comedies, set in Vienna or Paris or even mythical kingdoms, where you could 'get away with it.'" That is as good an explanation as any of the artistic transformation that Lubitsch underwent when he stopped making spectacles shortly after coming to America and began focusing almost exclusively on comedies and comedy-dramas about sexuality, the kind of Lubitschean films with which he is most associated today. In the Roaring Twenties, a greater erotic freedom began revitalizing the American screen. The women's suffrage movement, the disillusioning effects of the Great War, and other forms of social upheaval had a liberating effect on women's abilities to express their sexuality and act with greater independence. This revolution, not achieved without strong and sometimes violent pushback from conventional moralists and censors, would be reflected in and influenced by films in both Europe and the United States, notably those directed by Lubitsch, who was ahead of his time in portraying liberated women. He set the gold standard for subtlety and sophistication in presenting adult sexual behavior on-screen.

In an indication of how one era's sophistication and subversiveness can be interpreted as the opposite in a later time and place, to some casual or narrowly ideological viewers today, *The Marriage Circle* may appear to simply endorse the hypocrisy of the double standard and condemn the aggressive female who selfishly tries to disrupt her friend's happy marriage. Many viewers seem to expect a filmmaker to offer characters as role models who exemplify the moral orthodoxy of the present day rather than as flawed subjects for critical observation of a flawed social system. Such biases tend to blind some viewers to how *The Marriage Circle* examines marriage critically and does not hold up any of his characters, even Charlotte, as a paragon of virtue.

While acknowledging the existence of the double standard as a fact of life even in such a sexually liberated time as the Roaring Twenties, *The Marriage Circle* offers an often-satirical and sometimes earnestly dramatic critique of the problems surrounding marriage, partly because of the double standard, and examines the ambiguous social role of the newly "liberated" woman during that period of social disruption. The survival of a marriage such as that of the Brauns, who clearly love each other and want to be faithful, depends on overcoming a succession of deceptions, misunderstandings, the uncertain ability or desire of the husband to withstand temptation, and varying degrees of innocence or willful ignorance on the part of the wife as well as her tolerance and forgiveness, for a time, of his indiscretions. Despite the fragile nature of the marital relationship in a Lubitsch film, it is seen as worth preserving. But Charlotte's disillusionment over her "ideal" marriage eventually leads her to be more assertive, manipulating Franz into submission while she tells him, "I'm as guilty as you," even if he refuses to believe it and it isn't entirely true.

Although Florence Vidor's Charlotte is a dignified character who believes in and defines the old-fashioned virtues of fidelity in marriage, her initial security and smugness are challenged systematically until the climactic moment when she is forced to recognize, with utter disgust, that her husband and her best friend are having a dalliance. It can be argued that Charlotte is the central character of the film, not Franz, and that it revolves around the path she takes toward understanding the true complex nature of marriage rather than her initially idealized notion of it. Vidor plays the role straight, not comedically; the comedy comes from Charlotte's misunderstandings and her initially limited perspective. Lubitsch greatly admired Vidor, whom he directed again in his 1928 film, *The Patriot*. In a 1933 interview, he explained the complexity of character he captures through her in *The Marriage Circle*: "She is the essence of refinement. Under the right circumstances, her type might defy the rules of chastity, but never the rules of decorum. She has a very sensitive, intelligent mind. There is constant conflict between thought and emotion with her."

Lubitsch clearly admires Charlotte's strength of character and her intelligence in handling the threat to her marriage once she belatedly recognizes it. Her slowness to comprehend that threat is related to her innocence and her overly trusting character, but she manages to surmount those weaknesses and take charge of the situation to her own satisfaction, driving Mizzi away, forcing the sheepish Franz into fidelity, and declaring that the marriage will be on an equal basis from now on. But Charlotte's susceptibility to Gustav's flattery and her own mildly flirtatious behavior with him are seen as less threatening to the survival of the marriage than her husband's actions, and therefore as comical, partly because they are somewhat subconscious and because her would-be lover, while as ardent as Mizzi, is shown as somewhat pathetic and ineffectual.

And yet *The Marriage Circle* never goes so far as to make Gustav a figure of utter absurdity as Lubitsch's 1932 Maurice Chevalier/Jeanette MacDonald musical remake, *One Hour with You*, does with the role of the wife's suitor. Lubitsch was planning to only produce that film, with George Cukor directing, but when he was dissatisfied with the early rushes, he took over the principal directing duties. Cukor's more naturalistic style with actors had clashed with Lubitsch's penchant for extreme stylization; Cukor was awarded the credit "Assisted by" only after he sued Paramount. *One Hour with You* portrays Charlie Ruggles's Adolph as a fatuous simpleton, thus making any notion of genuine dalliance between him and the wife unthinkable. The musical treats as out-and-out comedy what the original portrays as mostly serious. In *The Marriage Circle* we are allowed to imagine the possibility that Charlotte might go off with Gustav if her marriage were to fall apart, though such a denouement would seem a letdown for her because of the doglike nature of his devotion and her obvious preference for the more charming if somewhat oafish Franz.

Casting is indeed critical in a Lubitsch film. The offbeat casting of Monte Blue as the husband makes Franz's romantic fumblings seem more ridiculous than serious, yet not entirely absurd, because his relationship with Charlotte shows the kind of mutual devotion that is based on the acceptance of flaws as well as virtues. But his portrayal is nevertheless much more broadly comical than Charlotte's; that is partly a way of making Franz's temptation to stray seem less serious and partly a way of satirizing his weakness. Lubitsch makes Blue seem smug and clownish in his behavior and appearance; his wide eyes and droopy mouth are accentuated by epicene makeup, and Franz takes a smugly patronizing attitude toward his wife that ultimately has her play him as a fool while she discovers her own hidden strengths.

A strapping, athletic actor who was half Native American (his birth name was Gerard Montgomery Bluefeather) and began as a stuntman, Blue was usually cast as a more dramatic and romantic leading man in the 1920s. But Lubitsch, who often played with stars' images for comic effect, brings out a latent goofiness in the actor not only in this film but also in *So This Is Paris* (1926), a more purely comedic romp, and presumably in the lost 1925 comedy about divorce, *Kiss Me Again*, the disappearance of which is particularly regrettable because Lubitsch, along with many reviewers, considered it one of his best films. Lubitsch originally cast Warner Baxter as Franz in *The Marriage Circle* but fired him after the first eight days, remarking, "He looks like a detective" (the film already had a detective character, played by the suitably glum Harry Myers, who is hired by Josef to get the goods on his wife). Judging from Baxter's other work, Lubitsch must have been frustrated with trying to get much humor out of the dour actor, and so he was fortunate to find Monte Blue and keep him around for other films.

The people in *The Marriage Circle* are not impossibly glamorous as the characters are in many romantic comedies; they are much like the people watching the film. Lubitsch has it both ways by casting American actors, both "common" and "classy" performers, playing both high and low comedy in a continental setting—Vienna, "still the city of laughter and light romance" as the opening intertitle reassures us. That promise is a bit deceptive, for though the film is by definition a comedy, since it deftly manages to provide believably happy endings for all five people in this intricate circle of romantic disillusionment and renewal, it plays as much as a drama as it does a comedy. The issues it treats could not be more important—trust, fidelity, passion, and their opposites—but they are approached lightly, a paradox that puts Lubitsch in the company of such fellow humorists and moralists as Oscar Wilde and G. K. Chesterton. As Chesterton remarked, "It is so easy to be solemn; it is so hard to be frivolous." The deft, sometimes deceptive duality of comedy and drama with which Lubitsch treats romantic and sexual situations in the seminal *Marriage Circle* and in his subsequent work, a form of playing with audience expectations in order to keep the work fresh and unpredictable, is a key component of his style and protean achievement.

Some of the people involved in *The Marriage Circle* had their reasons for being able to relate so well to their roles. Schmidt's play was brilliantly adapted by Bern, a German-born screenwriter and director. In 1930, as Bern's biographer E. J. Fleming notes, "Lubitsch gave an entertaining interview discussing [the irony of the] apparently confirmed bachelor [Bern] writing a script about relationships and marriage. Everyone in the film was having marriage issues: Monte Blue and Marie Prevost divorced [other people] during filming, Adolphe Menjou, cameraman Charles Van Enger and Creighton Hale shortly thereafter, and finally Lubitsch himself." Florence Vidor divorced her husband and frequent director, King Vidor, the year after *The Marriage Circle* was released. Lubitsch quipped to a Los Angeles newspaper, "Everybody is divorced but Paul Bern, who wrote the script. And he isn't married." Lubitsch was not actually divorced at the time he made the remark in June 1930, but his wife, Leni, had filed for divorce earlier that month. The couple broke up after Lubitsch discovered that she was having an affair with his frequent screenwriter Hans Kräly. And while that situation resembled a darker version of one of Lubitsch's cinematic romantic triangles, Bern's story ended with a deception more tragic than anything in *The Marriage Circle*. In one of Hollywood's most notorious scandals, Bern's common-law wife, Dorothy Millette, murdered him in September 1932, two months after his marriage to Jean Harlow. MGM covered up the truth about Bern's murder by maligning his sexual potency in an effort to protect Harlow, a somber Hollywood fable in the same genre as Wilder's *Sunset Blvd.*

Substituting the unfunny Warner Baxter with the antic Monte Blue could help explain why Lubitsch puts such emphasis on the husband's ridiculousness in *The Marriage Circle*. Lubitsch mocks Franz's attempts at husbandly dignity while he struggles to deal with a woman who keeps flinging herself at him in a rather irrational way. Mizzi's mad desire for the klutzy, suavity-deficient Franz seems explicable only as jealous revenge against her "best friend," Charlotte, for having what superficially appears to be such a placid and happy marriage. While Franz is often silly and Gustav pitiable, so too, in a different way, is Mizzi, the would-be wild flapper, a minx who would be better off aiming her charms at a man who is more readily available.

A former Mack Sennett Bathing Beauty, Prevost employs her considerable skills as a comedian as she toys with Franz, but she also plays Mizzi with a fierce relish that the audience can choose to regard as amusingly "naughty," somewhat demented, or both; she flings off a scarf in a garden to show Franz that she is hot on a cold night in a memorable Lubitsch Touch of genuine eroticism. Prevost brings a sense of desperation (a word Mizzi actually uses in a letter to Franz) to her character's sexual longing, a misdirected passion that makes Mizzi seem more confused than liberated. Mizzi's husband's excessive coldness also gives us some sympathy for her. She seems masochistic in her futile attempts to throw herself at a man she can't have, efforts that bring her only contempt from the other characters until she becomes the (resilient) butt of the film's concluding gag in which she winds up with Gustav merely because he is available, the extra man in the story. (Prevost would go on to appear for Lubitsch as a playboy's mistress in *Three Women* and as Blue's estranged wife in *Kiss Me Again*. She appears charmingly zaftig in these films, but she committed suicide in 1937 at age thirty-eight by starving herself when her increasing weight caused her problems getting work in Hollywood.)

In 1924 Lubitsch wrote a revealing article discussing how he had to cure actors of bad habits from their earlier work. He wrote that "the hardest task of the director" is "to show the actors how to portray these characters on the screen. The trouble with many of the actors today is that they have just a small number of stock gestures and set facial expressions which they repeat over and over again, no matter what the situation really calls for." Prevost seemed to be offering an explanation of Lubitsch's curative methods when she told Harry Carr of *Motion Picture Classic* on the release of *The Marriage Circle* in February 1924,

> I never realized what acting really meant until I began to hear Mr. Lubitsch's voice coming to me from behind the camera. He deals in subtleties that I never dreamed of before. His marvelous technique consists of elements and effects that I never heard of before. At first it was terribly discouraging. He made me do simple scenes—just coming in and out of rooms—fifteen or twenty times. At first it seemed as tho [*sic*] there wasn't any sense to it at all. Then it began to dawn upon me what the art of acting was all about, and it seemed intolerably and impossibly difficult. Then I began to see as he saw it. He is a tremendous and wonderful artist. To act even one scene under his direction is not only an education but a revelation.

In keeping with *The Marriage Circle*'s realistically unidealized, if questionable, portrayal of the double standard in 1924 Vienna (and implicitly America), male indiscretions are regarded as laughable but forgivable, but Mizzi's flirtations are met with harsh responses from everyone but Gustav. Not only is she the target of righteous outrage from Charlotte when she realizes she has been betrayed, Mizzi is also despised by her own husband as well as by the man she is scheming to seduce. In the film's most oblique but biting touch—a primarily verbal gag hidden in the German language of the director and screenwriter—Franz writes to Mizzi what he intends to be a kiss-off letter, ironically addressing her as the *Hochwohlgeborene Frau Mizzi Stock* (the Honorable Madame Mizzi Stock). Josef, her soon-to-be ex-husband, tosses the letter in front of her at the breakfast table with a withering look.

Charlotte's propriety does not preclude sexual fantasies of her own, although it keeps her from consciously acting on them. This can be viewed as a concession to the American audience and Lubitsch's careful avoidance of censorship; he knew where to draw the line in a story rife with potentially objectionable elements. Showing a flagrantly philandering wife and having the couple remain together at the end would have been difficult if not impossible to get away with at the time. But Lubitsch uses Charlotte's strength of character as a foil for the other, weaker characters even as he suggests that she too is susceptible to temptation. He directs Vidor with great finesse, making her appear superior to her childish husband, overly trusting in a way that threatens to destroy her marriage, and somewhat reckless (innocently or not) in encouraging Gustav's ardor. Drawing explicitly from the Freudian psychiatry that had become fashionable by the 1920s, *The Marriage Circle* shows Charlotte explaining away a seemingly innocently mistaken episode of kissing and embracing Gustav by pretending at first that it was only a dream (as the title of the source play puts it). But in describing that incident as a dream, she is revealing that she has more of a subconscious desire for such pleasures than she can bring herself to admit. She eventually tells Franz, albeit deliberately misleadingly, "Gustav's kiss was no dream—it was real." *The Marriage Circle* also calls humorous attention to the vogue for Viennese psychiatry by having Franz and Gustav practice that profession; their shingle reads "SPECIALISTEN FUR NERVOSE LEIDEN" ("SPECIALISTS IN NERVOUS SUFFERING").

While lightly satirizing Charlotte's obliviousness to her own desires and her husband's wandering impulses, in some respects *The Marriage Circle* anticipates the darker but also dreamlike exploration of extramarital impulses in Schnitzler's *Dream Novella* and Stanley Kubrick's film adaptation, *Eyes Wide Shut*. An ambiguous sensual incident occurs in *The Marriage Circle* when Charlotte, in the aftermath of a nocturnal quarrel with Franz, tries to make up with him. Thinking he is outside when she sees a man's silhouette through the door (even though Franz has actually gone off with Mizzi), she mistakenly calls Gustav into the house and invites him to kiss her. She does so while lounging in a chair with an arm outstretched and her eyes (wide) shut. Upon realizing the man's true identity, she sends him away not with anger but with embarrassment—and, in private, a self-satisfied smile. How much are Charlotte's misunderstandings only that, and how much are they accurate perceptions of her situation?

There is an even more provocative, more openly ambiguous hint of the wife's less than absolutely faithful impulses earlier in the film in one of Lubitsch's first uses in Hollywood of what would become his signature door shot. Generally in a Lubitsch film, we can easily infer what kind of illicit behavior is going on between a couple behind a closed door. That is part of the fun, the game the director is playing with the audience and the censors. But in this case, when Charlotte visits Franz's office unexpectedly and discovers evidence of possibly compromising behavior on his part, Gustav goes behind a door to "console" the weeping Charlotte, as he is asked to do by her unsuspecting husband. Lubitsch holds the shot considerably longer than expected before suggestively fading out. We simply do not know what is happening behind that door, which makes this touch all the more unusual and significant. And it shows what a powerful effect Lubitsch could make with the timing of his editing. The very indirection of the shot makes us think more about Charlotte's depth of character. It allows us a subtle opportunity to consider that perhaps she is not as innocent or incapable of infidelity as she initially seems. If she is getting a bit of her own back here, the film would support a reading that the turnabout is fair play, part of the "circle" of its title.

The dramatic possibility that some actual physical contact may go on behind that closed door helps counterbalance, to some extent, the more obvious flirtations of Franz. We the audience are privy to them thanks to Lubitsch's otherwise allowing us a more omniscient point of view even as Charlotte takes a comically long time to catch on to the dismaying truth about her best friend's dalliance with her husband. Whether or not Franz actually consummates his flirtation with Mizzi is only hinted at, though there is a strong possibility that he may be doing so when he disappears into her apartment for a suspiciously long period. The initial period of time is carefully clocked by the detective hired by her husband to collect evidence for a divorce action; the rest is left implicit in the fact that Franz returns home around dawn, acting apologetic. Franz's behavior is far more flagrant than Charlotte's, but Lubitsch's subtle use of the door shot with her and Gustav in the office allows us to speculate, as we might wish, that she may be getting a bit of revenge, a quid pro quo for Franz's behavior. Lubitsch makes clear that she deserves consolation for the way she is treated, and Franz's behavior is even worse than she knows since she does not realize at that point who the other woman is. This is far from Lubitsch's first use of doors for sexual innuendo—he does so in some of his German films—but it helps point the way for how, inspired by the need to outwit American puritanism, he will use doors for such purposes many times in his Hollywood work, including in later scenes in *The Marriage Circle* (such as when Franz, storming out of Mizzi's apartment, pushes his way even more comically through no fewer than four doors). Lubitsch told Douglas Fairbanks Jr., the star of his last film, *That Lady in Ermine*, "Doors [are] as important as the actors."

The intricately oblique pattern of glances and gestures and the deployment of objects that Lubitsch uses to tell the story are best seen in the early series of scenes gradually leading up to Charlotte's discovery that Franz is deceiving her. This cinematic pattern is an almost entirely visual tour de force and must have been one of the main reasons the film was greeted with such excitement by its contemporary admirers. The couple's happy state is shown in a loving ritual ingeniously conveyed by Lubitsch's elliptical treatment of their break-fast. After they are shown gazing wistfully at each other, there is a close shot showing an eggcup, a coffee cup, and their hands. The hands start tapping the egg and stirring the coffee. But breakfast is quickly pushed aside as the couple embrace, and only their torsos are seen in the background of the shot, their faces remaining off camera. This droll sequence using food and drink as objects of foreplay anticipates Lubitsch's suggestive use of breakfast delicacies to convey other sensual appetites in the "Breakfast Time" number in his musical *The Smiling Lieutenant*.

The director also uses an intricate floral motif in *The Marriage Circle* to develop Charlotte's growing suspicions that Franz's behavior may stem from something even worse than indifference. As Gustav's car pulls up at the house, Franz and Charlotte are shown embracing in a wider shot, and then Charlotte goes to the patio to clip roses for her husband to take to his office. Her ardent suitor down below tips his straw hat lovingly as Charlotte, innocently enjoying the flirtation, drops a rose to the ground by "accident," another Freudian touch. Gustav smells the rose suggestively, again to her amusement. She goes back inside and gives Franz the bouquet of roses, but as he embraces her, he carelessly lets them fall to the floor, suggesting how shallow his love for her is compared with hers for him. After he departs, Charlotte leaves the frame as Lubitsch holds on the flowers briefly for unspoken emphasis. Gustav brandishes her rose behind Franz's back as they drive off. Charlotte's laugh-ter vanishes as she discovers the mess of flowers on the floor and stands like a disconsolate statue at the fade-out.

While Gustav is busy at the office with a chattering female patient whose neurotic complaints comically infuriate him ("Anyone who talks so much can't be sick," he says, thumping his desk), a mysterious woman in a veil enters Franz's office. She unwinds her facial covering, revealing herself to be

Mizzi, and sits brazenly on his desk. She plays with his hair and strokes his forehead. Gustav enters and sees them from the back, embracing; Franz, head turned, tells him to leave as the woman's hand waves him away. The disconsolate Gustav naturally assumes that Franz is having a romantic visit from Charlotte. But he is immediately surprised to find Charlotte sitting in the waiting room, holding her bouquet of flowers. Angered at her husband's carelessness, she has come to present the bouquet again, "to teach him not to throw my roses away." Gustav, behaving like the audience as we watch a Lubitsch film, puts two and two together in his mind with delicious deliberation and makes four without the director spelling it out. Lubitsch's style fully flowers here.

This realization of Franz's betrayal of Charlotte makes Gustav smile slyly: he sees his opening. But he is too much of a gentleman to usher Charlotte into Franz's office, which would cause the kind of direct confrontation Lubitsch prefers to avoid as long as possible, increasing the suspense. (It is no coincidence that *The Marriage Circle* made such an impact on Hitchcock because it is a master class in how to create visual suspense as well as how to dissect romantic problems between couples, an obsessive concern of Hitchcock's films; Hitchcock also paid a perverse tribute to Lubitsch by having Joseph Cotten's psychopathic, woman-hating Uncle Charlie called "the Merry Widow Murderer" in *Shadow of a Doubt*.) While Charlotte is in Gustav's office, she is delighted to see her rose in a glass on his desk. Mizzi leaves by another door after an awkward embrace in which she and Franz knock over a vase containing some other flowers. Charlotte, hearing the noise, is ushered into Franz's quarters where she hands him her bouquet and tries to straighten up his hair. His guilty expression is emphasized during the sequence in an unusually large close-up, and Gustav is shown from behind, scratching his head. Charlotte, seeing the new floral mess, becomes upset all over again. Franz lies that a "nervous man" knocked them over. Accusingly, Charlotte holds up a woman's glove. Franz sheepishly explains, "But I have many patients!" Charlotte, who has now added up the math in *her* head, realizes that her husband may be deceiving her, yet she still remains ignorant of Mizzi's involvement. And then comes the scene of Gustav going behind the door to "console" Charlotte.

This virtuosic series of scenes performs many functions smoothly, gracefully, and with a clockwork precision in its staging, framing, and choreography that makes everything in the story seem logical and inevitable. The main narrative effect is to convey the disruption in what initially seemed a placid marital arrangement, at least in the eyes of the wife, whose complacency has now been shattered. Franz's continuing pattern of thoughtlessness and mendacity digs him ever deeper into a hole, while Mizzi's scheming and their mutual concealment of their growing involvement lay the foundation for Charlotte's still-misdirected suspicion. The suspense of how she will find out that Mizzi is involved is sustained even as the marriage starts showing signs of unraveling. Gustav's involvement in the midst of all this neatly intensifies his sadly futile role as the would-be seducer of Charlotte. But Lubitsch and Bern follow up not with a dramatic confrontation revealing Mizzi's perfidy and a clash between husband and wife, as would be the conventional expectation, but with a surprising reversal, playing another game with the audience and prolonging the suspense for further comical and emotional development. The film introduces an elliptical passage of time in which Charlotte's early suspicions are somehow "forgotten" as an intertitle assures us. The next scene shows Charlotte and Franz vowing not to quarrel again and embracing with relief that their marriage is safely back on track. They are about to throw a formal dinner party as if in celebration.

Charlotte's newfound trust in Franz—clearly based on a denial of reality—is quickly disrupted all over again in a very Lubitschean sequence of confusion over the place cards at the dinner table (a favorite device he will employ in later films as well). Charlotte imagines that Franz is trying to manipulate the cards so he can sit next to a certain Fraulein Pauline Hofer (soon revealed to be a ravishing, lissome young blonde, Esther "the American Venus" Ralston). The irony is that Franz has replaced Mizzi's place card with Fraulein Hofer's in another vain attempt to fend off Mizzi's relentless advances. Charlotte, in her increasingly seriocomic complacency, assumes the opposite, ironically forcing Franz to sit next to Mizzi, someone she thinks she can trust. By weaving this elaborate pattern of marital deceit, obliviousness, and misinterpretation, Lubitsch has established the "circle" that by constant turns will keep revolving, seemingly effortlessly, from comedy to nearly catastrophic drama. Charlotte's eventual realization of how seriously Franz has been deceiving her with her "best friend" leads to her attempt at retaliation.

She reveals to Franz that Gustav has been pitching woo and has even kissed her (this is when she says, "Don't ask my forgiveness—I'm as guilty as you . . . Gustav's kiss was no dream—it was real").

The ultimate joke, revolving the film back from drama to comedy, is that when she forces Gustav to confess what he did with her, Franz smugly eggs him on behind Charlotte's back, refusing to believe his friend or his wife. But the joke is now on Franz, though more from our point of view than his. And now that Charlotte thinks she has established a new level of parity with her freshly tamed, or at least temporarily domesticated, husband ("Fifty-fifty," she tells him), Mizzi is exiled to the street, with Gustav chasing like a pet dog after her automobile as she beckons to him.

Conveying such a complex pattern of emotional interchanges—loving, suspicious, deceitful, and hurt—with a minimum of intertitles, Lubitsch created a dazzling tour de force of seriocomedy that showed everyone in Hollywood what the word "direction" really means. Small wonder that *The Marriage Circle* was hailed by *Photoplay* for having "the characters themselves reveal the story, which runs smoothly along to its logical ending. There is no straining for effects. . . . It's all very simple, very human and immensely entertaining." Robert E. Sherwood, later a noted playwright and screenwriter, praised the film's "fragile grace," writing in *Life*, "Ernst Lubitsch is, in many ways, the greatest director of them all. He has a delicately tuned sense of comedy, great control of the forces of drama, and an instinct for literary construction." When *Film Daily* in 1927 asked ten leading directors to name their favorite films, Lubitsch picked *The Marriage Circle*, declaring,

> In this production I was experimenting. . . . My desire was to create a story that would reflect life as it is lived by thousands of married couples—just everyday people that we meet all around us. In back of the idea was a desire to create a new form—a different technique. . . . I mean the processes employed in developing a story along natural, human lines, with the characters all flesh and blood people who were just a little bit bad and not too good. . . . There was suspense—interest—comedy—human beings reacting to given situations as they do in life. . . . There is not one single change I would make if I had to do it again.

THE RIDICULOUS AND THE TRAGIC

A measure of how unconventional and groundbreaking *The Marriage Circle* appeared in its day is in a comment in *Moving Picture World*. While praising Lubitsch for handling "a rather daring and sensational theme with simplicity and directness," the trade paper observed, "So different is this picture that its boxoffice appeal is difficult to gauge. With its distinctly continental flavor and atmosphere and with the code which surrounds married couples weighing lightly on the conscience of several of the characters, although there is no great moral transgression, the theme is snappy and skims on thin ice and will not appeal to the conventionally minded, [and] its subtlety and wit may also be over the heads of certain classes of patrons." Lubitsch's American films, including this one, were never boxoffice barnburners. A Lubitsch film was generally a succès d'estime that turned a modest profit; as this early review suggested, his films tended to be better received in the more sophisticated markets than in what *Variety* used to call the "stix." The films did well enough at the boxoffice to keep him bankable, and his reputation as a star maker and as a director who could be relied upon to bring out the best in every actor also meant a great deal in Hollywood. His peers in Hollywood and the reviewers were his greatest champions, gratefully recognizing how he advanced the medium and admiring his skills with their connoisseurs' taste.

Lubitsch's agility in adapting to the cultural mores of a new country was a talent he had honed when making films in Germany that were aimed at an international market, the United States in particular. His careful study of the American market, the world's largest at the time and the artistic terrain he was aiming to occupy, was refined in Hollywood with a clever exile's cunning and adaptability as he bent the American system of production to his own ends. If Lubitsch, as a consequence, had to be careful to walk a fine line between tweaking American puritanism and blatantly, self-destructively offending it, a critic who would find him at fault for doing so would seem to want him to be a different person, and one without a long, successful, and influential career. Lubitsch rather quickly evolved subtle means of portraying characters and situations in ways that would enable him to entertain and, to some extent, enlighten American audiences while maintaining his artistic and commercial freedom to a degree shared by few other directors. These stylistic means included relying more on visual suggestiveness than on more easily interpreted and reductive intertitles as well as encouraging his actors to explore nuances in their characters that kept them from being easily categorizable and (in some quarters) objectionable.

With his ability to make lightning transitions from comedy to drama and back again, to see people from all sides, Lubitsch defies categorization and keeps his films creatively unsettling, just as his films usually defy categorizing characters as simply good or bad. If a character such as Mizzi might seem an exception with her shameless disruption of her best friend's marriage, the kind of behavior that would be condemned by puritanical moralists and feminists alike, Lubitsch qualifies Mizzi's "badness" by making her seem too harshly dismissed by her husband and pathetically desperate for love (or at least affection) and by having her take advantage of the flaws in the Brauns' marriage. Both Franz and, to a lesser degree, Charlotte, are partially culpable for any success Mizzi temporarily achieves in disrupting their marriage. Indeed, as Graham Petrie notes, "Relationships which are resolved or held together in this manner, on a basis of self-deception, deliberate deceit, or a refusal to acknowledge facts, cannot be said to be particularly healthy." But to blame the problems in the Brauns' marriage purely on Mizzi, even if she is "shallow, opportunistic, and disloyal," as Petrie puts it, is largely to miss the central point of the film. She is a flawed person but also a handy catalyst for Franz's weaknesses and deceptions. In Hitchcock's terms, she is the Mac-Guffin, "the device, the gimmick, if you will, or the papers the spies are after. . . . It doesn't matter what it is."

In a Lubitsch film (or in real life), a Mizzi can always be found by a husband who has a roving eye. The equivalent character played by Genevieve Tobin in the musical remake *One Hour with You* is even more brazen, partly because the husband played by Chevalier has fewer struggles with his scruples than the husband in *The Marriage Circle*. *One Hour with You* is an entertaining romp, subversive in its relative tolerance of adulterous impulses, but a minor film, on a different level of complexity, seriousness, and achievement from *The Marriage Circle*, which stands as an example of Lubitsch at his best.

As Molly Haskell observes in her insightful 1974 book *From Reverence to Rape: The Treatment of Women in the Movies,*

Lubitsch's greatness was largely self-concealing: It lay in an ability to blend different elements—satire, musical comedy, and melodrama, for example—in a manner so effervescent that genius was mistaken for mere "touch." At the same time, he created women characters of depth and complexity whose originality was glossed over in the general designation of "Continental sophistication." But Lubitsch's worldliness was as deceptive as his touch. If anything, it was in going against the grain of the polished surface, in the hints of awkwardness with which he invested his men and women, that they—particularly the women—acquired complexity.

Lubitsch's belief in the existence of such a thing as a good marriage is not achieved at the expense of blindness to human weakness in *The Marriage Circle*. The study of human weakness is, after all, ingrained in the nature of comedy. Twenty-four centuries ago, Aristotle wrote in his *Poetics*, "As for Comedy, it is (as has been observed) an imitation of men worse than the average; worse, however, not as regards any and every sort of fault, but only as regards one particular kind, the Ridiculous, which is a species of the Ugly. The Ridiculous may be defined as a mistake or deformity not productive of pain or harm to others; the mask, for instance, that excites laughter, is something ugly and distorted without causing pain." When Mizzi, Franz, and other characters in a Lubitsch film are being merely ridiculous, they are comic; when they are causing pain, they approach tragedy. The best of Lubitsch's works often combine these two modes in a delicate equilibrium with a skill few other film directors have ever managed to approach. So trying to define the characters in his films, however admirable or reprehensible their behavior may be, by merely assigning labels or by expecting them to be role models for any particular period would not only be ridiculous but would also miss what Lubitsch is all about.

In the perfection of his style in *The Marriage Circle*, which remains one of his masterpieces in its precision and incisiveness and wisdom, Lubitsch shows as clearly as in any other film that he is a moralist in the Noël Coward sense of the word rather than the puritanical one: more tolerant of weakness but more exacting about deliberate choices about how men and women should behave toward each other. Since Lubitsch clearly believes that the Brauns' marriage, however imperfect, has value, this undoubtedly makes him romantic. Does that also make him conservative? In the eyes of Petrie and Kaplan and others, it does, and thus simplistically implies his disqualification from the ranks of major artists. But we need to look at artists for who they are, not who we might wish them to be.

Audiences, reviewers, and fellow filmmakers alike recognized that *The Marriage Circle* paved a road for a more mature, more truthful understanding of subject matter that was too often trivialized or sensationalized on American screens. That, as much as its stylistic brilliance, accounts for the film's great influence in paving the way for a higher level of sophistication in the romantic comedy genre, giving Lubitsch the right to claim the title as true creator of the genre. And in so doing, *The Marriage Circle* set the pattern for the rest of his career, defining the terrain and style he would triumphantly make his own. It is a style with many imitators that none could surpass.

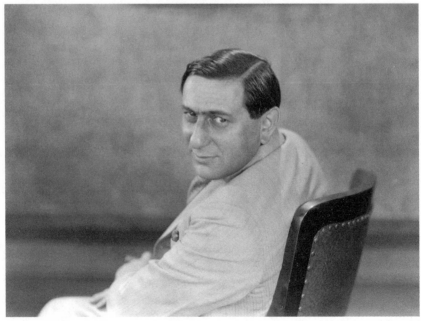

4

TIN CANS IN A WAREHOUSE?

L ubitsch's silent years ended with a rush of creative energy—eight films in the five years between 1924 and 1929, with three in 1924 alone. But though he was enjoying the freedom he had quickly earned in America, it seemed he was still trying in some ways to work out his identity. His films during that time vary widely in subject matter, style, and quality, ranging from some of the best work of his career to a couple of indifferent assignments. He was experimenting and testing his powers, which enabled him to grow as an artist, but while in the process of acclimating himself to his new country and a new film industry, it was almost as if he were asking *himself* who he really was.

Following *The Marriage Circle*, Lubitsch made three films before directing the other (existing) masterpiece of his American silent period, *Lady Windermere's Fan*. His 1925 adaptation of the celebrated 1892 play by Oscar Wilde is a tour de force for the sheer audacity of turning it into a silent film—and even more so because it was successfully done without using any of the

---

4.1 With May McAvoy (Lady Windermere) during the making of his audacious silent adaptation of Oscar Wilde's play *Lady Windermere's Fan* (1925). *(Warner Bros./From the collections of the Margaret Herrick Library, Academy of Motion Picture Arts and Sciences.)*

4.2 Portrait of Lubitsch at the time of his 1924 film *Forbidden Paradise*. *(Famous Players-Lasky/ Paramount.)*

play's many familiar epigrams—but it is also one of Lubitsch's most delicately played, finely nuanced, and poignant works. Lubitsch and screenwriter Julien Josephson chose to heighten the drama rather than the comedy of the play. They arguably improved upon this classic work in transforming it from stage to cinema and giving it a contemporary setting. Building on Lubitsch's triumph the previous year with *The Marriage Circle*, *Lady Windermere's Fan* further consolidated his reputation as a master Hollywood director.

But the creative path between those two superb films was somewhat erratic, and the vagaries of film survival make it hard to trace in any definitive way. His three intervening films, *Three Women*, *Forbidden Paradise*, and *Kiss Me Again*, exercised different aspects of his talent. They deserve brief study for their diversity and the light they shed on his development although these films are among his most obscure today. *Kiss Me Again* is not known to exist; the other two are very hard to see, and one of those, *Forbidden Paradise*, has been in poor condition though it is in the process of restoration.

The light tone that counterbalances the essentially serious nature of *The Marriage Circle* is only intermittently present in *Three Women* (1924), making it seem an odd hybrid, far less sure-handed and satisfying. Although *Three Women* was also made for Warners, and a good 35 mm print exists, the film is available for viewing today only in archives, for reasons that are unclear, or in inferior bootleg prints. It is one of Lubitsch's few films to take place entirely in the United States even though he had declared his intention as a Hollywood director to do "modern stories about American life." That ambition was strangely deflected, perhaps after he came to recognize how constraining Hollywood censorship could be; instead, most of his films offer disguised, oblique comments on American sexual mores. *Three Women* is set in New York high society and at the University of California, Berkeley (represented by a student bungalow filmed against Southern California hills). The film lacks some of the characteristic Lubitschean finesse partly because it does not have his familiar layer of continental mores and manners to offer an ironic overlay. Despite occasional felicities, *Three Women* seems blunt and heavy-handed in a way that Lubitsch films seldom are.

It starts promisingly as a pointedly insightful satire of a wealthy middle-aged Park Avenue woman, Mabel Wilton (Pauline Frederick), worrying about her looks and sexual appeal; she is initially seen fussing with a scale over a few extra pounds and anxiously getting herself ready for a society ball in a lonely-looking apartment of bleakly empty luxury. The theme of feminine insecurity is intensified by the arrival of her sprightly eighteen-year-old daughter, Jeannie (May McAvoy), a coed whose unwanted presence offers a harsh perspective on maternal neglect and selfishness. The mother's competitiveness toward her daughter might have been a promising setup for an examination of two stages of women's lives in a shallow upper-class society that views women unforgivingly as sexual objects. But instead, the film (adapted by Hans Kräly from the novel *Lillis Ehe* [*Lillie's Marriage*] by Iolanthe Marees) becomes a predictable melodrama as both women become successively involved with a penniless, money-grubbing seducer, Edmund Lamont (Lew Cody). This mustachioed fellow leers relentlessly and is so obviously slimy that he seems to sport the very word "cad" in blinking warning lights on his forehead. How different *Three Women* might have been if this character had been cast and performed in a more ambiguous way, with some genuine charm and attractive qualities mixed in with the cynicism—if Lamont, in short, had been played by Adolphe Menjou. *Three Women* would have benefited immeasurably from Menjou's genuine suavity and amused detachment, a style of behavior that, as can be seen in his character's contemptuous treatment of his wife in *The Marriage Circle*, was capable of dark inflections.

But largely lacking such nuances, *Three Women* is a tedious morality play that looks and feels routine, as if any competent director could have handled it almost as well as Lubitsch. Why did he regress from his lightly ironic treatment of dramatic material in *The Marriage Circle* to this kind of shallow melodramatic fare? Perhaps he wanted a change of pace as he often tended to do; perhaps he lacked a feeling of genuine creative involvement and was simply filling time between more challenging projects. *Three Women* displays Lubitsch's intermittent tendency to forsake his comic talents for overly sober dramaturgy. But in his best work, he is able to deftly and often inextricably combine comedy and drama rather than treating those two modes of storytelling as distinct.

As Lamont works his wiles in *Three Women*, one thing leads to another, with both mother and daughter behaving foolishly and blindly; they finally get the picture after he dumps Mabel to marry Jeanne and reflexively takes a mistress (Marie Prevost, looking as unhappy as the other women in a role that amounts to little more than an afterthought). *Three Women* resolves the situation with a thudding lack of imagination unworthy of Lubitsch: the previously frivolous Mabel turns into an avenging angel, unsuccessfully confronting and then killing the remorseless, blackmailing Lamont. Lubitsch makes a gesture at his characteristic oblique storytelling by showing the murdered man collapsing in shadow on a wall as Mabel goes in and out of frame to pull and fire a gun from a desk drawer. That visual touch was probably intended to help distance the audience from the essential ugliness of the situation, but the effect, though flamboyant, fails in that purpose. Following a trial almost entirely conveyed through ellipsis, Mabel is exonerated by an all-male jury (shown simply by the foreman shaking his head without need for an intertitle), a verdict it apparently reached because of her victimhood and social status. Mabel's reckless act is excused by Lubitsch because she supposedly has repented her earlier neglect of Jeanne and killed Lamont to save her daughter, the kind of conventionally moralistic flourish more typical of DeMille than Lubitsch. While we could read a less sentimental, more venal motive of revenge into Mabel's actions, which would be more in keeping with her narcissistic personality, this film, unusually for Lubitsch, does not seem very interested in exploring ambiguities.

Though it has intermittent felicities—a spare, even severe visual elegance; the occasional bravura sequence; and a daring, even ostentatious avoidance of intertitles in favor of extended visual storytelling—*Three Women* is notably stingy with Lubitsch Touches and the kind of visual ellipses that marked the elaborate development of his style in *The Marriage Circle*. *Three Women*'s clumsy construction, uncertainty of tone, and lack of inspiration are in striking contrast to the sparkling creative excitement generated by his approach to sexual deception in his previous film. While in *The Marriage Circle* the wife's slowness to realize how her husband is deceiving her is a credible result of her misplaced trust in him and her marriage, in *Three Women* both the mother and the daughter seem exceptionally dense to be unaware that Lamont is exploiting their loneliness to get his hands on their money. The way Lubitsch gets that point across to the audience when Lamont first sees the mother at a society ball—by having him leer at her tiara and other jewels in a series of close-ups—is mildly amusing but uncharacteristically crude.

Where *Three Women* occasionally comes alive is in its sardonic as well as compassionate treatment of Mabel's anxiety over aging and Lamont's indifference to her feelings. This theme is most acutely played out when, in anticipation of what she thinks will be a romantic tryst, she carefully arranges the mise-en-scène of her sitting room, adjusting the lighting from various directions to keep it low and flattering while burning incense to heighten the romantic ambience. But when Lamont enters, he snaps on a bright light and, having thoughtlessly spoiled her mood, promptly sets about his business of conning her out of her money. Lubitschean grace notes such as these are rare in *Three Women*. Perhaps the film's most significant place in his career was as a rehearsal for his far more subtle and moving depiction of a troubled mother-daughter relationship in *Lady Windermere's Fan*, which also features the winsome McAvoy but in a much more focused, mature, and complex characterization. If the routinely melodramatic material of *Three Women* inhibited and defeated Lubitsch, the rich source material of the Wilde play would stimulate his best creative impulses.

ANOTHER BIG HEAD OF POLA

Forbidden Paradise, the third Lubitsch film released in 1924, is a distinct change of pace after *Three Women*. An experimental film that plays daringly with genre expectations, *Forbidden Paradise* is a loose, loopy comedy set in a mythical kingdom straddling the modern day and what seems like the eighteenth century. It is a playful riff on some of the legends about Russian czarina Catherine the Great. Pola Negri, who had come to Hollywood a little before Lubitsch in 1922, reunites with the director as Katerina, providing one of the film's numerous points of connection with his German spectacles. But *Forbidden Paradise* seems positively surreal in its approach to history. The czarina wears dazzling modern gowns and sports a bobbed 1920s hairdo, and her suave, cynical chamberlain (Menjou) rides through the countryside in an open automobile to defeat a threatened rebellion by brandishing a checkbook as his very modern weapon of choice.

Lubitsch indulges his stylistic and narrative whims with abandon in this delightful film. Negri is much more relaxed and natural than she was in the German spectacles, bringing a sense of modernity and spontaneity to her sexually liberated character, and the film's light tone and playful style make the mood infectious (Negri's more subdued style was anticipated in Lubitsch's last German film, *Die Flamme*). *Forbidden Paradise* was adapted by Hans

Kräly and Agnes Christine Johnson from the play *The Czarina* by Lajos Biró and Melchior Lengyel (Lengyel would also provide the story material for Lubitsch's *Angel*, *Ninotchka*, and *To Be or Not to Be*).

Forbidden Paradise seems like major Lubitsch, but it is hard to judge it more definitively until its restoration by the Museum of Modern Art is released. This lavish Paramount production was neglected by the studio, as were most silent films (perhaps in this case because it was remade in 1945 by Twentieth Century-Fox as *A Royal Scandal*). *Forbidden Paradise* has survived in Czechoslovakian and Russian archives as well as at the George Eastman Museum in Rochester, New York, and in the American Film Institute collection at the Library of Congress. The Cinémathèque Française undertook partial restorations in 1963 and 2010 from an incomplete Czech print. Some scenes have been missing entirely; unofficially circulating DVD copies are of a poorly duped condensed version that is missing more than one-fifth of its original seventy-eight minutes (the MoMA restoration, from two Czech archive prints, will have more footage but will still be incomplete). Mordaunt Hall's *New York Times* review describes in detail how the czarina has her long black hair bobbed before her distraught ladies in waiting, "and the women in the audience at this point appeared to be holding their breath," but in the prints that have been available, we see only a basket of shorn hair being carried out of her chambers. Other scenes survive in various prints but are chopped into fragments.

The film's most incisive Lubitsch Touch has the rebel general (Nick De Ruiz) clutching his sword when confronted by the chancellor but relaxing his grip when Menjou's cigar-holding hand, also in close-up, pulls his checkbook from a coat pocket. But the scene goes by so quickly in some dupe copies that it is barely intelligible. In the best archival print that has been available in Europe, the rhythm of those intercut close-ups is graceful and makes its point as wittily as one might expect from Lubitsch at his best.

The vaguely Russian (or Balkan) sets by Hans Dreier are at once impressive and bizarre—Katerina's castle is decorated with elaborate conical set pieces that look like giant artichokes—yet, at least in the available prints, the sets are deployed in the narrative eccentrically. Contrary to convention, but as Lubitsch sometimes does, we are not given wide establishing shots of the castle until late in the film when Katerina is running around desperately, a tiny figure in huge empty halls, as her rebellious army masses outside, joined by the mutinous palace guards. The rebellion is quickly and humorously dispelled when Menjou returns from the rebel headquarters to report that he has bought them off, and they all declare renewed fealty to the czarina. Until that point, the action, so to speak, takes place mostly in the czarina's intimate, relatively modest private quarters, mostly her boudoir, office, and antechamber. It is impossible to know whether this reversal of the usual style of visual exposition is a result of the condensing of the film or an innovative stylistic device; that it could be at least partly the latter is suggested by Lubitsch's employment of a similar method in some of his other films.

Unlike in his German spectacles, which sometimes draw comedy from history but are still essentially dramas, the political level of *Forbidden Paradise* is a deliberate joke. The czarina does not seem unduly despotic—at least we do not see much of her effect on the common people—but her troops are whipped into rebellion by a male chauvinist soldier who objects to their being commanded by a woman, an attitude the film treats as absurd. Many of Katerina's soldiers didn't seem to object to her rule earlier, especially since she rewarded her sexual conquests with the "Order of the Star," pinning large medals in the shape of starbursts on their tunics. The doltish young leading man, Alexei (Rod La Roque), a lieutenant promoted to head of the palace guard because the czarina desires him, is so proud of his star that his chest actually swells, bursting a button. There is a charming comic touch when the diminutive czarina pulls a stool over with her foot so she can stand on it when she kisses him. Alexei's mood is soon deflated when he attends a banquet filled entirely with officers wearing identical medals. The young officer is already wrestling with conflicted emotions over Katerina's seductive tactics since he is engaged to one of her ladies-in-waiting, Anna (Pauline Starke), but that subplot does not seem to count for much emotionally in *Forbidden Paradise*. Lubitsch would usually do more with those kinds of complications—most of his films revolve around love triangles—but perhaps they are diminished here because we are missing scenes; in any case, La Roque's dull presence as the distractingly pretty male ingenue is a weakness in the film.

Josef von Sternberg, in his far more baroque and kinkier 1934 film about Catherine the Great, *The Scarlet Empress*, a Paramount film starring Marlene Dietrich, borrowed the medal gag. At one point, Sternberg has Catherine, leering ironically, take a star from the chest of one lover in the palace guard and pin it on another while saying, "For bravery—in *action*." In contrast with Lubitsch's sympathetic portrayal of Katerina as a warm, easily amused, affectionate, sometimes desperately lonely woman (albeit what would later be considered, in chauvinist terms, a nymphomaniac), Dietrich's Catherine is a rampantly voracious sociopath, taking revenge for the way she was mistreated in an arranged marriage to a lunatic. She uses her sexual wiles to exercise brutal political power while reveling in sadomasochistic relationships with the men under her control, including her deranged husband, the Grand Duke Peter (Sam Jaffe), whom she has assassinated after he becomes Emperor Peter III. To embellish the production values of his already wildly flamboyant film, Sternberg also borrowed some long shots from Lubitsch's 1928 Russian-set Paramount silent film, *The Patriot*. Those shots, now otherwise missing from the existing fragments of *The Patriot* itself, ironically caused Lubitsch's ire not because they were borrowed from his own work but because he did not recognize the footage and, while serving as head of production at Paramount, mistakenly used it as an example to criticize Sternberg for being too extravagant.

Lubitsch's mischievous mixing of periods in *Forbidden Paradise* is his way of comically illustrating the saying *"plus ça change, plus c'est la même chose."* Nevertheless, he is dealing in *Forbidden Paradise* with a country that evokes elements of his father's ancestral homeland, the site of the recent Bolshevik Revolution. Lubitsch presents that land as one ruled by barbaric methods of varying political ideologies in *Ninotchka*, his occasionally stinging 1939 satire of Stalinism and czarism, and in *The Patriot*, whose storyline justifies the assassination of the mad Czar Paul I, Catherine's son. The mockery of the political goings-on in *Forbidden Paradise* reflects some of Lubitsch's skepticism about his ancestral land, whose anti-Semitism and despotism had caused his father to flee to Germany, but it conveys the director's views in a more lightly satirical vein than *The Patriot*. Katerina may be a tyrant by profession, but she is an oddly sympathetic one, devoted primarily to her own pleasure and amusement in toying with men. When one (Alexei) finally denies her, she simply turns, with the encouragement of her pimpish chamberlain, to a new sex object, the Spanish ambassador. The film ends with a Lubitsch door gag as the ambassador leaves her chambers wearing the ubiquitous star.

The available evidence indicates that Lubitsch reverted to the style of his German spectacles for the last time when he returned to the subject of

Russia four years later in *The Patriot*. All but a few minutes of that once-heralded silent film and its trailer are lost, but those fragments indicate a stylized drama with the kind of grandiose settings and flamboyant performance by Emil Jannings that also characterize the German spectacles. Again, it is hard to judge a film that is not complete, but the operatic style of *The Patriot*, a film celebrated in its day (it received one of the first nominations for best picture by the Academy of Motion Picture Arts and Sciences), does not wear as well to contemporary eyes as the romping, insouciant style of *Forbidden Paradise*. That silent comedy is far more appealing than its 1945 remake, *A Royal Scandal*, which Lubitsch prepared but was too ill to direct (Otto Preminger took over that duty). Talk-heavy, ponderous in its humor, and laboriously plotted, *A Royal Scandal* shines a spotlight on the contrasting virtues of the silent version. The world-weary Tallulah Bankhead gives a campy performance as the czarina that pales in contrast to the spirited, genuinely sexy jollity of Negri's characterization.

If *Forbidden Paradise* is something of a throwback for Lubitsch, or a peculiar hybrid between his German and American silent styles, it also contains visual elements that reflect significant transitions in his stylistic development. Conveying subtle overtones of loneliness and melancholia in its use of space, it shows the czarina often alone in her oversize settings, at times an ironically small and desolate figure. His German spectacles do not use their gargantuan settings to dwarf or diminish the protagonists. But in Hollywood, the small figure of Mary Pickford in *Rosita*, the impoverished street singer, finds herself adrift in large, lavish sets. *The Marriage Circle* effectively opts for more intimate, simpler settings, but in *Three Women*, Pauline Frederick's lonely quarters, with their large entryway and sitting room, reflect her isolated, self-centered nature. And after the visually striking use of cavernous spaces in *Forbidden Paradise*, the characters in his next film, *Lady Windermere's Fan*, are dwarfed by unusually high ceilings and improbably large doors. The tiny, bewildered heroine, May McAvoy, and the dramatically helpless male characters seem visually overwhelmed by their upper-class settings, adrift in their empty, relatively unadorned "luxury," a source of rich visual irony for Lubitsch. Perhaps this trend in his style was a sly observation on the contrasting extravagance and the emotional and cultural emptiness of the life he saw around him in America and specifically in Hollywood.

A MISSING LINK

Before tackling *Lady Windermere's Fan*, Lubitsch made another marital comedy for Warners, *Kiss Me Again* (1925). By all accounts it was a triumph. Herman Weinberg in his 1968 book *The Lubitsch Touch* goes so far as to write, "It may well be Lubitsch's most dazzling work." How much more frustrating that this is a lost film. From Weinberg's memory and contemporary reviews, it seems that *Kiss Me Again* was a piquant variation on *The Marriage Circle*, casting Monte Blue and Marie Prevost as an unhappily married Parisian couple who, in the process of cynically cooking up reasons to justify a divorce, wind up reuniting. Even more tantalizingly, this is the only Lubitsch film whose cast included Clara Bow, at the peak of her sensual vivacity. Playing the secretary of Blue's divorce lawyer, Bow's Grisette has designs on the client.

Loosely adapted by Kräly from the venerable 1880 Victorien Sardou-Émile de Najac farce *Divorçons!* (*Let's Get a Divorce*), *Kiss Me Again* was indifferently remade by Lubitsch himself in 1941 as *That Uncertain Feeling*, starring Melvyn Douglas and Merle Oberon. However *Kiss Me Again* might hold up if we could see it today, it obviously did not share the obvious flaws of the independently made sound-era remake—an uninspiring, even irritating cast saddled with a lackluster, verbose script and production values depressed by visual drabness. *That Uncertain Feeling* suffers from a general lack of vitality, a rare problem for Lubitsch but perhaps a sign that he recognized the project's marked inferiority to the original version and was only going through the motions creatively (by contrast, Lubitsch's changing of *The Marriage Circle* to a musical, *One Hour with You*, gave that remake more of a raison d'être and made it a fresh creative challenge). *That Uncertain Feeling* seems like a second-rate imitation of the master that could have been directed by someone else.

Kiss Me Again received exceptional reviews, even including some from highbrow publications that were beginning to take up Lubitsch as a model of sophistication, far transcending the norms of Hollywood entertainment. Ted Shane wrote in the *New Yorker*, "It is Continental high comedy done in the Central European manner with Germanic harshness and irony of attack. It is as far from America as Mr. Lubitsch is above the sophistication of Mr. Will H. Hays. . . . As a result we have startling pantomime and a hilarious picture." Richard Watts in *Theatre Magazine* described *Kiss Me Again* as "just about the finest of all photoplay high comedies. The appeal of the picture is almost entirely an intellectual one. There is no attempt to tug at your heart-strings. Every effort is aimed at the intelligence." Lubitsch himself, in a 1947 letter to Weinberg surveying his career, published in *The Lubitsch Touch*, listed *Kiss Me Again* among his favorite films of his American silent period, along with *The Marriage Circle*, *Lady Windermere's Fan*, and *The Patriot*.

It is not surprising that the team of the phlegmatically foolish Blue and the wanton Prevost (at least as they appear in their screen images for Lubitsch) would create a comically incompatible couple on-screen in *Kiss Me Again*, but the satirical point of this story is how even in the Roaring Twenties they have to go along with the letter of the law to create a provocation for their divorce. The neglected wife, the delectably named LouLou Fleury, whose husband, Gaston, smugly takes her for granted is having a romantic dalliance with a long-haired, long-fingered bohemian pianist, Maurice (John Roche). Lubitsch and Kräly jazzed up the suitor from the rather wooden forester of the original play. *Divorçons!* seems laborious today in its extended machinations around a theme that was daring for its time, the campaign for reinstatement of divorce in France (which occurred four years after the play was first produced). While Lubitsch's French characters can take for granted the more liberal social climate of the 1920s, the drama still turns on a revelation of character.

To provide a suitable legal excuse for divorce, Gaston is advised by his lawyer to strike his wife, but he cannot bring himself to do the deed. Previously she had found him unexciting and complacent, but now his gentlemanly attitude starts to win her back. For both parties, though, increasingly desultory dallying takes place before they reunite (Gaston takes up with Grisette to make LouLou jealous). The ending sounds like a delicious Lubitsch Touch: Gaston emerges from his bedroom to tell the lingering Maurice to tone down his piano playing and then closes the bedroom door on his wife's rejected suitor. The gag is amiably recycled in *That Uncertain Feeling*. Not the least of the remake's failings is that the husband actually does slap the wife in the remake, though he has to get drunk to do it. That change reflects the influence of the somewhat brutal screwball comedy genre in which Lubitsch had dabbled three years earlier with the even more offensive *Bluebeard's Eighth Wife*.

Some sense of what contemporary reviewers perceived as the special quality of *Kiss Me Again* is evident in an article on Lubitsch by Matthew Josephson titled "Masters of the Motion Picture" in a 1926 issue of *Motion*

Picture Classic magazine. Josephson, who would become a noted writer, editor, and author of books on literary and economic subjects, indicates in his appreciation of Lubitsch that the director has carried the art of pantomime and its cinematic employment for visual storytelling to a higher level in this, his fifth American film. In both *The Marriage Circle* and *Kiss Me Again*, writes Josephson,

> There is less glitter to dazzle your eyes. The nature of these films is simpler as the highest art is nearly always the simplest. . . . There is a sequence running several thousand feet in which the husband and wife, Monte Blue and Marie Prevost, discuss with their lawyer the most sensible method of getting their divorce. The pantomime here is tremendously funny without having any of the dynamic farce of the Harold Lloyd buffoonery. The face, hands, body of Monte Blue suddenly become an instrument that flickers before the camera lens with infinite fantasy. The film offers a brilliant psychological portrait of these frivolous but extremely human characters. . . .
>
> Lubitsch is analytical, and prefers to film a few highly concentrated moments. . . . Lubitsch's great stunt is that he gets all these effects with such simple means, with such *reasonable* material; like the framework of the old domestic triangle. He is so intelligent and competent as he moves from one bit of business to another that he makes pantomime, which is too often mere dumb show, have a much greater range of meaning.

"A WARNER BROTHERS CLASSIC OF THE SCREEN"

Not long before his death in 1947, Lubitsch discussed what he felt was the transitory nature of his life's achievement. The occasion was a unique work session with his longtime screenwriter Samson Raphaelson. The writer had composed a funeral tribute in 1943 when Lubitsch had nearly died of a heart attack. The document was leaked to Lubitsch, much to Raphaelson's embarrassment, but in a deliciously seriocomic real-life Lubitsch Touch, the director set about revising and polishing it with his writer. The work was going fairly smoothly with only some friction when Lubitsch objected to exaggerated accounts of flaws in his table manners and sartorial taste. But when Lubitsch came to the part reading, "However great the cinema historians will eventually estimate him, he was even bigger as a person," he remarked, with "a touch of bitterness" as Raphaelson recalled, "What historians? They'll laugh at you. A movie—any movie, good or bad—ends up in a tin can in a warehouse; in ten years it's dust. You're smart that you stick with the theater, Sam. What college teaches movies? But drama is literature. Your plays are published. Someday a student gets around to you—you have a fighting chance."

That discussion, of course, is fraught with ironies. Lubitsch's disillusionment and underrating of his own craft was typical in those days for filmmakers, who had to deal with the reality that their work was so insufficiently valued. And though Raphaelson thought of himself primarily as a playwright—he was a diligent and masterful screenwriter, though he admittedly did not take that job very seriously—it is his work with Lubitsch for the screen that defines his own legacy, much to his later surprise and chagrin. He complained, "To think that I should be remembered for the bloody movies! It's simply absurd!" And Lubitsch fortunately was mostly wrong about whether his own work would last. Like most people of his time, inside or outside the film industry, he thought film was a disposable art form. Frank Capra told me they thought of movies like newspapers—tossed on a porch, read briefly, and then thrown away. Lubitsch did not foresee that film study, including the study of eras long past, would become a major field in academia and elsewhere or that great advances would be made in film preservation despite the many losses we have suffered over the years. It is sad to know that such a great filmmaker thought his work was so ephemeral. We can take comfort from knowing that it is not even though it deserves to be much better known today. *Lady Windermere's Fan* is a sterling example of Lubitsch's greatness, abundantly deserving of the publicity encomiums it received from Warner Bros. at the time.

When Lubitsch made his audacious silent adaptation of Wilde's play, he and Warners gave every indication that they at least *hoped* their work would last and, indeed, that it would rival the theatrical classic on which it is based. The studio gave the 1925 film a rare road-show release at elevated ticket prices, and the opening titles in Gothic lettering proclaim it "A Warner Brothers Classic of the Screen." The silent film version famously does not use any actual Wilde epigrams in its intertitles. That radical decision by Lubitsch and screenwriter Julien Josephson may have smacked of arrogance in the face of a seemingly impossible challenge or at least a droll artistic stunt, but more crucially, it also served as a declaration of independence for the much younger art of the cinema.

It continued a trend in Lubitsch's work, already remarked on both favorably and not by reviewers, to minimize intertitles in order to concentrate on the interplay of glances between characters. As the glories of the silent medium were nearing their end, Lubitsch had so mastered the art of screen pantomime that he hardly needed intertitles to convey what people were saying, even in the most subtle and sophisticated of dramatic or comedic scenes, as he masterfully demonstrates in such films as *The Marriage Circle* and *Lady Windermere's Fan*. His aversion to using titles was almost as strong as that of F. W. Murnau, who famously had minimized titles in his 1924 German classic *Der letzte Mann (The Last Laugh)*. Lubitsch's style was so artistically supple that most audiences seemed to have no problem following his stories. In a December 1923 interview with the *New York Times* soon after the release of *Rosita*, Lubitsch talked about how in working with his screenwriter he habitually "mapped out carefully beforehand every detail of direction of the production." Then, he said,

> I try to exclude titles wherever possible. I want all action, where it is feasible, to explain itself without titles to interrupt the suspense, which is so often killed by the insertion of words. For a modern realistic drama, we must have spoken titles, but even those should be made to read just as one speaks in real life, and not according to the stiff conversation of books. The ideal manuscript [that is, scenario] is one without titles, but it is not for today or tomorrow, but in a couple of years or infinitely longer. This has nothing to do with pictures as they are produced nowadays. In our titles we borrow from the stage or the novel. Later we will have discovered the modern picture style.

Wilde's *Lady Windermere's Fan* contains quite a number of his most noted epigrams, including "History is merely gossip"; "We are all in the gutter, but some of us are looking at the stars"; and "In this world there are only two great tragedies. One is not getting what one wants, and the other is getting it." Lubitsch and Josephson, undaunted by their source, replace the playwright's verbal wit with equally brilliant pantomime. The intertitles by

Maude Fulton and Eric Locke are often witty but in a less showy way than Wilde's dialogue. The first title sets the tone of quiet irony and social satire: "Lady Windermere faced the grave problem—of seating her dinner guests," a social situation with sexual overtones that is often the subject of merriment and drama in Lubitsch's films. Wilde's plays are studded with so many spectacular witticisms that those lines sometimes stand out in ways that can seem jarring, taking us out of the narrative at hand, although it is hard to object to such riches or to question the validity of his original and enduring style. But it is also true that the stage version of *Lady Windermere's Fan*, along with its frequent flourishes of satirical wit, relies heavily on expository dialogue and has its characters speak lengthy soliloquies, spelling out their motives and concerns, making the author's messages extremely explicit. Lady Windermere tells her husband late in the play, "I don't think now that people can be divided into the good and the bad as though they were two separate races or creations. What are called good women may have terrible things in them, mad moods of recklessness, assertion, jealousy, sin. Bad women, as they are termed, may have in them sorrow, repentance, pity, sacrifice."

Although Lady Windermere's acknowledgment of the gray qualities of human behavior and morality can be seen as anticipating some of the essence of Lubitsch's tolerant worldview, such a highly verbal approach is better suited to the theater, which has to create its milieu more through words than settings and cannot jump around as nimbly as a film or employ the full panoply of visual shorthand and expressiveness that were Lubitsch's stock-in-trade. Even Anton Chekhov, another master of oblique storytelling, felt the need for frequent exposition in his plays, which in other respects epitomize the subtlest character development. Rather than using Wilde's didactic mode to convey that playwright's characteristically caustic ironies about morality, Lubitsch trusts the audience more, as he always does. He is out to show the audience, with dazzling artistry, just how subtle and complex the cinema can be in conveying the nuances of character and social interaction. His stunt of eschewing Wilde's epigrams calls attention to the importance he placed on showing that pantomime can be the equal of clever dialogue or even superior to wordplay. Lubitsch told the *New York Times*,

> Playing with words is fascinating to the writer and afterward to the reader, but on the screen it is quite impossible. Would much charm remain to

long excerpts from Wilde's play if the audience had to ponder laboriously over the scintillating sentences on the screen? Motion pictures are essentially words translated into human action, which should flow smoothly from start to finish, developing each step in the story easily, naturally and without inconveniencing the mind of the spectator, who should never have to wait for written titles to understand what is going on. The more complicated the plot the clearer and more decisive the photoplay should be.

This silent film masterpiece demonstrates that motion pictures can be spoken of in the same breath of respect as the finest theater. It triumphantly proved in 1925 that the new art form was capable of its own infinitely rich delicacy of expression, particularly in the hands of such a masterful director. That is why Lubitsch was so highly regarded by his peers and even by many literary critics in those days when intellectuals tended to scorn the movies as a low-level, vulgar form of entertainment for the unwashed masses.

Not only that, but *Lady Windermere's Fan* has survived the ravages of time unusually well for a film of the silent period. An estimated 90 percent of silent films have been lost, and many of the surviving ones are not in good shape. But this Lubitsch gem still looks sparkling in both theatrical prints and the best available copies on DVD. The delicate visual shadings of cinematographer Charles Van Enger—whose work with Lubitsch also included *The Marriage Circle, Three Women, Forbidden Paradise*, and *Kiss Me Again*—are not blurred or muted today in *Lady Windermere's Fan*. The unusual sets by Harold Grieve—with their high ceilings and doors that suggestively engulf the London socialite characters, particularly the heroine played by the lovely, wispy McAvoy—retain their expressive combination of uncluttered elegance and subtle social satire.

Silent pantomime (always accompanied by music) in many early films may have been "too often mere dumb show," as Matthew Josephson noted in his commentary on *Kiss Me Again*, but it evolved in the hands of great directors into sublime artistry. *Lady Windermere's Fan* is the best extant demonstration of how Lubitsch, in Josephson's words, "is so intelligent and competent as he moves from one bit of business to another that he makes pantomime . . . have a much greater range of meaning." The former stage actor D. W. Griffith, whom Lubitsch emulated and then surpassed in his own historical epics, helped create the techniques of screen acting in his Biograph shorts. In a relatively short time, Griffith developed the use of body language, gestures, and facial expressions into an art perfectly suited for the intimacy of the camera. Griffith's 1919 masterpiece *Broken Blossoms*, a poetic dramatic feature about interracial romance with Lillian Gish and Richard Barthelmess, is a case in point. As Andrew Sarris eloquently observes in *The American Cinema*, "When Richard Barthelmess first confronts Lillian Gish in *Broken Blossoms*, the subtle exchange of emotions between the two players would defy the art of the greatest novelist." *Photoplay* reported in 1922 that Lubitsch considered *Broken Blossoms* "one of the screen's immortal classics."

After his humble beginnings as a broad knockabout comedian, grimacing and gesticulating wildly for the camera, Lubitsch learned more delicate ways from Reinhardt, Griffith, Stiller, and Chaplin. Lubitsch equaled their best work in purely visual storytelling before the silent era reached its end, just as it was reaching its pinnacle of achievement. Mary Pickford aptly noted in 1931, "It would have been more logical if silent pictures had grown out of the talkie instead of the other way round." Lubitsch may never have surpassed the intricacy of his system of emotional and comedic exchanges among the characters in *The Marriage Circle*, but the way he refined that method of conveying character with quiet looking and behaving and minute changes of facial expressions in *Lady Windermere's Fan* was equaled only by Griffith and Chaplin at their greatest. Lubitsch would go on to use sound with equally innovative creativity and expressiveness, but there will always remain something ineffable and irreplaceable about his best silent work. As Pickford put it toward the end of that era, "Talking pictures are like lip rouge on the Venus de Milo."

Pantomime, as Lubitsch employs it, proves perfectly suited for the themes of *Lady Windermere's Fan*, which centers around a secret, something unmentionable between Lord Windermere (Bert Lytell) and his wife. The secret is that Lady Windermere's mother, whom she thinks is dead, has returned to blackmail the husband so that his young wife doesn't learn the truth about her. Mrs. Edith Erlynne (Irene Rich), who abandoned the child to run off with a lover, was later abandoned herself and pursued a career as a notorious woman of affairs. She blackmails the aristocrat out of financial desperation. He says of his wife in the play, "I dare not tell her who this woman really is. The shame would kill her." The film instead has him tell Mrs. Erlynne directly, "She worships her dead mother. The truth would kill her!" Although in the play Mrs. Erlynne comes close at the end to telling all to her daughter, in the film that is never a real option. Even though the film updates the play to the 1920s, Lubitsch's view of high society is that its strict formal adherence to black-and-white standards of morality would still prevent that from happening, even though society is portrayed in the film as thoroughly hypocritical and insincere. That milieu's code of alleged morality papers over all manner of covert indiscretions that everyone may know about but no one publicly acknowledges. That is an even harsher view of high society than the portrait Wilde offered in 1892, perhaps since Lubitsch was more of an outsider in that world than Wilde was, even if the playwright would become ostracized from society just a few years later with his own sex scandal.

The interplay of looks and gestures in Lubitsch's version of *Lady Windermere's Fan* is mostly in conveying the characters' evasiveness and lies; and the director constantly shows us the truth behind the deceptions. This conflict is sometimes the stuff of comedy, comedy of a bitter sort, but mostly of drama in the Lubitsch version. Partly because of its elimination of Wilde's epigrams, the film focuses more intently on the powerful truth that it takes a fragile tissue of lies to preserve a marriage and a naïve young woman's way of looking at the world. Several people risk their own reputations to protect the dubious innocence of Lady Windermere, who is shown to be hovering on the edge of infidelity herself. Her husband's act of intended goodwill in paying blackmail is undertaken not without sympathy for Mrs. Erlynne, whom Lubitsch portrays in a nonjudgmental light, generous and somewhat admiring, as a regretful but practical woman who is philosophically resigned to her state while cleverly trying to outwit the prudes who condemn her as a fallen woman. But Windermere's clandestine meetings with Mrs. Erlynne and his payments to her are misinterpreted by gossips and eventually by Lady Windermere herself as evidence of an affair between her husband and the notorious woman.

The misunderstanding almost destroys the marriage and tempts the young woman to run off with her lovelorn suitor, the dashing, suavely insinuating Lord Darlington (Ronald Colman). Early in the film, Darlington is emboldened by thinking that Lord Windermere is unfaithful, a suspicion conveyed in a sardonic Lubitsch Touch when Darlington passes a letter from Mrs. Erlynne to Lord Windermere surreptitiously in close-up so he can hide it as he deceives his wife. After the husband departs, Darlington declares his love for the neglected Lady Windermere in a scene shot with a daringly unusual use of space. He walks to the far end of a huge study to make his declaration rather than sit beside her on a couch in the foreground of the frame. From his distant bench, Darlington tells her with a wry smile, "Lady Windermere, I think I have a bit of news that might interest you." This prompts the anxious young wife to make the long walk (elided with a quick cut) to sit with him, asking "What?" twice in pantomime, with a quizzical, imploring expression. "I love you!" he says seriously. Rather than have her walk away indignantly as a conventional director would do, Lubitsch has Lord Darlington walk slowly and sadly by himself to the other end of the room as Lady Windermere sits pensively at the fade-out, a small and enigmatic figure. This directorial display of the expressive powers of mise-en-scène conveys a complex blend of mutual attraction and cautious retreat by the young married woman. And the staging helps convey the emotional gulf that separates these two characters. Darlington eventually passes along to her the falsehood about her husband's affair, believing it to be true and hoping it will further his chances. Though a more plausible suitor than Dr. Gustav Mueller in *The Marriage Circle* and one who stirs genuine if conflicted interest in the married woman he desires, Darlington is ultimately a failure at his mission, a melancholy figure.

In this web of deceit, Mrs. Erlynne ironically comes off best because she is most honest about her situation and because she not only feels regretful but also has a genuine concern for her daughter's emotional well-being. In a truly great performance by Irene Rich—a largely unheralded actress best known today as a minor member of the John Ford Stock Company—Mrs. Erlynne is shown by Lubitsch in a highly complex, richly textured, unstereotyped light as a warmhearted but eminently practical woman with no illusions about life. Rich's performance helps give the lie, if any such evidence were needed, to Pickford's claim that "Lubitsch was a man's director, he had no sensitivity about women." The camera often lingers in unbroken takes on Mrs. Erlynne's lightning shifts of emotion as she absorbs blows of pain and humiliation but rebounds with wit and aplomb. Lubitsch admires her cleverness (what the film calls her "polished wits") and her ability to manipulate the situation so masterfully (like the director himself). Lady Windermere is shown as what Wilde calls a narrow-minded "puritan" who has to be taught a lesson about the gray nature of human morality. Lords

Windermere and Darlington are not condemned by Lubitsch for their dubious actions; they too act mostly out of genuine regard for the emotionally fragile Lady Windermere, and Lubitsch sees his characters as three-dimensional people whom he cannot help loving because of as well as in spite of their very human flaws. These characters often convey mixed emotions that defy simplistic categorization and capture the finely nuanced feeling of real life, a major achievement in a silent film that is perhaps made possible in part by the relative absence of words. Lubitsch's characteristic use of ellipses and partial perspectives helps convey the film's interplay of concealment and revelation. The Lubitsch Touches have more to do with the conflicts between emotional needs and class strictures than with sexuality per se.

Lady Windermere seems arrested in a childlike state as well as trapped in her social status. That her romanticized vision of her long-absent mother is false is ironically what sustains her ability to preserve her own marriage. But though she never learns Mrs. Erlynne's true identity, Lady Windermere very belatedly comes to appreciate the woman who perpetuates the deceit. When Lady Windermere, outraged by her husband's apparent infidelity as well as somewhat bored by his stolid nature and susceptible to the younger man's flattery and flirtation, tries to run off with Darlington, Mrs. Erlynne willingly makes herself an object of scandal again, sacrificing her own chances for social acceptance to prevent her daughter from repeating her own disastrous mistake. She convinces her daughter that her husband has been faithful and retrieves her daughter's fan from Darlington's apartment, pretending it is hers. Secretiveness, reticence, and the consequences of elaborate misunderstandings and lies not only fit the art of silent film especially well but are essential to this film's concentration on what can't be discussed in polite (or hypocritical) society, why it can't be, and what would happen if it were. If only the husband could tell the wife the truth about Mrs. Erlynne, it would be a much different story and a much different society. Lubitsch analyzes these hypocrisies as unrelentingly as a surgeon with a scalpel. Lady Windermere, chastened by her injustice to Mrs. Erlynne, is tempted to reveal her own dalliance to her husband, but the older woman insists that she keep that secret: "Don't tell him! You would kill his love—and spoil the only decent thing I ever did."

Lady Windermere's Fan, as Wilde indicates in his stage directions, is a comedy that constantly hovers on "a note of deep tragedy"; Lubitsch's heightening of the dark elements of the play is not uncharacteristic of a director who frequently veered into stark drama while also, as he does at the end of this film, restoring the comic balance by generously giving the "fallen" but heroic woman a happy ending. The film clears up the "misunderstanding" (by restoring the lies) and reunites Mrs. Erlynne with her somewhat dim-witted but handsome and game suitor, Lord Augustus Lorton (Edward Martindel). Their relationship, like that of the Windermeres, flourishes on deceit, and Mrs. Erlynne, as the last shot of the film indicates when her hand reaches out to close the door of their cab, is firmly in control. Making its moral points largely visually, the film jettisons Wilde's didactic sub-title, *A Play about a Good Woman*, and its last line, Lady Windermere's comment to Lord Augustus about Mrs. Erlynne: "Ah, you're marrying a very good woman!" The most overtly moralistic the film becomes is in a scathing visual touch showing the heads of three wizened old-lady gossips rising one after another into the frame to glare at Mrs. Erlynne when she arrives at the Windermeres' party without invitation. Behind them is a tapestry of Jesus defending the "woman taken in adultery," in the parable in which he tells her accusers, "He that is without sin among you, let him first cast a stone at her."

Lady Windermere's Fan, even if its character roundelay is not as intricate as that of *The Marriage Circle*, is just as much if not more of a visual tour de force. The most spectacular example in the later film and one of the high-lights of Lubitsch's career is the racetrack sequence. Shot in Toronto to give it a suitably British flavor, and somewhat akin to George Cukor's highly styl-ized "Ascot Gavotte" sequence in *My Fair Lady* (1964), Lubitsch's sequence offers a dazzling array of point-of-view shots from every possible direction, sometimes dissolving from one to another, as high society directs its furtive, or flagrant, gaze toward Mrs. Erlynne like a Hydra with many eyes. She makes a spectacular entrance, alone, elaborately done up in an elegant dark dress and feathered turban designed to attract that kind of attention to her-self as a mature sex object in this aristocratic but crass marriage market. She struts back and forth as man after man in formal garb studies her with bin-oculars or naked eyes, and women do their part with binoculars or lorgnettes. But in displaying herself, Mrs. Erlynne also reveals her vulnerability to the camera and to Lord Windermere while stirring the lustful attentions of Augustus as she does so.

Lubitsch directs most of his attention to the box in which the Windermeres sit with Darlington and Augustus. Windermere rebukes the three
elderly female voyeurs in defense of Mrs. Erlynne, much to the discomfort
of his wife, a situation Darlington observes wryly and is determined to exploit.
Augustus is thoroughly delighted to see Mrs. Erlynne being the cynosure of
every eye. The elaborate sequence ends with a brief series of shots that anticipate pop art: Mrs. Erlynne walks from the racetrack under an exit sign with
a giant pointing finger. She draws Augustus relentlessly in her wake, just as
she intends, while Lubitsch puckishly changes the size of the frame to gradually box them in as the image fades out on the beginning of their relationship. This is one of the rare occasions that Lubitsch used this framing device
in America even though he had gone wild with it in his German farce *The
Wildcat*, getting it mostly out of his system.

The racetrack sequence not only brings together all the strands of the
plot of *Lady Windermere's Fan* but also dazzlingly connects rampant voy-
eurism with unbridled, if somewhat covert, social hypocrisy. In so doing,
the sequence implicates the cinema audience as voyeurs by making us share
the multiple glances, furtive or not, of these pompous, hypocritical society
men and women who cannot resist ogling Mrs. Erlynne despite their supposed disdain for her. There are few more virtuosic demonstrations than this
of the power of what Hitchcock called "pure Cinema," whether in Lubitsch's
work or anyone else's.

The contemporary critical response to *Lady Windermere's Fan*, though not
unanimous, included some remarkable appreciations of the true nature of
Lubitsch's achievement in equaling Wilde as well as an understanding that a
genuinely faithful film adaptation of a literary work often has to rework the
original substantially to fit the new medium. These appreciations, coming
from the relatively new but already prestigious literary journal the *New Yorker*
and the eminent literary critic Edmund Wilson, show how Lubitsch was
already held in special regard during only his third full year in America. *New
Yorker* reviewer Ted Shane thought Lubitsch had succeeded "magnificently" in
his audacious mission: "He has attempted and succeeded in transfilming a
Wilde without use of a single tinseled Wildean epigram from the play, rather
trusting to his own great sense of cinematic wit and the dramatic. The result
is a Wilde of wondrous characterization and situation, well interspersed
with pictorial wit, acted by the usual splendid hand-held lubitschean [*sic*]

actors." Wilson, who had also admired *Kiss Me Again*, found *Lady Winder-mere's Fan* to be "a very attractive film" visually, in Lubitsch's "most distinguished manner," praising his "theatrical ingenuity" and calling his subtle shooting style "as effective as ever."

The prominent French film historian Georges Sadoul, in his 1959 *History of World Cinema*, pronounced it "Lubitsch's best silent film, [full of] incisive details, discreet touches, nuances of gestures, whose behavior betrays the character and discloses the sentiments of the personages. With Lubitsch a new art carried on the subtleties of Marivaux, and the comedy of manners made its debut on the screen."

HEADING TOWARD SOUND

Lubitsch's subsequent silent work seems somewhat anticlimactic after his two midtwenties masterworks and the highly lauded *Kiss Me Again*. But we cannot be entirely sure without more evidence than we now have of *The Patriot*. He followed his essentially dramatic version of *Lady Windermere's Fan* with a divertissement playing with the subject of adultery in a thoroughly jocular manner, *So This Is Paris* (1926). That Warner Bros. film touches lightly, with little emotional investment in the characters this time, on the kinds of extramarital temptations familiar from *Lady Windermere's Fan* and *The Marriage Circle*. But the auteurist similarities extend to having the clownish Monte Blue returning from *The Marriage Circle* to play another doctor husband, Paul Giraud, drawn again to dally outside wedlock—this time more enthusiastically with an old flame, Georgette Lallé, a free-spirited married woman played by the fetching Lilyan Tashman.

Lubitsch often liked to rework his previous material from new angles in the classic pattern of themes and variations. *So This Is Paris*, adapted by Kräly, not only echoes the director's immediately preceding Hollywood films but is a loose, unofficial remake of his 1917 German film *The Merry Jail*. That film's source, Julius Roderich Benedix's play *The Prison*, is uncredited in *So This Is Paris*, which is credited instead to an 1872 French vaudeville play, *Le réveillon* (*The Midnight Supper*) by Henri Meilhac and Ludovic Halévy. Both plays provided material for *Die Fledermaus*. The common situation is that of an errant, drunken, philandering husband who is sentenced to a brief jail term for insulting an official while his wife, herself caught in a potentially compromising situation, is rescued by her suitor's going to jail in his place, and the husband and another woman go out on the town together. The farcical complications in *So This Is Paris*—which is much funnier than *The Merry Jail*—are resolved with a marital reconciliation similar to that of *The Marriage Circle*, involving the husband's smug misunderstanding of his wife's actual flirtation with another man. Lubitsch deftly caps the jokes in *So This Is Paris* with a facetious "Moral: When you appear at your window put on your shirt."

The reference is to the opening sequence in which Madame Suzanne Giraud (Patsy Ruth Miller), after an orgasmic experience reading a "hot" romance about an Arabian sheik, imagines that she sees such a man, partially disrobed, menacing a woman in an apartment across the way. A series of drolly elliptical point-of-view shots expresses another very Lubitschean misunderstanding as we realize that what Suzanne is actually witnessing is Georgette's feline husband, Maurice Lallé (André Beranger), practicing a seemingly violent "Apache [pronounced *Ah-pahsh*] Dance" with her. That strange fad, which originated in the Parisian underworld (the "Apache" for which the dance was named), links the supposed savagery of Native Americans with the spectacle of a pimp and his prostitute enacting a mock-violent sexual ritual. The dance is also spoofed by Lubitsch in one of the sketches he contributed to the 1930 omnibus film *Paramount on Parade*, with Maurice Chevalier and Evelyn Brent as the husband and wife violently acting out their conflicts in their bedroom as foreplay. The Apache Dance and the soft-porn-for-housewives of the sheik genre are not the only "naughty" cultural trends of the Roaring Twenties that Lubitsch has fun with in *So This Is Paris*. The film also pays spectacular tribute to the Charleston craze in the film's wildly frenzied climax at a Parisian Artists Ball.

That sequence is one of Lubitsch's most elaborate tours de force. He frames it with Suzanne at home listening to a transmission of the ball on her radio, with some of the words from the program superimposed on the images of her. Among Lubitsch's numerous precursors of the imminent coming of sound, this clever device cues his staging of another full-fledged musical number in a silent film as he had done seven years earlier with the "Foxtrot Epidemic" in *The Oyster Princess*. The Charleston contest is brilliantly rendered in avant-garde visual fashion by Lubitsch, cinematographer John J.

Mescall, art director Harold Grieve, and the film's uncredited editor, with fast cutting, fast dissolves, superimpositions, wildly tilted angles, and the elaborately sexualized interaction of a large group of lavishly costumed dancers dancing with abandon in a giant ballroom lit by swaying, flashing lights, all to the beat of a black jazz band. Lubitsch manages again to convey the rhythmic intensity of music in the silent medium through his visual staging and montage (with the help of live musical accompaniment in the theaters showing the film).

The next dance, only briefly glimpsed in semidarkness, leads into one of the film's rare moments of pathos as the revelry dissolves to a shot of Suzanne's solitary feet moving in rhythm while she listens to the radio, enraptured, her head back and her eyes closed, unaware that her husband is out tripping the light fantastic with Georgette. The news of her husband winning the Charleston contest with Georgette soon reaches Suzanne over the radio. She takes revenge by going to the ball in a mask to lure her drunken husband home, declaring that she will be the "Big Boss" in the household from now on—a "victory" Lubitsch conveys with a gag visual effect of Paul shrinking to tiny dimensions and slinking out of the room. The film also plays with an even more blatant series of Freudian gags involving Paul's cane, first as his intended weapon to thrash Maurice but eventually disappearing down the ineffectual husband's throat in a nightmare of phallic symbolism.

Although the cast is charming and the staging deft and often witty, *So This Is Paris* conveys the sense of Lubitsch marking time with a piece of relative fluff between other films that engage him at his best, that is, on deeper levels of interwoven comedy and drama. The theme of the dallying husband and the flirtatious wife being able to reunite happily only because they both have guilty secrets to hide is recycled with little at stake in *So This Is Paris*. This favorite Lubitschean conclusion conveys his sophisticated, very continental recognition that marriage depends partly on both partners repressing their wandering instincts. But more tolerance is again demanded from the mildly errant wife, whose flirtations are depicted as reluctant and as such less culpable than those her husband far more actively pursues.

In the context of Hollywood in the repressed climate of late 1920s due to the studios' defensive response to scandals, this denouement reflects the hypocrisies of the double standard that seem far more apparent and more dubious to viewers today. Lubitsch does his best to subvert that form of sexist hypocrisy by slyly suggesting that the wives in these situations may have hidden impulses that they might do more to act out if only they were not so socially constrained. *So This Is Paris* hardly supports much serious analysis, but after Lubitsch's masterful achievements in blending comedy and drama with such profundity in *The Marriage Circle* and *Lady Windermere's Fan*, he was entitled to a bit of jolly diversion. Kristin Thompson notes in her book on Lubitsch, "As Lubitsch and Warners were parting ways, the firm essentially buried his farewell film, *So This Is Paris*. It was released in a haphazard way." *So This Is Paris* still suffers from neglect. It appears at festivals occasionally in a well-preserved and restored print from the Library of Congress but has not been available on homevideo since an inferior-quality VHS edition went out of print.

BITTERSÜSS

As he often did, Lubitsch, after this romp, reverted to weightier dramatic fare, the 1927 MGM silent *The Student Prince in Old Heidelberg* (aka *Old Heidelberg*). By then he had left Warners. In the wake of the studio's growing unhappiness with his films' relatively low profitability, there was an acrimonious dispute over Lubitsch's remaining contractual obligations. Although his five films for Warners were made on modest budgets, ranging from $212,000 (*The Marriage Circle*) to $320,000 (*Lady Windermere's Fan*)—the equivalent of $3 million and $4.375 million in 2017—and though none lost money, they did not do particularly well at the boxoffice despite their critical acclaim. Their American audiences were relatively highbrow, and the European boxoffice grosses on his Warner Bros. productions were unspectacular.

Warners' executives increasingly complained to the director that his work was too sophisticated to achieve wide popularity. Harry Warner wired his brother Jack, "HIS PICTURES ARE OVER PEOPLE'S HEADS." Harry wasn't just talking behind Lubitsch's back, for he told the director, "YOU HAVE PICKED YOUR OWN STORIES AND MADE YOUR OWN PICTURES WITHOUT INTERFERENCE BUT MADE THEM TOO SUBTLE THE WORLD WANTS THRILL AND ENTERTAINMENT." It seemed that Lubitsch was caught between two poles of expression and was still struggling to firmly establish his creative personality as an international filmmaker working in Hollywood.

Studio executives kept harping on the need for Lubitsch to make what they called a "big picture," and he would counter by complaining that Warners did not have the resources or the stars to enable him to do so. Although he actually was happy making his more intimate pictures and was not looking to return to spectacles, he replied peevishly and more than a bit sarcastically to Harry, "IT IS VERY UNFORTUNATE FOR ME THAT FOR PAST THREE YEARS I HAD NEITHER MEANS NOR CHANCE TO MAKE BIG PICTURES AND YOU HAVE NO ONE BUT YOURSELF TO BLAME THAT MY TALENTS ARE WASTED THUSLY." Eventually a complicated exit deal was worked out in which two bigger studios, MGM and Paramount, took over his contract. Lubitsch was able to raise his salary to $125,000 per film, more than double what he had been making at Warners, while waiving any further profit participation on the films he had made for that studio.

Eyman's Lubitsch biography details the history of these complex negotiations:

> In 1923, Harry and Jack Warner had needed Ernst to give their shoestring operation some credibility. But, by the end of 1926, the premiere of John Barrymore's *Don Juan*, accompanied by a Vitaphone sound track, had driven the price of Warners stock from $8 a share to $65. Lubitsch had served his purpose and gotten them the critical attention Harry wanted, albeit without the profits Jack lusted over. . . . Jack and Harry Warner had undoubtedly assumed that Lubitsch would pull a much larger audience in Europe than he had, but the European returns on his Warner productions were never more than $90,000 apiece; the knowing attitudes about the heavy chains of matrimony that struck Americans as so delicious probably struck many Europeans as business as usual. While Lubitsch's pictures outdrew other Warner productions in Europe, they also cost more.

Warners claimed that its sole reason for parting ways with Lubitsch was that it wanted to concentrate on Vitaphone sound films. Although Warners soon upended the industry with the first part-talking feature, *The Jazz Singer* (1927), a film Lubitsch himself had wanted to make, their decision to let Lubitsch go shows a remarkable lack of foresight, for within three years, he would become the most adventurous and advanced maker of talking pictures. After engineering Lubitsch's departure, Harry Warner wrote of the director's contract in a letter to his brother Albert, "It is a lucky star that this is off our hands, because I think it is the worst lemon we have on our hands, so thank the Lord this is over."

The Student Prince in Old Heidelberg, starring Ramón Novarro and Norma Shearer, was Lubitsch's first film under his new deal outside Warners. This beautifully mounted and crafted MGM film was the kind of "big picture" that the director had not been able to make at his old studio, a tragic romance set in the early twentieth century in the mythical kingdom of Karlsburg as well as in the German town of Heidelberg, the site of the celebrated university. Somewhat resembling *Rosita* in its production values but with a more bittersweet mood (in German, *bittersüss*), it appealed to many filmgoers and most reviewers, but it lost money because of its high cost, $1.2 million. The film remains an undeservedly obscure title in the Lubitsch canon despite its exquisite craftsmanship and considerable emotional power. Perhaps its underrating is due to it lacking the usual sarcastic edge of Lubitsch's comedy. There were also some reports of production difficulties, which made it seem even less characteristic of the director. But that change of style, its straightforwardness and emotional sincerity, was intentional. Lubitsch told interviewers at the time, "*Old Heidelberg* is something new for me. I got tired of frothy French farce comedies—and maybe the public is tired of those too. . . . I tried for simplicity. It's a tender, romantic story, and I treated it that way." To the last comment, his interviewer responded, "Then it won't be anything like *Forbidden Paradise*, say." Lubitsch said, "Not in the least!" he explained, "There I was above my characters, looking down at them, laughing at them. Here I'm on the same level with them, I'm one of them."

Lubitsch was never above some pragmatic degree of commercial calculation, however, so he may have been changing his tone in hopes of seeking the wider audience that Warners had taken him to task for not having. This was one of the intermittent stylistic shifts that helped him remain viable in Hollywood. His intermittent attempts at straight drama and his constant effort to explore new ground help account for his remarkable versatility and range. After Lubitsch returned from shooting location scenes in Heidelberg (he also visited Berlin), he was interviewed for *Cinema Art* magazine by Robert Grosvenor, who wrote, "His gifts of comedy have been most utilized in his American career so far. Yet Mr. Lubitsch would very much like to make serious pictures. 'You ask me what I should like to do next. I will tell you: a real picture. To me a "real" picture is one in which character is consistently developed.' . . . He has never made a serious picture of American life and is afraid that if he were to do so he might be criticized for dealing, as a foreigner, with matters of which he had not sufficient intimate knowledge."

It is easy to underrate or dismiss *The Student Prince in Old Heidelberg* because it is not "typical Lubitsch" and because another first-rate director could also have made a good film from the material. Erich von Stroheim rejected the project, though his version would have been considerably different from Lubitsch's, just as his mordant 1925 silent *Merry Widow* for MGM is dissimilar in tone from Lubitsch's 1934 MGM musical version, which appears more romantic on the surface but is actually a sharp critique of sexual cynicism. Another reason for the obscurity of Lubitsch's late silent *The Student Prince in Old Heidelberg* could be that its provenance and even its title have caused some confusion, reflecting its complex pedigree and making it somewhat complicated to discuss. The film was adapted by Kräly from a 1901 German play, *Alt Heidelberg* (*Old Heidelberg*) by Wilhelm Meyer-Förster, and from his 1898 novel version, *Karl Heinrich* (the novel is the only source listed in the film credits, and no author is listed). The play served as the basis for the popular 1924 Sigmund Romberg operetta *The Student Prince*, with book and lyrics by Dorothy Donnelly.

The original *New York Times* review of the Lubitsch film on September 22, 1927, gave no fewer than three variants of its title. The paper had reported on September 4, "The original [production] title of this subject was *Old Heidelberg*, but acquisition by the producers of the rights to the music of *The Student Prince*, based on the same story, was followed by a change in title. The full title will be *The Student Prince in Old Heidelberg*." That deal followed a legal dispute with MGM earlier in the year involving the German playwright and a German film company. The 1927 posters call the film *The Student Prince in Old Heidelberg*, but the surviving prints give the title simply as *Old Heidelberg*, as it appears on the 1986 Thames Television/MGM version with an original orchestral score by Carl Davis. It is a truism that if a film title is hard to remember and repeat, it hurts the film's reception.

Although Lubitsch had pulled off the feat of filming Wilde without epigrams, and though he had filmed musical sequences for his pictures before, he wasn't trying to make a silent musical here. The film, for which no accompanying orchestral score survives, does show characters doing some singing, including in a joyously raucous scene set in a Heidelberg beer garden, but the only song identified is the venerable academic song "Gaudeamus Igitur." Critics who value Lubitsch primarily for his supposed cynicism toward love—always a misunderstood and oversimplified view of his work—would not be favorably disposed toward his sincere exploration of sentiment here. The film is without a tongue-in-cheek safety net and almost devoid of sentimental excess, except in one floridly expressionistic love scene on a hillside that left the director dissatisfied even after reshooting it. There are humorous touches, particularly in the early part of the film—such as when the child heir apparent, played by Philippe De Lacy, arrives wide-eyed and frightened in his sailor suit at a train station after a ridiculously over-the-top display of regal pomp—but even they have their poignancy, as is typical of Lubitsch at his best.

The lovely characterization by Jean Hersholt of the crown prince's tutor and surrogate father figure, Dr. Jüttner, a Lubitschean figure with his constant cigar-smoking, haimish warmth, and subtle sense of irony toward his position, is always tinged by intimations of loneliness and mortality. In one funny but disturbing scene, the aging tutor, ill in bed, is taking medicine while also smoking a cigar and drinking wine. That is something of a premonition of Lubitsch's own premature physical decline, and it was probably not coincidental that Lubitsch had lost his father, Simon, in 1924. The director was not present at his father's death and was unable to return to Berlin for the funeral; in *The Student Prince in Old Heidelberg*, we learn of Jüttner's death in a moving Lubitschean ellipsis, implying that his pupil was unable to be with him because of his royal duties.

While leavened by romantic interludes and comical moments—some resembling the rustic humor of *Kohlhiesel's Daughters*, a Lubitsch romance largely set in a country inn with female characters who are barmaids—the film is deeply sad overall. It is the story of a young man doomed, ironically, to a helpless, powerless, loveless state of entrapment, unable to follow his own romantic inclinations because of his royalty. This kind of story has been told often but seldom better than here. Lubitsch's sense of class barriers was always acute, and his own rise from humble origins to world renown helped inform his keen understanding, through inversion, of the conflicts Novarro's Karl Heinrich must face in his miserably impersonal grooming for kingship. The sincerity with which Lubitsch and his cast approach the familiar story accounts for its transcendence of clichés.

Andrew Marton, the film's editor and later a renowned second-unit action director, reported that Lubitsch "never thought that Ramón Novarro or Norma Shearer was the right casting for the film, but the studio insisted and he was stuck with them. Lubitsch did marvelously with them, actually, but not to his exacting standards." Even if that was the case, the stars are so appealing under Lubitsch's sensitive handling that it would be hard to imagine anyone else in the roles of Karl Heinrich and Kathi, the Heidelberg barmaid with whom he falls in love. John Gilbert, who starred in Stroheim's *Merry Widow*, was considered for Karl Heinrich, but as splendid an actor as he was, the more sophisticated and world-weary Gilbert would have been hard-pressed to summon up the innocence and vulnerability Novarro brings to the part with such seeming effortlessness.

Novarro was then a major star and romantic heartthrob; he had recently played the title role in MGM's epic *Ben-Hur*. He was Mexican, and the *New York Times* reviewer of Lubitsch's film, Mordaunt Hall, considered Novarro "a little too Latin in appearance for the role" of the Teutonic prince. But that objection seems narrow-minded, for Lubitsch brings out the gentle qualities of the handsome actor and the simplicity of Karl Heinrich's discovery of love in a country inn after a lonely childhood in a castle—another Lubitsch set whose high ceilings and doors make ironic points by dwarfing the protagonist. The sweetness of the characterization of a prince hopelessly in love with a commoner is touching, as is the boyish pleasure he takes in being accepted as just another student, one of the "Corps Saxonia." No doubt if contemporary reviewers had known that Novarro was gay as well as a "Latin lover," that too would have become the subject of biased criticism, but Lubitsch uses Novarro's endearing diffidence to help capture the shyness of the character. (Novarro's film career faded after the early 1930s. In 1968 he was the victim of a grisly slaying by two gay hustlers.)

The young and lively Norma Shearer, in her earthier period before her screen persona turned grand and somewhat remote, relaxes into the role of Kathi, a young woman with a shy, innocently fetching smile but a forthright sexuality. Shearer was romantically involved with MGM's young production chief, Irving Thalberg, and married him later in 1927. "The first

week of shooting was bumpy," Gavin Lambert reports in his biography of
Shearer.

Norma had never worked before with a director who refused to let actors
rehearse at length and in detail because he believed it made them less spontaneous. She also disliked his technique of acting out a scene, then expecting her to imitate him. By now she had fixed her own approach to a role,
which was to immerse herself completely in it until she felt secure. Lubitsch's
method gave her no time to reach this point of security; the result was a
tantrum and a phone call to Thalberg, asking him to come over to the set.
He listened to both sides, then quietly told Norma that "everyone has a lot
to learn from Mr. Lubitsch."

Tactful, and typically shrewd, the comment implied that Norma was
not flexible enough and risked becoming a prisoner of habit. She took the
point, stilled herself of caution, liberated her sense of adventure, and pro-
ceeded to give one of her finest silent movie performances in one of the
director's best silent movies. "I flatter myself I opened a door for her,"
Lubitsch said.

The Lubitsch Touches that linger in the mind are when Kathi guilelessly
shows the prince around his humble suite at the inn, giving him a pound
cake she has cooked (which he digs into voraciously while alone) and demonstrating the bed for him. She pats it strenuously before bouncing up and
down on it as he watches through an open doorway, his eyes rolling toward
the ceiling in a blend of embarrassment and joy. A short time later, as she is
alone, making the bed, Lubitsch and cinematographer John Mescall light
the scene with only a candle to movingly convey her sensual longing as she
smoothes out the pillow. The prince glimpses her again from the half-open
doorway; then she spies the partially eaten cake, a suggestion of his sexual
appetite for her.

Lubitsch's always sure-handed sense of how to use objects for expressive purposes, highlighting their importance through significant glances,
is evident throughout, again leaving him little need for explanatory intertitles. When Kathi, in the first of their two farewell scenes, packs Karl
Heinrich's school sash in a leather case embossed with the royal crest and

then takes his school blazer off him and replaces it with a formal coat, such details are as moving as the characters' fervent embrace. The most elaborately inventive Lubitsch Touch is the half-satirical, half-ecstatic tracking shot as Karl Heinrich playfully pursues Kathi through a grove of trees; in each of a succession of clearings, we see her half-heartedly putting him off until the camera comes to a sudden stop on a suggestively empty space. A dachshund runs into the shot from the opposite direction, sees something offscreen, and with perfect comic timing, dashes away. The two young lovers come back into the frame; what happened during the ellipsis is deliciously implicit and helps explain why, when the couple move onto a hillside for further lovemaking, it is Kathi we see kissing him first, violating any remaining vestige of royal protocol.

Lubitschean moments such as these are often more effective than conventional love scenes, which the film generally employs with restraint. But it misguidedly pulls out all visual stops for the highly artificial romantic scene on the hillside. Filled with daisies rippling in the wind, the scene climaxes with Karl Heinrich seeing a shooting star; unusually for Lubitsch, the overly obvious staging suggests that he does not trust the actors to convey the emotions but has to resort to scenery and visual effects instead, allowing the pathetic fallacy to run rampant. Although it was rumored that MGM had John M. Stahl reshoot the scene, Marton said that Lubitsch chose to redo it himself, but he never liked it. The *Times'* Mordaunt Hall wryly described the scene as "more humorous than appealing." Far more effective is the passionate, simply filmed scene of the prince kissing Kathi farewell in the hotel, both knowing their transient happiness is doomed because he must marry the princess who has been chosen for him instead. As Lubitsch's German spectacle films frequently did, the story focuses on the tragic conflict of love versus duty.

Karl Heinrich's powerlessness to follow his own desires is accentuated by the film's running motif of oblivious common folk remarking variations on "It must be wonderful to be a prince!" That bitter irony is capped by an old couple telling each other as they watch the wedding carriage pass, "It must be wonderful to be a King!" We do see the young queen briefly from the outside of the carriage, but Lubitsch pointedly omits any close-up of the bride and keeps her offscreen even when Karl Heinrich glances her way with a dutiful smile. Then he turns back toward the camera, staring forlornly straight ahead at the fade-out. Lubitsch reportedly had to battle MGM to preserve this devastatingly bleak ending.

THE END OF AN ERA

The Patriot remains a conundrum in film history, one of the most tantalizing of (mostly) missing pictures from the silent era. A critical and commercial success, *The Patriot* received an Oscar nomination for best picture, the only film with such a distinction that is largely lost today, with only a few minutes of footage and the trailer surviving.

The 1928 Paramount film seems a late-silent throwback to the historical spectacles that made Lubitsch's international reputation. Set in eighteenth-century Russia, it deals with the mad Czar Paul I, son of Catherine the Great, and his assassination by Count Pahlen (the title character). *The Patriot* was adapted from the play *Der Patriot* by Alfred Neumann, which was based on a story by Dmitri Merezhkovsky, and the English stage adaptation by Ashley Dukes. This material might have offered Lubitsch the opportunity for another grandly filmed but more mellowed reflection on the themes of power and human fragility that he had explored in his German spectacles. He was also, it should be recalled, a Russian citizen and had made a tongue-in-cheek takeoff on Czar Paul's mother, *Forbidden Paradise*, so he had a personal connection with the country, however distant he may have felt from it emotionally. But the surviving evidence and contemporary reviews indicate that *The Patriot* was more akin to *Madame DuBarry*—a drama with some comic elements—than to *Forbidden Paradise* or his later romantic comedy/political satire *Ninotchka*, which is partly set in the Soviet Union. Jannings's portrayal of the stooping, cowering czar in the extant footage also bears a resemblance to Lubitsch's expressionistically twisted performance as the insanely jealous hunchbacked clown in *Sumurun*, though Jannings was a far superior actor.

In 1934 Lubitsch fondly recalled *The Patriot* as "a daring experiment. . . . It certainly is true that only a big studio can afford to experiment." What he meant by calling the film an "experiment" is not entirely clear; he was probably not referring to its partial use of sound, which was added by Paramount after the shooting without his involvement. Contemporary reviews of *The Patriot* describe it as being primarily in the tragic mode that Lubitsch periodically attempted when he was in a restlessly ambitious mood, although it was laced with some comical moments. Jannings's performance was much admired while being described as extravagantly and operatically grotesque. The surviving few minutes of footage from *The Patriot* held in the Munich Film Museum as well as the three-minute trailer and scene stills display handsome production values, but they also make the film, and Jannings's acting in particular, seem wildly overblown and devoid of humor unless of the grotesque or unintentional variety. Trailers can be deceptive, since they tend to select the most extreme moments of a film, and the brief preserved footage also bears out that impression, but it is impossible to judge *The Patriot* on that sketchy evidence.

Herman Weinberg, who saw the film, describes some effective quicksilver transitions from zany to psychotic behavior in Lubitsch's depiction of the czar, including a running gag of his putting his mistress's Pekingese outside the door of the boudoir when he is randy until, in exasperation, he throws the dog out a window. A contemporary reviewer, Richard Watts of the *New York Herald Tribune*, wrote,

> Not the least of Jannings' feats was his ability to make Paul at the same time a homicidal maniac, a boorish clown and a pitiful, moving human being. . . . Though the picture is essentially a tragedy, Ernst Lubitsch, who directed, has made, at least half of it, that sort of sly, brilliant sex comedy that mocks the czar's amorousness without ever obtruding on the tragic mood of the drama. . . . The prankish Lubitsch, whose chief directorial joy it is to be ironically facetious in his attitude toward screen amorousness, has, at it happens, made these scenes with the supposedly ponderous Jannings the latter's finest.

Paramount spared no hyperbole in its trailer for *The Patriot*, calling it "THE PERFECT MOTION PICTURE . . . The World's Greatest Dramatic Star, EMIL JANNINGS, IN HIS MOST DISTINGUISHED ROLE . . . Superbly Directed by the Master Producer ERNST LUBITSCH . . . With Spectacular SOUND EFFECTS—You HEAR as well as SEE! . . . As REAL as Life *and ten times more thrilling!* . . . The heart-rending drama of a man who slew his best friend *to save a nation!* . . . The screen's most glorious achievement to date!"

Some of those extravagant claims were echoed by some contemporary observers. *Variety*'s reviewer found that "many elements combine to give *The Patriot* a valid claim to greatness," including the "magnificent" performance by Jannings, an "excellent" story, the "almost flawless" cast, and a physical production "rich in beauty." The reviewer recognized the Lubitschean approach in commending Lewis Stone's Pahlen for being "pictured as a suave man of the world rather than the paragon of virtue as legendary heroes are usually presented." In the view of the *New York Times*' Mordaunt Hall,

> There is, as a matter of fact, hardly a flaw to be found in the whole picture. It is a gripping piece of work with subtle touches that answer at times the purpose of comedy. . . . Emil Jannings gives even a finer performance than he did in [the 1925 German silent film] *Variety*. Superlatives flow to one's mind as one thinks of his depiction of Czar Paul's different moods without borrowing any tricks that he has previously displayed in other screen efforts. There is not here the slightest sign of overacting and yet Mr. Jannings has probably attacked the most difficult role of his career.

The only elements criticized by the *Times* reviewer were overly loud music, mad laughter, and agonized bellowing from the czar "that might better have been left to the imagination." *Variety*, reviewing the film months earlier, had found that the soundtrack had been "managed inconspicuously. There is no dialog." But things had changed during postproduction as studios rushed to add more sound to capitalize on that new fad. Jannings objected to another actor dubbing lines for him, so those were eventually removed, but the German star obtained a termination of his contract with Paramount as a result of this experience, and he returned to Europe. Lubitsch left no comments on the addition of sound, although, from the description of the crudity of the grafting, it is likely he also was displeased.

In addition to its Academy Award nomination for best picture, *The Patriot* received four other nominations, tying it with Raoul Walsh's early-sound Western *In Old Arizona* to lead the competition (the nominations were not official, but the films that had been under consideration were revealed after the ceremony). *The Patriot*'s other nominations went to Lubitsch as director (Frank Lloyd won for *The Divine Lady*), Lewis Stone for best actor

(Warner Baxter won for *In Old Arizona*), Hans Dreier for art direction (Cedric Gibbons won for *The Bridge of San Luis Rey*), and Hans Kräly for best screenplay, the only statuette won by the film. At that second Academy Awards ceremony on April 3, 1930, which included films released in both 1928 and 1929, the execrable 1929 MGM musical *The Broadway Melody* was chosen as best picture. By any rational measure, the best musical of 1929 would be Lubitsch's *The Love Parade*, but that baffling injustice could have been caused by an anomaly of the Oscar voting calendar. Lubitsch's groundbreaking film was released after the unusual August 1928–July 1929 eligibility period. It was nominated in the following Oscar race but lost to the classic 1930 World War I film *All Quiet on the Western Front*, whose director, Lewis Milestone, was also honored over Lubitsch.

Emil Jannings, who was not nominated for his starring role in *The Patriot*, had won the first Oscar for best actor the year before for Josef von Sternberg's 1928 Paramount film *The Last Command* and 1927's *The Way of All Flesh*. Susan Orlean claims in her 2011 biography of Rin Tin Tin, the movie-star dog who made more money for Warner Bros. than Lubitsch ever did, "Rinty received the most votes for Best Actor [in that competition]. But members of the Academy, anxious to establish the new awards as serious and important, decided that giving an Oscar to a dog did not serve that end, so the votes were recalculated, and the award was diverted to Emil Jannings." Lubitsch said he suggested (without credit) the story of *The Last Command*, about a Russian general who, in exile after the revolution, is reduced to being a Hollywood extra and dies while going mad during a battle scene, believing himself back in action. This caustic, moodily atmospheric film was inspired by the story of an actual general whom Lubitsch had met, and the ironies are recognizably Lubitschean, evocative of his tragic historical spectacles, with a meta and compassionate twist about the illusory world of filmmaking. Lubitsch said in a 1941 interview that he did not seek credit after learning that Jannings had passed off the story as his own, though it was credited to playwright Lajos Biró, who received an Oscar nomination for best original story (Biró had collaborated on the play Lubitsch adapted as *Forbidden Paradise*).

Tastes can change drastically in hindsight—and many films that were celebrated in their day and honored by the Academy fail to hold up over time—but any commentary on *The Patriot* today can only be idle guesswork unless a complete print of the film ever emerges. At the least, it can be said that with all the kudos it received in its day, *The Patriot* would have been a fitting vehicle for Lubitsch to make his exit from the (mostly) silent cinema. His enduring fondness for the film somewhat ambivalently included thoughts of a remake. He told the *New York Times* in 1936 that he was considering doing it again with Charles Laughton in the Jannings role: "Ah, Laughton would be good in that part! He would be magnificent!"

ANTICLIMAX

The director unfortunately followed the ambitious *Patriot* with a conventional romantic melodrama set in a Swiss Alpine village in 1806, *Eternal Love* (1929), based on Jacob Christopher Heer's 1900 novel *Der König der Bernina* (*The King of Bernina*). The film seems to be a belated afterthought to the rapidly vanishing silent era and is a prime contender for Lubitsch's worst surviving film. *Eternal Love* is a dull and lugubrious affair even with the usually dashing John Barrymore in the starring role.

Barrymore seems subdued and depressed, with a perpetually stunned expression under his alpine hat as if to telegraph to the audience, "What have I gotten into here?" With its absence of wit and its efficient yet impersonal style, *Eternal Love* could have been made by dozens of other directors. Perhaps the ethereally romantic Frank Borzage could have done something with it. The film does not even look much like Lubitsch's work, with restless camera movements taking the place of his characteristically subtle intercutting of facial glances and expressive use of objects. Evidently Lubitsch, like John Ford and others, was going through a period of Murnau influence. Murnau had been imported to Hollywood by Fox in the wake of his international success with *The Last Laugh*, and he continued his adventurous work with the moving camera and other expressionist effects in his 1927 American film, *Sunrise*. But Lubitsch's stylistic effort to embellish his weak material in *Eternal Love* falls flat. He makes uninspired use of natural settings (in Canada) for picture-postcard effects that are jarringly juxtaposed with glaringly phony mountain sets filmed back in the Hollywood studio.

More distressingly, the asinine plot seems entirely atypical of Lubitsch, who usually avoided conventional moralizing. *Eternal Love* requires Barrymore's roguish huntsman, Marcus Paltram, to marry a conniving low-class vamp (Mona Rico) who has ensnared him into a drunken night of sex. He has to reject the woman he loves, Ciglia (Camilla Horn), the virginal blonde niece of the local minister. It is hard to fathom why the supposedly rebellious individualist Marcus would give in to such a self-defeating arrangement, even in a rustic village in 1806 with villagers who form a lynch mob like those in a Frankenstein picture. And what does a plot like this have to do with Lubitsch? Such a lot of *mishegoss* over a one-night stand. The only element that vaguely interests the director is Ciglia's continuing to love Marcus after she marries his petulant rival, Lorenz (Victor Varconi), but her deceitful attitude toward Lorenz is used more to advance the plot than to bring out character nuances. *Eternal Love* contrives to make things right, at least by mindlessly delirious Hollywood romantic standards, by having Marcus and Ciglia walk off into an avalanche in an embrace to die in the throes of eternal love. The perfunctorily expressed religiosity of the story is another element alien to Lubitsch's worldly viewpoint.

Released by United Artists in May 1929 with a synchronized Vitaphone musical score and sound effects, *Eternal Love* was fatally out of synch with the already far-advanced trend toward talking pictures. But worse than that, it is a mere potboiler, a pointless and ridiculous afterthought to Lubitsch's stellar silent career. The man who had made the farce *Romeo and Juliet in the Snow* took on this assignment because he owed one more picture to United Artists. He had been working on a more promising project about high-society thieves called *The Last of Mrs. Cheyney*. Based on a play by Frederick Lonsdale, with a script by Kräly, it was intended for Barrymore, but the rights were sold to MGM, and it was filmed with Basil Rathbone and Norma Shearer with Sidney Franklin directing. Lubitsch and Barrymore, both unhappy over that development, switched quickly to the mountain yarn, then called *Avalanche* or *King of the Mountain*. Realizing there was little to appeal to him in the story, Lubitsch did not try to do anything except get through the unpleasant task.

Eternal Love was a lost film until a print was rediscovered in the Mary Pickford collection in the 1990s and restored by the UCLA Film and Television

Archive even though no original 35 mm nitrate materials exist; it was released on DVD in 2001. Why it and not *The Patriot* had to turn up is another of the many regrettable twists of film history. Billy Wilder once remarked that even Lubitsch occasionally made a bad picture. He pointed out that Lubitsch made something called *The Mountain King* with John Barrymore. Wilder didn't remember the final title correctly. But he did remember the picture.

A REAL-LIFE ROMANTIC MELODRAMA

What is saddest about this utterly undistinguished film is that it marked the end of Lubitsch's partnership with Hans Kräly, one of the most fruitful and important writer-director collaborations in the history of cinema. Their work together covered an astonishing twenty-nine films, including many classics, over a period stretching back to 1915. The way the collaboration fell apart would have been rejected as a plot twist for one of their movies on the grounds that it was too tawdry and trite.

Lubitsch and his wife, Helene (Leni), who had married in Berlin in 1922, legally separated on June 5, 1930. She filed for divorce on June 10, and it was granted thirteen days later. Leni testified that her husband was "99 percent in love with his work and had no time for home." The *New York Times* added, "There were other circumstances—temperament and unpleasant names— Mrs. Lubitsch testified." Lubitsch was an admitted workaholic. He said in 1938, "I think I am possessed only of a fascination for the work I have chosen to do. I am so engrossed by the production of a film that I literally think of nothing else. I have no hobby, no outside interests; and want none. If this is a sign of 'mad genius,' then I suppose I am guilty." They reached a settlement in which Leni was granted ownership of their Beverly Hills home and $150,000 in cash.

But there was more to the story. In the spring of 1930, Lubitsch had discovered that his longtime screenwriter was having an affair with Leni. After the divorce, Lubitsch had an unpleasant public encounter with Leni and Hans on a dance floor. At a benefit party thrown by Mary Pickford and Douglas Fairbanks on October 4, 1930, Lubitsch was dancing with actress Ona Munson, one of the women he dated in the wake of his marital breakup. He thought Leni and the man who had cuckolded him were mocking his dancing all evening, so he hit Kräly in the chest, then Leni slapped Ernst, and people had to pull them apart.

"They taunted me into it," said Lubitsch afterward. ". . . They continually taunt me. This was the third time. They mimic me when I dance. They laugh at me. He made remarks in German that aren't in the dictionary as they passed me."

Although Kräly professed not to understand the cause of the fracas, Leni told the press after the divorce and the incident that their breakup was due to "jealousy." She claimed that Lubitsch

> always accused me of making fun of him and talking about him when we were married. It's always the "great Lubitsch" with him. He wants everybody to do as he bids. No man or woman had anything to do with our divorce. If there had been a man he had plenty of opportunity to so charge when the divorce was filed. He is just jealous. Even though we are divorced, he doesn't want to see me out with another man. I guess he wants me to go to a convent or something. Lubitsch and Kräly were the best of friends up until the divorce. Now he doesn't want any of our friends to be my friends since we have parted. They can be his friends but not mine. I am sorry this had to happen. . . . I admire him as a great artist, which he is. But he should never be married. If he had been living in Germany I would have divorced him long ago.

That embarrassing public donnybrook was a rare moment of scandal in Lubitsch's life, but he was seen as the aggrieved party, the one with whom Hollywood sympathized. Lubitsch went on making Lubitsch pictures with hardly a hitch, but Kräly's career never recovered. The director soon found another longtime screenwriting partner, Samson Raphaelson, who proved a more congenial as well as eminently loyal collaborator. Director Henry Koster, a refugee from Nazi Germany who came to Hollywood in 1936, claimed, "Lubitsch insisted that Kräly become blacklisted, and from 1932 until I came in 1936, Kräly couldn't pay his rent. He had invested his money and lost it all. He was in bad shape, and I took him." Koster hired Kräly to work on the script of the first American film he directed, *Three Smart Girls* (1936), though without credit, and he gave Kräly screen credit for the "idea" of *One Hundred Men and a Girl* (1937) because Kräly was in severe trouble, and he had helped me work on it, so I gave him the credit. . . . All the Europeans used to stick together. . . . A year or so after *Three Smart Girls*, I was in a steambath sitting next to Lubitsch. I thought, I'll try once. I said, "Ernst, I feel terribly sorry for Kräly." And he started shouting at me, and said, "I don't want you ever to mention that name again." So I couldn't get them together. When Lubitsch died in 1947, I was one of the pallbearers. I saw, in that little chapel in Forest Lawn, way in the back, Kräly standing, crying. It was very touching. Kräly died three years later.

After his marriage to Leni broke up, the director's ill fortune in love would continue to shadow his life in sadly ironic contrast to the ideal romantic world he conjured up on-screen. Raphaelson said, "He liked women who treated him badly."

THE SOUND OF THINGS TO COME

"Sound revolutionized the accepted theories of silent films," Lubitsch said in the 1930s. Unlike some silent directors who would not or could not adapt to this revolution in the industry, Lubitsch soon found himself creatively stimulated and indeed completed as an artist by the opportunities offered by adding sound to pictures.

In the same year that he closed his silent career, 1929, the director reclaimed his artistic leadership with the dazzling sound film *The Love Parade*. This musical starring Maurice Chevalier and Jeanette MacDonald made supple and imaginative use of the new medium even with the handicap of a largely static camera encased in the soundproof boxes used in that transitional period. *The Love Parade* can be fairly credited with creating the musical genre on film. Despite *The Broadway Melody*'s best-picture Oscar, that otherwise-forgotten film is a creaky museum piece, a backstage story with poorly choreographed stage numbers. *The Love Parade*, on the other hand, remains just as lively and original today, a musical conceived for the screen, with its musical numbers fully integrated into the story and advancing it with innovative cinematic wonders.

Lubitsch's early sound career, like his glorious days as a silent filmmaker, would be a period of continual experimentation, technical achievements, and artistic tours de force. It would be a period of more focused energy that brought sharp definition to the term "Lubitschean" and brought him to the pinnacle of his artistic powers. His highly sophisticated uses of the medium for comedic, dramatic, and musical effects in the Depression era would elevate him well beyond the level of any of his peers in that uncertain time for the film industry.

5

"GIVE ME A MOMENT, PLEASE"

When the movies officially began to talk and sing in 1927 after a series of tentative and often-failed experiments, that technological and artistic revolution caused consternation among many in Hollywood and beyond. There were those who worried it would destroy the art of film, which had just been reaching its pinnacle. And there were others who simply worried that the talkies would put them out of a job. Lubitsch was not among those who were anxious about the future of the medium. After all, as Jean Douchet observed, Lubitsch himself had "invented the musical" in 1919 with the "Foxtrot Epidemic" sequence in his German film *The Oyster Princess*. That raucous, syncopated tour de force had anticipated the uses to which the cinema would put sound when the medium finally caught up with Lubitsch eight years later with Warners' sensational part-talking, part-singing Al Jolson feature, *The Jazz Singer*.

The fact that Lubitsch wanted to direct the schmaltzy tale of Jewish family life in New York showed the alacrity with which he embraced the new technology that gave other directors such anxiety. He was deprived of that opportunity partly because his films had been losing favor with Warners.

5.1 AND 5.2 Bawdy postcoital innuendo: the "Breakfast Time" song in *The Smiling Lieutenant* (1931), with Claudette Colbert and Maurice Chevalier (frame enlargements). *(Paramount.)*

Journeyman director Alan Crosland made *The Jazz Singer* instead. Lubitsch, undaunted, set out to make far better musicals of his own. He poached Samson Raphaelson, the playwright of *The Jazz Singer*, who loathed the film version and who became Lubitsch's regular screenwriter for a fruitful creative partnership in the final two decades of the director's career. Although Raphaelson's first love was the theater, and he tended to look down on movies, he admitted to being enamored of one that he had seen—Lubitsch's *The Love Parade*.

By the time Lubitsch plunged headlong into the talkies in 1929 with that Maurice Chevalier/Jeanette MacDonald musical, he arguably already had more experience with "sound" on film than any other major director. Not only had Lubitsch blithely filmed operettas as silent movies—*The Merry Jail* (loosely based on *Die Fledermaus*) and *The Student Prince in Old Heidelberg*—he also had made a cinematic takeoff on a celebrated opera, *Carmen*. In *So This Is Paris*, Lubitsch had staged the lavish Charleston contest sequence that echoes his "Foxtrot Epidemic" while pulling out all cinematic stops to let the audience savor the sights and sounds of another spectacular musical number.

The new sound technology stimulated Lubitsch to fresh artistic solutions as he discovered his true motion picture style. Some theoreticians and filmmakers thought sound would best be used for purposes other than merely "pictures of people talking," to use the disparaging words of another great director who started in silents, Alfred Hitchcock. In a famous 1928 statement on sound film, Soviet directors and theoreticians Sergei Eisenstein, Vsevolod Pudovkin, and Gregori Alexandrov argued that sound could best be used in counterpoint with visuals, an idea that was played with for a while in Hollywood and elsewhere but gradually dropped. *The Patriot*, though a critical success, suffered with audiences to some degree for its studio-added sound effects and dialogue, because they were quickly getting used to pictures with actual talking scenes. Lubitsch's last silent film, *Eternal Love*, belated and forgettable though it is, also has a synchronized musical track. When he made his first full picture with dialogue and music, Lubitsch found it almost second-nature to put sound on film. Like John Ford, Howard Hawks, and Frank Capra in America and René Clair and Jean Renoir in France, Lubitsch was one of the directors who understood that the coming of sound enhanced their art and expanded its range. These directors reveled in their new ability to use the medium in more supple and expressive ways than they had been able to do before.

The addition of sound added the final essential tool to Lubitsch's aesthetic kit. Sound enabled him to develop the more complex and even more nuanced style we most associate him with today. Sound solidified the Lubitschean approach of the cinematic magician whose deft Touch enables him to suggest almost anything without having to come right out and say it even while actors are talking or singing or while the soundtrack is making other kinds of comments on the proceedings. With his characteristically oblique way of telling a story, Lubitsch did not fall into the pitfalls of the early talkies that relied on actors standing or sitting around, laboriously telling the stories largely with dialogue. Sound in some ways freed Lubitsch to be even more deftly allusive and suggestive. And Lubitsch would be responsible for creating the musical genre in its true cinematic sense, not as a mere recording device for stage numbers but as a medium for the integration of songs and narrative.

His style reached its most elaborately audacious levels of visual intricacy and near abstraction in his films of the 1929–1934 period, when sound became fully established. His triumphant debut in the talkies, *The Love Parade*, is a thoroughly artificial, stylized musical set in the mythical monarchy of Sylvania. Chevalier's Count Alfred Renard, partly as punishment for his rampant philandering in Paris, is forced to become prince consort to MacDonald's Queen Louise and experiences the same kind of subservience and extreme power imbalance that women commonly endured in marriage at the time. The story is told in large part through the vocal talents of the romantic leads and other performers, including the servants played by the astonishing Lupino Lane and Lillian Roth, who contribute a wildly acrobatic sexual routine set to music ("Let's Be Common"). The earthy servants, with their mocking echo of the romance of the central characters, are borrowed from Mozart (Papageno and Papagena in *Die Zauberflöte* [*The Magic Flute*]), and Mozart had been influenced in such humor by Shakespeare, whose work Lubitsch knew well. So Lubitsch was drawing on the masters in drama and music to bring a new vitality to the film medium. A hit that mightily advanced the development of musicals, *The Love Parade* was the first of several musicals Lubitsch made in the early sound period. This cycle of films, including three parts of the revue

Paramount on Parade (1930) and the features *Monte Carlo* (1930), *The Smiling Lieutenant* (1931), *One Hour with You* (1932), and *The Merry Widow* (1934), took full and increasingly artful advantage of the screen's newfound ability to speak and sing and make joyful noise.

During that period, Lubitsch also made a few nonmusicals. These are some of his most remarkable achievements and include what is perhaps his most unusual film. In 1932 alone he made not only *One Hour with You* but also his masterpiece, the romantic comedy *Trouble in Paradise*, as well as a memorable comic sketch in the episodic film *If I Had a Million* and the anomalously somber antiwar drama *The Man I Killed* (aka *Broken Lullaby*). Lubitsch followed those films with the thematically daring romantic comedy *Design for Living* (1933), a free adaptation by Ben Hecht of Noël Coward's play about a bohemian ménage à trois, a film as cheekily irreverent in its approach to acclaimed material from another medium as Lubitsch's reimagining of *Lady Windermere's Fan*. Lubitsch's early sound period represents a creative explosion of diverse cinematic styles, one of the most dazzling runs of achievement any director has ever achieved in half a decade of work.

Aside from the reported awkwardness of the postsynchronized soundtrack in *The Patriot*, which Lubitsch had nothing to do with, his early sound films betray almost no sense of the limitations that stymied many other directors and make many films of that period look like clunky antiques today. In the transitional period, when many people worried that visual storytelling had been thrown out the window in favor of people stiffly sitting around talking into microphones, Lubitsch acted as if there were no problem at all. And for him, there was not. He worked around the potentially awkward limitations of primitive motion picture sound, which included the initial confinement of the camera in a large glass booth (called an "icebox"), restricting its ability to move or even pan, and the sound recordist in an elevated booth. Early talkies often used three cameras for visual variety but with a single soundtrack for a scene until sound editing was eventually introduced. Often, if music was needed in a scene, the orchestra had to play directly on the set during the filming as it did for some scenes in *The Love Parade*. Yet Lubitsch's groundbreaking musical still seems effortless in its smoothly entertaining style, pacing, and delivery, from the cleverly deceptive opening onward. If the camera remains largely static, not even panning much, unlike in Lubitsch's subsequent musicals, his always-precise style of blocking and editing scenes makes us hardly notice.

The film begins with the jaunty song "Ooh La La" by Jacques (Lupino Lane), the valet for Chevalier's military attaché character. As Jacques sets the table for a romantic dinner, he caps it off by deftly whipping away the table-cloth without spilling anything and makes his grand exit. In the context of its time, this magical opening seems to be a flourish that Lubitsch uses to tell his viewers, "You ain't seen (or heard) nothin' yet." Then follows a seemingly melodramatic scene with an outraged husband breaking in on his wife having a tryst with Alfred, her false suicide attempt, Alfred blithely stashing the gun in a drawer full of other pistols, some dialogue in French as the ambassador from Sylvania orders Alfred out of Paris, the revelation that Alfred has been cuckolding the ambassador, and all this leading to a song presented directly to the camera, with Alfred confiding in the audience about his sexual escapades. Hardly allowing the audience to catch its breath, Lubitsch tops this series of bravura words-and-pictures-and-music gags with Alfred singing a fond farewell to Paris ("Paris, Stay the Same") while we see an array of beautiful women listening in the street below and in surrounding windows. Then the director tops *that* with the valet singing his own farewell to servant girls, with a similarly expansive montage of responses, and finally, in a wry mockery of the new medium, Lubitsch has the count's dog bark his own romantic farewell to his bevy of grateful bitches. Lubitsch's virtuosic display of stylistic devices in this dazzling array of scenes announces to his audience his full command of the sound-and-visuals medium, a preview of further delights to come.

Lubitsch compensated for the sound medium's initial limitations by devising innovative ways of taking the static shots of characters singing and talking—static shots that are actually extremely lively in terms of performing content, giving more autonomy to the actors—and surrounding these with clever forms of contextualizing montage. In so doing, he constructed multi-layered sequences that combine audio elements with the intricately suggestive, witty visual language he had mastered in the silent cinema. Sound added a fresh layer to the Lubitschean language of suggestiveness, giving him many additional ways of conveying innuendo, including with ironic contrasts of picture and sound, as well as with music and sound effects playing over more fluid shots that were filmed silently. As the technology of sound improved by making the iceboxes mobile and with the development of camera blimps to muffle noise, the camera was gradually freed from its glass prison. It could move again with the freedom it was accustomed to enjoying in the late silent era—a development that was fully underway by the time of the supremely graceful musical *The Smiling Lieutenant* (even if one can occasionally hear the noise of the camera dollying in that film, shot at Paramount's Astoria Studios in New York, where Paramount briefly tried to establish an eastern production base).

Lubitsch appears to have decided, with his characteristic shrewdness, that making musicals was, at least during that period of change, the best way to take immediate advantage of the gifts of the sound medium while minimizing any temporary obstacles. The inherent artificiality and stylization of the genre, its ability to soar beyond the mundane confines of settings and story, its blithe obliviousness to the strictures of realism, and its roots in the tradition of the European operetta, which he knew so well (especially the Viennese operetta), enabled Lubitsch to play and experiment with sound in ways that seem almost effortless technically. Because of Lubitsch's theatrical background as an actor, both as a component in the fully integrated visual/aural stage style of Max Reinhardt and as a participant in the more raucous and casual format of the Berlin cabaret, his use of sound seems entirely natural. The characteristic rhythms of the dialogue in his films, which resemble music and sometimes even function as spoken song lyrics, are a by-product of that long theatrical experience, which honed his uncanny sensitivity to the nuances of acting. Lubitsch's oft-remarked-upon penchant for acting out all the parts for his actors was his way of ensuring that they would follow his preferred rhythms, which are integral to the humor and emotion of his work. Even though he spoke with a heavy German accent, he managed to impart a distinctively Lubitschean flavor and tone to the line readings and dialogue exchanges of many disparate actors in his talking pictures. And Lubitsch's fifteen years of directing more than fifty films of all kinds prior to 1929, from slapstick comedies to romances to historical spectacles and intimate chamber dramas, had given him full rein to explore the multidimensional properties of the medium well before he was given the additional tool of sound.

Lubitsch's experimentation in his early musicals is as audacious as that of King Vidor—who made the all-black *Hallelujah* partly on Southern locations in 1929, breaking all the rules of studio-bound filmmaking—or René Clair or Rouben Mamoulian. Clair's 1930 musical *Sous les toits de Paris* (*Under the Roofs of Paris*) earned worldwide acclaim for its cutting-edge liberation of the camera and microphone for poetic purposes. The influence on Lubitsch seems evident even though both directors were already working along parallel lines in different countries. Mamoulian, an Armenian who had left Georgia after it was taken over by the USSR, applied his extensive theatrical experience and penchant for daring stylistic innovation to such early musicals as *Applause* (1929) and *Love Me Tonight* (1932). He sometimes directly borrowed and adapted devices from his stage work, such as his celebrated rhythmical orchestration of morning sounds from the play *Porgy* (1927) for the bravura opening sequence of *Love Me Tonight*. Mamoulian was also a pioneer in refusing to be bound by the rule that the unwieldy camera couldn't be moved. *Love Me Tonight* draws inspiration from Lubitsch's prior experimentation, and its casting of Chevalier and MacDonald makes the connections obvious (in fact, both Lubitsch and Raphaelson had been involved in that project during its early stages).

It is sometimes claimed that Mamoulian's *Love Me Tonight* outdoes Lubitsch at his own game. Tom Milne, in his 1969 critical study of Mamoulian, somewhat predictably calls it "the Lubitsch film that Lubitsch was always trying to pull off but never quite did." One suspects that Milne and others who have echoed his remark were never especially fond of Lubitsch in the first place. Clair and Mamoulian attracted more highbrow attention in their day than Lubitsch did for their brilliant yet showier and sometimes pretentious experimentation in those and other films of the early thirties (such as Clair's 1931 *Le Million* and Mamoulian's 1933 *Queen Christina*). At the same time, Lubitsch was working more humbly, in the spirit of a popular artist, practicing cinematic sleight of hand designed to make even the most difficult feats seem nonchalant and, most of all, amusing.

Because of their unpretentiously experimental nature, Lubitsch's early sound films have rarely been given their full historical due. But now we can see that they are as adventurous in their stylized use of the medium as those of any other groundbreaking director from that era. Their particular charm comes as much as anything from the sense that the director's innovative style is predominantly at the service of his own pleasure and that of his audience. His musicals have none of the longueurs that mar *Love Me Tonight* in its middle sections despite Mamoulian's use of slow motion, zooms, and other devices that were unusual at the time. Lubitsch is not only a more adept storyteller than Mamoulian, less focused on cinematic tricks for their own sake, but also more concerned with keeping his romantic leads and their emotional concerns in the center of the action. Mamoulian has a tendency to stray onto tangents. When Lubitsch looks away from his central characters, it is usually to contrast and intercut them comically with the antics of their servants, who serve as counterpoint to and commentary on the main actions. In a 1972 essay on Lubitsch's musicals, Andrew Sarris wrote,

> I have no desire to argue with the persuasive defenders of Rouben Mamoulian's *Love Me Tonight* as the best of the "Lubitsch-like" musicals. Nonetheless, I would not trade Lubitsch's daringly subdued and scintillatingly circular treatment of "The Merry Widow Waltz" as a prison-cell *pas-de-deux* for all the slow motion and showy camera angles in *Love Me Tonight*. Lubitsch makes of *The Merry Widow* the last musical of a certain spirit and style to be made on this planet. And it is his intimation of a genre's mortality and the sad smile that goes with the intimation that makes Lubitsch ultimately inimitable and ineffable.

If audiences are mostly attracted to musicals to see and hear the singers and dancers, Lubitsch was happy to give his casts the most glittering showcases while simultaneously delighting the spectators with amusingly offbeat ways of telling stories. If the storylines of his musicals often seem extremely slight or deliberately silly, that is part of the director's winking at the audience and part of the secret of their success. Not only do these films liberate the camera and soundtrack to the utmost extent possible in their time, they avoid overly weighty plot material to help free Lubitsch to play with the medium and its conventions while exercising his stylistic faculties with rigorously disciplined abandon. As one of the minor, unsympathetic characters in *Monte Carlo* puts it while watching an opera that reflects the plot of the film, "It's a silly story, only possible with music."

That opera, *Monsieur Beaucaire*, ends unhappily in the film, unlike the actual 1919 André Messager opera of that title, which was based on the novel by Booth Tarkington. But Lubitsch does not leave his audience in a downbeat state. His romantic couple—Jeanette MacDonald's impecunious Countess Helene Mara and Jack Buchanan's Count Rudolph, who woos her while masquerading as her hairdresser—uneasily watch the opera for cues about how they should behave. Rudolph reacts by speaking for Lubitsch: "I don't like that ending—I like *happy* endings" (an echo of the husband's comment in Stiller's *Erotikon*). Lubitsch obliges Rudolph, the audience, and himself by uniting the couple for a celebratory song as they head off into the uncertain future on a train. Together they reprise MacDonald's famous "Beyond the Blue Horizon" number from earlier in the film, a number that attracted a great deal of attention in that early sound period, for an elaborate montage of peasants watching from fields intercut with the train racing past with the warbling MacDonald. The kind of self-reflexive commentary that Lubitsch and screenwriters Ernest Vajda and Vincent Lawrence work into the ending sequences of *Monte Carlo*—among many such moments in Lubitsch's films of this period—is a sign of the director's sure-handed sophistication and confident self-mockery, his ability to play with musical genre and romantic screen conventions in a way that seems postmodern *avant la lettre*.

But it is telling that as Lubitsch moved along in the genre, he gradually began to intertwine comedy and emotion in his finest manner, treating the love triangle of *The Smiling Lieutenant* with disturbing complexity that challenges the viewers' emotions. The blithe philandering lifestyle of Lieutenant Niki von Preyn (Chevalier), as a member of the Vienna palace guard, is complicated when he falls in love with an independent woman who is a violinist in an all-girl band (Claudette Colbert) and then a prim, sheltered princess (Miriam Hopkins) falls for him. Princess Anna, from the backward mythical kingdom of Flausenthurm, insists on taking Niki home as her subservient husband, and he must comply, unhappily, on the orders of his ruler, Emperor Franz Josef I.

Lubitsch had long wanted to make a film adaptation of the source operetta, *Ein Walzertraum* (*A Waltz Dream*) by Leopold Jacobson and Felix Dormann, with music by Oscar Straus, which is based on the novel *Nux, der Prinzgemahl* (*Nux, the Prince Consort*) by Hans Müller. The director had planned to make a silent version in Germany in 1922 and again in Hollywood in 1925; Ernest Vajda and Samson Raphaelson adapted the material for *The Smiling Lieutenant*. Its pattern for a hard-to-resolve love triangle prefigures the following year's *Trouble in Paradise*, a romantic comedy in which the viewer is equally drawn to both women—Miriam Hopkins and Kay Francis—in the triangle with Herbert Marshall's suave international jewel thief. As a result, the final choice Marshall makes is as melancholy as anything Lubitsch has given us, despite that romantic comedy's upbeat finale. The somewhat similar ending of *The Smiling Lieutenant* is presented, somewhat unsatisfactorily, as less emotionally troubling although it is not without its moments of *tristesse* before the forced, overly exuberant fade-out.

A LUBITSCHEAN *SHAMPOO*

The 1930 *Monte Carlo* is not the best of Lubitsch's musicals; in fact, it is the one that seems the most remote from today's sensibilities. But of all his musicals, only *Monte Carlo* has an entirely satisfying resolution in dramatic/comedic terms. That is because the film, even more than the others, is entirely self-conscious and self-reflexive, fittingly for a blithely lighthearted tale about role-playing and the absurdities of class issues. This relaxed, visually free-wheeling musical is Lubitsch's 1930 equivalent of the brilliant 1975 Warren Beatty/Robert Towne/Hal Ashby film *Shampoo*, which is similarly about a hairdresser who uses his trade as cover for his true interest, seduction. But in *Monte Carlo*, as the audience knows from the start, Rudolph (Buchanan) is an entirely inept fake hairdresser, a count who masquerades as a servant ("Rudy") to woo the impoverished countess. After narrowly escaping being married to an elderly, cadaverous aristocrat, MacDonald's Countess Mara has come to the gambling resort of Monte Carlo in a desperate attempt to recover her solvency while masquerading as a grand lady of means. Although *Trouble in Paradise* is sometimes said to be Lubitsch's first film to reflect the realities of the Great Depression, *Monte Carlo* also touches on them, if obliquely.

Rudolph's elaborate charade, conducted because he immediately realizes that the countess is in no mood for romance, includes secretly bankrolling her gambling as well as some deliciously sexual byplay when she oohs and ahs as he shampoos her hair and massages her scalp—the crowning Lubitsch Touch is his cut to her maid (ZaSu Pitts) listening, scandalized, from behind a closed door. Rudolph's game lasts until nearly the end of the picture, when he reveals himself as a fellow aristocrat, enabling the countess to relax her inhibitions and accept him as her natural love partner. The countess's previously snobbish mistreatment of Rudolph as a mere lackey is gracefully and satirically pardoned by having the title character in the opera *Monsieur Beaucaire* sing, "There is nothing to forgive; / Being a lady of propriety, / You just obeyed the dictates of society." Beaucaire walks out on his lady because he doesn't believe she truly loves him. But when Rudolph expresses his preference for a happy ending, the director is not only puckishly playing to his audience but also toying in a most sophisticated manner with the expected conventions of the genre and "the dictates of society."

There is little attempt at emotional involvement with the characters in *Monte Carlo*, a film of unadulterated gaiety and frivolity, whose romantic themes are further qualified (at least for more "knowing" modern audiences) by having such an effeminate leading man. It is hard to take the notion of a sexual relationship between Rudolph and the countess seriously. Buchanan was a dapper, quintessentially elegant stage and film actor of Scottish descent, best known now perhaps for his role as a flamboyant stage director (modeled on Orson Welles) in the 1953 Vincente Minnelli musical *The Band Wagon*. But his sweet-tempered, cultivated, fey screen persona is at an opposite pole from the brazenly macho sexuality flaunted by Chevalier in other Lubitsch musicals. As sexual attitudes have evolved since then, that distinction is to some extent in Buchanan's favor, since Chevalier's exuberant sexism, although qualified by Lubitsch's ironic touches and ridiculous in its extremity, can be grating at times.

Lubitsch is clearly aware of the artifice involved in Buchanan's on-screen relationship with MacDonald and plays along with the gag; *Shampoo* does much the same by having Beatty's character exploit the stereotype of hairdressers as gay so that he can quietly seduce his married female clients without their husbands realizing. The most telling moment of Lubitsch's tongue-in-cheek humor in *Monte Carlo* comes when the countess haughtily complains that Rudy is "not a man at all," by which she ostensibly means to insult him as a mere servant. Buchanan's character, becoming indignant, almost gives away his faux-hairdresser game at that point by exclaiming in his most effete tones, "What's this? I'm not a *man?*" The director, who had played with gender roles and bisexuality in such sophisticated, advanced ways in his 1918 German comedy *I Don't Want to Be a Man*, is comfortable enough with all variations to gently kid any kind of sexuality. Too often, however, viewers today feel free to mock Buchanan's less-than-"manly" manner in homophobic terms. That and Buchanan's theatricality are reason the euphemistic word "quaint" pops up more frequently with this film than with the other Lubitsch musicals. But the comparative lack of a strongly defined gender contrast between the man and the woman in *Monte Carlo*, while it makes for a certain parity between the sexes that is easier to establish than in Lubitsch's other musicals, also makes the film seem less challengingly contentious and less consequential than some of the others.

The best Lubitsch musicals walk a riskier emotional tightrope. Those that do not also include the risqué sketches in *Paramount on Parade* and the inferior musical remake of *The Marriage Circle*, *One Hour with You*, a glossy but uneasy collaboration between Lubitsch and George Cukor. Maurice Chevalier's Dr. André Bertier, ostensibly happily married to Colette (Jeanette MacDonald), is thrown by the arrival of her "best friend," the saucy Mitzi (Genevieve Tobin), a shamelessly determined seducer. Mitzi eventually wears down André's defenses and puts the survival of his marriage in jeopardy. But the conflict is unsatisfactorily trivialized in comparison with the complexity of the silent masterpiece. *One Hour with You* determinedly avoids the dramatic underpinnings of its predecessor, which, for all its jollity, deals with the subjects of adultery and marital fidelity in deeply serious ways. There is nothing inherently wrong with films taking light approaches to their subjects, but in this case, the difference is so glaring that it diminishes one's pleasure and makes *One Hour with You* seem overly concerned with avoiding the implications of its subject matter.

On the other hand, the underlying seriousness of the character relationships and gender issues raised in *The Love Parade*, *The Smiling Lieutenant*, and *The Merry Widow* allows for many lively, delightful moments of both drama and comedy with thought-provoking conflicts. But in the end, that more ambitious dimension in Lubitsch's musicals remains somewhat uneasily handled. Lubitsch and his writers make many telling satirical points about power relations between men and women while also giving the scenes some emotional weight, but the highly artificial stories tend to be resolved in awkwardly overdetermined, simplistic ways. This problem reveals conflicts between the films' more complex ambitions and the genre conventions that even Lubitsch's films had to follow to be viable in the Hollywood commercial marketplace of that period. This was even the case despite the freer climate before the Production Code began to be enforced strictly in the late stages of production on *The Merry Widow*.

"DIFFERENT AND GOOD"

Among the many enduring charms of Lubitsch's musicals are the audacious and clever ways he finds to film the musical numbers. His skill in integrating them into the storylines is one of the reasons his "talent and originality are stupefying," as Orson Welles put it. Lubitsch's musicals showed the rest of the industry how to make musicals more than just song revues or backstage stories with musical numbers interspersed. *The Love Parade* is just as entertaining as ever today but seems to exist in a different aesthetic world from the creaky relic of that same year, *The Broadway Melody*, which won the best-picture Oscar. Lubitsch's film was fully recognized in its time for its startlingly innovative nature, which pointed the way forward for his colleagues as well as for his audiences. His musicals paved the road for, among others, the Fred Astaire/Ginger Rogers films of the Depression era, in which the couple's love scenes are their dances, expressing their feelings in ways that words cannot (even those of the great songwriters who contributed to those films, such as Cole Porter and Irving Berlin).

Lubitsch's stage background and cultural affinity with the Viennese operetta tradition as well as his amateur love of piano playing helped him navigate the transition from silents directly into musicals with apparent effortlessness. But as was always the case with his work, he fully recognized the differences between theater and film and cleverly played with theatrical conventions in cinematic ways. Lubitsch puts across songs and dances with a playful wit equal to his silent touches. He especially enjoys intermingling singing with recitative, the method of "talking on pitch" popularized later by Rex Harrison in the stage and film versions of *My Fair Lady*. Not only does talking a song allow performers with limited vocal talents (such as Colbert and Hopkins) to shine in Lubitsch films, but in scenes with more skilled singers, it also enables the director to orchestrate the full range of verbal and musical expression available in the sound film.

In a 1931 protoauteurist article on "The Style of Ernst Lubitsch" in the New England journal *Hound & Horn*, Kenneth White wrote of Lupino Lane's dazzling opening song number in *The Love Parade* that it "snapped the picture off as if it had been flung out by a rubber-band." After Chevalier's more serious song lamenting his forced departure from Paris, having the servants and even the dogs mockingly echo him is another way Lubitsch announces right from the start that he is going to play with the fresh form of the musical medium to amuse his audience (and himself). As White puts it, Lubitsch "did not let [the song] die out but multiplied its effects in a comic mood to carry the farce that much farther." Experimentation in movies always goes down easiest with audiences if it is cloaked in humor, as Lubitsch demonstrates throughout his work. Screenwriter Samson Raphaelson recalled, "I never caught Lubitsch ever thinking in terms of a formula; that is, he wouldn't say, 'How can ve use a door in this scene?' Never once would he say that. He would face the problem and say, 'Vat do ve do here? How do ve lick dis? How do ve say it vit style? How do ve say it *different*? How do ve say it *different* and *good*? Different and true?'"

Here are some of the many other ingenious devices, *different* and *good*—sometimes simple, sometimes highly intricate—that Lubitsch uses in his musicals to play with song numbers while simultaneously advancing his narratives:

• Buchanan and MacDonald sing a love duet over the telephone in *Monte Carlo*, their first actual "conversation." At first outraged by his cheeky vocal intrusion while she is trying to sleep, she becomes entranced by his crooning of "Give Me a Moment, Please." A few days later, Count Rudolph hears another man singing the same song and raving about how beautiful Countess Mara looks in the morning. The count takes offense until he learns that the man is her hairdresser—giving him the idea to masquerade as "Rudy" the hairdresser, thus triggering the film's basic story device by using a song as the bridge.

• In the sexy "chamber music" duet in *The Smiling Lieutenant* ("While Hearts Are Singing"), Colbert's Franzi plays her violin and talks her song to Chevalier's Niki at his piano. Because Colbert talks the lyrics, we wonder whether she can sing at all until she unexpectedly comes out with her beautifully sung line, *"Live for today"*—a coup de théâtre by Lubitsch (or more precisely, a coup de cinéma).

• Different kinds of musical love scenes are daringly intercut to develop the bizarre romantic triangle in *The Smiling Lieutenant*: Franzi and Niki waltz in a secluded ballroom, accompanied by her all-girl band, while singing lasciviously about their lovemaking schedule during his free time from Princess Anna. This dissolves to the prim and shy Anna excitedly expressing her desire for Niki and her deluded view of his character to her ladies-in-waiting in a rhythmical talking song ("I see him now, so *modest* and so *gentle*, so sentimental") while Lubitsch wickedly cuts back and forth to Franzi making almost violent love to Niki as they speak and sing their wild passion (she vows, "I'll thrill you 'till I kill you, you son of a gun!").

• In *One Hour with You*, MacDonald and Tobin, in their reunion scenes, share contrasting thoughts about men and marriage (Tobin's Mitzi thoroughly cynical, MacDonald's Colette glowing and naïve). They exchange viewpoints in rhyming dialogue, underscored by music, connected with a series of dissolves (echoing a similar but silent sequence of the two women "friends" in *The Marriage Circle* chattering in an amusing series of fast shots linked by dissolves without intertitles). Lubitsch pivots gracefully from comedy to tenderness in the musical remake when Colette breaks into song to pay tribute to her marriage ("Day after day / We will always be sweethearts").

• Mitzi makes advances on Dr. Bertier in *One Hour with You* by pretending to be ill so that he has to make a house call, and the doctor reciprocates in their duet (him singing, her mostly talking, *almost* singing), which is loaded with racy double entendres about how she can feel better by trying "a real hot application, three times a day."

• While MacDonald's Sonia, the title character in *The Merry Widow*, sings the romantic showpiece "Vilja Song" in her ripest trilling tones, Chevalier's Count Danilo woos her, puckishly playing Cyrano de Bergerac by having his valet join her in a rich baritone. This auditory and visual gag, kidding the venerable song as well as the stars for their differences in vocal styles, is taken to a further comic level when Lubitsch incongruously dubs an accomplished male singer (Allen Rogers) into the mouth of the valet, who is played by a character actor the audience knew well for his comically squeaky voice, Sterling Holloway.

"GIRLS, GIRLS, GIRLS"

Among its other virtues, the musical genre enabled Lubitsch to romp as freely as he ever did, if not more so, with sexual subject matter. The elaborately bawdy sequence at the Paris nightclub Maxim's in *The Merry Widow* is perhaps the consummate example. Count Danilo's cavorting with his

"Maxim's girls" in risqué song, dance, and dialogue—including the uproari-ous "Girls, Girls, Girls" number—is as explicit as any pre-Code Hollywood film could be about philandering and prostitution. But shortly after the PCA was formed, the baleful arrival of the new Code came on July 15, 1934, near the end of shooting on *The Merry Widow*. During postproduction, the film brought Lubitsch into serious conflict with the censors. From that point on, his career and his filmmaking style were radically changed.

Lubitsch's lavish production of *The Merry Widow* is his loose reworking of the celebrated 1905 Viennese operetta composed by Franz Lehár, *Die lustige Witwe*, about an aristocratic ladies' man who is expected to marry a wealthy widow for reasons of state but balks because he truly loves her. The book and lyrics for the operetta are by Victor Léon and Leo Stein, who adapted the story from an 1861 play by Henri Meilhac, *L'attaché d'ambassade* (*The Embassy Attaché*). Stroheim had directed a dramatically intense, elaborately textured 1925 silent version for MGM, starring John Gilbert and Mae Murray. Stro-heim focuses mostly on the backstory of how the young woman becomes a wealthy widow through often-grotesque circumstances that leave her deeply jaded; her successful wooing by Prince Danilo becomes the film's romantic third act. Lubitsch's highly idiosyncratic interpretation of the material, set in 1885, is a much lighter and yet still romantically passionate adaptation. It vividly demonstrates how two master filmmakers can achieve a wide varia-tion in tone while working with the same material. Both black-and-white films were shot by the same cinematographer, Oliver T. Marsh, whose work is strikingly brighter, sweeping, and more "colorful" for Lubitsch, while he gives Stroheim's film a suitably moody and oppressively cluttered look, even while brilliantly highlighting the widow's jewels as she is ogled by a suitor in an expressionistic variation on a Lubitsch Touch from *Three Women*.

Although a piece of profound personal filmmaking, the Lubitsch version of *The Merry Widow* was also, paradoxically, a supreme product of the MGM factory system. The project went through a long and unusually involved pre-production process lasting several years before Lubitsch committed to direct and produce. That process included complex negotiations over the rights, many writers working on script treatments and drafts, and Chevalier's attempts to force MGM to hire a leading lady other than MacDonald, whom the actor by then actively disliked (he considered her prudish and hypocritical; she called him "the fastest derrière pincher in Hollywood"). Chevalier by that time was also uncomfortable working with Lubitsch and looking forward to returning to France, so that contributed to the preproduction complications. Lubitsch did not agree to come aboard the project until December 1933, and he managed to achieve an unusually high degree of creative control for a director working at MGM under its strong-willed production chief, Irving Thalberg.

A measure of what Lubitsch had to overcome at his new studio and under its factory system is suggested by veteran screenwriter Anita Loos, who was brought aboard by the wary Thalberg to do some uncredited script doctoring:

> Irving was always worried about [Lubitsch's] tendency to neglect the human element in a story. Any love scene Ernst directed might just be warming up when his camera would zoom away [*sic*] from the sweethearts to focus on a pair of fancy bedroom slippers, the hero's pearl-buttoned spats, or an ornate piece of bric-a-brac. I was instructed to keep reminding Ernst that his plot concerned the human heart and not the prop department. Ernst grudgingly accepted my aid on the script . . . but as soon as work got under way, I found him obsessed by an idea of the widow owning a pair of poodles, one snow-white and the other coal-black; a gimmick that kept interrupting the love story.

In fact, the transformation of the widow's Pekingese dogs (not poodles) from black to white via a dissolve in a sequence also showing her wardrobe changing color is one of the most delicious Lubitsch Touches in the film, and it does not interrupt the love story but helps give it impetus by graphically depicting Sonia's transformation of mood as she readies herself for romance. The condescending attitude Thalberg and Loos displayed toward Lubitsch's stylistic signature was a sign of Hollywood's changing attitude toward a director who needed no reminding that "his plot concerned the human heart."

Lubitsch had left Paramount because it had gone into receivership in 1933; it fell into bankruptcy in 1935. His films contributed to the studio's financial malaise: *The Man I Killed*, *One Hour with You*, and *Trouble in Paradise*, all released in 1932, lost money domestically, a combined total of $870,000 (his only boxoffice success that busy year was as a contributor to the omnibus film *If I Had a Million*). His 1933 film *Design for Living* had to be made for a relatively modest $563,000, a little more than *Trouble in Paradise* ($520,000) but considerably less than the financial disaster *The Man I Killed* ($890,000). Moving to the more stable MGM, albeit partly out of necessity, enabled him to command greater financial and technical resources. He was able to work with his trusted collaborators Vajda and Raphaelson on the droll and incisive shooting script of *The Merry Widow*; the lyrics are by Richard Rodgers and Lorenz Hart, with additional lyrics by Gus Kahn.

A French version, *La veuve joyeuse* (1935), was filmed simultaneously at MGM since Chevalier could perform in his native language and MacDonald was also adept at singing in French; some of the secondary players were replaced for that version. It closely follows Lubitsch's mise-en-scène for the English version and is also credited to him, although an unidentified French director actually supervised the shooting along with a French dialogue director. Specially reworked versions were also prepared for the English and Belgian markets (the latter with French dialogue) to avoid offense to royalty. With all that complicated production history and the film's sumptuous sets (which won Oscars for art director Cedric Gibbons and his associate Fredric Hope), it is no wonder that *The Merry Widow*, with a final cost of $1,605,000, was one of MGM's most expensive films up to that time. Five years after its release, it was carried at a loss of $113,000 in worldwide returns.

In both Germany and Hollywood, Lubitsch loved to make humor out of the spectacle of multitudes of women cavorting with a lecherous man. Such surreal comedy amplifies the director's fascination with sexuality that extends beyond conventional coupledom and with gags involving multiplying elements. Anticipating Chevalier's characters in *The Merry Widow* and the other Lubitsch musicals, Paul Heidemann's Lieutenant Alexis ("Alex the Seducer") in the 1921 German silent *The Wildcat* bids a memorably raucous farewell to a literal horde of women when he is transferred to another post. Alexis's army of lovers rush from every direction and surround his open car. Ironically, they are rioting not with anger but with unrestrained lust; soldiers keep trying to scatter them, including by dumping mice from a sack, a variation on the sexist gag at the end of *The Doll* when Ossi shows herself to be a real woman by being frightened by a mouse. Although the women in *The Wildcat* are less frightening than the mob of would-be brides chasing Buster Keaton in *Seven Chances* (1925), Lubitsch's sequence, with its multiplicity of gags, could have become a sexual-fantasy-turned-nightmare. But Lubitsch characteristically treats the outlandish situation with blithe humor. Alexis calmly and complacently blows the female crowd a kiss and thanks them for bringing him happiness. Women line the streets as his car drives away, anticipating the opening of *The Merry Widow* in which Chevalier's Count Danilo marches in a military parade. He sings about the joys of "Girls, Girls, Girls" as women wave at him and blow kisses from every direction. In *The Wildcat*, Lubitsch even fills the screen with a gaggle of flag-waving little girls in white dresses, waving to Alexis as they all shout, "Goodbye, Papa!" But that farewell sequence is an extended, isolated gag that does not dominate the movie.

Danilo in *The Merry Widow*, on the other hand, outdoes any past or future Lubitsch rake in his sustained ability to juggle an almost incredible multitude of grateful women without any unpleasant consequences—at least until he runs into "Fifi." The wealthy widow, Sonia, pretends to be a common Maxim's girl in order to teach him a lesson in love. Before that, when Danilo makes his triumphant appearance at Maxim's, the prostitutes carry on in a sexual frenzy, hoisting him in their arms on the dance floor like a conquering monarch, leaving little to the imagination about what they all might be getting up to behind closed doors in the private rooms upstairs. As he does with the mob scene in *The Wildcat*, Lubitsch milks that delightfully outrageous sequence at considerable length, pushing the envelope and shocking the sensibilities of the increasingly emboldened PCA. (Jean Renoir pays homage to Lubitsch's *Merry Widow* in his 1937 classic *La Grande Illusion* when the German and French aristocratic characters played by Stroheim and Pierre Fresnay swap stories about their pre–World War I sexual adventures in Paris and discover they both were involved with the same woman at Maxim's, Fifi.)

"DEFINITELY . . . SUGGESTIVE"

During postproduction on *The Merry Widow*, the censors, girding for battle with Lubitsch, objected to Maxim's being portrayed as a virtual brothel. They recoiled at the spectacle of Danilo, as a male sex object, nearly being torn to shreds by a bevy of eager conquests. PCA chief Joseph Breen had initially approved the film under pressure from Thalberg. Some retakes were made during production to avoid censorship at a cost of more than $100,000, but Breen otherwise gave in to Thalberg's defense of the lavish production.

After the Catholic Legion of Decency was formed in May 1934, one of the first films it condemned for viewing by its millions of members was Lubitsch's 1933 Paramount film *Design for Living*. The legion was also a leading force in bringing the PCA into existence and installing the staunchly Catholic, anti-Semitic Breen as its head. According to Maureen Furniss's study of Lubitsch's relationship with the Code, *Design for Living* and *The Merry Widow* "were used by the Legion of Decency and the PCA as specific examples of the moral delinquency against which their fight for further censorship control within the industry was waged." Lubitsch continued to be a target of the censors over the next couple of years while his directing career went on hiatus and he was working as Paramount's production chief, partly so he could reevaluate where he stood in the industry in light of the strictures of the new Code. As Furniss notes,

> Because of censorship, Lubitsch was experiencing some difficulty in terms of his marketability. Beginning in 1935, Paramount was largely unsuccessful in their efforts to attain new [Code] Seals for [reissuing] his films. Lubitsch's work was, therefore, affected by the PCA insofar as his early [sound] films could not be rereleased under the new Code enforcement. In August 1935, *Design for Living* and *Trouble in Paradise* were the first films to be denied approval for re-issue. The next January, *The Love Parade* was also rejected. This must have been very frustrating for Lubitsch and no doubt affected his image at the studio in terms of his money-earning capacity. . . . In 1936, *The Smiling Lieutenant* was also rejected for rerelease by the PCA. *Monte Carlo* (Paramount, 1930), however, became the exception to the rule as it was allowed to be rereleased in September 1936.

After the New York premiere of *The Merry Widow*, as a result of pressure from the Legion and one of its organizers, Martin Quigley, the Catholic publisher of the *Motion Picture Herald*, Breen belatedly insisted on thirteen cuts in the film, totaling about three minutes, to tone down some of the bawdiness. MGM ordered that these cuts be carried out by all its distribution offices before the film went into national release. On October 22, eleven days after the premiere, Breen wrote his boss, Will Hays, saying, "The picture as it now stands is not the light, gay, frivolous operetta which it is intended that it should be but rather the typical French farce that is definitely bawdy and offensively—in spots—suggestive. . . . I am now of the opinion that we made a mistake in approving this picture as it now is. . . . I am frank to confess to you that after having seen the picture on Friday I was very greatly worried that I had ever passed this picture." Fortunately, the version of the film now in circulation is Lubitsch's original version, since the negative was not cut when the film was censored in 1934, only the initial release prints.

SEX AND LOVE

The censors seemed oblivious to the fact that Lubitsch's take on *The Merry Widow*, with all its wild carrying-on and raucous humor, offers some of his most serious meditations on the distinctions between sex and love. In an elaborate bravura sequence early in the film, Sonia sits at her desk and lies in bed, writing in her diary, singing and speaking about her yearning for romance, her lonely widowhood, and her complicated feelings about Count Danilo after discovering he is actually a notorious playboy ("It was all just a fleeting dream / Men are not, *not* what they seem"). Her face is superimposed in cameo style on the diary pages over a period of several days until she becomes "fed up with Marshovia" and declares, "There's a limit to every widow." Then her wardrobe and her dog comically morph from black to white as she prepares an excursion to Paris. This style of advancing the narrative in innovative visual and auditory ways shows how deftly Lubitsch can tell a story while allowing the character to express both her deepest and most mutable emotions through song.

Far more than the other characters Chevalier plays in the previous Lubitsch musicals, Danilo is made to confront the negative implications of his heedless attitude toward women. After he gaily sings, "I'm going to Maxim's, / Where all the girls are dreams," his flamboyant but recklessly unfeeling approach to the opposite sex is played to the hilt by Lubitsch. Danilo sings "Girls, Girls, Girls" at the nightclub while dancing with a seemingly endless parade of sexy, gaudily dressed, rather cheap-looking women. The Maxim's sequence is so extreme in showing them throwing themselves at Danilo without a trace of jealousy that it becomes a prolonged and quite hilarious, though biting, joke about the dehumanizing fantasies of the male libido. In addition to mocking Danilo's outrageous egomania, the number suggests that he cheapens *himself* by gleefully turning into a male sex object. Chevalier's characters complain when women try to do that to him in *The Love Parade* and *The Smiling Lieutenant*. Chevalier's characters learn an ironic lesson from Lubitsch's treatment of sexual objectification in those films, but in *The Merry Widow*, Danilo has to learn in a more emotionally painful way how the opposite sex feels about being put in that position.

The carousing song at Maxim's was anticipated by Lubitsch's delirious fantasy routine "The Rainbow Revels" in the 1930 revue film *Paramount on Parade*. In that sketch (originally filmed in two-strip Technicolor, although it now exists only in black-and-white), a Parisian chimney sweep played by Chevalier literally ascends into the heavens with a bevy of beautiful, scantily clad woman as he sings "Sweepin' the Clouds Away" while taking his harem "up on top of a rainbow." This metaphor for multiple, orgiastic orgasm is a Lubitschean spoof of a giddy Busby Berkeley musical number, with these women as syncopated sex objects celebrating Chevalier's incredible virility. Another Lubitsch number in that film, "Origin of the Apache," combines sex and violence by showing a married couple, Chevalier and Evelyn Brent, wildly stripping off each other's clothes and tossing them into artfully composed close-ups while the director allows us to imagine their naughty behavior offscreen. The gag is that "proper" married couples can and do behave as violently in their sex lives as the criminal classes are assumed to be doing with the greater freedom allowed by their lower status. The outrageously overblown satirical sketches Lubitsch contributed to *Paramount on Parade* allow him free rein for some of his less inhibited sexual impulses as he apparently works off the excess excitement provided by the licentiousness of the new medium.

But after four years to mellow out from these early forays, in *The Merry Widow* the director treats sexual license more seriously, examining the emotional consequences of male abandon. The interchangeability of three women in Danilo's harem at Maxim's is amusingly conveyed when they greet him in close-ups, each saying a separate syllable of his name: "Da-," "-ni-," "-lo!" But the frolicking comes to a sudden halt when he is given the emotional equivalent of a rough slap in the face by both MacDonald and the director. She had been captivated by his courtship back home in Marshovia until she discovered what a fraud and philanderer he is. So she bitterly mocks his low tastes by masquerading as the glamorous but common "Fifi." After playing along with his smug, well-practiced seduction routine in a private upstairs dining room, she reveals that she is not the prostitute he callously assumes she is but the socially proper, emotionally discerning widow he had been ordered to seduce to keep her fortune from leaving Marshovia. Sonia is no floozy but a mature woman uninterested in a casual fling, especially when she realizes that Danilo has been assigned to seduce her for her money rather than for herself.

This confrontation comes after the most breathtakingly beautiful camera movement in all of Lubitsch's work, the gracefully sweeping shot that follows first Sonia dancing alone and then the couple, in serpentine paths as they dance around the private room to the sublime strains of "The Merry Widow Waltz." The camera, on its dolly in this long take, manipulated by Hollywood technicians at their most virtuosic, acts almost as a partner in a ménage à trois. The theme of sexual infidelity, and all the conflicts it implies, is one of Lubitsch's favorite romantic situations; here his camera, by dancing with the couple, allows us to participate viscerally, as more than mere voyeurs. When Danilo glibly tries to complete his standard seduction process by pretending he loves Sonia, she has finally had enough. She breaks the spell by telling him with contempt, "You 'great lover'—you don't even know what love is!"

With that well-deserved insult—delivered in the final on-screen pairing of Chevalier and MacDonald, reflecting their contentious offscreen relationship—Danilo is brought back to reality by being made to experience a somber coming-to-terms with the shallowness of his Don Juan personality. It is a key moment in the evolution of Lubitsch's musicals. That character development is far removed from any of Chevalier's more callous dealings with women in the previous Lubitsch musicals, which often blithely celebrate his characters' sexual adventurism as the filmmaker's way of thumbing his nose at the puritanical nature of American society. In those earlier films, Lubitsch invites us to revel in Chevalier's shameless shenanigans, and the French actor's blasé charm helps lure us into complicity, but that is not the case as *The Merry Widow* begins to dig deeper emotionally. (Chevalier went back to France soon after making that film, dissatisfied with his Hollywood typecasting as a brassy boulevardier. He disgraced himself during World War II by entertaining the Nazis, leading Jean-Luc Godard to have Jean-Paul Belmondo's character tell Jean Seberg in *Breathless*, "You Americans are so dumb. You adore Lafayette and Maurice Chevalier. They're the stupidest of all Frenchmen.")

The Merry Widow determinedly advances the emotional story of Danilo learning to respond more genuinely to Sonia's affections. The lavish use of mirrors to multiply the dancers at the Embassy Ball is part of the most visually opulent musical extravaganza in Lubitsch's body of work, even more spectacular than the "Foxtrot Epidemic" in *The Oyster Princess*, the Charleston sequence in *So This Is Paris*, or the cancan and other dancing at Maxim's. *The Merry Widow* moves the operetta's embassy scenes from the opening to the middle of the story. Lubitsch and cinematographer Oliver Marsh go all out here with geometric visual patterns, almost abstract use of black-and-white contrasts in settings and costuming, overhead camera angles, swooping crane shots, and more than two hundred dancing extras. The sequence plays a succession of musical numbers ostensibly straight but also showing off the director's cinematic resources for the cognoscenti (and his boss at MGM, Irving Thalberg). Lubitsch adds even more dimensions to the Embassy Ball with his clever editing style. The number is continually interrupted by comic interludes and serious romantic scenes. Lubitsch creates a disturbing sense of claustrophobia around Danilo and Sonia in a series of scenes in which the couple waltzes alone before they are continually swallowed up by crowds of other dancing couples and keep trying to get away. It is the closest he ever came to a group-sex scene. The couple's frustrated search for privacy (a symptom of the frequent Lubitschean conflict between love and duty) becomes a key dramatic element in their relationship, culminating in their heavily monitored wedding in a jail cell, another Lubitsch musical ending with a sting to it.

Discerning students of Lubitsch may sense some sending-up of the growing Hollywood trend for outlandish musical numbers in his handling of the ball. It challenges Busby Berkeley at his own game but does so with elegance rather than jazzy flash. At one point Lubitsch allows his central couple to disappear entirely in the crowd while jamming the other anonymous dancers into an even more claustrophobic mirrored corridor, making them execute highly unlikely maneuvers, filmed from an overhead angle that turns the scene into as much of a kaleidoscopic pattern as an actual dance. Showing the mass of dancers as virtually identical automata moving in Berkeley-like visual patterns is Lubitsch's commentary on the artificiality and phoniness of the formal embassy culture in comparison with the more intimate, fluid, and spontaneous musical duets of Sonia and Danilo. They are trying to work out, in private or semiprivate, a more ad hoc kind of relationship than their formalized high society usually allows.

This elaborate sequence and Lubitsch's bravura in interweaving the dancing with other elements of the stylized narrative represent the director's lavish farewell to the musical genre. When Lubitsch returned to the form much later, at the very end of his career, for the frothy nostalgia piece *That Lady in Ermine*, based on a German operetta, it seemed a tinny echo of his earlier musicals. That laboriously unamusing Technicolor film is one of the saddest final works of any great director's career, seeming to represent the loss of all the qualities that made him great.

So it is really *The Merry Widow* that represents Lubitsch's last word in musicals, one of the peaks of his achievement, albeit an imperfect one because of its unsatisfying forced resolution. Having the romantic couple get married in jail may have seemed to Lubitsch a cleverly bleak irony, but it is the culmination of an increasingly constricting third act in a film that starts out as a joyous romp and gradually, awkwardly darkens, a shift in tone that in itself conveys dissatisfaction with the genre's limitations in conveying the depths of emotion his best films evoke.

Adapting *The Merry Widow*, an unusually tender and thoughtful, time-tested operetta with exquisite music, into his most complex and graceful vein of romantic comedy and drama brought Lubitsch to a level of heightened seriousness. The film takes us to the point of no return emotionally in a genre that usually tends to resist such levels of involvement. Perhaps that is one reason why he decided to leave the musical behind after this one. In effect, by 1934 he had said all he had to say in that genre. That decision lasted for nearly the rest of his career, until he misguidedly went out with a feeble imitation of his better musicals, dying during the production of *That Lady in Ermine* in November 1947. He explained in an interview that April, shortly after receiving an honorary Oscar, why he had abandoned the genre years before: "One gets tired, one changes. When one has a personal style it is like one's handwriting—he can't get away from it. I had done so many musicals . . . that I felt the need of a different approach. But I had none. So . . . I returned to an earlier métier, comedy of the sophisticated sort."

But part of the reason Lubitsch stopped making musicals was more practical and market-driven. The commercial failure of his highly expensive MGM film came at a time when the Depression was making the mass audience turn away from the traditional operetta to the unglamorous proletarian romantic comedy. That new trend was exemplified by Frank Capra's sleeper hit of the same year, *It Happened One Night*, a comedy about an oddly matched couple roughing it on a cross-country bus ride. Audiences were delighted by the proletarian comedy of a snooty heiress (Claudette Colbert) being humanized by a footloose reporter (Clark Gable). Colbert, the French-born actress who could pronounce "genre" correctly and was used to the luxury of Lubitsch's work and similarly stylish films, admitted that she had a hard time adjusting to the Capra film's more ordinary settings and costumes and the characters' "seedy" appearances. She came to appreciate the new style, but only grudgingly. Capra was a Lubitsch admirer, and his celebrated deployment of the "Walls of Jericho" gag at the motel as sexual shorthand (including for the ending, with a closed door and a trumpet blowing) amounted to adapting the concept of the Lubitsch Touch to a lower-class setting. But the "common man" protagonists of Capra's films seemed more in keeping with the times than the more rarified characters who tended to populate Lubitsch's films.

Lubitsch's move from the financially shaky Paramount to the more prosperous MGM for *The Merry Widow* was temporary but still disruptive to his career. Although he had gone to MGM for security and to command greater resources, it was a sign of the times that his expensive film still lost money while doing twice as well in Europe as it did in America. That commercial flop was followed by Lubitsch's longest period of directorial inactivity since he had begun in 1914. He spent an unhappy year between February 1935 and February 1936 as Paramount's production head and as a producer, supervising other directors' films. Lubitsch's decision to move on from the artificial glory of the musical genre—and his hiatus from directing—allowed him time to reassess his stylistic approach in the light of the new Production Code that threatened to put him out of business as a filmmaker. He had also stretched the musical form to its limit, especially in its sexual and emotional expressiveness, while managing to avoid turning his back almost entirely on the lighthearted escapist qualities that usually make musicals popular. But the effort was getting more strained, the mixture more uncomfortable.

While visiting New York for the premiere of *The Merry Widow* in October 1934, Lubitsch told *Times* film critic Andre Sennwald that

> this present [censorship] campaign, I must admit, has caused me to worry about the future. . . . If I were to film my old [*sic*] picture, *The Patriot*, today, it would be impossible for me to make it true to life as I see it. I would be in trouble at once. We will be crippled in our artistic efforts to present a candid and accurate view of life. When the effect of the campaign is to fight the free and truthful expression of the artist, which is a fundamental definition of the function of art, then the campaign becomes dangerous and the development of an artistic cinema is impeded. . . . I can work with almost complete freedom on light, flimsy [*sic*] stories like *The Merry Widow*, but it would be impossible for me to produce a film which pretended at any profundity in story and character. . . . I should like nothing better than to take $400,000 of their money and produce a film version of *Faust*, just for the satisfaction of having it censored and of hearing the censors inform the public that Goethe is an immoral writer.

LUBITSCH AND THE DOUBLE STANDARD

While tolerance of adultery in a Lubitsch pre-Code musical or romantic comedy can be refreshing in its impudence and candor, the director, as a result, sometimes runs up against obstacles he has difficulty resolving, despite all the clever narrative twists he and his screenwriters can muster. William Paul's critical study *Ernst Lubitsch's American Comedy* (1983) makes a telling point about that structural problem in the musicals, which, as he notes, is a symptom of deeper thematic issues. In writing about "the musicals that deal with courtship," Paul observes that they

> clearly move their characters toward a not always willing acquiescence in the status quo. The social order that dominates at the beginning of the film continues to dominate in the end. In other words, with the musicals the plot patterns of the historical tragedies have been introduced into the comedies, so that the happy endings toward which the musicals always move seem both facile and forced. . . . The resolution of the conflict is

generally confused, partly as a result of trying to make a bleak plot pattern conform to the optimistic expectations of the genre.

Paul omits *One Hour with You* from his discussion, even though it makes the problem most starkly apparent when Chevalier's married man is torn between two women and chooses marital fidelity in the end after committing adultery. In that case, the faithful wife's having to cheerfully accept the double standard to preserve her marriage seems far from the happy ending it is intended to be. Instead, it comes off as an unjust form of submission. And it is worth noting that this unusually simplistic happy ending was part of a reshoot after some negative reactions to the film at a preview.

As Paul suggests, the "bleak plot patterns" Lubitsch uses to make satirical and dramatic points in some of the musicals—*The Love Parade*, *The Smiling Lieutenant*, and *The Merry Widow* to varying degrees—could just as well lead to unhappy resolutions. But if the films are to conform to the audience's generic expectation of an ending with the couple happily united, there is little alternative to having the character(s) who are threatened with drastic consequences settle for their "not always willing acquiescence in the status quo." The genre requires that their acquiescence be presented in a manner that at least *seems* voluntary as well as jolly. But the compromises made to achieve these ends seem to modern viewers to be less than satisfactory because they involve the banishment of a déclassé partner who does not fit the status quo (notably, and most painfully, Colbert's alluring but self-sacrificing Franzi in *The Smiling Lieutenant*) or because they contrive to reestablish a dominant patriarchal order in private even when the man is officially outranked by his royal female partner in *The Love Parade*. In *One Hour with You*, the abrupt resolution involves the wife and husband addressing the camera directly as she deliberately accepts her husband's past infidelity as a fair equivalent ("Fifty-fifty") of her own supposed "dreams" of romance. Telling the audience, "And you adore him . . . What would you do?" she embraces her errant husband on the fade-out. That is a far less emotionally complex resolution than Lubitsch achieves with the shaky marriage in *The Marriage Circle*. It is also a pathetic, self-deluding sham on the wife's part here, since the man who has been trying to woo her (Charlie Ruggles) is presented as a sexless clown rather than as the serious, more plausible suitor of the earlier film. The original ending of *One Hour with You* included MacDonald accepting the supposed "fifty-fifty" arrangement but then had Chevalier ducking out of their bedchamber and trying with comical lack of success to justify himself to the audience as he relates his encounter with Mitzi in her apartment ("Now I'm sure the *ladies* may believe me. But the *gentlemen* may say, 'Did you really drink brandy?'"); MacDonald was not in that final scene. It is hard to accept her even more categorical papering-over of the issues in the reshoot for the release version, just as the ending of *The Merry Widow* is hard to accept as entirely happy when marriage is literally presented as a form of incarceration.

Lubitsch's continental tolerance of adultery, a position rare in Hollywood filmmaking, accounts in part for the special quality of his films and their provocative nature. His films suggest that occasional straying from monogamy can reinvigorate a marriage or lead to a happier relationship with a partner (as in *Trouble in Paradise*). That subversive attitude may still be unacceptable to many viewers today; it certainly surprised my San Francisco State University students when I taught a course dealing with his work, though it intrigued them. A female student raised the question of the double standard in his films and accurately noted that the director's tolerance of adultery extends only to the male partner's carrying-on. I pointed out that in the Hollywood of Lubitsch's time, films found it almost impossible to show women being adulterous and getting away with it, but that double standard remains a limitation of his work today. And yet when seen in the context of his times, Lubitsch's work seems far more sexually adventurous than the norm. Indeed, it seems so even by contrast with much of today's American filmmaking.

Another issue, related but not identical, is that Chevalier's cheerful sexism as a performer in these films is (up to a point and with certain crucial qualifications) supposed to be part of his charm, an attitude that seems to require a certain suspension of disbelief today if it does not automatically induce tongue-clucking disapproval. If you look at Chevalier from another vantage point, Lubitsch is using his cocky self-assurance as a device for having fun with and often mocking male nymphomania. Chevalier can easily slip from cheerful bonhomie into a preening and leering delivery of songs and dialogue that can be amusing or off-putting, depending on personal taste and on how much the films allow us to enjoy his verve and sheer delight in performing. One way Lubitsch succeeds in persuading us of Chevalier's appeal is by pushing the cockiness of the performer to such ludicrous extremes that his sexual braggadocio becomes a joke, an ironic commentary on the flaws of the male ego. We are also encouraged to find a level of insecurity in these characters, which sneaks in around the edges and begins to qualify their rampant egotism, as does the pointed criticism and disdain that some of the female characters express toward Chevalier's preening. In the better films, such as *The Love Parade, The Smiling Lieutenant,* and especially *The Merry Widow,* the Chevalier character's ego is eventually deflated, and his moral sense is belatedly awakened as he genuinely falls in love with women or at least acquires more empathy for women. Even when Chevalier is at his most lubricious, Lubitsch always uses the character's relationships with women to explore the kind of moral issue he finds most compelling: how men and women should treat each other. The films do not propose simple answers to the questions they raise around this issue, but they do offer clear attitudes toward the subject, exploring areas of human conduct that are often conveniently ignored or swept under the rug in other Hollywood films of that period.

Although the sexual power situation is reversed in *The Love Parade,* Lubitsch paints himself into a corner with the submissiveness that Chevalier's Count Alfred must endure as the prince consort. Even if his situation ironically makes us recognize the injustice women endure in marriage, Lubitsch, screenwriters Ernest Vajda and Guy Bolton, and the actors strain to find a conclusion short of having the couple separate, which would be unthinkable for the genre. Since Alfred is married to a queen whose power over him is nearly absolute, the only possible resolution to keep him happy is to have the couple reach a private sexual détente that involves role-playing behind the scenes. Queen Louise willingly pretends to be submissive toward him as long as her public does not see it that way. But, despite our privileged position, peeking behind the palace walls, how much of a chance do we believe this compromise might have to work? Can this game playing actually balance the two conflicting forms of power in their relationship? Such a resolution, though cleverly handled, seems half-hearted dramatically, depending too heavily on the willing suspension of disbelief the musical genre offers. This uneasy solution also papers over the disgruntled squabbling that pervades the lengthy postmarital section of the film; that sour tone continues to leave the viewer with a bitter taste beyond the ending. The paean to monogamy in the song that gives the film its title, with Alfred cataloguing his former lovers and claiming they are all subsumed in his "love parade" of a queen, is charming but hard to swallow, despite Chevalier's most earnest and graceful effort to sell the concept to his newly beloved Louise as he tries to convince her and us that he now intends to be entirely faithful.

MacDonald has considerable appeal as a lovely, womanly, supremely dignified leading lady in these films. Lubitsch, who was reportedly smitten with her, also takes every possible occasion to display her lush figure in underwear, emphasizing the saucier side of her personality. These winning attributes of the female star go some way in helping us suspend our disbelief over whether her dubious romance with Alfred in *The Love Parade* can succeed. The queen's initially imperious manner, which includes wearing a military uniform, has already been delightfully undercut by the director showing her eagerly reading through a dossier of Alfred's scandalous conquests while smoking up a storm and briefly ducking out in the middle to surreptitiously powder her nose. MacDonald's light-operatic singing voice is another matter of taste for today's audiences, but if one enjoys her delicate vocal talents, their tones of maturity, sophistication, warmth, and affection help Lubitsch convince us that she can overlook the tendency of her favored male in *The Love Parade* to wander so egregiously. But MacDonald's Sonia in *The Merry Widow* has a more realistically difficult time dealing with the rampantly promiscuous nature of her mate, which helps make that later work a considerably richer and more complex film emotionally. Danilo's philandering is repellent to the widow he has been delegated to seduce. Sonia struggles with her love for him despite his errant character while he is conflicted because his growing romantic attraction to her can only survive if he is willing to surrender his independence and become monogamous.

The comparative parity between the romantic couple in *Monte Carlo* is an exception to this problem because MacDonald's countess and Buchanan's count have little trouble once his posing as a hairdresser is exposed, and they accept each other as partners, partly because they are both aristocrats, even if she remains impecunious, and because he seems to have an unlimited supply of ready cash to support them. But *Monte Carlo* also falls into the "status quo" situation common to marriage in that period, making it workable only because the husband has the dominant financial power. That neither partner seems to object to that imbalance is a symptom of the social mores and, given the artificiality of the genre, the relationship is not especially objectionable to the audience today, except for an uneasiness that these characters are not well suited sexually. And yet a relatively unerotic marriage between the count and countess could well be a pragmatic success in reconciling that period's marital conventions.

If Lubitsch and his writers in the musicals sometimes become boxed in by genre expectations, censorship strictures, and the need to work out happy endings to potentially bleak or even tragic situations, they try to meet that need by using their best tools: irony, reversals of narrative expectations, and other ways of winking at the audience. They also benefit from the complexities of the character relationships. The films work through many variations, both amusing and piquant, on these themes of power imbalance between the sexes and on the fraught subject of class differences between men and women, including monarchs and subjects who happen to be their spouses. So in criticizing the endings to some extent, we should not overlook the many ways in which these films use the very problems they raise to make trenchant satirical and emotional comments; the uneasiness of the endings is part of the price they pay for their ambition. Rather than merely being cynical in supplying happy endings, Lubitsch, to his credit, often tries to encompass both modes of storytelling within a single film while trying to balance what the audience wants (a necessary component in his survival as a popular artist) with the deeper feelings he wants us to experience.

For example, when Colbert's Franzi in *The Smiling Lieutenant* realizes that she cannot overcome the social barriers involved in being a mistress to the husband of a princess, it is not because a woman did not have the option in such a society to remain a mistress. It is because Franzi is a romantic who wants to have Niki to herself rather than share him with his wife. This is her choice and one that speaks well of her. After a mutual crying session with Anna over Niki, Franzi decides to take the dowdy, old-fashioned, but essentially attractive young princess in hand and educate her about how to be sexually appealing to her husband. Franzi surrenders her position as mistress while doing a generous deed for both husband and wife. The scenes of Franzi working the transformation are delightful despite, and partly because of, their underlying poignancy. "Let me see your underwear," she tells Anna before they share a delicious piano duet, "Jazz Up Your Lingerie." The two women, playing and singing together in an unbroken two-shot, discover a joyous female camaraderie (ironically, since the two actresses reportedly did not get along on the set). Then Anna, in a series of dissolves, silently changes her hairstyle and wardrobe to become a slinky modern jazz baby, much to the eventual surprise of her husband. At the climax of that process, Anna is shown striking a sultry pose in a short negligee in a shadowy composition by cinematography George J. Folsey that shows off her figure in a teasing peek-aboo fashion. Franzi and Anna share a tender sisterly embrace as Franzi is about to leave: Franzi says to the newly sexy Anna, "Be a good girl," and Anna laughingly replies, "I won't!" The long shot of Franzi as she slowly walks out of the story through the palace hall, gallantly waving goodbye to Anna without looking back, has tragic overtones of self-sacrifice and lost love that linger in the mind after the film ends "happily."

Some viewers criticize *The Smiling Lieutenant* for supposedly being conventionally moralistic by banishing Franzi. Sarris, usually a great admirer of Lubitsch, makes that criticism in his 1972 essay on the director, perhaps somewhat defensively since it was a time when male film critics were still struggling to come to terms with the women's movement. Sarris writes that *The Smiling Lieutenant* is

> gravely flawed by the contradiction between the director's exquisitely flavorsome treatment of Claudette Colbert's *demimondaine* and the puritanical resolution of the plot to allow Miriam Hopkins's prissy princess to come out on top for the sake of the presumably sacred marriage contract. Indeed, the Colbert character must even contribute to her own romantic downfall by advising her rival how to snare the Smiling but straying Lieutenant (Maurice Chevalier) with a song about sexy underwear, as if the elective affinities were merely consumer goods and textbook tactics.

But by having Franzi say to Anna at the end, "Girls who start with breakfast don't usually stay for supper," the film is sadly playing off the words she said to Niki the first night they met, when she objected to his trying to seduce her prematurely. Franzi is simply stating a fact of life in her society. Lubitsch is not being puritanical but realistic. He does emotional and dramatic justice to the material by allowing us to have equal sympathy for the two equally alluring women in the film (as he will do in *Trouble in Paradise*) and by making clear that Franzi's surrender to convention is not what she would choose if she could see another alternative she would find emotionally viable. The somewhat overwrought comical tag of Niki emerging from the marital bedchamber to exult directly to the camera about the joys of fidelity does seem forced, even if it is preceded by another deliciously Lubitschean scene of innuendo. Anna has pretended to insist that she and the suddenly excited Niki play checkers instead of make love (her pointed reminder of how she had to play checkers with her father when Niki rejected her on their wedding night). But Niki tosses the checkerboard onto the bed, and in a saucy two-shot, they give each other a silent look of love and lust. Lubitsch's camera tracks slowly toward the bed, taking the place of the characters, as it moves with sensual suggestion. But while it may seem implausible that Niki could so easily forget Franzi, we do not. Lubitsch tries to compensate by having Anna reveal such an appealing side to her personality, even if that cannot fully satisfy the viewer in this bittersweet finale, a sign of Lubitsch's irreconcilable and unconventional honesty within a highly artificial genre.

Earlier in the film, Niki's rejection of Anna was so harshly expressed that the audience was made to become uncomfortable with how unfairly she was being treated by her husband. His excuse is that he has been tricked into the marriage—his smile at Franzi during a royal parade was misinterpreted by Anna as smiling at her, and she forced her father, the king, to enlist the support of Emperor Franz Josef in forcing Niki to marry her. The painful scenes of Niki's sexual rejection of Anna after their wedding draw the film closer to tragedy and away from comedy, which is not a flaw in the film but a sign of its ambition, even if such realistically mixed-up emotions go uneasily with the genre. This is similar to the way *The Love Parade*, after the uproarious opening sequences, darkens in tone when Alfred succumbs to the humiliations of marriage to a queen. Lubitsch does his best to wring some good jokes from the situation, such as having the minister say at the wedding, "I pronounce you wife and man." The viewer is invited to note the irony of a man's discomfort over the kind of subjugation that women then were supposed to take for granted, but as the marriage drags on, Alfred's moping becomes less and less amusing, and Lubitsch has to contrive an elaborate pact between the couple to barely pull off a satisfying finale.

The ending of *The Merry Widow* requires even more elaborate contrivances to unite the former Don Juan with the widow, who has apparently managed to tame him. When the civil and religious authorities connive to marry them in jail, cynically collaborating for the financial benefit of Marshovia, the ironies are too heavy-handed to be as amusing as Lubitsch intends. As a trapdoor turns to provide the incarcerated couple with champagne glasses and rings, with a band playing "The Merry Widow Waltz" in the corridor outside, we are literally shown the plot mechanics turning to enable the story to cobble together a happy ending. Lubitsch is trying to have it both ways by mocking social institutions while gratifying his audience's expectations for an upbeat finale, but in doing so in such a blatant fashion, he seems to be condescending to the audience, something he rarely does elsewhere.

Nevertheless, the ability to play with the conventions of a genre, enabling us to examine and experience their deeper levels, is usually one of Lubitsch's greatest artistic strengths. He pulls it off to some extent in the poignant resolution of *The Smiling Lieutenant*. And the emotional complexity of *The Merry Widow*'s long sequence in the private room at Maxim's between Sonia and Danilo, bringing him to a deeper understanding of what love means, shows Lubitsch at his finest, taking a farcical sexual situation and turning it inside out to examine its morality. The haunting sequence lingers in our memory despite the film's unsatisfactory ending.

Lubitsch took many risks in critically examining the relations between men and women in such a lighthearted genre and at a time when few viewers were questioning gender power imbalances. Looking at these films purely from a modern perspective can skew our understanding of how clever and indeed subversive much of their satire actually was and still is. That these musicals play so well today, despite our occasional misgivings about some sexist elements and some indulgence in the long-discredited sexual double standard, is a tribute to their unusual levels of sophistication, their visual and verbal wit, the verve and charm of the performers, and the way the master director blends all these elements with such brilliance and gusto. His films celebrate unconventional women and forms of gender-bending and sexual freedom that were far ahead of their time. And his treatment of women was already seen as unusual from the viewpoint of his time. Paramount pointed out in a 1938 press release, "The women in his pictures always are smart; he's never yet used a dumb one in any cast of his."

WHEN THE BUTTER WAS ON THE TOAST

Somewhat sadly, despite his later achievements, the 1929–1934 musicals along with the early-thirties romantic comedies *Trouble in Paradise* and *Design for Living* are the last hurrah for the bawdiest Lubitsch. Aside from a few lapses into overly blatant jabs in the ribs, Lubitsch creatively revels in the myriad joys of innuendo in those films, offering some of his most amusing plays on sexual libertinism. The kind of flamboyant sexual carrying-on showcased in *The Merry Widow* is in a direct line of stylistic succession from Lubitsch's German silents such as *I Don't Want to Be a Man*, *The Oyster Princess*, *Madame DuBarry*, and *The Wildcat*. Although the Lubitsch Touch became more refined after he went to Hollywood, his subtler stylistic elements were not thrown out the window willy-nilly when sound arrived. The coming of sound did encourage, occasionally, a far more brazen approach to sexual innuendo. But in many ways, the addition of sound, while giving him more license, also gave Lubitsch a wider range of options for suggestive cleverness without necessarily having to be overtly lewd.

The all-girl band in *The Smiling Lieutenant* bills itself as the Viennese Swallows. Since it takes a moment of thought to register the audacity of that joke, it is amusing rather than simply lewd. There are many varying levels of interplay between overtness and covertness in that delightfully sexy film. The initial exchange between Niki and Franzi when he takes her to his apartment is frankly adult while still partaking, mostly, of the director's trademark obliqueness. On the way there, the incipient couple discuss the joys of playing their "duet" together in obviously suggestive terms ("I play the *piano*," Chevalier says with a leer), but when they get down to the actual playing, it is more romantic and tender than blatantly physical.

The film turns more explicit when they kiss after the duet and Niki asks Franzi if she wants to see him again. Attracted but trying not to be too easy, Franzi suggests dinner the following evening. He replies that he cannot wait twenty-four hours—"I'm so *hungry*"—and suggests they skip right to breakfast. She replies, somewhat hesitantly and touchingly, "First tea—and then dinner—and maybe . . . maybe breakfast." Although having him announce "I'm so *hungry*" lacks even the verbal wit of the Viennese Swallows, their banter about food and drink gradually becomes more in tune with the more cleverly oblique Lubitschean style, leading to the glorious "Breakfast Time" song, one of the highlights of his body of work.

There is no racier song in the cinema than that astonishing, delectable song (music by Oscar Straus, lyrics by Clifford Grey), presented in an unbroken two-shot. Chevalier and Colbert exchange double entendres over breakfast following their (unseen) first night of lovemaking. As Billy Wilder put it, "The butter was on the toast and not the ass" as they eye each other with charming affection. Chevalier sings, "You put kisses in the coffee, such temptation in the tea . . . You put 'It' in every omelet . . . You put passion in the prunes," and Colbert matches him, with such colorfully suggestive remarks as "I find romance each sweet entrancing moment, every time you touch the spoons" and her pièce de résistance in this menu of lasciviousness, "I'm *gone* when you invade the marmalade!" When the couple is finally about to kiss, Lubitsch discreetly fades out; he has already told us everything we need to know.

Bawdy exchanges such as these are what audiences today relish about pre-Code films, but though adult sexual banter on the screen was soon forced to become less explicit (one reason *The Smiling Lieutenant* vanished for many years), Lubitsch was so supple in his style that he could function just as well whether allowed to be frankly bawdy or under stricter censorship. When the Studio Relations Committee, the arm of the MPPDA in charge of policing film content in the pre-Code early 1930s, was discussing Lubitsch's suggestive treatment of sexuality in *Trouble in Paradise*, it recognized that his unique style would enable him to circumvent most such problems. The SRC's Jason S. Joy wrote to Paramount, "Of course we realize the light Lubitsch touch is rather the all-governing factor insofar as domestic censorship is concerned." That is a key admission and insight in explaining Lubitsch's ability to circumvent Hollywood censorship. The respect the censors and the studios had for his genius and for his ability to play the game (and outwit them) was the reason he got away with as much as he did. The trick for him and other directors in succeeding with sexual humor in that system, and even under the much stricter PCA from 1934 onward, was always to keep it amusing: it is not crude if it is witty. But the changing marketplace of the Depression era and the strict enforcement of the Code were soon to bring about major strategic shifts in Lubitsch's career and in his characteristic approach to filmmaking.

When the pre-Code Lubitsch was allowed to be bawdy through innuendo, his special comic style was in its full flower. There is no more brilliant Lubitsch Touch than the famous one in *The Merry Widow* conveying how old King Achmed discovers that his young queen has been cheating on him with Count Danilo by realizing that he is buckling on the wrong sword belt. But Lubitsch, characteristically, is not content to leave it at that; he extends the gag to deal lightly with the emotional implications of this unorthodox triangle. The next Lubitschean twist is that under normal circumstances, this would merely be the king's unpleasant discovery of his wife's infidelity, but in this situation, it is a matter of diplomacy to be dealt with on a practical basis by the three parties involved. The further comic implication is that the elderly king knows he has to do *something* to keep his wife satisfied as long as the outward proprieties are observed. So the three conspire to cover up the problem by "pretend[ing] to be social," murmuring false pleasantries to fool anyone in the royal court who might overhear them. This is the delightful kind of Lubitsch topper Wilder celebrated as the "superjoke." Wilder used this very sequence to explain the nature of the Lubitsch Touch to American Film Institute students. Such gleefully bawdy moments, which manage to circumvent the expected outrage demanded by conventional moralists, are not only as hilarious as anything in Lubitsch but also as clever, subtle, and flattering to the audience's intelligence as anything in his most evanescent silent work.

Still, the license Lubitsch and other filmmakers were given to be more explicit about sexual matters with the coming of sound was something of a mixed bag. Sometimes, as noted above, the double entendres in these pre-Code musicals are not even double entendres but blatant expressions of sexuality of a kind that the extremely subtle late-silent Lubitsch films, notably *The Marriage Circle* and *Lady Windermere's Fan,* had tended to avoid. The early Lubitsch films in Germany, it should be recalled, often indulge in broad, crude humor that can, nevertheless, be refreshingly raucous—and is elevated to art in such delightfully orchestrated sex farces as *Kohlhiesel's Daughters* and *The Oyster Princess*—but is largely devoid of the subtlety of expression he gradually developed in his Hollywood silent comedies and dramas. Nevertheless, getting around American censorship constraints, as writers and directors were increasingly forced to do after 1934, made them be more creative, so it actually had some beneficial effects on their work. By the time of *Trouble in Paradise* in 1932, Lubitsch had fully and triumphantly established his style, making a film as subtle and risqué as anything he had accomplished in the silent era. One reason that film seems the epitome of his style is that it keeps such a perfect balance between outright sexual statement and innuendo. His experience making musicals for the three previous years seems to have been a major factor in helping him hone the style and cinematic language he needed to strike such a balance in another genre.

John Ford told Peter Bogdanovich that talking pictures were "much easier to make than silent pictures. I mean, silent pictures were hard work. . . . [It was] very difficult to get a point over. You had to move the camera around so much." Of all directors, Lubitsch was best able to disguise how hard he worked to get his most subtle points over, whether in silents or in sound. His innuendo in silent pictures works so well partly because he makes it so easy for the audience to read. He finds ways of speaking the unspeakable in those silent films, of "getting a point over" by making characters' motives visible without the need for dialogue or for many intertitles. Avoiding overt verbalization of story points is one of his means of cleverly getting around the strictures of censorship in the best of his talking pictures as well. That, in turn, is a major part of the appeal of his humor and of what made critics and audiences recognize and hail his rare degree of artistry.

When the unspeakable can be spoken, more or less, and even with witty obliqueness in dialogue or lyrics, there always remains the danger that it can lose some of its appeal to the intelligence of the audience, the quality that makes Lubitsch, at his best, so special. The intricate comic business in *The Marriage Circle*, of the wife trying to prevent what she thinks is her husband's roving eye by manipulating the place cards before their formal dinner party only to have her maneuvers backfire because she has suspected the wrong woman, is less amusing when repeated in *One Hour with You* since nuances that had been purely visual in the silent version are spelled out with dialogue. And we can see the deleterious effects of the coming of sound in the off-putting introduction to Chevalier at his smarmiest in *The Smiling Lieutenant*. Wearing his pajamas and a cocked, shiny military cap, rolling his eyes and licking his incongruously rouged lips, even sticking his thumb in his mouth to blow it like . . . a trumpet, Lieutenant Niki boisterously croons, "Toujours l'Amour in the Army." He has just dismissed his sexual conquest for the night, and this is his postcoital song of rampant male boastfulness: "We give the girls a rat-a-tat-ta-ta when we go out campaigning . . . / We're the boudoir brigadiers," and so on.

This number is more grotesque than amusing, a display of male chauvinism at its most flagrantly self-regarding. It is hard to find any irony or wit in Niki's crudely raunchy business and warbling, and it takes a while for the character to win us back. But Lubitsch's musicals far more often find genuinely clever ways of dealing with sexual matters. When they do, they are exhilarating in their sexual candor in joyful ways that would soon become more difficult to express with the strict enforcement of the Code. Even though *One Hour with You* is markedly inferior to *The Marriage Circle*, with its sexual bluntness and relative simplistic characterizations, it can be argued that an intricately expressive Chevalier song such as "Oh, That Mitzi!" is as witty a way of conveying Dr. Bertier's conflict between marital fidelity and his temptation to stray as the innuendo in the silent version. The song's very directness—with the doctor addressing the audience as confidants, delivering the song looking straight into the camera ("I love Claudette; I haven't weakened yet, / But oh, that Mitzi!")—serves as an example of how filmmakers could express themselves more simply and efficiently with the coming of sound. But Chevalier's singing soliloquy about his moral conflict achieves genuine wit because of the brilliance of the lyrics (by Leo Robin) and the actor's droll panache in putting them over to a bouncy tune by Oscar Straus: "To stay—or go—I really can't decide, / But this I know, we can't all three be satisfied." The static nature of the unbroken take here is effective because it lets the camera serve as a neutral observer for Dr. Bertier's unsuccessful wrestling with his conscience. Underneath the playful surface of the song, there is genuine feeling, the kind of emotional conflict that brings out the best in Lubitsch.

If, when we think of Lubitsch, it is often the risqué early-thirties musicals and the equally racy *Trouble in Paradise* that come to mind, that is partly because his style had to be modified so drastically after *The Merry Widow*. Besides turning away from the lavishly opulent settings and camerawork of those musicals when the Depression era made audiences more prone to identify with proletarian characters and everyday situations, Lubitsch's post-1934 style largely abandoned the intricate, almost giddy stylistic flourishes that are most pronounced in his musicals and *Trouble in Paradise*. Lubitsch's style eventually took a 180-degree turn away from visual gags and innuendo into the "invisible" camerawork that prevailed in classical Hollywood. Although social and commercial factors influenced that development in his career, perhaps he would have had to take a new turn in any case after having reached such heights of suggestive stylization. The pre-Code *Trouble in Paradise* stands as the most elaborately oblique film of his career, the quintessence of the Lubitschean form of cinematic storytelling. Late in life, Lubitsch wrote, "As for pure style I think I have done nothing better or as good as *Trouble in Paradise*."

6.1 Miriam Hopkins and Herbert Marshall as thieves getting romantically involved in Lubitsch's masterpiece, *Trouble in Paradise* (1932). *(Paramount/From the collections of the Margaret Herrick Library, Academy of Motion Picture Arts and Sciences.)*

6

"IN TIMES LIKE THESE . . ."

Ah, yes, I remember it well—the first time I saw a Lubitsch film. It was during the late 1960s, in the early days of my growing absorption in film, when I watched a 16 mm print of *Trouble in Paradise* on the University of Wisconsin campus in Madison. I remember that after watching Lubitsch's 1932 romantic comedy, in pure rapture as it zipped along with breathtaking wit and verve for eighty-three minutes, I thought, "I've just seen this guy's masterpiece."

The reason for my immediate reaction—which has been borne out by time—was that I realized, "Nothing could ever be more perfect." At least no romantic comedy could ever hope to surpass the grace, elegance, charm, wit, intricacy, and audacity of this triangular love story involving a romantically involved pair of jewel thieves, Gaston Monescu and Lily (Herbert Marshall and Miriam Hopkins), and a wealthy Parisian businesswoman, Mariette Colet (Kay Francis), to whom Gaston confesses, "I came here to rob you, but unfortunately I fell in love with you." Just as Lubitsch more or less invented the musical, he deserves credit for shaping the emerging form of the romantic comedy genre with this gemlike piece of work, which remains the summit of the form all these years later. I was astonished above all at his ability to make us care equally for the two women, thus complicating our emotional responses beyond any conventional morality, while somehow managing to pull off an entirely satisfying and bittersweet resolution. And I was awed by the sheer stylishness of this intimate spectacle, the way the director moves his human chess pieces around the glowing art deco sets with such ease and fluidity and yet keeps his people so gloriously, lusciously alive.

Trouble in Paradise tells its story with so many brilliant stylistic devices, including a nonstop parade of memorable Lubitsch Touches, so many surprising moments of suggestive obliqueness, and so many ingenious narrative twists, that it would take a monograph to catalogue them all. Among the innumerable sly ellipses that help make this film so supremely Lubitschean is not showing the opera itself during the key sequence of Gaston stealing Mariette's expensive purse at the opera house. We see the audience and the conductor but only hear bits of the opera; in a delicious touch, the pages of the conductor's sheet music turn rapidly as singers off camera segue directly from "I *love* you" to "I *hate* you." And it is not until the very end of that sequence, when the rest of the spectators are all gone, that we see Gaston exiting the men's room with his usual sangfroid. Before that, he is shown holding a pair of opera glasses before his eyes, studying his prey. In a wry point-of-view shot framed through the glasses, the camera moves from the purse up to Mariette's lovely face and then back down to the purse, giving us a direct identification with Gaston's thought processes and revealing what is most important to him at that moment.

Most remarkably, as Peter Bogdanovich explains in his 2003 introduction to the Criterion DVD edition,

> You never see anybody. Every other director would see her put it down and somebody grab it. You never see *anything* being stolen in the picture, and it's about thieves! You never see it, because he's much too sophisticated to [show] somebody actually *steal* it. . . . They used to refer to Lubitsch's editing as "invisible," because you don't know how he does it. . . . The first time you watch it, you're not really aware of how this is happening to you. You're taken into the hands of a master storyteller.

The film's economy and precision of style were breathtaking for me to contemplate as a first glimpse of Lubitsch's genius, and they remain just as impressive on each viewing of *Trouble in Paradise*. François Truffaut declared in his 1968 essay on Lubitsch, "If you said to me, 'I have just seen a Lubitsch in which there was one needless shot,' I'd call you a liar. His cinema is the opposite of the vague, the imprecise, the unformulated, the incommunicable. There's not a single shot just for decoration; nothing is included just because it looks good. From beginning to end, we are involved only in what's essential." That's what *Trouble in Paradise* conveyed to me then and what it still conveys: the essence of the man and his art. How did I recognize, on my first encounter with Lubitsch, that I had seen the consummate perfection, the epitome of his style? To paraphrase what Jacques Rivette once wrote of Howard Hawks, the evidence on the screen is the proof of Lubitsch's genius: you only have to watch *Trouble in Paradise* to know that it is a perfect film. Although now, fifty years later, when I have finally managed to see all the rest of the surviving Lubitsch works, forty-seven films that exist in whole or in part, I have not seen any that surpasses *Trouble in Paradise*.

COMMUNICATING THE UNSHOWABLE AND UNSPEAKABLE

What is "pure style" in the context of Lubitsch? It can only partially be explained by Hitchcock's phrase "pure Cinema," which he applied particularly to Lubitsch as a way of saying that Lubitsch, his fellow graduate of silent pictures, told stories more with the camera than with what Hitchcock called "pictures of people talking." Yet I have always believed that Hitchcock somewhat overemphasized his case for visual storytelling, because some of the most memorable and moving elements of his own films are scenes of people talking.

Just think of the haunting scene of Janet Leigh and Anthony Perkins sharing a quiet dinner in Norman Bates's office at the Bates Motel shortly before he kills her in *Psycho*. They "just" sit and talk, but the camera angles, the decor, the interplay between the actors, and the dialogue itself all form a unity of style. That style conveys a tentative human connection Norman craves yet cannot have and a generosity of spirit Leigh's Marion Crane offers him only to have him brutally attack her a few moments later because Norman cannot bear his sexual attraction to her and is compelled to punish and obliterate her for it. The talk scene is crucial to the overall meaning of the film; without it and the poignant sense of failed human connection it conveys, the shower murder, despite being the epitome of "pure Cinema," would be a stunt, a montage of brilliantly conceived and edited shots existing mostly in a vacuum.

Lubitschean cinema mostly lacks the violence of Hitchcock's worldview but shares the same acuity and intensity of character observation. Indeed, Lubitsch's films helped show Hitchcock how to express even the most unshowable things on-screen in suggestive ways that are all the more powerful for not making the action fully visible (the shower murder itself is an example because Hitchcock could not show full nudity or actual penetration of flesh by knife). For Lubitsch, "action" is mostly human interaction. Even when he made silent pictures, he spent much of the time showing people talking, and we fully understand, without much need for intertitles, what they are conveying to each other. When talkies came along, Lubitsch embraced them for offering endless new ways of showing people interacting with words as well as with gestures, looks, and body language. "Pure Cinema" or "pure style," then, for Lubitsch, can be as much a matter of the words that are spoken on-screen and how they are spoken as it is of pictures. Focusing our attention on people talking involves us in the intricacies of human relationships—the area in which Lubitsch most excels—rather than distracting us with stylistic flourishes. This is what Truffaut means when he insists, "Nothing [in Lubitsch] is included just because it looks good."

Though he uses the camera with rare expressiveness and often lets it tell the story in a silent or sound montage sequence, he is not in the business of simply showing off beautiful decor and costumes as centers of attraction or performing an innovative tour de force for its own sake with movement and montage à la Mamoulian. As much as Lubitsch has in common with some elements of Oscar Wilde, the director would not agree with the Wilde epigram "In all unimportant matters, style, not sincerity, is the essential. In all important matters, style, not sincerity, is the essential." Lubitsch would not distinguish between style and sincerity or indeed draw a sharp distinction between important and unimportant matters; nor should we in assessing his work. Wilde himself points out, "Those who see any difference between soul and body have neither. . . . It is only shallow people who do not judge by appearances."

Lubitsch's style in *Trouble in Paradise* is a direct outgrowth of his experimentation with the interplay of sound and pictures in musicals. It would not have been possible without that evolution. Although it is not a musical per se,

Trouble in Paradise represents the outgrowth of Lubitsch's immersion in that genre during the pivotal years when films were transformed by the coming of sound. He could not have achieved its level of "pure style" without having first formalized his own personal concerns within that new genre of musical filmmaking. *Trouble in Paradise* is romantic comedy set to music, with its blending of elaborate visual shorthand and exquisitely timed, rhythmically paced dialogue and musical accompaniment that ranges from wry and puckish to bittersweet. The film even introduces one of its major characters (Madame Colet) with a singing radio commercial. Crooned by Tyler Brooke (who had sung charmingly for Lubitsch in *Monte Carlo*), this delightful ditty about her Paris *parfumerie*, Colet et Cie., accompanies lustrous close-ups of beautiful women dabbing themselves with her fragrances and long shots of workers leaving her swanky factory (this gently satirical montage might be seen as Lubitsch inventing the form of the television commercial). *Trouble in Paradise* has a witty, multilayered musical accompaniment by W. Franke Harling, who is best known as the composer of "Beyond the Blue Horizon" from *Monte Carlo*. Harling's underscoring is unusually sophisticated for an early sound feature. Eschewing the crude overemphasis and frequent use of "Mickey Mouseing" (imitating action with music) that was more common in scoring during that formative period, Harling uses a variety of evocative motifs for the characters and situations, a method that would not be perfected by most film composers until later in the decade. He applies his musical commentary meaningfully yet lightly and often unobtrusively.

Harling helps make possible Lubitsch's adroit use of visual montages, also including Mariette going about her self-indulgent day with her servants, merchants, and suitors, a sequence soon echoed by one of Gaston briskly taking over every compartment of her life, implicitly including her sex life, as suggested in an unabashedly lewd shot of Mariette, in short shorts, bending upside down in a gymnasium exercise and coyly soliciting his approval. Lubitsch puts these elliptical sequences together with fast, sharp wipes and other editing devices that, along with the music, not only carry the narrative in a condensed manner but, in the process, offer droll commentary on the characters much as the song numbers/montages do in his musicals.

A carryover from the musicals is also evident in this film's strong comedic/dramatic emphasis on game playing. Not only are the two jewel thieves masquerading as aristocrats, and then as respectable white-collar working people, but the film's serious underpinnings emerge most movingly after Gaston and Mariette fall in love, when he is forced to drop the pretenses and choose between her and Lily. That situation is acted out toward the end in a sequence of game playing between them that gradually turns more candid. When Mariette pretends she does not know about Gaston's thievery, she is testing him to see whether he really intends to betray her and put his desire for money ahead of his desire for her, which, sadly, he does. Their game breaks down as the film finally shows its full emotional hand, with the couple facing this conflict in which sexual and romantic passions collide with monetary compulsions and the unresolved business of Gaston's continuing love for Lily. This virtually insoluble conflict, and the deft but bittersweet way in which it is resolved, is the true subject of *Trouble in Paradise*, the moral dilemma underlying a seemingly amoral tale about a couple of thieves getting away with their crimes in the pre-Code era. The story's dramatic turn, which resembles the direction in which Lubitsch would take the early frivolity in his 1934 *Merry Widow*, is resolved in a scene when the two would-be lovers reconcile themselves to the unpleasant facts. The gallantry with which they handle the situation, Mariette's in particular, makes *Trouble in Paradise* perhaps Lubitsch's most emotionally affecting film. Both here and in *The Merry Widow*, men who are toying with women's passions are forced to face the consequences of their deceptions and recognize their own deeper emotional natures.

The musicals' concentration on the romantic intrigues of aristocrats is inverted to some extent in *Trouble in Paradise*, in which the two jewel thieves are only masquerading (at first) as members of the upper class, a situation from which Lubitsch derives a great deal of delightful humor. The hilarious playacting between Gaston and Lily as pseudoaristocrats during their first dinner in the Venice hotel room comes to a head when they discover, to their mutual delight and ours, that they have been robbing each other of a watch, a wallet, a brooch, a purse, and most improbably, even her garter. Lubitsch is dealing with two members of the criminal class—Gaston proudly tells Mariette that he is a "self-made crook" after pretending to be "a member of the nouveau poor"—yet the director is still operating in the high-society milieu of the musicals, which gives the film some surprisingly socially conscious tensions. As the film frequently reminds us, there is a Depression right outside these fancy hotel, mansion, and perfume factory settings. "In times like these . . ." is a constant refrain in the dialogue, usually spoken ironically. The characters' incessant talk about money is the engine that drives the film, just as it drives them to desperate actions. And our initial impression of Madame Colet as a frivolous wealthy woman undergoes steady change as the film progresses, revealing her to be the most truly sympathetic and generous person in the story, a characteristically Lubitschean irony.

As we have seen, Lubitsch, contrary to the image presented by some of his critics, was not a complete stranger to political dimensions in his work before 1932. His historical spectacles deal with political upheaval, however obliquely, in relation to the times in which they were made, and he had made his commercially unsuccessful antiwar satire, *The Wildcat*, in Germany in the aftermath of the Great War. But *Trouble in Paradise* was a demarcation point in his career, marking an overt shift into a more socially aware context. The film was made at the nadir of the Great Depression, almost three years after the stock market had crashed. It was a time when one-quarter of the American public was unemployed, banks were failing daily, filmgoing was in a serious decline, and Lubitsch's home studio, Paramount, was in grave financial jeopardy, on the verge of going into receivership. These changing conditions compelled the director to make some significant shifts of emphasis in this and two of his other 1932 films, *The Man I Killed*, his film about a French soldier suffering guilt over his service in the Great War, and his segment in the compilation film about ordinary people becoming improbably rich during the Depression, *If I Had a Million* (that year's musical *One Hour with You* was an exception to this tendency in Lubitsch, remaining firmly set in an obliviously luxurious milieu). The more realistic social background that became increasingly foregrounded in Lubitsch's work by 1932 would help bring about a major evolution in his subject matter and style over the years to come.

"DOING THAT, WITHOUT DOING THAT"

Lubitsch's approach to social themes is different from that of any other director. As usual, he tends to address them with indirection, setting us up for light entertainment and gradually, in his roundabout manner, turning the story into something more substantial. The degree to which he revels in "pure style" is evident with a bawdy Lubitsch Touch in the very credit sequence of *Trouble in Paradise*, when the word "Paradise" dissolves in over a shot of a bed after "Trouble in . . ." This is followed by the famous touch in the opening scene that establishes Venice as the story's "romantic" location by showing a garbage man emptying a pail into a gondola and paddling off into the Venice night. This opening helps to establish *Trouble in Paradise* as a nonstop lesson in how to avoid clichés. The cliché was Lubitsch's *bête noire*, the hurdle he always pushed his writers to help him jump over en route to something astonishing. Samson Raphaelson explained the reasoning behind the canal gag and the creative process behind the Lubitsch Touch in general: "We wanted to introduce Venice. Just say that you're in Venice. Now, pictorially, the conventional way of saying that is to open on a long shot of Venice, medium shot of wherever you want to be, and close shot on the canal and the house, and then you go inside the house or hotel or whatever it is. That's a conventional way. Now, Lubitsch would sit and say, 'How do we do that, without doing that?'" Raphaelson explained how they decided to open on a house, and "you don't know where it is. It could be any European—or maybe even a Brooklyn—middle-class street. It's dawn. There are trash cans, garbage cans, in front of the house, and you hear the clatter of the cans, and along comes the garbage man." The writer described the way they gradually expand the viewer's worldview to take in the garbage gondola, and only then do "you see the whole glory of the Venice Grand Canal as the camera steps back."

Add the superjoke of having the gondolier singing "O sole mio" in his beautiful baritone voice, and as Raphaelson said,

> Well, that's a Lubitsch touch. That's how Lubitsch would bring you into Venice. . . . He worked for it, you see. We spent about—oh, maybe three days getting that opening shot. He wouldn't be content unless we got a brilliant opening shot. . . . [He would often say], "How do ve get into it? How do ve open? It gotta be brilliant!" . . . Now, other times, he started right away, he didn't want to get a brilliant opening shot. Here he felt he wanted it. He wanted to open with laughter and with style—and style, of course, is the essence of Lubitsch.

"How do we do that, without doing that?" is one of the best summations of Lubitsch's working method. In this instance, as in many other moments in his work, he reverses the conventional order of shots to put the establishing shot last in a sequence instead of first. He often does that, notably in his historical films, which are prone to withholding full views of the palace or the big street set or the film's other major element of production value or atmosphere until the director has first given us tighter, more intimate views of the setting or settings. There is a certain irony involved in this stylistic strategy; it deflates the importance of the fancy, expensive, grand locations in favor of closer views of the characters in all their human flaws, virtues, and idiosyncrasies. Showing Venice through the vantage point of a garbage gondolier is also Lubitsch's way of telling us, right at the start of *Trouble in Paradise*, that he is going to be mocking conventional views of romance, making us wallow a bit in the muck of life as it is really lived; a little later in the film, he puckishly cuts back to the garbage gondola in the midst of a love scene.

Perhaps the most extreme example of a Lubitschean stylistic tour de force, a way of "doing that, without doing that," is the clock sequence in *Trouble in Paradise*. Lubitsch conveys Gaston and Mariette's romantic evening entirely through dissolves to a series of different clocks, with changes in lighting and music to help convey the passing time and mood and offscreen dialogue laid over the clocks to convey the delicate drama of the situation. Here, perhaps, we could say that Lubitsch out-Mamoulians Mamoulian with his showiness, and yet this sequence is at the crux of the story, letting us ponder the growing romantic interplay between Gaston and Mariette, along with Lily's mounting jealousy, from an aesthetic distance, as if putting us in the minds of the three characters. The stylized presentation conveys the intricacy of Gaston's partly deceptive, partly sincere romancing of Mariette. Showing the scenes through clocks (however elegant they and the lighting are) emphasizes the detached, mechanical style of Gaston's wooing. But focusing obliquely on the essence of what is happening is also a means of being discreet and treating the offscreen situation with delicacy. As much as we watch and listen with admiration to the unique way in which Lubitsch conveys the romantic evening, the film keeps us focused on the tentative, ambiguous nature of the couple's growing emotional involvement through the words we hear and not primarily on the mechanisms of clocks, bells, and chimes.

Most subtly, the emphasis on time conveys a subliminal sense of the transience of this relationship, our realization that as time clicks inexorably on, the couple are doomed to part even though Mariette does not yet know it.

This theme of the evanescence of romance (which will be picked up again toward the end of the film) is as movingly conveyed here as it is throughout Max Ophüls's classic 1950 adaptation of Schnitzler's *La Ronde*, a film in which the characters compulsively ask each other, "Quelle heure est-il?" ("What time is it?"). Scene after scene in *Trouble in Paradise* unfolds with such ingenuity and freshness, as Truffaut pointed out, because Lubitsch "racked his brain" to enable us to participate in working out the plot, and he did so largely by avoiding the use of clichés in telling his story.

As an example, Truffaut cites the deliciously delayed series of scenes that convey, with mounting hilarity, the gradual process by which Edward Everett Horton's pompous, dense would-be playboy, François Filiba, finally remembers where it was he has previously met Gaston. Filiba and the equally clueless Major (Charlie Ruggles) form a running punch line in the film with their frustrated wooing of Mariette, who keeps this pair of eunuchs around in order to toy with them and perhaps to avoid hurting their feelings by banishing them from her life. So Filiba has other reasons for being angry at the suave gentleman who appears out of nowhere to act as Mariette's private secretary; as the woman who accompanies Filiba to Mariette's garden party drolly puts it, "*He* says he's her secretary. *She* says he's her secretary. Maybe I'm wrong—maybe he *is* her secretary." Filiba mutters to her in confusion and frustration, trying to recall where he might have met Gaston. He gives a series of befuddled takes and double takes at the party before he *almost* remembers. He angrily jams a cigarette into an ashtray shaped like a gondola (with the soundtrack reprising "O sole mio" as an instrumental). He looks as if he is about to see the light, but Lubitsch is not about to let the joke end this quickly; he milks Filiba's distress for more laughs in different scenes before topping it all with the superjoke.

After more dithering by Filiba, he remarks to party guests that Gaston is "Insignificant. He's a secretary, always *was* a secretary, always *will* be." The Major casually remarks, "Funny—the first time I saw him, I thought he was a doctor!" At this, Filiba jumps up, finally recalling how he was robbed and knocked over the head in a Venice hotel a year earlier by Gaston, who was masquerading as a doctor. And yet Filiba's thought process is not spelled out so prosaically. All he says is, "*Tonsils! Positively tonsils!*" The screenplay indicates, "(Major and Mariette think the man has gone insane)." As master screenwriters do, Raphaelson and Lubitsch have laid careful preparations for this series of gags that pays off late in the film. We viewers know that the film is harkening back to a tour-de-force sequence in which the prefect of the police and hotel manager and his staff excitedly confer (in Italian) about how the "doctor" came to examine Filiba's *"Tonsille!"*

Some time later, Gaston, who has just been hired by Mariette, meets the Major and tells him she is under too much strain to see him. The Major, mistaking his manner for the real thing, replies, "Just as you say, doctor." Lubitsch relies on the audience to piece together all these parts of the puzzle. The film is so subtle that it does not even show the actual robbery of Filiba in his hotel room, only its immediate aftermath, with Filiba keeling over twice, the shadowy Gaston escaping and stripping off his disguise, and two call girls whom Filiba had summoned to his suite angrily complaining about his failure to answer their knock on the door. Even though they speak entirely in Italian, we get the drift of what is happening with the women whom Filiba later tells the police were his "two—uh—two business associates." When Lily confronts Gaston toward the end of the film, saying, "Come on—be brilliant! Talk yourself out of it—bluff yourself in!" we can't help but think of Lubitsch constantly giving himself the same challenge and triumphantly meeting it in every scene.

PERFECTION

"Trifles make perfection," said Michelangelo, "and perfection is no trifle." Lubitsch's singling out one of his own films for its pure style suggests that he felt he had achieved a distillation of his artistic methodology, an ultimate precision that his other films, for all their qualities, do not quite achieve. Previous Lubitsch films to which the word "perfect" can fairly be applied—such as *The Oyster Princess*, *The Marriage Circle*, and *Lady Windermere's Fan*—contain many memorable and audaciously conceived sequences and litanies of breathtaking touches. They are fully satisfying achievements in their genres or in their clever combinations of genre elements. But Lubitsch almost always works at such a level of accomplishment that even when his films are uneven or flawed, they are filled with so many dazzling moments and scenes that the flaws often seem relatively minor.

Following the example of his theatrical mentor Max Reinhardt, Lubitsch, by the time of *Trouble in Paradise*, had perfected a style that brought all his dramatic and pictorial devices into play at the same time. The truism that style equals content and is not some kind of separate entity applies to Lubitsch at his most elaborately stylized as much it does to the work of any other artist. And yet in trying to define the perfection of his style in *Trouble in Paradise*, by analyzing gags, touches, sequences, or the entire flawless construction of the story, there is some other quality that remains elusive. This is the essence of what film historian James Naremore calls the "ineffable" nature of Lubitsch. Welles said something similar to Bogdanovich: "I think more highly of Lubitsch as the years go by, all the time. . . . There was a sort of spirit that pervaded his films that you can't analyze." Welles did not comment on specific Lubitsch films that impressed him, but Patrick McGilligan's biography *Young Orson* reports that one of the films Welles watched on a visit to New York in 1932, when he was about seventeen, was *Trouble in Paradise*. Welles then spent a couple of years vainly pursuing Raphaelson, who was also a playwright, for help in trying to launch his own career in the theater.

While it is true that Lubitsch's work is difficult to analyze, if I were to accept the argument that it *cannot* be analyzed, I would not be writing this book. Truffaut does not seem to agree with Welles's head-shaking wonderment, writing instead that Lubitsch's "cinema is the opposite of the vague, the imprecise, the unformulated, the incommunicable." So what exactly is it that Lubitsch communicates that no one else can, and how does he communicate it in this, the most perfect of his films? What precisely is the substance that expresses itself lucidly in his ineffable style?

Perhaps the difficulty comes with any attempt to reduce Lubitsch's meaning to words. As with any good film, the screenplay is only a blueprint, a guideline. This is true even though Raphaelson's scripts were so precisely written and detailed, composed with Lubitsch's constant input, and followed with a fidelity rare in the film industry. But if the films are in a sense "directed on paper" and can be analyzed on paper, in a deeper sense the process of reduction to words before or after shooting omits something crucial, something evanescent that takes place in the moment of filming. A critic can suggest by description and analysis what Lubitsch is conveying, but the essence is a matter of nuance and implication. In keeping with his characteristic love of ellipsis, some of the deepest meanings are between the lines or even between the scenes.

A good example is one of the funniest and yet most touching moments in *Trouble in Paradise*. It comes when Gaston, unmasked as a thief, is preparing to leave Mariette, despite his growing love for her and her loving trust in him. He calls a flower shop and, in his most dulcet tones of regret, orders five dozen red roses to be sent to Madame Colet: "And attach a card: 'In memory of the late M'sieu Laval.' [That is the alias he gave her.] Tomorrow morning—ten o'clock." There is a pause as he listens and says, "What? Oh— charge it to Madame Colet." According to Raphaelson, those last two lines were added on the set during the shooting; he does not specify whether Lubitsch himself added them. They make all the difference. They transform what would otherwise have been a conventionally sentimental scene into something more complex and Lubitschean. A simple farewell gesture would not be entirely true to Gaston's character. We laugh at his cynicism, but in so doing, we realize that it does not negate his gesture of sending the roses or the message on the card; it intensifies the emotion by defining it more sharply. Mariette is a rich woman, after all, and this is not a matter of money; who pays for the roses does not change the sentiment. But the touch also emphasizes that what separates them is partly their financial situations. This fine balance between sentiment and cynicism goes to the essence of Lubitsch and his worldview. This is what Sarris calls the "counterpoint between sadness and gaiety that represents the Lubitsch touch."

Another moment, related in tone, that helps define the Lubitschean worldview, comes early in the film when Gaston, returning the expensive purse he has stolen so he can collect the reward from the unsuspecting Mariette, makes an inventory of its contents. Noting that he has read a love letter to her from the Major, Gaston offers "one suggestion, Madame. *Not* the Major. I don't mind his grammatical mistakes. I'll overlook his bad punctuation. But the letter has no mystery—no bouquet . . ." He murmurs the words "no mystery—no bouquet" while leaning close to her for the first time and in a wistful, loving tone. This is unmistakably the voice of Lubitsch, whose films all have that "mystery," that "bouquet," a quality that, as much as anything, characterizes his Touch. And though we can perceive the fragrance of a bouquet, it is an evanescence, not something tangible. Yet we perceive it with our senses. It communicates, it can be analyzed, but it remains somewhat mysterious, somewhat ineffable. The Touch can be conveyed in a gesture, a composition, an ellipsis, or an intonation.

The wide variety of actors, whether of great or limited ability, who appear in Lubitsch films almost always do so to their best advantage. He manages to bring out qualities in them that may be latent and are sometimes apparent only when they work for him. When I first saw Kay Francis in *Trouble in Paradise*, I found her so soignée and delectable that I began seeking out more of her films. But I realized, to my dismay, that she is usually flat, dull, and obvious in her period glamour, lacking the deftness, sparkle, and sophistication of her Madame Colet. Miriam Hopkins, on whom Lubitsch had an unrequited crush, is as delightful in *The Smiling Lieutenant* and *Design for Living* as she is in *Trouble in Paradise*. But over time, this consummate Lubitsch leading lady, who combines delicate whimsy with an admirably fierce strength of character, became a rather hard-edged performer, the veneer of southern-magnolia charm she displays in his films gradually wilting and turning unpleasantly into steel. In 1933, at the time he was making *Design for Living*, Lubitsch offered a shrewd analysis of Hopkins's contradictory personality, suggesting both his attraction for her and the frustrations she caused him: "Her type is an irresistible siren. Her almost baby face gives no hint of the tigerish possibilities of her emotions. If she cared enough, she could be all things to a man, a wife, companion, and mistress, but Miriam will seldom care enough. She is a self-sufficient person in many ways, loving her books, loving her solitude." *Photoplay* reporter May Allison Quirk, who did this interview discussing Lubitsch's views of his actresses, observed, "He knows more about feminine psychology than any man I have ever met. That, in itself, is disconcerting."

British actor Herbert Marshall, a theater veteran whose speaking voice is always as elegantly musical as it is in *Trouble in Paradise*, has a certain stiffness that Lubitsch expertly uses to help convey the impeccable manners and sangfroid of Gaston's phony aristocratic persona. Lubitsch even makes a wry, cheeky in-joke of Marshall's literal woodenness: the actor had an artificial leg from his service in World War I, which is probably why the director keeps throwing in shots of Gaston racing nimbly up and down a curved staircase, scenes played by a smoothly integrated double. Kidding aside, it was a rare tribute to Marshall's consummate suavity in *Trouble in Paradise* that Lubitsch, who usually acted out all the parts for his players, admitted that he did not have to do so in this actor's case. *Variety* reported in October 1932, "Following the preview of his latest picture *Trouble in Paradise*, Ernst Lubitsch told friends that he deserved no credit for the performance of Herbert Marshall, from legit [the stage], who drew a rave from everyone present. Lubitsch said that Marshall was the one actor in his experience who did not need direction. Nine times out of ten direction would probably spoil Marshall's work, stated Lubitsch."

FREUNDSCHAFT

The emphasis on style in discussion of *Trouble in Paradise* by Lubitsch and his admirers has tended to obscure the central achievement of his greatest film. That lies in its humanity, the degree of intense emotional involvement we come to have with the people involved in the filmmaker's favorite situation, a three-way love relationship.

Lubitsch's films play endless variations on triangles and other complicated forms of sexual and romantic intrigue. The precarious relationships Gaston maintains with Lily and Mariette are among the subtlest, most nuanced in the director's body of work. Lily's fraught relationship with Mariette as both employee and romantic rival is more broadly comical yet similarly intricate in its blend of role-playing and genuine emotion. Because the film is so stylized, the characters at first may seem like marionettes the director is manipulating, with the winking complicity of the actors, to comment wryly on their interactions. That distancing effect, crucial to the film's comedic tone, sometimes gives it a semiparodistic feeling, such as in Gaston's playacting with Lily during their initial romantic dinner, which disorients the audience until they start leveling with each other about being professional thieves. That tongue-in-cheek approach gradually melts away as the emotional issues between Gaston and the women he loves come to the forefront. Gaston smoothly controls both women as he exploits Mariette and uses Lily as an accomplice, but only until the game becomes untenable. Then he must make his choice between them and, more important, win back the respect of each woman. Lily plays a critical role in provoking the final resolution of Gaston's relationship with Mariette, as well as her own relationship with him, in the film's most dazzling, brilliantly written and acted sequence.

For our heightened quality of involvement with these characters, we need to give a considerable share of the credit to screenwriter Samson Raphaelson. A solid case can be made for Raphaelson as the finest, most congenial, and most creatively enriching of Lubitsch's writers. Their collaboration spanned nine films from 1931 to 1947, including some of the director's

best-loved classics. In examining the crucial nature of Raphaelson's contribution to Lubitsch's work, we will be able to understand more clearly how
the director worked with writers and what he needed and drew from them.

Raphaelson, who always considered himself primarily a playwright, came
to Lubitsch's attention with the 1925 play on which *The Jazz Singer* was
based. Because Lubitsch wanted a strongly emotional approach to the adaptation of a grimly sentimental 1925 French play by Maurice Rostand, *L'homme
que j'ai tué* (*The Man I Killed*), he recruited Raphaelson, who had little experience in screenwriting but adored *The Love Parade*. Raphaelson and Ernest
Vajda wrote *The Man I Killed* (*Broken Lullaby*) in 1931 from an English adaptation by Reginald Berkeley, but the film was not released until the following year, following Raphaelson's more successful second collaboration with
Lubitsch on *The Smiling Lieutenant*. *Trouble in Paradise*, the high point of
their work together, came during only the second year of their collaboration.
They went on to make such other memorable films as *The Merry Widow*,
Angel, *The Shop Around the Corner*, and *Heaven Can Wait*.

Raphaelson has written at length about his working relationship with
Lubitsch in his insightful and witty essay "Freundschaft" (the German word
for "friendship"), first published in the *New Yorker* in 1981. But he leaves most
of the details of exactly how they collaborated mysterious, as he also tended
to do in interviews. He was not being coy but being true to the nature of collaboration in films. There are rare instances in the essay and in his interviews
in which he will note specific contributions by each of them. But it is often
hard, if not impossible, to determine exactly who did what in their writing
process, and that ultimately is an idle quest in such successful joint creative
endeavors.

As Raphaelson points out, Lubitsch "wrote some of my best lines, and I
supplied some typical Lubitsch touches. I did not keep score, and I never
came home from work with details lingering in my mind." But as Raphaelson said in his 1967 interview for Weinberg's book *The Lubitsch Touch*, Lubitsch
"thought like a writer" and had the greatest respect for his screenwriters.
Raphaelson said he wrote most of the dialogue, and yet Lubitsch "was better
able to write a line, if he had to, than any other director who ever existed."
Once, to Raphaelson's amazement, Lubitsch sent a car to bring him to location so he could approve the change of a single line of dialogue, a gesture the
writer appreciated both because it was unique to Lubitsch and because the

director understood how one change might affect something else in the script that he had overlooked. In the final analysis, said Raphaelson, "We wrote it together, that's all. You couldn't trace it. If the problem was, 'How do we get into this scene?,' whoever finally found it wasn't necessarily the author of it because he might not have found it if the other hadn't said two words before. . . . We had the most fabulous collaboration. Utterly. I don't know why I didn't realize I was in heaven."

It is commonplace for directors to claim they deserve writing credit on their films and for critics, under the influence of auteurism, to routinely assume the same whether it is true or not. But in the case of Lubitsch, there is no doubt that such is the case. Billy Wilder, who collaborated on the scripts of Lubitsch's *Bluebeard's Eighth Wife* (1938) and *Ninotchka* (1939), declared, "I think that all the pictures that he made should have his name as a collaborator, at least on the script. You don't just sit down and write, 'Lubitsch does this.' You come up with twenty suggestions, and he picks the one that makes a Lubitsch touch. . . . What he did was purify, and that was what made him a great writer." Wilder further declared, "If the truth were known, he was the best writer that ever lived. Most of the 'Lubitsch touches' came from him." According to Eyman's biography of Lubitsch, he liked to think of himself as a writer and would sit at the writers' table at the Paramount commissary. But after the silent period, Lubitsch almost never took screen credit as a writer, and he rarely tried to take credit away from his writers in interviews. Being known as a great director was enough. He was also smart enough to recognize that being discreet about his role in the writing process was the better part of valor. Howard Hawks, one of the important directors who acknowledged Lubitsch as a major influence, was seldom reticent about discussing his contributions to the scripts of his films. He told me, "I practically always work in a room with the writers." But his approach to screenwriting resembled Lubitsch's in one crucial way: when I asked Hawks, "Why do you so rarely take a writing credit on-screen?" he replied, "Because if I did, I couldn't get such good writers to work with me."

In 1937, while shooting *Bluebeard's Eighth Wife*, Lubitsch explained his method of working and the paramount importance that he placed on the writing process:

You give extraordinarily careful attention to the script. As you write the script, you cut the film, you build the sets, you light your players, you design their wardrobe, you set the tempo, you delineate the characters; all of this in your mind, of course. In writing a script, you are creating, inventing. I like to do it so thoroughly that when I finish the script, I breathe a sigh of relief. Creation is the most intense sort of work, the most satisfying. And for me it is virtually all done in the script. What remains is just the execution of an idea. . . . Friends frequently ask me about the "Lubitsch" touch. I don't know what the "Lubitsch" touch is. But whatever it is, I'm sure that it must be in the script.

Such a painstaking process of preparation was what enabled Lubitsch to edit his films quickly, within only a few days in the silent era, somewhat longer in the era of sound, but always with remarkable efficiency. Herbert Howe of *Photoplay*, after observing Lubitsch at work in Germany, wrote,

If Lubitsch is a fast stepper on the "set" he certainly is a shimmie [*sic*] dancer in the cutting room. You would imagine that he was mad at the film. He tears at it and until you almost think you hear him growl. . . . [*Die Flamme*] required about three days to cut and assemble. Any other director I've ever observed would take two weeks for an ordinary program feature. *The Loves of Pharaoh*, originally in ten or twelve reels, required less than a week. This faculty for rapid cutting must be attributed to a supernatural memory, one which carries the story so perfectly that lightning decisions are possible.

Since editing is, in effect, the final stage of the scriptwriting process, it is not surprising that Lubitsch remained in full control there too. Gottfried Reinhardt, Max's son, who worked with Lubitsch as an assistant director on *Design for Living* and later became a producer and director, recalled, "He really did everything himself. He even cut the film himself; he may have been the only director who did that. I never met any director who actually went into the cutting room with scissors and cut their own films but Lubitsch."

However much credit Lubitsch deserves for the writing of his films, and hence for the conception of all the elements in them, there is a noticeable distinction in the scripts Raphaelson wrote for Lubitsch. The best of their films together have an intricacy of structure and a depth of characterization that are rivaled in Lubitsch's work only by the screenplays of *The Marriage Circle* (by Paul Bern); *Lady Windermere's Fan* (Julien Josephson); *Design for Living* (Ben Hecht); *Ninotchka* (Charles Brackett, Wilder, and Walter Reisch); and *To Be or Not to Be* (Edwin Justus Mayer). Aside from *Ninotchka* and *To Be or Not to Be*, which are based on original stories by Melchior Lengyel, these other films have plays as their sources, as is also the case with all the films that Raphaelson wrote for Lubitsch. Lengyel, who also wrote the plays on which Lubitsch based *Forbidden Paradise* and *Angel*, said, "Writing for Lubitsch is just kibitzing."

Trouble in Paradise is based on a 1931 Hungarian play by László Aladar called *A Becsuletes Megtalalo* (*The Honest Finder*), with an adaptation by Grover Jones. The play, which Raphaelson said he did not read, was supposedly inspired by the exploits of a notorious Hungarian swindler and thief named Georges Manolescu. Regarded as something of an emblematic symbol for the corrupt aspects of the Weimar Republic, Manolescu wrote two autobiographies and helped write two silent films based on his exploits. He was also the inspiration for Thomas Mann's unfinished 1954 novel *Confessions of Felix Krull, Confidence Man: The Early Years*, based on a short story the author wrote in 1911. While *The Honest Finder* and other plays Lubitsch adapted for his films provided some of their basic structure, the director and his writers generally took a free approach to adaptation, using the situations mostly as springboards for their own invention, even (and most notoriously) in the cases of the much-transformed plays *Lady Windermere's Fan* and *Design for Living*.

Praising those screenwriters from the sound era for the delicate nuances of their work with Lubitsch should not be considered a slight on Hans Kräly, the director's other major screenwriter. Before their unhappy breakup for personal reasons, Kräly wrote most of Lubitsch's work in both Germany and Hollywood from 1915 through 1929. Those films are often virtuosic but tend to be more broadly sketched in tone and characterization than the later classics, which is not a flaw in Kräly's smart, boldly stylish, endlessly imaginative screenplays but makes them distinct from the more finely observed character portraits that Raphaelson provided in his collaboration with the director. Lubitsch, when given the new tool of sound, had evolved into a position of needing a writer from the theater who could help him with the process of analyzing people's behavior more three-dimensionally.

Raphaelson was a Chicago-educated New York native who had turned to playwriting after working in journalism and advertising. He admitted that he tended to look down on his film writing and take it for granted, even the scripts he wrote for Lubitsch. "I was terribly patronizing to Hollywood," he said in 1977. The irony that Raphaelson is now known and celebrated though his films was not lost on the writer, who lived until age eighty-nine and came to see the Lubitsch films recognized as classics while his plays were mostly forgotten. Raphaelson died in the same year (1983) that three of his Lubitsch scripts (*Trouble in Paradise*, *The Shop Around the Corner*, and *Heaven Can Wait*) were published with an appreciative introduction by *New Yorker* film reviewer Pauline Kael. Raphaelson's condescending attitude toward his Hollywood work—and even, to some extent, toward Lubitsch, whom he concedes he often took for granted despite his reluctant admiration for the director's genius—was partly a by-product of the times, when movies were undervalued by most of the critics and intelligentsia and plays and novels were regarded as real writing. With perhaps a note of self-criticism, Raphaelson admitted that every time they finished a script, he "rushed back to my 'real' life" in the theater. And he wondered in hindsight whether he was to blame: "How did [Lubitsch] take my obvious lack in movies?" Looking back over his time with Lubitsch, Raphaelson conceded, "What an emptiness it might have been if I hadn't met him."

The fate that worried Lubitsch—that his work would end up as "dust . . . in a tin can in a warehouse"—fortunately has not come true for much of his oeuvre, although for decades even *Trouble in Paradise* was hard to see. It was not approved for theatrical reissue in 1935 by the Production Code Administration because of the censorship regulations that had been tightened in 1934. Although some 16 mm prints eventually circulated for nontheatrical viewing (which is how I first saw it in the late 1960s) as well as archival 35 mm prints, Lubitsch's masterpiece was never released on VHS. It only resurfaced for home viewing on laserdisc in 1997, in a Criterion set called *The Lubitsch Touch*, and on DVD in 2003. So it took a while to disprove what Raphaelson worried about while writing *Trouble in Paradise*: "Who's going to remember a movie?" Film historian Molly Haskell, discussing the censorship problems that Lubitsch worked so hard to circumvent, believes that the reputation of this great film has suffered because certain segments of the motion picture audience still resist the sexual frankness of his films. "The Production Code didn't come out of nowhere," she observed in 2010. "It represented the thinking of most people in this country who were uneasy with it. It's one of the reasons I think *Trouble in Paradise* has never gotten the attention it deserves, because it is really about sensuality and morality."

CRAFTSMANSHIP

Of the numerous screenplays Raphaelson wrote for other directors besides Lubitsch, it is no coincidence that the best known of these is for an Alfred Hitchcock film, *Suspicion* (1941), the story of a naïve bride who suspects that her new husband may be trying to kill her. Despite a compromised ending, *Suspicion* is an intimate work of suspense built around the dark complexities of a marital relationship (Raphaelson wrote it with longtime Hitchcock collaborator Joan Harrison and Alma Reville, the director's wife, from a Francis Iles novel, *Before the Fact*). In analyzing what Raphaelson brought to his working relationship with Lubitsch, it is worth quoting one of Hitchcock's observation on screenwriting that illuminates why both he and Lubitsch were able to make good use of Raphaelson's talents in adapting works for the screen. The two directors had strong similarities in their approaches to screenplay development, which are attributable to their common foundation in silent cinema and their passion for what Hitchcock called "pure Cinema" as well as their shared belief in the critical importance of preproduction planning.

Both always went into production with a carefully written script from which they would rarely deviate. Both worked closely with their writers while not taking writing credit. Unlike Lubitsch, Hitchcock performed that collaboration in two distinct phases. He would usually develop a lengthy, detailed treatment with Reville before turning to another writer to flesh out the storyline and add depths to the characterization. Lubitsch tended to start with a play, often of an obscure European vintage, whose basic outline he would simply recount to his writers rather than let them read it. Then they would transform the germ of the idea in fresh ways from page one, always working from the beginning and not continuing until it was *"terrific,"* as Lubitsch liked to say. The intense planning Lubitsch and Hitchcock lavished on their films in preproduction was a function of the creative attention they both placed on structure and, along the way, on the cleverly developed, often self-contained, and virtuosic sequences for which they became famous. And both relied to a large degree on their writing collaborators for help in developing the people in the stories, although Lubitsch, at every stage of his work, was more focused on his characters as driving forces than Hitchcock tended to be, with his greater focus on the mechanics of suspense devices, although it should be noted that Hitchcock's work with actors is considerably underrated.

Because these two great directors needed to work with writers who could help them develop characters within fairly rigidly controlled situations and scenes, they preferred working with screenwriters who were also playwrights. When Hitchcock was asked in a 1964 interview whether he preferred to work with a novelist or a playwright on screenplays, he replied, "I will say the playwright rather than the novelist is more important, because you need *scenes*, playing scenes. There's people who are from the theater who can write playing scenes for you. . . . Compression and economy belongs to the playwright. It doesn't belong to the novelist. You know, he can go on for a thousand pages." Raphaelson's work with Lubitsch gives abundant illustration of how that playwright excelled at "writing playing scenes." If we fondly remember the many Lubitsch Touches (often purely visual) in the films they made together, and the marvelous bon mots Raphaelson wrote—such as Mariette's remark to Filiba, "You see, François, marriage is a beautiful mistake which two people make together. But with you, François, I think it would be a mistake"—the underlying character interactions are of equal if not greater importance. The poignant final sequences involving Mariette's unmasking of Gaston, their mutual chagrin at his admitted betrayal of her, their tender yet still amusing gestures and words of farewell, and the rapturously comical ending in which Lily recovers the upper hand after "buying" Gaston back from Mariette constitute the finest sustained passage in Lubitsch. This breathtakingly constructed series of scenes owes a great deal to the oblique, unconventional comedy-drama of the dialogue exchanges and to the surprising yet believable character twists that were masterfully put on the page by Raphaelson in a script Lubitsch filmed with remarkable fidelity and brought to vibrant life with his actors.

And yet in one of the most wrongheaded instances of a screenwriter undervaluing his own work, Raphaelson said in 1973 that *Trouble in Paradise* "was just another job and it never occurred to me that I was making history."

He said he preferred *Heaven Can Wait* and *The Shop Around the Corner* because "I cared more about those people than I did about the people in *Trouble in Paradise*. I thought the people in *Trouble in Paradise* were just puppets." Raphaelson's ambivalence toward both the film medium and Lubitsch probably indicates that he harbored some resentment about realizing that he was a much better writer when he worked with Lubitsch. Aside from *The Jazz Singer*, Raphaelson's play about generational conflicts in a Jewish family, which was adapted for the screen in ways he did not approve of, his three best-known plays—*Accent on Youth* (1934), *Skylark* (1939), and *Jason* (1941)—are subtly developed portraits of romantic and/or marital relationships. Raphaelson's sense of structure is solid and displays a fondness for clever third-act turns and inversions. In that, we can see structural similarities with his work for Lubitsch. Raphaelson said that when he started writing plays, he realized, "That's what my life has been—technique. Craftsmanship." But though Raphaelson's plays are well crafted and their dialogue often amusing, the repartee is sometimes arch and largely lacks the sharpness, drollery, and sparkle we find in his scripts for Lubitsch. The plot twists of the plays, while ingenious, tend to be overly telegraphed and ultimately come off as mechanical and rather tedious devices for the purpose of scoring thematic points.

Even though Raphaelson's plays take advantage of the greater candor about sexuality that was allowed onstage in that era compared with the more oblique approach writers and directors were compelled to take in Hollywood, they tend to provide surprisingly conventional resolutions to their risqué sexual situations and entangled relationships. Despite their sophisticated repartee, Raphaelson's mostly upper-class characters tend to give in to the demands of social expectations rather than rebel against them. Kael observes, "Raphaelson's writing is different in his plays; his comedies don't have a comic vision—they're not really light-headed in the way that his best work for Lubitsch is. They aspired to be more than comedies; there was always a serious kernel—a moral nugget, wisdom. Lubitsch freed him from the literate playwright's obligation to have 'something to say.'"

Raphaelson's reliance on theatrical conventions in his plays seems unimaginative in contrast to the brilliant playing with convention that distinguishes his screenplays for Lubitsch. Partly for that reason, his plays seem antiquated while the Lubitsch films he wrote are timeless; they transcend their period settings in ways that the plays fail to achieve. Raphaelson revealingly admits in "Freundschaft" that his more casual approach to screenwriting made him freer with his imagination and that Lubitsch, more fully attuned to the fanciful salvos of wit, seized upon this trait with alacrity: "From the first, I found that a certain kind of nonsense delighted him. I would toss in preposterous ideas—'Here's a bad example of what I mean'—while we were struggling over a scene. He encouraged such nonsense . . . rampages of invention in what was known as his style, a style I loved and never ceased loving—for him, not for myself." Raphaelson mentions that he suggested the delightfully absurd touches in the early dinner scene between Gaston and Lily when they discover their common bond as thieves. He playfully spun the zany gags of the couple revealing that each has stolen items from the other's clothing—including the notion that Gaston has somehow managed to remove her garter without her realizing it. Raphaelson assumed that the impossibility of such gags made them unusable, but Lubitsch, to his surprise, put them in the script: "He loved my wild doodle" of Lily giving Gaston his watch and saying, "It was five minutes slow, but I regulated it for you." The result is one of the most delightfully offbeat scenes blending comedy and romance in the director's work.

It is noteworthy that Raphaelson admitted, "I would never have written any of that material in a play of my own," an indication that Lubitsch was the dominant partner in their collaboration. Despite the license Raphaelson had onstage to be franker in some ways, or at least more blunt, about sexual relationships than he could in movies during that era, he suffered by holding back the better part of his creativity, his more antic side. And as Kael puts it, because he felt less serious while working for Lubitsch, Raphaelson "could try out the irresponsible thoughts that came to mind. He could trust his impulses, his instinct. But the freedom didn't carry over when he went back to working in the theater. In the plays he held down his own affections, warmth, passion."

As for the kinds of personal touches Lubitsch would bring to their work together, Raphaelson gives a revealing glimpse of one memorable example that helps define what a director can add to a screenplay. In the scene near the end of *Trouble in Paradise* as Mariette and Gaston embrace and kiss without her realizing that he is preparing to leave her, Lubitsch added while shooting some haunting elements of visual poetry. During the embrace, Mariette murmurs, "We have a long time ahead of us, Gaston—weeks, months, *years*."

Lubitsch came up with the idea of cutting away from a two-shot of the couple to use this dialogue as part of a montage of reflections of Gaston and Mariette. We see them first in mirrors hanging over a bed and on her makeup table and then in shadow on the bed as they *nearly* kiss again in silhouette, before Mariette, back in the two-shot, turns her head away from him. The extreme poignancy of the dialogue—Mariette's mistaken assumption of permanence in a relationship that she does not realize is about to end harshly— is not simply illustrated by Lubitsch's visual additions but given its deeper, definitive meaning by the visual context in which it is placed. The reflections, the shadows rather than substance, simultaneously convey what is false about the relationship and what it could have been. These bittersweet visual elements show how Mariette has fallen for the illusion of her "romance with a crook," as Lily caustically calls it a little later in the film. Such visual layering adds a considerable note of complexity to the already touching dialogue by Raphaelson, showing what film can do that the theater cannot.

"It is striking in the context of Lubitsch's films that Mariette and Gaston never do sleep together," William Paul points out in his book on Lubitsch's American films. "Even after the introduction of the new Production Code in 1934 Lubitsch seemed able to introduce adulteries into his films without having to punish his characters for their sexual desires, so the omission here has nothing to do with censorship or desire to conform to dominant mores. The embrace in the mirrors is in fact the actual consummation of the affair, and this alone could justify the elaborate shooting style at that moment. Gaston and Mariette have had their moment, itself a kind of eternity that removes them from all the temporal and spatial coordinates of everyday reality."

NO EASY SOLUTION

Throughout much of *Trouble in Paradise*, we are drawn ever more deeply into Gaston's seemingly irreconcilable conflict: he loves two women, and we share his feelings for both of them. The women are quite different yet equally alluring; Lubitsch does not make us pick sides. The majesty of the film is that it offers no easy solution. Usually in films about love triangles, the situation is rigged in favor of one rival or the other. But Lubitsch refuses to do this. He carries that refusal right through to the end, not stubbornly but because it is his nature to be so generous. That generosity of spirit, above all, is the special quality of *Trouble in Paradise*.

Initially we are enchanted by Miriam Hopkins's brittle, sexy, comical behavior as Lily. She seems all the more appealing to Gaston, and to us, when he unmasks her true identity as a professional thief. She, in turn, is delighted to learn that he is the notorious Gaston Monescu, self-described as "the man who walked into the bank of Constantinople and walked out *with* the bank of Constantinople." Lily's madcap blonde persona, her saucy, sprightly gamine quality, masks a fierce shrewdness and amoral practicality that comes out mostly when she is in private with her partner in love and crime. But as captivated as we are with her reckless charm, as soon as Gaston becomes involved with Mariette, first by robbing her and then as her private secretary so that he can steal more from her, our sympathies become conflicted. With him, we are falling under the spell of the dark-haired, sinuous, elegant beauty and her serene, more mature womanly charms, reflected in her opulent art deco mansion settings by Hans Dreier and her slinky costumes by Travis Banton. Gaston's dilemma becomes ours. We are suspended for most of the film in the heady but worrisome state of loving both women at the same time and not knowing what to do about it any more than Gaston does. To borrow the lyric sung by Maurice Chevalier when he is weighing adultery versus fidelity in *One Hour with You*, "But this I know, we can't all three be satisfied." In watching *Trouble in Paradise*, we only know that this suspenseful romantic state, this precarious balance between high society and lower-class life, cannot last forever. The suspense is as intense as anything in Hitchcock.

Complicating our feelings beyond the realm of conventional morality is essential to Lubitsch's vision of the relations between men and women. There are no simple ways to describe the principal characters in his films, no simple judgments offered. Neither "good" nor "bad" but realistically gray, his characters are flesh-and-blood, three-dimensional human beings, whose company we are free to enjoy without feeling compelled to judge them or choose between them. *Trouble in Paradise* is the supreme example. Lubitsch's subversiveness in dealing with sexuality and romance is part of what keeps his work so alive today. His undercutting and mockery of the traditional screen conventions for depicting romantic involvements give his films the complicated sense of real life. The lightly fantastic trappings of his films help him get away with his challenging of those conventions.

As James Naremore observes, "Lily is not only shrewd but also multilingual, sharp as a whip, and admirably self-reliant; Mariette, on the other hand, is a wealthy, pampered, but isolated and vulnerable woman who deserves romance and who needs Gaston to help rescue her from the unsympathetic characters who feed off her." Lily's pluck and wildness are appealing, and her resourcefulness and loyalty to Gaston constantly win our sympathies, including when he is off betraying her with Madame Colet, and she expresses her anguish in a uniquely Lubitschean way—by humming a tune in various registers, from giddy to distraught, as she packs their trunks for their escape, an example of the film's numerous ways of having characters "speak" without using English dialogue. Nor are we encouraged to judge Mariette, who gracefully defies stereotypes of the frivolous rich woman, even, remarkably enough, when she superficially seems to embody them. She is first seen in her perfume factory, playing the role of the shallow, unconcerned widow to confound her all-male board of directors' attempts to cut workers' salaries in a time of financial crisis. But we recognize the shrewdness and goodwill that motivate Mariette's game playing with these callous businessmen, and we see numerous other examples of her genuine kindness, generosity, and vulnerability throughout the film. Lubitsch characteristically avoids easy sentimentality by also showing her enjoying her riches without any trace of guilt. Immediately after rebuffing the attempt to cut salaries, she indulges her luxurious impulses by buying an absurdly expensive bejeweled handbag, the film's MacGuffin (the Hitchcockian term for an apparently insignificant plot device that propels the story along and carries deeper meanings as it does).

Lubitsch keeps calling our attention to Mariette's casual enjoyment of her wealth while the rest of the world suffers from the Great Depression, quietly insisting on the point yet not condemning her for her status per se but drawing a distinction between what she owns and how she behaves. The way she treats the people around her (including her workers), not her wealth, is his barometer of her character. Lubitsch mocks conventional socially conscious filmmaking (and even anticipates such a scene in Frank Capra's 1936 *Mr. Deeds Goes to Town*) by having a wild-haired Bolshevik (Leonid Kinskey) burst into Mariette's mansion to berate her in Russian with a bogus quote from Leon Trotsky: "Any woman who spends a fortune for a silk purse is a sow's ear." Gaston enters to command the Bolshevik to depart (also in Russian). Lubitsch is no Marxist, no ideologue, and yet the film clearly spotlights the imbalances and injustices of capitalism, including in this satirical scene. Gaston's self-defense when caught stealing from Mariette is partly to point out that she has been robbed systematically for years by the elderly head of her board of directors, Adolph J. Giron (C. Aubrey Smith), whom she hesitates to turn in to the authorities. Gaston responds in a caustic tone, "I see—you have to be in the Social Register to keep out of jail. But when a man starts at the bottom and works his way up, a self-made crook, then you say, 'Call the police, put him behind bars.'"

Lubitsch's satire of revolutionary rhetoric and moral relativism in *Trouble in Paradise* is not an avoidance of social consciousness but in fact part of his most persistent strain of political commentary on the Depression. When characters continually mention how "in times like these" one thing or another must happen, that is Lubitsch and Raphaelson's way of focusing our attention on the social determinism that rules even the lives of these seemingly reckless, carefree characters. Gaston wryly consoles Lily at a low point in their fortunes by spouting Herbert Hoover's already ridiculous 1932 campaign slogan, "Prosperity is just around the corner" (the film was released on October 21 of that year, just eighteen days before the epochal election in which Franklin D. Roosevelt trounced Hoover in a landslide, and it had its New York premiere on the very day of the election). These jibes and the scene with the Bolshevik, with its gag about Trotsky, still a contemporary figure for Lubitsch's audience, are only the most obvious signals of the film's unusually rich political nature. By this low point of the Depression, when filmgoers' tastes were changing in response to the world crisis, Lubitsch had already internalized the necessities he discussed in 1939 with the *New York Sun*: "We can't make pictures in a vacuum now. We must show people living in the real world. No one used to care how characters made their living—if the picture was amusing. Now they do care. They want their stories tied up to life. . . . Now [a character] must have a job, or else the fact that he doesn't work becomes the important thing about him."

What Eyman's Lubitsch biography takes from this statement is that after making the screwball comedy *Bluebeard's Eighth Wife* in 1938, Lubitsch "suddenly realized that the world had changed around him. He could no longer get away with the delightful irresponsibilities displayed by the characters in *Trouble in Paradise*." That is a serious misreading of Lubitsch's 1932 romantic comedy. The film is actually deeply concerned with how its characters make their living, whether or not they work at conventional jobs. This is a film constantly focused on money, not only on the central plot devices of thievery and embezzlement but also on the intricacies of salaries, corporate and personal monetary transactions, the prices of luxury objects, the trading value of illicit goods, Gaston's blaming his need for a job as Mariette's secretary on his problems with "the stock market—a bank crash," and on and on. While making his plans to rob the wealthy businesswoman by cracking her wall safe at her mansion, Gaston disingenuously lectures her in his most businesslike tone, "In times like these, when everything is uncertain, every conservative person should have a substantial part of his fortune within his reach." Furthermore, the themes of money and sex are intertwined throughout the film, in the characters' behavior, often explicitly in their dialogue, and sometimes in the visual double entendres such as penetrating a rich woman's purse and wall safe and (at the end) stuffing money into a purse on another woman's lap. The drives for sex and money may cause conflict but are inextricable in Gaston's seduction and betrayal of both women. His claim to Lily about Madame Colet, that "her whole sex appeal is in that safe," is a (partial) lie but makes that very linkage. It is echoed when Lily, taking matters in hand with consummate cleverness, announces a convoluted but emotionally satisfying business deal to settle the romantic transaction. She caustically gives back to Mariette both the stolen money and Gaston, but then she buys him for herself with Mariette's own money—and then takes the money with her. As Lily tells Gaston before she walks out in disgust, "This is what I want—this is real—money—*cash!*"

Aaron Schuster offers a thoughtful commentary on the film's often-overlooked political dimensions and its modern relevance in his 2014 essay "Comedy in Times of Austerity," from the Slovenian collection *Lubitsch Can't Wait: A Theoretical Examination*:

If *Ninotchka* (1939) is a film about communism and *To Be or Not to Be* about fascism, *Trouble in Paradise* is a comic treatment of the worst economic crisis the world has seen, the Great Depression. These three films, the most socially conscious in Lubitsch's oeuvre, form a kind of trilogy which deals with the crisis of capitalism and its two historic solutions: fascism and communism. And "in times like these," of budget cuts, bank busts, and Eurozone bailouts, the film's study of capitalist manners has only gained in relevance. Indeed, *Trouble in Paradise* is perhaps the ultimate comedy for times of austerity: for that reason alone it should be required viewing today. This does not mean, however, that one should expect any kind of straightforward critique or moral sermon from Lubitsch; the point is not that beneath all the entertaining banter and funny reversals there lies a serious message—again, the serious message is already there in the comedy itself. . . .

No one in the film is spared, the satire cuts in all directions, but Lubitsch's sympathy is clearly for the classy "self-made" criminals over the hypocrite institutional crooks. In this radical comedy, "the thieves not only get away with the loot but actually go on to a charmed life of more thievery" [as William Paul observes in his book on Lubitsch]—an astonishing ending for a Hollywood picture of that era. But we should add that the other thieves will presumably have a happy end too: Giron will be safe (a hushed-up scandal, a golden parachute), Madame will go on with her shopping sprees, and the board will have its way. Everyone is stealing, and no one is punished—that, in a nutshell, is Lubitsch's portrait of the times.

Although, like Gaston, we are carried along for most of the film, happily not having to make the choice between Mariette and Lily, the plot finally compels us, and him, to do so. The plot may appear thin in *Trouble in Paradise*, as in most Lubitsch films, but it represents the strictures of social order. Even if Gaston and Lily are outlaws, they are part of that corrupt high society because they live on its fringes, cynically reaping its benefits at the same time they are robbing it blind. As in *Monte Carlo*, Gaston must leave Mariette because he has to obey "the dictates of society." A lady of propriety, Mariette must also obey those dictates, although with sadness and despite her impulses to rebel. Even her wealth does not give her the license to continue carrying on her illicit romance with a thief. Gaston leaves Mariette's employ because otherwise there is no way of preventing this "self-made crook" from going to jail and disgracing Mariette in the process. That social imperative, however hypocritical, fortuitously solves his personal romantic dilemma. Although he and Mariette recognize that their love affair "could have been marvelous.—Divine.—Wonderful," it would be impossible for him to remain in such an ambiguous and dangerous position socially and legally. Life with Mariette is only a fantasy for Gaston. Madame Colet's wealthy, cocooned existence is alluring yet ultimately unattainable, a pretty dream that would have become untenable for both her and Gaston. He may be returning to Lily partly by default, but we (along with all three of them) recognize that the two thieves are perfectly paired personally as well as professionally.

As the plot of *Trouble in Paradise* races headlong to its climax once Gaston has been exposed as a thief, Lubitsch and Raphaelson build up to the real moral dilemma at the heart of the film. The primary question is not whether or not or how a crook should be punished, nor is it the class issue of whether he is a jewel thief or a distinguished member of society. Those are ironic sidelights to what most interests Lubitsch. The genuine moral dilemma the film raises is, How should Gaston treat Mariette?

In the film's intricate, sixteen-minute finale, an astonishing tour de force of screenwriting and direction, Gaston is forced to admit he has been exploiting Mariette's affections all along. And though he loves her, he still loves Lily. He does not offer an outright apology to either woman—Lubitsch characteristically prefers to treat Gaston's expressions of regret obliquely, as in his ordering flowers to be sent to Madame Colet—but he is forced by both women to confront his mistreatment of them. That chastened recognition, and how he deals with it, is the film's dramatic core, one that in another film could result in tragedy but here gives a cathartically astringent tone to the comedy. Gaston looks pained and ashamed when Mariette says sadly, "You wanted a hundred thousand francs. And I thought you wanted me." Gaston's parting gestures and words to Mariette—such as his admission that he came to rob her but fell in love with her—show that he genuinely cares for her and, more important, that she cares for him despite everything.

After Lily settles the deal, Gaston hurries out after her. The camera holds on Mariette at the closed door and moves in toward her and it. She looks chagrined as she hears him running away. She moves back to sit and mourn but allows herself a moment of hope when she hears Gaston's footsteps again as he runs back up the stairs. The door opens, and he comes over to her and announces, "Goodbye." This seriocomic reversal of expectations, with the accompanying emotional letdown, is oddly touching. The couple's mutual expressions of regret that he must leave are followed by his saying, with seeming smugness, "Do you know what you're missing?" She smiles and nods, her eyes closed, clearly (and elliptically) calling up sublime romantic images.

"No—*that's* what you're missing," he says matter-of-factly, pulling from his coat pocket a string of pearls that Lily has coveted. Gaston does not have to tell Mariette that he still loves Lily but conveys it with that new theft and the gallant, admiring, yet rueful way he suggests, "Your gift to her." What is astonishing is that Lubitsch manages to make what might have seemed a brazen gesture into a shared token of sympathetic understanding. In perhaps the most moving single moment in a Lubitsch film, Mariette, with a tender smile and consummate grace, acquiesces, "With the compliments of Colet— and Company." Insurance will cover the loss, but it will not cover her loss of Gaston.

Mariette's generosity and philosophical acceptance help assuage Gaston's feelings of guilt, absolving him in our eyes while further ennobling her. The contrast between the clichéd expectations we once had of her character and her actual humanity makes a heart-piercing point. Her behavior restores the moral order Lubitsch maintains, with his absolute balance between our respect for both women as well as in his satirical (and seriously meant) equation between the profession of jewel thief and the institutionalized thievery of the world of high finance. This is the opposite of an escapist conclusion. Mariette's generosity is tinged with visible melancholy and a similar note in her voice that lingers, along with her and Gaston's other belated but welcome expressions of regret, in the film's otherwise-uproarious happy ending.

Now that the seemingly insoluble problem the film has set up—Gaston having to choose between the two women—has been resolved with breath-taking skill, it can be capped with a perfectly satisfying ending love scene in the inimitable Lubitsch high-comedy style, with a nod to the tradition of silent-movie pantomime. Gaston and Lily are heading off together in a taxi-cab at night, into an uncertain, rootless future. Humorously reprising their mutual revelations of robbery from the opening scene, they exchange items they have lifted from Madame Colet and each other. Finally, Lily reveals that she even has the MacGuffin, the bejeweled handbag, and Gaston tri-umphantly thrusts the stolen wad of money into Lily's own small black purse, nestled in her lap, the film's raunchiest Lubitsch Touch. If leaving Mariette was an imperfect solution for Gaston's romantic conflicts, ending his fantasy that he could have both women in his life, the film is able to make this com-plex resolution work precisely because Lubitsch underscores rather than downplays its emotional impact on all three central characters. Gaston has had to face the truth with Mariette and make amends with her. He also has to heal the hurt he has caused Lily. She reestablishes their equality in their loving partnership as thieves by buying him and then stealing from him again. No avoidance of reality or papering-over of plot holes has been necessary to make this happy ending possible, as was the case in some of the Lubitsch musicals, which generally lack this film's sense that its problems have been worked out in the most mature, inevitable way.

Despite Gaston's disappointment that his dual life cannot continue, he opts for the only practical solution. Lily is a peripatetic adventurer who is more suited to him than the languid, somewhat complacent, if kind and generous Mariette. We enjoy Lily's adventurous amorality and endless resourcefulness. Mariette, with all her charm, was only a dream for Gaston because of the impossibility of a settled existence. But the ending in the taxi, bringing Lily and Gaston back together—an echo of their first night of lovemaking—has a bittersweet undertone. Their riding off into the night also reminds us of the ending of Ernest Hemingway's quintessential Lost Generation novel, *The Sun Also Rises* (1926), with the two dispirited lovers in a Paris taxi. Lady Brett says, "Oh, Jake, we could have had such a damned good time together," and Jake replies, "Yes. Isn't it pretty to think so?" Gaston might well be thinking such thoughts about Mariette while riding off to his precarious, impermanent future with Lily. As Raphaelson once put it, "The so-called happy ending of a high comedy should have a sardonic overtone because there is no such thing as a happy ending for an intelligent writer."

MASTERFUL SUCCINCTNESS

The trend toward political commentary in Lubitsch's work was also evident in his brief but masterful contribution to Paramount's compilation film *If I Had a Million*, which features segments by eight directors. It was premiered in New York on November 18, 1932, shortly after the election of President Roosevelt. Based on the 1931 novel *Windfall* by Robert D. Andrews, the film is among those from the early thirties that comment most directly on the Depression's impact on both ordinary citizens and wealthy people with a social conscience. The framing story has an eccentric, angry, dying tycoon (Richard Bennett) defying his financial advisers and heirs by giving away part of his fortune to strangers. The segments' tones vary: most of them are broadly comedic, but one is starkly tragic, about a man on death row, and another, set in a home for impoverished old ladies, movingly combines pathos with a wish-fulfillment happy ending (that segment may have inspired Orson Welles's original ending for his 1942 film *The Magnificent Ambersons*, set in a shabby boarding house with Agnes Moorehead suffering the effects of what Welles called "impecunious" old age; Bennett, considerably aged, is that film's Major Amberson).

Lubitsch's contribution to *If I Had a Million*, which is placed as comic relief immediately after the death-row segment, is generally considered the film's highlight. He avoids the obvious commentary on social conditions evident in some other segments, and his segment is unique because it is almost silent. There are only three brief lines of dialogue. Visual Lubitsch Touches abound and carry most of the meaning in its two minutes and thirteen seconds of running time. Some sources refer to Lubitsch's segment as "The Clerk," but no such title appears on-screen. The clerk, working in an insurance company, is one Phineas V. Lambert, played by Charles Laughton. The director has anarchic fun with the fantasy of what an ordinary man would do with a check for a million dollars, an astronomical sum for audiences of 1932 (the 2017 equivalent would be $18.5 million). But the farcical elements express Lubitsch's empathy for anyone who would rebel against the system if only he could find the resources to do so, a crucial element in the director's satirical social viewpoint.

Lambert is a meek, mustachioed little man who is seen working among a field of desks after the camera gradually finds him in a seemingly desultory tracking shot. He is mechanically working on papers when a messenger delivers an envelope. In a delightful ironic touch, Lambert casually sweeps it aside until he is finished with his task at hand. He opens the envelope and, upon finding the check, fails to show the expected visual reaction, looking mildly put out by his discovery. He rises from his desk and plods up a steep staircase with his usual methodical pace. Lubitsch shows him going through a series of doors displaying increasingly pompous titles ("ADMINISTRATION OFFICES," "SECRETARY TO THE PRESIDENT," "THE PRIVATE SECRETARY TO THE PRESIDENT," and "MR. BROWN / PRESIDENT"). Before entering the final door, Lambert checks his appearance in a mirror as if preparing to go onstage.

He knocks. A voice is heard: "Come in." Lambert enters and asks, "Mr. Brown?" His boss asks, "Yes?" Lambert responds in close-up with an eloquent raspberry before the segment fades out. No further commentary is needed on the use to which he has decided to put his new freedom.

Billy Wilder told me in 1978, "Naturally, I would have liked to direct anything by Lubitsch; I would be very happy if I just would have directed the two-minute skit he did with Charles Laughton in *If I Had a Million*." Another admirer of that skit was Japanese director Yasujiro Ozu, who included a clip from it in his silent 1933 tragedy *Woman of Tokyo*, about an office worker prostituting herself during the Depression to help put her brother through a university. Her brother watches the Lubitsch segment on a date, and Ozu shows us almost all of it, including even Lubitsch's writing and directing credits, though the happy ending is elided. Ozu had begun his career as a director of comedies, often in the vein of American cinema, and was strongly influenced by Lubitsch even before making this somber film. Komatsu Kitamura, the screenwriter of four Ozu films, reported in 1930, "We worked through the night drinking Japanese wine and Bordeaux from the 1800s and listening to gramophone records of *The Love Parade*." Donald Richie writes in his critical study *Ozu* that *The Marriage Circle* had an "enormous" impact on Japanese directors of that period and a "decisive" effect on Ozu's shooting style, helping him develop his similar penchant for oblique and unexpected kinds of reaction shots. Lubitschean methods of elliptical storytelling can be seen throughout *Woman of Tokyo*, which also includes a direct homage to the opening of *The Marriage Circle* (with a man complaining about a hole in his sock). Ozu uses the Lubitsch vignette from *If I Had a Million* to underscore the monotony of the life of an office worker, a mood he often evoked and one that would be disrupted if he had included Lubitsch's fantasy ending.

But despite Lubitsch's influence on these and other major filmmakers, my showing of his segment from *If I Had a Million* to a large film production class was a dispiriting sign of how little his ironic style is in synch with today's audiences. I used the segment as an example of how to tell a story simply, quickly, elliptically, and with a minimum of words. The students reacted to the film without laughing and with mostly blank expressions. One student blurted out, "Is that *it*?" I quoted what Wilder had said—to even greater incomprehension. "But all of that . . . is too mild," Wilder also said of the Lubitsch segment and of his mentor's other work. "It is witty. It is beautiful, for me. . . . But this is not the age for it."

Lubitsch's characteristically droll and oblique approach to a grave social issue, which helps make *Trouble in Paradise* such a trenchant satirical commentary on the Depression, is similarly evident in his deft contribution to *If I Had a Million*. The somewhat uncharacteristic touch of vulgarity with the concluding raspberry would not have been out of place in his German work, but it is surprising here from the man who had since become known in America as the master of sophisticated comedy. The jarring, unexpected nature of that proletarian touch contributes to its hilarious effect. For Great Britain, where the raspberry was then regarded as unspeakably crude, it had to be replaced by a specially shot version in which Laughton whistles instead.

"TRÄUMEREI"

The Man I Killed is usually regarded as the most anomalous film of Lubitsch's career—a stark antiwar preachment about a French war veteran tormented by guilt over his killing of a German soldier during World War I. The film is mostly as lugubrious as that makes it sound, but it is worth remembering that Lubitsch made a number of overtly "serious" films in his career to demonstrate his skills to the many critics who, then as now, underrated the art of comedy, despite his towering reputation. Yet *The Man I Killed* stands out as his last such effort in America, probably because it flopped so resoundingly at the boxoffice. Future Lubitsch efforts with weighty subject matter—most notably his 1942 World War II film *To Be or Not to Be*—would be in a seriocomic vein, and even then he would receive a barrage of attacks for supposedly making light of Nazism. Of course, anyone who knows Lubitsch's work well realizes that even his "light" works, his romantic comedies and musicals, can be and usually are serious in their own less pretentious way.

There is little doubt that Lubitsch is at his best when he works in comedy or approaches heavy subject matter with a seriocomic perspective, not when he goes all-out for pathos. *The Man I Killed* is not only heavy-handed, pretentious, and overly rhetorical but also uncharacteristically overindulgent in its approach to acting. Phillips Holmes tears a passion to tatters in the lead role of the anguished veteran Paul Renard. The callow Holmes seems inadequate for the demands of the role, however inherently sympathetic Paul's quest for redemption may seem and however grim the irony that the actor himself would be killed in World War II in a 1942 plane crash while serving in the Royal Canadian Air Force.

The Man I Killed is among a number of Hollywood films that sought to go beyond jingoism once World War I had begun to recede into history and tried to stir some sympathy for the defeated German people. The classic example is *All Quiet on the Western Front*, the 1930 Universal talkie directed by Lewis Milestone and based on the best-selling novel by German author Erich Maria Remarque. *All Quiet* has a memorable lead performance by Lew Ayres as a sensitive German youth who is swept up in combat only to become disaffected (Ayres became a conscientious objector in World War II); that film's indictment of militarism and the graphic nature of its battle scenes retain their power to move us today. *All Quiet* was preceded by John Ford's *Four Sons*, a moving 1928 Fox silent (with sound effects and one word of German dialogue) about a Bavarian family whose sons wind up fighting on both sides of the conflict.

All Quiet was a substantial commercial and critical success, the Oscar winner for best picture, and a bête noire for the Nazi propagandist Josef Goebbels, who led disruptive protests against Milestone's pacifist film in Germany. So though Lubitsch's almost unrelentingly grim *The Man I Killed* may seem an odd project for Paramount to have financed in the depths of the Depression, it was riding the wave of *All Quiet*, and it was also the year (1932) that Paramount filmed Ernest Hemingway's World War I novel *A Farewell to Arms*, with Frank Borzage directing Gary Cooper and Helen Hayes. In 1933 Ford would make his first great film, *Pilgrimage*, a drama for Fox about an American mother who sends her son to die in World War I rather than lose him to the woman he loves but later tries to expiate her guilt while visiting his grave in France. The subject of disenchantment with militarism was not so far out of the commercial mainstream during the dark days of the early thirties as *The Man I Killed* might make it seem.

Despite its mostly leaden nature and writing, directing, and acting that veer into the flagrantly obvious—tendencies placing it far outside the characteristically Lubitschean realm of subtlety, violating so many of the principles that make him a great filmmaker—there are strongly personal elements in *The Man I Killed* that make it, intermittently, strangely compelling. This is a passionate outcry by a German American director who feels the subject deeply, almost too much so for its effect on his artistry. Along with its emphasis on German suffering, and in particular on the grieving parents of dead soldiers, the film looks German militarism squarely in the face (as does Lubitsch's 1921 antimilitarist farce *The Wildcat*, in a more surrealistic vein, which also flopped). *The Man I Killed* paints a disturbing picture of the xenophobic, mostly unrepentant older generation whose bitterness over their country's defeat makes them yearn for a revenge match with the victors. Lubitsch sends an urgent warning to his 1932 audience that another major war is coming. Paul tells a priest that during the last war, "Nine million people got slaughtered, and they're already talking about another war. And the next time, there'll be ninety million! And the world calls that sane. Well, then I want to be insane!" (The film was not far off in that prediction; modern estimates are that sixty to eighty million people died in World War II.)

The father of the dead soldier, Dr. Holderlin (Lionel Barrymore), abandons his kneejerk hatred of the French when affected by Paul's humanity. After listening to his belligerent cronies at a rathskeller, the doctor makes a passionate outburst: "Who gave them bullets and gas and bayonets? We, the fathers, here and on the other side. We're too old to fight, but we're not too old to hate. *We're* responsible. When thousands of other men's sons were killed, we called it victory and celebrated with beer. And when thousands of our sons were killed, they called it victory and celebrated with wine. *Fathers* drink to the death of *sons*. Ah, my heart isn't with you any longer, old men. My heart's with the young, dead and living, everywhere, anywhere." As James Harvey writes in *Romantic Comedy in Hollywood*, this "is, after all, a film about a monstrous fact: about the corruption of sons by their war-loving fathers, about the hatred of the old for the young." The film reflects Lubitsch's sober view of the increasingly fascist trend in contemporary German politics and his disenchantment with his former homeland. It is no coincidence that this film was released the same year that Lubitsch made what would be his final visit to Germany, the year before the Nazis seized power. Lubitsch reveals here how much he was haunted by Germany, by his loss of his homeland, his loss of his parents, the memory of the previous world war that he and his fellow countrymen had lived through, and the specter of an even more devastating war to come. And perhaps also by survivor guilt over having been a noncombatant because of his Russian citizenship.

The film's political message is delivered in a blunt, overly rhetorical manner, as if too anxious to make sure its points are understood. Raphaelson felt uncomfortable, and later somewhat apologetic, about writing such an unabashed, largely humorless cinematic sermon in his first collaboration with Lubitsch. The writer recalled that he and the director had fundamental differences over the story:

> The nature of our quarrel, if you can call it that, was the hero. I felt the last thing that person should do if he wanted to help was to go anywhere *near* that family. What could he do for them? I thought he was a self-important, self-pitying son of a bitch. I wanted to change the situation, the character, all of it. But Lubitsch was sure. He'd say, "No, Sam, *wait*—you'll see it on the screen, it'll be up there." That was the only time he ever said that to me. On every film after that one, we had a tacit understanding that when one of us objected to something, we'd work on it until we *both* liked it—partly, I think because he realized he had been wrong about *The Man I Killed*. The picture came out, and you *didn't* see it up there. . . . The whole thing gave me the creeps, in fact.

The opening sequence, a visual and aural tour de force of symbolic antiwar rhetoric, was highly acclaimed in its time and for many years was distributed by the Museum of Modern Art as a short subject to demonstrate the art of montage in early sound films. Still impressive up to a point, the sequence, set on the first anniversary of the Armistice, is nevertheless too heavily ironic in its schematic contrasts between a religious service to commemorate the war dead and the militaristic pomp that profanes the ritual. But a more characteristically Lubitschean tone gradually works its way into the film, blending the antiwar fable with the subtler genre he was more comfortable with, the romantic comedy-drama.

After Paul goes to the small German town to seek out the parents of the man he killed, intending to ask forgiveness, he hesitates and pretends he was a friend of their son, Walter (Tom Douglas), in Paris before the war. Paul finds himself accepted as a surrogate son by the old couple (Louise Carter plays the mother) and falling in love with his victim's former fiancée, Elsa (Nancy Carroll). Their romance, though rather grotesque under the circumstances, like the rest of this morbid film, gradually blossoms in a manner that Lubitsch persuades us is believable. These two young people who share a common loss might shore up the ruin of their cultures and the emotional deadness of the Holderlin household out of sympathy, understanding, and a need to find a new cause for living. But it takes most of the film's running time before the almost-crazed Paul can admit his true identity and confess his guilt to Elsa.

Surprisingly, she accepts him, a development of which we are persuaded by Carroll's delicate, unsentimental playing and Lubitsch's shift into a lower-key mode of storytelling that is more congenial to his personality. However, Elsa persuades Paul to keep up his lie to the elderly doctor and his wife, that he was simply a friend of their dead son: "They must never know the truth. . . . You're not going to kill Walter a second time. You're going to live, for them." The ending is touching and disturbing in equal parts, with Paul playing Robert Schumann's haunting "Träumerei" ("Dreaming") on the dead youth's violin as Elsa plays the piano (Lubitsch again expresses love through a musical duet, as in *The Smiling Lieutenant*). In a complex shot uniting all the characters—panning from Paul to Elsa as she goes to the piano, moving in on her unlocking it, before returning to Walter's parents, looking in both directions as they listen to the young people playing—Lubitsch fades out on the old couple, embracing in a two-shot, comforted in their obliviousness. So, despite its tendency to spell out its message, *The Man I Killed* is another Lubitsch film that revolves around ellipsis, in this case a giant emotional ellipsis in the story, a failure to fully confess a festering guilt about an absent character whom everyone obsesses over. That omission and the characters' shared evasion of reality gradually become the film's essential subject. That astringent Lubitschean element helps the film partially overcome its otherwise-clumsy dramaturgy and oppressive sentimentality.

There is not much opportunity for humor in Lubitsch's approach to his story, but there are moments that come alive because he temporarily drops his veil of solemnity. The most charming sequence—which also, characteristically of Lubitsch's best work, has melancholy overtones—is Paul's promenade through town with Elsa. People in shops keep opening doors to spy on the scandalous sight of the Frenchman courting the hometown girl. After several shots of gossips and voyeurs in doorways and windows and an almost-abstract shot of an opening door without people in it, Lubitsch holds on the unsuspecting couple in a long tracking shot as they walk quietly, with the sounds of ringing bells heard from every direction, signifying more unseen people spying at them. Along with clocks, bells are a dominant motif, linked with mourning and sacred rituals from the opening church sequence, and yet here Lubitsch turns that aural motif into chilling dark comedy. This very Lubitschean device is a glimpse of the better film he could have made if he had not been so intent on wringing the hearts of the audience but had focused even more on the young couple's healing romance. Yet the fact that *The Man I Killed* essentially revolves around a lie—even while it argues, as Elsa convinces Paul, that the lie is more compassionate than the truth— makes one wonder how successful this romance can ever become. Ending on a questioning note of emotional fragility, with the young and old couples sharing a state of delusion, makes the final sequence the most genuinely moving one in the film.

It must be noted that as wildly overdone as much of the film seems to us today, it was highly regarded in its time. Although Dwight Macdonald, writing in *The Symposium*, dismissed it as a "Teutonic tearjerker," most reviewers were rapturous. Mordaunt Hall wrote in the *New York Times* that Lubitsch, "the masterful German director, has turned his attention from frivolous comedies to an ironic, sentimental post-war film drama . . . [that is] further evidence of Mr. Lubitsch's genius, for, while it is tearful, its story is unfurled in a poetic fashion. . . . Each sequence is fashioned with sincerity and great care." Robert E. Sherwood hailed it in the *New York Post* as "the best talking picture that has yet been seen and heard," and William Boehnel in the *New York Telegram* wrote, "A film that in its humanity, quiet comprehension and the sympathy which he brings to his characterizations, has never before been equaled for effectiveness on the screen."

Such overreactions can be ascribed to a variety of factors—the film's sense of timeliness; the tendency of reviewers, then as now, to be inordinately impressed with films that wear their socially conscious natures on their sleeves; the usual overrating of drama versus comedy; and the goodwill that Lubitsch brought to this obviously personal effort as the leading Hollywood director of his day. Perhaps we also need to keep in mind that while the frantic acting style of Phillips Holmes seems terribly overstated by today's standards and a far cry from the more effectively underplayed style of such quintessential Lubitsch actors as Adolphe Menjou, Ronald Colman, and Herbert Marshall, the theatrically flamboyant style that Holmes exemplifies was considered at the time the acme of conventional dramatic acting, for better or worse. The audience predictably "stayed away in droves" from this film (as Samuel Goldwyn would put it) even though Paramount, in a panic shortly after the New York opening, changed the title to *Broken Lullaby*. Ostensibly, they did so because they thought *The Man I Killed* sounded like the title of a gangster film, but probably also because *Broken Lullaby* sounds less disturbing and does not give away the mystery. The beautifully made 2016 French version, *Frantz*, directed by François Ozon, avoids the problems of the original film (see the Epilogue for further discussion).

Lubitsch learned a lesson from *The Man I Killed*—the old adage, "A cobbler should stick to his last"—but he also managed to send a fervent warning about contemporary German rearmament to those who could hear it and gave vent to his horror over the world's ever-increasing tendency toward mass slaughter. Nevertheless, in hindsight that desperate message seems mixed, both antiwar and subtly isolationist, a complicating factor that works against the film's artistic and political intentions while contributing to its unresolved, unsettling quality, what James Harvey called "its appalled tone." Like his protagonist, Lubitsch finally does not know where to turn with this tragic vision of human nature except to play a mournful, dreamy song on his violin.

FANCY DANCING

"The story of three people who love each other very much" was Noël Coward's description of his play *Design for Living*. That is a quintessential Lubitschean situation. The director had already worked endless variations around threesomes and other exotic sexual relationships. So it was not a stretch for him to film the play, even if an unabashed ménage à trois was outré even by pre-Code standards; this 1933 Paramount film would be banned from reissue by the Breen Office in 1935 after censorship had tightened considerably. That Lubitsch filmed a Coward play and changed it considerably in the process proved controversial with reviewers, but the matchup was salubrious. Coward and Lubitsch, two specialists in high-style, witty comedy, shared a delight in mocking and subverting bourgeois values, and yet the play and film versions of *Design for Living* are quite different in emphasis.

Lubitsch's film is a lighthearted romp, adapted for the screen by the supremely irreverent, cynically romantic screenwriter Ben Hecht, whose creative influence on this dialogue-driven film is unusually strong for a Lubitsch collaborator. The film version is, in fact, even more daring and unconventional than Coward's more brooding and anxious take on this essentially comic material. "I hope your heart will not be broken to know that we are completely rewriting it," Lubitsch told an interviewer in August 1933. But on its release that November, the film was faulted by reviewers for such cheeky alterations of the source, including using only one line of Coward's dialogue, the toast "Good for our immortal souls!" Lubitsch and Hecht also made many major structural changes.

To forestall the criticism, Lubitsch explained just after completing the shooting,

> In my experience as a director I never have observed a motion picture photographed with an eye to absolute fidelity of stage form which reached within a mile the quality of that play. The reason for this is that the screen is an art form in itself. True that it is related to stagecraft, but it is by no means the same. With this in mind, I analyzed *Design for Living* before the Ben Hecht script was written, and decided on an individual treatment which preserves the plot and essence of Noël Coward's drama and at the same time affords an expression that is distinctly cinematic. A strictly photographed copy of a stage play, regardless of how excellent it may be as such, is to me, a second-rate substitute for the original, singularly void of imagination, zest and creative ability of the picture maker.

Lubitsch's public affirmation of film being "an art form" (put forth in a Paramount press release) was unusual for that era, when such talk by a Hollywood director was often taken as a sign of elitism and unforgivable pretension, risking the kind of backlash that damaged the careers of such forthright cinematic artists as Erich von Stroheim and Josef von Sternberg. Lubitsch was usually cagier about discussing his ambitions as well as more instinctively a popular artist. But his move back into heavy drama with *The Man I Killed* the year before making *Design for Living* was a further sign of his still-nagging need to be taken more seriously. The sharp decline in his boxoffice record in 1932, at the nadir of the Depression, perhaps made him all the more defiant in declaring his artistic ambitions with *Design for Living*. He clearly believed strongly in the bold steps he was taking with the material and wanted the public and reviewers to know how he felt. Being widely regarded by his peers and reviewers as Hollywood's most accomplished director allowed him to insist on being recognized as an artist on the same level as a great playwright or novelist. But the mixed response he would receive with *Design for Living* and the financial problems Paramount and other studios were having, along with his own shaky commercial status and the imposition of the strict new Code, would prove challenging to his ambitions and force him to reevaluate his approach.

The director wisely advised Hecht to dramatize the backstory of Coward's play about the impoverished beginnings of the three principal characters, a playwright (Fredric March), a painter (Gary Cooper), and their muse (Miriam Hopkins), an interior decorator in the play but a commercial artist in the film. Coward's *Design for Living* starts with the playwright character already a success (offstage) in London. Coward's preoccupation is mostly with what Tennessee Williams later called "the catastrophe of success," the psychological and practical problems that arise once a person's goals have been achieved. Coward shows the disillusioning effect on the male characters of their commercial corruption, the woman's opting out of the ménage à trois for a safer option (marriage to a staid businessman), and the threesome's absorption in work at the expense of their interrelationship. Lubitsch and Hecht, on the other hand, start by showing how the characters meet on a train in a lengthy silent sequence that seems designed to assert the primacy of film over the stage. "What do we have the camera for?" Lubitsch had said in 1932. "Why talk about things that happen, or have happened? Show them! Let the camera build up the sequence—for which the dialogue is the climax!" Considerable focus is placed on the part of the story Coward does not dramatize, the two men's struggle to achieve success and the characters' lives in bohemian Paris digs. The comedy-drama in the film of the threesome's formation and of the men establishing themselves in their fields makes it much more meaningful when the characters veer off in conflicting directions, personally and professionally, and eventually come back to their senses. Unlike in the play, we get the sense that the two men are rather mediocre talents; Hecht, a playwright himself, knowingly and hilariously skewers the pomposity of March's playwright character in particular. As a result, the men's corruption is less of an issue on-screen; for all the characters' talk about art, what is more at stake is their independence, the importance of not giving in to stifling social expectations.

Much of *Design for Living* is confined to Lubitsch's "Paris, Paramount." Like *Die Flamme* (*Montmartre*), which also deals with bohemian life and art in Paris, *Design for Living* is beautifully designed but economical in its artificial settings and pointedly claustrophobic. That creates a paradoxical visual contrast with the characters' attempts to live unfettered by social conventions. The film is elegantly designed by Hans Dreier and lit by Victor Milner, both of whom had teamed with Lubitsch on *Trouble in Paradise*. *Design for Living* is something of an inversion of that film—instead of a man involved romantically with two women, we have a woman involved romantically with two men, a much more scandalous situation in terms of the moral standards of the time. And in a sharp visual contrast with the swanky Parisian milieu of *Trouble in Paradise*, the first part of *Design for Living* is set mostly in the characters' shabby garret, with some prolonged stylized shots taken from outside the windows looking in. The effect is at once constricting and amusing, visually conveying the tensions involved in the storyline.

One of the choicest Lubitsch Touches has Hopkins's Gilda, unable to choose between the two men, throwing herself histrionically on their couch, raising a cloud of dust—a gag Lubitsch likes so much he does two variations on it. After March's Tom and Cooper's George have climbed up in the world, the characters move into swanky quarters in London and Paris, and the third act, unusually for Lubitsch, is set in the United States. Gilda unwisely tries to settle down into what used to be called a "New York marriage" with her dull, sexually ambivalent boss, Max Plunkett (Lubitsch's favorite eunuch, Edward Everett Horton). But her two "hooligan" boyfriends gleefully disrupt the marriage and induce her to run away with them from Plunkett's home in Utica, New York. Like *Trouble in Paradise*, *Design for Living* ends in a taxicab at night, with the three characters (rather than the other film's two) vowing to return to their former bohemian ways. They may be deluded about how successfully they can turn back to the past, but this joyously uninhibited ending is somewhat less "equivocal" than Coward's (to borrow his description). His characters laugh uproariously at their situation as the curtain comes down, which, as he notes, can be interpreted in varying ways according to the inclinations of the audience.

While the film of *Design for Living* is not as dazzling an achievement in the romantic comedy genre as *Trouble in Paradise*—the originality of the later film comes more from its situation, daring dialogue, and characterizations than from its more subdued narrative and filmic style—it represents a considerable improvement over Coward's original. Reviewers at the time, burdened with the prejudice of assuming that a prestigious theatrical work must be superior to a film version, particularly one that jettisons so much of the original, did not agree. They mistakenly assumed the changes weakened the play, a criticism that, it should be noted, was not made with Lubitsch's similarly brazen reworking of Wilde's *Lady Windermere's Fan*; in that case, the director probably earned a pass because it was a silent film, so substantial changes would have been more expected. Reviewers in 1933 also found it jarring that Coward's sophisticated European male characters—roles he wrote for himself and his friends Alfred Lunt and Lynne Fontanne, the reigning theatrical couple of the time—were transformed into three Americans (with Gilda keeping her name but the men being renamed from Otto and Leo to George and Tom while Ernest is renamed Max). Cooper plays considerably outside his already-developing taciturn type as the loquacious, often-irascible George, and the usually dour March is given as much lightness and charm as Lubitsch could coax from him, while Hopkins's folksy Georgia accent and thoroughly American manner are a far cry from Fontanne's grande dame style, but with all the compensations of Hopkins's saucy, seductive appeal.

Raphaelson passed on writing the screen adaptation, perhaps daunted by the challenge of rewriting Coward since he was a second-rank fellow playwright, although he rationalized the decision in other ways as well. He wondered, "What the hell can I do to add to Noël Coward?'" He "wished Lubitsch wouldn't do it. I was fed up with that whole milieu by then" and thought that Lubitsch should be fed up as well. Raphaelson asked himself, "He's so good; why doesn't he expand and deepen?" But the writer admitted in hindsight, "I failed to realize that this is what he's got." Lubitsch initially encountered difficulties adjusting to Hecht's more independent way of collaborating although they eventually accommodated to each other's personalities. The more equal balance of power between Lubitsch and Hecht (Hollywood's leading screenwriter for many years), unlike the imbalanced (if more harmonious) partnership between Lubitsch and Raphaelson, helped make *Design for Living* as much a writer's film as a director's. Hecht's brand of dialogue—brassy, impudent, always brilliant, raucously American—is much different in tone from the languidly sophisticated witticisms uttered by Coward's threesome. Hecht's writing is also more biting and sarcastic than Raphaelson's gentler form of romantic comedy. *Design for Living* often feels like a preliminary sketch for the screwball comedy genre that would soon displace the earlier brand of romantic comedy, with Hecht himself helping provide some of the choicest examples, such as *Twentieth Century* and *Nothing Sacred*. Screwball comedies tend to feature tougher and more aggressive female characters who control and humiliate weaker men, and the genre often involves physical mayhem between the sexes. Lubitsch's attempt to enter the screwball domain in 1938 with *Bluebeard's Eighth Wife* would result in one of his least characteristic, most abrasive films.

Lubitsch's wisdom in making radical changes in *Design for Living*—while keeping the basic situation of that provocative play—is hard to dispute. It is hard to reread the play today without finding it a dispiritingly pale forerunner of a much livelier film. The structural improvements made by Lubitsch and Hecht draw on an aspect of filmmaking in which the director always excels. Besides rectifying the play's awkward opening—with its lengthy discussion of a character we have yet to meet, and whose success is not dramatized but already a given—Lubitsch and Hecht incorporate many other important events the play keeps offscreen or deals with rather vaguely. Coward seems to avoid some of the dramatic issues that arise only to be brushed aside, but Lubitsch and Hecht confront them head-on. Sometimes to a fault: like *The Man I Killed*, this screenplay tends to spell things out too much although that same explicitness helps underscore how rebellious the characters are. *Design for Living* is, for the most part, an infectiously liberating film; the overall impression we get from the play is often the opposite whether or not Coward intended it to be so. Instead, he shows the messy emotional and practical complications of the characters' unorthodox lifestyle, especially the men's angry jealousy, which is treated more insouciantly by Lubitsch and Hecht. Because the play appeared when homosexuality was illegal in England, Coward may have felt somewhat constrained in his ability to be as free as he wanted with the sexual aspects of the threesome, especially with the distinctly gay overtones in the two men's relationship in his play (if not in the film, which treats it more as a relaxed male friendship). Gilda often seems an afterthought in the play, and she is given lines disparaging her gender and her own femininity. "I don't like women at all, Ernest; and I like myself least of any of them," she declares at one point, launching into a detailed catalogue of what Coward considers feminine flaws. Lubitsch, on the other hand, is a director who always appreciates and celebrates women, so his Gilda is more sympathetic.

Although working in a more constrained medium, Lubitsch had so far mastered the art of innuendo that his film version, paradoxically, feels much franker, looser, and less worried about sexuality than the original. There is always less Sturm und Drang surrounding sex in Lubitsch's cosmopolitan cinema than in film or stage works by others, and that is a major component of his originality. With less emphasis on the male bonding and a stripping away of the play's overt misogyny, the film is considerably more heterosexually romantic, albeit in Hecht's wisecracking vein, revolving around Hopkins's glorious performance in her expanded role as the sexually adventurous Gilda. Gilda's off-and-on, sometimes-simultaneous involvement with both men is unapologetically experimental sexually, almost astonishingly so for a 1933 film. This is the case even though the film has Gilda declare "No sex!" and insist that they all make a "gentleman's agreement" to avoid that complication. Anyone who knows Lubitsch can easily picture him winking broadly at that hilarious ironic touch. Although it disarmed the literal-minded censors in the Studio Relations Committee (SRC), the industry censorship body at the time the film was made, the more sophisticated members of the audience are clearly meant to regard that gambit as a joke since avoiding sex is a flagrant impossibility under such risqué circumstances.

Coward claimed, in a filmed introduction to a 1964 British television production of the play, "*Design for Living* as a title is ironic rather than dogmatic. I never intended for a moment that the design for living suggested in the play should apply to anyone outside its principal characters, Gilda, Otto, and Leo. These three glib, overarticulate, and amoral creatures force their lives and problems into fantastic shapes because they cannot help themselves." But it hardly seems accidental that many people have taken the play as a prescription for a rebellious, bohemian lifestyle. While it is true that Coward depicts his three characters as idiosyncratic creatures and their "design" as largely ad hoc, scattered, and awkward, it is otherwise hard to see the play as ironic. It seems clearly on the side of the characters' defiant, outspokenly antibourgeois libertinism. As Otto tells Gilda in the play, "We are different.

Our lives are diametrically opposed to ordinary social conventions; and it's no use grabbing at those conventions to hold us up when we find we're in deep water. We've jilted them and eliminated them, and we've got to find our own solutions for our own peculiar moral problems." Coward's curious statement about the title being ironic may be another sign of his defensiveness toward the material, even at such a late date. This is what D. H. Lawrence meant by "Never trust the artist. Trust the tale. The proper function of a critic is to save the tale from the artist who created it."

Lubitsch's film makes it abundantly obvious where its sympathies lie, with these "hooligans" who defy conventional middle-class morality. What both the play and the film are doing, in fact, is proposing the kind of situational ethics and highly individual morality that we are familiar with from Lubitsch's entire body of work, a moral "design" his characters arrive at empirically and not abstractly. While Lubitsch does not overlook the emotional difficulties involved in two men loving the same woman, he does not view it as an exhilarating dilemma bound to end in tragedy, as Truffaut does in his 1962 film *Jules et Jim*, which is strongly influenced by *Design for Living* (despite the major differences between Hopkins's warm and sensible Gilda and Jeanne Moreau's alluring but psychotic Catherine). Lubitsch's viewpoint on his characters' attempt to work out their own way of living together outside the bounds of traditional marriage and coupledom is generous and admiring. While some jealousy enters the picture, as it is bound to do in such a situation, the characters muddle through and find ways of putting it mostly behind them. Although *Design for Living* had to do some fancy dancing to get around the censorship it faced even a year before the Code was strictly enforced, and though its degree of feminism is qualified, it by and large pulls off its difficult balancing act with surprising frankness.

When Gilda first visits the men's messy apartment after flirting with both of them separately, she explains her modus operandi: "A thing happened to me that usually happens to men. You see, a man can meet two, three, or even four women and fall in love with all of them. And then by a process of—uh—interesting elimination, he's able to decide which one he prefers. But a woman must decide purely on instinct, guesswork, if she wants to be considered nice. Oh, it's quite all right for her to try on a hundred *hats* before she picks one." Tom interrupts, "Very fine. But which chapeau do you want, madame?" She looks down and says with humorous resignation, "Both." She goes on to describe her feelings for each of the men with delightfully Lubitschean (or Hechtian) hat metaphors. As Molly Haskell comments in *From Reverence to Rape*, "The number of sacred cows gaily demolished by the film—premarital virginity, fidelity, monogamy, marriage, and, finally, the one article of even bohemian faith, the exclusive, one-to-one love relationship—is staggering."

Most of that is true, although the film is less radical than Haskell's assessment in one important respect. Reflecting the limitations of gender power roles in films at that time—even in the rarified, highly sophisticated world of a Lubitsch movie—Gilda, for all her boldness, is self-effacing in a way that modern audiences cannot help finding problematic. When she lays out the ground rules for the three-way relationship, including the supposed avoidance of sex, she tells the men, "It'll be grand. . . . We're going to concentrate on work—your work—my work doesn't count. . . . I'm going to be a mother of the arts!" She kisses each man on the forehead, reiterating, "No sex. [They all join hands.] It's a gentleman's agreement." Although those last two lines seem tongue-in-cheek on Lubitsch's part, in telling the men that "my work doesn't count," Gilda is conforming to convention. We should not expect the heroine of a 1933 film to behave like a woman from the twenty-first century, but Gilda raises higher hopes than most female characters did even in that relatively enlightened and realistic pre-Code era. As a result, her self-effacing, even self-sacrificial dismissal of her own work seems a dispiriting concession to the gender limitations of her times.

Lubitsch does put somewhat more emphasis on Gilda's artistic ability than Coward does, starting with the film's bravura opening, the sustained silent sequence in the train compartment in which she sketches clever caricatures of the two sleeping men. When they wake, they all speak French for a while until the first English line of dialogue is heard: Gilda exclaiming, "Oh, nuts!" Although this sequence immediately establishes Gilda as a fellow artist, her supposed inferiority in that area is emphasized by the way she devotes her talents to illustrating tacky advertising projects for Max and then sells out to marry him rather than pursue her own interests. Despite having her finally throw over that unfulfilling bourgeois lifestyle and run off at the end with Tom and George for another try at some kind of ménage, the film still has Gilda reverting to being the "mother of the arts," acting supportive of the men rather than being truly independent.

Perhaps Lubitsch is trying to take a realistic view of the difficulties of sustaining a ménage à trois in that society, even more so for a woman than a man, but since Gilda's decisions are portrayed as voluntary on the part of this character who thinks of herself as determinedly unorthodox, her way of resolving these personal and professional conflicts is a distinct limitation in *Design for Living*. Gilda's settling for third place in the relationship conflicts with the way the film otherwise revolves around her and celebrates her spirit and sense of sexual liberation. Her career self-abnegation also seems disappointing in contrast with the denouement in *Trouble in Paradise*. Although both films are concerned with how unconventional sexual relationships can be pursued within formidable social strictures, *Trouble in Paradise* seems more genuinely daring and provocative, even if it does not go so far as to propose a ménage à trois as the solution for Gaston's dilemma.

But too much stress can be put on the literal mechanics of the relationship in *Design for Living*. How the characters try to achieve a practical balance between their romance and careers is probably less important than their sense of audacity and experimentation, the qualities that appeal most to Lubitsch. As Haskell notes, the film has more transcendent issues on its mind than sexuality per se, and these go deeply into the nature of the attraction between men and women as both friends and lovers: "The candor and innocence of the relationships . . . enable the film to go beyond sex to its true spirit which is not carnal but romantic, the collusion of kindred souls, of blithe spirits in a working relationship that works. . . . Perhaps the greatest and fullest relationships, like the greatest art, come from the imaginative, rather than physical, exchange of sexual characteristics, from a spiritual, rather than literal, identification of one sex with the other."

"NO 'COMPENSATING MORAL VALUES' "

The threesome running off together at the end of *Design for Living* is still surprising to see in the overall context of American filmmaking. As Kim Morgan writes in her 2011 essay on the film,

One cannot imagine this happening in a motion picture aimed at the masses today (unless it was meant to be darkly humorous, or played as a kinky kick), but since *Design for Living* isn't interested in hopped-up thrills, we're not clutching our pearls, startled by the finale; we're actually in a state of swoony wonder. A year after the film's release, however, the newly stringent Production Code Administration was all a-dither over the thing. Not only was the film banned by the Catholic Legion of Decency [a major force in pressuring the industry into enforcing the Code], but it was also denied a certificate by the PCA for rerelease [in August 1935]. It was now a pre-Code naughty.

Yes, but even so, the question still remains for viewers today: Just how did Lubitsch get away with this in 1933? Although the film was made before the imposition of what Andrew Sarris aptly described as "airtight" Hollywood censorship, the SRC was not entirely asleep at the switch even if the strictures it did impose, after initially judging the script to be unacceptable, seemed somewhat toothless and clueless, perhaps deliberately so. How *Design for Living* was pushed through the Hollywood system offers a case study of the finesse with which Lubitsch and his supportive studio managed to run rings around the censors to bring highly unconventional material to the screen.

Lubitsch spoke openly about how daring the film was and did so in an unusually expansive manner. Following a preview whose responses, Paramount reported, left him "highly optimistic," Lubitsch said while completing the final stages of editing, "I almost have the idea that a whole new philosophy of screen romance will be inaugurated by the general theme of the picture, and by one fetching expression of truth in particular. I refer to the situation in which Miriam Hopkins addresses Fredric March and Gary Cooper in which she discloses her duplicity and confesses that she loves both of them." Lubitsch went on to quote her speech about how "a thing happened to me that usually happens to men" and how she feels that a woman similarly should be able to try out different partners. Lubitsch continued,

Not only does this frank philosophy violate all the traditions of the past, but I believe it will find a sympathetic understanding with the audience. I think that it will not only provoke them, but also satisfy them in the same way Mae West does. After all, boil her confession down and it is merely the story of a woman with no inhibitions; a woman who does on the screen what all the male Don Juans have been doing for ages—and attractively.

Heretofore, the picture industry has complacently sat back and allowed the screen to maintain that romance for screen women meant a love which led to a singleness of coupling—heroines had to be in love to enjoy bedtime stories. Now we have a picture which upsets that. The woman in our triangle contends that her sex is entitled to a liberty that only men have enjoyed in the past. And when you say that, you say something that is as entertaining as it is provocative.

Of course, I'm not able to explain this to you with full justice to the situation as it is developed in the story of *Design for Living*. Relating it this way makes it sound like something that is usually left unsaid. But to have a pretty woman speak such lines with sincerity and charm gives the picture an entirely different complexion.

Pugnacious in the face of the threatened imposition of strict censorship on his and others' filmmaking, Lubitsch was just getting warmed up over what he considered an important step he was taking in the freedom of the screen. In another press release, he expounded on what he thought were the social causes for the newfound license he was enjoying (all too briefly, as it turned out). He paid tribute to the salutary influence of Coward and other playwrights on audience tastes and to what he saw as a loosening of the old puritanism in American life. Paramount reported that Lubitsch "believes this sudden metamorphosis of public taste is due to the younger generation's tolerance of the essential weaknesses of human nature. Also the older generation's sincere wish that their offspring grow up as liberal-minded men and women." Lubitsch said with defiant overoptimism,

I think the present custom of parents teaching the facts of life to their children at an early age is responsible for the success of the theater today. Without those new and wider views, motion pictures and the stage would have to confine their art to the traditional, old theme of a love which led to a singleness of coupling. But creative artists of the theater—the writers, actors and producers—can't thrive on outworn patterns. And the public's new acceptance of freedom in love comes as a life-saver to the theater.

It is the greatest and most vital forward step the entertainment world has taken since the days of the ancient Greeks. It gives broader scope and freer reign to the motion picture director who strives to achieve something different in lines of truth.

Shortly after Coward's play opened in New York that January, several months before the film began shooting, the SRC scented trouble. It declared in an internal memorandum, "Despite the author's excuse for the unconventionality of the characters' actions on the ground that they are artists and responsible, accordingly, to their own code of morals, it is somewhat doubtful whether a motion picture audience would take that viewpoint, and a motion picture treatment would be faced with that basic difficulty." After reading the script for Lubitsch's production, the censors insisted there had to be "at least two bedrooms" in George and Gilda's posh apartment, and that when George, after returning from a trip, unexpectedly discovers Tom there, Tom has to emerge from George's bedroom (still wearing his tuxedo from the night before) and not from Gilda's. Furthermore, in the two men's first apartment, there has to be "sufficient accommodation for three to live separable in the apartment and live up to their bargain of no sex." Those cosmetic changes were easy enough for Paramount to make and hardly got in the way of Lubitsch's innuendos. The layouts of the apartments are not stressed in the staging, but Lubitsch flouts the censors by having George return from a trip to discover Tom in one of the bedrooms in the apartment shared by George and Gilda, and after we are shown a close-up of a breakfast table with evidence of a meal consumed by two people, Tom readily admits to George that he spent the night with Gilda. The censors worried over smaller details as well. They did not want Gilda to say she was happy to be a "law-abiding citizen again," since that would have suggested that she had enjoyed illicit sex in the past. And they fretted over whether a theatrical producer would come off as too effeminate (Lubitsch dealt with that by casting Franklin Pangborn, the screen's foremost "sissy" character actor, as if to thumb his nose in their faces), and they even worried that the French would be offended by having Gilda caricature Napoleon as wearing only a union suit.

Dr. James Wingate, the head of the SRC before it evolved into the PCA, argued on the film's behalf to censor Joseph Breen, "The basic story—three people who find out there is something more important in life than sex, a lesson they learn by suffering when they do wrong, should be satisfactory under the code." During that time, when the SRC was still inclined to roll over to studios' creative wishes, Breen bought Wingate's dubious claim, and with the dual bedrooms and the "No sex" line, the censors were appeased enough to give *Design for Living* a seal. Still, the film was cut by fourteen minutes after being previewed. And after the PCA was formed in 1934, Breen was harsh in his condemnation of the film.

Not only was it barred from reissue in 1935, but when RKO raised the idea of a remake in 1940, Breen complained to that studio, "It goes without saying that the [Lubitsch] picture we saw this morning is definitely, and specifically, in violation of the Production Code on a half dozen counts, because it is a story of gross sexual irregularity, that is treated for comedy, and which has no 'compensating moral values' of any kind. That is the basic objection to the story as a whole." Breen also vetoed another attempt by Paramount to reissue the film in 1944, writing to a studio executive, "You will please have in mind that this particular opus, *Design for Living*, was one of the pictures which contributed much to the nation-wide public protest against motion pictures, which flaired [*sic*] up early in 1934, and which resulted in the formation of the Legion of Decency." But in the same year Breen wrote that letter, the inscrutable PCA somehow allowed the release of Preston Sturges's wildly salacious, hilariously blasphemous, and politically subversive sex farce *The Miracle of Morgan's Creek*, which Lubitsch greatly admired; James Agee wrote of that film, "The Hays office has been either hypnotized into a liberality for which it should be thanked, or has been raped in its sleep."

Design for Living is in some ways another transitional film for Lubitsch. Despite his hopeful statements, it was his last film released before the imposition of draconian censorship, and the tightened enforcement of the Code had much to do with the drastic changes his style underwent after *The Merry Widow*, the racy musical with which he followed *Design for Living*. But Lubitsch's style already showed signs of evolution in *Design for Living*. Perhaps as a conscious form of counterpoint to its flagrantly daring content, the film is relatively restrained visually, much less flamboyant than *Trouble in Paradise* and Lubitsch's other early sound pictures. And partly because it is so dialogue-driven, *Design for Living* is filmed with a less active camera, often in three-shots or two-shots and long takes, and with the camera functioning as a dispassionate observer. That relative neutrality works well for the themes of this story, and *Design for Living* is shot with the elegance one always associates with Lubitsch. But it seems in retrospect that with *Trouble in Paradise*, Lubitsch had gone almost as far as he could possibly go with his extremely stylized manner of storytelling. Although *The Merry Widow* is something of a return to that elaborate style, it represents its final flowering.

The simplification that began to dominate Lubitsch's style with his next film as a director, *Angel* (1937), was a further step in being more visually discreet in a period of increased censorship as well as a function of financial limitations and changing tastes. The Depression-era audience had become more interested in proletarian stories and more utilitarian, "invisible" forms of direction and production design; musicals set in mythical kingdoms and other fanciful frolics became less popular. Paramount's financial problems in the early thirties, which stemmed partly from the trend for grittier filmmaking, and Lubitsch's own weak boxoffice pattern in 1932 had helped prompt him to economize by making *Design for Living*, whose intimate scale allowed for a relatively modest budget ($563,000). With that film it became apparent that he was concentrating more on people talking than on using his camera to make points with the ostentatious touches for which he was celebrated even if he includes some characteristically Lubitschean flourishes (such as the opening silent sequence, the dust gags, and the ingenious visually and verbally metaphorical connections drawn between Tom and his typewriter). The more unobtrusive visual approach that began with *Design for Living* eventually, by the late 1930s, became Lubitsch's preferred style. In the aftermath of his last-ditch sexual frolicking, the Code forced him to become even more subtle in his means of expression, a radical change in style that was spurred by the outré subject matter of *Design for Living* and became a necessity after he ran into problems with the censors in the late stages of *The Merry Widow*.

With that expensive musical a boxoffice flop, Lubitsch took a hiatus from directing for more than two years, from the fall of 1934 until March 1937. He seems to have done so partly in order to reconsider his artistic approach in light of the new censorship strictures and his flagging boxoffice appeal. During that period of uncertainty in his career, he surprised Hollywood by accepting the position of head of production at Paramount, a move that lasted only a year and did not work out well for either him or the studio. When he returned to directing with *Angel*, Lubitsch's style, in a sense, became more safely conventional, employing the invisible storytelling methods that had been perfected by the Hollywood system.

But if Lubitsch lost something in abandoning his most visually stylized approach for a more subdued kind of filmmaking, the evolution of his work after the midthirties also demonstrates an increasingly self-effacing absorption in his actors and in the way they embody the storytelling through their interactions. It can be argued that this greater subtlety represents an advance in his directing. His invisible staging and blocking in such films as *Angel*, *Ninotchka*, and *The Shop Around the Corner*, when studied carefully, is as masterful in its complexity and sophistication as his earlier, more obviously virtuosic works. The later films help demonstrate the adage that sometimes the greatest art is that which disguises its artistry.

7

MASTER OF THE INEFFABLE

·

Lubitsch's self-imposed hiatus from directing in order to take stock of his career in the wake of industry changes, including the boxoffice decline of his films and the rise of censorship, led him to become a studio executive on February 4, 1935. Douglas W. Churchill of the *New York Times* somewhat hyperbolically called the move "the most interesting experiment in Hollywood history." But the year Lubitsch spent as head of production at Paramount was, by all accounts, an unhappy experience. Although the studio made a profit during his brief tenure, he did not prove a good fit for the job. The temperament that made him gently controlling on the set—"He did not allocate responsibility," as actor Robert Stack put it—was seen as overly autocratic in the front office, where he had to delegate some of his responsibilities, as any executive must do, as well as deal with lesser or very different talents whose foibles made him impatient.

A number of the films he supervised were too expensive or major disappointments at the boxoffice, such as Norman Taurog's revue *The Big Broadcast of 1936* and Leo McCarey's comedy *The Milky Way* (starring Harold

7.1 AND 7.2 "Garbo Laughs" was the famous ad line for *Ninotchka* (1939), with Greta Garbo and Melvyn Douglas, who breaks down her Russian reserve at a Paris restaurant. *(MGM/From the collections of the Margaret Herrick Library, Academy of Motion Picture Arts and Sciences.)*

Lloyd). Nor was Lubitsch's track record for supervising more highbrow entertainment much more successful. The one enduring classic he helped supervise during his tenure as production chief was a film maudit, Josef von Sternberg's *The Devil Is a Woman*, a flamboyantly stylized, extremely personal work that took that director's tortured relationship with Marlene Dietrich into avant-garde territory. The 1935 film was a flop that caused great turmoil at the studio, leaving Sternberg in disrepute and Dietrich's career in disarray. But it was in postproduction when Lubitsch took the job, so his input was minimal other than changing the title, against Sternberg's wishes, from *Capriccio Espagnol*, in an attempt to make this art-house curio more commercially attractive to the English-speaking audience. McCarey's splendid comedy Western *Ruggles of Red Gap* was released shortly after Lubitsch took the job, so it cannot be counted as his achievement in any way. But Henry Hathaway's uncharacteristically fantastical *Peter Ibbetson*, starring Gary Cooper and made during Lubitsch's brief tenure, was a succès d'estime and went on to become a minor cult film. Nevertheless, most of the productions Paramount turned out during Lubitsch's tenure, other than Cecil B. DeMille's formulaic spectacle *The Crusades*, were potboilers.

Gottfried Reinhardt recalled that when Lubitsch became Paramount's production chief, "all of Hollywood thought it was a weird choice. . . . Lubitsch was a particularly bad idea because he was incapable of delegating authority. . . . He was a loner, he had to be a loner, to work his own way." It seemed that Lubitsch, adrift in his true profession, took the job partly out of uncertainty over what to do next and because it appeared to offer a new level of prestige in Hollywood at a time when he felt vulnerable. That he may have needed such reassurance, important by Hollywood standards but not so much to the outside world, may seem strange in retrospect. Despite his faltering commercial track record during that financially troubled period, Lubitsch was still widely regarded as being among the handful of most important Hollywood directors. And yet younger talents were rising, most notably Frank Capra, who had been paying his dues directing a wide variety of pictures for Columbia for seven years before his 1934 romantic comedy, *It Happened One Night*, became a runaway hit and the first film to sweep all five major Oscars, while Lubitsch's lavish, stylistically dazzling *Merry Widow* was suffering relative boxoffice neglect.

The handwriting was on the wall for Lubitsch and Hollywood: the market for high-style, ultrasophisticated romantic comedies and musicals was constricting as the newer, rougher, more proletarian kind of comedy was beginning to dominate those genres. There is no evidence that in taking a break from directing Lubitsch planned a permanent retirement from his primary job, which he had been carrying out so masterfully for more than twenty years in two countries. But assuming the demanding, even grueling executive post at Paramount, supervising sixty films a year for a studio that was just emerging from bankruptcy, did demonstrate a strong degree of ambition and commitment.

Churchill of the *Times* tempered his excitement over Lubitsch's new job in a March 1935 article by presciently expressing skepticism about how such a strongly individualistic talent would be able to work with ordinary mortals: "His assumption of the Paramount throne is, frankly, an experiment, and Hollywood has ever been just a little shy of experiments. Perhaps, quite unconsciously, the lads of the town fear him. . . . To triumph in an argument with him it is necessary not only to be a good debater . . . but to have and to be able to prove ability. Lubitsch knows all the answers." Lubitsch tried to assure the interviewer, "I can't contribute much to sixty pictures a year, but I can give a little to each. . . . The screen would be pretty dull if all directors made pictures alike. I haven't any intention of injecting my personal tastes into anyone's work." But he distinguished between the "script shooters," competent directors who merely followed the carefully prepared studio scripts, and the small number of "creative" directors. And he sent a clear signal that he and Paramount had no continued tolerance for Sternberg's artistic experimentation: "There was a time when directors thought that by making silly camera angles and dissolves they were geniuses. They didn't know how to tell a story and they covered up with a pseudo artistry. . . . They impressed for a short time, but their day is over. No man is a genius unless he can deliver honest entertainment." Churchill noted, "He named no names, but those familiar with recent history at Paramount can possibly divine the subject of his comment."

With that somewhat philistine attitude (Sternberg bitterly said he was "liquidated by Lubitsch"), Lubitsch unfortunately signaled that Paramount was in for a dull time under his watch, as indeed proved to be the case. "The Lubitsch regime at Paramount has been slow in starting," Churchill noted in a follow-up piece that May. Elsa Schallert observed in the *Los Angeles Times* that Lubitsch "was more or less wedged between the machinery of a passing regime and a new order. There was the usual chaos and uncertainty. He spoke in pat, noncommittal phrases. Mere words tossed literally over the left shoulder. . . . Mr. Lubitsch reminded one of a newly elected monarch sitting watchfully and cautiously on his throne, wondering whether or not his crown was on straight." When she visited again six months later, however, she found a "marked change in attitude and spirit of Mr. Lubitsch himself. He again talks as he formerly did. He is at once more the dynamic, positive, aggressive man that I have known for many years. The highly informed, acute mind—the sharp humor, the biting irony—all of these qualities were abundantly evident." But that buoyancy did not last much longer.

Just how miscast he was in his new role can further be gauged by the 1936 romantic comedy *Desire* starring Dietrich and Cooper. This was the one film during his tenure as production chief on which Lubitsch put his name as producer, indicating an unusual degree of personal involvement and investment of reputation. But the director was Frank Borzage, a respected specialist in ethereal love stories, and the main title card bills it as "A Frank Borzage Production." Some accounts suggest that Lubitsch may have directed some scenes, but his touch is not evident in this thoroughly mediocre film. He is on record pointing to his hiring of Borzage and two other top directors for Paramount, King Vidor and Lewis Milestone, saying it would be "presumptuous of me to try and dictate to these three. . . . I'd be too shrewd for that." Still, *Desire* bears some superficial resemblance to Lubitsch's work as a director. Some of his key behind-the-camera collaborators worked on it, and one of the several screenwriters, Edwin Justus Mayer, would later write Lubitsch's classic *To Be or Not to Be. Desire*'s storyline about a small gang of jewel thieves pretending to be aristocrats in Paris and Spain bears some resemblance to that of *Trouble in Paradise*. But that is where the similarities end.

Desire is glossy and well-shot, with two leads at the peak of their physical beauty. But it is an overly contrived, largely unfunny romantic comedy whose attempts at humor are often irritating; one extended "gag" involves a car horn that keeps going on and off until you want to scream. Even worse, the film is bereft of any genuine romantic chemistry between Dietrich and Cooper. That is particularly strange given the sparks the pair had struck a few years earlier in Sternberg's *Morocco* (1930). In *Desire*, Dietrich does her professional best to be charming and alluring in her duplicity. She looks spectacular, wearing an impressive array of contemporary fashions. Cooper is dapper but ill at ease in the vaguely defined part of an American automobile engineer who is, in effect, stalking Dietrich on his vacation in Spain while she uses him as a stooge to help smuggle stolen jewels. Cooper reacts to Dietrich's wiles with the kind of uncomfortable, embarrassed, schoolboyish chortle he began to adopt around this time, a mannerism the actor unfortunately would exhibit for the rest of his career. The settings for *Desire* are a patchwork of location shots in France and Spain filmed by Lubitsch's longtime associate Eric Locke combined with frequent shots of the two lovers driving in front of a process screen. That constant artifice is especially distracting for a film about a lengthy road journey. So, from a production point of view, *Desire* squanders a first-rate team of stars because of a weak story, a tepid screenplay, and lackluster shooting methods. The feeling left by *Desire* is of a film without a strong hand at the tiller either as director or producer.

Perhaps that is adequately explained by Lubitsch's distracted state at the time. But the film's pallid nature also stems from Paramount's attempt, led by Lubitsch himself, to create a new screen persona for Dietrich apart from Sternberg. *The Devil Is a Woman*, the last of that director's great run of eight films with her, had failed spectacularly at the boxoffice. It is the most unrelentingly sumptuous and baroque of all their collaborations, outdoing even *The Scarlet Empress* in its extreme stylization. Like *Desire*, *The Devil Is a Woman* is set in Spain, although in the earlier years of the century, and is a rarified allegory with Dietrich playing a heartless temptress cruelly toying with men. The long-standing enmity between Sternberg and Lubitsch, stemming mostly from a series of instances of professional friction, predated Lubitsch's becoming his boss. Paramount no doubt would have put an end to the increasingly uncommercial and ever more elaborately baroque Sternberg/Dietrich cycle even if Lubitsch had not been in charge.

Dietrich and her mentor were also showing strains in their working relationship, but Paramount's attempt to tone down the ever-increasing stylization of her vehicles and make her seem more like a "regular" star was not only a sad reflection of the studio's failure to appreciate the artistry of her Sternberg films but also a doomed attempt to recast a unique exotic star into roles for which various actresses could have been interchangeable. As a result, in *Desire* she seems lost in a pedestrian vehicle, still an ultraglamorous presence but bereft of the elaborate trappings that set off her beauty so exquisitely in the Sternberg films. *Desire* looks thin, underpopulated, and underdesigned as if in contempt of Sternberg.

Lubitsch's unhappy reign at Paramount came to an end with his abrupt firing on February 7, 1936. The lack of warning made him unhappy, although many in Hollywood could have predicted his ouster, and we can be grateful it drove him back to his true métier as a director. Despite his hurt feelings over this humiliation, Lubitsch realized he was far better off not being a studio executive and returning to the job in which he actually excelled. Paramount papered over the embarrassment with press releases stressing that positive aspect. "Please tell people that I'm first and last a director," Lubitsch said.

> During the past two [*sic*] years I have been sitting behind a big desk, having connection with the production of pictures only through other persons. . . . All of the pictures that I've had anything to do with during the past two years were directed by somebody else, and it has been necessary for me to work sort of by remote control, which hasn't pleased me at all. . . . For me, this has been all work without any fun. I derive my greatest enjoyment from being right on the set in the midst of activity around the camera. That's creative, and nothing else gives as much satisfaction. . . . I look forward to getting back into my old duties with a great deal of relish.

Before doing that, however, he recuperated by setting off on a lengthy European and Russian honeymoon with his second wife, Vivian Gaye. Born Sanya Bezencenet, the tall, icy blonde, who was twenty-seven when they married on June 27, 1935, in Phoenix, Arizona, was a London native of Russian descent. She was a graduate of the London School of Economics, and as an obituary reported when she died at the age of 102 in 2010, "She and a friend, Patricia Nathan, reinvented themselves as a Hungarian film star 'Sari Maritza' (Ms. Nathan) and her manager 'Vivian Gaye.'" Vivian was also an actress and was working as a writers' agent in Hollywood when Lubitsch met her; she sold him the rights to the German play on which *Desire* was based. According to Eyman, Vivian "would come to be almost universally loathed by Lubitsch's friends," who tended to think of her as a blatantly ambitious, snobbish adventurer. Their ultimately unhappy marriage led to divorce in 1944; Lubitsch, she said, had lost interest in her. Vivian later became the wife of Lane Timmons, who supervised U.S. aid to the French forces during their war in Indochina in the 1950s and was the American ambassador to Haiti when they married in 1964. Lubitsch's mismatched marriage to Vivian was another sorry episode in his romantic history, which contrasted so starkly with his filmic fantasies, and it helps explain why he threw himself so fervently into those artificial romantic worlds as a form of compensation. But the marriage did produce a daughter, Nicola Annepatricia Lubitsch, born on October 27, 1938, on whom Lubitsch doted for the remaining nine years of his life.

Lubitsch's first film as a director after his debacle as a studio executive, *Angel* (1937), stars Marlene Dietrich, which is somewhat ironic in light of his clash with Sternberg. Dietrich, who had a strong sense of how to control her image, did not see entirely eye to eye with Lubitsch during the production. But with his creative energies rekindled, Lubitsch was able to rectify all the missteps of *Desire* by casting Dietrich in a far more emotional, truly romantic role in one of his subtlest, most enigmatic films. *Angel* would mark the true beginning of a fascinating new creative period in which Lubitsch redefined himself artistically for the rest of his career. Lubitsch said at the time, "The official billing on the picture will be 'Marlene Dietrich in an Ernst Lubitsch production, *Angel*,' directed by Ernst Lubitsch. All of the honor is the first phrase, my agent tells me, but all of the fun is in the second."

STRETCHING THE POWERS OF SUGGESTION

No other Lubitsch film approaches its story with the extreme degree of obliqueness that we see in *Angel*. It is almost an experimental film in that regard. This tour de force is the director's adroit way of getting around the challenge of filming material that may have seemed almost unfilmable in that era under the Code. Based on a play by Melchior Lengyel, with a screenplay by Samson Raphaelson from an adaptation by Guy Bolton and Russell Medcraft, *Angel* is the discreetly scandalous story of a married woman, Lady Maria Barker (Dietrich), who seeks a sexual adventure after being neglected by her politely boring British diplomat husband, Sir Frederick (Herbert Marshall). While visiting a Parisian "salon" that, with perfect ambiguity, could be seen as a gambling establishment, a social club where affairs are arranged, a high-class brothel, or all three, Maria meets and falls in love with an American during a brief fling. Tony Halton (Melvyn Douglas) has not met her husband but turns out to have a connection with him, a deliciously oblique one, a shared lover named Paulette in Paris during World War I; that history foreshadows the more consequential dilemma on which *Angel* turns. Once the seemingly impossible situation of her enigmatic alliance with Tony is revealed to Frederick, the drama focuses on the married couple's attempts to work out a modus operandi.

Lubitsch's long-standing fascination with three-cornered romantic relationships is not treated lightly this time but with a high degree of emotional intensity. This does not mean overwrought drama with on-the-nose dialogue exchanges, as was the case, uncharacteristically, with *The Man I Killed*. The acting and dialogue in *Angel* are low-key and exquisitely subtle. The directing, for the most part, is emphatically unemphatic. The characters, due to a combination of deceit, discretion, social constraints, and censorship, can barely begin to describe their feelings in words, despite being highly articulate, sophisticated people. Out of that necessity and in response to the other influences that had been operating on his career and in Hollywood in general, Lubitsch was able to evolve an even greater level of subtlety in storytelling than he had attempted before. James Harvey's comment on *Trouble in Paradise* applies even more so here: "It's as if [Lubitsch and Raphaelson] had set out to test the expressive limits of indirection." Going beyond *The Marriage Circle* and *Lady Windermere's Fan* in its dexterous, between-the-lines dealing with suggestive sexual material, *Angel* spins an inextricably expressive web of dialogue and pictures. It often uses looks between the characters to convey the deeper meanings of seemingly casual or flippant remarks that can only hint at the drama unfolding and the emotions beneath these characters' tightly restrained exteriors.

The eyes have it in *Angel*, particularly Dietrich's, wide and festooned with lashes that function like windshield wipers, batting away emotional storms. If a character tries to come out and say something directly, such as Tony telling Maria during their first dinner that he loves her, it is treated more as a chess move than a call to obvious action. In the film's most darkly amusing irony, when Maria bluntly tells Frederick as they have breakfast, "Someone is in love with me. I'm crazy about him. I've decided to leave you," Frederick either does not hear her or does not believe her, a sign of the complacency that is the real problem with the marriage and has caused her to seek excitement elsewhere. She prefaces this revelation with, "I might say I'm a neglected wife," and he readily admits it; he assumes she will accept that neglect as part of the price of being married to a man of the world who keeps getting telegrams sending him hither and yon on vaguely defined but supposedly crucial diplomatic missions (to borrow Graham Greene's sarcastic comment on the Ronald Colman character in Capra's 1937 *Lost Horizon*, these messages "fall with an odd sound on ears accustomed to more dispensable Foreign Secretaries"). Lubitsch avoids dating his film too much or provoking political controversy (despite the talk of impending war, an inevitability by that year) but also indicates a certain disdain for political intrigue by keeping these matters so sketchy.

Some key dramatic action apparently happens in the gaps between scenes of *Angel* although to what extent is left somewhat ambiguous. Do Tony and "Angel" (Tony's term of endearment for Maria) consummate their passion that first night together between the scenes we do see, the dinner at the restaurant and an abortive late-night tryst in a nearly empty park? Or is that consummation a boastful lie on Tony's part? We get the "information" obliquely when Maria quizzes her husband about what Tony told him about his evening with a mystery woman. It seems to be an assumption on Frederick's part that Tony and the woman had sexual relations, and Maria's pointed question is perhaps an indication that it could be true. However, Frederick's belief that the couple dined at Tony's apartment, with all the innuendo that conveys, is contradicted by our having seen them in a private dining room after their more public dinner at the same restaurant. Did the sexual affair take place in that private room as Danilo's trysts do in *The Merry Widow*? In this private room, post-Code, we do not see a bed or a couch, but there may be one just offscreen, and we do see them kissing. The high degree of excitement and tension and intimacy displayed by Tony and Maria when they meet again might suggest, without words, that they *were* physically intimate in some way even if they did not have intercourse. But how much does the truth matter in this instance in comparison with the emotional stakes involved in the romance? As with much else in *Angel*, of greater and lesser magnitude, these issues are left to us to ponder. The film's deeper concern is not with carnal knowledge but with Maria's feelings for Tony and how they affect her marriage.

Despite Lubitsch's best efforts to work around Code strictures, some of the film's extreme obliqueness evidently had to do with censorship imposed *after* the film was shot. "For reasons that are unclear in PCA documentation, the film had to be recalled and reedited after it was initially approved and released," Maureen Furniss wrote in her study of the influence of the Code on Lubitsch's work.

> It seems, however, that a Legion of Decency review may have been a motivating factor. In a letter to [chief censor Joseph] Breen, the PCA's Geoffrey Shurlock noted, "John [Hammell of Paramount] stated that he assumed that our letter accepting the [previous] changes would not clear up the Legion of Decency's attitude. I told him of course that I assumed this to be correct; that their listing was an entirely separate matter." The cost of recutting and rescoring was, according to Shurlock, "staggering." He noted that the expense was "of course most regrettable, but nevertheless it contained a ray of comfort for us, inasmuch as they will probably be very careful in the future to avoid any recurrence of this regrettable incident." It appears that Lubitsch and his producers did become more careful after *Angel*, as Shurlock had predicted. In any case, PCA files for the remainder of Lubitsch's films show a marked decrease in censorship problems, although *That Uncertain Feeling*, *Ninotchka*, and *That Lady in Ermine* experienced some difficulty during the early stages of approval.

The interactive relationship between Lubitsch and his audience—an element more central to his work than perhaps any other director's, even Hitchcock's—has seldom been as vital as it is in *Angel*. Truffaut best explains this trait: "There would be no Lubitsch without an audience—but, watch out—the audience is not something apart from his work; it is *with* him in creating, it is part of the film. On Lubitsch's sound tracks, there are dialogue, sounds, music, and our laughter—this is essential. Otherwise, there would be no film. The prodigious ellipses in his plots work only because our laughter bridges the scenes. In the Lubitsch Swiss cheese, each hole winks." Truffaut described a Lubitsch film as a "game" played by three parties, "Lubitsch, the film, and the public." *Angel* is not one of the laugh-out-loud Lubitsch pictures, nor is it one of his entirely "serious" dramas. It adopts techniques more familiar from his comedies than from his outright dramas, ellipsis and suggestion, while treating somewhat gently a subject of the utmost emotional seriousness. In that, it is more effective than a more strenuously serious film such as *The Man I Killed*, and the smooth blending of comedic and dramatic techniques in *Angel* defines the successful approach of Lubitsch's evolved later style, which is more restrained stylistically than his earlier work. *Angel* does have a constant undercurrent of wit in its extremely oblique way of telling the story. The film's discretion becomes breathtakingly suspenseful and funny when this woman who has a one-night fling with a man finds him showing up as a luncheon guest at her home with her unsuspecting husband. She knows; the lover knows; the husband does not know. We know much of what has happened, but not all. Some of the backstory remains pointedly secretive, hidden away by Lubitsch to enhance the mystery of the emotions passing between "Angel" and Tony and, eventually, between Maria and her husband.

Truffaut cites the famous luncheon sequence in *Angel* as one of his foremost examples of celebrating Lubitsch's storytelling method. What is delightfully audacious and characteristic is that we do not see the actual luncheon. Instead, in the most stylishly comical Lubitsch fashion, we understand it through the reactions of the servants. The imperious butler, Wilton (Ernest Cossart), whom Lubitsch kids for his pomposity, is in an anteroom supervising the two table waiters. The waiters bring the plates back from the dining room quizzically for close examination. First comes the plate of Lady Barker. She has hardly touched her food. The staff wonder if there is something wrong with the veal. Then back comes the plate of Tony Halton. He has not eaten his meat either but chopped it, with apparent obsessive-compulsive anxiety, into little squares. And finally comes the plate of the master, Sir Frederick. His plate is empty. So there is nothing wrong with the meat. Something else is terribly wrong, and the shrewd servants, along with the audience, discern this from Lubitsch's wry use of food to express inner states of being. Frederick's appetite shows that he is blithely complacent in his ignorance of what is troubling his wife and guest.

A little earlier, while Tony was chatting casually with Frederick before Maria's entrance, Tony spotted a portrait in a frame on the piano, but it was turned away from the camera. Tony asks Frederick if it is Lady Barker and leaves their two-shot to go take a look. For a longish time, Lubitsch just holds on the husband and the empty space Tony has occupied as Frederick casually mixes them drinks. We are left to imagine Tony's thunderstruck reaction to discovering the terrible coincidence that Angel is the woman married to his newfound friend. How much more effective, then, when Maria joins them soon thereafter, that she and Tony are perfectly blasé, outwardly at least, determined not to tip their hands. Lubitsch's oblique approach to this revelation avoids showing predictably overwrought reactions and instead enables us to study the intricately subtle nonverbal responses Tony and Maria display privately to each other in the midst of the three-cornered dramatic situation that this meeting has brought about. We also study Frederick to wonder what will happen when he learns the truth we are privileged to know. So we become the fourth party in this situation. And even before the elliptical scene with the photograph, we had been let in on the central drama. When the social-climbing Tony introduces himself to Frederick at a party and wangles an invitation to the country house of this illustrious man, not knowing, unlike the audience, to whom Frederick is married, we can anticipate what will ensue, even if we cannot imagine how Lubitsch will show it.

It is no surprise that Hitchcock regarded Lubitsch as one of *his* masters: every action, every look, every inflection that follows for the rest of *Angel* keeps us in a state of (happily) agonized suspense. Hitchcock defined "suspense," as opposed to "mystery," as letting the audience in on things the characters do not know: "To my way of thinking, mystery is seldom suspenseful. In a whodunit, for instance, there is no suspense, but a sort of intellectual puzzle. The whodunit generates the kind of curiosity that is void of emotion, and emotion is an essential ingredient of suspense. . . . Whenever possible the public must be informed." Suspensefully waiting to see how characters will deal with situations that we can partially anticipate, we are enabled to have insights into their behavior that we otherwise would not have. Lubitsch's mastery of suspense in *Angel* is brilliant, and it is more than a game; rather, it is in the service of revealing the complexities of human character. We understand that just as Maria is playing a role as Angel, she is also offering a performance as the dutiful wife; like so many other Lubitsch characters, she is trapped in her social role but handles it with aplomb for her own developing purposes while she tries to "obey the dictates of society," as the opera scene in *Monte Carlo* puts it. We watch to see how Maria plans to wiggle out of the dilemma or turn it around for her own benefit. In the process, we come to learn about the depths of her personality even as she is realizing them herself.

Her attempt to deny that she is Angel when she is alone with Tony confuses him briefly but inevitably fails to succeed. After resisting his entreaties for another meeting, she tentatively agrees to see him again at the Paris salon. But by the time of that rendezvous, Frederick has found out about their clandestine relationship. The way Lubitsch shows this is especially ingenious. During the romantic dinner Tony had with Angel on their first meeting, a restaurant violinist improvised a tune Angel aptly calls "lovely" (this plaintive Frederick Hollander piece expressing the couple's romantic feelings is, like so much else in the film, pointedly nameless, as the violinist replies when Maria asks its title). And as often happens in Lubitsch romances, the music advances the story of the relationship. Maria absentmindedly plays the piece on the piano at home, rousing Frederick's aesthetic interest, which she carefully deflects before he can wonder too much about what it is. When Tony is visiting and starts to hum the same tune, she quickly cuts him off so Frederick will not recognize it and make the connection. Lubitsch, at that point, uses a flurry of unusually tight close-ups between Maria and Tony and an accelerated editing pace to express the danger involved and their shared realization that they must keep the tune a secret. But later, when Frederick (offscreen) calls Tony on the telephone and a butler goes to summon him, Tony is seen distantly through a doorway, playing the tune on a piano. All in the same dazzlingly inventive shot, Lubitsch pans back to the phone lying on the table and tracks in to a close-up, letting us imagine Frederick putting together all the pieces in his mind as the scene fades out.

The denouement also revolves around ellipses. These are Maria's way of demonstrating her feelings about the marriage and how Frederick should regard her. In ultra-Lubitschean fashion, the climax turns on interplay with an empty room and two doors. At the salon, Maria challenges Frederick about whether or not he will open the door to the next room to see whether another woman is in there as she claims, the actual Angel. This is her response to Frederick's angry demand upon learning the truth about her tryst, "What kind of life have you been leading? What kind of woman are you?" The mystery of Maria's true nature, and by extension the mystery of womanhood and love itself, is the principal focus of Lubitsch and Raphaelson's attention throughout the film. Preserving that mystery is the ostensible method Maria uses to force her husband to display trust or distrust, to let his feelings about her be known without him having what Othello calls "ocular proof" of whether or not she actually is the unfaithful Angel. But the director's emphasis on his female protagonist's mysteriousness is a form of respect for the depths of her character and her insistence on her individual identity beneath the role-playing—on her right to a dual identity, to the complexity of character that exists in all of us.

Before her marriage, Maria had some kind of friendship or other relationship, perhaps of a business nature, with the "Grand Duchess" who now runs the salon (Laura Hope Crews). This was evidently before the Russian woman opened the salon—if the two of them are telling the truth. Perhaps, as in other instances in the film, they are sharing a lie for the sake of appearances, a form of winking at each other to preserve their indiscretions. A virtuosic tracking shot introduces the salon as Tony enters it by letting us peek in a series of windows as the Grand Duchess arranges social introductions and supervises a gambling operation with a series of characters. Whether gambling is merely the cover for a brothel or whether the place is actually some kind of fancy social introduction club that skirts the edges of propriety is never made entirely explicit. We aren't allowed to hear the dialogue, and while we see some social activities between men and women, we don't see what goes on in the spaces between the various windows the camera passes. The true purposes of the Club de la Russe are left to our imagination; this is not the flagrant brothel masquerading as a Parisian nightclub that Lubitsch portrayed in *The Merry Widow* in 1934 before the censors went to work on that sequence and made such future representations in Hollywood films unthinkable. But the overriding impression for sophisticated viewers remains that the Grand Duchess is running a brothel; the ambiguity is there for plausible deniability to get around the censors. The point of the story would be diminished if the club were anything less than a brothel.

The challenge Lubitsch faced in marshaling all his powers of suggestion to imply what goes on at the club can be inferred from a statement about censorship he made in October 1934, around the time *The Merry Widow* opened and ran into its last-minute censorship problems: "No industry that lives from drama can exist if not permitted to deal with the urgent problems of the times, and it should not be forced to treat such problems in an unbelievable, fairy-tale manner. In my opinion, the present censorship drive will be successful only if it is liberal." By "successful," he presumably meant "doing the least amount of possible damage to artistic expression on the screen."

Why does Maria go to the club? We assume to meet a man, but it is all left unstated and discreet. *Angel* may not exactly be Lubitsch's version of Luis Buñuel's *Belle de Jour*; unlike Catherine Deneuve's title character in that 1967 film, Maria is not working at the establishment on a regular basis but apparently paying a single visit or her first in years. And if we want to believe that she just happens to hook up with a suave, handsome bachelor at a gambling salon/social introduction club without fully planning to cheat on her husband, the film allows us to do so. Despite the considerable difference between *Angel* and *Belle de Jour* in their degrees of explicitness, it is tempting to find affinities between those two films' examination of the taboo desires existing below the surface of a coolly proper married woman's life. As in Buñuel's film, and as there is so abundantly in the Sternberg/Dietrich films, there is even a hint of masochism in *Angel*. Maria tells Frederick she has dreamed of him beating her. He asks what she did in response, and she replies, breaking into a shy smile, "I'm afraid to tell you—I liked it."

Dietrich's foreignness makes a particularly strong contrast in the stuffy British manor house she inhabits as Lady Barker. Their different nationalities go largely unremarked on except for Maria's urging her husband to rekindle their romantic relationship by interrupting his busy routine to take her on holiday to a hotel where they had an early fling in Vienna. While helping Dietrich forge a less extremely eroticized but still exotic screen image in her post-Sternberg era, Lubitsch expressively uses her differences from Marshall's quintessentially proper upper-class Englishman to suggest a fundamental incompatibility that Sir Frederick cannot recognize. His complacency in not seeing this problem—like his inability to hear Maria's confession of infidelity—is so blatant that it becomes a form of satire. The oppressive decor of the Barker manor house is far removed from the sleek art deco settings of the previous Lubitsch talkies. Frederick's domain is characterized by heavy wooden doors and beams, low ceilings, few windows, and other features that contribute to making it feel not only musty but claustrophobic, a prisonlike setting from which Maria, we infer, is bound by a restless nature to escape despite her conflicting desire to be dominated (the impulse that drove her to find safety and respectability in a stifling marriage). But even the Paris salon is visually constricted by the tight camerawork and rendered unappealing with its bland, anonymous, barely furnished decor; the few shots of Paris streets are mostly stock or process shots, contributing to the film's entirely artificial feeling and lack of visual latitude.

In mostly jettisoning his trademark array of clever visual and aural touches for an unshowy visual style that generally conforms to the rules of Hollywood's standard invisible storytelling, Lubitsch throws more emphasis than ever before on the actors and the dialogue; their oblique dialogue is always pregnant with meaning. The camera is largely content to serve as a quiet observer of character interchanges. As in *Design for Living*, there are frequent and sometimes leisurely two-shots and three-shots, in keeping with Lubitsch's posture of discreet neutrality and his distinct lack of judgment toward his characters. They are allowed to exist in the frames without as much obvious directorial commentary as in his earlier films, whose greater reliance on elaborate montages intercutting shots of characters looking at objects and other people gives those films more highly directed, subjective points of view. But Lubitsch's seemingly scrupulous neutrality in *Angel* is just as much a stylistic choice as his previous intrusiveness. He directs our attention to telling details in less obvious ways while allowing us even greater freedom to make our own assessments of his characters. The more restrained camerawork of his new style, which he would follow until the end of his career in 1947, reflects a more emotionally open, if still carefully controlled, approach to directing. And style, as always, is in harmony with theme. Ironically, Lubitsch also reacted to the increasing pressures of censorship by adopting an even more flagrantly tolerant stance toward his characters. The director's increasingly generous, diplomatic view of human nature abounds in most of his late work, even in such a disturbing film as *Angel*.

Dietrich's glamour in *Angel* makes her stand out from the others in the film, providing its own statement of her independence. Maria is positioned as the center of our attention not only in plot terms but also as the exception to the film's overall visual grayness. Charles Lang, who previously shot *Desire*, lights Dietrich glowingly again here, with frequent backlighting of her blonde hair, and her glamorous features and outfits make her stand out like a beacon in a world of fog, a dazzling exception to a general run of drab characters. The Grand Duchess of the salon is not a high-blown Russian lady but is played by a dowdy American character actress, one of Lubitsch's comical casting-against-type affronts that George Cukor complained about after working with Lubitsch: "I admire Lubitsch very much, but he shot things in a highly stylized way that is simply not my own. And we had a different approach to language. Lubitsch never really spoke English very well, and it didn't finally matter in his case, but it led him to do things I couldn't do. For instance, he'd cast a very Middle Western actor like George Barbier to play the Emperor Franz Joseph"—actually, Barbier plays the king of the mythical kingdom of Flaustenthurm in *The Smiling Lieutenant* and the king of Marshovia in *The Merry Widow*—"This is something he'd never have permitted in German, where he was sensitive to the nuances of speech."

Sir Frederick's diplomatic exploits are chronicled in the kind of exigent headline montages reserved for characters of world importance in 1930s films, but he seems a rather dull technocrat who submits to having his life driven by urgent telegrams and speaks with calculatedly casual vagueness about what he actually does to make himself so indispensable to the state. Marshall is all crisp propriety and impeccable manners but with the conspicuous absence of the sly charm of his Gaston Monescu. And with Melvyn Douglas you always feel as if there is something vital missing. Though a suave and intelligent actor, he lacks the supreme star allure of a Gary Cooper or Cary Grant and gives the sense of filling in for one of the era's better leading men (as indeed he does in *Ninotchka*, for which Lubitsch wanted Grant but could not get him). But it is also possible to see that Douglas's second-rate quality helps his leading ladies shine more brightly by contrast and take more command of the screen.

The dazzling Maria seems conspicuously out of place in her husband's country manor house. She does not want to be regarded as a mere wife, an appendage to Sir Frederick, but as a woman who values both the marriage and her sense of personal freedom. She wants both, she wants it all, and we want it for her. She is unfailingly polite to Frederick but needs him to respect her as much as the director does even if, unlike Lubitsch, Frederick barely pays attention to her. Maria has to risk her marriage to get his attention, and she finally resorts to a dramatic ultimatum to force her husband to care at least as much about her as he does for the fate of Yugoslavia. When Frederick, finally aroused by learning of her apparent infidelity, shows up at the salon, she tells her husband, "Now, Frederick—if you go into that room, I'm afraid our marriage is over. . . . On the other hand, if you don't go in at all, you'll be a little uncertain. You won't be quite so sure of yourself, or of me. And that might be wonderful."

It is possible to see the film's happy ending as simply a compromise with the Breen Office, a reaffirmation of a troubled marriage, a way of reestablishing the conventional status quo. But it is more complex than that. Unable to help himself, Frederick opens the door. When he finds the room empty, he realizes by indirection that his wife indeed is the notorious Angel. She is an errant wife who has thereby admitted her betrayal of him. But despite her ultimatum, that is not the end of the marriage. For once looking sheepishly undignified, Frederick comes back to find her with Tony. After giving Tony a withering look, Frederick tells her, "You see, Maria, in the last few moments, I've thought more about our married life than in all the years we've been together." We have no doubt of this. With resignation, he goes to leave the establishment. Lubitsch tracks with him as he heads toward the door leading to the street, hoping against hope that she might follow him to their planned romantic reconciliation in Vienna.

We do not see Maria leave Tony inside. Instead she enters the tracking shot and joins Frederick by the arm, neither of them looking at the other as they exit the salon to pursue a life of considerable ambiguity and uncertainty. So the marriage is preserved despite Frederick's admitted distrust of his wife. He has made her promise that her Angel persona will no longer make an appearance, but this should not be taken as definitive, for Lubitsch has rarely been one to condemn adultery outright. *Angel* is consistent with his other films that view adultery in a mostly favorable light, perhaps even as an enhancement to a marriage that badly needs some excitement. Frederick tacitly admits this by going back to her, as she does by taking him back. Perhaps *Angel* suggests that the trade-off for the pleasure of being married to Marlene Dietrich is letting her nip off to a Parisian brothel every so often without asking any questions about it. So is this ending actually a way of restoring the "normality" of the marriage, a sop to the Code and American conventionality? Or is it Lubitsch's more continental way of respecting the true complexity of a marriage, as his protagonist defines it, as a matter of uncertainty that can be "wonderful"? I think it is both, though the marriage is only normal if the definition of that term is stretched well beyond conventional morality.

Lubitsch again manages to have his way with the Breen Office and twist social strictures to his own purpose. He knows how to outwit the censors and avoid unduly offending his audience with an ending that seems to preserve the status quo they want to cherish but also makes the relationship true to life's complexities, more realistically gray, not a black-and-white matter of blind trust or distrust. Frederick has learned the kind of lesson in life that Lubitsch characters are often made to learn, not the kind of moral lesson taught in churches or Hollywood boardrooms but the enlightening experience of a work of art, a nonmoralistic lesson based on empirical evidence of human conduct and interaction. The married couple, starting their lives over, go off together to explore the mysteries of each other's personalities (hers admittedly being far more mysterious than his). They will build their future together day by day, moment by moment, rather than assume that anything is permanent and not expect anything from each other beyond a commitment to make the effort.

This represents a very Lubitschean openness and generosity toward his characters' complex sense of their personal freedom. Having the marriage break up over Frederick's distrust would have been a simpler and less ambiguous ending, one that would have left Maria "punished" and alone yet in control of her own destiny. Having her depart arm in arm with Tony was impossible; in the Hollywood of 1937, a married woman could not go off happily with her lover even after her husband has left her. But a truly conventional ending would have had her chastened in some way; this film does not do so. *Angel* makes it clear that Maria values her marriage, and the film never takes the easy way out of making Frederick an ogre. As always in Lubitsch, the dice are not loaded, and the love of the game, the serious game of sexual and emotional affinities, is what matters.

THE MASTER STUMBLES

With his next two films, Lubitsch continued experimenting while still following most of the tenets of invisible Hollywood visual style. Hollywood—and particularly Paramount, his longtime base of operations—was beginning to consider him somewhat old hat in the changing commercial climate. Partly as a reaction to the tightened Code, the general tone of screen comedy was shifting from sexual suggestiveness to sexual aggression. So Lubitsch responded by reaching out to a newly minted team of writers. Charles Brackett and Billy Wilder gave Lubitsch's work the infusion of acerbic timeliness that the director needed to help him through this uncertain juncture in his career. But despite the writing team's arduous months of work with Lubitsch on their first collaborative effort, *Bluebeard's Eighth Wife* (1938), the working relationship among the three had not yet meshed in an artistically satisfying way. In examining the qualities that go into making the career of a great director, it is also instructive to study how even a master can stumble badly. And Brackett and Wilder's influence on Lubitsch, especially Wilder's, provides a valuable case study in the director's way of working with writers; Brackett and Wilder were considerably different from Raphaelson in the worldviews and writing styles they had to offer.

With *Bluebeard*, Lubitsch awkwardly dove into the current trend of screwball comedy with mostly unfunny and lamentable results. The film uncongenially adopts the conventions of the screwball genre and is thus uncharacteristically harsh in its treatment of sexual relations in a manner alien to Lubitsch's better instincts. Despite a lively performance by Claudette Colbert as a freewheeling, down-at-the-heels French adventurer, *Bluebeard* often comes off as cruel and misogynistic in showing her being manhandled by Gary Cooper, who clumsily plays an American millionaire playboy, Michael Brandon. Lubitsch should have learned from *Desire* not to cast Cooper in this kind of film, a mistake Wilder also made in *Love in the Afternoon* (1957); as Wilder later noted, although Cooper was actually a rake in real life, audiences would not accept him as one after his wholesome screen image had been formed. Colbert's character in *Bluebeard*, Nicole de Loiselle, gives her own punishment to her husband in spades; as Sarris wrote, her "excruciatingly sadistic performance . . . reflects the horrible torture inflicted on sex comedy after censorship reared its ugly head." The actress's considerable charm and usual breeziness make the film somewhat palatable despite its gratuitous unpleasantness.

But the director spectacularly regained his artistic bearings with his glorious 1939 romantic comedy *Ninotchka*. The imbalance in his collaboration with the screenwriters was rectified, and their differing strengths proved complementary. On *Ninotchka*, Brackett and Wilder collaborated with Wilder's former Berlin colleague and fellow Viennese Walter Reisch, who was probably a leavening influence. Wilder had previously worked with Reisch on the uneven but often-captivating Lubitsch-influenced 1932 German film *Ein blonder Traum* (*A Blonde Dream*), a poignant musical romance set against the grim social conditions of the Depression era.

Ninotchka stars Greta Garbo as a hardboiled Soviet commissar whose latent vulnerability and humanity emerge in a romance with a gigolo (Melvyn Douglas) during her trade visit to Paris. That film is based on a story by Melchior Lengyel, the Hungarian writer whose plays had served as the source material for Lubitsch's silent *Forbidden Paradise* as well as *Angel* and who would also provide the story for *To Be or Not to Be*. As the Lengyel connection would suggest, *Ninotchka* harks back in some ways to Lubitsch's silent historical comedy-dramas in blending political events with intimate sexual intrigue; *Forbidden Paradise*, from Lengyel's play *The Czarina*, is also based on a Russian theme. But *Ninotchka*'s viewpoint was very timely and au courant even if an updated title card had to be added when World War II broke out shortly after the previews. The film's incisive, hilarious satire of the clash between communism and capitalism—with capitalism and luxury winning out over regimentation and austerity, naturally enough for Lubitsch—is so sophisticated, so intelligently written and played, that *Ninotchka* is one of the rare Hollywood anticommunist films that can be watched today not with embarrassment but delight.

Ninotchka is justly celebrated as one of the warmest, most endearing of romantic comedies. As such, it stands in stark contrast to *Bluebeard's Eighth Wife*. Some of the political acumen of *Ninotchka*, along with some of the asperity of *Bluebeard*, can be attributed to the influence of Wilder, the brash young European émigré, rather than to his considerably older, more genteel, and conservative writing partner, Brackett. First teamed by Paramount story editor Manny Wolf in August 1936 specifically to work with Lubitsch on *Bluebeard*, Brackett and Wilder went on to have a long and fruitful, though contentious, partnership. *Ninotchka* would bring the team their first Oscar nominations as well as the first for Reisch.

Wilder's background as a reporter in Vienna and Berlin made him an acute social observer, a trait that elevated his work in German newspapers and films above the formulaic during the turbulent Weimar period, which helped form his caustic sensibility. "Billie" Wilder, as he was then known, learned how to navigate the perilous waves of political and cultural upheaval as a screenwriter for the leading German studio, UFA, in the time before the 1933 Nazi takeover. According to Brackett's diaries, Lubitsch was familiar with Wilder's German work before he hired the team to collaborate with him. Wilder's most successful screenwriting in Berlin was on *People on Sunday*, the 1930 antiromantic slice of life shot on a shoestring budget in natural settings in and around the city, and on his endearingly comical 1931 screenplay about a youthful street gang capturing a thief, *Emil and the Detectives*, based on the novel by Erich Kästner. The last screenplay Wilder wrote in Germany, *Was Frauen träumen* (*What Women Dream*), an uneasy 1933 comedy about a female kleptomaniac in Berlin whose jewel thievery is protected by a wealthy older suitor, is a direct, though far inferior, homage to *Trouble in Paradise*. It not only lacks the assured high style of a genuine Lubitsch film but also suffers from the dark mood of impending danger that was descending when it was made. By the date of the film's German premiere, April 20, 1933, Hitler was running the country, Wilder had fled to Paris en route to Hollywood, and his name had been removed from the screen credits because he was Jewish. Although Wilder was largely frustrated with his work for UFA, the skill he began developing there for interweaving trenchant contemporary sociopolitical commentary with popular entertainment values became one of his vital contributions to *Ninotchka*.

Wilder would become Lubitsch's most celebrated acolyte, always holding up Lubitsch as his mentor and sporadically trying to emulate his style overtly. But Wilder, a more caustic filmmaker, had to take a roundabout route to fully return to his Lubitschean roots in his later work even if that background influenced him throughout his Hollywood directing career. There was a conflict in Wilder between the elegance he cherished in Lubitsch, partly as a throwback to the bygone ideals of their common cultural heritage, and his own harsher sensibility. It is one of the bitter ironies of his career that after he fled fascism and emigrated to America in 1934, the first few film assignments he was given in Hollywood, as a refugee struggling to establish himself while learning to write in a new language, were even less suited to his talents than the mostly formulaic fare he had been given to write at UFA. Initially in Hollywood, he was typecast as a writer of pseudo-European light comedies and frothy musicals, and his early American scripts are considerably more banal and compromised than most of his German work. It was only after Paramount fortuitously teamed Wilder with the upper-crust American Brackett that the immigrant screenwriter was able to start escaping the straitjacket that had bound him during the first decade of his career in two countries with very different political systems but remarkably similar film industries. But even after he began working with Brackett, Wilder still had to work on some trivial projects while the team battled with Paramount for assignments to more substantial material.

The European backgrounds that Wilder and Lubitsch shared gave them the cosmopolitan sensibility with which they revolutionized American sexual comedy in their different eras of dominance and with their different ways of lancing abscesses of sexual hypocrisy. Wilder remarked in 1970, "If I look back and if I say, 'Well, who would I like to be were I not myself?' I would have to say, naturally, Lubitsch." Even though Wilder often tried to channel Lubitsch, the acolyte had to face the fact that the task was quixotic: "Occasionally, I look for an elegant twist and I say to myself, 'How would Lubitsch have done it?' and I will come up with something and it will be *like* Lubitsch, but it won't *be* Lubitsch." Lubitsch was not often as overtly caustic or blunt as Wilder, but his satirical jabs could be as sharply pointed when he wanted them to be. His films' dominant tone was romanticism, but it was always strongly seasoned and qualified with an acidulous dose of irony. Wilder's work as a writer/director was both celebrated and flayed by critics and audiences for its supposed "cynicism." He had an unsentimental view of women (unusual for his time and place and enough for some to consider him a misogynist), but he had an equally unsentimental view of men. Wilder's jaundiced attitude toward human nature—"Is everybody in this world corrupt?" cries the young East German communist in his 1961 film *One, Two, Three*, to which a Soviet commissar replies, "I don't know everybody"—did not mean he was heartless. It did not preclude a Lubitschean generosity toward ordinary human foibles and a deep streak of unreconstructed romanticism. That tendency, seen sporadically in his occasional uneven attempts to make Lubitschean pictures, came out fully in his late work as a reaction against other filmmakers who were reveling in shock, crudity, and brutality.

But despite the deep cultural connections between Wilder and Lubitsch, there were also substantial differences between their sensibilities. That was already evident in the way Wilder's pugnacious approach infiltrated itself into the unaccustomed roughhousing of *Bluebeard's Eighth Wife*, which seems so atypical of Lubitsch and so uncongenial to his talents. Wilder claimed in his 1999 interview book with Cameron Crowe, "Lubitsch was never blunt, you know—it was never right *in your face.*" Except, notably, in this one instance.

The assignment working with Lubitsch represented major career breakthroughs for Brackett and Wilder, who eventually became so linked in the public eye that they became celebrated as "BrackettandWilder." Brackett had more distinguished literary credentials than his junior partner. Forty-four years of age to Wilder's thirty when they were teamed, Brackett had published short stories in the *Saturday Evening Post*, had been drama critic for the *New Yorker*, and was a novelist before coming to Hollywood in the early 1930s. One of his novels, *Entirely Surrounded* (1934), satirized the Algonquin Round Table of sophisticated New York wits; he hovered on the periphery of that institution. But Brackett's novels did not receive much acclaim, and his early screenwriting career was mostly undistinguished, the work unsatisfying to his tastes. Nevertheless, he was a respected figure in Hollywood, president of the Screen Writers Guild in 1938–1939, and his conservative, establishment, old-American bona fides gave Wilder not only a leg up in Hollywood status but also protective coloration.

"The anomaly of their relationship is that two more antithetic personalities would be hard to find," Lincoln Barnett observed in a 1944 *Life* magazine profile of the team.

> Brackett is something of a blue blood . . . a congenital Republican with liberal instincts, Wilder is a fervid New Dealer with leftist leanings. . . . Wilder is galvanic, facile, prolific with ideas, endowed with visual imagination. Brackett is critical, contemplative, gifted with a graceful literary style and cultivated taste. When Wilder sparks off a salvo of suggestions, Brackett sorts good from bad and imparts to the best of them adroit terms of action and phrase. The exquisite, lambent dialog that is the hallmark of all of their pictures is generally ascribed to Brackett although Wilder, despite his accent, has a keen ear for the American idiom and an acute sense of the flexibility of words. They complement each other in other ways. Wilder is cynical, taut, acidulous, a realist. Brackett is urbane, gentle, fanciful. Wilder is an instinctive dramatist who envisages story ideas through the camera's mobile eye: "I'm a celluloid maniac," he says. Brackett is primarily a novelist, attuned to niceties of continuity and construction.

Shortly after they began working together, Brackett wrote in his diary that Wilder was "a hard, conscientious worker, without a very sensitive ear for dialogue, but a beautiful constructionist. He has the passion for the official joke of a second-rate dialogist. He's extremely stubborn, which makes for trying work situations, but they're stimulating." Construction was a craft Wilder had learned in Germany both as a journalist and as a screenwriter for hire. And though he always felt somewhat insecure in his English, there have been few greater wits in Hollywood history; his screen dialogue would become celebrated for its flair and style. Wilder's lingering anxiety about his adopted language was one of the reasons he always wanted a partner in addition to his gregariousness and restless discomfort about writing alone. Eventually, after twelve years of a fertile but increasingly abrasive partnership—Sarris aptly described Brackett as "older, more highly educated, more socially prominent than Wilder, but pathetically and vulnerably dependent"—Wilder broke up with Brackett and found a more culturally and professionally congenial partner in I. A. L. Diamond. As a result, Wilder's social critiques sharpened, and his treatment of sexuality became bawdier.

The Brackett and Wilder team's working relationship with Lubitsch seems to have been largely harmonious even if the director proved a hard taskmaster and often made them redo their work in a search for perfection and greater hilarity that remained elusive in the case of *Bluebeard*. Wilder was jealous of how harmonious Brackett at first seemed to be with Lubitsch. One time Wilder "shouted indignantly" at his partner, "For Christ's sake, what is this? He apologizes to you! You and he will be making a baby together before the picture is through!" Lubitsch had only a passing relationship with Wilder in Hollywood before they worked together. Wilder told Crowe that Lubitsch "never wanted to work with a German, because he did not want to get the reputation that he only works with Germans. Actually he wanted to have Brackett." But though the highly assimilated Lubitsch kept many of his fellow German émigrés at an arm's length in Hollywood so that he would not become overly identified with foreign filmmaking, he did have some prominent collaborators from Europe before Wilder, including Hans Kräly, Ernest Vajda, Henry Blanke, production assistant Eric Locke, and costume designer Ali Hubert. Lubitsch also helped support refugees from Europe to Hollywood through the generous cooperative fund that he and Austrian émigré agent Paul Kohner spearheaded in the film industry. Despite his initial roadblock with Lubitsch, Wilder quickly ingratiated himself through his talent and diligent adulation, and they eventually became close friends, even living together for a while after Lubitsch had one of his heart attacks in the 1940s.

MEETING CUTE, MARRYING UGLY

Bluebeard's Eighth Wife is based loosely on the 1921 play *La huitieme femme de Barbe-bleue* by Alfred Savoir, a Polish Jewish émigré to France. The "bluebeard" in the play is an American named John Brown, "the richest man in the world." The same year brought an English adaptation by Charlton Andrews, *Bluebeard's 8th Wife*. A silent film version, now lost, was made in 1923. It was directed by the not-usually-witty journeyman Sam Wood and starred Gloria Swanson, who would become Wilder's Norma Desmond in *Sunset Blvd.* The leading lady of Andrews's stage version of *Bluebeard* was Ina Claire, who costars in *Ninotchka* as Garbo's romantic and political rival, the White Russian émigré Grand Duchess Swana.

In a posthumous tribute to Lubitsch, Brackett and Wilder recalled, "To write for Ernst Lubitsch was an education, a stimulus, a privilege, but it was no cinch. . . . He was apt to approach each portion with the terrifying statement, 'This scene must be *hilahrious.*' Thereupon, all minds involved focused on making the scene *hilahrious* and were held to that task with a kind of pneumatic-drill steadiness until, by George, the scene became *hilahrious.*" It is evident in retrospect that any strain they encountered early on was more between their sensibilities (especially Wilder's) and Lubitsch's. The writers evidently toiled conscientiously to entertain audiences with the misadventures of the much-married, sexually feckless cad played by Gary Cooper. Just before they wrote the script, Cooper had captivated audiences in quite a different role as the naïvely romantic small-town man who gets wised up through heartbreak in Capra's *Mr. Deeds Goes to Town*; Cooper's role in *Bluebeard* seems especially ill-matched to his already developing star persona as a likable naïf.

Perhaps Lubitsch thought he could pull off another modern version of *The Taming of the Shrew*; he had already used Shakespeare's comedy as a partial model for his 1920 German farce with Emil Jannings, *Kohlhiesel's Daughters*.

But *Bluebeard* is far from as good-natured as that film is about the war between the sexes. Cooper's Brandon, a seemingly incorrigible male chauvinist who expects women to go along with his every whim, is a more worldly figure in the Lubitsch gallery of characters than Jannings's Peter Xaver in the rustic silent comedy. But Michael is actually clueless about women, and when he struggles to understand how to deal with the opposite sex, he is shown consulting the text of the Shakespeare play, a comical but somewhat ambiguous touch by the director. Although the malleable Peter is ironically tamed by Henny Porten's shrewish variant in *Kohlhiesel's Daughters*, much to the delight of the audience, Michael's reading *The Taming of the Shrew* for pointers about handling women simply prompts him to go berserk and physically attack his latest wife, Nicole.

Bluebeard's Eighth Wife also contains allusions to Lubitsch's *Madame DuBarry* and compares Michael to Henry VIII, the psychopathic, six-time-wed English king in *Anna Boleyn*, whose marital misadventures are not treated comically. In *Bluebeard*, all but one of Michael's previous seven marriages have ended in divorce; he assures his understandably anxious new bride that the other ex–Mrs. Brandon died "a natural death." Nicole says with understandable exasperation to this smug American fashion plate, "You buy wives, just like . . . like shirts—and after you've worn them, you toss them away."

While conducting business at his bank in Nice on the French Riviera, Michael is tricked into another marriage by Nicole, the impecunious but feisty daughter of a French marquis (Edward Everett Horton). The marquis has been seeking business deals of his own with Brandon, and he basically pimps out Nicole to Brandon to save his seedy old family from destitution. Wilder's career-long fascination with themes of prostitution—both literally and in many social variants—shadows this ostensibly comical situation in *Bluebeard*. Nicole is no gold digger, however, but a struggling con artist trying to navigate the shoals of the Depression while keeping as much of her self-respect as the situation allows. Although she can be seen as subtly prompting the millionaire's attentions, she has our sympathy because she is getting back at Michael after he presumptuously proposes marriage with barely any wooing. She negotiates her own lucrative prenuptial agreement (here the film is definitely ahead of its time) and marries the callous American to teach him a much-needed lesson. She does not intend to consummate the deal before driving him to divorce her and collecting her settlement.

After much mutual antagonism and some wavering on Nicole's part, the irascible Michael winds up in a French mental hospital wearing a straitjacket in this comedy of hostility, which leaves viewers with a bitter taste, in a manner uncongenial to Lubitsch. The director seemed to acknowledge this when commenting on the ending to the *New York Times*, "Subtlety, ha? Don't tell them there's a sledge-hammer in it." Anticipating what would happen to the genres he helped create, the romantic comedy and the musical, Lubitsch had noted in 1937, "The Lubitsch touch is the direct opposite of the equally famous sledgehammer touch. The sledgehammer touch comprises a technique equally difficult to achieve. As befits its name, it carries a terrific sock, a sock which in fact stuns the audience. The sledgehammer touch is the one which inspired the well-known and age-old comedy line, 'Hit me again, I can still feel it.' . . . I do not think audiences need to have a point driven home with a sledgehammer."

Nicole's claim that she and Michael are now on an equal basis and her supposed falling in love with him despite it all are never remotely convincing, although she gets off a drolly acerbic Wilderish quip: "Why do you think a woman puts a man into a straitjacket? Because she loves him." *Bluebeard's Eighth Wife*, and indeed, the whole screwball genre, revels in sexual antagonism. Such films follow the observation of the psychiatrist in Howard Hawks's 1938 *Bringing Up Baby*, one of the leading exemplars of the genre, that "the love impulse in men very frequently reveals itself in terms of conflict."

Michael, a Michigan native, is one of the first of numerous "Ugly Americans" pilloried in Wilder's work for their kneejerk arrogance and rudeness, infuriatingly smug sense of entitlement, and abysmal ignorance of more civilized European values. But rather than presenting this millionaire as a walking Brechtian alienation effect, a heel like some of Wilder's later protagonists who dare the audience to try to identify with them, this confused film enlists Cooper in an utterly charmless performance that must have baffled many of his contemporary admirers. In one of the film's many misjudgments, Lubitsch prods this consummate underactor to overact, bellow, and snarl throughout. As Frank S. Nugent wrote in his *New York Times* review, "Put seven divorced wives behind Mr. Deeds, each with a $50,000-a-year settlement, and it becomes pretty hard to believe that he's just a small boy at heart—which is [supposedly] the principal charm of Paramount's gangling hero." There is little that is actually funny in Michael's contentious relationship with Nicole and nothing amusing in his physical abuse of her, including slapping, near-strangling, and painful spanking. Although such elements are unfortunately common in the screwball genre, the genre also somewhat paradoxically valorizes aggressive women. Nicole does get the opportunity to slap Michael back. She also bites him, and both of them pummel her hapless suitor, Albert (David Niven), who is pressed into service as Michael's secretary. Niven has little to do but look bewildered, a sad waste of that splendid comic actor who nevertheless regarded Lubitsch as "the masters' master." Nugent felt that Lubitsch was directing with "brass knuckles" and that some amusing sequences and supporting players "do not entirely compensate for the arid and barren stretches which not even Lubitsch could make yield light comedy. . . . In these days it's bad enough to have to admire millionaires in any circumstances; but a millionaire with a harem complex simply can't help starting the bristles on the back of a sensitive neck."

What does the Production Code as revised in June 1934 say about the kind of situation this film deals with? The Code specified that "special care be exercised in the manner in which the following subjects are treated, to the end that vulgarity and suggestiveness may be eliminated and that good taste may be emphasized." Among the subjects so enumerated was "the institution of marriage." Listed among "Repellent Subjects" was "the sale of women, or a woman selling her virtue. . . . Such subjects are occasionally necessary for the plot. Their treatment must never offend good taste nor injure the sensibilities of an audience." One hesitates to endorse any purposes of that thoroughly repellent Code that did so much to throttle the mature treatment of sexuality on-screen, but *Bluebeard's Eighth Wife* demonstrates what could happen when filmmakers set out to flout parts of the Code without compensating subtlety or wit. Lubitsch and Wilder usually managed that feat triumphantly, making it a driving force in their success, as it was for Preston Sturges, whose *Miracle of Morgan's Creek* is perhaps the most audacious example of subverting the Code. *Bluebeard's Eighth Wife* falls far short of Sturges's spectacular achievement. When seen today, the Lubitsch film seems merely a curiosity for trying to pass off as comedy a flagrantly amoral story that disregards some of the Code's intent yet apparently was approved (after some haggling) because it stemmed from a successful European play. Hollywood has always had somewhat different standards when it comes to literary adaptations, especially from foreign material, which seem to give cultural validation to subjects otherwise considered untouchable; Lubitsch's habit of setting his films mostly in Europe is a reflection of that stratagem.

The unusually nasty, bizarrely offensive trailer Paramount concocted for *Bluebeard's Eighth Wife* concentrates on violence between the sexes as a selling point and seems to be deliberately trashing previous notions of the Lubitsch Touch. Employing Lubitsch for the last time after his return to directing from his unsuccessful stint as an executive, the studio apparently thought that once-sparkling phrase had become a commercial liability and needed radical updating. Entitled *"HOW TO HANDLE YOUR EIGHTH WIFE!"* the trailer starts by demonstrating what it calls Michael's "superb technique" of marching angrily down a hallway and smashing a vase before pushing open a door and slapping Nicole. A title card proclaims, "COOPER CLUNKS COLBERT. In Ernst Lubitsch's latest story of a man who fell in love early and often—and still knows nothing about women!" The trailer goes on, "In case you missed the finer points of the *Lubitsch touch*, WE REPEAT THE LESSON"— this time they are *both* shown slapping each other. "You'll learn plenty about handling Sweethearts—when you see . . . ERNST LUBITSCH'S *BLUEBEARD'S EIGHTH WIFE*." Part of the grotesque "love scene" in which a tipsy Nicole chomps onions in an effort to repel her husband's advances and overcome her own attraction to him is followed in the trailer by further examples of physical violence. It is hard to imagine Lubitsch approving a trailer that goes out of its way to denigrate his entire career. Such a sales pitch appears to be an act of desperation for a studio that had lost faith in its former star director in a drastically changing boxoffice climate. Fortunately, Lubitsch soon departed that uncongenial home for another studio, MGM, where he would make two of his best pictures.

The thematic license Lubitsch was able to get away with in *Bluebeard* does not help him illuminate sexual relations in any new or liberated way but actually represents a regression in his approach because he was trying too hard to bend with changing tastes in comedy that were antithetical to his strengths. This coarse film demonstrates by indirection how much better off he was artistically, even under the Code, having to work with his characteristic obliqueness, as he had done in such a heightened way with *Angel*. *Bluebeard's Eighth Wife* even has an uncharacteristically clumsy, graceless visual style. The process photography of European locations, again shot by Lubitsch's assistant Eric Locke, is inserted into the action with such glaring crudity that even 1938 audiences who were used to such conventions must have been stunned. It is one of the few Lubitsch films that look like they were directed by someone else, someone indeed with a "sledgehammer touch." For that development in *Bluebeard*, we surely have another overpowering artistic personality, Wilder, more than partly to blame. As masterful a filmmaker as he would become, Wilder's influence on this film early in his Hollywood career can only be described as deleterious. In his collaboration with Lubitsch and Brackett so soon after having to flee Germany, with a war against fascism looming, and with fear for the safety of his mother and other family members in Europe (some of whom would be killed in the Nazi Holocaust), Wilder was evidently and understandably in a particularly harsh state of mind when he worked on the script in 1936. That asperity eclipsed his own romantic tendency and overwhelms even Lubitsch's general goodwill toward his characters.

Bluebeard's Eighth Wife is not without some incidental felicities in its snappy dialogue and innuendos and some bright Lubitschean sight gags. Wilder cited an especially memorable touch that comes right at the beginning. As Michael stops outside a clothing shop in Nice, he sees a sign in the window:

MAN SPRICHT DEUTSCH

SI PARLA ITALIANO

ENGLISH SPOKEN

AMERICAN UNDERSTOOD

Wilder recalled Lubitsch taking a pencil and adding that delectable final line; in the film, the camera tilts down to emphasize it. "A tiny little joke, but it meant everything," recalled Wilder. And he told Crowe, "We had no joke there before. He just added that, and said, 'Go ahead and structure the picture, I'm shooting [*Angel*], but I'll give you an hour here and there.' And we wrote that picture. Lots of Lubitsch ideas in the picture, lots of Lubitsch suggestions. My [major] contribution was in the beginning." Wilder may have been trying to distance himself from the picture with those retrospective remarks. But the beginning he refers to is one of the most famous "meet-cutes" in film history.

A meet-cute was a gimmick much prized by Hollywood screenwriters in the Golden Age who strove mightily to find clever ways of getting male and female characters together. Wilder kept a notebook to jot down story ideas, and he paid special attention to meet-cutes. So when he and Brackett first met with Lubitsch, he was ready with one that delighted the director. When Michael goes into the shop to buy pajamas, since he is what Wilder calls a "very stingy" millionaire who sleeps only in pajama tops, he insists on paying half price and not buying the pants. This causes great consternation among the store personnel. It is resolved after Nicole comes in, sizes up the situation, and offers to buy the bottom half for a man she knows who does not wear pajama tops. This naturally piques Michael's interest, and ours, in Nicole's sex life and, as Crowe notes, makes us imagine them partially unclothed together (although it eventually turns out she is buying the pants for her father, the marquis).

Wilder recalled how Lubitsch embellished on that memorable gag:

> Lubitsch, of course, would always find a way to make something better. He put another twist on that meeting. Brackett and I were at Lubitsch's house working, when during a break he emerged from the bathroom and said, What if when Gary Cooper comes into the store to buy the pajama top, the salesman gets the floor manager, and Cooper again explains he only wants to buy the top. The floor manager says, Absolutely not, but when he sees Cooper will not be stopped, the floor manager says, Maybe I could talk to the store manager. The store manager says, That's unheard of! but [the vice-president] ends up calling the department store's owner, whom he disturbs in bed. We see the owner in a close shot go to get the phone. He says, It's an outrage! And as the owner goes back to his bed you see that he doesn't wear pajama pants either.

Actually, Lubitsch uses a wide shot of the old man getting out of bed to put over the gag with more immediate comic effect. The script adds a wry political touch by having the owner say, "Oh, no, no, never, never! Well, that is communism!" The harried floor manager explains to Michael, "The consequences might prove disastrous. Now, our president says we've had enough trouble in Europe as it is." The connecting comic elements that Lubitsch added involving the frantic store personnel hark back to his silent

German comedies about shopkeepers and point forward to *The Shop Around the Corner.*

But after that sparkling opening, the rest of *Bluebeard* plods tiresomely through its grating plot mechanisms to engineer Nicole's unlikely triumph over Michael, a development that seems barely able to survive the quick fade-out on a perfunctory Lubitsch door gag involving his old reliable Edward Everett Horton. When Brackett saw *Bluebeard's Eighth Wife* again with Wilder five years after its release, he admitted in his diary, "It is terrible! Screwball comedy, long sequences to almost practically no dramatic purpose, climax sequences so brief as to be choppy—a really embarrassing picture, but it brought back a lot of fond memories of Lubitsch."

NINOTCHKA

It is surprising in retrospect that *Ninotchka*, one of Lubitsch's defining masterworks, came together for him in such a haphazard way. It was not a film he initiated or set out to make. During Brackett's hiatus between work with Lubitsch on *Bluebeard* and *Ninotchka*, the screenwriter recorded in his diary a June 3, 1938, luncheon at a Hungarian restaurant with the director, "who has no studio commitment, a rather terrifying thought, since one would think that he would have been made quantities of irresistible offers."

The film Lubitsch wanted to make at that time was *The Shop Around the Corner*, an adaptation of a 1937 Hungarian play by Miklós László (listed in the film's credits as Nikolaus Laszlo) entitled *Illatszertár* (*Drugstore*), also known as *Parfumerie* or *Perfume Shop*. The sparkling screenplay that Samson Raphaelson wrote for the film (which eventually reached the screen in 1940) is the piquant love story of two feuding sales clerks (Margaret Sullavan and James Stewart) in a prewar Budapest leather goods and gift shop. They exchange lonely hearts letters without realizing they are seducing each other with literary language that is absurdly but delightfully opposite to their hostile daily interaction. The script rings deeply true with its compassionate understanding of human foibles and its ironic insights into the contradictory impulses underlying romantic relationships. Lubitsch's degree of devotion to *The Shop Around the Corner*, with its lovingly insightful portrait of life in a modest shop-keeping establishment, reflects his nostalgia for his youth in Berlin with the family tailoring establishment of S. Lubitsch and the early silent films that put him on the map, *The Pride of the Firm* and *Shoe Palace Pinkus*. Lubitsch bought the rights to the play himself in July 1938 and offered Raphaelson a one-third share in the property, telling the screenwriter he was hoping to make the film with private capital. The director entered into a partnership with the prominent agent Myron Selznick, and they offered the project to Paramount and other studios but initially found no takers. That was a sign of Lubitsch's diminished boxoffice luster as well as a reflection of the way the bumptious screwball craze had, at least temporarily, dampened studios' taste for the gentler kind of romantic comedy that *Shop* represents.

Lubitsch's emotional investment in this affectionate tribute to working people and his own past is illustrated by his comment to Weinberg in 1947, "As for human comedy, I think I was never as good as in *Shop Around the Corner*. Never did I make a picture in which the atmosphere and the characters were truer than in this picture." His frustration over the difficulty of persuading studios to back the film was expressed in a November 1938 letter to Raphaelson: "Here I am sitting with what I consider the best script I have had in a long time in my hands, and am forced, through all kinds of manipulations, into one postponement after another. You have no idea of all the trouble and headaches I go through."

For the time being, Hollywood did not want the kind of atmosphere and characters the script depicted—unglamorous people getting by day to day in faraway Budapest, but in a shop that could just as well have been on Main Street, USA. With some notable exceptions, including the films of Frank Capra, William Wellman, Raoul Walsh, and other directors who dealt with the so-called common man, Hollywood in the Depression era was still less interested in working-class verisimilitude than it was in glamour. It would be necessary for Lubitsch to first make *Ninotchka*—a film steeped in glamour, set mostly in swanky Paris hotel suites and showcasing the world's most lustrous star in a story worked around the advertising slogan "Garbo Laughs!"—to earn the green light from MGM for his little picture about "little" people. But since both films are among Lubitsch's finest, the price MGM exacted was eminently worth the bargain.

Ninotchka was initially developed at Metro in 1937 by producer Gottfried Reinhardt from a three-sentence pitch by Melchior Lengyel: "Russian girl saturated with Bolshevist ideals goes to fearful, capitalistic, monopolistic

Paris. She meets romance and has an uproarious good time. Capitalism not so bad, after all." That is pretty much the theme and tone of the film, which eschews the allusive, oblique approach that Lubitsch had developed to such a virtuosic degree in *Angel*. *Ninotchka* comes directly to its points, and yet not simplistically and always with a level of wit rarely equaled in Hollywood filmmaking. Along with Raphaelson's impeccable script for *Trouble in Paradise*, *Ninotchka* is at the summit of romantic comedy writing, with the added element of more explicit political satire that has seldom if ever been equaled in Hollywood.

Along with its narrative clarity, *Ninotchka* once again shows Lubitsch eschewing his former brand of ostentatious visual pyrotechnics; it goes beyond the standard strictures of invisible studio storytelling to a rare degree of transparency. But *Ninotchka*'s seeming visual simplicity is deceptive, employing a magician's form of indirection, for it displays some of the most elegant and graceful camera movements and editing of Lubitsch's career. Many scenes involve subtle, barely noticeable reframing with tracking and dolly shots, many more than in *Angel*, which relies more on montage than on camera movement to construct its points. *Ninotchka*'s transparency in a narrative sense can be attributed partly to the influence of Wilder, who always believed in making films as lucid as he could achieve (at least on the surface, if not always in subtext). That was a trait the more highbrow Brackett did not find entirely congenial, complaining to his diary in 1941 of "Billy's terrifying neurosis that everything isn't crystal clear to the audience." Both as a screenwriter and a director, Wilder took to heart Lubitsch's gag of making "AMERICAN UNDERSTOOD." But if he was less oblique than Lubitsch, Wilder also followed Lubitsch's example in allowing the audience to add up "two plus two" to appreciate wit without spelling it out. What Wilder once said of Lubitsch is true of his own films as well, and it encompasses even the supreme sophistication of *Ninotchka*: "His technique is clear to the last village idiot, but he makes him feel that he is very smart."

Wilder and Brackett were brought on to *Ninotchka* rather late in the development process. Lengyel had written an expanded story outline, and the project acquired a total of ten writers along the way. Bernhardt had commissioned scripts from Jacques Deval (the French playwright and codirector of a Paris-set comedy about Russian exiles, *Tovaritch*) and the celebrated American playwright S. N. Behrman, who had contributed to the Garbo films *Queen Christina*, *Anna Karenina*, and *Conquest*. George Cukor, Lubitsch's unhappy collaborator on *One Hour with You*, was originally slated to direct *Ninotchka*. The versatile, consummately stylish MGM director was justly renowned as an actors' director—especially celebrated for his brilliance with actresses—and had scored a triumph with Garbo in the 1937 *Camille*. But Cukor departed for the more prestigious assignment to direct *Gone With the Wind*, from which he was eventually fired, instead winding up making MGM's film version of Clare Boothe Luce's bitchy all-female play *The Women*, a project for which Lubitsch had also been considered. Cukor's influence survives in *Ninotchka* primarily in the casting of Ina Claire, best known as a stage actress specializing in brittle comedy, to play the exiled Russian Grand Duchess.

When Lubitsch, in this elaborate game of studio musical chairs, was offered *Ninotchka*, he saw an opening for his pet project, agreeing with the proviso that MGM make the two-picture deal that guaranteed he could produce and direct *The Shop Around the Corner*. Raphaelson was disappointed that their earlier financial arrangement on *Shop* had to be scrapped and he had to settle for less than his usual salary on the modestly budgeted production. *Shop* was filmed in only twenty-seven days in late 1939 for $474,000, compared with the $1.3 million cost of *Ninotchka*. Raphaelson later complained, "Alas, it all ended with Lubitsch succumbing to the vast resources of M-G-M, where he transposed his independence." That was shortsighted of Raphaelson, who nevertheless always considered *Shop* one of their best collaborations.

Lubitsch would have hired Raphaelson to adapt the Lengyel idea for *Ninotchka* if his favorite screenwriter had not been busy on a play. Instead, the director worked for a while with Walter Reisch, who changed what Ninotchka is trying to peddle in Paris from a Russian nickel mine to diamonds, prompting Lubitsch's explanation, "You can photograph them sparkling on the tits of a woman." Finally, Lubitsch felt the need to pep up the romance with more biting topical humor of the kind Brackett and Wilder were so agile in providing. The film's political savvy is clearly one of their principal contributions. And this time, perhaps partly thanks to Reisch, Wilder's old friend from Europe, Brackett and Wilder were able to make romantic conflicts endearing rather than merely abrasive even though the couple in *Ninotchka* are so starkly opposite in their ways of life.

In a rare tribute to a director, Brackett, Wilder, and Reisch actually petitioned MGM to put his name on the *Ninotchka* screenplay credits with them, but the studio declined. Not only would such a gesture have disrupted the delicate balance of power between writers and directors in the studio system, but it came at a time when the Screen Writers Guild was especially concerned with protecting its hard-won right to determine writing credits, which it achieved with its recognition by the major studios in March 1939, almost exactly five months before *Ninotchka* had its Hollywood premiere on October 6, 1939. But *Ninotchka*, like the other films of Lubitsch's later period that eschew technical dazzle for deeper character insights, can fairly be regarded as a writers' picture as much as it is a director's picture. There is nothing wrong with that, and Lubitsch was too big a man and artist to feel threatened by his writing collaborators. Instead he welcomed the opportunity to enhance his work by delving deeper into the mysteries of the human personality.

METAFILM

Among the many qualities that make *Ninotchka* such an unusual and enduring classic is the way it functions as a kind of metafilm. It is simultaneously a supreme example of a romance, a comedy, and a political satire as well as an overt commentary on those three interlocking elements. The most sophisticated aspect of the running commentary on genre by Lubitsch and his writers is that it plays out so naturally as part of the storyline, with the characters sharing insightful thoughts and feelings about the ideological differences that drive them as well as about the very nature of comedy and romance. As a piece of what could be called premature postmodernism, *Ninotchka* is decades ahead of its time and yet so lucid in its analysis of these elements by highly articulate, sophisticated characters fully aware of the social roles they are playing it never feels arch or comes off as overly self-conscious as too many postmodernist works tend to do.

Ninotchka was also Lubitsch's timeliest film up to that point in his career even though, paradoxically, it has proved timeless in its emotional appeal. That is due in part to its high degree of stylization; its setting in the MGM equivalent of "Paris, Paramount"; and the glossy lighting by Garbo's longtime favorite cameraman, William Daniels. Although the film makes many topical references to world politics and mockingly includes pictures of Joseph Stalin being carried at a May Day parade as well as characters giving the Hitler salute, it is at the same time a pure visual confection of the MGM factory and its backlot. In that sense, *Ninotchka* is a product of capitalist cultural engineering at its most adroitly artificial, wrapping its unusual political satire in a protective cocoon of entertainment.

The film achieves all this while treading on what was then risky ground. It finished shooting on July 27, 1939, and as it was going through previews in August, the signing of the German-Soviet Nonaggression Pact on August 23 shook the world (and left-liberal Hollywood politics) to their foundations. The outbreak of World War II when Germany invaded Poland on September 1 necessitated the addition of an anxiously nostalgic prologue card, carefully setting the film in the days just before the war. The opening shot is a wide view of Paris that could open any one of hundreds of films. But that view—with unobtrusive sacred undertones, taking in two famous churches, the Basilica of Saint Clotilde with its twin spires and the Eglise Notre-Dame de-l'Assomption de Paris but *not* the Eiffel Tower—is overlaid with "THIS PICTURE TAKES PLACE IN PARIS IN THOSE WONDERFUL DAYS WHEN A SIREN WAS A BRUNETTE AND NOT AN ALARM—AND IF A FRENCHMAN TURNED OUT THE LIGHT IT WAS NOT ON ACCOUNT OF AN AIR RAID!" That opening combination of picture and words is a bittersweet, very Lubitschean way of acknowledging the coming of the Second World War, and the words make the familiar picture-postcard view of Paris seem freshly poignant.

The humorous depiction of the female Soviet special envoy's clash with the capitalist system before she succumbs to its temptations could have raised the ire of audiences after the German-Soviet Pact was signed and her government was in bed with Hitler for political expediency in a time of war. But any concerns that the film's potentially off-putting topicality in dealing, however lightly, with the clash between violently opposed political systems might diminish the boxoffice were allayed when *Ninotchka* had its successful release in November. That it went over so well with audiences in that tense early wartime period is a tribute to its sophistication. *Ninotchka* is never reductive in its treatment of the conflicting ideologies of its two central characters, and even though it is an unabashed piece of soft-sell propaganda for the more appealing aspects of capitalism, it also sharply mocks capitalist corruption, and it does not push its anticommunist message in the obnoxious way that most Hollywood films on the subject have done. But *Ninotchka* is also one of the rare films of its period to directly acknowledge the evils of Stalinism, with frequent audacious and accurate references to the purge trials, wholesale executions, famine, and other draconian aspects of the regime. One of the first remarks Garbo's Nina Ivanovna Yakushova makes in the film, when asked how conditions are in her country, is, "The last mass trials were a great success. There are going to be fewer but better Russians." (Brackett commented in 1952, while defending the film's political viewpoint during the McCarthy era, "This happens to be a line tossed into the script by Ernst Lubitsch, but I spring to its defense with ardor, as would Billy Wilder. Could a single sentence better compress the inhuman Russian point of view? Could that point of view be held up to ridicule in a healthier way?")

Despite such chilling lines, Ninotchka is an appealing character because she manages to transcend her initial ideological limitations and biases and embrace the universal pleasures of life. Ninotchka's seduction by the Parisian gigolo Count Leon d'Algout, the kept man of the exiled White Russian Grand Duchess, is inextricable from the contrasting ways of life the new couple represent and from their negotiations over the jewels, but they find common ground in matters of the heart. The film's sympathetic but trenchantly observed depiction of the life of a gigolo is largely attributable to Wilder's most celebrated piece of journalism, "'Herr Ober, bitte einen Tänzer!': Aus dem Leben eines Eintänzers," or "'Waiter, Bring Me a Dancer!': From the Life of an *Eintänzer*." While struggling to sell stories to Berlin newspapers and magazines, Wilder had written that four-part series of articles for the *B.Z. am Mittag* in 1927. It vividly details in movie-like scenes his often-humiliating but mordantly amusing experiences working as an *eintänzer*, a "tea dancer" for ladies at two prominent hotels, the Eden and the Adlon. Wilder undertook the job of a sort of pseudogigolo while out of work as a journalist, both to survive and to provide print material. The masterful series and the "scandal" it caused "made him famous overnight," according to his German biographers Andreas Hutter and Klaus Kamolz. As a result of that formative Berlin experience, gigolos and kept men of various kinds often figure prominently in Wilder's work, part of his pervasive theme of prostitution, which he always handles with great complexity and ambivalence.

Sex and money are inextricably intertwined in *Ninotchka* as well as in many of Wilder's other screenplays, and in this case, the romantic couple manages to transcend their financial battle. The royal jewels of the czarist regime that Ninotchka has come to Paris to sell in order to feed her people (she calls them "the tears of old Russia") become the MacGuffin that, as in Hitchcock's work, serves as the conduit for this film's essential concentration on cross-cultural romance. Leon's role in trying somewhat playfully to negotiate for the jewels with Ninotchka and her fellow commissars, Buljanoff, Iranoff, and Kopalski (delightfully played by Felix Bressart, Sig Rumann, and Alexander Granach), quickly becomes secondary to his more complex negotiations with Ninotchka over the terms of their relationship. This very Lubitschean approach, exalting sensuality and emotion over political rigidity and economic barriers, echoes his earlier historical comedy-dramas and is part of his characteristic open-mindedness. In placing the emphasis on love and comedy, he enables the film to avoid ideological narrowness by skewering the flaws of communism, capitalism, and czarism with nearly equal relish and acuity. At heart, Ninotchka's succumbing to the pleasures of love and the creature comforts of Paris while coming to realize the arid nature of her life in Moscow is consistent with Lubitsch's basic fondness for luxury over austerity and for individualism over regimentation.

As a Russian citizen who became a naturalized American in 1936, and as a Jew who still to some extent had to function as a refugee and citizen of the world, Lubitsch knew whereof he spoke in his criticisms of both the Soviet and czarist regimes. He had been sobered by a visit to Stalin's USSR while on his honeymoon in early 1936 with his second wife, Vivian, née Sanya (whose father was Russian). Lubitsch was said to have modeled Ninotchka's initially humorless character as a slavish communist ideologue on the actress and writer Ingeborg (Inge) von Wangenheim, whom he visited in Moscow. She was the wife of Gustav von Wangenheim, who had acted for him in *Kohlhiesel's Daughters* and *Romeo and Juliet in the Snow*. They had been living in Moscow since 1933 as dedicated adherents of communism. When Inge finally caught up with *Ninotchka* in the 1970s, she proved its validity by denouncing the film in her memoirs as a "counterrevolutionary concoction." Lubitsch drew from that experience of Stalinism in his bleakly accurate satirical depiction of Ninotchka's life back home as one of deprivation, a lack of privacy, and miserable conformism. In a May 1936 interview with the *New*

York World-Telegram, Lubitsch commented, with a touch of his characteristically oblique humor, "The theaters over there are crowded. Maybe it is because of the congested living conditions—you know each person is allotted only ninety square feet of space which not only makes for crowding but for arguments. People have to go out and there is less friction." And yet the film also allows Ninotchka fervent and intelligent defenses of the better aspects of the theoretically egalitarian system she represents and passionate criticisms of the cruelties of czarism. Her last line has her proclaim in close-up, "No one shall say Ninotchka was a bad Russian!" Her complex personality makes her a bridge between cultures for the audience, helping enlighten them beyond the usual stereotypes of communism and capitalism.

She comes to represent Everywoman in her need to find a livable existence in a time of world chaos and uncertainty. Ninotchka's moving plea for some measure of personal happiness, delivered to Leon in her hotel suite with a tongue loosened with tipsiness from her first encounter with champagne, resonated with audiences in those early days of the war and retains its impact today: "Can I make a speech now? Comrades! People of the world! The revolution is on the march! I know—bombs will fall. Civilization will crumble. But *not yet, please.* Wait. What's the hurry? Give us our moment. Let's be happy."

MGM's trailer for *Ninotchka* took the time-tested Hollywood safety measure of cloaking a serious theme in frivolity, though not entirely ignoring the film's adroit blending of ingredients; the trailer positioned the film mostly as romantic comedy and milked its novelty for all it was worth. Though Garbo was primarily a tragedienne, she had laughed before on-screen (such as in Rouben Mamoulian's 1933 *Queen Christina*), but *Ninotchka* was a departure since it was her first outright comedy. The trailer begins with a shot from the film's greatest set piece, the restaurant scene in which Leon, after doggedly telling joke after joke in a vain attempt to make the obdurate Ninotchka laugh, finally succeeds only by losing his temper and taking a pratfall that *he* at first ironically refuses to see as funny. After a reaction shot of other patrons roaring at the sight of Leon sprawling on the floor, Lubitsch gives us a glorious shot of Ninotchka caught in the midst of her uncontrollable throes of laughter, a moving moment of liberation. The trailer proclaims, "*Garbo Laughs* AND THE WHOLE WORLD WILL LAUGH WITH HER. . . . THE *Garbo* YOU'VE BEEN WAITING SO LONG TO MEET! SINGING . . . LAUGHING . . .

Swinging FROM ONE ESCAPADE TO ANOTHER. ONLY *Garbo* COULD HAVE PLAYED IT! ONLY *Lubitsch* COULD HAVE MADE IT!" [That title plays over a silent shot of a smiling Lubitsch in his director's chair.] . . . THE ONLY TEARS YOU'LL HAVE . . . WILL BE TEARS OF LAUGHTER!"

Ninotchka lives up to its extravagant billing in offering Garbo's most enchanting performance, her most wide-ranging in mood, an indelible triumph even in a great career that had seen such landmarks as *Queen Christina*, Clarence Brown's *Flesh and the Devil* and *Anna Karenina*, and Cukor's *Camille*. Kenneth Tynan's famous comment about Garbo—"What, when drunk, one sees in other women, one sees in Garbo sober"—is never more applicable than in this effervescent performance, with Lubitsch cannily bringing out all the enigmatic actress's most unexpectedly variegated qualities. When he was introduced to Garbo in 1932, Lubitsch exclaimed, "Mein Gott, mein Gott, Greta!" Unabashedly hugging and kissing the reclusive star, he asked, "Greta, why don't you tell those idiots in your studio to let us do a picture together? Gott, how I would love to direct a picture for you." He went on, "How vunderful Greta and I vould be together. Ve vould make a vonderful picture." Garbo was already a fan of Lubitsch's films, her biographer Barry Paris reports; she had been especially taken with his silent comedy *So This Is Paris* and its costar Lilyan Tashman, who became her lover. Although it took seven years for Garbo and Lubitsch to get together professionally, she opted for Lubitsch on *Ninotchka* when MGM asked her to choose between him and her *Grand Hotel* director, Edmund Goulding. *Ninotchka* rings several humorous variations on her trademark declaration as the Russian ballerina Grusinskaya in *Grand Hotel*, "I want to be alone"; this running gag is no doubt the influence of Wilder, whose work is replete with movie jokes.

Lubitsch and Garbo had some creative friction during the shooting, the actress sometimes finding him too controlling and exuberant and the director finding her "probably the most inhibited person I have ever worked with." But this incandescent pairing of director and actress brought out the liveliest and most delicate qualities in both. As early as 1932, Lubitsch had claimed some ability to see through her aloof façade, if incompletely. Insisting that she was no "mystery," he said, "She is a real Swede, and I have known many Swedes. They are shy, afraid to meet people. It is natural for them to keep in the background. But Garbo—she has a fine sense of humor. She is pleasant company, once you get to know her. That is the problem." In a 1938 interview, Garbo looked forward to what she realized would be a transforming opportunity to work with Lubitsch on a film that was more lighthearted than her usual vehicles: "I am tired of period pictures and I want to do something modern now. My next film is to be a comedy. . . . Will I be allowed to keep my lover in it? Certainly I am hoping so. Don't you think it is high time they let me end a picture happily with a kiss? I do. I seem to have lost so many attractive men in the final scenes." Her close friend Mercedes de Acosta, the Spanish poet and dramatist, wrote that during the time when she was making *Ninotchka*, "Never since I had known her had she been in such good spirits. She had been shooting the first gay picture she had ever done, and Lubitsch was directing it. '[It is] the first time I have had a great director since I am in Hollywood,' she said. Greta was a changed person; [she] laughed constantly. She would imitate Lubitsch's accent. . . . It was fascinating to see how by playing a gay role rather than a sad one how her whole personality changed."

Ninotchka is at her gayest in her romantic scenes with Leon, but she is no giddy fool. She is given serious and thoughtful patriotic defenses of her homeland, its "tremendous achievement" in modernized technology and its bringing power to "the masses" by deposing the tyrannical czarist regime and the old aristocracy. Lubitsch explicitly views the barbarism of that former regime as a system that had to be overturned even if what replaced it was far from ideal and in fact engaged in mass murder, as the film acknowledges. The White Russian viewpoint is represented and espoused with sour nostalgia by Grand Duchess Swana, who rules pathetically over a posh but constricting hotel suite in Paris and tries vainly to hold on to Leon; Ina Claire, with her ostentatious theatrical style, makes Swana at once imperious, cruel, pathetic, and ridiculous. The film differentiates itself from her selfish and retrograde motives by offering many principled barbs against the Soviet attempts to impose a collectivist regimentation contrary to human imperfection. The tone is set early on by Leon's quip when he meets Ninotchka on a Paris street, "A *Russian*! I *love* Russians! Comrade, I've been fascinated by your five-year plan for the last fifteen years."

And though Lubitsch never leaves us with any illusions about the murderous nature of Stalinism, as some Hollywood films about the USSR in that era tended to do propagandistically or with romantic indulgence, he does not do so by glossing over the flaws and injustices of capitalism. The dialogue is as sharp as a scalpel throughout as it satirizes all sides of the ideological divide.

When a Parisian jeweler smoothly assures the commissars that he expects to take a loss on the transaction involving their crown jewels, two of them mutter to each other knowingly, "Capitalistic methods. . . . They accumulate millions by taking loss after loss." Ninotchka proves as adept at skewering Leon's cultural assumptions as he is of hers, declaring when he tries to pitch woo at their first encounter,

> NINOTCHKA: I have heard of the arrogant male in capitalistic society. It is having a superior earning power that makes you that way. . . . Your type will soon be extinct.

But when he follows her to the top of the Eiffel Tower, which she wants to inspect as a technological achievement, he tries to impress her instead with Paris's aesthetic beauty, and she begins to soften:

> NINOTCHKA: Now, don't misunderstand me. I do not hold your frivolity against you. As basic material, you may not be bad. But you are the unfortunate product of a doomed culture. I feel very sorry for you.
> LEON: Ah, but you must admit that this doomed old civilization sparkles. Look at it. It glitters!

The endearing humanity of Lubitsch's three comical comrades, Buljanoff, Iranoff, and Kopalski, who join Ninotchka in her rebellion and wind up defecting with her, is a key element in the film's remarkable ability to make the American audience look beyond its deeply ingrained cultural stereotypes about communism. Lubitsch achieves a remarkable rapport with those actors, particularly Felix Bressart and Sig Rumann, who went on to be regulars in his films. Bressart, a refugee from Hitler who had appeared in numerous German films, became a Lubitsch surrogate figure and virtually his on-screen conscience with his warm-hearted and droll performances in *Ninotchka*, *The Shop Around the Corner*, and *To Be or Not To Be*. Rumann (later Ruman), a gifted comedian who emigrated to the United States from Germany in 1924, gives an indelible performance as the absurd yet still sinister Nazi colonel "Concentration Camp" Ehrhardt in *To Be or Not To Be*, as well as appearing in Lubitsch's *That Uncertain Feeling* (1941) and the 1945 Lubitsch production *A Royal Scandal*.

Frank Capra told me one of the secrets of his films was to give the villains their best arguments rather than treat them as cartoonish. *Ninotchka* owes much of its political savvy and sophistication to giving all sides the best arguments that the writers and Lubitsch can muster for them. The film respects the intelligence of the audience to make up its own mind about the relative merits of each character's behavior in a very Lubitschean spirit of generosity. Ninotchka, after gradually succumbing to the capitalistic pleasure principle, learns to poke fun at her previous pretensions to an impossible, bloodless purity. The initially frivolous Leon offers wry, self-mocking defenses of his mostly worthless but enjoyable and basically harmless lifestyle as Swana's kept man. Even Swana's pitiless diatribes about peasants and fond tributes to violent Cossack repression are mixed with laments about how everything she had was taken away from her during the revolution. It is precisely that vestige of humanity that lifts her character from the level of an exasperating plot contrivance and gives her the weight she contributes to the film's unstable balance of powers.

It is often said that romantic comedy thrives on the barriers placed between a potential couple. And that one reason for the decline of the genre in later years has been that there are fewer (or less obvious) social barriers than there were in the heyday of the genre in the 1930s. *Ninotchka* benefits from three kinds of barriers to romance: the stark sociopolitical differences between Ninotchka's sternly committed communist functionary and Leon's representative of the decadent pleasures of capitalism, Ninotchka's initially complete absence of humor in contrast to Leon's habitually wry nonchalance, and her seeming lack of interest in love and romance contrasted with the fact that wooing women is Leon's stock-in-trade. "You are something we do not have in Russia," she tells him, adding, "That's why I believe in the future of my country." The couple's three formidable hurdles to genuine emotional and political freedom are all overcome in synchronicity since, in this film's viewpoint, they all revolve around a fundamental conflict between dispassion and passion.

When Ninotchka is exposed to the literally and figuratively warmer atmosphere of Paris, her defenses collapse like dominoes, revealing the vulnerable woman underneath. In the 1992 documentary interview of Wilder by German director Volker Schlöndorff, conducted partly in German, Wilder comments in that language, "And we know this woman has been—" and

Schlöndorff interjects, *"beschädigt,"* meaning "corrupted" or "damaged." Wilder does not disagree; he probably saw it that way to some extent as his mordant worldview would indicate. The way he puts it in another interview is that "she has fallen into the trap of capitalism, and we know where we're going from there." Lubitsch, in a significant contrast, regards her evolution more ambiguously and more positively. Ninotchka's transformation is carefully developed through two elaborately constructed sequences revolving around her discovery of romance and laughter. That evolution is metaphorically encapsulated with one of Lubitsch's most brilliant Touches, what Wilder called "the famous Lubitsch key scene."

As often happened when they were stuck on a scene, the director would come up with the solution. Wilder recalled: "We worked weeks [in Lubitsch's house] wondering how we could show that Garbo, in *Ninotchka*, was becoming bourgeois—that she was starting to become interested in capitalist things. We wrote a bunch of different things." Then one day when they were having a story conference, Lubitsch went to the bathroom. Eventually he came out, declaring, "Boys, I've got it. I've got the answer. It's the hat!"

It is a three-step gag. On her arrival in the Paris hotel, Ninotchka is shown passing a funny-looking conical women's hat in a lobby display case and saying smugly, with a shake of her head, "How can such a civilization survive which permits their women to put things like that on their heads? It won't be long now, comrades." Later, there is a second, silent stage of the buildup: Ninotchka simply passes the showcase and shakes her head silently at the ridiculous hat. Lubitsch finally shows that she has changed by having her lock the door of her suite, kneel in front of a small chest, open a drawer, and take out that very hat. She puts it on and studies herself quizzically in a mirror, head in hand, astonished and a little chagrined over how she has been transformed. That moment works so beautifully because it has been carefully prepared. Wilder remarked of this Lubitsch Touch, "That's not a screenwriter's idea. It's the idea of a plastic artist." He also said, "It's funny, but we noticed that whenever he came up with an idea, I mean a really *great* idea, it was after he came out of the can. I started to suspect that he had a little ghostwriter in the bowl of the toilet there. . . . I guess now I feel he didn't go enough."

After her liberation via Paris and Leon and the hat, Ninotchka throws open a hotel window, telling her fellow commissars, "I always felt a little hurt when our swallows deserted us in the winter for capitalistic countries. Now I know why. We have the high ideal, but they have the climate." Under this curative influence, she is able to give full vent to her romantic feelings for Leon rather than merely offer the scientifically expressed admission of their first encounter, "Chemically we're already quite sympathetic." Although she is not a sexless prude, she views what Leon calls "the divine passion" as a purely biological function—telling him, "Your general appearance is not distasteful. . . . I acknowledge the existence of a natural impulse common to all"—until his ability to do more than just woo her, to make her laugh, finally liberates all her inhibitions.

By contrast, Cyd Charisse's Ninotchka in *Silk Stockings*, the 1957 musical remake directed by Rouben Mamoulian, *is* fiercely prudish before her transformation, her hardened attitude a reflection of the Cold War era's more rigidly condemnatory attitude toward communism. Charisse is able to convey Ninotchka's change of heart with her breathtakingly graceful dancing in an autoerotic equivalent of *Ninotchka*'s key scene, substituting silk stockings for the hat, but her acting otherwise consists mostly of granitic stares. *Silk Stockings* has its charms and amusements but tends to be glacial where *Ninotchka* is warmhearted. Fred Astaire, for all his dancing genius, is always a rather diffident romantic partner on-screen, and it is cruel for any actress, especially one of Charisse's limited range, to be asked to reprise one of Garbo's greatest roles. The repressed nature of the character in the Lubitsch version may keep her from smiling and laughing at first but never gives her a stone face; Lubitsch never conceals the sensitivity Garbo conveys with the subtlest nuances of her facial expressions and sidelong eye movements. The director makes full capital of the most expressive face in screen history; her deadpan expressions in *Ninotchka* are as fully alive with wry humor and obliquely unsentimental emotion as Buster Keaton's.

Ninotchka's exposure to the Parisian pleasures of romance, luxury, and the capitalism that makes them possible leads her to question the system that has made her a robotic slave to her political duties. Her high life in Paris makes her miserably dissatisfied with her lack of privacy and comfort back in her comically overpopulated one-room Moscow apartment. Leon, for his part, throws away his self-indulgent existence and parasitic dependence on the Grand Duchess for an uncertain but potentially far more fulfilling future as Ninotchka's partner as a fellow exile in Constantinople with their three old comrades, who have opened a Russian restaurant (although the film's final touch is to show Kopalski already picketing Buljanoff and Iranoff, claiming unfair labor practices). The cleverness and grace with which the screenplay interweaves these personal and political strands with seeming effortlessness make *Ninotchka* one of the triumphs of screenplay construction.

The lengthy scene of Ninotchka's first visit to Leon's apartment and her gradual seduction is elaborately verbalized, in keeping with the characters' almost stifling self-awareness. The nature of romance is dissected and celebrated in this offbeat love scene that is explicitly *about* the nature of romance. Realizing he is dealing with someone whose approach to sexuality presents itself as staunchly rational, Leon employs all his rhetorical wiles to convince Ninotchka that romance actually exists, that there is more to sex than mere physical attraction. The film's use of a gigolo in arguing for the mysteriously emotional components that make sex more than a purely mechanical function is paradoxical as well as peculiarly persuasive. Leon goes through an eloquent litany on the theme of "Birds do it, bees do it," but with the pointed question of why all the world's creatures not only mate but in the process also feel something more: "Oh, Ninotchka, Ninotchka, surely you feel some slight symptom of the divine passion? A general warmth in the palms of your hands, a strange heaviness in your limbs, a burning of the lips that isn't thirst but something a thousand times more tantalizing, more exalting, than thirst."

Here is the characteristic Lubitsch concern with how men and women should treat each other, the essence of the director's unconventional moralism. As is characteristic of a Lubitsch film, the moral is conveyed through indirection and irony, here with a reversal of stereotypical gender roles, the man passionately speaking up for emotional involvement and the woman arguing for a more pragmatic approach. In Lubitsch's world, if biological impulses are realistically acknowledged, and they are far more so in his work than in most American films, romance still rules, even over ideology and world conflict. And what is romance to Lubitsch? Something akin to what E. M. Forster wrote in *Howards End*: "Only connect . . ." People in Lubitsch's films find common ground and mutual respect in their shared humanity. If this ideologically opposed couple who seem so cynical in their different ways are able to come together on an equal basis, that is perhaps the supreme test of the romantic impulse in his work, and the characters are so complex that there is no need of the usual Lubitschean complication of serious emotional competition from a third party. The third party getting in their way is not a person but ideology itself.

Ninotchka, who has been listening intently but skeptically in Leon's apartment to his impassioned sales pitch for romance, acts unpersuaded, but the wary fascination we detect in her eyes alerts us otherwise. Her eventual response to Leon's lengthy speech is droll. She says simply, "You're very talkative." Exasperated, Leon abandons his seemingly vain attempt at verbal persuasion and takes the risk of kissing her. He does not even know how much of a risk he is taking, for before leaving his apartment, Ninotchka will confess to once having kissed a young Polish lancer when she killed him. Surprising both Leon and us, Ninotchka likes the kiss he bestows on her, murmuring that it was "restful." She commands, *"Again."* Garbo invests the word with tremendous sensuality. Lubitsch by now has cut to an overhead angle and holds on it as the couple indulge in their second kiss, a more fervent coming together. This piquant camera angle moves us because it makes the characters more vulnerable, less in control of their passions than they appeared in the prolonged eye-level two-shots that preceded this gently privileged view. Favoring the now-complaisant Ninotchka, the camera seems to caress the couple as it looks down protectively from its slight overhead angle. She even takes charge of the situation by wrestling Leon into submission, prompting *him* to mutter, "Again" (as Wilder would call it, the Lubitschean superjoke). If the couple has not yet reached a state of full détente, they are prepared to enter into one with the consummate Lubitsch Touch in a memorable scene that soon follows.

Despite Ninotchka's willingness to indulge in sexual pleasure, Leon is frustrated by her stubborn refusal to smile or laugh, her seeming lack of a sense of humor. Leon is acting on behalf of the director when, determined to break down her resistance, he pursues Ninotchka to a workers' bistro, pretending he is a regular customer (a ruse the proprietor soon dispels by heartily welcoming him as a new patron). Just as the kissing scene is about the nature of romance, the restaurant scene is explicitly about the nature of comedy. Lubitsch and his writers (and cast) set about demonstrating what comedy is all about. The scene becomes the director's testament to his art, much like the ending of Preston Sturges's 1941 comedy *Sullivan's Travels* in which a Hollywood comedy director (Joel McCrea) who wants to make more "serious" fare goes on the road to learn about real life and is taught by an audience of fellow chain-gang convicts watching a Mickey Mouse cartoon why laughing is more important.

Lubitsch stages the restaurant scene mostly in prolonged two-shots of Leon and Ninotchka at their table, occasionally punctuated with reaction shots of working men having lunch. The two-shots give us the opportunity to study Leon's and Ninotchka's reactions closely and simultaneously, in effect allowing for reaction shots within a single prolonged shot. The resistance to the temptation of cutting is a signpost in Lubitsch's evolution, for it gives each character equal weight in the scene, drawing them together visually even while they are still at odds ideologically. Douglas's performance is at its best in his determined, if misconceived, assault on Ninotchka's fortress of stolidity. Like a cheap vaudevillian, Leon thinks the way to prod Ninotchka into laughing is by telling her a series of jokes. She may be humorless (so far), but she is also too intelligent to fall for his feeble gambit. Some of his jokes do not seem funny at all, even if he were not telling them badly. One that is funny becomes so garbled in his retelling that it loses its point. What is actually funny is Leon's fumbling attempt to be funny and his exasperated, increasingly irate, even panicky response to Ninotchka's stubborn refusal to laugh other than to give him a contemptuous "Ha-ha." Lubitsch is showing us something that is key to his work and indeed to that of any first-rate comedy director: the essence of comedy is not joke telling. Jokes may be amusing enough on their own, but comedy that stems from character is funnier as well as deeper and potentially more moving. Leon's purpose, however, is serious, to prod Ninotchka into "having a good time for the first time in your natural life" by smiling. "At anything. At the whole ridiculous spectacle of life, at people being so serious. Taking themselves pompously, exaggerating their own importance. If you can't think of anything else to laugh at, you can laugh at you and me."

Coming at such a perilous time in world affairs, this fervent plea for the crucial value of laughter carries the weight of a subversive political statement. Both the romance and the comedy express the film's political message, which is what makes *Ninotchka* successful in uniting those three strains with such rare dexterity. As Lubitsch put it in his 1947 letter to Herman Weinberg, "As to satire, I believe I probably was never sharper than in

Ninotchka, and I feel that I succeeded in the very difficult task of blending a political satire with a romantic story." Lubitsch and his writers are trying to focus the audience on the enduring truths of lovably fallible individual human nature rather than on the collective insanity of the wider political conflicts that keep Leon and Ninotchka apart and are threatening to tear the world around them from its foundations. *Ninotchka* does not make its point about "the whole ridiculous spectacle of life" the easy way, by sticking its head in the sand and pretending that the world outside the theater is not on the verge of collapse and that real ideological barriers do not exist. Instead, as Ninotchka's tipsy speech in the hotel conveys, the film rests its case for the crucial importance of human contact precisely on the audience's awareness of the perilousness of the world situation. Ninotchka's moving plea, "Give us our moment," is her eventual response to Leon's challenge in the restaurant to think "of the moment in which we're living? The only moment we ever really have?"

The restaurant scene encapsulates how Lubitsch, when pressed, defined the approach he took to life. He told *American Cinematographer* interviewer Mollie Merrick not long before his death in 1947:

> What exactly, you ask me, is the Lubitsch touch? It's the king in his bed-room with his suspenders hanging; it's the gondola hauling garbage in Venice while the gondolier sings romantically in the moonlight; it's the husband bidding his wife a melancholy good-bye and then dashing madly for the nearest telephone booth. It's naughty and it's gay. It's based on the theory that at least twice a day the most dignified of human beings is ridiculous.

Ninotchka, with its transparent, unaffected visual style and its camera always in the perfect place to tell the story, feels perfectly natural, even with its artificial "Paris, MGM" visual style. It mostly avoids interrupting the narrative with the kinds of emphatically noticeable Lubitsch Touches that sparkled throughout his earlier work and came to dominate it stylistically in the early 1930s. Aside from the key scene with the hat and a few other standout touches such as the elaborate gag in which a parade of waiters and cigarette girls keeps coming and going from the closed door of the corrupted commissars' suite, Lubitsch Touches are subsumed mostly in the character interchanges. That led Richard J. Anobile, who edited a 1975 photo book of *Ninotchka* images and dialogue, to complain, "Lubitsch's direction of *Ninotchka* is plain and unobtrusive. He has a sense of scene—and the film is basically only a series of prolonged scenes, but one would be hard pressed to consider his style cinematic. Lubitsch's *Ninotchka* could easily have been a stage play." Ignoring the fact that Lubitsch came from the theater and that his work was always a blend of "pure Cinema" and theatrical devices adapted in cinematic terms, Anobile is drawing the spurious distinction between film and theater that was common in that formative period of film studies; it was a rhetorical ploy to claim primacy for film over the stage, a gambit that now seems unnecessary and belittling to certain directors, including Lubitsch.

Anyone who studies *Ninotchka* and Lubitsch's other late work carefully and without such a constricting predisposition will recognize that his lively camera and seemingly effortless but masterfully fluid staging, while it may draw from theatrical devices, is nothing like a mere photographed play. Only those who make the simplistic claim that dialogue scenes per se are not cinematic would still argue otherwise. And that argument would miss most of the qualities of late Lubitsch and the writercentric, actorcentric, character-based nature of his mature masterpieces. Such a misreading of his late work is partly a misguided overreliance on the shallowness of the expression "Lubitsch Touch," which the director himself found limiting as it became more of a vague marketing ploy. As can be seen in Paramount's manhandling of that clichéd, often reductively applied phrase in promoting *Bluebeard's Eighth Wife*, it had largely outlived its usefulness by the time Lubitsch changed his style to become unobtrusive in the midthirties. It can be said most accurately that instead of containing occasional Lubitsch Touches, the whole of *Ninotchka* is a seamless Lubitsch Touch.

And yet life has a funny way of providing its own distinct Lubitsch Touches. One that Wilder always fondly remembered came after a preview of *Ninotchka* in Long Beach. On the way back, the writers were riding with Lubitsch in a studio limousine, and the director was studying the comment cards filled out by audience members. Wilder recalled,

He had this very serious expression as he was reading, and you could tell that it was pretty positive. Well, he gets to this one card and he just stares

at it for a while and then he breaks into this howl of laughter. He was rock-
ing back and forth on the seat and pounding it with one hand. We were
looking at each other and wondering what the hell was so funny. Finally, he
hands me the card and this is what it said:

"Great picture. Funniest film I ever saw. I laughed so hard, I peed in
my girlfriend's hand."

8.1 Jack Benny (in Nazi uniform, as the Polish actor Joseph Tura) and Lubitsch share a laugh on the set of the 1942 black comedy *To Be or Not to Be*. *(United Artists/From the collections of the Margaret Herrick Library, Academy of Motion Picture Arts and Sciences.)*

8

THE AGING MASTER

As Lubitsch aged and his health declined in the 1940s, he deepened his explorations into the intricacies of human character, light and dark. In most (but not all) of the later films, there is an increased urgency, a heightened concern with mortality and the other inescapable turning points of life, as well as a benign sense of acceptance. Andrew Sarris wrote that the 1943 *Heaven Can Wait*, a comedy about a dead man looking back over his mostly aimless but enjoyable life, was "in the mellow manner of later Lubitsch." Indeed, the final seven years of Lubitsch's career saw his embrace of life expand even more generously beyond the amused tolerance he had always displayed toward human nature.

The major exception to the benign pattern in his late work is *To Be or Not to Be*, his astonishingly dark and corrosive yet wildly funny 1942 film that assails all the audience's preconceptions about how such a momentous political subject as Nazism should be treated on-screen. Ferociously attacked in some quarters at a time when the very concept of black comedy was barely understood, that film was indignantly defended by its maker, who marshaled his unique strengths as an artist in the passionate service of his most personal convictions. It is the Lubitsch film that resonates mostly deeply with modern audiences, who are more fully attuned to its blend of mocking ferocity than most viewers in its day could manage to be.

Most of Lubitsch's forties work is epitomized, however, by the warmly affectionate tone of his comedies *The Shop Around the Corner*, *Heaven Can Wait*, and his last completed film, *Cluny Brown* (1946). These are the gentle works of a master artist giving us his richest, most rounded, most profoundly understanding portrayals of human beings. The benevolently paradoxical spirit of loving someone because of his or her flaws, not in spite of them, pervades most of Lubitsch's later work.

HOW CHARACTERS MAKE THEIR LIVING

"Which of his movies is most like him? *The Shop Around the Corner*," Lubitsch's niece Ruth Hall told his biographer Scott Eyman. "It's so European; it contains the most of what he was, all the types, the people that were his friends, the people he loved."

The director who made his name with portraits of royalty in his German historical films and glamorous characters living in high style on Hollywood sets returned to his more modest roots with his depiction of Matuschek & Company, the Budapest shop that reflects the life lived by most of his audience. Lubitsch's shift to this humbler, haimish milieu seems effortless. As the French critic Jean-Georges Auriol pointed out, the director's characteristic concern for serving his audience made him resemble the solicitous proprietor of a compact, highly specialized, lovingly run establishment. The cozy little store in *The Shop Around the Corner* is so personal to the director because it so strongly evokes both the firm of S. Lubitsch, his family's women's clothing shop at Berlin's 183 Schönhauser Allee (just around the corner from Ernst's birthplace), and the filmmaker's early cinematic reflections of that milieu in *Shoe Palace Pinkus* and *The Pride of the Firm* (the film directed by Carl Wilhelm that made Lubitsch a star). Farcical as those silent comedies are, they share the same roots as *Shop* with their bumbling but ambitious apprentices, anxiously conscientious clerks, and irascible yet lovable bosses.

Nostalgically giving himself a rare on-screen line of dialogue in the charmingly offbeat trailer for his 1940 comedy-drama, Lubitsch emerges from the front door of the shop onto the "Budapest, MGM" street to join Frank Morgan, who is in character as Mr. Matuschek. The actor's salesman's spiel for the film is interrupted by the dapper, cigar-smoking director tapping him on the shoulder with mock impatience and pointing to his watch. Morgan responds, "Ladies and gentlemen, I want you to meet Ernst Lubitsch, our director, the man who gave you a Garbo in *Ninotchka* who made you laugh and who now gives you a Morgan who makes you laugh—" Lubitsch deadpans, "I *hope*!" Lubitsch's appearance in this trailer for a film that draws so much from his early days reminds us that he first broke into public view as an actor—playing the clownish go-getters Siegmund Lachmann and Sally Pinkus, brash but endearing shop boys who climb their way to success in their little worlds by mastering the rituals of serving the fickle public and manipulating their tyrannical bosses, just as filmmakers must do. The cocky errand boy Pepi amusingly played by William Tracy in *The Shop Around the Corner* is a direct descendant of Siggy and Sally, down to the bowler hat he affects when he gets promoted (it is a tribute to Lubitsch's skill with actors that Tracy is so charming here yet so insufferably obnoxious the following year under John Ford's direction in *Tobacco Road*).

Shop defied initial Hollywood indifference to find immediate popularity with the mass audience who saw themselves reflected in it, and over time it has become one of the director's most beloved films. Lubitsch's triumph stems from his common touch in knowingly depicting working-class life as well as his masterful deployment of all the cinematic skills he had been honing throughout his long career. With its gracefully unobtrusive camerawork in confined spaces, its precise yet relaxed deployment of a small but diverse and shrewdly assembled ensemble of actors, and its perfectly judged balance of comedy and drama, *Shop* is Lubitsch's most discreet tour de force of art concealing art.

Auriol notes, "Lubitsch's first little theater was his father's shop, where he learned to observe and criticize mankind, at least on the surface, and to make fun of what he regarded as grown-up child's play." As in the silent comedies that re-create the atmosphere of that family establishment, Matuschek & Company is a kind of theater, a stage on which to impress and manipulate the moods of the buying public. The deliberately limited spatial geography of the film enhances that theatrical feeling. But Lubitsch's adroit use of the limited floor space and side rooms is highly cinematic in the natural way it transforms an MGM set into a little world. *Shop* can be studied as a model of how a director can work marvels of versatility with his camera. Lubitsch often pans from a single shot of a character to take in a group shot or two-shot, sometimes pulls back in a semicircular arc to follow complex patterns of action, moves in subtly to emphasize character interactions, and knows just how often to punch in an emotion with a close-up. The cinematographer, as in *Ninotchka*, is Garbo's favorite, William Daniels, and though *Shop* has the requisite MGM glow and some lovely backlighting of Margaret Sullavan's offbeat beauty, it studiously avoids the ravishingly romanticized qualities Daniels brought to his Garbo films. The constantly bustling form of theater that the life of a shop resembles is comically displayed in the histrionics of Mr. Matuschek, the slickly polished sales lines and routines of his clerks, and their clever manipulation of the customers (as well as the customers' occasional resistance). But the human dramas in *Shop* are not as obviously theatrical as the stage-management shenanigans of Siegmund or Sally in the silent comedies. There is no equivalent here of the extravagant fashion shows staged by those characters. The film instead resembles a slice of daily life in the working world.

The change in Samson Raphaelson's masterful film adaptation from the perfume shop in Miklós László's source play, *Parfumerie*, to a mostly leather-goods establishment is a move away from luxury to utilitarianism; as one of the workers emphasizes, this is a shop catering to middle-class customers. The change in milieu makes it pointedly unlike the ritzy settings of most of Lubitsch's 1930s films. While *Shop*'s comic routines tend to be centered in the interchanges with the customers and the rapid mood swings of Mr. Matuschek when customers enter or exit, the deeper dramas are among the workers and between them and their volatile boss. The frequent sparring between Klara Novak (Sullavan) and Alfred Kralik (James Stewart), the clerks who ironically don't realize that they are romantic correspondents in their private lives, and Mr. Matuschek's misplaced suspicions about one of his employees carrying on an affair with his wife keep the shop in a constant state of tension as the film walks a fine line of suspense. In a rare instance for a Lubitsch film, adultery is not treated as amusing or liberating but as the cause of near tragedy (*Angel*, in a sense, prepares us for this). Unlike Adolphe Menjou's Professor Stock in *The Marriage Circle*, who also hires a detective to spy on his faithless wife but does so gleefully, Mr. Matuschek's situation leads him to a suicide attempt—filmed from outside a door, a somber Lubitsch Touch the director will echo in a black-comic way with the suicide attempt of Sig Ruman's Nazi commandant in *To Be or Not to Be*. Perhaps this reversal in Lubitsch's treatment of adultery and the great empathy we feel for Mr. Matuschek in Frank Morgan's majestic performance are attributable to the unusually close emotional affinities the director felt with the character's situation. The shop owner's feeling of betrayal by someone close to him echoes what happened when Lubitsch learned that his first wife, Leni, was having an affair with his longtime screenwriter Hans Kräly. But Lubitsch is not simply settling scores; as an artist, he is exploring the full complexity of such a situation. The emotionally unhinged Mr. Matuschek unjustly thinks Kralik is the culprit, but Kralik is his most loyal employee, and the lover of the boss's wife is actually the shop's fashion plate, the hypocritically unctuous Ferencz Vadas, played by Joseph Schildkraut.

The strained atmosphere of Lubitsch's little shop, which makes the film's comic situations often hover close to personal disaster, is heightened by the film's keen awareness of the economic anxieties of the workers, their fears of losing their jobs and their need to placate their unstable boss in a marginal business at a time when, as one of them points out, "millions of people are out of work." The most humane character, Pirovich, played by Lubitsch's wise, droll, cigar-smoking alter ego Felix Bressart, freely admits that he has to submit to Mr. Matuschek's abusive behavior because he must keep his job at all costs to support his wife and child—and yet Pirovich shows great character when he cannot stand by and allow Mr. Matuschek to falsely abuse his friend Kralik. Lubitsch's state of mind in making this heartfelt tribute to working people and the milieu from which he emerged is evident from his comment in 1939 that audiences now wanted more than amusement, they cared about "how characters made their living."

Raphaelson's brilliant adaptation of *Parfumerie* takes a solidly built but rather bluntly verbose play, with its more refined milieu, and adds layers of richness, color, and wit to the characterizations. Raphaelson and Lubitsch also straighten out a couple of major dramatic flaws in the source material. *Parfumerie* begins with the lead female character already working in the shop and jousting with her male counterpart, but the film more effectively delays her entrance for ten minutes even though Sullavan is top-billed as Klara Novak. Klara is looking for work at the outset, quite desperately, and after Alfred politely informs her that there are no openings, she cleverly improvises a sales ploy for a female customer. In one of the few obvious Lubitsch Touches in the film, her ingenuity helps Mr. Matuschek unload a dubious product, a cigarette box that maddeningly keeps playing "Ochi Tchornya" (the traditional Russian folk tune whose title translates as "Dark Eyes"). There is a similar comic device in *Shoe Palace Pinkus*, with Lubitsch's Sally improvising a ploy to fool a female customer into buying a pair of shoes that are the wrong size for her, a flattering device that leads to the woman's financing his takeover of the store. In *Shop*, Alfred has already pointed out the drawbacks of the cigarette box to Mr. Matuschek (he is proven correct when the stock eventually has to be discounted), but the boss is so impressed by Klara's skill as a saleswoman that he hires her on the spot.

Klara's bright wits and adaptability enhance her characterization and help lay better groundwork for the evolution in her relationship with Alfred. Initially polite, he resents learning that she is a job seeker rather than a customer and quickly shifts to pulling rank on her. Her showing him up with the music box and his somewhat petty resentment of her salesmanship ploy establish their professional and personal antagonism. His resentment of her glibness and insincerity is brought out in this interaction. But his instinctive graciousness upon meeting her, even a hint of attraction ("If it were up to me, I'd put you to work right away"), helps make credible their eventual rapprochement. Late in the film, she admits that she also felt an early attraction to him before he turned abusive. And though the workplace relationship between Klara and Alfred is mostly contentious, it has moments of civility as counterpoint. By contrast, the characters' hostility in *Parfumerie* is so extreme and unrelenting throughout, as well as less motivated, that it makes the play rather unpleasant.

Lacking the advantage of Lubitsch's cinematic toolbox, the play lays out its points far more explicitly and contains a number of long speeches, but Raphaelson's script follows his and the director's characteristic method of obliqueness. This is especially valuable and revealing because the basic plot device of the central characters misjudging each other makes every line and nuance of their antagonism all the more piquant. There are so many unspoken feelings in *Shop*, in the Alfred/Klara relationship but also in the subplot involving an adulterous affair, which is the subject of workplace gossip but can only be fitfully acknowledged by those directly involved. Lubitsch remarked of Mrs. Matuschek, "The proprietor's wife never appears, yet she's very important, almost the most important character in the picture." That is an exaggeration but a revealing one from this director who lives by ellipsis.

The love/hate relationship between Klara and Alfred and their trouble with understanding and conveying their true feelings, a deep-seated conflict between the sexes, often arises in screwball comedies as well as romantic comedies in which barriers and misunderstandings of all kinds prevail. But as nasty and cruel as the couple occasionally are to each other in *Shop*, this film avoids the sour tone of *Bluebeard's Eighth Wife*. The dialogue and camerawork in the shop scenes subtly reveal dual levels of personality in each of the two "mismatched" lovers over and above the central irony that they are sharing romantic thoughts on paper in their anonymous correspondence while seeming to despise each other in person. In addition to being amusing, that plot device reflects a schism between the conscious and subconscious feelings of men and women in personal relationships. The squabbling between the characters gives the film a certain astringency that, while not overdone, helps keep it from tipping over into the sentimental traps inherent in the material. *Shop* exemplifies the old joke (sometimes attributed to James Thurber) that the war between the sexes will never be won because there is too much fraternizing with the enemy.

The stark contrasts between what Alfred and Klara think they feel about each other and what they (or their other selves) actually feel provide many opportunities for glimpses of sexual and emotional repression. The gender tensions are remarkably modern and help account for the film's increasing popularity in recent years. In today's world, the issues surrounding a workplace relationship between a male authority figure, Alfred's head clerk, and a female subordinate would be even more fraught than they appear in this 1940 workplace. But *Shop* draws its drama from those very issues and is fully cognizant of feminist concerns. A large part of Klara's resentment of Alfred is how he controls her ("You've taken my personality away—you're a dictator") and how he condescends to her ("a good little worker like you"). She repeatedly declares that she resents working "under" him, a locution that carries a sexual undertone Lubitsch and Raphaelson avoid foregrounding despite the comic effect it might carry in their other work. Because the film offers a metaphor of the shop as a family (Mr. Matuschek calls the shop "my home," Pirovich reminds him that Kralik "was almost like a son to you," and so forth), there is a possible suggestion of an even deeper taboo—incest—lurking within its sexual tensions. Even though Mr. Matuschek is the lonely and isolated father figure, Alfred fancies himself usurping that role, telling

Klara, "I feel almost like a father to our little family." Beyond his irritating pretensions toward paternalism, Alfred presents himself simultaneously (if subconsciously) as both a lover and substitute father to Klara's daughter figure, so it is no wonder she feels such a deep sense of discomfort around him.

"My problem is what one might call 'psychological,'" the understandably confused young woman touchingly admits. Since we are privy to this conflict within her, and since Alfred becomes aware of it before she does, we simultaneously study her struggles in a comical/dispassionate way while sympathizing with her dilemma. So much of this is revealed visually, not verbally. That is a major reason why *Shop*, despite being mostly filmed in confined spaces like a play, never feels stagey. A character undergoing Klara's kind of subconscious confusion is a ripe subject for Lubitsch's probing yet kindly camera and his career-long preoccupation with sexual innuendos and complex role-playing. As a result, Klara's snide remarks toward Alfred at work and even her devastating put-down of him in the pivotal café scene, when she calls him "you little insignificant clerk," never forfeit our sympathy for her. It is a difficult balancing act that Lubitsch and the actress pull off beautifully. Sullavan's delicate charm and humor on-screen always stemmed partly from her neurotic traits, palpable insecurity in relationships, wide-eyed vulnerability, anxiously refined quality (including her theatrical mid-Atlantic accent), and sweetly tremulous voice with its exquisite inflections. Listen to the way she tells Alfred at the end that she has come to realize that in the romantic drama she has helped create, she is not an imperious actress playing a part: "Well, you see, I was a different girl then, I was really rather naïve. All my knowledge came from books, and I just finished a novel about a glamorous French actress from the Comédie-Française. That's a theater in France. . . . You see, my mistake was I didn't realize that the difference between this glamorous lady and me was that she was with the Comédie-Française, and I was with Matuschek & Company." She admits that when she began to find Alfred attractive, "I got psychologically mixed up." And when she learns the truth about their penpal romance, she tells him, "Psychologically, I'm very confused, but personally I don't feel bad at all." Sullavan's casting in a comedy always carries an undertone of melancholy, for the actress had her own psychological problems; she suffered from depression and eventually died of a barbiturate overdose that was ruled accidental.

Much of what bedevils Alfred and Klara is their shared idealism and its inevitable clash with the depressing reality of their daily lives, a situation with which Lubitsch's audience could readily identify. The romance stems from the couple's stubborn conviction that there is something better than their routine at Matuschek & Company and that somewhere out there is the ideal lover. That is the quintessence of romanticism. And if the basic plot device in the play and film—that this couple who are clearly meant for each other cannot stand each other in person—seems contrived, no one who sees the film feels that to be a problem, for the psychological underpinnings of the characters are so true, so real that we accept and enjoy the irony all the more. Lubitsch deeply believes in the romantic ideal and makes us believe in it here. But he does so while keeping us fully aware of how ideals are likely to be disappointed if belief in them is too easily discarded when reality clashes with the ideals. Dealing with two lovers who cannot see each other or themselves clearly gives Lubitsch the opportunity for one of his most acutely observed examinations of his core theme of how men and women should treat each other and so often do not.

There is real pain behind the key characters' behavior, most palpably in Mr. Matuschek's agonized reaction to his wife's cheating on him but also in the two romantic leads. Klara's desperation for a job at the beginning carries urgency and conviction, and her need for a partner and a better life is a reflection of the emptiness of the sales routines and patter she employs and the drab existence we briefly glimpse in her rooming house. Alfred has inchoate ambitions, never as focused as those of the social-climbing characters in the early Lubitsch farces but more realistically portrayed as his suffering from the "quiet desperation" Thoreau discerned in most people's lives. It is the same kind of yearning for a better life that Klara conveys with more fervent candor. Alfred's festering frustration and the rage we see just below the surface of his outwardly urbane and polite personality are symptoms of his profound unhappiness with his lot in life. His modest ambitions to be a store manager and his pathetic pride in being head clerk of the little shop are further signs of his feelings of inadequacy and of how poorly he understands them until Klara enters his life. So, when she delivers her harsh judgment in the café, Lubitsch holds on a silent reaction shot of Alfred for an unusually long time. We register the terrible sense, as he does, that she is right, and he is indeed a "little insignificant clerk." That is his worst nightmare, his secret, wretched inner view of himself.

Frank Capra was a great admirer of Lubitsch—"Ernst Lubitsch was the complete architect of motion pictures. His stamp was on every frame of film—from conception to delivery"—and this painful café scene foreshadows a pivotal moment that helps push Stewart's George Bailey to a suicide attempt in Capra's 1946 *It's a Wonderful Life*. The corrupt businessman Mr. Potter (Lionel Barrymore) sneeringly calls George "a warped, frustrated young man, a miserable little clerk crawling in here on your hands and knees and begging for help." George's despondent act is provoked by his realization that this description is essentially true. And in *Shop*, Alfred provokes Klara's vicious comment with his cruelty toward her in the café. When he arrives for the long-awaited rendezvous with his romantic pen pal and finds to his chagrin that the woman waiting for him is actually Klara, he fails to tell her the truth about himself and, out of disappointment, takes a seat at her table uninvited and taunts her romantic desires and cultural pretensions: "Now let me tell you something, Miss Novak. You may have very beautiful thoughts, but you certainly hide them. As far as your actions are concerned, you're cold and snippy like an old maid. And you're gonna have a tough time getting a man to fall in love with you."

The intimations of Stewart's despair in his iconic role in *Wonderful Life* are conveyed in his reaction when Klara condemns Alfred in the café scene. This is a remarkable sign of how Lubitsch managed to penetrate into an aspect of Stewart's persona he had not fully revealed even in the Capra films that had made him a newly minted star by 1940. Stewart's screen image before *Shop* was still largely that of an innocent, although his Senator Jefferson Smith in Capra's *Mr. Smith Goes to Washington* (1939) is brutally wised up and forced to tap into a fierce resilience that draws from his inner complexities and strength of character. In that great performance, Stewart conveys the dark underside of idealism, the bitter disillusionment that drives Smith to the point of despair before he is able to surmount it. Those twin poles of idealism and despondency became foundational in the actor's screen image. The darkness that became even more pronounced in Stewart's persona after World War II is usually attributed to his experience as a U.S. Army Air Forces bomber pilot in the war as well as the changed postwar environment. But inklings of that dark side were already visible to Lubitsch, such a shrewd judge of human character, by 1940; Lubitsch could see Stewart's inner compulsions even before he went to war.

Alfred has his gentle side, the part that writes romantic love letters and is capable of careful politeness and diplomacy toward his coworkers. He is a fairly well-educated man, even if he thinks Zola wrote *Madame Bovary*, and Klara has to correct him (the references to Flaubert's novel and to Tolstoy's *Anna Karenina* subtly connect the main storyline with the film's subplot about adultery). Alfred's sensitivity and literary aspirations draw from the aspects of Stewart that convinced Capra to cast him rather than Gary Cooper as Mr. Smith. As Capra put it, "Gary Cooper was an honest man, but he wouldn't know an idealist if one came up and hit him. He had a native honesty and decency about him, but it was on a lower level than Jimmy Stewart. Jimmy could deal with an idea." Capra noted that Stewart, for all his aw-shucks common-man qualities, was actually a graduate of Princeton. But the other side of Stewart's persona is evident in Smith's moments of depression and rage and in Lubitsch's depiction of Alfred's similar frustrations. Those flaws are similar to the torments that afflict not only George Bailey but also the even more violently troubled characters Stewart plays in his 1950s Anthony Mann Westerns and Alfred Hitchcock psychodramas. That evolution in Stewart's character helped make him what Sarris called "the most complete actor-personality in the American cinema." Stewart's great range was demonstrated by how he adapted with such ease to the disparate screen worlds of Capra, Mann, Hitchcock, and Ford, becoming a central figure in each of those major directors' work. And considering how different the cosmopolitan Lubitsch is from those filmmakers, it is perhaps most remarkable that Stewart fits so perfectly into the Lubitsch milieu, a tribute both to the actor's range and to Lubitsch's sensitivity with his performers.

It is almost a wonder that the couple in *Shop* could ever find common ground, but the film convinces us that they actually have a chance at happiness, perhaps because their insecurities are so related. The actors' personalities gave them a special rapport on-screen that led these MGM contract players to star in four films together (the others were *Next Time We Love*, *The Shopworn Angel*, and *The Mortal Storm*); Sullavan's nurturing of Stewart's talent has been credited as crucial to his career during that formative period. The couple's coming together at the end of *The Shop Around the Corner* is a beautifully written and acted scene of Alfred revealing his other identity. He does so by audibly completing the message he conveyed to Klara in a love letter from her pen pal that she is reciting. "You?" she says with astonishment, just like the recovered blind woman finally recognizing the Tramp as her benefactor at the end of Chaplin's silent classic *City Lights.* "'Dear Friend?'" Klara adds in wonderment, using the salutation she and Alfred have employed in their letters. The feeling we get in the unresolved ending of *City Lights* is ambiguous but mostly bleak. In *Shop*'s restrained happy ending, there is a similar, though less foreboding element of precariousness about what kind of life these two people will have together in a most uncertain world. In the real world outside "Budapest, MGM," Hungary would join the Axis powers later the same year the film was released. Lubitsch's achievement in this cinematic fairy tale is to make us hope and believe his young lovers will live happily ever after, but the fairy tale has such a realistic foundation and is so determinedly unsentimental that we clearly recognize how tentative its conclusion is, just as in life itself.

RUNNING ON EMPTY

Maybe Lubitsch was creatively depleted after making two consecutive masterworks, one of which he struggled to bring to the screen, for he followed *The Shop Around the Corner* with *That Uncertain Feeling* (1941), one of his weakest films. An updated remake of his lost silent romantic comedy *Kiss Me Again* (1925), which was regarded as one of his finest films from that period, the sound version is so indifferently made and so devoid of inspiration that it is one of the few Lubitsch films that look as if any halfway competent director could have turned them out. Lubitsch was evidently marking time, for he had no new creative ideas to bring to this surprisingly shoddy independent production.

His wobbly standing in the industry as it entered the 1940s is evident in his leaving MGM to make two independent films for United Artists. The project began in 1939 as a four-picture partnership with veteran producer Sol Lesser (best known for his lucrative string of Tarzan movies) to make films costing only $400,000 apiece, but Lesser pulled out after *That Uncertain Feeling* failed at the boxoffice. Fortunately for Lubitsch, the Hungarian-born British producer Alexander Korda stepped in to help produce the second UA film, *To Be or Not to Be*, which became another landmark in Lubitsch's career. The innovative, swashbuckling Korda was temporarily based in Hollywood because of the uncertain state of the British film industry during the war and because he was clandestinely serving as an agent of the British government. He had been involved peripherally with *That Uncertain Feeling* by helping ensure the participation of his wife, actress Merle Oberon.

That Uncertain Feeling—the vague title refers to a bored married woman's temptation to stray sexually—and its silent predecessor are based on the French play *Let's Get a Divorce* by Victorien Sardou and Emile de Najac. Unfortunately, for the remake, Lubitsch failed to achieve any noticeable creative rapport with screenwriter Donald Ogden Stewart or with Walter Reisch, who receives an adaptation credit. That uncharacteristic conceptual failure perhaps points to a lack of genuine engagement on Lubitsch's part in remaking his earlier success. He had worked well with Reisch on *Ninotchka*, and Stewart was known for his sophisticated screenplays for romantic comedies, including the George Cukor films *Dinner at Eight*, *Holiday*, and *The Philadelphia Story*. Stewart's colorful pedigree included membership in the Algonquin Round Table and the fact that he served as the model for a character (Bill Gorton) in Ernest Hemingway's classic 1926 novel *The Sun Also Rises*. Stewart was a political activist, a self-described Marxist, and the cofounder and first president of the Hollywood Anti-Nazi League. But there is little of his or Lubitsch's customary wit, character insight, or social observation in *That Uncertain Feeling*, which feels rushed, mechanical, and never remotely believable.

It also looks unusually cheap for a Lubitsch film. The Park Avenue apartment of Jill and Larry Baker (Merle Oberon and Melvyn Douglas) is tastelessly decorated, like something out of a mass-market magazine of the period, and cramped-looking. The camerawork does nothing to enhance the film's visual appeal. And though this is one of Lubitsch's rare films set in the United States, he shows no real interest in the New York setting that enlivens so many other romantic comedies and screwball comedies of that period. The characters are as dreary as the scenery. Jill's supposed predicament is that she wants more from her tepid marriage than her dullish insurance executive husband can give her, but her character never rises above the level of a shallow, pampered housewife (in a better movie, that might be the satirical point). Her husband's ploy of encouraging her to get a divorce so she can marry her eccentric paramour, a wildly egocentric concert pianist (Burgess Meredith), is supposed to show Larry's urbanity and cleverness; Larry thinks his willingness to give her a divorce will bring her back to her senses. He is able to transcend petty jealousy until the divorce wheels actually begin to turn. But there is little at stake emotionally here even if the film makes a stab at tugging the heartstrings (with a sudden rush of schmaltzy music) when Larry recalls their happy moments together and Jill belatedly shows regrets. But since Larry seems so blasé for most of the film and Jill is so vapid, we do not really care whether they get back together or not, and that is fatal for a romantic comedy. Other than the Nazis in *To Be or Not to Be* (Sig Ruman's ironically droll characterization excepted) and Henry VIII in *Anna Boleyn*, Meredith's Sebastian is perhaps the most obnoxious and insufferable character in Lubitsch's body of work, utterly charmless, self-centered, and borderline insane, but Jill does not come off much better in her pointless pseudorebellion that almost wrecks her marriage. The marriage may not be worth saving, but this is a film in which the other actors are so irritating that the film actually makes us long for Melvyn Douglas to come on the screen with his relaxing brand of easygoing blandness.

Since we cannot see *Kiss Me Again*, it is hard to know why it was such a success in contrast to *That Uncertain Feeling*. Perhaps the intervening period of time was partly responsible for the collapse in quality between the two films. *That Uncertain Feeling* suffers from being structured around antiquated divorce customs that it make it unfunny and sometimes offensive but could have seemed more quaintly comical in a silent film taking place in the very different world of 1925. The New York divorce laws governing the characters in *That Uncertain Feeling* still require a co-respondent or actual evidence of cruelty, so Larry is forced to slap his wife in front of a witness, a legal secretary (Eve Arden) with whom he is carrying on an affair (the far livelier Clara Bow played that role in the original, with Monte Blue and Marie Prevost as the married couple). To carry out his unpleasant task, Larry has to get drunk. This is painful rather than amusing, although Lubitsch and Douglas try to make the moment of the passing slap seem as perfunctory as possible. Although this film is not as flagrantly offensive as *Bluebeard's Eighth Wife*— it is less aggressively violent and is oddly indifferent to marital fidelity rather than actively misogamic, and Larry, unlike Cooper's Michael Brandon, is no misogynist—*That Uncertain Feeling* comes off as another sour exercise of a veteran director misguidedly trying to be au courant by the debased standards of the era.

While it is baffling that Lubitsch could have made such a weak film after two successive career highlights, perhaps the root cause of its failure lies not in the slipshod production values or the recycled nature of the story. At the onset, *That Uncertain Feeling* seems as if it could be a bright satire on the early 1940s fad for psychoanalysis—Jill seeks help because of a case of hiccups, treated by the director, of course, as a mild double entendre—but the film largely abandons that track, showing little interest in exploring her actual psychological conflicts over sex and marriage. Perhaps that is because Lubitsch had just made another film that had dealt in a far more sophisticated way with the dilemma of a young woman torn between her conscious and subconscious desires. Even if *The Shop Around the Corner* is not explicitly about psychoanalysis, in that film Lubitsch had exhausted most of what he had to say, at least for the time being, on the subject of a woman's conflicted feelings over love, romance, and her individual identity. In retrospect, *That Uncertain Feeling* seems a mere time filler in Lubitsch's career as he recharged his creative batteries in the midst of a string of great films. The next one he would make must already have been preoccupying him, demanding the most profound creative engagement of his career.

"MORTAL LAUGHTER"

No Lubitsch film is more discussed today, and perhaps more admired, than *To Be or Not to Be*. While many of his works languish in neglect, this film is widely shown and analyzed by scholars. The reasons for the discrepancy are not hard to see. Lubitsch's black comedy about Nazism was so audacious and so far ahead of its time that the incomprehension and sometimes-vicious attacks it provoked in 1942 are seen as badges of honor today. Black comedy is a mode of satire that has become increasingly popular over the intervening decades as the world has veered ever more deeply into *Dr. Strangelove* territory, but that kind of storytelling was little known and scarcely understood at the time Lubitsch made his film. Its dizzying blend of genres—farce and romantic comedy and wartime spy drama all wrapped in a reflexive narrative that blends playacting with life-or-death suspense—made it baffling to some reviewers at the time. Today we are more attuned to films that play with the medium, change modes, and use comedy for serious purposes. So we admire and revere *To Be or Not to Be* as a film that expresses its moment in time with the utmost emotional urgency and yet seems timeless in its ability to stand at an ironic distance, commenting on its subject matter with the most trenchant satire.

To Be or Not to Be deals with a troupe of hammy Polish actors who outwit the occupying Nazi forces early in World War II (the film begins in August 1939, just before the outbreak of war) by using ingenious theatrical ploys that constantly blur the borders between reality and playacting as they put their lives on the line for the sake of national survival. Lubitsch's background as a secondary member of the Max Reinhardt troupe gave him a privileged perspective that lends great credence and wit to this film's portrait of the complexities of backstage life and the idiosyncrasies of actors. And as a Jewish émigré from Europe, Lubitsch had a deep personal stake in this story. Among its other unusual aspects, it offers the most explicit portrayal of a Jewish character (Felix Bressart's Greenberg) in any of his films since Lubitsch himself stopped playing Meyer from Berlin and other comical Jewish characters in German silents. In a strange and bitter irony, Berlin journalist Bella Fromm, who had interviewed Lubitsch on his last trip to Germany in 1932, reported in her diary entry for March 17, 1933, "Hitler is inordinately fond of motion pictures. He spends many hours every night in his private movie room. It takes two or three full-length pictures a night to satisfy him. Once after seeing a picture in which Felix Bressart appeared, the Fuehrer said: 'This fellow is wonderful. A pity he is a Jew.'"

And in a master stroke of daringly unconventional casting, Jack Benny has the central role in *To Be or Not to Be* as the supremely vain Joseph Tura, "that great, great Polish actor" who may be ridiculous as Hamlet but becomes a genuine hero at the instigation of his unfaithful but supportive wife and leading lady, Maria Tura (Carole Lombard). Casting Benny as the star of a film about resistance to Nazism was cheeky in itself, for despite his great popularity on the radio, his film roles had been forgettable, and having a comedian as hero, especially a Jewish comedian, made the film's approach seem all the more subversive. (After making *To Be or Not to Be*, Lubitsch shot about ten days of retakes on a Benny comedy for Fox in 1942, *The Meanest Man in the World*, an inconsequential, only mildly amusing vehicle. In that adaptation of a 1920 play by George M. Cohan, Benny plays a small-town lawyer who moves to New York City and tries unsuccessfully to live up to what he thinks is the big city's expectation that he should be nasty. Released in 1943, the film is credited to director Sidney Lanfield.)

By all accounts, Lubitsch had a more intense involvement in the writing of *To Be or Not to Be* than he did with most of his films thanks to its unusually personal subject matter, but he also had especially gifted collaborators. The original story is credited to Melchior Lengyel, who had generously said, "Writing for Lubitsch is just kibitzing." The brilliant screenplay of *To Be or Not to Be* is by Edwin Justus Mayer, a veteran playwright and screenwriter (including on Lubitsch's production *Desire*) and a member of the Hollywood Anti-Nazi League. Mayer's contributions to this one-of-a-kind Lubitsch work were clearly substantial. In his 2002 monograph on the film, British playwright and screenwriter Peter Barnes points out affinities between its black-comic approach and that of Mayer's 1928 play *Children of Darkness*. Set in London's eighteenth-century Newgate Prison, the play is a "steely, tragic comedy . . . like a lost Restoration play, edged with terror." Mayer's intricately constructed, breathtakingly ingenious, wildly funny and yet unsentimentally moving screenplay ranks with the best of Raphaelson's work for Lubitsch. Raphaelson declined Lubitsch's offer to write *To Be or Not to Be*, explaining, "I didn't have it in me to make gags about the Nazis, in 1941." As Barnes notes, "With all his special gifts, Raphaelson would have been wrong. He did not have the touch of the abyss in him which black comedy needs to be wholly successful. Raphaelson's work has a priceless wit, sublime airiness and sly humour but it would not have fitted in the world of Colonel Ehrhardt," the grotesquely funny and yet still sinister Gestapo chief played so brilliantly by Sig Ruman.

The fact that the film was released at the lowest ebb in the Allied counteroffensive against Hitler (March 1942) made Lubitsch's blend of farcical comedy and darkest drama seem especially bizarre and reprehensible to his detractors. The most prominent commentator unsettled by the film's "jangled moods and baffling humors" was the *New York Times*' perennially clueless reviewer Bosley Crowther, who wrote,

To say it is callous and macabre is understating the case. Perhaps there are plenty of persons who can overlook the locale, who can still laugh at Nazi generals with pop-eyes and bungle-some wits. Perhaps they can fancy

Jack Benny, disguised behind goggles and beard, figuratively tweaking the noses of the best Gestapo sleuths. . . . But it is hard to imagine how any one can take, without batting an eye, a shattering air raid upon Warsaw right after a sequence of farce or the spectacle of Mr. Benny playing a comedy scene with a Gestapo corpse. Mr. Lubitsch had an odd sense of humor—and a tangled script—when he made this film. . . . As it is, one has the strange feeling that Mr. Lubitsch is a Nero, fiddling while Rome burns.

The very traits deplored by contemporary viewers such as Crowther and others are justly hailed today as evidence of the film's daring and originality. *To Be or Not to Be* was an astonishing act of courage for any filmmaker to make in 1941–1942, particularly for a German Jewish émigré, and it is as audacious aesthetically as it is politically. The "jangled moods" Crowther complained about are a large part of what makes the film so unsettling and challenging for any audience, and such a mélange was rarely attempted in that era of filmmaking. *To Be or Not to Be* jumps freely, though not capriciously, among the genres it invades, mingling its broad farce, romantic comedy, and sinister and violent war drama, replete with references to concentration camps and other forms of Nazi brutality. Most boldly, the film often blends these seemingly disparate elements within the same scenes, making Gestapo officers buffoonish as well as savage, getting laughs in the midst of heart-stopping suspense, and blending dramatic political intrigue with lightly played elements of adultery and sexual jealousy. The comic elements coexist with scenes of the greatest emotional urgency, especially when a Jewish member of the Theatre Polski, Greenberg, gives heartfelt renditions of Shylock's classic speech about anti-Semitism from Shakespeare's *Merchant of Venice*. All these elements are crucial to the worldview *To Be or Not to Be* represents in reflecting its lawless times and are inseparable from the film's unique impact on the viewer.

Lubitsch's films, from the beginning of his career, always involve a direct interchange with his audience, a crucial factor in his allusive approach to filmmaking. *To Be or Not to Be* is perhaps the supreme example of his respect for the audience's intelligence. In this respect, it is worth noting that even though the film caused a scandal in the press, many members of the public may have had a more positive, open-minded attitude. Taking the rare step of issuing a public defense of one of his films after Crowther attacked *To Be or*

Not to Be, Lubitsch wrote an article in the *Times*, pointing out that the American public had embraced the film and could understand the difference between comedic and dramatic scenes. Responding to Crowther's complaints about his mixing of genres and supposed bad taste in making a comedy set during the Nazi takeover of Warsaw, Lubitsch admitted that he had avoided the usual modes of cinematic storytelling and instead had made a film "with no attempt to relieve anybody from anything at any time; dramatic when the situation demands it, satire and comedy whenever it is called for. One might call it a tragical farce or a farcical tragedy—I do not care and neither do the audiences."

Although Lubitsch was trying to be sanguine about the film's reception, it undoubtedly suffered to some extent in its public response from being released on March 6, 1942, not long after Pearl Harbor (the December 7 attack took place while it was in production) and in the aftermath of Carole Lombard's death in a plane crash on January 16 while on a war bond sales drive. Orson Welles claimed, in my presence during the taping of his television talk show pilot *The Orson Welles Show* in 1978, that Lombard's plane was shot down over Nevada by the Nazis and their agents. A confidant of President Franklin D. Roosevelt during the war, Welles reiterated that claim to Henry Jaglom, saying that the plane was "full of big-time American physicists, shot down by the Nazis. . . . The people who know it, know it. It was greatly hushed up. . . . No one wanted to admit that we had people in the middle of America who could shoot down a plane for the Nazis." According to the exhaustively researched 2014 book *Fireball: Carole Lombard and the Mystery of Flight 3* by Robert Matzen, the official accounts of the crash are inconclusive, suggesting the possibility of pilot error and overloading that caused the plane to collide into a mountain in the darkness. Matzen writes that investigations by the FBI and the Select Committee on Air Accidents in the United States "could never pull together enough threads to make a case for sabotage." But Matzen admits that Welles's account "can still produce chills," and the possibility is suggestive in light of the controversial subject matter of the film Lombard had just completed and the fact that she was the first Hollywood star to undertake a bond drive in the war.

To Be or Not to Be is sometimes regarded as a boxoffice failure—United Artists, which gave up on it after Lombard's death, took a preemptive write-off less than four months after it opened—but it actually grossed twice its production cost of $1 million. In another era, the film undoubtedly would have been more thoughtfully received and had a wider success. But it is precisely because *To Be or Not to Be* came out when it did that it is so extraordinary and so valuable as a time capsule of a great artist's highly personal, idiosyncratic response to a world crisis. That the film was crafted with an ad hoc blend of styles in response to an unprecedented situation is part of what makes it seem so fresh today. As Truffaut wrote, "An hour later, or even if you've just seen it for the sixth time, I defy you to tell me the plot of *To Be or Not to Be*. It's absolutely impossible." Indeed, each time you see the film, it is as if you have never seen it before. The only other work that has that effect on me is Richard Condon's astonishing 1959 novel, *The Manchurian Candidate*, which is similarly unsettling in mixing Cold War horrors with surrealist black comedy and seems completely new each time I read it. Sometimes shifting generic gears back and forth so radically is the only way to get to the heart of a monstrous situation that defies conventional logic and morality.

Lubitsch had spent his career figuring out clever ways around the censors and brazenly dealing with subjects that were considered unshowable or unspeakable. Most of what he had to get around before this was the taboo of dealing with sexuality in an adult way, a field in which he was the acknowledged master. But with *To Be or Not to Be*, he broke the boundaries of what was considered acceptable dramatic discourse in dealing with an even more incendiary topic, the menace of fascism. Not only was the United States still in the throes of isolationism when the film went into production, but the Hollywood film industry, in response to that pressure as well as fear for its European market, had largely avoided dealing directly with the Nazi menace in previous years. There were some notable exceptions, including Anatole Litvak's 1939 *Confessions of a Nazi Spy*, Charles Chaplin's 1940 *The Great Dictator*, Frank Borzage's 1940 *The Mortal Storm*, and even the Three Stooges' 1940 short *You Nazty Spy!* with Moe as the dictator of Moronica. Chaplin's brave frontal assault on Hitler, thinly disguised as Adenoid Hynkel, dictator of Tomania (Chaplin also plays a Jewish barber who doubles for the dictator), helped pave the way for Lubitsch and broke the largely intact industry taboos on the use of the word "Jew" and against identifying characters as Jewish. Although *To Be or Not to Be* does not use the word "Jew," a Hollywood film industry evasion that was also typical of the political rhetoric and journalistic coverage of the war and of what we now call the Holocaust, the film clearly identifies Greenberg as Jewish from his first scene, in which he says to a ham actor in the troupe, "What you are, I wouldn't eat." Lubitsch makes the Jewish actor's brave, rebellious responses to the Nazis a major thematic thread.

President Roosevelt, who was doing all he could to draw his isolationist country into war, was "very enthusiastic" about *The Great Dictator*, according to Kevin Brownlow's research. Although Roosevelt kept a low profile on the subject and did not attend the New York premiere (but sent his son Franklin D. Roosevelt Jr.), the president evidently urged Chaplin to make the film in the face of widespread opposition from his Hollywood colleagues who were anxious not to put the industry so far out front in combating Hitler. Partly because of its novelty but also because of its expert, deeply felt blend of comedic acuity and rhetorical passion, Chaplin's film played a significant role in enlightening audiences about the Nazi menace at a time when most Americans did not want to see their country enter the war. The German Jewish émigré film critic Rudolf Arnheim could just as well have been writing about *To Be or Not to Be* when he praised Chaplin's satire of Hitler: "Charles Chaplin is the only artist who holds the secret weapon of mortal laughter. Not the laugh of superficial gibing that self-complacently underrates the enemy and ignores the danger, but rather the profound laughter of the sage who despises physical violence, even the threat of death, because behind it he has discovered the spiritual weakness, stupidity, and falseness of his antagonist."

Despite the ground broken by Chaplin's popular blend of satire and drama, the critical response to *To Be or Not to Be* proved how unspeakable a subject Nazism could still be for comedy. Nazi Germany by early 1942 was in such ascendancy that the democratic nations were facing the real possibility of defeat. The war had been raging in Europe for two years when Lubitsch began shooting the film in October 1941, and the mass killing of Jews was well underway and was being reported in the press (if sketchily and not widely enough believed by the public, due in part to the inadequate emphasis given to the subject by the *New York Times* and other newspapers). Yet it is important to keep in mind that the United States was not yet at war until nearly the end of filming. By launching the project in such an uncertain period, "with no attempt to relieve anybody from anything at any time," Lubitsch was offering a particularly daring challenge to his American audience, which was still largely isolationist until Pearl Harbor. He not only wore his heart on his sleeve politically but also took the risk of being considered offensive and distasteful in dealing with subject matter that would in fact be abhorrent if treated in any other way.

By showing a group of artists managing to do what many then thought virtually impossible—defeating the Nazis—Lubitsch was demonstrating the power of artistry and intelligence over brute force, of laughter over terror, of humanity over cruelty. The film is about resistance to tyranny but uses the special weapons of theater and mockery to help overcome it. There has always been a debate about whether ridiculing evil is the best way to counteract it, or even a valid way. Chaplin himself expressed qualms, writing in his 1964 autobiography, "Had I known of the actual horrors of the German concentration camps, I could not have made *The Great Dictator*; I could not have made fun of the homicidal insanity of the Nazis." Hitler argues in his 1925–1926 book *Mein Kampf* that it is "absolutely wrong to make the enemy ridiculous" because it fails to prepare "the individual soldier for the terrors of war" and the ferocity of the opposition. As a result, thought Hitler, "His desire to fight, or even to stand firm, was not strengthened, but the opposite occurred. His courage flagged." Hitler praises English and American propaganda of World War I for its efficacy in representing the Germans as barbarians: "After this, the most terrible weapon that was used against [the individual soldier] seemed only to confirm what his propagandists had told him; it likewise reinforced his faith in the truth of his government's assertions, while on the other hand it increased his rage and hatred against the vile enemy."

It is a disturbing irony that Hitler modeled much of his highly effective war propaganda on the American method of demonizing the "Hun" in World War I, as devised primarily by public relations specialists Edward Bernays and Walter Lippmann. Deborah Lipstadt points out in her 1986 book, *Beyond Belief: The American Press and the Coming of the Holocaust 1933–1945*, that part of the reason it was hard for many Americans to believe that the mass killing of Jews was underway in World War II, in addition to the inadequate news coverage of those events, was that the overstated Allied propaganda of the previous war and the backlash against its exaggerations and lies had made many readers wary of believing such lurid accounts. The effect of propaganda on soldiers also differs to some extent from its effect on noncombatants, including much of the wartime audience attending films, which have a powerful effect in shaping their views of the enemy. Despite all the Allied propaganda during the war and the incomplete coverage of Nazi atrocities in the press, it would take the cinematic evidence of the death camps in newsreels after their liberation at the very end of the war in Europe in April 1945 to convince many skeptical members of the public of the full extent of Nazi evil.

Hitler, of course, may have had an ulterior, personal motive for not wanting to be regarded as ridiculous, but more dispassionate observers have long argued about the relative efficacy of comedy versus the frontal attack. I would contend that satire is as valid a weapon against totalitarianism in art or in political rhetoric as the more "serious" mode of address. Neither should cancel out the other; both are useful, and both can have enduring artistic value. Undercutting the suffocating solemnity with which dictators surround themselves to maintain their power is a valid way of tearing them down. Lubitsch's film uses humor to make the Nazis seem less invincible than they seemed to many at the time while also making them seem human in their fallibility rather than simply monstrous. That choice helps to account for some of the controversy the film aroused as well as its unusual insights into the totalitarian mindset.

Even though the full horrors of what the Nazis were doing were not known when Chaplin made *The Great Dictator* in 1939–1940, and though the Holocaust, as we know it today, was not yet fully underway, the persecution of the Jews in Germany was an open book by the time Chaplin and Lubitsch made their films. To name just three milestones in that respect, the Nuremberg Laws restricting the rights of Jews had been enacted in 1935; the nationwide Kristallnacht pogroms took place in November 1938; and in January 1939 Hitler told the Reichstag that another world war would mean "the annihilation of the Jewish race in Europe." An alert reader of the news who was paying careful attention to the reports out of Europe, sketchy and marginalized as they were, who was not in denial and cared to find out about what was happening, would have known a fair amount about the widespread murder of European Jews by 1940–1941. The depiction of Nazi violence and the persecution of Jews and other peoples on-screen in *The Great Dictator* and *To Be or Not to Be* and those films' references to concentration camps clearly demonstrate that Chaplin and Lubitsch did have a considerable understanding of what was happening in Nazi-occupied Europe even though the extermination camps did not become operational until 1942. The Wannsee Conference, at which the plans for the Final Solution were formalized, took place on January 20, 1942, when *To Be or Not to Be* was in postproduction. The fact that the Chaplin and Lubitsch films were made at the moment in history when the events they were portraying were actually occurring gives those films much of their potency. One only has to look at the 1983 remake of *To Be or Not to Be*, a Mel Brooks production starring Brooks and his wife, Anne Bancroft, to see how crucial that element is to the power of Lubitsch's film; the remake, though enjoyable and fairly similar to the original, suffers from a lack of urgency. It seems inconsequential because of its safe distance from the actual events.

The gravity with which Lubitsch viewed the situation in Europe when he made his film can be gauged by his vow never to return to his native Germany once Hitler took power and his forbidding the speaking of German in his house. "He wrote Germany off," his niece Evy Bettelheim-Bentley recalled. "He wanted nothing more to do with it." Lubitsch became a member of the Hollywood Anti-Nazi League, which had been founded in 1938 by a left-liberal coalition and included some conservatives among its members as well. But Lubitsch's trip to the USSR in 1936 had caused him to be phobic about association with some on the Left, even in such an important cause. Austrian-born screenwriter Salka Viertel, who ran a Hollywood salon of European exiles and was later blacklisted, recalled in her 1969 autobiography, *The Kindness of Strangers*,

> Ernst Lubitsch told me that he was withdrawing from the Anti-Nazi League because it was dominated by communists. He advised me to do the same. I begged him to reconsider . . . [and said that] the Popular Front was the only way to fight Fascism. "I know it from a reliable source that the Reds are controlling the Anti-Nazi League," insisted Lubitsch, and he mentioned a few names which made me laugh. "But, Ernst," I said, "what all these people do is sit around their swimming pools, drinking highballs and talking about movies, while the wives complain about their Filipino butlers." "I am only warning you," he said. "I am getting out." "And I am staying." The difference in our beliefs never influenced our friendship.

Nevertheless, in October 1939 Lubitsch prominently rejoined the anti-fascist cause when he helped Paul Kohner set up and run the European Film Fund, which drew funding from Hollywood filmmakers to provide sustenance and find jobs for refugees from Nazi Germany. Lubitsch also helped members of his own family escape from Germany to the United States. During the war, he served as an air raid warden in his Bel Air neighborhood, wearing a helmet and causing comic consternation one night. As Lubitsch's longtime secretary, Steffi Trondle, recalled, Walter Reisch "had forgotten to close his blackout curtains and Ernst Lubitsch, the air raid warden, called, in that accent of his, 'Walter—your lights! You have forgotten!' and Walter replied, 'Ach, yes, was gibt?' ['Ah, yes, what is happening?'] [Director] Meryvn LeRoy, hearing this, yelled from his window, 'German paratroopers have taken over!'"

Lubitsch's opposition to both communism and fascism stemmed from his fundamental, deeply felt, unambiguous antiauthoritarianism. His making of *Ninotchka* reflected his revulsion toward Stalinism after seeing it up close. Hollywood was torn politically by the signing of the German-Soviet Pact in 1939. Anti-Nazi League president Donald Ogden Stewart, who would work with Lubitsch two years later, was among those in Hollywood who began to doubt Stalinism as a result of the fallout from the pact. As Stewart wrote in his 1975 autobiography, when he turned away from the newfound sentiments for peaceful accommodation of many on the Left, "I found myself reviled by the Right and suspected by the Left." Stewart would be blacklisted in 1950, removing himself to London. Lubitsch's concern about leftist influence in the Anti-Nazi League did not prevent him from working with Stewart, a self-described Marxist, on *That Uncertain Feeling* in 1941, partly, perhaps, because of their shared antipathy toward Stalinism. Stewart wrote of his collaboration with Lubitsch, "It was a fluffy bit . . . but I had always wanted to work with Ernst and we had a lot of fun putting it together. Once more, politics were politely relegated to occasional bits of kidding. Lubitsch, a Berliner of the '20s, knew his political onions, and craftily mocked my starry-eyed innocence. Anyway, I was pleased that as a writer I had made good with the maestro."

Toward the end of Lubitsch's life, he was deeply troubled by the postwar Hollywood Red Scare designed to purge leftists and intimidate liberals. The studios imposed the blacklist just five days before his death in November 1947, shortly after a contentious series of hearings before the House Committee on Un-American Activities (HUAC), which would result in the Hollywood Ten, the first to be blacklisted, being sent to prison for contempt of

Congress. Lubitsch did not live to see the more widespread firings and ostracism of many others on the Left during what Hollywood Ten member Dalton Trumbo called "the time of the toad," but he had an immediate and instinctively negative reaction to the firing of the Ten. According to Herman Weinberg, two days after the imposition of the blacklist, during a Thanksgiving celebration at Jeanette MacDonald's house, Lubitsch—just three days before he died—kidded around and "was his old ebullient self again," seeming recovered from his heart problems. But he did get serious at one point when the subject of HUAC came up. "This mad-dog committee infuriated him, and he took a strong unequivocal stand against it."

Lubitsch's leap into controversial political filmmaking with *To Be or Not to Be*—a far more confrontational film than *Ninotchka*—can simply be explained as stemming from his natural loathing of Nazism. After making *To Be or Not to Be*, he spent a week in October 1942 directing *Know Your Enemy: Germany* at Fox for Capra's U.S. Army propaganda unit, the film that was rejected and reshot as *Here Is Germany*. Lubitsch had always been a highly assimilated Jew, both in Germany and in the United States. His daughter, Nicola, says in Robert Fischer's 2006 documentary *Ernst Lubitsch in Berlin—From Schönhauser Allee to Hollywood*,

> The Jewish element with my father is kind of puzzling, only in that when I talk to my cousin Evy, it was so not present in his life, in his family life. Obviously they were Jewish, but totally, totally secular. And just in what I know of my father and look[ing] at his later work, and in what I've heard from my mother, his taste, his sensibility, it was not Jewish. And I mean that in the kind of sense that his early comedies were so ethnic, that obviously must have been a niche that he saw he could fill. But I don't think it was the reality in the house.

Perhaps, as is often the case with members of succeeding generations in relating to their ethnic backgrounds, Lubitsch's daughter to some extent downplayed the influence of Ernst's Jewish heritage on his development as a man and an artist. His early films draw on that background so strongly that it seems he was driven by more than mere careerism to play Jewish characters self-mockingly, in part as a form of self-defense, acting clownish and playing up to the majority in order to function and succeed in that society.

But his eventual downplaying of that element of his personality and background, a development coinciding with his abandonment of his acting career, meant that his work in America was largely nonethnic in nature, at least overtly. Nevertheless, from the mid-1930s onward, the increasingly direct provocations by the Nazis were pushing Lubitsch to a greater consciousness of his Jewishness and may have helped persuade him that he could not avoid the subject of Nazism in his films.

After the Nazi regime stripped him of his citizenship in 1935 and banned his films from *Design for Living* onward, Germany made it even more personal. The 1940 German propaganda film *The Eternal Jew* singled out Lubitsch as one of the prime symbols of what Nazis thought was wrong with international Jewry, along with "the Jew [*sic*] Charlie Chaplin . . . a deadly enemy" and "the Jewish stage dictator Max Reinhardt." This vile film, which among its many other offenses literally depicts Jews as rats, makes twisted use of the newsreel footage of "the Jew Ernst Lubitsch" smiling benignly on his last trip to Germany in 1932. Lubitsch, whom the Nazis noted "was hailed as a German film producer," was probably singled out for such abuse because of two factors that the film conspicuously avoided mentioning, his success in America and his popularity as a silent film comedian for playing lovably bumptious Jewish characters, a cultural phenomenon the Nazis particularly deplored. *The Eternal Jew* claimed, "Jews consider portrayal of the disreputable and repellent particularly fertile ground for comic effect." The Nazis' attack on Lubitsch became yet more personal when, as Barnes notes in his monograph on *To Be or Not to Be*, "Hitler had Lubitsch's face plastered on posters at railway stations as an example of a truly degenerate non-Aryan. There really is such a thing as bad publicity."

Under the circumstances, comedy was the best tool Lubitsch, like Chaplin, possessed—"the secret weapon of mortal laughter"—to fight the regime that had taken over his former German homeland and was out to conquer all of Europe and his father's Russian homeland. Lubitsch's masterful use of comedy to counterpoint the drama of organized and improvised resistance by the Polish acting troupe draws on his special talents and full set of skills to cover the material from the widest possible perspective. Comedy, as always with Lubitsch, was an ingratiating way to win over the audience to what he wanted to tell them, including some bitter truths. About a year after the film's release, he said, "It seemed to me that the only way to get people to hear about the miseries of Poland was to make a comedy. Audiences would feel sympathy and admiration for people who could still laugh in their tragedy. What is the only picture that is still remembered from the last war? It's not Griffith's *Hearts of the World*, or any of those sad ones. It's Chaplin's *Shoulder Arms*." Perhaps the failure of the overly earnest *The Man I Killed* had helped change Lubitsch's thinking on how best to approach the subject of wartime atrocities on-screen. That film's pacifism also was jettisoned when *To Be or Not to Be* had to confront a far different kind of world war.

In mixing genres and including some especially outrageous and controversial lines of satirical dialogue for the Gestapo chief, Colonel Ehrhardt—his quip, "What he [Joseph Tura] did to Shakespeare we are doing now to Poland," and his delighted boast, "So they call me 'Concentration Camp' Ehrhardt?!"—Lubitsch was taking his audience outside their normal comfort zone and staking his reputation on his ability to communicate the urgency of his feelings toward this subject matter. He was also taking the even riskier step of making a monstrous figure such as Colonel Ehrhardt seem recognizably human. In Ruman's superb, multifaceted comic performance, there is no doubt about Ehrhardt's brutality—he casually refers to torture, with a smirk, as "a little physical culture" and has people shot on the flimsiest of premises—but he is recognizably one of us, a vainglorious bureaucrat, skittish with anxiety about pleasing his superiors, a man who enjoys his little jokes even about the Führer, and a bug-eyed, bulky middle-aged buffoon who is convinced he is catnip to the ladies. Colonel Ehrhardt's insecurities echo Tura's, but Tura cleverly plays on the Gestapo chief's to outwit him. Lubitsch's keen insights into the insecurities of actors also enabled him to show the commonality between them and the Nazis, who are portrayed as playacting both lethally and vaingloriously.

Making Nazis human was not calculated to be a popular approach when blatant propaganda was the rule of the day, but it was part of Lubitsch's strategy to show that even these self-proclaimed supermen could be defeated. He wanted to counteract the tendency toward defeatism that underlay much of the United States' isolationism and the fear engendered by Nazi conquests early in the war as well as the intimidating way Nazis were portrayed on-screen. Lubitsch explained in his *Times* article that he had eschewed the clichés of explicitly showing Nazi brutality, which in any case would have not been his style. Instead, he characteristically allowed the viewer to imagine the Nazis' methods through their joking references to torture and concentration camps. He wrote that the Nazis in his film did not display their sadism overtly because they "passed that stage long ago. Brutality, flogging and torturing have become their daily routine. They talk about it with the same ease as a salesman referring to the sale of a handbag."

The film's mostly positive reception by viewers both then and now shows that Lubitsch did not lose his popular touch despite his career ups and downs during that period and whatever his detractors were saying about *To Be or Not to Be*. The film's ability to shake people up and make them think in new ways was a demonstration of his keen ability to touch a nerve. If the film's eccentric mixture of genres and modes of addressing the audience seemed not to be what some people expected from Lubitsch, then they did not know him well enough or fully realize what he was capable of doing. Perhaps he did not realize that potential himself until he made this film, one of those works that shows an artist going beyond his usual limits.

To Be or Not to Be was a film "ripped from the pages of today's headlines" and dealt with a level of evil that even the psychotic despots in his historical dramas, Emil Jannings's King Henry VIII in *Anna Boleyn* or his Pharaoh Amenes in *The Wife of the Pharaoh*, could not have imagined in their most megalomaniacal fantasies. But *To Be or Not to Be* is not a complete departure for the director. Since so much has been written analyzing the film, it might be most enlightening for this study of Lubitsch's career to discuss not the obvious question, How is this film unlike any other Ernst Lubitsch film? but instead to ask, How is this film profoundly characteristic of Ernst Lubitsch? (Readers of my biography of Steven Spielberg may recall that I asked the same question about his Holocaust drama *Schindler's List*, which was widely considered a departure for that filmmaker but, in a similar way, drew on themes he had been exploring throughout his career. In an odd coincidence, when we see the appointment book of the Gestapo chief in *To Be or Not to Be*, the next visitor listed after Maria Tura for December 16, 1941, is someone named "Schindler." Oskar Schindler was working with the Nazis at the time to manipulate them into letting him save his Jewish workers in Kraków, although Lubitsch could not have known this.)

To Be or Not to Be synthesizes the various kinds of storytelling Lubitsch had mastered at various stages of his career—farce laced with Jewish humor, romantic comedy involving adulterous intrigue, and historical drama interwoven with scandalous sexuality—and it carries to an nth degree his penchant for having characters engage in self-conscious role-playing. It is instantly recognizable as a Lubitsch film for the oblique nature of his storytelling, the complex and playful interchange with the audience, the characteristic trait Truffaut defines with his quip, "In the Lubitsch Swiss cheese, each hole winks." Lubitsch keeps one or more steps ahead of us at all times in the elaborate narrative game that *To Be or Not to Be* constitutes and challenges us to keep up with it. Much of the humor comes from the farcical nature of the elaborate character games and phony setups the Polish acting troupe employs to outwit the Nazis, replete with disguises, false beards, doubling of characters, and confusion between the stage and reality. Lubitsch's vast and intimate knowledge of the theatrical profession and his love of the interplay between life on and off the stage enable him to move effortlessly from one form of role-playing to another, both for comedy and for breathless life-and-death stakes, sometimes simultaneously. The film is replete with what Othello calls "hairbreadth 'scapes i' th' imminent deadly breach." This edgy combination of comedy and drama is incarnated in the dreamily self-absorbed persona of Maria Tura, who is always playacting in one way or another, whether inappropriately strutting her glamour onstage at a rehearsal for the anti-Nazi play *Gestapo* and being reprimanded for her bad taste, consciously but casually flirting in her dressing room with a young suitor, or deceiving a Nazi spy as she plays a provocative double agent with all the earnestness she can muster (most effectively).

The film's adulterous triangle is treated as romantic comedy in the classic Lubitsch tradition. Maria carries on her blithe dalliance with a handsome aviator, Lieutenant Stanislav Sobinski (Robert Stack), while her jealous husband fumes helplessly. Lubitsch treats this subplot with benign amusement as he often does in his work. Here the cuckolded husband grudgingly accepts the status quo to preserve the marriage since he is so insecure both as a man and as an actor that he relies on his spouse and costar for constant reassurance. His patience is hilariously tested (as only Jack Benny's can be) by Maria's repeated use of the first line of Hamlet's soliloquy as a cue for her lovers to exit the audience and head for her dressing room. But it is Maria's flirtatious nature, initially the subject of light comedy, that eventually enables her to become a skillful spy in the resistance when a slippery Nazi agent, Professor Siletsky (Stanley Ridges), makes moves on her with fatal consequences for the would-be seducer. That turn from comedy to stark drama blends the archetypal Lubitschean adulterous triangle with the genre of historical drama he mastered early in his career. His expertise in bringing history to life comes back into play in his smooth integration of dramatic scenes involving the Gestapo, the SS, and Hitler with the kind of behind-the-scenes sexual and political intrigue that was also a hallmark of his silent German spectacles.

The turning point in *To Be or Not to Be* is Joseph Tura's sudden decision to put his life on the line for the cause. This moment of truth occurs when he finds his wife in what looks like a compromising situation with the aviator, but the two of them are actually talking about the urgent necessity to kill the Nazi agent, Siletsky. Putting aside his jealousy for the moment, Tura surprises them, and us, by volunteering to carry out the execution himself. He does not understand much about the situation he has fallen into, and he does not know anything about Siletsky other than what they tell him, but he trusts them implicitly and finds it in himself to be a patriot, risking his life for his country. The comical cuckold makes the instinctive decision to become a hero. Benny's exquisite comic timing makes this major leap in his character entirely credible. This man with so many human failings, this second-rate ham realizes that he needs to serve a cause bigger than himself, and his demonstration of faith in his compatriots and willingness to sacrifice his life if necessary form the basis of that momentous decision. In his reckless willingness to trust, Tura becomes one of those rare men who, as James Hilton writes in *Lost Horizon*, are "doomed to flee from wisdom and become a hero." Thus, the various strands of the film come together in a thrilling dramatic climax that is as moving as it is strangely humorous. "I hate to leave the fate of our country in the hands of a ham," says the troupe's producer/director, Dobosh (Charles Halton), who comes up with most of the ingenious anti-Nazi plotting. But the decision to participate in active resistance even makes Tura a better actor: faced with the exposure of his Nazi disguise and imminent death at the hands of the Gestapo, he saves himself and outwits the Nazis with brilliant improvisations, Lubitsch's tribute to the ability of actors to transcend the script.

The film is seamless because, in the late stage of a such a long and varied career, the director was so practiced in every aspect of these varied forms of filmmaking that he could synthesize them in various ways and switch gears from one form to another with perfect ease. Only Lubitsch could have pulled off this feat so smoothly because such a disparate set of generic tools is seldom found in the body of work of a single filmmaker, particularly one uniquely positioned to do so at that time in history. In this confluence of Lubitsch genres and themes, one element stands out in fascinating contrast to his earlier work. The element of Jewishness that had been gently lampooned in his silent farces such as *Shoe Palace Pinkus* and *Meyer from Berlin* had to be starkly altered in the face what was happening in world history. The subject matter of this 1942 film compels Lubitsch to portray the persecution of the Jews with the utmost seriousness, and yet he finds room for Jewish humor in the most drastic circumstances.

THE REAPPEARING AND DISAPPEARING JEW

In the intervening years, because he had abandoned his early Jewish caricatures and assimilated into the filmmaking mainstream, Lubitsch had avoided obviously Jewish characters, although some of his characters, notably the ones Felix Bressart plays in *Ninotchka* and *The Shop Around the Corner*, can be identified as most likely Jewish despite not being identified as such. In *To Be or Not to Be*, however, Lubitsch makes the Jewishness of Bressart's Greenberg clearly identifiable and repeatedly brings this ostensibly minor member of the troupe to the forefront of the fight against the Gestapo and Hitler himself (the Führer appears, seen twice from behind, at a theatrical gala for Nazi officers in Warsaw). But even that aspect of the film is not a complete reversal of Lubitsch's previous work, for despite the essential grimness of these scenes, one of Greenberg's most important roles in the story is to continually remind everyone of the importance of getting a laugh. Even at moments of the gravest peril, this courageous Jewish character is heard saying, "It would get a terrific laugh," "A laugh is nothing to be sneezed at," and other variants thereof. He is speaking for Lubitsch, for whom laughter is one of the essential virtues of human existence. And Greenberg does so while others, including Dobosh, are too consumed in their struggle to see its ridiculous aspects. This reiterated reminder by Greenberg, insisting on the need for maintaining the great tradition of Jewish humor, is Lubitsch's most moving affirmation of how crucial laughter is in keeping the balance of civilization alive, especially in the face of brutality and totalitarianism.

Greenberg is a more sensitive, more philosophical, more thoughtful updating of some aspects of the characters Lubitsch used to play in his silent shop comedies: Greenberg is a lovable schlemiel who proves himself a mensch. The young men Lubitsch played knew they were the butt of others' humor but would not hesitate to stand out from the crowd and withstand ridicule or contempt to further their goals. For shmendriks such as Siggy Lachmann and Sally Pinkus, the goals were ambition and self-aggrandizement for the purpose of social advancement in a less-than-welcoming environment. In the murderously hostile environment of *To Be or Not to Be*, the goal is far more urgent: survival. Survival of the troupe, of Poland, and of the Jews. Greenberg is a spear-carrier whose great ambition has always been to play Shylock in *The Merchant of Venice*, the controversial play that has sometimes been regarded as anti-Semitic. Although Shylock is treated as a villain by the Christians in the play (if more ambivalently by Shakespeare) and schemes to retaliate in the harshest way, he is regarded as the hero by some modern commentators for his forthright and ferocious stand against the systematic oppression of his people, which Shakespeare expresses in powerfully eloquent language.

Lubitsch acquired his affinity for Shakespeare when he was a member of Reinhardt's stage company, acting in at least nine Shakespeare plays, including roles as the second gravedigger in *Hamlet* and Launcelot Gobbo, Shylock's comical servant, in *The Merchant of Venice*; Lubitsch may also have played Tubal, Shylock's Jewish patron, for Reinhardt, but that has not been verified. In *Cluny Brown*, Lubitsch has the Charles Boyer character, Professor Adam Belinski, a Czech refugee from Nazism who has found sanctuary in England, quote the famous line from *The Merchant of Venice*, "The quality of mercy is not strained." As a film director in Germany, Lubitsch had made loose cinematic adaptations of *The Taming of the Shrew* (as *Kohlhiesel's Daughters*) and *Romeo and Juliet* (as *Romeo and Juliet in the Snow*). Playing small parts in Shakespeare plays helped Lubitsch identify fondly with the spear-carriers played by Bressart and Tom Dugan in *To Be or Not to Be*, who are reminiscent of Rosencrantz and Guildenstern in *Hamlet* in their function as a seriocomic chorus. Lubitsch uses Shakespeare in *To Be or Not to Be* with warm fellow feeling as a spokesman for human values in a world sorely bereft of them. The film also holds up Shakespeare as representative of British culture in a time when England stood almost alone in fighting the Nazis. The young aviator, Sobinski, is a member of one of the Polish squadrons of the Royal Air Force, and most of the troupe wind up finding a haven in England. *Cluny Brown* similarly rallies Shakespeare to the anti-Nazi cause by having Professor Belinski, shortly before the war, quote the playwright's celebrated patriotic tribute to England from *Richard II*: "This royal throne of kings, this scepter'd isle / . . . / This other Eden, demi-paradise."

Three times in *To Be or Not to Be*, Bressart's Greenberg recites parts of Shylock's famous speech about the humanity of Jews. The speech reads in the original, "Hath not a Jew eyes? Hath not a Jew hands, organs, dimensions, senses, affections, passions? Fed with the same food, hurt with the same weapons, subject to the same diseases, healed by the same means, warmed and cooled by the same winter and summer, as a Christian is? If you prick us, do we not bleed? if you tickle us, do we not laugh? if you poison us, do we not die? and if you wrong us, shall we not revenge?" Greenberg's magnificent delivery of this speech while in peril for his life, surrounded by (real and fake) Nazis in the hallway of the theater outside Hitler's box, is the dramatic highlight of the film. It is perhaps the most powerful scene in any Lubitsch film.

Yet even Lubitsch was unable to use the word "Jew" in that famous speech in 1942 in an anti-Nazi film. "Hath not a Jew eyes?" is changed to "Have we not eyes?" It seemed that Chaplin's use of the word was a special case, for while both *The Great Dictator* and *To Be or Not to Be* were United Artists releases, Chaplin partially owned the company, so he had more freedom. As Bill Krohn notes in his 2007 history of Hollywood and the Shoah, although in *To Be or Not to Be* Lubitsch went as far as he could to identify Greenberg's cultural heritage, "Lubitsch's solution to the taboo on references to the Shoah is not to use the taboo word at all . . . while having Greenberg ring all the changes on the most famous denunciation of anti-Semitism ever written, which undercuts the Nazis' tasteless jokes about concentration camps by its threefold iteration." But Hollywood studio chiefs still maintained their shameful taboo on verbally identifying Jews as Jews until after the war, when the 1947 films *Gentleman's Agreement* and *Crossfire* brought the word and the issue of anti-Semitism into the open. The playwright and screenwriter Lillian Hellman, a target of the postwar Red Scare, wrote in the December 1947 issue of the *Screen Writer*, just after the blacklist was instituted, "Naturally, men scared to make pictures about the American Negro, men who only in the last year have allowed the word Jew to be spoken in a picture; men who took more than ten years to make an antifascist picture, those are frightened men. And you pick frightened men to frighten first. Judas goats; they'll lead the others, maybe, to the slaughter."

Still, the essence is clear when Greenberg confronts the image of Hitler with Shakespeare's words. Greenberg represents the Jewish people on-screen at this point in history, and he heroically rises to the occasion. At the climax of the speech, Bressart emphasizes the word "revenge" in a magnificent close-up as he faces down (a double for) Hitler and then lunges at him. It is the crowning moment both for Greenberg and for Bressart as actors, and it may cost Greenberg his life, a sacrifice he is willing to make as a resistance fighter, using words as his weapons. Joel Rosenberg points out in his 1996 essay, "Shylock's Revenge: The Doubly Vanished Jew in Ernst Lubitsch's *To Be or Not to Be*," that as a result of his heroic action, Greenberg disappears from the film at the end of this scene. "Revenge," significantly, is the last word he utters. We last see him being led off by (fake) Nazi guards in an oblique Lubitschean allusion to what must be his actual fate.

That is made chillingly clear in the film's penultimate scene, for when the rest of the troupe has triumphantly escaped to the British Isles, Greenberg is not present. This is the most disturbing of all Lubitschean ellipses, the more so for his absence not being remarked upon by his self-centered fellow actors. Lubitsch counts on us to notice it for ourselves, and not everyone does: Barnes incorrectly claims in his monograph on the film that "the whole company escape to England—no-one is left behind. This is what 'fraternity' means." But disappearance is a running motif in *To Be or Not to Be*, both comically and tragically, as it is a primary subject in all films dealing with the Holocaust, the disappearance of six million Jews and several million others. As Rosenberg writes, "To have included [Greenberg] would have diminished the aura of ever-present danger against which the comedy of the film gains its peculiar force, and perpetuated a lie about the situation of the Jews. Greenberg's absence tells us that all victories in this film have had their price, and that the enemy portrayed here is a real one. Moreover, it tells us that even within the ranks of anti-Nazi Poles (and perhaps ersatz Nazis of Tura's sort), the Jew was seen as expendable." That emphasis on Jewish presence and absence falls with great significance on the most prominent overtly Jewish character in a

Lubitsch film since his own Meyer from Berlin brought amusement to German audiences, Jews and Gentiles alike, in a more innocent time. Although Greenberg vanishes from the world of *To Be or Not to Be* and from the world of 1942 Europe beyond the cinema, his sense of humor lives on in our memory after the film ends. For as Bressart's Buljanoff tells Ninotchka, "They can't censor our memories."

THE CENSOR FORBIDS

The other crucial aspect in Lubitsch's work called into play in *To Be or Not to Be* is the director's engagement with the problems of censorship. Throughout his career, his outwitting of industry censors was a constant factor in developing the oblique storytelling methods at the center of his art. As Rosenberg notes, Lubitsch incorporates this battle with censorship into the storyline of *To Be or Not to Be* and gives it an even more overtly political dimension than usual. The film is critical of Hollywood by implication for its inadequate representation of Jews and Nazism, and in a wider sense, it links artistic censorship to fascist repression of free speech and thought. Early in the story, the Theatre Polski production of *Gestapo* is interrupted by a Polish foreign office representative who bans it on the grounds that "it might offend Hitler." That craven act, which raises immediate objections from Joseph Tura and other members of the troupe, is symbolic of the issues the film raises involving resistance versus collaboration. The troupe's resentment over being censored is similar to the way creative artists in Hollywood responded to censorship by the anti-Semitic Joseph Breen and the timidity of the studios. The ingenious way the Poles get around the edict, by staging what is in effect their own real-life version of *Gestapo* to fool the Nazis, is suggestive of the elaborate ruses Lubitsch employed against censorship in the staging of his films.

War itself is discussed in terms of who controls "the show." As the troupe huddle together in the basement of the theater during the first air raid after the Nazi invasion, Tura says bitterly, "Well, anyway, we don't have to worry about the Nazi play anymore." Another member of the troupe says, "No, the Nazis themselves are putting on the show now, and a much bigger one." And Maria responds, "There's no censor to stop them." Fascism, as the film shows in many ways, is the ultimate form of censorship. And so Lubitsch makes his antifascist film by rallying artists against Hitler and demonstrating how serious playacting can be in the face of mortal danger. That his artists triumph, however tenuously, is the film's way of encouraging the audience to have faith that the people of the world can ultimately conquer the evil powers that are represented and mocked on-screen through the eloquent artifice of Lubitschean cinema.

As Rosenberg points out, the film's use of the theater milieu helps it function as a thinly disguised reflexive critique of the strengths and weaknesses of the American film industry:

> If the Polski Theater is virtually crawling with hidden and not-so-hidden Jews [including Benny, who is not identified as Jewish in the film but was known by many viewers to be an American Jew], then Lubitsch has shaped himself, among other things, quite an adequate metaphor for the situation of Jews in American film. Indeed, Lubitsch sustains throughout the film a triple dimension to the situation of censorship set forth in the story: the Polski Theater is censored from presenting an anti-Nazi play; Greenberg is more or less censored from playing Shylock; and American filmmakers, for the past decade or so, had been effectively self-censored, by various internalized taboos, from representing Jews and Jewish experience—and, in more recent times, from dramatizing the plight of European Jewry or portraying the war against Hitler, whatever else it was, as a Jewish struggle. These taboos are systematically violated in the film. . . . And in offering us (or, I should say, offering up) Greenberg, Lubitsch made telling allusion to the doubly vanished Jew: the Jew who was then disappearing from Europe, and the Jew who, in that otherwise noble era of classic Hollywood cinema, had all but disappeared from the American screen.

The highly unusual nature of *To Be or Not to Be* stems partly from the fact that it was not a product of the studio factory system but a maverick independent production. United Artists was a distribution company that did not own a studio lot but contracted with outside producers and was known for giving them wide latitude. *To Be or Not to Be* was produced by Lubitsch, with Alexander Korda presenting, through a subsidiary that UA set up for the production and funded with a loan from the Bank of America. Working on the fringes of the system, although with the benefit of an important distributor, was a key factor for Lubitsch in ensuring his relative, though not complete, creative freedom. Not only could he not use the word "Jew," but even after finishing the film, Lubitsch had to outwit UA to get it to the public in the way he wanted.

UA wanted to change the title because they considered an allusion to Shakespeare too highbrow, even if the allusion is to the single most famous line by the world's greatest playwright. Lubitsch hilariously plays on that status by having Tura need a prompter to give him the line when he makes his initial uneasy entrance as Hamlet (Lubitsch himself had played a prompter in a 1912 Reinhardt production of *Don Juan*). Lubitsch countered UA's meddling with *To Be or Not to Be* by puckishly suggesting changing the film's title to *The Censor Forbids*, both an allusion to the suppression of *Gestapo* and another dig at the Hollywood system. Then he covertly orchestrated a protest campaign by Benny and Lombard against the proposed title change. One of the last acts Lombard performed in her life was to send a telegram to UA from a train on her bond tour, declaring, "I consider the title *The Censor Forbids* suggestive and definitely question its good taste. It in no way conveys the spirit of the picture and is unbecoming to an organization as important as United Artists. So strongly do I feel about this that had the picture been offered to me under [that] title, I definitely would not have accepted the engagement."

It's not clear whether she was in on the joke, but UA relented under this barrage of clever Lubitschean misdirection, and he was able to keep the multilayered title he wanted, one that is simultaneously serious and a gag. *To Be or Not to Be* expresses the existential nature of the struggle against fascism as well as foregrounding the importance of theater and artifice. It also plays off the comical Lubitsch Touch that bookends the subplot of Joseph Tura's cuckoldry, his wife's suitors walking out on cue when he speaks those words during his big moment onstage. And so the title gracefully alerts us to the mixture of dark and light strands in this extraordinarily ambitious, intricately woven, daringly original film. Unusually up-to-the-minute though it was for a Lubitsch film, *To Be or Not to Be* was not so much a film for 1942 as it is a film for the ages.

9

THE DOOR CLOSES

A medicine cabinet door opens as the protagonist's voice tells us, "This is me at seventy." We see bottles of pills filling every shelf of the cabinet as the camera pulls back abruptly, as if in a puckish visual gasp. One of the funniest Lubitsch Touches in *Heaven Can Wait*, this compact transitional gag is emblematic of the director's penultimate film in that it treats lightly a somber subject: mortality. When you think about the gag, it becomes more serious than it seems at first, and so does the film itself. *Heaven Can Wait* was released shortly before Lubitsch had a severe heart attack in September 1943, the first of several that led to his untimely death in 1947 at age fifty-five. As if he already knew his days were numbered, this comedy-drama is clearly designed as the director's testament film, a summing-up of his attitudes toward life, love, sexuality, youth, aging, and death. It also offers his most direct critique of the puritanism and materialism of American life along with a rousing defense of continental-style hedonism in opposition to bourgeois morality.

9.1 Lubitsch acting out a scene for his players, as he typically did, on the set of his mellow late comedy-drama *Heaven Can Wait* (1943), with Don Ameche and Gene Tierney. *(Twentieth Century-Fox/From the collections of the Margaret Herrick Library, Academy of Motion Picture Arts and Sciences.)*

9.2 The door closes. The death of Henry Van Cleve (Ameche) in *Heaven Can Wait*, as the camera retreats from his sickroom (frame enlargement). *(Twentieth Century-Fox.)*

Only Lubitsch could have made a film treating mortality and adultery with such a delicate touch. This gorgeous three-strip Technicolor box of cinematic chocolates was his first use of color other than his dabbling with two-strip Technicolor in 1930 for "The Rainbow Revels" segment in the revue film *Paramount on Parade* and his retakes for the dismal Jeanette MacDonald musical *The Vagabond King*. The brightly variegated surface and mellow tone of *Heaven Can Wait* convey a largely benign acceptance of the messy complexities of life, marriage, and death. But there is also a waxy, cold feeling to its deeply saturated Technicolor, an atmosphere of death in the midst of life. Jean-Luc Godard observed in 1996, "The first Technicolor, and Technicolor, still today, is more or less the color not of real flowers but the flowers on funeral wreaths." We witness moments of bittersweet tension in the cradle-to-afterlife saga of aimless, wealthy playboy Henry Van Cleve (Don Ameche), and the story and style carry a gathering melancholy. The director and his screenwriter Samson Raphaelson resolve the dark undertones by force majeure (the film is adapted from the 1934 Hungarian play *Szuletesnap* [*Birthday*] by Laszlo Bus-Feketé).

A lifelong New Yorker with a family mansion on Fifth Avenue, Henry has a long and mostly successful marriage to a placid, stunningly beautiful woman from Kansas, Martha (Gene Tierney), who is remarkably indulgent of his wayward tendencies. Despite his unfaithfulness to Martha, who is always portrayed sympathetically, Henry's sensual enjoyment of life and essentially gentle, if self-centered, personality redeem him in the director's eyes from a life that Henry admits is "one continuous misdemeanor." Humorist Robert Benchley, narrating the film's trailer, says of Henry, "His collar was stiff, but his ideas were flexible." Benchley calls Martha "the jewel of the Van Cleve household . . . a paragon of beauty, culture, and virtue—but a nice girl in spite of it."

Unusual for Lubitsch because of its American setting and long time span (1872–1942), *Heaven Can Wait* pays close attention to sociopolitical details of the family saga, their mores and cultural values, and the class system they inhabit. With its episodic, sprawling structure, it is a film that seems determinedly, defiantly old-fashioned in style and subject matter. It takes place largely in the "quaint" decades before it was made and amusingly recalls the customs of bygone days, including those Lubitsch had explored and celebrated during his previous two decades in America. At a point in Hollywood history when Preston Sturges's anarchic, bawdy comedies such as *Sullivan's Travels*, *The Palm Beach Story*, and *The Miracle of Morgan's Creek* were pushing the envelope of the Production Code more strenuously than Lubitsch ever dared, the relaxed, even dawdling nature of *Heaven Can Wait* and its nostalgic tone are a tacit acknowledgment by the director that he had become somewhat passé. In that, Lubitsch resembles the middle-aged Henry, who, as he moves out of his prime, can no longer pass as the reckless philanderer of his youth but has become a graying, paunchy, somewhat depressed rake who frets about his waning appeal to women. A cynical showgirl, Peggy Nash (Helene Reynolds), sarcastically responds to his note asking to visit her, which she mistakes for a sexual advance, by saying it has "all the quaintness of bygone days." She calls him "the great cavalier of the Gay Nineties . . . a kind of retired Casanova!" Henry has spotted Peggy in a *Ziegfeld Follies* musical number, "The Sheik of Araby," which satirically evokes the artificially exotic atmosphere of Lubitsch's silent "Oriental" films. Sung by a sheik to his harem, the song symbolizes Henry's egotistical and indulgent self-image, and yet the tune plays quietly and ironically under the ensuing scene with Martha. Martha, for her part, departs from her usual sweet-naturedness and gets some of her own back by similarly describing him as a "retired Lothario" and kidding him about his potbelly.

This Twentieth Century-Fox film's opulent Technicolor visual style—usually reserved in those days for musicals and other escapist entertainment—is employed by Oscar-nominated cinematographer Edward Cronjager in the service of bittersweet nostalgia akin to that of Orson Welles's 1942 saga of a doomed wealthy family from the Midwest, *The Magnificent Ambersons*. Lubitsch was transporting his wartime audience out of the contemporary scene he had been exploring in his last few films and into a more contemplative realm of his memory and imagination. Although *Heaven Can Wait* charms the viewer with its veneer of period nostalgia, Lubitsch complicates and critiques that feeling with his satirical depiction of the narrow-minded social conditions of the time and the spoiled insularity of the wealthy protagonist. The film's opulently colorful depiction of the privileged Van Cleve family lifestyle is further qualified by the subtly claustrophobic staging. It is shot largely in studio sets of the family mansion, whose forbidding stone exterior and cluttered and gaudy interior decor (art direction by James Basevi and Leland Fuller) satirically reflect the dismal aesthetic taste of the upper class of those times.

The other major setting, the midwestern home of Martha's parents, the Strables (Eugene Pallette and Marjorie Main), goes beyond bad taste into active grotesquerie. The Strables' small-minded mean-spiritedness, the corpulent Mr. Strable's profession as one of America's leading meatpackers, and their monstrosity of a Gothic nouveau riche estate are scathingly depicted as a comic nightmare from which Martha feels compelled to escape. Her horrid background helps explain why she would stay married to Henry, who, although hypocritical, is at least amiable. One of the film's wittiest and most offbeat comic sequences has the Strables' African American butler, Jasper (Clarence Muse), relaying messages between the squabbling old couple as he moves from one end of their long breakfast table to the other, diplomatically rephrasing their hostile comments and trying to make peace between them. The multitalented Muse, who was a lawyer offscreen and always managed to bring dignity to his roles in a time when African American actors were seldom treated with full humanity on-screen, is given the opportunity by Lubitsch to play a character of shrewd intelligence as well as great charm and warmth. Jasper's kindness and sensitivity and his coddling of his childish employers are all that keep the Strables human when their errant daughter returns home after having been cruelly ostracized for eloping with Henry.

The Van Cleve milieu, though more comfortable than the Strable abode, is stifling in its own way, with few improvements in social attitudes or decor over the years. Their Fifth Avenue home, mostly seen in a large, theatrical-looking drawing room with a balcony surrounding it, begins to feel like a museum or a prison. Counterpointing the gaiety of individual scenes, the film sustains its subtle undertone of melancholy throughout. The inexorable sadness of passing years is conveyed in classically Lubitschean ellipses by having family members silently disappear between almost every episode. Their presence remains emotionally felt in dialogue and in oil portraits that replace their physical selves. Andrew Sarris said that as he aged, he realized that the film, particularly with its emphasis on the afterlife, is "all about not wanting to lose the people you love." Standing out significantly among the family portraits in later scenes is the recurring compositional presence of the late Grandpa Van Cleve, the raucous, sympathetic family patriarch and Henry's surrogate father figure, played by that splendid character actor Charles

Coburn in one of his most amusing and endearing performances. Seeing Henry's ancestors "living" with him conveys the constant weight of the past, which is both reassuring and onerous. The device is carried even further in Lubitsch's final film, the Betty Grable musical *That Lady in Ermine* (1948), which he was in the midst of shooting when he died. In that dispiriting Technicolor frolic, the ghosts of the sixteenth-century ancestors of a nineteenth-century Italian countess come to life out of their palace portraits to help her vanquish an invading army. Lubitsch's increasing fixation on the past was never more apparent than in that film, although (partly because Otto Preminger completed it in heavy-handed fashion, but also due to Lubitsch's weakened creative juices) it is but a pale shadow of the genuinely witty and engaging treatment of the past in *Heaven Can Wait*. Late in that film, when the elderly Henry creeps back into the house after an all-night bender, his son aptly remarks, "You look like a ghost."

In *Heaven Can Wait*, the saga of a pampered, essentially futile family who, for better and worse, represent the values of a vanished society, Lubitsch was reviewing, sarcastically but indulgently, not only the changing times but also the span and preoccupations of his own life and career. *Heaven Can Wait* contains numerous references to previous Lubitsch films that help make it seem like a compendium of his work. This is most meaningful in the dream of mortality, nostalgically filled with Lubitschean motifs, that the bedridden Henry relates just before he succumbs to a sudden return of belated sexual passion. Henry is a generation older than Lubitsch, who was only fifty-one when he made the film. But because Lubitsch "worked like a dog, bled himself white, died twenty years too early" (as Truffaut put it), the director seems like Henry's contemporary. Henry is a Lubitsch alter ego, a fellow representative of a more gracious time and privileged milieu in which idle pleasure seeking could be seen as a virtue and continuous misdemeanors could more easily be excused.

Henry tests our acceptance of him by defying conventional norms: he never has a job, he devotes his life to selfishly gratifying his sensual pleasures, and though he truly loves Martha, he takes a casual attitude toward his marital vows. Lubitsch can keep us engaged with such a flawed character because this is a film that celebrates every manner of unorthodoxy and quiet rebellion against conventional social mores. When the director, shortly before his death, wrote his letter to Herman Weinberg looking back over his career, he stressed these unusual aspects of *Heaven Can Wait* while also seeming somewhat defensive about what made it special:

> I consider it one of my major productions, because I tried to break away in several respects from the established moving picture formula. I encountered partly great resistance before I made this picture because it had no message and made no point whatsoever. The hero was a man only interested in good living with no aim of accomplishing anything, or of doing anything noble. Being asked by the studio why I wanted to make such a pointless picture, I answered that I hoped to introduce to a motion picture audience a number of people, and if the audience should find them likable—that would be sufficient for its success. And as it turned out, I was fortunately right. Besides, I showed the happy marriage in a truer light than it is usually done in moving pictures where a happy marriage is only too often portrayed as a very dull and unexciting by-the-fireplace affair.

After setting himself a nearly impossible task in making a seriocomic film about Nazism, Lubitsch was trying to pull off a feat almost as difficult within the Hollywood system in making *Heaven Can Wait*—a film about a Don Juan who nevertheless is happily married over a period of many years. Lubitsch had to convey that paradox within the sexual strictures of the Code as well as persuade audiences that Henry's dual nature is believable and forgivable. If this was an enormous challenge for Lubitsch, it is an even greater challenge for audiences today to deal with, since the film shows the marriage surviving because Martha accepts the double standard that allowed men of that era, especially wealthy men, to fool around while the wives had to remain virtuous. That aspect of the film partly reflects the hypocritical nature of marital relationships in the periods it depicts, but it is also clearly endorsed by Lubitsch. The cosmopolitan attitude toward adultery that runs throughout his work—a very un-American perspective, at odds with his adopted country's essential puritanism—is stretched to the limit in *Heaven Can Wait*. "One has to remember that the censorship was airtight in those days," Sarris pointed out. ". . . Nothing could be explicit . . . and so, looking at it today, it seems so genteel, but even so, there were people who felt that this was a little frivolous and irresponsible, too pleasure-loving, too antipuritanical." And some still do, which helps account for the film's uncertain critical status.

Heaven Can Wait is oblique about Henry's sexual transgressions, never showing him doing any actual philandering even though other characters (including his wife) make pointed reference to his extramarital dalliances. This style, even more elliptical than usual for Lubitsch, stemmed from factors beyond the director's trademark innuendo about sexual matters and the need to tiptoe around the Code. Introducing ambiguities and plausible deniability for Henry keeps him a likable figure when he could easily have become repellent. Some commentators have even suggested that since the film is so vague about Henry's Don Juan-ism, he may be a bit of a fraud in that department, a man whose flirtatious reputation far exceeds the ineffectual reality or is partly imaginary. Perhaps. The film can almost sustain that interpretation, and it may help explain why Martha puts up with Henry's wandering nature so blithely after the painful episode ten years into their marriage when she tries to leave him because of his philandering. Martha is lured back into acceptance by his neediness, her grudging fondness for him despite it all, and the comical intervention of Grandpa Van Cleve, a roguish old man with a somewhat excessive fondness for Martha. Even after fleeing Henry, Martha defies expectations by telling her former fiancé, Henry's cousin Albert Van Cleve (Allyn Joslyn), who is still carrying a torch for her, "I don't want anybody to get the impression that I've been the victim of ten years of misery. Nothing of the kind! On the contrary, I can say there were moments in my marriage which very few women have been lucky enough to have experienced."

One of the most unusual ellipses in Lubitsch's work is that he does not show those crucial first ten years of the couple's marriage. Henry elopes with Martha after literally sweeping her off her feet at the party for her engagement to Albert, a staid corporation lawyer who tellingly compares himself in fine detail to a suit of clothes that is not flashy but wears well, one of Raphaelson's most wryly metaphorical Lubitsch Touches and a fitting throwback to Lubitsch's roots in the clothing business. Leaving Albert is the first rebellious act Martha performs in the film, a considerable social transgression for that period and a sign of her streak of independent thinking and her strong desire for a truly happy marriage. In some ways, she is as impatient with bourgeois strictures as Henry and Lubitsch himself; and if neither Henry nor Martha has the excuse of being an artist, unlike Lubitsch, at least they make an art of enjoying life. The film goes right from the engagement party to Henry's discovery that Martha has escaped to her parents' home in Kansas on their tenth anniversary and is seeking a divorce. The anniversary coincides with Henry's birthday, making a doubly festive occasion supremely painful. The central structural device of the play that Lubitsch and Raphaelson were adapting is to follow the womanizing protagonist through a series of birthdays representing crucial stages in his life. It is likely that part of what attracted Lubitsch to this story is precisely that it is built on ellipses, and *about* ellipses, making the audience fill in its many gaps and ponder their own attitudes toward the characters, reserving their own judgments so that Lubitsch does not have to come down hard on Henry. The artificiality of this episodic structural device provides a distancing factor in the film's presentation of its protagonist, enabling us to evaluate him critically even as we are invited to revel in his misbehavior.

This partial distancing is heightened by the period setting, the use of flashbacks, Henry's often-ironic narration, and the story's fantasy elements, including the stylized candy-box color. All this helps Lubitsch, while working in an American setting, achieve a similar effect to his usual device of setting his risqué stories safely in another country. As L. P. Hartley wrote in his 1953 novel *The Go-Between* (later filmed), "The past is a foreign country: they do things differently there." The flashback structure of *Heaven Can Wait* gives Henry's life a sense of predetermination, making him seem helpless to break out of his habitual patterns. The film is bookended with audaciously funny scenes in Hell, where the suave Devil (Laird Cregar) presides like the host of a luxury hotel. Heavyset, suggesting that he is a sensualist like Henry, the Devil is nattily dressed in a cutaway, and his large office (evocative of a Hollywood studio executive's showy quarters) is elegantly but eerily decorated in shimmering shades of blue and silver with bright-red phallic pillars. Henry resignedly presents himself in Hades at the beginning of the film because of his sexual peccadilloes, which he assumes disqualify him from heaven. American films touching on the afterlife usually content themselves with showing a dreamy but deadly version of heaven, so framing this film in the netherworld is another subversive touch as is the film's very title.

In a wry twist only Lubitsch could have gotten away with in 1943 Hollywood, the Devil, addressed by Henry as "Your Excellency," is a sympathetic character, urbane and filled with compassionate understanding for human vice, much like the director himself. The Devil pardons Henry at the end of the film, dispatching him to the place he euphemistically refers to as "Above." That exoneration stems from the Devil's acknowledgment that Henry has committed no major crime worthy of perdition, as he himself reluctantly admits. His Excellency, with a roguish glint in his eye, tells Henry that "several young ladies" will testify that "you've made them all very happy" and adds more soulfully that Martha "will plead for you." It is no coincidence that early in his career, Lubitsch, befitting his sometimes devilish sense of humor, had played Satan twice, one of the times in stylish modern garb, urbane and charming like Cregar's character, in *Doctor Satansohn*.

Since in *Heaven Can Wait* we are not made privy to scenes showing the early progress of the marriage of the incorrigible rake to the lovely but innocent young woman from Kansas, we have to glean the causes for Martha's disenchantment from what she says and does in her subsequent confrontation with Henry at her parents' home. Henry is at his worst in this section of the film, petulant and childish and self-pitying. While trying to lie his way out of evidence Martha has found of his betrayal—a bracelet he bought for another woman, the cause for Martha's wanting a divorce—Henry inadvertently reveals that he was seen having tea at the Plaza Hotel with a pretty young lady. But he still expects Martha to forgive and forget and resume their married life. She parries his excuses with ease and cutting remarks: "Oh, Henry, I know your every move. I know your outraged indignation. I know the poor, weeping little boy. I know the misunderstood, strong, silent man—the wounded lion who's too proud to explain what happened in the jungle last night." The daring decision by Lubitsch and Raphaelson to elide the early development of the marriage and zero in so quickly on Martha's unhappiness over Henry's infidelity makes her more sympathetic and controlling and complicates our identification with her husband. It also ensures that our attention for the rest of the film will never lose sight of the shaky foundations on which the marriage is based. Even though Lubitsch was portraying what he considered a "happy marriage," he makes us aware that he regards such an achievement as being based on compromises, deceits, and betrayals.

Shortly after meeting Martha, Henry describes her to his mother (Spring Byington) as a creature out of a "fairy tale. It's like a waltz by Strauss, like a minuet by Mozart." This choice of words in Raphaelson's script is telling, for along with its more obvious fantasy elements and stylization and allusions to previous Lubitsch films, the film portrays Martha as something of a figure out of Henry's imagination and the marriage itself as a form of wish fulfillment. Gene Tierney, who looks impossibly beautiful in Technicolor, is perfectly cast since she always seems to be floating through her films in a serene, dreamlike state. When she enters the engagement party, Lubitsch's camera rushes breathlessly toward her into a stunning close-up. Martha is the Ideal Woman from a traditional male point of view, loving, accepting, and forgiving, mostly without reservations. But it is important to her character's credibility that we do see her trying to leave Henry early in the story and that she gently makes fun of him as he ages. She tells him that after he and Grandpa Van Cleve brought her back from Kansas, "I still didn't feel that you really belonged to me—and only to me. . . . And then one day I noticed that you began to have a little—well, just a little tummy. Then I knew I was safe. From that moment on, I knew that you were really mine. That you'd settled down." This needling echoes the crass gold digger Peggy Nash's verbal jab at his waistline. As the script indicates, Henry is "crushed" by his loving wife's implication that he is hors de combat in the war between the sexes, no longer a viable Lothario, but it scores points for Martha in our estimation. She is fully aware of his character flaws even as she accepts him as he is.

There is no getting around the fact, however, that the film, like Henry himself, comes down on the side of the double standard, as do some other Lubitsch films. Not only does the marriage endure only because of Martha's forbearance, but Henry makes clear that he could not tolerate any corresponding infidelity on her part. When she gets a telephone call from a man late in the story, Henry becomes insanely jealous only to be chastened to find that the man is her doctor. She has been concealing a serious illness, whose nature is elided, and not long afterward dies offscreen in another discreet ellipsis. The last we see of Martha, she is waltzing with her husband on their twenty-fifth wedding anniversary. Henry is telling us in voiceover, "It was the last time we danced together. There were only a few more months left for Martha, and she made them the happiest of our lives together." The camera, which has been following them gracefully as they dance, pulls back to an elegiac overhead angle before the scene fades out. It is one of Lubitsch's most poignant touches, an emotional tribute to Martha, her importance to Henry, and their enduring marriage, ended only by death.

Heaven Can Wait could easily be called sexist by today's standards for implying that the double standard is the sine qua non for a happy, enduring marriage. That attitude reflects the times that Lubitsch depicts in the film. And however advanced and cosmopolitan he was in his films' acceptance of adultery, the wives in his films are never allowed the same license as the husbands only partly due to the hypocritical "moral" standards of Hollywood censorship. The wife played by Florence Vidor in Lubitsch's silent masterpiece *The Marriage Circle* is allowed to have sexual fantasies and even to kiss a man she is not married to, but she does that only by accident and never consciously acts out her fantasies. The husband strays but is allowed to get away with it and still keep his wife's loyalty; Lubitsch rarely punishes characters for their flaws. He tends to suggest, as he does there, that a bit of dalliance can be good for a marriage. But his films, in their portrayals of marriage, tend to be sexually conservative in employing the double standard with more than obligatory conformity to the Code; they do so with genuine enthusiasm.

This is especially crucial to *Heaven Can Wait* because it is centered around this very issue of the wife's acceptance of her husband's habit of wandering and because it takes place over a much longer time period than his other films tend to, examining changing sexual mores as it progresses. One could argue that Martha is free to accept him as he is and is being pragmatic about preserving her marriage and privileged way of life, a not uncommon situation among the wealthy. But she is offended when her husband tries to buy her back in Kansas with an expensive bracelet. Her rejection of this bribe is a sign that she has self-respect and is not a gold digger like Peggy Nash, whom Henry later pays off to break up with his adult son, Jack (played as suave and compassionate by Michael Ames). But it is clear that Martha makes the trade-off of inequality for comfort and security as well as for the intermittent affection her relatively guileless husband is able to bring to the marriage. She tells Henry late in their life together that she is "the happiest woman in the world." The film's implication that such a compromise is necessary for a marriage to work and for the wife to be happy can be seen as cynical or realistic, depending on one's point of view.

That Martha is not portrayed as a more independent woman and not, anachronistically, as a feminist role model is problematic for some modern viewers. Even Raphaelson, in a 1977 discussion with an audience at the Museum of Modern Art, seemed uncomfortable with *Heaven Can Wait* in that period when the women's liberation movement had upended traditional ways of thinking about marriage. Raphaelson said, somewhat defensively, "Well, my wife liked it very much. . . . But I got a little tired of the variations on lechery. . . . About three-fourths of the way through, I feel, 'Come on, Henry. Skip the next chick of your dreams. Let's not donate all the charm to Grandpa. What does Grandpa like about *you*, anyway, beyond your bungling infidelity?'" Raphaelson's failure to mount a strong defense of his and Lubitsch's film reflects a certain half-heartedness that the director probably would not have shared even at that late date; Lubitsch was always the less conventional member of the team, less inclined to bow down to what now would be called political correctness. The screenwriter, contradicting his qualms about Henry, also said he would have preferred to see the character depicted more openly as a philanderer, whooping it up drunkenly with showgirls: "I'd like an edge to him, personality, flavor."

Raphaelson recalled that Twentieth Century-Fox vetoed a scene he had written in which

> this cavalier fellow became an old man; he was kind of a sexy old guy, he got into a mess with the nursemaid of his grandchild, or something, and this was a scene of grisly humor, inspired completely by Lubitsch; it came out of his knowledge, out of his European savvy. Once I got the idea, I was delighted and helped him express it. But it was so harsh, it was so mean, that [studio chief Darryl] Zanuck said, "We can't possibly dare to use this." It was the only time anything by Lubitsch was ever—that we both thought was good—that was ever rejected by the head of a studio.

According to Robert Carringer and Barry Sabath in their book on Lubitsch, "The original plan called for Henry to get married again in his late fifties to a young, blonde, golddigging manicurist, whose whole crude family moves into the Fifth Avenue mansion [as in *Rosita*]; Jack was finally to kick them out when he came back on his father's sixtieth birthday and saw how cruelly they were taking advantage of the old man." Raphaelson and

Lubitsch rewrote this as the scene of the lonely Henry trying to persuade his son to hire a young woman as a "reader," a far more gently humorous scene that deftly conveys the sadness of Henry's persisting but futile lechery. It includes an especially poignant Lubitsch Touch of Henry absentmindedly pulling a book from his bookcase and finding it is the one Martha was buying when they first met, *How to Make Your Husband Happy* by Dr. Blossom Franklin ("a forbidding-looking woman with glasses," the script calls the author of this Victorian sex manual). The earlier script version Zanuck vetoed, Raphaelson commented, "was a vicious scene which [Lubitsch] didn't fully realize was vicious because he so loved lecherous old men, so he made him the way he knew such old lechers were—and the way he liked him."

Heaven Can Wait with a more flagrantly lecherous Henry would have been a different film and a much less interesting one as well as a project impossible to get past the censors in 1943. Zanuck was probably right to veto that scene, and Lubitsch was wise to resist depicting Henry carousing outside his marriage. The virtues of Lubitsch's comparative discretion in the finished film stand in relief against conventional notions of how to depict a Don Juan. Don Ameche's soft-spoken, kindly persona works resoundingly in the film's favor. Even if the Fox contract player, best known for *The Story of Alexander Graham Bell* (1939), may have been a lesser actor than some of the others considered for the role (including Joseph Cotten, Fredric March, and Rex Harrison), Ameche's lack of macho aggression helps makes Henry appealing. The actor's vocal rhythms often seem like a subtle carryover from Lubitsch's previous work with Jack Benny's schlemiel in *To Be or Not to Be*, enhancing the sense that Henry is also rather foolishly pompous and naïve. Lubitsch's elliptical presentation of *Heaven Can Wait*'s narrative, in addition to allowing Henry to seem more harmless (Martha calls him "my obstinate little boy"), enables us to share Martha's mature, if arguable, perspective that sexual fidelity may not be the most important component of a marriage. Lubitsch always knew what he was doing in depicting the nuances of gender roles, as his sophisticated body of work shows in abundance, and he was conveying his viewpoint about how difficult it can be to sustain a long marriage.

To fully accept *Heaven Can Wait*, a viewer needs to see the wisdom of Martha's serene point of view about her marriage and to view Henry with the same indulgence that she and the director grant him. For some viewers in today's world, which in some ways, ironically, is even more prudish than the world of 1943, that can be too much of a stretch, and the film may seem less than fully satisfying, less defensible. Perhaps *Heaven Can Wait* would have been a more challenging film if it had granted Martha more freedom or at least an occasional desire to have a life of her own outside their marriage after she returns to Henry. But the film is what it is, a reflection of the times it depicts and the period in which it was made as well as an expression of Lubitsch's unconventional, continental perspective on fidelity.

Heaven Can Wait is his romantic vision of marriage as an alliance between two imperfect people, the man flawed by his sexual appetites and the woman by her tolerance. In a discussion between the married critics Andrew Sarris and Molly Haskell that was included on the 2005 Criterion Collection edition of the film, Haskell said that when she first saw the film in the 1970s, she had "resented this womanizing figure," but over the years she had come to be "more indulgent" toward Henry, like Martha and the other women in the film, beginning with his mother, who spoils him throughout her life. Haskell said of the Van Cleve couple, "It's a very unconventional marriage, which somehow suited both people in it, and that's sort of hard for people to accept. . . . This sense of discretion and tact within a marriage—that's something that went out the window [in modern society]. . . . There's so much [in the film] that's kept under the surface for the good of the marriage." Sarris added, "It is. It's Lubitsch, and he's unique, and somehow people [in his day] tolerated him, but they didn't really understand him."

Heaven Can Wait's oddities and omissions can also be partially explained by the fact that it is something of a Lubitsch psychodrama, whose decoding helps us better understand his approach to the subject. The great irony of his life, as Eyman's biography shows, is that this director who created some of the screen's most alluring romantic imagery was, in his personal relationships, largely unsuccessful with women. As we have seen, his first marriage ended abruptly when his wife Leni cheated on him with his screenwriter Hans Kräly, blaming Lubitsch's workaholic tendencies for her infidelity. His second marriage, by all accounts, was less than ideal because his wife Vivian was a social climber who was snobbish toward her husband's relatively humble roots. She was regarded by his friends, including Raphaelson, as not his intellectual equal, even if that may not have bothered Lubitsch unduly.

Between marriages, Lubitsch tended to pursue actresses and other women his friends thought were beneath him in most ways, just as Henry chases after showgirls and other women who are mere playthings and do not threaten his love for Martha. Lubitsch may have displayed a lack of self-esteem by aiming low in his love life, with unhappy results. To compensate for that dismaying emptiness, he tended to idealize romantic relationships in his films. *Heaven Can Wait*, with its rosy and somewhat unreal portrait of marriage and its mysterious ellipses, especially the lacunae regarding Martha's feelings, is a wish-fulfillment fantasy Lubitsch wants us to indulge in with him. Martha's endlessly forgiving nature may represent his own desire for the kind of tolerance he habitually displays toward others and may not always have received from the women in his life. As he described what seemed his ideal woman, in contrast to his frustrations over Miriam Hopkins, "If she cared enough, she could be all things to a man, a wife, companion, and mistress." For Lubitsch, mutual tolerance is perhaps the supreme virtue. As Peter Bogdanovich wrote of *Heaven Can Wait*, "It is Lubitsch's 'divine comedy': no one has ever been more gentle or bemused by the weaknesses of humanity."

Among the other elements that make *Heaven Can Wait* a Lubitsch psychodrama is its affectionate portrayal of the hearty and droll Grandpa Van Cleve, who, as Lubitsch's daughter, Nicola, said, was "totally modeled on my grandfather," the master tailor Simon Lubitsch. And much like Martha, Lubitsch's mother, Anna, appears to have been a more reliable, stable character than her husband, who "liked pretty ladies." Anna played a major role in running the firm of S. Lubitsch; Martha's job is to preserve and keep the family home intact. Grandpa Van Cleve is not uncritical of Henry but tends to indulge him over the decades because he identifies with the personality traits that others look upon as flaws. In a rare moment of reproach and wistful regret, Grandpa tells him, "If a woman like Martha runs away from her husband, there must be a reason. Now, look here, Henry. You were the only Van Cleve I ever really cared about. I loved you; you were like me—at least I thought so. You were all the things I wanted to be. You did the things I wanted to do, and didn't. And now you've let me down."

Unlike Henry's more conventionally responsible father and son (Louis Calhern and Michael Ames), who both work in the family business, Henry's ability to live out an idle existence is made possible by Grandpa, the man who amassed the family fortune. But Grandpa is already too old when we first meet him to whoop it up anymore other than through acts of harmless mischief or vicarious pleasure. He is, however, the spirit of the family, the most humane and multifaceted of the Van Cleves, which is why Lubitsch repeatedly emphasizes his enduring presence in compositions, including his portrait, which is continuing to oversee Henry's activities from beyond the grave. In addition to being a tribute to Lubitsch's father, Grandpa also speaks and acts for Ernst Lubitsch himself, who poured most of his energies into his work and was perennially unlucky in love, unlike Henry, who blunders his way through an aimless life but is rewarded for his relatively guileless sensuality by both the director and Martha. The protagonist's lack of growth, his perpetual childishness, could account for why the setting of the family home changes so little over the years; it is Henry's refuge, maintained in his self-image, frozen in time like his Grandpa's portrait and himself, supported by their family wealth and his wife's anchoring influence.

The idealized life of the somewhat dubious family in *Heaven Can Wait* is a magical blend of the happier elements of Lubitsch's life story and what he lacked but wished he could have had. That accounts for the film's ability to persuade us, with consummate charm and grace, of the value of its improbably likable central character and his ability to succeed with women, or at least with the one woman he truly cares about. Ever the ladies' man, even in death, Henry says to the Devil at the beginning of the film, before the flashbacks begin, "Perhaps the best way to tell you the story of my life is to tell you about the women in my life." His admission that he feels unworthy of Martha is balanced by the generous way she has treated him throughout their life together, an attitude wholeheartedly endorsed by Lubitsch's other surrogate figure, the Devil. Despite the qualms we may have about the storyline and whatever preconceptions we might bring to our view of Henry, *Heaven Can Wait* is an endearing fairy tale because it is Lubitsch's most embracing statement about life. That wholehearted tolerance of human foibles is what he wanted to leave us with in this, his testament film. That accounts for why it is more sentimental than Lubitsch's earlier work tended to be.

Among its other virtues, *Heaven Can Wait* has the greatest death scene in the history of cinema. Fittingly, it involves an ellipsis behind a closed door. This storytelling shorthand evokes nostalgia for Lubitsch's entire body of work while treating even death with the lightness of his fabled Touch. When the elderly Henry, inside the bedroom, relates his dream to a nurse, it summarizes his life at the same time that it recapitulates emblematic highlights of Lubitsch's career and evokes some of his trademark hedonistic personal habits, blurring the boundaries between the director and his protagonist. As the scene starts, right after the gag about the crowded medicine cabinet, we are outside the door of Henry's sickroom. Henry's son and his wife emerge and leave for the night, expressing concern about his well-being to a doctor, who reassures them. Lubitsch dissolves inside the room. We see the pajama-clad, white-haired elderly invalid lying in bed asleep, attended by a nurse who is almost as old as he is. She taps his wrist to wake him so she can put a thermometer in his mouth. He reflexively begins patting her hand indulgently and murmuring. But as he wakes, the old playboy, true to form, winces when he sees her homely face and glasses. Henry pushes her hand away as she tries to put the thermometer in his mouth with her other hand—a wry allusion to and twist on a celebrated Lubitsch Touch, the doctor's wrist flip after the errant best friend in both *The Marriage Circle* and *One Hour with You* takes his hand but her husband enters unexpectedly. Henry's nurse tries to put the thermometer in his mouth again, but he crankily pushes it away and relates his dream:

Oh, what was that dream all about? Oh, I was having such a good time! What was that all about? Oh, yes—the door opened, and a man stepped out of a rowboat. He said, "Henry, I've come to take you on a trip from which you'll never come back." And I said, "My good fellow, if I ever take a trip like that, it'll be in a deluxe cabin and not in a dinky little rowboat that doesn't even have a bar." So I threw him out, rowboat and all. And what do you think he did? He came back with a big luxury liner, floating on an ocean of whiskey and soda. And instead of funnels, there were big black cigars.

And on top of the bar, sitting in a lifeboat, was the most beautiful blonde, wearing a Merry Widow costume. She dived into the whiskey and swam right over to my bedside. "Henry," she said, "how about a little dance?" And the man from the boat took an accordion out of his pocket and he played the "Merry Widow Waltz." The girl held her arms out to me and she started to dance. Well, with him playing, and her dancing, and me up to my neck in whiskey anyhow, well, I put my arms around that beautiful girl and was just about to dance with her when, of all people, you cut in—you, yes, you! Oh, go away and take that thermometer with you. Ohh . . .

A knock on the door. The butler announces, "The night nurse is just arrived." The older nurse takes her medicine bag and leaves. Lubitsch cuts outside the door and tracks with her along a balcony to a big round mirror in a gilt frame. It is flanked by two large vases that look like burial urns for the ashes of Henry and perhaps Grandpa, with a display of orange flowers between them. The homely nurse looks into the mirror and primps. She exits, and we hold on the mirror. We hear her exchange greetings off-camera with another woman. Then, as if the mirror is an object out of a Disney fairy tale, the "wicked witch" is magically transformed into an improbably gorgeous, voluptuous young blonde nurse. Entering the frame of the mirror, she flounces her luscious locks, giving herself a satisfied little smile as she pushes out her chest. She goes into the sickroom with her black bag.

The door closes.

We hold on it, and after a brief pause comes the ultimate Lubitsch Touch, what I described in 1992 as "an elegantly resigned gesture by a man closely in touch with his own impending mortality": we hear the soft strains of "The Merry Widow Waltz" playing on an accordion, a tune that, as Sarris pointed out, is associated with "this whole idea of death in the midst of merriment—and that is the key, I think, to the Lubitsch style, the Lubitsch Touch." Another pause, and the camera gracefully starts pulling back and downward, in the direction of Hell, where the old man mistakenly thinks he deserves to go. The camera descends ever more rapidly, past a staircase, into the hallway below, as the romantic music is picked up by an orchestra. We dissolve to a craning shot in Hell, heading farther downward to Henry sitting with the Devil, looking dejected, but then finishing his life story with a happy flourish. Along with the classical allusions to the rivers Styx and Acheron, and to Charon, the ferryman of Hades, who rows people from the land of the living to the underworld realm of the dead, and the personal Lubitschean allusions to his cherished vices of cigars and whiskey, we have the wistful evocation of one of his most sublimely romantic movies, *The Merry Widow*.

Henry asks His Excellency, "Who could ask for a more beautiful death?"

LUBITSCH WITHOUT LUBITSCH

Lubitsch's final years were shadowed by his increasingly threatening heart problems. Although he continued working at Fox, he completed only one film as a director in his last four years. On July 4, 1946, Charles Brackett wrote in his diary after visiting Lubitsch's home with actor Richard Haydn, "There has been an appalling change in Ernst. He seems to have shrunk, his lips were blue and he talked wildly and incessantly in a thin, throaty voice that wasn't his voice." Lubitsch suffered his fatal heart attack on November 30, 1947, on a Sunday off from making *That Lady in Ermine*, for which he was posthumously given solo directing credit even though Otto Preminger shot the last few weeks and removed some of the material that Lubitsch had filmed. Before that dismal finale, Lubitsch had prepared two other projects he was also unable to bring to fruition, the period comedy *A Royal Scandal* (directed by Preminger, 1945) and a period melodrama, *Dragonwyck* (the 1946 directing debut of Joseph L. Mankiewicz). None of those three films remotely lives up to Lubitsch's standards, and he did not even put his name on *Dragonwyck* as producer. But in the midst of this daunting, largely depressing period, Lubitsch did manage to complete one last gem, *Cluny Brown*.

Filmed from December 1945 through early February 1946 and released that June, it is a modest and endearing tale of a British plumber and serving girl (Jennifer Jones) who finds her true place in the world with the help of her rootless Pygmalion, a Czech refugee intellectual (Charles Boyer). Even if it is not on the same level of ambition and achievement as Lubitsch's masterpieces of the early forties, *Cluny Brown* is a pleasing swan song for his great career. While making it after his enforced period of absence from the director's chair, he said, "I feel like a dancer with a broken leg who suddenly can dance again." We will save a detailed discussion of *Cluny Brown* for the end of this chapter since it is Lubitsch's return to form, the way the director would have wanted to be remembered.

After *Heaven Can Wait*, which finished shooting in April 1943 and was released that August, Lubitsch had planned to return to the kind of film that had made his name in Germany and he had dabbled with intermittently during his early years in Hollywood, the historical comedy-drama interlaced with sexual intrigue. *A Royal Scandal*, filmed in late 1944, is a remake of his brilliant 1924 comedy *Forbidden Paradise*, the Pola Negri film loosely inspired by the sexually voracious Russian empress Catherine the Great. Lubitsch prepared an overly talky adaptation of the play by Lajos Biró and Melchior Lengyel, *The Czarina*, with Bruno Frank and *To Be or Not to Be* screenwriter Edwin Justus Mayer, but the director's doctors advised him against the stress of shooting the film himself. Lubitsch had to hand over the reins to Preminger. Aside from their shared cultural background (Preminger was an Austrian Jew), it is hard to think of two more dissimilar filmmakers coexisting in Hollywood during that era. Lubitsch's light touch contrasts with Preminger's lumbering lack of humor. Lubitsch's jovial yet firm way of exerting control on the set was at a far remove from Preminger's bullying and blustering. Lubitsch's ironic reliance on intercutting and gracefully staged character interplay within a tightly controlled storytelling perspective are at an opposite pole from Preminger's so-called neutral method of shooting scenes in longish takes, usually in two-shots, carefully balancing opposing viewpoints. The clash between their cinematic styles—even though Lubitsch was on the set throughout the filming of *A Royal Scandal* and helped rehearse the actors—makes the film a mishmash, far inferior to the silent classic on which it was based. One can only imagine how frustrated Lubitsch must have felt to not be in full creative control.

A Royal Scandal plays like a weak imitation of Lubitsch. The remake does away with the original film's audacious mixture of time periods and sets itself squarely in Catherine's eighteenth-century court. But Sternberg and Dietrich had already staked out cinematic ownership of that turf in their astonishing 1934 film *The Scarlet Empress*, and the sexual pursuit of a young officer by the empress in *A Royal Scandal* seems tepid and tedious in comparison with Dietrich's outrageously lurid erotic adventurism. The production values of *A Royal Scandal* are considerably down the artistic scale from those of Lubitsch's silent original, with the action taking place in a few generic interior sets and with exteriors glimpsed only in shoddy backdrops outside the palace windows. Most ruinously, the empress saucily incarnated by the young vamp Negri is played in *A Royal Scandal* by the much older Tallulah Bankhead, whose jaded persona, husky voice, masklike face, and theatrical manner of phrasing make the film seem even more flat and tired than Preminger's mise-en-scène (one of Bankhead's first lines, unfortunately, is "I look awful"). Garbo had been sought for the lead, and she would have raised the emotional stakes in another Russian role for Lubitsch, but she had been retired from the screen since 1941.

The reliable presence of such delightful Lubitsch character actors as Charles Coburn and Sig Ruman keeps *A Royal Scandal* from being unwatchable, but the male lead (William Eythe) is callow and overwrought even for the meager demands of his role as Catherine's boy toy, whom she succinctly characterizes as an "idiot." Preminger's graceless staging and frequently unmotivated camera movements add to the feeling that this was a project executed by people who were merely going through the motions of material that they realized had seen a better day. Putting the leaden *A Royal Scandal* side by side with the scintillating *Forbidden Paradise* would be a perfect way to demonstrate the special qualities of the silent film medium that had been lost with the coming of sound. But unfortunately, *Forbidden Paradise*, like some of Lubitsch's other major early films, has been hard to see in recent years, perhaps partly because it was remade; Hollywood often tried to obliterate the originals to prevent unfavorable comparison. Lubitsch's decision to remake a film that had found its ideal form earlier was a blunder, and even if he had been in charge behind the camera, it is unlikely he could have done much to make *A Royal Scandal* more than a time filler, a considerable comedown after the highly original and captivating *Heaven Can Wait*. Because of his waning physical and psychological energies after his 1943 heart attack, his ability to remain fresh and lively as a creative artist was in jeopardy, as, indeed, was the very continuation of his career. His doctor cut his daily cigar intake from twelve to fifteen a day down to five, and sometimes he only chewed on them.

Lubitsch was only fifty-four when he completed filming *Cluny Brown* in February 1946, but he seemed much older. Though his rapidly advancing end helped him imbue that film, like *Heaven Can Wait*, with a serene grace, he faltered badly in his choice of material with *Dragonwyck* (released in April 1946) and *That Lady in Ermine* (released posthumously in August 1948). *Dragonwyck* is a lugubrious *Jane Eyre* knockoff based on a popular novel by Anya Seton and adapted by Joseph Mankiewicz, a long-established Hollywood writer and producer who was known for his erudite dialogue and sophisticated characterizations (among his writing credits were the omnibus films *Paramount on Parade* and *If I Had a Million*, to which Lubitsch contributed). Set in mid-nineteenth-century Connecticut and New York, *Dragonwyck* is the story of a governess (Gene Tierney) menaced by a psychotic employer (Vincent Price) who becomes her second husband. It plays to some of Mankiewicz's strengths but seems oddly unsuited to Lubitsch. The best explanation for why Lubitsch chose to film it—again, he had to turn over the directing reins because of his health—might be his penchant for veering occasionally from his true métier of sophisticated comedy into more ostensibly prestigious and "serious" subject matter. The story also bears a superficial similarity to Lubitsch's 1922 German silent *Anna Boleyn*, another largely humorless film about a wife murderer.

Mankiewicz, never much of a visual stylist, managed to carry off a creditable directing debut with the help of Fox's great cinematographer Arthur C. Miller, whose shadowy lighting gives the film whatever haunting qualities it actually possesses. Unlike *A Royal Scandal*, which suffers from Preminger's rat-a-tat-tat pacing of dialogue (the characters often sound as if they are reading from the telephone book), the mostly outlandish, derivative *Dragonwyck* benefits from Mankiewicz's customary fluidity with the spoken word. But though it is a more accomplished piece of studio craftsmanship than *A Royal Scandal*, both films show how important Lubitsch's characteristically musical dialogue rhythms, his impeccable sense of visual pacing, and his unique ability to control the tonal blend of comedy and drama were to making the films he directed stand out from the usual run of Hollywood entertainment. Although Lubitsch was known for rigorously preplanning his films and collaborating intensively with his writers, as polished as his scripts are, his Touch was not entirely contained within their pages. The undistinguished direction of these two 1940s films that he only produced demonstrates how much his work depended on the moment-by-moment execution of his conceptions on the set. A Lubitsch film without Lubitsch directing is not really a Lubitsch film.

Samson Raphaelson glumly recalled what happened when Lubitsch summoned him back to Hollywood to write the film that became *That Lady in Ermine*, the director's final project: "I began finding fault the moment I saw what he was up to—just another variation on the old Lubitsch fun-in-a-castle triangle. He thought the stuff was great, and I felt that he was kidding himself." They had a "hollering session" over it. But Raphaelson realized by midday that Lubitsch was "a very sick man plodding along on formula and I couldn't fight him. What I had to do there was deliver what a worn-out man expected and I did it as an act of compassion. . . . I don't think I fooled him. Looking back, I believe he knew precisely what we were doing, shared my viewpoint, but preferred survival to glory."

Although filmed as *This Is the Moment*, Lubitsch's final project did not capture the vitality of its moment in time but was a sad attempt to go back to the past and fantasize about dead people. Set in a nineteenth-century principality, it was the director's only return to the musical genre after his magnificent *Merry Widow* in 1934. But not only were Lubitsch's creative powers waning by 1947, the world had changed irrevocably since the war, making everything about this project seem culturally passé. The film is acutely embarrassing in its execution. Based on the 1919 operetta *Die Frau im Hermelin* (*That Lady in Ermine*) by Rudolf Schanzer and Ernst Welisch, which had been filmed twice before, this musical fantasy deals with a countess whose ancestors come back to her life from their palace portraits to help her outflank a dashing Hungarian invader as her predecessor had done more violently with an invading duke three hundred years earlier.

The project was originally developed by Lubitsch at Fox in 1943. Irene Dunne, mature, dignified, and possessed of a lovely light-operatic voice, was considered for the dual roles of Countess Francesca and her ancestor Angelina. Lubitsch imagined Charles Boyer as the male lead, another dual role. Dunne might have lent the project some of the combination of lightness and gravity it needed. Lubitsch subsequently proposed a reunion with Jeanette MacDonald instead, but her day as a star had mostly gone. Tierney was also considered, but Lubitsch wound up saddled with Fox's most popular star of that era, the World War II pinup girl Betty Grable, whose singing and dancing are mediocre and whose acting skills are minimal. She comes off as petulant, dim-witted, and hopelessly adrift as a middle-American naïf who has been incongruously planted in a foreign period setting. Her commonness is ill fitting with the character's nobility. Not walking away from the project when Grable was cast was a misjudgment on Lubitsch's part, but he wanted to work, and with time running out, he was no longer the stubborn fighter for quality he had been in days gone by. The dispirited going-through-the-motions mood seemed to infect most people involved in the project, despite its expense, $2.4 million, the highest budget of Lubitsch's career, which he was granted because Fox thought Grable's stardom would gain luster from his prestige. Even the songs by Leo Robin and Frederick Hollander, who had made such memorable contributions to earlier Lubitsch films, are weak. And though Raphaelson was feigning interest in order to humor his old friend and collaborator, he should have tried harder with the verbose, painfully unfunny script. The writer's exasperation seems to come through when Grable is yammering away to her costar, Douglas Fairbanks Jr., and he stops her by saying, "Countess, may I make a suggestion? Why don't you keep quiet?"

What attracted Lubitsch to this feeble project? Probably, at this precarious stage in his existence, he was drawn to its delirious blurring of the line between life and the afterlife. But by treating the theme of mortality as a musical fantasy extravaganza, the film becomes far more stylized than *Heaven Can Wait* and with a major diminution of emotional impact. After the relatively subdued *Cluny Brown*, Lubitsch seems to have felt the need to cut loose with his camera in a manner reminiscent of his zany German comedies such as *The Oyster Princess*, *The Doll*, and *The Wildcat*. In July 1947, three months before beginning production on *That Lady in Ermine*, he told Mollie Merrick of *American Cinematographer*,

> Unfortunately we have neglected the camera greatly in the last few years. We have failed to tell the story in visual terms. Naturally the spoken word is a terrific asset and carries great power; but we have become so engrossed in words we have neglected to take full advantage of the dramatic power of the visual approach. In my next picture I hope we will have a chance to give more space again to visual effects. I hope to take full advantage of dialogue and speech, but also I'd like to give enough room for the valuable things we learned and have partly forgotten from the silent days of the motion picture.

But then Lubitsch, far removed in time from his early experimental days, seemed to betray some uncertainty about how far to go in that direction: "It should not be handled with camera tricks. Fantasy can never be put over that way. My ghosts will be very corporeal people who will move and talk and react just like other actors in the picture. . . . If you seek to emphasize your story situation with trickery, you fail because you cannot achieve a dynamic effect in a picture if you let your audience become conscious of the mechanism behind motion picture making."

Beyond that aesthetic confusion between wanting to strike out in another direction and feeling an emotional urge to make a nostalgic retreat to his past, there was a deeper level that clouded Lubitsch's judgment. The surprising clumsiness of *That Lady in Ermine* perhaps reflects his unsettled state of mind as he was being forced, with increasing urgency, to contemplate his own mortality. The device of Francesca's ancestors coming out of their portraits to help her defend her principality comes off as leaden whimsy. The film's recycling of the power conflict from *The Love Parade* between a female ruler and her male consort (Cesar Romero) lacks the emotional resonance that formerly underpinned Lubitsch's comical treatment of gender imbalance. The director's fascination with the intricacies of adulterous triangles suffers further because of the cardboard characterizations of the countess and her consort. Fairbanks makes a valiant effort in the role of the Hungarian hussar, Colonel Ladislas Teglas, who becomes enraptured by Francesca but is befuddled by the supernatural goings-on. Fairbanks makes his part work by playing it straight, as comedy should be played. But the filmmakers think it is amusing to have Colonel Teglas constantly yelling at subordinates, including ones standing right next to him. This is derived from the running gag with Colonel Ehrhardt shouting "Schultz!" in *To Be or Not to Be* (most hilariously after Ehrhardt fails to shoot himself offscreen), but it becomes irritating when it is repeated incessantly rather than saved for choice moments as in the earlier film. Lubitsch's sense of humor seemed to vanish in *That Lady in Ermine* along with the subtlety that had long made his direction so distinctive. When asked on the set by a *Los Angeles Times* interviewer why he had gone back to the musical genre, Lubitsch admitted, "One gets tired."

On the afternoon of Sunday, November 30, Lubitsch died of a coronary thrombosis, caused by four years of atherosclerosis, in his bathroom after having sex with a prostitute. Billy Wilder, who arrived soon afterward, said Lubitsch's factotum, Otto Werner, paid her and whisked her out the door. When Lubitsch was pronounced dead at 2:45, he had a slight smile on his face. Indeed, "Who could ask for a more beautiful death?" With unintended gallows humor, *Daily Variety*'s banner headline the following day announced,

"LUBITSCH DROPS DEAD." At least we have the consolation that it is hard to imagine a trade paper giving any other director's obituary a banner headline then or now. Hollywood's state of shock was palpable when it lost the man who had singlehandedly transformed its output into a more mature art form. Perhaps John Ford best expressed what Lubitsch had meant to the industry: "None of us thought we were making anything but entertainment for the moment. Only Ernst Lubitsch knew we were making art."

Later on the day Lubitsch died, Wilder, "looking like a heartbroken cherub," and Brackett joined what the senior partner in the writing team called "the German contingent"—including Marlene Dietrich, Otto Preminger, Henry Blanke, Gottfried Reinhardt, Miklos Rosza, and Salka Viertel—for an informal wake at Walter Reisch's house. Brackett confided to his diary, "We were all happy at the suddenness and lack of suffering with which the end had come—it was so on the cards that he would suffer long and painfully. We talked of his great, great gifts to the art of picture-making, the greatest any of us knew."

Lubitsch was buried at Forest Lawn Memorial Parks & Mortuaries in Glendale, California, on December 4, after a funeral held before what "seemed to be most of the industry," Brackett wrote. He gave the eulogy, saying that Lubitsch had helped teach the "raw, gawky, stumbling" film medium "how to carry itself as becomes a personage of the world, how to wear it like a boutonnière, and how to imply droll, wonderful things without saying them at all. . . . He was no wild, impractical poet clashing with the businessmen who make picture history, but he was an unmitigated artist, blessedly incapable of meeting a standard of taste which wasn't his own." Jeanette MacDonald sang "Beyond the Blue Horizon" from *Monte Carlo* as well as a song Lubitsch had written for his daughter, Nicola, "It's a Beautiful Day." The simple metal grave marker reads, "ERNST LUBITSCH / 1892–1947 / BELOVED DADDY."

The next day, the lugubrious, tyrannical Preminger again stepped in, opportunistically, to finish an abortive Lubitsch project, which he treated with something less than the respect the late director deserved. It is sometimes reported that Lubitsch had shot only a few days on *That Lady in Ermine*. But according to Carringer and Sabath in their book on Lubitsch, he had begun shooting on October 20, 1947, and Preminger finished the filming from December 5 through January 5, 1948; Lubitsch shot thirty-six days,

Preminger twenty-six. Preminger reshaped the film's storyline to some extent, either to fit his own dubious sensibility or simply to get the job over and done with. He dropped Lubitsch's opening and ending as well as two musical numbers and reshot some other Lubitsch footage "because it was too subtle," Fairbanks recalled. Carringer and Sabath note, "In a final scene Francesca leads the ancestors in a dance as they all sing, 'Ooh, what she'll do to that wild Hungarian!' (Lubitsch's original plan called for a final scene where Francesca pours herself a glass of wine, remembers her beautiful dream with the Colonel, and finally takes off the ermine coat to reveal what she wore to the Duke's tent. This was eliminated by Preminger.)"

An Otto Preminger musical is almost a contradiction in terms. Even the usually inventive choreographer Hermes Pan, best known for his symbiotic work with Fred Astaire, somehow could not do any better here than having Francesca's ancestors repeatedly traipse around the palace lobby in circles. The film often looks like a high school play. All that makes it (barely) watchable is Leon Shamroy's lush cinematography, draping the funereal proceedings in his characteristically bold, glossy Technicolor shades.

Rather than dwell any longer on this leaden parody of Lubitsch, it is more pleasing to remember the master going out with his last completed film, the delectable *Cluny Brown*.

"SQUIRRELS TO THE NUTS"

Cluny Brown is among the few films Lubitsch adapted from novels. As such, it has more social texture than his usual source material from the stage. He mines British author Margery Sharp's charming novel for a loving yet often mocking portrait of the follies of his native Europe on the brink of war. The 1944 bestseller, set in 1938 England, pokes fun at the insularity and isolationism of that country's ruling class in the run-up to World War II. Sharp was serving as a British army education lecturer when she wrote this graceful, gently satirical book. Peace had just come when Lubitsch made the film version in late 1945 and early 1946, which made the film even more reflective and ironic.

Cluny Brown (Jennifer Jones) is a plumber's niece whose unorthodox personality gives her a yen for worldly experience outside her stifling London working-class environment. She has her own passion for plumbing, which was viewed in that society as an unbecoming job for a woman but marks her as something of a feminist pioneer—and gives Lubitsch the opportunity for some of his more raucous double entendres, such as having her say, "One good bang might turn the trick in a jiffy. . . . Why don't you let me have a whack at it?" As punishment for her ambitions, the plucky young woman is sent by her uncle into domestic service with a snobbish and crushingly dull upper-class family in their country manor, Friars Carmel. Cluny's problem, repeatedly emphasized by other characters, is that, like Eliza Doolittle in George Bernard Shaw's *Pygmalion*, she doesn't know her "place." She has internalized that criticism and badly wants to find out where she belongs. So does Charles Boyer's Adam Belinski, the exile from Nazism who finds temporary refuge as a guest at the manor. The guileless Cluny and this foreign intellectual, so different in background but so similar in their predicaments as outsiders, find themselves gravitating toward each other almost without realizing it and after putting up some resistance to their fated union.

Sharp has a keen eye for social observation and an engaging way of depicting eccentric but believable characters. Her romantic tale owes a further debt to Shaw in its sarcastic portrait of the British gentry through the Carmel parents, who are clueless about the coming war. Sir Henry Carmel (Reginald Owen) is an amiable dolt, and Lady Alice (Margaret Bannerman) covers her hauteur imperfectly with a veneer of politeness. Their feckless son, Andrew (Peter Lawford), is anxiously concerned about the world situation but does not know what to do about it except to write letters to the *Times*. Andrew's elusive inamorata, an aristocrat everyone calls the Honorable Betty Cream (Helen Walker), is a knockout who flirts with young men like a cat taunting flies for her amusement. *Cluny Brown* could have been quite caustic in its mockery of these smugly insular characters, but Sharp treats the story in a disarmingly casual, light-spirited, relaxed style. She gives us a window into the British class system by focusing on a déclassé ugly duckling whose journey into the fringes of high society exposes its inadequacies and, ironically, liberates her from the shackles of her own narrow existence.

The Carmels and Belinski, in their differing ways, are drawn to Cluny's unaffected goodness and help her find her place, the Carmels by showing her where she does not want to stay and Belinski by showing her where she needs to go. Cluny never quite becomes sophisticated until she manages to get out of her native country—her gawky callowness is part of her appeal—and her adventurousness is attractive to Belinski as well as to us. Jennifer Jones brings more physical glamour to the role than it has in the novel, which emphasizes how physically plain Cluny is in order to give her a further element of sympathy. Jones has a rough-hewn commonness to her screen personality that Lubitsch carefully molds into a charmingly earthy portrayal even if her British accent is sometimes shaky. At the end, Cluny and Belinski flee to America, escaping the dead end of the stifling British class system and finding a happy and prosperous new life together. This fairy-tale ending for an unlikely couple, united by their need for a society that allows them the freedom to be themselves, offered consolation to the reading public in a perilous time of war and did so again for film audiences in the uneasy postwar climate.

Lubitsch embraces the novel's political satire with glee, sharpening it at some points but softening it at others out of his characteristic kindly indulgence toward his characters. The director brings to the story his own keen sense of class differences, but his satire is good-natured. The Belinski character is more romantic and kinder as well as more emotionally vulnerable in Lubitsch's elegantly nonchalant reshaping of the material. The screenwriters, the Russian-born Samuel Hoffenstein and American-born Elizabeth Reinhardt (no relation to Max), had previously collaborated (with Jay Dratler) on Preminger's haunting 1944 film noir, *Laura*. *Cluny Brown* contains little of the friction between Belinski and Cluny that in the novel is caused by his jealousy over her misguided engagement to another man, and Belinski's intellectual condescension toward her is jettisoned entirely. In the mellow late stage of Lubitsch's career, this man of the world becomes another alter ego for the director, a wryly romantic refugee from a crumbling Europe. Belinski treats his female partner with emotional generosity and eventually finds success in the New World as a popular novelist (specializing in crime), much as Lubitsch did as a popular filmmaker in Hollywood. Belinski's predicament as a rootless, homeless outcast receives greater emotional emphasis than in the novel; the film largely takes his point of view, though the female writer's novel takes Cluny's, and the change of emphasis gives the story more urgency because of Belinski's situation as a political refugee and makes their offbeat romance more believable.

Lubitsch changes Belinski from a Pole to a Czech, making him an unofficial representative of a country that was betrayed by Britain in the Munich Agreement, which was signed the year in which the story is set. An antifascist professor from Prague, this writer and philosopher on the run from Hitler has lost his own tenuous place in European society. Although not identified as Jewish, Belinski embodies the outsider status of the Wandering Jew (he is one of the implicit Jewish characters Joel Rosenberg points to in Lubitsch's films). In the person of Belinski, Lubitsch is able to express the brutal rejection he and his people suffered with the coming of Nazism and the rootlessness he must have continued to feel even after finding his own haven in the United States. But Lubitsch was able to transform his more painful feelings into a poignant charitableness toward both his characters and British society, flawed though they all may be, and even though Andrew impatiently tells his father that he is "sitting on a volcano."

Cluny Brown often resembles a Jean Renoir film in its satire of class issues, its sympathetic treatment of outsiders, and its approach to transcending those social barriers as well as in its fluid, graceful camerawork that emphasizes group interaction with natural ease (the elegant cinematography is by Joseph LaShelle, whose work also includes *Laura*; Billy Wilder's *The Apartment* and *Kiss Me, Stupid*; and John Ford's *7 Women*). Casting an unwavering eye on the hypocrisies of the wealthy but still seeing them with some affection as fallible human beings is what Renoir also does in *The Rules of the Game*, his great 1939 film about masters, servants, and hangers-on in a country manor house. Lubitsch concentrates on the theme that Renoir said was at the heart of his work: "My preoccupation is with the meeting, how to belong, how to meet. . . . It's very strange that it is what is often missing in a movie, very often—I believe, in this world, that we proceed in little groups. You must belong to a little group. That doesn't mean that you lose your individuality, not at all. Belonging to a little group helps you to find it."

Cluny, as a member of the Cockney working class, has felt excluded from any fruitful place in her society, and she yearns for some place that better fits her individual needs and allows her to express her quirky personality. But, as an orphan raised by mostly uncommunicative and emotionally undemonstrative relatives, she has no idea where she will find that place until she and Belinski form a "little group" together, augmented at the end by her pregnancy. That genuine family bond alleviates the loneliness that she felt earlier and that almost led her into a ruinous union with a stuffy local chemist in the town of Friars Carmel, Mr. Wilson (Richard Haydn), before she impulsively agreed to run away with Belinski. Lubitsch's intersection with Renoir in this contemplative comedy helps underscore the bond the two expatriate European masters share. They are unsentimental humanists who understand and respect the complexities of how "everyone has his reasons," as Renoir's Octave tells us in *The Rules of the Game*, while pointedly prefacing his oft-quoted remark with, "On this earth there is one thing that's terrible." Lubitsch, who, as Renoir said, "invented the modern Hollywood," is a more dedicated humorist than the French director, but they share career-long concerns with how individuality struggles to coexist with the inescapable demands of class structures.

The atmosphere of stifling class distinctions at Friars Carmel is quickly established upon Cluny's arrival. When she meets Sir Henry and Lady Alice, Cluny is greeted warmly because they mistake her for a guest of an aristocratic friend. But when they realize she is a mere servant, they quickly and deftly change their demeanor, Lady Carmel ringing a bell for Cluny to be taken to her quarters. In this bitterly satirical scene, Cluny is succinctly taught her place, a rigid role further reinforced by the housekeeper, Mrs. Maile (Sara Allgood), and the butler, Mr. Syrette (Ernest Cossart), another pair of outspoken Lubitsch servants who comically define the social structure of a film's setting. These two are, if anything, stricter than the Carmels in enforcing the rules of the game, and Lubitsch pokes fun at their stiffness and their mindless collusion in their own entrapment. They lack the gentility and polite veneer the Carmels have been trained to possess, and that Lubitsch regards as something of value, since manners, in his worldview, are so crucial to the happy functioning of life. Even though Sir Henry and Lady Alice are depicted as idle fools, Lubitsch spares them his sharpest tools of satire, just as Belinski is inclined to focus on their kindness and hospitality rather than on their obvious flaws. And the film acknowledges that when war comes, Sir Henry will be among the patriotic Britons rising belatedly to the occasion, following his idealistic son's eager example.

Although the working life at Friars Carmel is not particularly onerous for Cluny, it is emotionally unsatisfying for this restless young woman, who turns her attention to the conventional notion of finding a place as a bourgeois housewife. Unfortunately, the man who makes himself available is a thoroughly pompous prig, Mr. Wilson the chemist, hilariously played by Haydn with nasal line readings and a perpetually pinched face. Mr. Wilson lives with his elderly mother (Una O'Connor), a gargoyle who communicates only by clearing her throat in different registers, among the funniest of many Lubitsch gags involving the inventive substitution of other sounds for dialogue. In the novel, Mr. Wilson is depicted more three-dimensionally and sympathetically as a "tragic chemist," a widower who lost his wife in an auto accident, but that element is removed in the film. Lubitsch has nothing but mockery for a man who is so smug and ungenerous toward Cluny.

Cluny does not know enough about life to realize that her place as Mrs. Wilson would reduce her to a far more subservient role than she already occupies. She is roughly forced to that conclusion when the plumbing breaks down in the Wilson loo during their engagement party and she cannot resist fixing it. This mortifies Mr. Wilson and his snobbish middle-class guests, although the young son of one couple is enraptured by Cluny and cannot understand why all the adults are beating a hasty departure. It is only when Belinski, who has been admiring her from a gentlemanly distance, takes a more active interest in courting her that Cluny gradually, if almost subconsciously, comes to recognize her true place. It is in the kind of defiantly individualistic life he leads and in their shared nomadic roles as exiles in the more egalitarian country across the ocean ("Oh, it's so good to talk to someone who's out of place too," she tells him). Although Lubitsch had come to America voluntarily ("one of the talented ones," as Wilder wryly called him), he had to put his homeland forever behind him when the Nazis took over, so he identifies with the forced exile of Belinski and his desire to find a better life in the United States. *Cluny Brown* memorably defines the bohemian philosopher's view of the world in Belinski's passionate speech to Cluny early in the film (which is not in the book). It comes as close as any verbal statement in Lubitsch's work to explicitly providing his philosophy of life:

Nobody can tell you where your place is. Where's my place? Where is anybody's place? I'll tell you where it is. Wherever you're happy, that's your place. And happiness is a matter of purely personal adjustment to your environment. You're the sole judge. In Hyde Park, for instance, some people like to feed nuts to the squirrels. But if it makes you happy to feed squirrels to the nuts, who am I to say, "Nuts to the squirrels"?

Belinski has been adopted by the Carmels by grace of Andrew's political fervor: the callow young aristocrat dabbles in socialism and melodramatically fantasizes a far more dangerous escape from the Nazis than Belinski actually had to make. In the novel, Belinski has been roughed up by the Nazis more brutally than is suggested in the film, but Sharp also has Belinski modestly deflating people's notions of his heroism. Andrew fancies him "one of Hitler's worst enemies," but Belinski insists that he is in no more danger than everyone else in the world. Much as Lubitsch does with Joseph Tura in *To Be or Not to Be*, the director characteristically avoids the noble posturing of most Hollywood films about the war, recognizing that genuine heroes do not brag about their courage. The director makes Belinski more of a quiet soul who simply wants to write his books in peace, much as Lubitsch might have wanted to keep enjoying making films in "Paris, Paramount" until the real Paris became off-limits because of Hitler.

In referring to the Nazis in *Cluny Brown*, Lubitsch avoids the harsh black comedy of *To Be or Not to Be*, which had to be so urgent because the war was actually underway when it was made. While filming *Cluny Brown* in the war's aftermath, Lubitsch took a more oblique tack, portraying Andrew and his friend and political comrade John Frewen (Michael Dyne) as well-meaning but shallow twits and having Sir Henry express a comically vague awareness of Hitler: "Oh, yes, he's written a book, hasn't he? . . . Sort of an outdoor book, isn't it? What's it called? Oh, yes, *My Camp*." To which Belinski offers a pointed comment on behalf of the German American filmmaker, "Yes. It's a kind of an outdoor book. The old German idea of sport. Not your kind of sport." A film set in 1938 England could have savagely satirized the aristocracy as rabid fascist isolationists, but Lubitsch is not after that kind of big game here. Instead, he depicts the Carmels as initially naïve but characteristic of a people whose collective bravery eventually helped defeat the Nazis. As Sir Henry puts it after expounding on his scant knowledge of Hitler, "We Carmels have never shirked our duty. No Englishman has or ever will. We'll see this thing through. We'll *show* that blighter." Lubitsch drops his mocking tone at this point to let us look beneath the surface to see the hidden reserves of British strength even in a shameful time of appeasement.

In keeping with Lubitsch's ironic approach, not only is the exiled Belinski even less politically engaged than in the novel but the film softens his personality further by stripping away his initial haughtiness toward Cluny and making him more consistently gentlemanly, if occasionally jealous. From their first meeting in London, when he admires her plumbing skills and discovers their bond of not having a place, he shows an indulgent fondness toward her even when she ignores his attentions in her misguided quest to become Mrs. Wilson. Ever philosophical, and older than in the book, Belinski expresses his intellectual distance from his setting in ironic phrasing and glances rather than by making obviously disapproving statements about the rigidity and narrowness of the life he finds around him. When he expresses gratitude to the Carmels for their hospitality by passionately quoting Shakespeare's *Richard II* to pay tribute to "this scepter'd isle," Belinski is momentarily chagrined to realize that his British hosts don't even know what he is talking about. He offers not one but two toasts to Shakespeare, an eternal touchstone to Belinski and Lubitsch if not to the playwright's benighted modern compatriots. But after making his speech, Belinski lets the moment go rather than despise them for their ignorance about their own cultural heritage. Lubitsch, the grateful refugee to America, is suggesting that foreigners often appreciate a place much more than those who are to the manor born. Belinski's place in that alien society, like Lubitsch's, is to help instruct the natives about their true heritage and to make their social mores more civilized.

Lubitsch further resists the temptation to unduly valorize Belinski by showing that underneath his gentlemanly veneer, this intellectual has, like most male characters in the director's work, a streak of lechery. After Cluny rebuffs his subtle advances, the frustrated, desperately horny Belinski makes a rather crude move toward another houseguest, the Honorable Betty Cream, barging into her bedroom while both are in nightdress. This young woman, with her hilariously delicious name (an ironic appellation like that of "the Honorable Madame Mizzi Stock" in *The Marriage Circle*), has all the conceit of narcissistic gorgeousness. Helen Walker, whose career would be blighted by the tragic effects of an auto accident on New Year's Eve 1946, is in her immortal glory under Lubitsch's deft hand: saucy, voluptuous, self-possessed. Betty Cream has the practiced savoir faire to parry Belinski's would-be suave thrusts with cutting comebacks of her own, a talent that is all the more impressive since he is played by Hollywood's epitome of the continental lover, Boyer. The scene goes well beyond the novel's more casual portrayal of Belinski's pursuit of Betty Cream, and it has some of the astringency of the lecherous scene that Fox would not let Lubitsch film for *Heaven Can Wait*. Lubitsch and his writers execute a neat comic-dramatic reversal by having this scandalous situation end with Lady Carmel sending the servants to their rooms and taking Belinski's place in Betty Cream's bedroom, instructing the young woman of her duty to marry Andrew post-haste. Knowing the rules of the game herself, the nubile but hitherto foot-less Betty, who has been stringing both Andrew and John along for her own amusement, docilely obeys the older woman, as well as what Lubitsch's *Monte Carlo* calls "the dictates of society," and settles down to help produce the next generation of Carmels.

This plot twist, as clever as any in a Shakespearean comedy, clears the way for Belinski to depart Friars Carmel and have Cluny chase him to say good-bye at the train station. The film resolves its complicated but seemingly nat-ural romantic intrigue with dual (offscreen) weddings. "Get in," Belinski commands Cluny, motioning to the train compartment, and she obeys, agree-ing to follow him to their new address, "General Delivery." The tone of this scene is not one of male dominance but of tenderness and the sense of an inevitable and benevolent destiny achieved by both parties. Lubitsch grace-fully wraps up the story with a nostalgic tribute to his roots in silent film. The couple are shown through the window of a bookstore on New York's Fifth Avenue, the newly stylish Cluny proudly explaining in pantomime to a gath-ering crowd that her husband has written the best-selling novel displayed in the window. She faints, and Belinski, also in pantomime, explains to a policeman and the rest of the crowd that she's going to have a baby. As in Shakespeare, the metaphors of fecundity and rebirth are celebrations of life reasserting itself. It's especially poignant to witness this ending while know-ing that it is the true swan song of a great director who was approaching death when he made the film but whose body of work is one long joyous celebration of life.

10.1 Breakfast time with the screen's new sexual freedom: *Avanti!* (1972), a Lubitschean romantic comedy by his protégé Billy Wilder, with Jack Lemmon and Juliet Mills. *(United Artists.)*

EPILOGUE

The Importance of Being Ernst

Speaking of *Trouble in Paradise* in 2003, Peter Bogdanovich noted that although Lubitsch's masterpiece had been made decades earlier, it still seems far more mature in its approach to sexuality and romantic relationships than anything being made in modern Hollywood. Bogdanovich said ruefully, "You think to yourself, 'This was made in 1932—for general audiences. What *happened?* When was America that sophisticated? When was the *world* that sophisticated? And how could we have gone so far in the other direction?'"

Lubitsch's influence on Hollywood storytelling and on fellow directors who regarded him as their master was pervasive in his heyday, but it had already begun to wane at the time of his death in 1947. Lubitsch's run of success was much longer than those of most of his contemporaries, although by his later years, his eminence as a director of romantic comedies was being challenged by the rise of Frank Capra, Preston Sturges, Billy Wilder, Gregory La Cava, Mitchell Leisen, and other upstarts who seemed more directly in tune with the changing times of the Depression era and World War II. Sturges admired Lubitsch, as demonstrated by the references to him in his 1941 comedy-drama about Hollywood, *Sullivan's Travels.* When the impoverished actress wannabe Veronica Lake asks Joel McCrea's director character to introduce her to Lubitsch, Sullivan peevishly replies, "Who's Lubitsch?" This backhanded tribute shows how confident Sturges was that Lubitsch's name was a household word. But Sturges's raucous, more overtly bawdy comedies helped make Lubitsch seem old-fashioned by the time of *Heaven Can Wait* two years later, as he himself clearly recognized.

History suggests that Lubitsch's subtle mode of dealing with sexuality could not have survived, even in his hands, much beyond his lifetime. The played-out feeling of his final film, *That Lady in Ermine*, seems to show that he knew he was running out of ideas or losing his grip on the changing marketplace even though he was only fifty-five when he died during production. The world was radically different during and after the war, and Hollywood's new look was film noir, a genre Lubitsch's most distinguished protégé, Billy Wilder, the hardboiled former Vienna and Berlin newspaperman, could easily relate to with *Double Indemnity* (1944) and other films. But Lubitsch, with his specialty of brightly lit and buoyantly played fantasy romances, was not temperamentally suited to that genre, although the startling departure of *To Be or Not to Be* suggests that he could have continued to go darker in his own way. It is tempting to wonder whether, if he had survived to make films in the radically changed cultural climate of the 1960s, he might have tried to push the envelope much farther than he had in that black comedy, going with the times, even if not as far as Wilder did. But such speculation is probably misleading since the essence of Lubitsch was antithetical to the modern tendency to let it all hang out on-screen, for better or worse. Lubitsch had already radically transformed his style three times to adapt to changing times and social conditions, but it is unlikely he would have been willing or able to radically transform it again as the world and filmmaking turned grittier and more explicit. As Wilder put it in 1975, Lubitsch "would have had big problems in this market."

Wilder and some other directors in the '40s and '50s continued to emulate aspects of Lubitsch's style from time to time, with varying degrees of artistic and commercial success. Wilder went Lubitschean in films ranging from his romantic comedy *The Major and the Minor* (1942), his darkly unfunny musical *The Emperor Waltz* (1948) set in the Austro-Hungarian Empire but filled with covert allusions to the Nazi Holocaust, and two uneven romantic comedies in the fifties starring Audrey Hepburn, *Sabrina* and *Love in the Afternoon*, to the brash, *Ninotchka*-quoting political satire *One, Two, Three* (1961) and the autumnal romantic comedy *Avanti!* (1972). Lubitsch's influence can be felt strongly in writer/director Ingmar Bergman's bawdy comedy *Smiles of a Summer Night* (1955). Although that classic film is laced with the Swedish filmmaker's darker inflections, it absorbs Lubitsch's lessons deeply in its complex interplay among social classes and its adroit blending of frolicsome sex farce and emotional elements, teetering on the edge of tragedy. *Smiles of a Summer Night* and *Avanti!* are probably the two most artistically successful filmic attempts to emulate Lubitsch since the master's death, although Wilder's film, unlike Bergman's, was a commercial and critical flop, demonstrating what a challenge it is to rekindle the Lubitschean ambience for more jaded modern movie audiences.

As Andrew Sarris wrote in 1972, Lubitsch is "ultimately inimitable and ineffable." It is too much to expect that any filmmaker today could fully re-create the values and context of the vanished world of Lubitsch's romantic comedies and musicals. It is enough of a reach for many viewers to immerse themselves in that world through his films. But some contemporary film-makers have continued to be deeply influenced by Lubitsch's work in ways large and small and occasionally attempt to adapt his style to modern subject matter, though usually without much popular success. Woody Allen has helped keep the romantic comedy genre alive through the years with his own elegantly neoclassical approach, especially in the iconic *Annie Hall* (1977) and the nostalgic yet also antinostalgic fantasy *Midnight in Paris* (2011), but for a diminishing audience. Romantic comedies and musicals self-consciously made in a retro style that succeed with modern audiences are more often a tribute to a school of filmmaking other than Lubitsch's, such as the acerbic, Sturges-like comedies by the Coen Bros. or Damien Chazelle's 2016 musical *La La Land*, a lovingly updated homage to the Astaire/Rogers films of the thirties and the MGM musicals of the early fifties.

The late French director François Truffaut subtly evoked Lubitsch in such diverse films as *Jules and Jim* (1962), *Stolen Kisses* (1968), *The Man Who Loved Women* (1977), and *The Last Metro* (1980). A passionate advocate in his splendid 1968 *Cahiers du Cinéma* essay "Lubitsch Was a Prince," Truffaut managed to express that appreciation on-screen without making his films seem like self-conscious homages. Above the typewriter Truffaut was using to write the screenplay for *The Man Who Loved Women* at the Beverly Hills Hotel, I saw that he had hung a photograph of Lubitsch. But I originally missed that obvious signal he was sending me of the influence on the film he was writing, a mordant comedy about a compulsive skirt chaser who has much in common with Henry Van Cleve in *Heaven Can Wait*, right down to his seriocomic death scene, reaching for a comely blonde nurse who is taking over the night shift from an older nurse. Truffaut's daughter Laura told me that when she was growing up, her father would have her and her sister Eva watch Lubitsch films on television with him so often that they would all recite the dialogue by heart. Laura also said that wherever her father traveled, he would go to bookstores and memorabilia shops to buy pictures of Lubitsch. Lubitsch's influence on Truffaut was so profound that it eluded detection by most reviewers, unlike the more overt homages by Bogdanovich in *At Long Last Love* (1975), *They All Laughed* (1981), and *She's Funny That Way* (2014) and by Jean-Luc Godard, whose deliberately klutzy postmodern musical *A Woman Is a Woman* (1961) has Jean-Paul Belmondo playing a character named Alfred Lubitsch.

Bogdanovich suffered a notorious flop with his elegantly filmed but lead-footed *At Long Last Love*, the most elaborate postwar Lubitsch homage, a lavishly produced musical set in the 1930s, shot in color but largely on black-and-white art deco studio sets. That stylish and ambitious but often imperfect homage was widely reviled, both for its actual flaws—such as the unabashed use of performers who are not at home in the musical genre—and, one suspects, for Bogdanovich's temerity in attempting to revive a long-lost tradition of filmmaking that was defiantly antithetical to the cynically unromantic seventies zeitgeist. Perhaps the film's biggest crime in the eyes of the lively but jaded "New Cinema" era was that it was a pseudo-Lubitsch film, in a style that was considered hopelessly passé and, paradoxically, beyond imitation. The inability of Godard's characters to sing and dance in *A Woman Is a Woman*, on the other hand, brought praise to the French director, but he did more winking at the audience in his art-house film than Bogdanovich did in his more emotionally sincere Hollywood extravaganza, which is much better than its reputation would indicate.

Bergman, a film buff and collector who admired Lubitsch's 1934 film of *The Merry Widow*, announced plans in the 1970s to direct his own film version of the 1905 Franz Lehár operetta, with Barbra Streisand or Diana Ross in the title role. But that nostalgic project was aborted in an era when the musical genre was most successfully represented by Bob Fosse's *Cabaret* (1972), a brilliantly morbid, decadently erotic, hyperkinetic portrait of Weimar Germany and the rise of Nazism. Most musicals since then, when they are made at all, have been downbeat and highly fragmented, using fast cutting that lets the camera do the dancing. The unabashedly romantic but somewhat melancholy *La La Land* attempted to reverse that trend, with its flowing camerawork, long takes, and framing that lets the dancers use their entire bodies. While following in the footsteps of French director Jacques Demy's stylized pastiches of Hollywood musicals, the operetta *The Umbrellas of Cherbourg* (1964) and *The Young Girls of Rochefort* (1967), *La La Land* reimagined the genre by approaching dysfunctional contemporary Hollywood from the perspective of romantic fantasy, a daringly postmodern balancing act, though only tangentially related to Lubitsch.

Boxoffice returns have shown that outright homages to Lubitsch are not as effective with modern audiences in reviving his style as films that incorporate Lubitschean ideas more organically into a filmmaker's own style, as Truffaut and Allen have done. The well-intentioned but uneasy attempts at tributes to Lubitsch in the seventies by Wilder and Bogdanovich demonstrated the difficulty in trying to recapture the master's mood and style. Wilder's lovely, hilarious, and often-touching romantic comedy *Avanti!* intelligently updates Lubitschean elements to a contemporary setting, blending them seamlessly with Wilder's own preoccupations. But audiences and most reviewers of its day snubbed it for being out of step with the times, when "romantic" was regarded as a dirty word. Such an audience could not care less about the romantic reawakening of a middle-aged American reactionary in Europe through his immersion into his dead father's adulterous lifestyle and a more gracious, vanished past that Wilder regards as superior in every way to modern American culture. "The Importance of Being Ernst" is the title I gave to an appreciation I wrote of *Avanti!* when it was released. The film's true subversiveness—the way it challenges modern cynicism about romance and its very Lubitschean insistence that a bit of adultery from time to time can be revivifying—was lost on the indifferent audience. "That was fine, but, you see, too soft," Wilder told me. "It is just too gentle. . . . So who cares? So he [the father] got laid. So big fuckin' deal, right? . . . All of that is gone: Lubitsch, Leisen, *Love in the Afternoon*."

The commercial failures of *Avanti!* and *At Long Last Love* and the general perception that such gentle character comedies are largely passé have continued to discourage most filmmakers, even those who admire Lubitsch, from attempting to mine his vein. Two literal remakes of Lubitsch films—the Mel

Brooks company's *To Be or Not to Be* (1983) and Nora Ephron's boxoffice hit *You've Got Mail* (1998), an updated adaptation of *The Shop Around the Corner*—did not provoke hostility but actually fall farther from the mark, missing the qualities that make the originals so memorable (as did the 1949 musical adaptation of *Shop*, *In the Good Old Summmertime*, which similarly transposes the story to the United States). The exception to this rule about remaking Lubitsch is *Frantz*, the movingly restrained 2016 film by French director François Ozon. *Frantz* improves on one of Lubitsch's rare misfires, *The Man I Killed* (*Broken Lullaby*), by dispensing with its overwrought theatrics and rethinking the storyline, telling it from the viewpoint of the female character and not giving away the reason for the male character's trauma at the beginning. Perhaps obliviousness occasionally can be an asset. In a sign of how little Lubitsch is known even by some film people, Ozon claimed he had never heard of the Lubitsch film when he started working on his adaptation of the source play by Maurice Rostand, *The Man I Killed*. "But when I saw Lubitsch's film," Ozon said, "I realized I wanted to do it differently."

Although there has been a striking resurgence of romantic comedies in twenty-first-century Hollywood, including some that try to deal with the intricacies of human relationships, most of these films tend to be gimmicky and crude, at a far pole from Lubitsch's example of treating sex and romance with subtle character observation and obliquely witty storytelling. They bear out the truth of what Lubitsch noted in 1937, that "the Lubitsch Touch is the direct opposite of the equally famous sledgehammer touch. . . . I do not think audiences need to have a point driven home with a sledgehammer."

A REPUTATION

Even if the Lubitsch Touch may seem largely AWOL in today's screen storytelling, it does have a devoted following among certain cinephiles in the United States and abroad. When fully appreciated, his films are not truly archaic, for they deal with timeless conflicts between the romantic impulse and unromantic sexual appetites, snobbery and commonality, opportunism and sincerity, honesty and dishonesty, kindness and cruelty. The modernity of his films stems from his high level of sophistication about the game of love and his shrewd critiques of social hypocrisy. A handful of Lubitsch films—especially *The Shop*

Around the Corner, *To Be or Not to Be*, and *Ninotchka*—are regarded as classics by connoisseurs of Golden Age cinema, and *Trouble in Paradise* inspires great devotion in those lucky enough to have seen it. Lubitsch films sometimes run on cable television, on streaming channels, and in film archives, yet not to the extent to which works by some other major directors from his era are showcased. Although a number of Lubitsch's films have been released on DVD or Blu-ray since the early 2000s, many of his American films are still unavailable in those formats, and most of his German films have never been distributed in this country in any form.

The general decline of cinephilia in recent decades is partly responsible for his eclipse, typified by younger viewers' widespread lack of interest in "old" black-and-white films. Bogdanovich has remarked that only in discussing films do people use the word "old" in relation to the arts: "Old movies are not old; there is no such thing as old Shakespeare. . . . In America we don't have a set tradition of American culture. So films get labeled as old or new." To casual observers, if they know him at all, Lubitsch's films can seem the kind of museum pieces that are easily disregarded as largely irrelevant to our contemporary concerns. Lubitsch's lack of pretension and his particular brand of subtlety and obliqueness—the very qualities for which he was celebrated in his time—tend to work against him now. But unless a viewer has a die-hard bias against films from the past and being immersed in the worlds they represent, encountering Lubitsch's genius can be a revealing experience. I have found that when people who do not have such hang-ups are exposed to his work today, they often respond with pleasure and excitement. Still, there is no doubt that he is a director whose reputation, once so exalted, badly needs rejuvenation.

The sheer delight of that discovery entails a recognition of how modern most of his work remains and always will be no matter how much times and fashions change. As Bogdanovich notes, the contrast between the sophistication of a Lubitsch film and much of what audiences are accustomed to seeing today can be shocking. Bogdanovich said in 2015, "I don't like to insult anybody, but I think it's no great piece of witticism if a joke depends on somebody having sperm in their hair or getting their equipment caught in a zipper. I'm sorry, it just isn't funny. It may be funny to some people because it's shock humor—and I'm not saying these people are stupid—but they just don't know any better. It's like you eat a certain kind of food and you think that's filet mignon." Although Lubitsch's films deal with societies long gone and social mores that may seem quaint in the abstract, the actual experience of watching and listening to the director's men and women interacting on-screen is a lesson in how acute his powers of observation are. Watching his films with an open mind makes us realize how the essence of human nature remains largely the same over time.

But so much else about the world has changed in the hundred years since Lubitsch began making films. The world of his films seems exotic, even fantastic today. And not only because society itself has evolved in ways Lubitsch and his characters could hardly have imagined. Lubitsch's psychological and social insights are drawn from highly stylized, artificial material, and his penchant for studio settings ("Paris, Paramount") further enhances his deliberate distanciation from mundane reality. The European and American milieus of his films are largely imaginary constructions or reconstructions. As Sarris observed, "The world he celebrated had died—even before he did—everywhere except in his own memory."

THE LOST ART?

So we return to the question raised in the introduction to this book, that of Lubitsch's legacy and whether it can survive. Styles of filmmaking have changed radically, and not just with the rapid-fire cutting, dizzying camerawork, and extensively unreal use of computer-generated imagery (CGI) that now characterize so many popular American films. In many ways, this is a different art form now from what it was in Lubitsch's time. In a peculiar historical irony, today's big-budget blockbusters offer viewers a high-tech return to the earliest days of the medium. Movies around the turn of the twentieth century were countering the theater and literature by offering a form of visual spectacle, what film historian Tom Gunning has called "the cinema of attractions," a carnivalesque spectacle sans narrative, "a series of displays, of magical attractions. . . . The story simply provides a frame upon which to string a demonstration of the magical possibilities of the cinema." By around 1906, several years before Lubitsch entered the movies, the medium came to be regarded as primarily a narrative form. However, Gunning notes that "the system of attraction . . . remains an essential part of popular filmmaking. . . . Clearly in some sense, recent spectacle cinema has re-affirmed its roots in stimulus and carnival rides."

Steven Spielberg and George Lucas are often blamed for that trend, but the reasons are more complex than the successful efforts of two popular filmmakers. The modern blockbuster cycle predated *Jaws* and *Star Wars*. Robert Wise's *The Sound of Music* (1965) and Francis Ford Coppola's *The Godfather* (1972) were blockbusters, and William Friedkin's megahit shocker *The Exorcist* (1973) helped lay the foundation for contemporary "spectacle cinema." Lucas has pointed out that *Gone With the Wind* (1939) is the mother of all blockbusters, and it was preceded by the 1914 Italian silent film *Cabiria* and D. W. Griffith's 1915 epic *The Birth of a Nation*. The new model of blockbuster filmmaking that emerged in the seventies to dominate the industry, while killing off the quirkier forms of personal filmmaking that enlivened the early years of that decade, had various root causes. Those include the changing demographics of filmgoing; the huge inflation of the costs of filmmaking (partly due to the inherently crooked nature of Hollywood accounting, which has made creative talent demand grossly inflated salaries up front); the almost prohibitive expenses of opening and advertising a film due to the increasing reliance on expensive television advertising, with its side effect of causing movies to be dumbed down to simple ad lines and aimed at the lowest-common-denominator mentality; and the resulting frenzied pacing, hyperviolence, coarsened attempts at comedy, and escapist unreality of so much popular filmmaking. Not all blockbuster movies, of course, are foolish: Coppola's *The Godfather* and *The Godfather Part II* (1974) are in a different aesthetic league from the mindless spectacles that followed. The *Star Wars* series Lucas personally created and his and Spielberg's *Indiana Jones* series are juvenile escapism, yet they seem like classical cinema now in contrast to the monstrosities typified by Michael Bay's mindless *Transformers* movies. Those ever-more-inflated spectacles consist of piles of indistinguishable metal slamming into each other to the accompaniment of ear-piercing noise. In such popular "entertainments," the notion of characterization is virtually irrelevant.

Along with the turn from narrative back to spectacle in big-budget filmmaking, the nature of romantic comedies has undergone a drastic evolution in recent years, reflecting the major shifts in society from the traditions in which Lubitsch worked. These shifts were already well underway before he died. Lubitsch imported much of his style from venerable European traditions, including the operetta and *Kammerspiel*, which no longer have much relation to American filmmaking. An art such as Lubitsch's seems lost to most people because it was the product of a long-gone time with much different social mores, particularly in terms of the class, gender, and sexual issues that so preoccupy Lubitsch and that in his work can seem both modern and outmoded. But Lubitsch was always a distinctive artist, the kind we would now call cutting-edge, and as such, he was "way ahead of his time," Wilder noted. And as the cinematic arts will continue to evolve in ways we can hardly imagine, it is possible that the stylistic pendulum could swing back in Lubitsch's direction, at least in the hands of some of the best, most adventurous filmmakers. Expecting society and culture not to change, whether for good or ill, is unrealistic, and filmmakers must reflect those changes or rebel against them. Simply imitating past masters is not a sufficient response to changing times, even if that imitation could also be construed as an act of rebellion, as were the ill-fated but still estimable *Avanti!* and *At Long Last Love*.

TURNING AWAY FROM LUBITSCH

Bemoaning the coarsening of our culture for the obsolescence of the Lubitschean style risks falling into the same traps that caused reviewers to attack Wilder's groundbreaking, often-outrageous films of the fifties and sixties for their supposed cynicism and indecency. In so doing, they overlooked Wilder's seriousness, his romantic qualities, and his bracingly sophisticated satire of social hypocrisy. To berate modern films and audiences for their general crudity is something of an overgeneralization, ignoring the occasional exceptions, and it can cause a critic and historian who decries the descent of Hollywood filmmaking from its former heights of sophistication to be mistaken for an old-fashioned reactionary. Any interviewer who listened to older directors discussing the new screen freedoms in the late sixties and early seventies (as I often did) had to sit through long, tediously clichéd diatribes about how sexually vulgar and hyperviolent everything had become. Those embittered veteran filmmakers, most of whom felt unjustly rejected by the system they had helped create, were onto some troubling seismic shifts in the medium, but they were also overreacting to social developments that had a somewhat freeing and cathartic effect on the previously inhibited Hollywood screen. The cultural upheavals of the 1960s that brought about the abolition of the increasingly irrelevant Production Code in 1968 helped open the door for more adult and realistic treatment of sex and other topics, a development that was necessary for Hollywood to keep up with changing times.

For a while, there was a new freedom of expression that led to many remarkable Hollywood films and foreign imports on American screens that examined sexuality and violence with increasing frankness. But for every *Bonnie and Clyde*, *The Wild Bunch*, *Carnal Knowledge*, and *Last Tango in Paris* that opened our eyes and ears to a more adult treatment of the disturbing realities of life, there were many films that simply exploited those new freedoms in stupid and ugly ways. Most damagingly, the greater license that was initially allowed by the collapse of the Code has not, by and large, led to a more sophisticated treatment of sexuality on American screens. The replacement of the Code by the Motion Picture Association of America ratings system was far from a panacea, and its dampening effect on mature filmmaking was exacerbated by a backlash that set in to restrict filmmakers in reactionary "family-friendly" ways. The ratings board is as hypocritical and prudish by modern standards as the old Code ever was. While encouraging an overindulgence in extreme violence and juvenile gross-out antics, the ratings system allows a far less adult treatment of sexuality and love than Lubitsch and Wilder and other directors were able to achieve by cleverly circumventing the strictures of censorship. This has contributed mightily to the jarringly coarse tone of most romantic comedies, such as Adam Sandler films, *Meet the Fockers*, *Sex and the City 2*, and *Bridesmaids*. Some latter-day romantic comedies, such as *The 40-Year-Old Virgin* and *Trainwreck*, manage to combine low humor with sharp character observation. And occasionally a modern romantic comedy is genuinely witty and charming without being crude, such as *Muriel's Wedding*, *Shakespeare in Love*, *Amélie*, and *Legally Blonde*. It is important to remember that Lubitsch's own joyous tendency toward leering humor was regarded as vulgar by some commentators. But Lubitsch was stimulated creatively by the way the Code forced filmmakers to avoid blatant displays of vulgarity and to find other ways of expressing sexual themes.

Lubitsch's often-unorthodox treatment of sexuality is far more daring than the kind of sophomoric stuff that often passes for audacity today. As his films demonstrate by indirection, it is hard to achieve his level of wit if you merely come out and say or show something sexual. The humor in romantic comedy, and its underlying poignancy, comes from how you frame it, from the attitude expressed. Compare the emotional subtlety and complexity of the finely balanced love triangles among three sophisticated adults in *Trouble in Paradise* and *Design for Living* with the juvenile tone of modern "bromances," stemming from their skittishness about adult sexuality and their blend of barely repressed homoerotic impulses with beautiful young women's improbable attraction to schlumpy young men. Lubitsch's droll treatment of cross-dressing and homosexuality in *I Don't Want to Be a Man* is still advanced a century later. Today's mishmash of arrested male development (the "Peter Pan Syndrome") and belittlement of female characters is not confined to bromances but is also reflected in the unrelenting escapist violence of the blockbuster trend of CGI spectacles and action movies that drives most contemporary American filmmaking today, aimed primarily at the adolescent and young-male market. Lubitsch could appeal to the more intelligent and sophisticated tastes in a mass medium with a wider range of audience members as long as he delivered popular comedic elements and clearly understandable storylines, even as he smuggled in his innuendos and double entendres along the way. He would suggest a teenage boy's sexual initiation by a French maid indirectly through comically suggestive dialogue and behavior in *Heaven Can Wait*, but he would not have been tempted to show a teenage boy desperately humping a pie in his family's kitchen, the comic centerpiece of the intermittently amusing 1999 hit *American Pie*.

Another case in point is the downward path of sophistication in boxoffice hits, ranging from *Pretty Woman* (1990) through *There's Something About Mary* (1998) to *Bridesmaids* (2011). *Pretty Woman*, a Disney (Touchstone) romantic comedy about prostitution, seemed fairly daring in its day, with Julia Roberts as the Hollywood hooker playing Cinderella/Eliza Doolittle to Richard Gere's corporate-raider version of Henry Higgins. As Bogdanovich noted, *There's Something About Mary* engaged in "shock humor" with its brief use of sperm as hair gel by the winsomely innocent Cameron Diaz. Both of these films, however, seem relatively tame and sweet-natured when stacked up against the crass sight gags about excretion and other rampant crudity that make *Bridesmaids* so repulsive. No doubt in the 2020s something will come along to top that entry in the rom-com genre by upping the gross-out ante and making even its excesses seem quaint.

A major change that has helped turn modern romantic comedies away from the Lubitschean style is a general decline in genuinely strong and complex women's roles. As Molly Haskell points out in *From Reverence to Rape: The Treatment of Women in the Movies*, the 1930s was the heyday of the classic "women's picture." Before television atomized the audience, people went to movies as a habitual pastime, often involving the entire family, and women usually made the choice of films. As Haskell notes, they often picked films with the many great, mature, and sophisticated female stars of the period, from Garbo to Katharine Hepburn and Bette Davis to Carole Lombard and Jean Arthur and Rosalind Russell, et al. But once families started staying home to watch television together, going out to the movies became more of a youthful dating ritual. Young men now tend to choose the pictures, resulting in a decline of female stars, especially mature women (along with the derogatory phrase "chick flicks" replacing "women's pictures"), despite the paradoxical fact that women have acquired much more social freedom over the years. It is an unfortunate fact that roles for women in American films reached their nadir and became most scarce during the period when the women's liberation movement was challenging sexual standards. The 1970s was a time when male buddy-buddy films dominated Hollywood filmmaking as a way of avoiding gender issues altogether. The situation has improved somewhat since then—it couldn't have gotten any worse—but films for mature audiences tend to be relegated to the niche market, and even if a few actresses manage to sustain longer starring careers than they did during the backlash years, good women's roles are still scandalously scarce in American films, decades after the women's movement brought about sweeping changes in society at large.

Lubitsch's films from the Jazz Age into the post–World War II years almost always provided stellar roles for strong, fascinating, challenging women. His fondness for complex female characters and his exploration of mature sexual themes are among the main reasons his films seem far more adult than most of today's fare. Perhaps most seriously, a loss of belief in romance itself now affects the climate for romantic comedies and the appreciation of Lubitsch. Books could be written on how the world has evolved from naïveté to disillusionment in the past hundred years, not only with regard to romance but also in just about every other aspect of life. Lubitsch's worldview can only be approximated through artifice, and filmmakers who make the best romantic comedies today often frame their stories as fantasies or dreams. Woody Allen's *Midnight in Paris* is a nostalgic fantasy that re-creates 1920s Paris and the Belle Epoque in order for a time-traveling Hollywood screenwriter to live out his literary dreams. In so doing, *Midnight in Paris* simultaneously criticizes nostalgia as a fruitless escape valve, appealing but a dead end.

An underlying yearning for old-fashioned romance can be detected as a strong, lingering element in some of the most popular modern films in the genre, such as *You've Got Mail* and *Pretty Woman*. Julia Roberts's hooker in *Pretty Woman*, ensconced in a Beverly Hills luxury hotel as a paid escort for an initially aloof businessman, admits, "I want the fairy tale." *You've Got Mail* brings back the tradition of epistolary courtship while updating it for the age of email and has Meg Ryan say to Tom Hanks at the end, "I wanted it to be you. I wanted it to be you so badly." Unfortunately, these films must struggle to make their stories believable while satisfying audiences' continued need for romantic happy endings, which modern social conditions have made increasingly difficult to accept. Filmmakers have largely failed to grapple intelligently with the creative opportunities presented by those changing conditions. After the couple's business relationship begins to turn emotional in *Pretty Woman*, the characters' sparks are replaced by sappy, clichéd scenes and songs celebrating their shallow and tenuous lifestyle in the hotel and other swanky settings. Lubitsch displays as much love of luxury as any other filmmaker, but there is more genuine sensuality in his characters' enjoyment of the high life than there is in a studied, materialistic, overly synthetic fairy tale such as *Pretty Woman*. The story conventions of Lubitsch's time help us accept his posh, unreal settings as part of the romantic game while also commenting on them satirically to provide layers of complexity that are largely absent from the screen today.

The dysfunctional nature of most male-female relationships in more recent romantic comedies, however, is a frankly realistic reflection of the breakdown of traditional social structures and roles in the postwar era, including upheavals in gender and family structures. While romantic comedies have always thrived on various forms of conflict between the partners, a sine qua non in the genre (and those were already exaggerated in the 1930s screwball subgenre, which Lubitsch could not master), contemporary romantic comedies throw up even more extreme, almost insurmountable roadblocks to romance, including all variety of sexual dysfunction, stunted or aberrational psychological conditions, and familial collapse. Although dysfunction, if handled with aplomb, can be entertaining, it can overwhelm a romantic comedy if it becomes too extreme, pushing a film from that genre into something far darker.

The Code, ironically, was a leavening, humanizing influence because it forced filmmakers to point their stories toward happy endings. Even if those sometimes seem forced—as they do in Capra's work, though usually not in Lubitsch's, except in most of his musicals—and though today's rom-coms slap unconvincing happy endings onto their disconcertingly muddled stories, the strictures under which Lubitsch operated offered a form of checks and balances, an anchoring in traditionalism that he brilliantly counterbalanced with his satire of social conventions. Truffaut once observed to me that serious filmmakers have always been caught in a fundamental conflict between the somber fact that life tends toward dissolution and death and the demands of the audience for a happy ending. That conflict, he suggested, cannot be entirely resolved. But the tension between those two poles, in the work of a talented director, can account for much of a film's power to move us. And as Orson Welles put it, "If you want a happy ending, that depends, of course, on where you stop your story."

Billy Wilder famously recalled how he and William Wyler walked silently to their car after Lubitsch's funeral: "Finally I said, just to say something to break the silence, 'No more Lubitsch.' To which Wyler replied, 'Worse than that—no more Lubitsch films.'" When I interviewed Wilder twenty-seven years later on the set of his 1920s newspaper comedy *The Front Page*, I asked if my supposition was correct that he had deliberately been trying to do Lubitsch pictures for the last several years. "I've been trying to do Lubitsch for 140 years," Wilder replied. I asked, "Closer and closer?" He smiled ruefully and said, "Like Lubitsch, not real Lubitsch. The time for Lubitsch is past. The subtlest comedy you can get right now is *M*A*S*H*. They don't want to see a picture unless Peter Fonda is running over a dozen people or unless Clint Eastwood has got a machine gun bigger than 140 penises. It gets bigger all the time, you know; it started out as a pistol and now it's a machine gun." And he told me four years later, anticipating future sociopolitical and cinematic developments, "Unless there is a man jumping out of the seventy-sixth floor with his ass afire, unless there is a wreck of sixty-four automobiles hit by a 747, they will not drop the popcorn bag."

The principal reason for the malaise in modern filmmaking, Wilder felt, was that "there is a different set of values today. Something which is warm and gentle and funny and urbane and civilized hasn't got a chance. There is a lack of patience which is sweeping the nation, or the world, for that matter. Noël Coward would not succeed today. It's all tough guys. It's all Telly Savalas. Today, you have to have a dirty jockstrap and a raincoat and be Columbo. They think it's very romantic. I think it's a lot of shit." I asked if he was bitter about that, and he said, "It's just a loss of something marvelous, the loss of a style I aspired to." What should a director do, then, give in and do what the audience wants? "You are not going to buck audiences at two or three million a clip, or you'll wind up on your keister. What good is it being a marvelous composer of polkas if nobody dances the polka anymore?"

THE FUTURE OF THE LUBITSCH LEGACY

But rather than simply decry the inevitable loss of the elliptical, suggestive, delicately satirical style that Lubitsch exemplifies, we could ask the questions: How would Lubitsch do it if he were here today? And is that question even relevant to modern filmmaking? Is the appeal of his work doomed to be limited to aficionados who seek out his work in esoteric venues? Perhaps that should be enough for any filmmaker who began more than a hundred years ago to expect with the passage of time. Lubitsch has been proven partly but not entirely wrong in his despairing comment to Samson Raphaelson that he would be ignored after his death because his films would be "dust." Some of his movies have indeed vanished, but even if most of today's moviegoers have never heard of him, his reputation among those who care about classical filmmaking, including some of his fellow directors, remains high. Some Lubitsch films are indeed even taught in colleges, contrary to his prediction. But is there any possibility that his style can be rekindled in the films that will be made by other directors in the future, whatever else films may look like?

With so much about filmmaking changing rapidly in our digital age, when even film itself has largely become obsolete, it is impossible for anyone to predict what the world of cinema will be like in ten or twenty years let alone another hundred years. Not only have filmmaking tools already undergone a major revolution, and methods of production have radically transformed, the system of distribution is also evolving in unpredictable ways. The only safe prediction is that we will get farther and farther away from the storytelling formats and delivery methods that we have been accustomed to for many years. Already, cinematic narrative, under the influence of younger audiences' impatient viewing habits, has been fragmenting from the feature format to shorter forms. The Internet is fast overtaking theaters as the preferred venue for watching films. Streaming video, binge viewing of television series, interactive storytelling, and other innovative methods of entertainment have been gathering force. With everything in such a state of flux, it may be idle to wonder what kind of influence Lubitsch, or any other classical filmmaker for that matter, may have in years to come. The late British filmmaker and critic Lindsay Anderson, while discussing his favorite film, John Ford's 1945 World War II drama *They Were Expendable*, once remarked that to make a film like that again, you would have to re-create MGM. Since it would be impossible to re-create the old Hollywood studio system, along with the culture that sustained it, it is quixotic to think that anyone can make "real Lubitsch" films again, as Wilder ruefully admitted after all his efforts. You would have to re-create Paris, Paramount. And the audience that wants it.

It would require an extraordinary degree of optimism, verging on delusion, to hope that some of the trends that have dumbed down our society in recent decades—the decline in our educational system, the widespread loss of interest in the past, the frenetic acceleration of the pace of life, the aggressive forces of political ignorance—will reverse themselves significantly in the years to come. Some of that damage may be irreversible. But one should never give up hope, even in the future. And it is possible that the excesses of theatrical filmmaking may swing so far out of control that a backlash eventually could upend the nature of that already-precarious economic and cultural system. Hollywood may be largely brain-dead and creatively moribund, far more so than even in the days when films were considered by snobs to be the lowest form of entertainment, but the cinema, like the theater, has always been a "fabulous invalid," perpetually reinventing itself. Cable television and streaming movies, the last refuge of cinematic storytelling that deals with people and dialogue, may help reverse the damaging trends of the increasingly obsolescent format of theatrical moviegoing.

Already we are seeing that the new digital technology is making it possible to shoot and edit a film for almost nothing if the filmmaker is so inclined and willing to work in what has been called a "no-budget" framework. A more minimalist style necessarily throws more emphasis back onto the script and the actors and away from elaborate action and spectacle. Independent filmmaking paradoxically offers more freedom than big-budget filmmaking, because with less at stake financially and more incentive to appeal to niche audiences neglected by mainstream filmmaking, writers and directors can operate with fewer creative restraints and enjoy more room for experimentation. The major problem for independent filmmakers has always been how to get their work seen by a mass audience, but with the Internet and other "new media" forms of distribution, that roadblock has already begun to disappear.

The result just might be a resurgence of interest in films that are more about people than special effects, more focused on narrative than spectacle, films that could more closely resemble the works of Lubitsch and his peers in the Golden Age while possibly making his light, playfully suggestive touch appealing again to general audiences. Popular tastes, in any case, are notoriously subject to reversal, and modernism periodically gives way to retro styles. Even in such a cutting-edge medium, it can be true that "everything old is new again." Furthermore, the accelerating pace of life has the positive effect of guaranteeing that styles change more rapidly than ever before. As Oscar Wilde wrote in 1885, "Fashion is ephemeral, Art is eternal. Indeed what is a fashion really? A fashion is merely a form of ugliness so absolutely unbearable that we have to alter it every six months!" So it may not be too much to hope that the more intimate, humanistic, and droll Lubitschean style could undergo a resurrection among filmmakers and audiences who are fortunate enough to study his work and learn from his example, not so much trying to counterfeit him but instead absorbing his influence into their own styles.

In his 1948 valedictory tribute, "Chez Ernst," French film critic and screenwriter Jean-Georges Auriol offered the charmingly apt metaphor of Lubitsch as the host of a sumptuous vintage restaurant:

> One could be sure to dine perfectly at "Ernst's," and the epicure was sure to find the same favorite sauces and garnishes. The service was always meticulous at "Ernst's," the proprietor correcting with a murmur the manner of one of his staff if his usual urbanity were about to slip into mere obsequiousness or his good humor into impertinence. A man could take his mistress to supper at "Ernst's" and see his wife there without the slightest chance of a scandal. Ernst could transform such a difficulty, or even possible sensation, into a slightly audacious farce. And Lubitsch's subtle handling of such a situation would cause some celebrities who were enjoying themselves in his establishment to say, "Ernst (the French usually called him Ernst), why on earth didn't you take up a diplomatic career? You would have made a first-class Ambassador."

Auriol suggested back then that the Lubitschean style might already be passé. He concluded by lamenting that Lubitsch's patrons knew that "'Ernst's' is closed on account of death. This particular restaurant will never be open again."

Lubitsch paid for his art with his health and suffered some indignities as he saw himself becoming obsolete in the industry he had once ruled. We can feel the pangs of that loss of influence and of the greater neglect that has followed it. But perhaps he should have been content to have defined an entire era of filmmaking—as the man who, as Jean Renoir put it, "converted the Hollywood industry to his own way of expression"—and perhaps that ought to be enough for us too. Whether or not Lubitsch's cultural influence can be revived remains an open question, and those of us who love him need to keep insisting on its importance. Even though there may be "no more Lubitsch films," there remain forty-seven of his own films that, through some miracle of film preservation, survive in whole or in part. They will remain new as long as there are new audiences to see them. And we can savor his work forever as long as we ensure that it continues to exist.

It's still open for business chez Ernst.

ACKNOWLEDGMENTS AND INFLUENCES

n the spring of 1992, to commemorate Ernst Lubitsch's centenary, I wrote a column for *Daily Variety*, "The Last Closed Door: 'No More Lubitsch,'" celebrating his achievements and wondering how and whether his legacy could endure in modern film viewing and filmmaking. Noting that Lubitsch's premature death "clearly marked the end of an era in Hollywood," a time when such witty, urbane, and humane directing and writing was still highly valued, I wrote, "All that was long ago, however. Seeing today's movies, you wonder how many people now working in Hollywood ever saw a Lubitsch film, or even know who Lubitsch was." The morning the column appeared, the phone rang. It was his daughter, Nicola, calling to thank me for appreciating him and his work. I cherish that moment. Her reaching out struck me as a gesture of kinship in our mutual hope that her father would be remembered as the great artist and man he was.

How Did Lubitsch Do It? has been another long journey, as my books often are. I steep myself in the subject's life and work and travel around the world to visit the places where he lived and worked. Johann Wolfgang von Goethe, the German poet and playwright whose *Faust* Lubitsch wanted to film as his first American project, once wrote, *"Wer das Dichten will verstehen, / Muss ins Land der Dichtung gehen"* ("Whoever wishes to understand a poet must go into the poet's land"). That meant I needed to go to Germany to visit the neighborhood where Lubitsch grew up, Berlin's fabled Scheunenviertel; to wander through the mazelike apartments where he and his family lived, going in and out of Lubitschean doors while absorbing that formative environment; and, thrillingly, to stand in the spotlights on the stage of Max Reinhardt's Deutsches Theater, where Lubitsch served his long theatrical apprenticeship. But for this book, since it is a critical study, not a biography, going into the poet's land most importantly meant seeing his films. That was not an easy task.

For many years, it was a source of great frustration to me that so few of Lubitsch's films were available for viewing in the United States. It has only been in the 2000s that a fair number of his films have come to homevideo, and even today, many of his films, especially ones he made in Germany, have to be hunted down through collectors. Some exist only in fragments or can be seen only in poor-quality prints. I revered Lubitsch from the day I first saw *Trouble in Paradise* in the late 1960s when I was running the Wisconsin Film Society at the University of Wisconsin–Madison. That post enabled me to rent the few Lubitsch films that were then available on 16 mm for viewing by our indulgent membership. But especially after reading Herman G. Weinberg's piquant valentine to the director, his 1967 book *The Lubitsch Touch: A Critical Study*, I was tantalized by reading about so many evidently marvelous films that I could not see. Eventually I realized that I had to write a book about Lubitsch if only to make it possible to see all his films—the ones that still existed, a considerable number for a director who began in the silent period.

I often decide to write a book because I want to right some kind of injustice or misunderstanding. I think of an exchange John Ford had in 1936 with Emanuel Eisenberg of *New Theatre* magazine. The interviewer asked, "Then you do believe, as a director, in including your point of view in a picture about things that bother you?" Ford replied, "What the hell else does a man live for?" When I feel that way about a subject, I can't let go of it until I feel I have made my contribution to doing it justice. Trying to clear away the fog of neglect and misunderstanding that has surrounded Lubitsch became one of my missions, one that only grew over time as my awareness of the neglect intensified. I wanted to contribute what I could to help restore this great artist to the place he deserves in our culture and world cinema in general—to remove that blank stare from people's faces. In my mind, the task with Lubitsch is about seeing what we can do to steer our collective cinematic consciousness back to the kind of civilized, sophisticated, humane, and above all, witty view of the world he shared with us from 1915 through his untimely death in the year I was born, 1947. Partly because he was not around in later years to burnish his legend as other directors of his generation were, and partly because the world has become so coarsened in his absence, we have too often been deprived of the benefit of Lubitsch's wonderfully seriocomic view of life, his tolerant embrace of humanity, the sheer fecundity of his aesthetic talent, and the healing power of his artistic vision.

Having the chance to finally study him in depth has been a constant joy for nine years. Following his creative compass has been an involved process because his body of work is so rich and varied, so much of it is not easily accessible, and it involved immersing myself in the culture of another country. I have long specialized in American cinema history, and so expanding my mental and physical horizons was an especially stimulating research and intellectual challenge. And there is an aesthetic hurdle to leap as well. As my colleague James Naremore pointed out when we discussed this book in 2015, it is not easy to write about Lubitsch because so much of what he does best is "ineffable." Indeed, much of what makes cinema a great art form is ineffable, and so trying to capture that intangible quality on paper as it relates to Lubitsch has been a lively task. Among its gratifying aspects is that it has taken me back to my roots as a writer of critical studies of great filmmakers. For many years I wrote biographies instead—of Frank Capra, Steven Spielberg, and John Ford, directors who badly needed critical biographies—but I realized that what was most needed with Lubitsch was not a biography but a close study of his work. And that meant *all* the work, both German and American.

There is a considerable body of writing on Lubitsch, of varying quality, and it has been useful for me to stand on the shoulders of the many diligent scholars who have preceded me, particularly those who have done the groundwork in biographical research. The German writer Michael Hanisch's research into Lubitsch's life and work in that country in two books has been invaluable and helps put him into his historical and cultural context. The 1984 compendium *Lubitsch*, edited by two other German scholars, Hans Helmut Prinzler and Enno Patalas, brings together a great deal of useful source material, and it is especially revealing on the pre-Hollywood period. *Ernst Lubitsch: A Guide to References and Resources* by Robert Carringer and Barry Sabath is a detailed and helpful map to his career. Scott Eyman's *Ernst*

Lubitsch: Laughter in Paradise, the only English-language biography of the director, offers factual groundwork on his life and some aspects of his work. Academic theses by Sabath (on Lubitsch's work with screenwriter Samson Raphaelson) and Jan-Christopher Horak (on Lubitsch's relationship to the German film industry) provide important source materials. But though the biographical facts about Lubitsch have been covered fairly well in these books, I felt the man was insufficiently interwoven with the work, which is one of the major tasks of a good critical biography.

Weinberg's impressionistic book *The Lubitsch Touch* (revised in 1971 and 1977) left many critical gaps to be filled, and much seemed to have been written from memory rather than based on recent screenings, but it served to catalyze my early scholarly inquiries into Lubitsch. It is still a book I savor for the deft ways it captures many of the evanescent charms of Lubitsch while situating him in his cultural context, perhaps more suggestively than any other book has yet done. The print and video commentaries on Lubitsch by Andrew Sarris, Molly Haskell, and Peter Bogdanovich brilliantly catch some of the elusive essence of Lubitsch, as does Raphaelson's fascinating reminiscence for the *New Yorker*, "Freundschaft," which was reprinted in the precious volume of his three published screenplays for Lubitsch.

Various book-length critical studies of Lubitsch have illuminated aspects of his artistic style and substance as well as his working methods, and some are more thought-provoking than others (William Paul's *Lubitsch's American Comedy* is an especially good study of the dramaturgy of those films, and the chapters on Lubitsch in James Harvey's *Romantic Comedy in Hollywood* do justice to his genius); the books by Sabine Hake and Kristin Thompson dealing in detail with Lubitsch's German period (as well as with some of his American work) provide helpful information about his working methods and cultural background. These precursors are duly acknowledged in my Notes on Sources. Yet, like the biographies, the numerous critical studies of Lubitsch often felt incomplete to me, despite their intermittent insights. Even they often seemed to miss the mark on what made Lubitsch's stylistic vision, and especially his humor, so delightful. It's hard to analyze humor, in any case, particularly when it is a rare sense of humor that manages to bridge continents and cultures. I also felt that the unique way Lubitsch expressed himself visually often did not receive enough emphasis, or conversely, that it was analyzed too formalistically, as if it could be detached from humor and emotion. Nor did I find that Lubitsch's European cultural context had been fully enough explored in most writings on the director, although Weinberg's study and books about his German period cited above are partial exceptions.

One of the major problems was that I did not find enough sense in any of the previous books of exactly how Lubitsch managed to straddle both cultures he inhabited while helping lead the German film industry into a period of world dominance and then transforming Hollywood with what Renoir called his "Berlin style." And so, when I launched this journey in 2009, the picture of Lubitsch's career remained fragmentary, like a ruined temple badly in need of reconstitution. The previous critical studies were mostly separated into books on his German career and books on his American career. There had not been a single critical study that looked at his career as a whole and in sufficient depth, drawing the connections and contrasts between the two cultures and film industries in which he worked. Not the least of Lubitsch's great achievements was that he was successively regarded by many people as the major director in both countries. So, when I set out to analyze the question of "How did Lubitsch do it?" I wanted to find out how he did so with such remarkable skill and influence in both his native and adopted lands.

In the process of that cinematic, historical, and intellectual journey, I have been aided and encouraged over the years by many other friends and colleagues in the international world of cinema who also revere Ernst Lubitsch and want to do what they can to keep his legacy a vital force in modern cinema. I am grateful to the people who helped me realize this dream project by making it possible for me to see his films, assisting with other forms of research, and discussing his work with me. One of the first was Herman Weinberg, with whom I corresponded in the sixties. Without my asking, he kindly sent me an advance copy of the jacket of *The Lubitsch Touch*, a gesture I view now as a kind of passing of the torch.

My former members of the Madison "film mafia" excitedly watched Lubitsch films with me long ago and helped form my cinematic consciousness; some of them I continue to learn from and value as friends, including Patrick McGilligan, Michael Wilmington, Gerald Peary, Danny Peary, Errol Morris, and David Bordwell. And the community of Los Angeles film aficionados to which I belonged for twenty-seven years was a source of constant inspiration. The late Ronald Haver programmed numerous Lubitsch films in lustrous 35 mm prints at the Los Angeles County Museum of Art, and

I was able to see others in screenings at Melnitz Hall at the University of California, Los Angeles. The UCLA Film & Television Archive holds, among other treasures, original Paramount prints of many Lubitsch films. An especially memorable occasion was when I went there with my friend and fellow critic Todd McCarthy to show Lubitsch's 1931 musical *The Smiling Lieutenant* to François Truffaut, who had never managed to see it before and brought Leslie Caron to the screening.

Truffaut, in turn, showed us the portrait of Lubitsch smoking a cigar that he kept above his desk in his room at the Beverly Hills Hotel where he was writing the screenplay for his 1977 film *L'homme qui aimait les femmes* (*The Man Who Loved Women*). Truffaut and I shared many cigars as we discussed our mutual fondness for Lubitsch, one of his favorite directors, about whom he wrote so passionately in his famous essay "Lubitsch Was a Prince." Those conversations were especially inspiring in those years when Lubitsch was in the critical wilderness. I miss my friend François deeply, but his influence hovers over this book, as does that of those other fellow Lubitsch admirers Jean Renoir and Orson Welles, two of my cinematic mentors. My later discussions with Truffaut's daughter Laura have revealed another bond we share in our love of Lubitsch.

After I decided to go ahead with this book, I traveled in March 2009 to the Filmmuseum im Münchner Stadtmuseum (the Munich Film Museum). I was able to see many of Lubitsch's films, especially the rare German ones, through the courtesy of the erudite film scholar who heads the museum, Stefan Drössler. He also showed me a documentary by Lubitsch scholar and former museum director Enno Patalas and a rare 1913 film directed by Max Reinhardt, *Die Insel der Seligen* (*The Island of the Blessed*). A member of Stefan's staff ably translated the German intertitles of the Lubitsch films for me. Stefan and I had many valuable talks about Lubitsch on that visit. Stefan's excellent article on Lubitsch's work with the German-American coproduction company EFA is a major contribution to Lubitsch scholarship.

Then, in 2010, I was invited to be the curator of a complete Lubitsch retrospective held by the Festival del Film Locarno (the Locarno Film Festival) in Switzerland, in conjunction with the Cinémathèque Française, where the retrospective also later played. I am grateful for the invitation from artistic director Olivier Père, to festival president Marco Solari, and to Carlo Chatrian, who supervised the retrospective with his coordinator Olmo Giovannini.

This event was invaluable for my research since we assembled the best existing 35 mm prints from throughout the world and showed every extant film (or fragment) directed by Lubitsch as well as films in which he acted. I contributed an essay on Lubitsch and notes on each of the films to the scholarly program booklet published by the festival. I introduced thirteen programs at the retrospective and hosted a question-and-answer session with Nicola Lubitsch, whom I met there for the first time. Our discussions of her father in Switzerland were delightfully warm and revealing. She has been enthusiastically supportive of this book and kindly gave me permission to quote her father's July 1947 letter about his career to Herman Weinberg. At the Locarno Film Festival, I also had the opportunity to discuss Lubitsch with many international filmmakers, scholars, and journalists, including Jean Douchet and N. T. Binh. Our communal love for Lubitsch's work was inspiring. I was surprised and touched to be chosen by the independent critics covering the festival for their Premio Boccalino d'Oro, "Al Personaggio più Significativo" (Golden Bowl Prize "To the Most Important Personage"), of the festival even though I felt the honor should have gone to Lubitsch himself.

Another key element of my research was my visit to Berlin in the summer of 2014 with my partner, Ann Weiser Cornell. Eszter Tompa, an actress and student who is well-versed in the German language and the world of film and theater, expertly guided me around the Lubitsch and Reinhardt sites in Berlin and translated for me. Eszter was industrious in talking our way into the Lubitsch family apartment building at 183 Schönhauser Allee and the Deutsches Theater. In our explorations of his old neighborhood, we also visited his birthplace, the former site of his parents' tailor shop (the firm of S. Lubitsch, now a beauty salon), and the Volksbühne Theater, where young Ernst also performed. I learned a great deal from Eszter about Berlin on that memorable visit and benefited from the hospitality of the current tenants of those apartments. Robert Fischer, whose many fine documentary films include the marvelous *Ernst Lubitsch in Berlin—From Schönhauser Allee to Hollywood*, was generous in telling me how to find the sites and sharing other information and thoughts about Lubitsch. While I was in Berlin, Robert also filmed a lengthy interview with me, *Perspectives on "Othello": Joseph McBride on Orson Welles*, at Das Bundesarchiv's Abteilung Filmarchiv (Federal Film Archive), where I did some research for this book and another one, with the assistance of Carola Okrug and other members of the staff.

The Criterion Collection and its producer Karen Stetler kindly invited me to do a twenty-two-minute interview for its 2011 *Design for Living* DVD and Blu-ray set, discussing the Noël Coward source play, the Ben Hecht screenplay, and the Lubitsch film. The Criterion sets of *Trouble in Paradise*, *Lubitsch Musicals*, *To Be or Not to Be*, and *Heaven Can Wait* have provided bounteous research. MCA/Universal Home Video's 1997 laserdisc set, *The Lubitsch Touch*, enabled closer study of films I had seen in 35 mm and 16 mm, and Kino Lorber's splendid 2007 collection *Lubitsch in Berlin* (which includes six of his films as well as Fischer's documentary) came along just at the right time to help me realize I could track down Lubitsch films that had been hard to see. The discussion of Lubitsch by Billy Wilder and Volker Schlöndorff in the English and German versions of the 1992 Schlöndorff/Gisela Grischow documentary *Billy, How Did You Do It?* is enlightening but unfortunately has been dropped for the American release version. In obtaining copies of rare films for repeated viewings in the course of my study of Lubitsch, I was aided by the people at the Locarno Film Festival and by other collectors around the world, especially Neil McGlone. My friend Elmar Kruithoff went the extra mile to provide assistance in obtaining copies of films, calling German archives and other institutions on my behalf, and coming up with copies of German books for my research. Elmar and his wife, Marianne Zandersen, who are good friends with Ann and me, opened their homes in Hamburg and Roskilde, Denmark, during our visits; their little son Peer was a cheerful multilingual companion as well, and I was touched when he saw my cluttered workspace in Berkeley and exclaimed, "*Schön* [beautiful]!"

Also going beyond the call of duty was the expert research librarian Howard Prouty of the Academy of Motion Picture Arts & Sciences' Margaret Herrick Library in Beverly Hills, who dug out and sent to me valuable articles, interviews, and press releases. My thanks to Bill Krohn for the research he did in the files of the Academy library, an institution that has served me so well for decades of work on my books. Ace researcher Barbara Hall pored through the library's remarkable photo collection to find and recommend Lubitsch stills and tracked down other information for me. Thanks also to Jeanine Braun, photographic archivist of the Margaret Herrick Library. Janet Bergstrom; Julia Riedel of the Deutsche Kinemathek, Berlin; and Marcel Steinlein of the Friedrich-Wilhelm-Murnau-Stiftung, Wiesbaden, enabled me to track down and obtain the use of the eloquent portrait of Lubitsch by

F. W. Murnau that appears in this book by permission of the Murnau-Stiftung. Mark Bishop and Derek Davidson of Photofest went the extra mile in enthusiastically finding and providing other photos. David E. Weingarten of Second Sight Video & Multimedia in Moraga, California, expertly made frame enlargements from Lubitsch films, and Phil Spruner of the A1 Photo & Video Lab in Berkeley transferred photos electronically; Jim Davidson, Dave's colleague at Second Sight, was also helpful, as he has been before.

I did research, as always, at the Wisconsin Historical Society in Madison, on the campus of my alma mater, the University of Wisconsin. That fabulous center of scholarship contains many important collections of films and papers, and they have done a great job over the years of organizing my own papers and making them accessible to other scholars (the papers for this book will eventually join those for my previous books). I am grateful to Mary K. Huelsbeck, assistant director of the Wisconsin Center for Film and Theater Research, for her work on my papers and other assistance, as well as to the now-retired Ben Brewster, Maxine Fleckner Ducey, and Barbara Kaiser for their work with me in the past. On my recent visits to Madison, I have enjoyed the company of two scholarly couples, Ben Brewster and Lea Jacobs, who gave me a copy of their Lubitsch bibliography, as well as David Bordwell and fellow Lubitsch author Kristin Thompson. My opportunities to speak at the campus Cinematheque on writing film books and on various directors have been highlights of my return visits to Madison.

The writings on Lubitsch by the late Andrew Sarris were among my early inspirations and helped inspire me throughout the writing of this book. Bruce Goldstein, the ace repertory director of New York's Film Forum, has invited me to participate in his programs and has shared his erudition on Lubitsch and other subjects (including providing translations of intertitles for German Lubitsch films). Others who have been helpful on this project include Ruth O'Hara, Joachim Hallmayer and Claudia Macaubas, Julie Kirgo, Victoria Riskin, Rex McGee, Pankaj Sharma, and Dave Kehr of the Museum of Modern Art, New York. Anton Kaes of the University of California, Berkeley, a major scholar of German film, offered important insights and encouragement. My son, John McBride, kindly gave me a copy of the collected works of Oscar Wilde and watched and shared his insights on many films with me. Marilyn Fabe of the University of California, Berkeley invited me to address the commencement ceremony of the graduating seniors from the university's Department of Film and Media and Department of Rhetoric in 2012; I was especially pleased that I shared the stage with my former film professor in Madison, Russell Merritt, who had become a member of the Berkeley faculty. Marilyn and her husband, Griffin ("Grif") Dix, and our mutual friends David and Pamela Benson, Victoria Nelson, and Carol Clover have participated in an informal viewing and discussion group in Berkeley, where I have had the benefit of their views as we have watched Lubitsch films together. Judy Schavrien, a longtime friend, also watched numerous Lubitsch films with me and offered many wise insights. Susan Oxtoby at the Pacific Film Archive in Berkeley has been a friend and has shown many Lubitsch films; thanks also to Becky Mertens for her hospitality there. My longtime agent, Richard Parks, who retired while I was in the process of writing this book, was always supportive and encouraging of the project.

My study of Lubitsch and the context in which he worked benefited from my interviews and conversations over the years with a number of his colleagues, including his foremost acolyte, Billy Wilder, who spoke to me at length about Lubitsch (once on the set of *The Front Page* and on another occasion when Todd McCarthy and I interviewed him for two days for *Film Comment*); Frank Capra; Rouben Mamoulian; Jean Renoir; Howard Hawks; John Ford; Edward Bernds; Gottfried Reinhardt; and Claudette Colbert. I also cherish a brief but memorable conversation I had with Ingmar Bergman when he came to Hollywood in 1975 with plans to make *The Merry Widow*. He and I fell into a spirited comparison of the Lubitsch and Erich von Stroheim versions, a discussion that his wife, Ingrid, confided was the highlight for him of an otherwise-dreary press conference.

My work in the final stages of writing this book was greatly aided by a sabbatical from San Francisco State University in the fall semester of 2015. For that opportunity, I thank our president, Leslie E. Wong; Sue V. Rosser, our former provost and vice president for academic affairs; Sacha Bunge, dean of faculty affairs and professional development; Daniel Bernardi, interim dean of the College of Liberal and Creative Arts and former chair of our Cinema Department; and his successors as chairs of the department and now School of Cinema, Professors Steven Kovacs and Britta Sjogren. The collegial support of my teaching institution is a mainstay of my career. I am grateful for the ongoing backing and encouragement of our university librarian, Deborah Masters, and Meg Gorzycki, our former faculty development consultant and now educational associate in academic technology. My students in the fall 2009 course I developed on "Romantic Comedy: Lubitsch and Wilder" provided thoughtful feedback on their films and a testing ground for my ideas. Pauline Lampert, a teaching assistant in that course, has gone on to become a valued friend and has had me as a frequent guest on her erudite film history podcast, *Flixwise*.

In a time when film studies are threatened on many fronts, I am fortunate to have found a congenial home for *How Did Lubitsch Do It?* at Columbia University Press through my old friend and esteemed colleague John Belton, the longtime editor of the Film and Culture Series in which this book appears. John's enthusiasm for Lubitsch and support for my work made its publication possible, and he offered many helpful and insightful editorial suggestions. He earlier wrote highly detailed, invaluable letters supporting my tenure and promotion process at San Francisco State University. Philip Leventhal, senior editor at the press, has been a keen and sympathetic source of strength in understanding the value of Lubitsch and the need for an in-depth study of his work. Copyeditor Abby Graves, indexer Silvia Benvenuto, and assistant production editor Marisa Lastres enhanced the book with their expertise and wise judgment. Lisa Hamm did the elegant design. I am grateful to other people who helped me to publication with their support and editorial advice, including Pat McGilligan, Walter Donohue, Rodney Powell, David Bordwell, James Naremore, and Molly Haskell.

Throughout the lengthy, arduous, but largely pleasurable process of writing this book, I had the enthusiastic support of my partner, Ann Weiser Cornell, an internationally recognized teacher and writer of books on emotional healing. She watched many Lubitsch films with me and shared her keen observations, making many fruitful suggestions about how to analyze them. Ann's familiarity with German culture and the language were of great help to me in understanding Lubitsch's native heritage, and our visits to Germany together have been memorable and delightful. As she has done for other books of mine, Ann also undertook the formidable task of reading the manuscript and making detailed and invaluable criticisms and suggestions. Without her involvement, this celebration of Ernst Lubitsch would not have been so deftly grounded or such a festive experience. I owe much gratitude to my beloved sweetheart not only for that generous contribution to my work but also for the daily joy she brings to our life together.

FILMOGRAPHY

Ernst Lubitsch's verifiable film credits include his roles as director, producer, screenwriter, and actor. Of the sixty-nine films Lubitsch directed (shorts as well as features), forty-seven are known to survive, although some are in fragmentary condition.

The films generally are listed in the order of release, although in some cases, when films were delayed for release until after World War I because of government censorship, they are listed in order of production. Many of Lubitsch's German films are lost or exist only in fragments. Films known to exist in whole or in part are indicated with an asterisk before the title. Many of his German films were short subjects. The running times of his silent films are inexact or unknown; camera speeds and the rate of projection varied extensively in the silent years. His first film that is considered a feature was *Die Augen der Mumie Mâ* (*The Eyes of the Mummy*) in 1918.

Information on films is drawn from books listed in the Notes on Sources, including the filmography by Wolfgang Jacobsen in Hans Helmut Prinzler and Enno Patalas, eds., *Lubitsch* (which is relied upon for release dates of German films, variously given in other sources); Robert Carringer and Barry Sabath, *Ernst Lubitsch: A Guide to References and Resources*; "Filmography" by Joseph McBride, in *Ernst Lubitsch* (booklet), Festival del Film Locarno; and Herman G. Weinberg, *The Lubitsch Touch: A Critical Study*; as well as from *The AFI Catalog of Feature Films*, American Film Institute (afi.com); the Internet Movie Database (IMDB.com); and the films themselves. Some films attributed to Lubitsch in various sources are unverified and are not listed here; see Prinzler and Patalas and Carringer and Sabath for information on those titles and on Lubitsch's stage work in Germany (1911–1918).

Filmography Key

EL	Ernst Lubitsch
DIST	Distributor
P	Producer
D	Director
S	Screenwriter and source material
*	an Extant work (in whole or in part)

GERMAN SILENT PERIOD (1913–1922)

1913

Die ideale Gattin (The Ideal Wife). DIST/P: Deutsche Bioscop GmbH; D: unknown; S: Hanns Heinz Ewers, Marc Henry; EL as actor only (billed as "Karl Lubitsch").

1914

Die Firma heiratet (The Company Marries a.k.a. *The Perfect Thirty-Six).* DIST: Union; D: Carl Wilhelm; S: Walter Turszinsky, Jacques Berg; EL as actor only.

Bedingung—kein Anhang! (Condition—No Dependents). DIST: Deutsche Bioscop GmbH; D: Stellan Rye; S: Luise Heilborn-Körbitz; EL as actor only.

Der Stolz der Firma: Die Geschichte einer Lehrlings (The Pride of the Firm: The Story of an Apprentice). DIST: Union; D: Carl Wilhelm; S: Walter Turszinsky, Jacques Burg; EL as actor only.

Fraülein Seifenschaum (Miss Soapsuds). DIST: Union; D: EL; EL also in cast. Though released after *A Trip on the Ice, Sugar and Spice,* and *Blind Man's Bluff,* this short, filmed in the summer of 1914, was the first film EL directed.

Fraülein Piccolo (Miss Piccolo). DIST: Luna-Film GmbH; D/S: Franz Hofer; EL as actor only. Completed by August 1914, banned for the duration of World War I, first shown in February 1919.

1915

Arme Maria—Eine Warenhausgeschichte (Poor Marie). DIST: Union; D: Willy Zeyn; S: Robert Wiene, Walter Turszinsky; EL as actor only.

Aufs Eis geführt (A Trip on the Ice). DIST: Malu-Film; P: Union; D: EL; S: Hans Kräly; EL also as actor.

Zucker und Zimmt (Sugar and Spice). P: Mátry-Lubitsch-Film; D: Ernst Mátry, EL; S: Mátry, EL, Greta Schröder-Mátry, based on verse by EL and Schröder-Mátry; EL also in cast.

Blindekuh (Blind Man's Bluff). DIST: Union; D: EL; EL also in cast.

*Robert und Bertram: Die lustigen Vagabunden (Robert and Bertram, or the Funny Vaga-
bonds). DIST: Union; D: Max Mack; EL as actor only.

Sein Einziger Patient (His Only Patient) a.k.a. Der erste Patient (The First Patient).
DIST: Union; D: EL; EL also in cast.

Der Kraftmeier (The Muscleman a.k.a. The Bully). DIST: Union; D/S: EL; EL also in cast.

Der letzte Anzug aka Sein letzter Anzug (The Last Suit). DIST: Union; D: EL; EL also in cast.

1916

*Als ich Tot War (When I Was Dead) a.k.a. Wo ist mein Schatz? (Where Is My Treasure?).
DIST: Union; D/S: EL; EL also in cast. The earliest surviving film directed by EL.

*Doktor Satansohn (Doctor Satansohn). DIST: Union; D/S: Edmund Edel; EL as actor only.

Der schwarze Moritz (Black Moritz). DIST: Union; D: Georg Jacoby; S: Louis Taufstein,
Eugen Burg; EL as actor only. A combined film and stage musical comedy.

*Schuhpalast Pinkus (Shoe Palace Pinkus). DIST: Union; D: EL; S: Hans Kräly, Erich
Schönfelder; EL also in cast.

Der gemischte Frauenchor (The Mixed Ladies' Chorus). DIST: Union; D: EL; EL also in cast.

Leutnant auf Befehl (Lieutenant by Command). DIST: Union; D: EL; EL also in cast.

Das schönste Geschenk (The Most Beautiful Gift). DIST: Union; D: EL; EL also in cast.

Der G.m.b.H. Tenor (The Tenor, Inc.). DIST: Union; D: EL; EL also in cast.

Die neue Nase (The New Nose) a.k.a. Seine neue Nase (His New Nose). DIST: Union; D: EL;
EL also in cast.

1917

Käsekönig Hollander (Royal Dutch Cheese). DIST: Union; D: EL; S: EL, Erich Schönfelder. Filmed in 1917 but banned for the duration of World War I; released probably
in March 1919.

*Der Blusenkonig (The Blouse King). DIST: Union; D: EL; S: EL, Erich Schönfelder; EL
also in cast.

*Hans Trutz im Schlaraffenland (Hans Defiance in Never-Never Land). DIST: Union;
D/S: Paul Wegener; EL as actor only.

Ossis Tagebuch (Ossi's Diary). DIST: Union; D: EL; S: EL, Erich Schönfelder.

*Wenn Vier Dasselbe Tun (When Four Do the Same). DIST: Union; D/S: EL; EL also in cast.

*Das Fidele Gefängnis (The Merry Jail). DIST: Union; D: EL; S: EL, Hans Kräly, based
on the operetta Die Fledermaus (The Bat) by Johann Strauss, libretto by Karl Haffner
and Richard Genée, and the play Das Gefängnis (The Prison) by Julius Roderich
Benedix. Loosely remade by Lubitsch in 1926 as So This Is Paris.

1918

Prinz Sami (Prince Sami). DIST: Union; D: EL; S: EL, Danny Kaden; EL also in cast.

Der Rodelkavalier (The Toboggan Cavalier). DIST: Union; D: EL; S: EL, Erich Schönfelder; EL also in cast.

Der Fall Rosentopf (*The Rosentopf Case*). DIST: Union; D: EL; S: EL, Hans Kräly; EL also in cast.

*Ich Möchte Kein Mann sein (*I Don't Want to Be a Man* a.k.a. *I Wouldn't Want to Be a Man*). DIST: Union; D: EL; S: EL, Hans Kräly.

*Die Augen der Mumie Mâ (*The Eyes of the Mummy*). DIST: Union; D: EL; S: Hans Kräly, Emil Rameau. EL's first feature-length film.

Das Mädel vom Ballett (*The Ballet Girl*). DIST: Union; D: EL; S: Hans Kräly.

*Carmen (*Gypsy Blood*). DIST: Union; D: EL; S: Hans Kräly, from the novella by Prosper Mérimée.

1919

*Meyer aus Berlin (*Meyer from Berlin*). DIST: Union; D: EL; S: EL, Erich Schönfelder; EL also in cast.

Meine Frau, die Filmschauspielerin (*My Wife, the Film Actress*). DIST: Union; D: EL; S: Hans Kräly, EL.

Das Schwabemädel (*The Girl from Schwabia*). DIST: Union; D: EL.

*Die Austernprinzessin (*The Oyster Princess*). DIST: Union; D: EL; S: Hans Kräly, EL.

Rausch (*Intoxication*). DIST: Argus-Film GmbH; P/D: EL; S: Hans Kräly, from the play *Brott och brott* (*There Are Crimes and Crimes*) by August Strindberg.

*Madame DuBarry a.k.a. *Passion*. DIST: Union; D: EL; S: Fred Orbing (Norbert Falk), Hans Kräly.

Der lustige Ehemann (*The Merry Husband*). P: Union; D: Leo Lasko; S: EL, from an idea by Richard Wilde.

*Die Puppe (*The Doll*). DIST: Union; D: EL; S: Hans Kräly, EL, loosely based on the story "Der Sandmann" ("The Sandman") by E. T. A. Hoffmann and the operetta adaptation *La Poupée* (*The Doll*) by Maurice Ordonneau and Edmond Audran, translated into German by A. E. Willner; EL also in cast.

1920

Die Wohnungsnot (*The Housing Shortage*). DIST: Union; D: unknown; S: Hans Kräly, EL.

*Kohlhiesels Töchter (*Kohlhiesel's Daughters*). DIST: Messter-Film GmbH; D: EL; S: Hans Kräly.

*Romeo und Julia im Schnee (*Romeo and Juliet in the Snow*). DIST: Maxim-Film Ges. Ebner & Co.; D: EL; S: Hans Kräly, EL.

*Sumurun a.k.a. *One Arabian Night*. DIST: Union; D: EL; S: Hans Kräly, EL, based on the pantomime by Friedrich Freksa; EL also in cast.

*Anna Boleyn a.k.a. *Deception*. DIST: Messter-Film GmbH, Union; D: EL; S: Fred Orbing (Norbert Falk), Hans Kräly.

1921

*Die Bergkatze (*The Wildcat* a.k.a. *The Mountain Cat*). DIST: Ernst Lubitsch-Film GmbH, in association with EFA; P/D: EL; S: Hans Kräly, EL.

1922

Das Weib des Pharao (*The Wife of Pharaoh* a.k.a. *The Loves of Pharaoh*). DIST: Ernst Lubitsch-Film GmbH, in association with EFA; P/D: EL; S: Norbert Falk, Hans Kräly.

1923

Die Flamme (*The Flame*) a.k.a. *Montmartre*. DIST: Ernst Lubitsch-Film GmbH for EFA; P/D: EL; S: Hans Kräly, from the play *Die Flamme* by Hans Müller (Hans Lothar).

AMERICAN SILENT PERIOD (1923–1928)

1923

*Test scenes for *Marguerite and Faust* a.k.a. *Faust*. Adapted from the play *Faust* by Johann Wolfgang von Goethe and the 1859 opera by Charles Gounod based on Michel Carré's Goethe adaptation *Faust et Marguerite*. Twelve minutes of tests filmed by EL in Hollywood for the Mary Pickford Company with several actors playing Mephistopheles.

Rosita. DIST: United Artists; P/D: EL, for the Mary Pickford Company; S: Edward Knoblock, from a story by Norbert Falk and Hans Kräly, based on the play *Don César de Bazan* by Philippe François Pinel Dumanoir and Adolphe Philippe Dennery.

1924

The Marriage Circle. DIST: Warner Bros.; P/D: EL; S: Paul Bern, based on the play *Nur ein Traum* (*Only a Dream*) by Lothar Schmidt. Remade by EL as *One Hour with You* in 1932.

Three Women. DIST: Warner Bros.; P/D: EL; S: Hans Kräly, from a story by EL and Kräly, based on the novel *Lillis Ehe* (*Lillie's Marriage*) by Iolanthe Marees.

Forbidden Paradise. DIST: Famous Players-Lasky/Paramount; P/D: EL; S: Hans Kräly and Agnes Christine Johnson, based on the play *The Czarina* by Lajos Biró and Melchior Lengyel. Remade (EL producing) in 1945 as *A Royal Scandal*.

1925

Kiss Me Again. DIST: Warner Bros.; P/D: EL; S: Hans Kräly, based on the play *Divorçons!* (*Let's Get a Divorce*) by Victorien Sardou and Emile de Najac. Remade by EL in 1941 as *That Uncertain Feeling*.

Lady Windermere's Fan. DIST: Warner Bros.; P/D: EL; S: Julian Josephson, based on the play by Oscar Wilde.

1926

So This Is Paris. DIST: Warner Bros.; P/D: EL; S: Hans Kräly, based on the play *Le réveillon* (*The Midnight Supper*) by Henri Meilhac and Ludovic Halévy. A loose remake of EL's 1917 film *Das Fidele Gefängnis* (*The Merry Jail*).

1926

The Honeymoon Express. DIST: Warner Bros.; D: James Flood, EL (uncredited retakes).

1927

*The Student Prince in Old Heidelberg a.k.a. *Old Heidelberg.* DIST: MGM; P/D: EL; S: Hans Kräly, based on the novel *Karl Heinrich* by Wilhelm Meyer-Förster and his play version *Alt-Heidelberg* (*Old Heidelberg*) and the operetta *The Student Prince* by Dorothy Donnelly and Sigmund Romberg.

1928

*The Last Command. DIST: Paramount; D: Josef von Sternberg; S: Lajos Biró, John F. Goodrich, based on a story by EL (uncredited).

*The Patriot. DIST: Paramount, Famous Players-Lasky; P/D: EL; S: Hans Kräly, from the play *Der Patriot* (*The Patriot*) by Alfred Neumann. Released in both silent and sound versions (with music, sound effects, and some dialogue). Several minutes of this film and the trailer exist.

1929

*Eternal Love. DIST: United Artists; P/D: EL; S: Hans Kräly, based on the novel *Der König der Bernina* (*The King of Bernina*) by Jacob Christoph Heer.

AMERICAN SOUND PERIOD (1929–1948)

1929

*The Love Parade. DIST: Paramount; P/D: EL; S: Ernest Vajda, Guy Bolton, based on the play *La prince consort* (*The Prince Consort*) by Léon Xanrof. Also released in a silent version and a French-language version, *Parade d'amour.*

1930

*The Vagabond King. DIST: Paramount; D: Ludwig Berger, EL (uncredited retakes); S: Herman J. Mankiewicz, based on the operetta by Rudolph Friml, Brian Hooker, and W. H. Post, and the play *If I Were King* by Justin Huntly McCarthy, from the novel by R. H. Russell.

*Paramount on Parade. DIST: Paramount; D: EL, Dorothy Arzner, Otto Brower, Edmund Goulding, Victor Heerman, Edwin H. Knopf, Rowland V. Lee, Lothar Mendes, Victor Schertzinger, A. Edward Sutherland, Frank Tuttle; S: Joseph L. Mankiewicz. A variety revue film with three segments by EL, "Origin of the Apache," "A Park in Paris," and "The Rainbow Revels." Also released in a French-language version, *Paramount en Parade*, directed by Charles de Rochefort; a Spanish version, *Galas de la Paramount*; and other European versions.

*Monte Carlo. DIST: Paramount; P/D: EL; S: Ernest Vajda, Vincent Lawrence, based on the play *Die blaue Küste* (*The Blue Coast*) by Hans Müller and episodes from the operetta *Monsieur Beaucaire* by Booth Tarkington and Evelyn Greenlead Sutherland, based on Tarkington's novel. Also released in a silent version.

1931

*The Smiling Lieutenant. DIST: Paramount; P/D: EL; S: Ernest Vajda, Samson Raphaelson, based on the operetta *Ein Walzertraum* (*A Waltz Dream*) by Leopold Jacobson and Felix Doermann, music by Oscar Straus, from the novel *Nux, der Prinzgemahl* (*Nux, the Prince Consort*) in *Buch der Abenteuer* (*Book of Adventure*) by Hans Müller. Also released in UK and French versions.

1932

*The Man I Killed a.k.a. *Broken Lullaby*. DIST: Paramount; P/D: EL; S: Samson Raphaelson, Ernest Vajda, based on the play *L'Homme que j'ai tué* (*The Man I Killed*) by Maurice Rostand and its American stage adaptation by Reginald Berkeley. Retitled *Broken Lullaby* shortly after release.

*One Hour with You. DIST: Paramount; P: EL; D: EL, "Assisted by" George Cukor; S: Samson Raphaelson. A musical remake of *The Marriage Circle*. Also released in a French-language version, *Une heure près de toi*.

*Trouble in Paradise. DIST: Paramount; P/D: EL; S: Samson Raphaelson, adaptation by Grover Jones, based on the play *A Becsuletes Megtalalo* (*The Honest Finder*) by László Aladar.

*If I Had a Million. DIST: Paramount; D: EL, Norman Taurog, Norman McLeod, Stephen Roberts, H. Bruce Humberstone, James Cruze, William A. Seiter, A. Edward Sutherland; S: EL, Claude Binyon, Whitney Bolton, Malcolm Stuart Boylan, John Bright, Sidney Buchman, Lester Cole, Isabel Dawn, Boyce DeGaw, Oliver H. P. Garrett, Harvey Gates, Grover Jones, Lawton Mackall, Joseph L. Mankiewicz, William Slavens McNutt, Robert Sparks, based on the novel *Windfall* by Robert D. Andrews. Episodic film; the EL segment, untitled, is sometimes referred to as "The Clerk."

1933

Mr. Broadway. DIST: Arthur Greenblatt Distribution Service, Broadway-Hollywood Productions; D: Johnnie Walker, Edgar G. Ulmer; S: Abel Green, Ed Sullivan; EL as himself.

*Design for Living. DIST: Paramount; P/D: EL; S: Ben Hecht, based on the play by Noël Coward.

1934

*The Merry Widow. DIST: MGM; P/D: EL; S: Ernest Vajda, Samson Raphaelson, based on the operetta *Die lustige Witwe* (*The Merry Widow*) by Franz Lehár, libretto and lyrics by Victor Léon and Leo Stein, who adapted the story from an 1861 play by Henri Meilhac, *L'attaché d'ambassade* (*The Embassy Attaché*). Also released in a French version, *La veuve joyeuse*, and versions for the English and Belgian markets.

1936

Desire. DIST: Paramount; P: EL; D: Frank Borzage (and EL, possible uncredited retakes); S: Edwin Justus Mayer, Waldemar Young, and Samuel Hoffenstein, based on the play *Die schönen Tage von Aranjuez* (*The Beautiful Days of Aranjuez*) by Hans Székely and Robert Adolf Stemmle.

1937

Angel. DIST: Paramount; P/D: EL; S: Samson Raphaelson, based on the play *Angyal* (*Angel*) by Melchior Lengyel and the English adaptation by Guy Bolton and Russell Medcraft.

1938

Bluebeard's Eighth Wife. DIST: Paramount; P/D: EL; S: Charles Brackett, Billy Wilder, based on the play *La Huitième Femme de Barbe-bleue* (*Bluebeard's Eighth Wife*) by Alfred Savoir and its American adaptation by Charlton Andrews, *Bluebeard's 8th Wife*.

1939

Ninotchka. DIST: MGM; P/D: EL; S: Charles Brackett, Billy Wilder, Walter Reisch, from a story by Melchior Lengyel.

1940

The Shop Around the Corner. DIST: MGM; P/D: EL; S: Samson Raphaelson, based on the play *Illatszertár* (*Drugstore*) a.k.a. *Parfumerie* (*Perfume Shop*) by Miklós László (a.k.a. Nikolaus Laszlo).

1941

That Uncertain Feeling. DIST: United Artists; P: EL, in association with Sol Lesser; D: EL; S: Donald Ogden Stewart, based on the play *Divorçons!* (*Let's Get a Divorce*) by Victorien Sardou and Émile de Najac. A remake of *Kiss Me Again*.

1942

To Be or Not to Be. DIST: United Artists; P: EL in association with Alexander Korda; D: EL; S: Edwin Justus Mayer, from a story by Melchior Lengyel.

Know Your Enemy: Germany. D: EL; S: Bruno Frank. EL made this dramatized documentary at Twentieth Century-Fox for Frank Capra's 834th Signal Service Photographic Detachment, Special Services Division, U.S. Army, in October 1942, but it was not released. The project was remade by the Capra unit as *Here Is Germany* (supervised by Gottfried Reinhardt, 1945), which was released by Warner Bros. in revised form as *Hitler Lives* (1945).

1943

The Meanest Man in the World. DIST: Twentieth Century-Fox; D: Sidney Lanfield, EL (uncredited retakes); S: George Seaton, Allan House, based on the play by George M. Cohan.

Heaven Can Wait. DIST: Twentieth Century-Fox; P/D: EL; S: Samson Raphaelson, based on the play *Születésnap* (*Birthday*) by Laszlo Bus-Feketé.

1945

A Royal Scandal. DIST: Twentieth Century-Fox; P: EL; D: Otto Preminger; S: Edwin Justus Mayer, adaptation by Bruno Frank, based on the play *The Czarina* by Lajos Biró and Melchior Lengyel. A remake of *Forbidden Paradise*.

1946

Dragonwyck. DIST: Twentieth Century-Fox; P: EL; D: Joseph L. Mankiewicz; S: Mankiewicz, based on the novel by Anya Seton.

Cluny Brown. DIST: Twentieth Century-Fox; P/D: EL; S: Samuel Hoffenstein, Elizabeth Reinhardt, based on the novel by Margery Sharp.

1948

That Lady in Ermine. DIST: Twentieth Century-Fox; P: EL; D: EL, Otto Preminger (uncredited); S: Samson Raphaelson, based on the operetta *Die Frau im Hermelin* (*That Lady in Ermine*) by Rudolf Schanzer and Ernst Welisch and its English-language adaptations. EL died while making this film.

NOTES ON SOURCES

See also previous bibliographies, including those in Herman G. Weinberg, *The Lubitsch Touch: A Critical Study*; Ben Brewster and Lea Jacobs, "Ernst Lubitsch," *Oxford Bibliographies*, Cinema Media Series, last modified February 25, 2016, published online and as an e-book; and Robert Carringer and Barry Sabath, *Ernst Lubitsch: A Guide to References and Resources*.

Biographical data on Lubitsch, unless otherwise specified, as well as film production and release dates, are from Carringer and Sabath, *Ernst Lubitsch: A Guide to References and Resources*; Hans Helmut Prinzler and Enno Patalas, eds., *Lubitsch*; Michael Hanisch, *Auf den Spuren Der Filmgeschichte: Berliner Schauplätze* [*In the Footsteps of Film History: Berlin Venues*]; and Scott Eyman, *Ernst Lubitsch: Laughter in Paradise*. See listings below; see also Filmography for further details.

Citations from books listed below in "Selected Books" are given in the notes sections with only the last names of the authors or editors. Other citations in the notes are given in full on the first mention and in shortened form thereafter.

Abbreviations

AFI	American Film Institute
AMPAS	Ernst Lubitsch file at the Academy of Motion Picture Arts and Sciences' Margaret Herrick Library, Beverly Hills
AMPP	Association of Motion Picture Producers
AP	Associated Press
BW	Billy Wilder
DV	*Daily Variety*

EL	Ernst Lubitsch
HR	*Hollywood Reporter*
JM	Joseph McBride
LAT	*Los Angeles Times*
MoMA	Museum of Modern Art, New York
MPPDA	Motion Picture Producers and Distributors of America, Inc.
NYT	*New York Times*

SELECTED BOOKS

Barnes, Peter. *To Be or Not to Be.* BFI Film Classics. London: British Film Institute, 2002.

Binh, N. T., and Christian Viviani. *Lubitsch.* Paris: Editions Rivages, 1991.

Brackett, Charles. *"It's the Pictures That Got Small": Charles Brackett on Billy Wilder and Hollywood's Golden Age* (Brackett's diaries from 1932–1949). Edited by Anthony Slide. New York: Columbia University Press, 2015.

Brownlow, Kevin. *The Parade's Gone By . . .* New York: Knopf, 1967.

Carr, Steven Alan. *Hollywood and Anti-Semitism: A Cultural History up to World War II.* Cambridge: Cambridge University Press, 2001.

Carringer, Robert, and Barry Sabath. *Ernst Lubitsch: A Guide to References and Resources.* Boston: G. K. Hall, 1978.

Crowe, Cameron. *Conversations with Wilder.* New York: Knopf, 1999.

Doherty, Thomas. *Hollywood and Hitler 1933–1939.* New York: Columbia University Press, 2013.

——. *Hollywood's Censor: Joseph I. Breen & The Production Code Administration.* New York: Columbia University Press, 2007.

Eisner, Lotte. *The Haunted Screen: Expressionism and the German Cinema and the Influence of Max Reinhardt.* London: Thames and Hudson, 1969. First published as *L'Ecran Démoniaque*, Paris: Encyclopédie du cinema, 1952; revised ed., Paris: Le Terrain vague, 1965.

Eyman, Scott. *Ernst Lubitsch: Laughter in Paradise.* New York: Simon & Schuster, 1993, 2015; Baltimore: Johns Hopkins University Press, 2000.

Festival del Film, Locarno, Switzerland. *Ernst Lubitsch* (booklet). 2010. Includes essay "How Did Lubitsch Do It?" and "Filmography," both by JM.

Frodon, Jean-Michel, ed. *Cinema and the Shoah: An Art Confronts the Tragedy of the Twentieth Century.* Translated by Anna Harrison and Tom Mes. Albany: State University of New York Press, 2010. Originally published as *Le cinéma et la Shoah: Un art à l'épreuve de la tragédie du 20e siècle*, Paris: Cahiers du Cinéma, 2007.

Gabler, Neil. *An Empire of Their Own: How the Jews Invented Hollywood.* New York: Crown, 1988.

Gemünden, Gerd. *Continental Strangers: German Exile Cinema 1933–1951.* New York: Columbia University Press, 2014.

Hake, Sabine. *Passions and Deceptions: The Early Films of Ernst Lubitsch*. Princeton, NJ: Princeton University Press, 1992.

Hanisch, Michael. *Auf den Spuren Der Filmgeschichte: Berliner Schauplätze [In the Footsteps of Film History: Berlin Venues]*. Berlin: Henschel Verlag, 1991. See esp. chap. on EL, "Ein Junge aus Der Schönhauser" ["A Boy from the Schönhauser"].

——. *Ernst Lubitsch (1892–1947): Von der Berliner Schönhauser Allee nach Hollywood [Ernst Lubitsch (1892–1947): From Berlin's Schönhauser Allee to Hollywood]*. Judische Miniaturen [Jewish Miniatures]. Berlin: Hentrich & Hentrich, Centrum Jüdaicum, 2003.

Harvey, James. *Romantic Comedy in Hollywood, from Lubitsch to Sturges*. New York: Knopf, 1987.

Haskell, Molly. *From Reverence to Rape: The Treatment of Women in the Movies*. 1st ed., New York: Holt, Rinehart & Winston, 1974; 2nd ed., with new preface, Chicago: University of Chicago Press, 1987; 3rd ed., with new introduction, and foreword by Manohla Dargis, Chicago: University of Chicago Press, 2016.

Heilbut, Anthony. *Exiled in Paradise: German Refugee Artists and Intellectuals in America from the 1930s to the Present*. New York: Viking, 1983.

Henry, Nora. *Ethics and Social Criticism in the Hollywood Films of Erich von Stroheim, Ernst Lubitsch, and Billy Wilder*. Westport, CT: Praeger, 2001.

Horak, Jan-Christopher. "Ernst Lubitsch and the Rise of UFA 1917–1922." MS thesis, Boston University, 1975.

Horowitz, Joseph. *Artists in Exile: How Refugees from Twentieth-Century War and Revolution Transformed the American Performing Arts*. New York: HarperCollins, 2008.

Horton, Robert, ed. *Billy Wilder: Interviews*. Jackson: University Press of Mississippi, 2002.

Kaes, Anton, Nicholas Baer, and Michael Cowan, eds. *The Promise of Cinema: German Film Theory 1907–1933*. Oakland: University of California Press, 2016.

Kaes, Anton, Martin Jay, and Edward Dimenberg, eds. *The Weimar Republic Sourcebook*. Berkeley: University of California Press, 1994.

Koszarski, Richard. *An Evening's Entertainment: The Age of the Silent Feature Picture, 1915–1928*. Vol. 3 of *History of the American Cinema* (Charles Harpole, general editor). Berkeley: University of California Press, 1990.

Kracauer, Siegfried. *From Caligari to Hitler: A Psychological History of the German Film*. Princeton, NJ: Princeton University Press, 1947. Revised and expanded edition, edited by Leonardo Quaresima, 2004.

Kreimeier, Klaus. *The UFA Story: A History of Germany's Greatest Film Company, 1918–1945*. Translated by Robert Kimber and Rita Kimber. New York: Hill and Wang, 1996. First published as *Die Ufa-Story: Geschichte eines Filmkonzerns*, München Wien: Verlag, 1992.

Lewis, Jon. *Hollywood v. Hard Core: How the Struggle over Censorship Saved the Modern Film Industry*. New York: New York University Press, 2000.

MacLean, Rory. *Berlin: Portrait of a City through the Centuries*. New York: St. Martin's, 2014. First published as *Berlin: Imagine a City*, London: Weidenfeld & Nicolson, 2014.

McBride, Joseph. *Two Cheers for Hollywood: Joseph McBride on Movies*. Berkeley: Hightower Press, 2017. This book includes JM article, "Shooting *The Front Page*: Two Damns and One By God," *Real Paper* (Boston), July 31, 1974; JM and Todd McCarthy interview with BW, "Going for Extra Innings," *Film Comment* (January–February 1979). The *Real Paper* article was published in somewhat different form as "*The Front Page*," *Sight and Sound* (Autumn 1974). Both pieces were also published in Horton, *Billy Wilder*.

Negri, Pola. *Memoirs of a Star*. Garden City, NY: Doubleday, 1970.

Novak, Ivana, Jela Krečič, and Mladen Dolar, eds. *Lubitsch Can't Wait: A Theoretical Examination*. Ljubljana, Slovenia: Slovenian Cinematheque; New York: Columbia University Press, 2014.

Paul, William. *Ernst Lubitsch's American Comedy*. New York: Columbia University Press, 1983.

Petrie, Graham. *Hollywood Destinies: European Directors in America, 1922–1931*. Revised ed. Detroit: Wayne State University Press, 2002. 1st ed., London: Routledge, Kagan Paul, 1985.

Pickford, Mary. *Sunshine and Shadow*. Foreword by Cecil B. DeMille. Garden City, NY: Doubleday, 1955.

Poague, Leland A. *The Cinema of Ernst Lubitsch: The Hollywood Films*. South Brunswick, NJ: A. S. Barnes, 1978.

Prinzler, Hans Helmut, and Enno Patalas, eds. *Lubitsch*. Munich: Verlag C. J. Bucher, 1984.

Sabath, Barry. "Ernst Lubitsch and Samson Raphaelson: A Study in Collaboration." PhD thesis, New York University, 1979.

Saunders, Thomas J. *Hollywood in Berlin: American Cinema and Weimar Germany*. Berkeley: University of California Press, 1994.

Smedley, Nick. *A Divided World: Hollywood Cinema and Émigré Directors in the Era of Roosevelt and Hitler, 1933–1948*. Bristol, UK: Intellect, 2011.

Thompson, Kristin. *Herr Lubitsch Goes to Hollywood: German and American Film after World War I*. Amsterdam: Amsterdam University Press, 2005.

Weinberg, Herman G. *The Lubitsch Touch: A Critical Study*. New York: Dutton, 1968; revised ed., 1971; 3rd revised and enlarged ed., New York: Dover, 1977.

Weitz, Eric D. *Weimar Germany: Promise and Tragedy*. Princeton, NJ: Princeton University Press, 2007; new and expanded ed., 2013.

PUBLISHED SCREENPLAYS

Anobile, Richard J. ed. *Ernst Lubitsch's* Ninotchka. Screenplay by Charles Brackett, Billy Wilder, and Walter Reisch, based on a story by Melchior Lengyel. A photobook with dialogue and frame enlargements. New York: Universe Books, 1975. The screenplay was also published in the MGM Library of Film Scripts, New York: Viking, 1972; University Reprints, 2002.

Raphaelson, Samson. *Three Screen Comedies by Samson Raphaelson:* Trouble in Paradise, The Shop Around the Corner, *and* Heaven Can Wait. Introduction by Pauline Kael. Madison: University of Wisconsin Press, 1983. Includes Raphaelson's essay, "Freundschaft: How It Was with Lubitsch and Me," first published as "Freundschaft," *New Yorker*, May 11, 1981.

DOCUMENTARY FILMS (CHRONOLOGICAL ORDER)

Patalas, Enno. *Ernst Lubitsch: Eine Lektion in Kino* [*Ernst Lubitsch: A Lesson in Cinema*]. Fernsehfilmproduktion, WEDR Westdeutsches Fernsehen (West Germany), 1971; revised version, 1982.

Schlöndorff, Volker, and Gisela Grischow. *Billy Wilder, wie haben Sie's gemacht?* [*Billy, How Did You Do It?*]. BW in conversation with Schlöndorff, Bioskop Film (Munich)/ Hessischen Rundfunk/Westdeutschen Rundfunk/Bayerischen Rundfunk, 1992. Shown on BBC-TV (UK) as *Billy, How Did You Do It?*, 1992, and released in the United States (without BW's comments on EL) as *Billy Wilder Speaks*, Kino International, 2006.

Molly Haskell and Andrew Sarris. Interview feature on *Heaven Can Wait*. DVD. Produced by Karen Stetler. The Criterion Collection, 2005.

Fischer, Robert, dir. *Ernst Lubitsch in Berlin—Von der Schönhauser Allee nach Hollywood* [*Ernst Lubitsch in Berlin—From Schönhauser Allee to Hollywood*]. Transit Film (Munich) and UFA, 2006. DVD in boxed set, *Lubitsch in Berlin*. Kino International, 2007.

Rosen, Peter, dir. *Strangers in Paradise: Hitler's Exiles in Hollywood*. Coproduced and written by Sara Lukinson and Peter Rosen. Westdeutscher Rundfunk Köln and Arte. DVD. Kultur, 2008.

Thomas, Karen, dir. *Cinema's Exiles: From Hitler to Hollywood*. PBS, 2009 (a German-French-American coproduction).

Bernard, Jean-Jacques, dir. *Lubitsch le patron* [*Lubitsch, the Boss*]. Written by N. T. Binh. Caïmans Productions, 2010. Feature on DVD of *L'Éventail de Lady Windermere* [*Lady Windermere's Fan*]. Paris, Éditions Montparnasse, 2010.

Joseph McBride: The Screenplay. Video presentation on the Noël Coward play, the Ben Hecht screenplay, and the EL film version of *Design for Living. Design for Living* DVD and Blu-ray editions. Produced by Karen Stetler. Criterion Collection. 2011.

INTRODUCTION: "HOW DID LUBITSCH DO IT?"

Books

Weinberg provides the quotes on EL from David Niven, and Jeanette MacDonald. How EL "played the game" and "find some new": Harvey. "A poignant sadness": Andrew Sarris, *The American Cinema: Directors and Directions, 1929–1968* (New York: Dutton, 1968). Noël Coward, "Morals": his play *Private Lives* (London: Heinemann, 1930). Frieda

Grafe, "The audacious artificiality": "Was Lubitsch berührt" ["What Lubitsch Touch?"], expanded version of article from *Süddeutschen Zeitung*, September 22–23, 1979, in Prinzler and Patalas. The EL retrospectives in Locarno, Switzerland, and Paris, 2010: Festival del Film, Locarno, booklet, *Ernst Lubitsch*. Gemünden on German exiles in Hollywood. Edward W. Said, "Reflections on Exile," *Granta* (Winter 1984), reprinted in his book *Reflections on Exile and Other Essays* (Cambridge, MA: Harvard University Press, 2000). EL remark on "Paris, Paramount" to Garson Kanin, quoted in Peter Bogdanovich, *Who the Devil Made It* (New York: Knopf, 1997). Criticisms of EL and his films: Eyman; David Thomson, *The New Biographical Dictionary of Film*, 6th ed. (New York: Knopf, 2014).

Articles

BW on EL sign in office *"How would Lubitsch do it?"*: Michael Blowen, "The Art of Billy Wilder," *Globe* (Boston), October 22, 1989, reprinted in Horton. Orson Welles's comment on EL: 1964 interview by Juan Cobos, Miguel Rubio, and J. A. Pruneda, *Cahiers du Cinéma*, April 1965, reprinted as "A Trip to Don Quixoteland: Conversations with Orson Welles," trans. Rose Kaplin, *Cahiers du Cinéma in English* no. 5 (1966), reprinted in Mark W. Estrin, ed., *Orson Welles: Interviews* (Jackson: University Press of Mississippi, 2002). Mervyn LeRoy quote upon presenting EL's honorary Oscar: Philip K. Scheuer, "Lubitsch Looks at His 'Oscar,'" *LAT*, April 6, 1947. Sarris, "to speak of Lubitsch" and "Lubitsch never won": "Lubitsch in the Thirties: Part One," *Film Comment*, Winter 1971–1972. Graham Greene calls EL "the witty playboy": his review of Frank Capra's *Mr. Deeds Goes to Town*, *Spectator* (UK), August 28, 1936, reprinted in Greene, *The Pleasure-Dome: The Collected Film Criticism 1935–1940*, ed. John Russell Taylor (London: Secker & Warburg, 1972). E. Ann Kaplan's comment on "Lubitsch's approach to sexuality": her essay "Lubitsch Reconsidered," *Quarterly Review of Film Studies* 6, no. 3 (Summer 1981). I. A. L. Diamond on BW and Arthur Schnitzler: Michiko Kakutani, "Billy Wilder Honored at Lincoln Center Gala," *NYT*, May 4, 1982, quoted in JM, "Thank You, Mr. Wilder: Billy Wilder, 1906–2002," *Written By* (May 2002). BW on EL, "His art is lost": BW, "Ave atque Vale," *Action*, November 1967, reprinted in Weinberg. BW on how EL "could do more with a closed door": Jon Bradshaw, "'You Used to Be Very Big.' 'I Am Big. It's the Pictures That Got Small,'" *New York*, November 24, 1975.

   EL a "dervish": Herbert Howe, "The Film Wizard of Europe," *Photoplay*, December 1922. EL, "Film is an art": EL, "Film-Internationalität," in Heinrich Pfeiffer, ed., *Das deutsche Lichtbild-Buch: Film probleme von gestern und heute* [*The German Photo-Book: Film Problems of Today and Yesterday*] (Berlin: August Scherl, 1924), reprinted as EL, "Film Internationality," trans. Michael Cowan, in Kaes, Baer, and Cowan. Philip French on BW et al.: *Observer* (UK), quoted in David Walsh, "Billy Wilder, Filmmaker and Satirist, Dies at 95," *World Socialist Web Site*, April 3, 2002, wsws.org. BW on the Lubitsch Touch as "a different way of thinking": Schlöndorff and Grischow documentary. "They'll love you forever": BW, "Wilder's Tips For Writers," in Crowe. François Truffaut, "Lubitsch était un prince" ["Lubitsch Was a Prince"], *Cahiers du Cinéma*, February 1968, reprinted in his book *Les Films de ma vie* [*The Films in My Life*] (Paris: Flammarion, 1975); reprinted, trans. Leonard Mayhew (New York: Simon & Schuster, 1978). EL usually smoked Upmanns: Raphaelson, "Freundschaft."

In addition to his Russian citizenship (see Eyman), EL became a naturalized German citizen after World War I, but his citizenship was revoked by Germany in 1935: "Lose Reich Citizenship," *NYT*, January 29, 1935; "Lubitsch To Be American," AP report, *NYT*, January 30, 1935; "Reich Blow at Lubitsch Fails Mark," unidentified newspaper, January 30, 1935, AMPAS. See chap. 2 notes for documents on EL's American citizenship. BW lost relatives in the Holocaust: Andreas Hutter and Klaus Kamolz, *Billie Wilder: eine europäische Karriere* [*Billie Wilder: A European Career*] (Vienna: Böhlau, 1998); Yad Vashem document on Wilder's mother, page of Testimony on Eugenia Wildar [*sic*: Eugenia Dittler Wilder Siedlisker], filed by her brother Mikhael Baldinger, May 12, 1957. BW's reactions to the Holocaust in his films: Nancy Steffen-Fluhr, "Palimpsest: The Double Vision of Exile," in Karen McNally, ed., *Billy Wilder, Movie-Maker: Critical Essays on the Films* (Jefferson, NC: McFarland, 2011). EL's parents' deaths and his loss of relatives in the Holocaust: Eyman.

Other Sources

Sign in BW's office, quotes from BW defining the Lubitsch Touch and on EL as "one of the talented ones": Schlöndorff and Grischow documentary in which BW and Schlöndorff are shown (in the German and British versions) visiting EL's grave at Forest Lawn Memorial Parks & Mortuaries in Glendale, California. Jean Renoir, "He invented": quoted in Peter Bogdanovich, video introduction to *Trouble in Paradise*, DVD, Criterion Collection, 2003. The 1940 Nazi propaganda film *Der ewige Jude* [*The Eternal Jew*], dir. Fritz Hippler. EL's family background and 1934 song "The Super-Special Picture of the Year" by the Yacht Club Boys: Fischer documentary. EL on his Touch from Paramount press releases, AMPAS: "I would like to know myself," February 3, 1938; "I have no words," release written by EL, March 25, 1938; "I want no misunderstanding," May 1937; "I cannot give you," from "Biography of Ernst Lubitsch," unspecified studio release; see also "Epilogue: The Lubitsch Touch" in Thompson. "When he thinks, he likes to pace": Twentieth Century-Fox press release, 1940s, AMPAS. François Truffaut and Nicola Lubitsch discussions with JM. James Naremore on EL as "ineffable": JM conversation with Naremore; Sarris also referred to EL as "ineffable" in "Lubitsch in the Thirties, Part II: All Talking! All Singing! All Lubitsch!," *Film Comment*, Summer 1972.

CHAPTER 1: "HERR ERNST LUBITSCH"

Books

History and culture of the Wilhelmine Empire and Austro-Hungarian Empire: Barbara W. Tuchman, *The Proud Tower: A Portrait of the World Before the War: 1890–1914* (New York:

Macmillan, 1966); Gabler; Michael Stürmer, *The German Empire 1870–1918* (London: Weidenfeld & Nicolson, New York: Random House, 2000); and Peter Gay, *Schnitzler's Century: The Making of Middle-Class Culture, 1815–1914* (New York: Norton, 2002). Weimar Republic history: Peter Gay, *Weimar Culture: The Outsider as Insider* (New York: Harper & Row, 1968); Kaes, Jay, and Dimenberg; Hans Mommsen, *The Rise & Fall of Weimar Democracy*, trans. Ellborg Forster and Larry Eugene Jones (Chapel Hill: University of North Carolina Press, 1996), first published by Frankfurt am Main/Berlin, Germany: Propyläen Verlag im Verlag Ullstein GmbH, 1989; and Weitz. EL's birth at 82A Lothringer Strasse in Berlin, January 29, 1892: Prinzler and Patalas, which reproduces his birth certificate; Hanisch's books, especially *In the Footsteps of Film History: Berlin Venues*, which gives a detailed portrayal of EL's neighborhood, the Scheunenviertel, and his family life and youthful activities. Hanisch reprints the August 9, 1911, announcement in the Berlin *Local Indicator* of EL and others joining the Max Reinhardt company; Prinzler and Patalas comment on Reinhardt's "Theater Magic." Eyman on EL's unhappy love life.

Mary Pickford complains about EL as "a director of doors": Brownlow. Works on EL in Germany include Hanisch's books; Hake; Thompson; and Horak. EL on rejection of *The Wildcat*: his letter to Herman G. Weinberg, July 10, 1947, published in Weinberg's article "A Tribute to Lubitsch, with a Letter in Which Lubitsch Appraises His Own Career," *Films in Review*, August–September 1951, reprinted in Weinberg, also reproduced in *Film Culture*, Summer 1962. Jean Renoir, EL's "Berlin Style": July 22, 1967, letter to Weinberg, in Weinberg's book. "We shall never see his like again": Sarris, *The American Cinema*. Walther Rathenau on Jews' status in Germany: MacLean. Lotte H. Eisner in 1967 criticizing EL's German comedies for Jewish humor and her remarks on other EL films: Weinberg; further comments are from Eisner, *The Haunted Screen*. Gemünden comments on Eisner and EL. Emil Jannings as Nazi supporter: Robert S. Wistrich, *Who's Who in Nazi Germany* (London: Weidenfeld & Nicolson, 1982). The praise for EL from Edmund Wilson and Dwight Macdonald is reported in Weinberg.

Sources on BW's background and career: Maurice Zolotow, *Billy Wilder in Hollywood* (New York: Putnam, 1977); Hellmuth Karasek, *Billy Wilder: Eine Nahaufnahme* [*Billy Wilder: A Closeup*] (Hamburg: Hoffmann und Campe, 1992); Kevin Lally, *Wilder Times: The Life of Billy Wilder* (New York: Holt, 1996); Ed Sikov, *On Sunset Boulevard: The Life and Times of Billy Wilder* (New York: Hyperion, 1998); Hutter and Kamolz; and Crowe.

Victor Arnold, including Alfred Kerr's comment "tormented by fear": Prinzler and Patalas; Hanisch, *In the Footsteps of Film History* (including the quote from Felix Hollaender's obituary of Arnold in the *Berliner Tageblatt*); EL on Arnold as "great influence" and admitting "if my acting career": EL 1947 letter to Weinberg. Harshly negative comments on EL's physical appearance are from the following sources, which are quoted in Hake: Oskar Kalbus, *Vom Wesen deutscher Filmkunst* [*On the Essence of German Art*] Vol. I (Altona-Bahrenfeld, Germany: Zigaretten-Bilderdienst, 1935); Curt Riess, *Das gab's nur einmal: Das Buch der schönsten Filme unseres Lebens* [*The Only Time There Was: The Book of the Best Films of Our Lives*] (Hamburg: Sternbücher, 1956); and Géza von Cziffra, *Es war eine rauschende Ballnacht: Eine Sittengeschichte des deutschen Films* [*It Was a Glittering Ball: A Moral History of the German Film*] (Frankfurt am Main: Ullstein, 1987). "Jewish milieu pieces," a phrase used by Julius Urgifi and Argus, the critic for *Cinematograph*: quoted in Hanisch, *Ernst Lubitsch*. That book discusses EL's film debut in *Die ideale Gattin* [*The Ideal Wife*], and it notes the repeated coincidence of EL's work with social revolutions, as well as EL's wry joke, "Ernst I have enough." The story about EL's father disparaging his face is from Riess, quoted in Hanisch, *In the Footsteps of Film History*. EL's comments about Jewish humor from his interview with Urgifi of *Cinematograph* (Dusseldorf), August 30, 1916, in Hanisch, *Ernst Lubitsch*.

Ferenc Molnár's 1910 play *A Testör* [*The Guardsman*], American edition, trans. Grace I. Colbron and Hans Bartsch, acting edition by Philip Moeller, foreword by Theresa Helburn (New York: Boni & Liveright, 1924). EL's *Know Your Enemy: Germany*: JM, *Frank Capra: The Catastrophe of Success* (New York: Simon & Schuster, 1992). EL costumed for *Where Do We Go from Here?*: photo in Weinberg, 3rd ed. The plays *Jacobowsky and the Colonel* by Franz Werfel and "American Play based on same" by S. N. Behrman were published in the same volume (New York: Random House, 1944).

Articles

Walter Benjamin on how nostalgia can be revolutionary: Terry Eagleton, "Waking the Dead," *New Statesman*, November 12, 2009. On how EL "registered the shock": Grafe. EL's article "American Cinematographers Superior Artists," *American Cinematographer*, December 1923. EL on "The modern movie" and "It is amazing": EL, "Our Chances in America," *Photo-stage*, May 17, 1924, written in April 1924, reprinted in Prinzler and Patalas. EL, "when I was a young man": Frank S. Nugent, "Movie Humor—No Laughing Matter," *NYT Magazine*, March 3, 1940. EL had expressed interest in filming *A Midsummer Night's Dream* before Max Reinhardt made it in 1935: *Motion Picture Classic*, 1934, AMPAS. Comolli's charge of anti-Semitism against EL: Jean-Louis Comolli, "*Der Stolz der Firma*," *Cahiers du Cinéma*, February 1968. Recollections of EL praying are from Hans Kräly quoted in Weinberg; Charles Van Enger quoted in Richard Koszarski, "Career in Shadows: Interview with Charles Van Enger," *Film History* 3, no. 3 (1989), which also contains the anecdote about EL having his acting bits printed up in rushes. John Ford's comment on EL acting out scenes for his cast is in JM's interview with Ford, "County Mayo Go Bragh . . . ," in JM, *Two Cheers for Hollywood*.

BW on paradox of EL's beginnings: Burt Prelutsky, "An Interview with Billy Wilder," *Michigan Quarterly Review* (Winter 1996), reprinted in Horton. Patalas on Eisner's attacks on EL as "Too Jewish-slapstick": Patalas, "*Trouble in Paradise*: Lubitsch Before the Touch," Criterion, criterion.com, January 6, 2003. Joel Rosenberg, "Shylock's Revenge: The Doubly Vanished Jew in Ernst Lubitsch's *To Be or Not to Be*," *Prooftexts* 16, no. 3 (September 1996). Descriptions of EL: Howe; and LeRoy in presenting his honorary Oscar in Scheuer, which also contains the reporter's description.

Other Sources

JM conversations with Nicola Lubitsch and Anton Kaes; JM interview with Gottfried Reinhardt on *Here Is Germany* for JM, *Frank Capra: The Catastrophe of Success*. Dedication ceremony (1992) of EL plaque at Berlin apartment building, 183 Schönhauser Allee: seen in Fischer documentary. The documentary includes Nicola's commentary on the firm of S. Lubitsch specializing in large women, on Simon Lubitsch as a model for Grandpa Van Cleve in *Heaven Can Wait*, and on autobiographical references in EL's work, as well as Evy Bettelheim-Bentley's commentary on the Lubitsch family (using audiotapes of Evy from the collection of Die Deutsche Kinemathek—Museum für Film und Fernsehen [The German Kinemathek—Museum for Film and Television]). JM 2014 visit to the Scheunenviertel neighborhood of Berlin, EL's birthplace, the Lubitsch family apartments, the former firm of S. Lubitsch, and the Max Reinhardt theaters, the Volksbühne Theater and the Deutsches Theater. JM interviews with tenants of the Lubitsch family apartment building and shops in the neighborhood (trans. Eszter Tompa, JM's guide in Berlin).

The Nazi propaganda film *The Eternal Jew*. Trailer for *The Shop Around the Corner*, on Warner Home Video, DVD, 2002. Bogdanovich on EL's work with actors: video introduction to Criterion DVD edition of *Trouble in Paradise*, 2003. EL's height is given in his Declarations of Intention (for American naturalization), U.S. Department of Labor, Naturalization Service, April 16, 1924, and June 23, 1933. T. S. Eliot, "The Love Song of J. Alfred Prufrock," *Poetry: A Magazine of Verse* (June 1915).

Press releases from AMPAS: EL autobiographical article, "I think it was music," "I like to laugh," "For 20 years," and "different stock companies," Paramount, March 25, 1938; "Those stories are pure fantasy," EL's claim that his parents encouraged his theatrical ambitions, "BIOGRAPHY OF ERNST LUBITSCH," studio unspecified, n.d. (1940s); EL on "In those days" and "more honest," "BIOGRAPHY OF ERNST LUBITSCH," studio unspecified, n.d. (1940s); "A small man," Twentieth Century-Fox, 1940s; "To be directed by Lubitsch" and EL on "If you make a study," studio unspecified, "BIOGRAPHY OF ERNST LUBITSCH," n.d., probably 1940s; Paramount description of EL as "the little man," February 3, 1938; EL "Especially famous," biography, unspecified studio, n.d., probably 1940s. Historian Dr. Jacob Rader Marcus on how German Jewish immigrants to America often "held Eastern Europeans in utter contempt": 1994 interview with JM for *Steven Spielberg: A Biography* (New York: Simon & Schuster, 1997).

CHAPTER 2: "WHO IS ERNST LUBITSCH?"

Books

Kracauer on *Madame DuBarry* (*Passion*) and EL's other spectacles as well as his German satires. EL's German style: Thompson; Hake. Expressionism and films in Weimar period: Kaes, Jay, and Dimenberg; Saunders; Weitz; Eisner on German cinema and expressionism in that era. UFA history: Kreimeier, including his report on German president Friedrich Ebert's visit to the set of *Anna Boleyn* in September 1920, with quote from Paul Eipper, from his *Tagebuch: Ateliergespräche mit Liebermann und Corinth* [*Diary: Atelier Talks with Liebermann and Corinth*], Munich, 1971.

Anti-German threats to EL in U.S. in 1921: "German Director, Lubitsch, Regarded Unkindly, He Says," *Variety*, February 3, 1922, cited in Petrie. EL calling *Kohlhiesel's Daughters* "typical German" and reference to that film, *The Oyster Princess*, and *The Doll* as his "most outstanding" German comedies: EL 1947 to Weinberg, which also includes his comments on *When I Was Dead*, the servant pacing the floor in *The Oyster Princess*, and *Montmartre* (the U.S. release version of *Die Flamme*). American films' influence on German cinema: Thompson. Influence of Mauritz Stiller's *Erotikon* on EL, and BW reporting what EL told him about it ("learned everything"): Crowe; see also BW's comments in Karasek. UFA history: Horak; Kreimeier.

Preview party for *Carmen*: Negri, *Memoirs of a Star* (a story told somewhat differently by Hanisch in Fischer's documentary). BW's reason for not casting Negri in *Sunset Blvd.*: Zolotow; Sikov. Eisner on EL's vulgarity: Weinberg. Raphaelson's "We just laughed our heads off": quoted in Eyman. Renoir regarding EL and "Berlin style": his 1967 letter to Weinberg. The life and death of Anne Boleyn: Susan Bordo, *The Creation of Anne Boleyn: A New Look at England's Most Notorious Queen* (New York: Houghton Mifflin Harcourt, 2013). Horak on *Anna Boleyn*. Petrie on Henny Porten. William Dean Howells to Edith Wharton on "What the American public always wants": Wharton, *A Backward Glance* (New York: D. Appleton-Century, 1934). Costs of D. W. Griffith films, 1915–1921: Richard Schickel, *D. W. Griffith: An American Life* (New York: Simon & Schuster, 1984). Simon Lubitsch "nearly in tears": Kräly's EL tribute in Weinberg.

Articles

"With the popularity": *Photo-stage*, May 1915; advertisement about EL, *Photo-stage*, June 1915. "Through Lubitsch": *Cinematographer*, quoted in Prinzler and Patalas. UFA (Universum Film AG), EFA (the Europäische Film-Allianz), and EL's filmmaking in Germany with Paul Davidson et al.: Stefan Drössler, "Ernst Lubitsch and EFA," *Film History* 21, no. 3 (2009). *Deception* (*Anna Boleyn*) publicity claiming EL was Bohemian: "Screen People and Plays," *NYT*, April 3, 1921. Drössler includes information on *Madame DuBarry* (*Passion*) advertised in New York without mentioning German origin (see also "Screen People and Plays," *NYT*, December 12, 1920, and advertisement for the film in same issue); protest of *The Cabinet of Dr. Caligari* in Los Angeles (see also "Riot over German Feature Picture: *Cabinet of Caligari* Egged on Coast," *Variety*, May 13, 1921); *Variety*'s claim EL was Polish (May 13, 1921); and EL's plans to adapt films by Viennese authors, citing "Deutschland-Oesterreich," *Der Film*, May 13, 1922. EL's plan to make *The Merry Wives of Windsor*: Prinzler and Patalas, citing note in *Photo-stage*, June 18, 1921.

Jan-Christopher Horak discusses the low cost of EL's German pictures in "Sauerkraut & Sausages with a Little Goulash: Germans in Hollywood, 1927," *Film History* 17, no. 2/3, The Year 1927 (2005).

EL, "No one will be surprised": EL, "My Two Years in America," *Motion Picture Magazine*, December 1924. EL's letter from Hollywood ("It is amazing"): "Our Chances in America," *Photo-stage*, Berlin, May 17, 1924, written April 1924, reprinted in Prinzler and Patalas. *Photoplay* on *Die Flamme*: Howe. *Variety* review of *Montmartre* (*Die Flamme*), July 9, 1924. EL on Negri as "savage": May Allison Quirk, "'All Women Are Sirens at Heart,' says Mister Lubitsch," *Photoplay*, August 1933. EL and earthquake: 1945 clipping, no source indicated, AMPAS. EL, "To come to America": "America Is Dream of European Artists, Says Lubitsch," *Exhibitors Herald*, January 14, 1922. EL, "Now I can make bigger productions": "Der deutsche Film in 1921," *Der Film*, January 8, 1921, translated in Drössler.

EL directing *Das Weib des Pharao* (*The Wife of Pharaoh*): John Walker Harrington, "Lubitsch, Master of Mobs," *NYT*, January 8, 1922. Friedrich Ebert at December 1, 1921, reception for *The Wife of Pharaoh*: Drössler. Alfred Rosenthal review of *The Wife of Pharaoh*: "Jannings contra Jannings," *Berliner Lokal-Anzeiger*, supplement *Film-Echo*, March 20, 1922, quoted in Drössler. *Variety* review of *The Loves of Pharaoh*: Rush, March 3, 1922; Dave Kehr review of restored version of *The Wife of Pharaoh*: *NYT*, October 18, 2012; Jan-Christopher Horak, "*The Loves of Pharaoh* (1921)," September 16, 2011, UCLA Film & Television Archive blog, cinema.ucla.edu; JM conversation with Drössler about his restoration work on the film. *Pharaoh* advertised as "THE MASTER WORK": *NYT*, Criterion Theater, March 5, 1922. Kurt Pinthus review of *Die Flamme*: *Das Tage-Buch*, September 22, 1923. EL, "To come to America": *Exhibitors Herald*, January 1922. EL, "Whoever continues," criticizing "politico-economic stupidities," "It is amazing," and "costume dramas" in his 1924 article "Film Internationality." EL, "Must film be art": EL, "Uns fehlen Filmdichtungen" ["We Lack Film Poetry"], *Das Tage-Buch*, September 11, 1920, trans. Alex H. Bush, reprinted in Kaes, Baer, and Cowan. EL first visit to U.S.: "Steamer Brings 15 German Diplomats . . . Foreign Movie Men Arrive," *NYT*, December 25, 1921. EL on Chaplin, "The best of all": Howe; EL on the influence of *A Woman of Paris*, "a marvelous production": "Lubitsch on Directing," *NYT*, December 16, 1923.

Other Sources

JM interview of Jean Douchet. Footage of President Ebert on the set of *Anna Boleyn* in 1920: Fischer documentary, also viewable at britishpathe.com. Evy Bettelheim-Bentley on EL as "absolutely apolitical": Fischer. Welles on Negri: his comments to JM and others on the set of *The Other Side of the Wind* (1970–1976). JM interview with Drössler on EL's "serious" projects and German career. EL characterization of German cinema ("the colossal"): Paramount press release by EL on national cinemas, December 10, 1936, AMPAS.

National Archives and Records Administration (NARA) U.S. immigration records for EL: Declaration of Intention for American citizenship, April 16, 1924 (U.S. Department of Labor, Naturalization Service), and June 23, 1933 (Department of Labor, Immigration and Naturalization Service [INS]); Petition for Naturalization, October 14, 1935 (INS); certificate of U.S. citizenship issued January 24, 1936 (U.S. District Court, Los Angeles). EL's December 3, 1922, departure to America with wife Helena or Helene ("Leni") Sonnet Kraus, and Heinz ("Henry") Blanke, and EL's marriage to Leni: EL's Petitions for Naturalization and Leni's Petition for Citizenship (INS), December 4, 1930 (also containing biographical information on her); Blanke accompanying them to America: his Declaration of Intention for naturalization (Department of Labor Naturalization Service), April 26, 1924; see also Eyman. BW living in Schöneberg: Wikipedia entry for Schöneberg.

CHAPTER 3: THE "BERLIN STYLE" IN HOLLYWOOD

Books

Renoir, "Berlin style": his 1967 letter in Weinberg. EL, "That's finished": to journalist Bella Fromm, quoted in her book *Blood and Banquets: A Berlin Social Diary* (London: Geoffrey Bles, 1943; New York, Garden City Publishing, 1944). EL contract with Warner Bros. 1923: quoted in Eyman. Thompson's "Epilogue: The Lubitsch Touch," on evolution of the phrase, quoting various sources, including the *NYT* review of *Anna Boleyn* (*Deception*), April 18, 1921; on *Lady Windermere's Fan*, *Film Daily*, December 6, 1925; and on *Three Women*, Charles S. Sewell, *Moving Picture World*, September 27, 1924.

EL, "We are groping" (on Chaplin), to unspecified interviewer in December 1923: quoted by Eyman. The influence of Stiller's *Erotikon* on EL: BW in Crowe; Howe; Petrie; and Weinberg on the influences of Chaplin and Stiller on EL. Hollywood censorship from early 1920s onward: books including Doherty; Lewis; and Koszarski. Background on *A Woman of Paris* shooting, release, and censorship from David Robinson's biography *Chaplin: His Life and Art* (New York: McGraw-Hill, 1985). Adolphe Menjou, "Because of the censorship," from Menjou and M. M. Musselman, *It Took Nine Tailors* (New York: McGraw-Hill, 1948).

Mary Pickford complains about EL in her autobiography, *Sunshine and Shadow*, and in Brownlow, *The Parade's Gone By . . .* Pickford's later antipathy to *Rosita* is also discussed in Brownlow's *Mary Pickford Rediscovered: Rare Pictures of a Hollywood Legend* (New York: Harry N. Abrams, in association with the Academy of Motion Picture Arts and Sciences, 1999), and in the introduction by Robert Cushman. Pickford's hiring of EL, disagreements over *Dorothy Vernon of Haddon Hall* and *Marguerite and Faust* (a.k.a. *Faust*) projects, anti-German protests against her hiring of EL, their relationship on *Rosita*, and her changing views of him: Pickford; Brownlow books; Eyman, *Ernst Lubitsch*; and Eyman, *Mary Pickford: America's Sweetheart* (New York: Donald I. Fine, 1990), also including Mitchell Leisen's story about EL on set of *Rosita*.

Pickford's letters to her attorney Dennis F. ("Cap") O'Brien on EL, quoted in Eyman, *Ernst Lubitsch*, which discusses EL's loan-out clause to work for Pickford in his

August 1923 Warner Bros. contract and quotes a letter from Pickford to EL, May 29, 1926, about his helping her on *Sparrows*. Information on United Artists (cofounded by Pickford): Tino Balio's books *United Artists, Volume 1, 1919–1950: The Company Built by the Stars* (Madison: University of Wisconsin Press, 1976), and *United Artists: The Company that Changed the Film Industry* (Madison: University of Wisconsin Press, 1987). Henry Blanke on EL feeling he was in "factory system": quoted in Eyman, *Ernst Lubitsch*. Pola Negri's friction with EL on *Die Flamme* was reported by Van Enger in Koszarski's interview.

Alfred Hitchcock defines the "MacGuffin" in Truffaut, with the collaboration of Helen Scott, *Hitchcock* (New York: Simon & Schuster, 1967), originally published as *Le Cinéma selon Alfred Hitchcock* [*The Cinema According to Alfred Hitchcock*] (Paris: Éditions Robert Laffont, 1966). Robin Wood on Hitchcock and "Pure Cinema": *Hitchcock's Films Revisited*, revised ed. (New York: Columbia University Press, 2002). Yasujiro Ozu influenced by EL and *The Marriage Circle* in particular: Donald Richie, *Ozu* (Berkeley: University of California Press, 1974); and David Bordwell, *Ozu and the Poetics of Cinema* (London: British Film Institute, Princeton, N.J.: Princeton University Press, 1988). Douglas Sirk on EL and *The Marriage Circle*: Jon Halliday, *Sirk on Sirk: Interviews with Jon Halliday* (London: Secker & Warburg, 1971; New York: Viking Press, 1972). Charles Chaplin's admiration for EL: Chaplin, *My Autobiography* (London: The Bodley Head, New York: Simon & Schuster, 1964). Oscar Wilde on "the one charm of marriage": *The Picture of Dorian Gray* (London: Ward, Lock, 1891). EL on *Heaven Can Wait*: EL's 1947 letter to Weinberg. Comments on *The Marriage Circle*: Petrie; Saunders. How EL "decided to make American audiences laugh" about sex: Weinberg. EL's conflict with George Cukor on *One Hour with You*: Sabath; Gavin Lambert, *On Cukor* (New York: Putnam, 1972), and rev. ed., ed. Robert Trachtenberg (New York: Rizzoli, 2000).

"It is so easy": G. K. Chesterton, "The Case for the Ephemeral" in *All Things Considered* (New York: John Lane, 1908). Screenwriter Paul Bern: Samuel Marx and Joyce Vanderveen, *Deadly Illusions: Jean Harlow and the Murder of Paul Bern* (New York: Random House, 1990); and E. J. Fleming, *Paul Bern: The Life and Famous Death of the MGM Director and Husband of Harlow* (Jefferson, NC: McFarland, 2009), with EL quote "Everybody is divorced" from his interview with the *Los Angeles Evening Herald Express*, June 30, 1930. Douglas Fairbanks Jr. quoting EL's comment "doors [are] as important": Weinberg. On "Lubitsch's greatness": Haskell. Aristotle's discussion of comedy in his *Poetics: On the Art of Poetry*, trans. Ingram Bywater, with preface by Gilbert Murray (Oxford: Clarendon Press, 1920).

Articles

EL on his final trip to Germany, 1932–1933, "visited the European studios": Barney Hutchison, "Hollywood Still Leads . . . Says Ernst Lubitsch," *American Cinematographer*, March 1933. On "Herr Ernst Lubitsch": *Motion Picture Herald*, November 1933. Germany revoking EL citizenship: see notes for Introduction; also see EL's U.S. immigration records cited in notes for chap. 2. Weinberg's conversation with EL in 1928: "A Tribute to Lubitsch, with a Letter in Which Lubitsch Appraises His Own Career," reprinted in Weinberg. Comments on *Deception* (*Anna Boleyn*): "Brought into Focus," *NYT*, April 24, 1921. EL on Chaplin as "one of the greatest artists": Robert Grosvenor, "Ernst Lubitsch Looks at Life and the Cinema," *Cinema Art* (October 1927).

"It's a little bit mean" and "wants to do modern stories": Howe. Complex loan-out arrangement of EL to Pickford and actors in screen tests for *Marguerite and Faust* (a.k.a. *Faust*) project: Drössler. Henry Blanke, "How many more": quoted in Eyman, *Ernst Lubitsch*. EL on *The Marriage Circle*, "I experienced a great change": "Lubitsch on Directing," *NYT*, December 16, 1923. EL's loan to Pickford, Negri arriving in Hollywood before EL and doing *The Spanish Dancer* after planning to star in his German version, *Karneval in Toledo*: Drössler; see also Negri. Pickford on hiring EL for *Rosita*: Edwin Schallert, "The New Mary Pickford: As Rosita She Is Doing Up Her Curls and Essaying a Real Grown-Up Heroine," *Picture Play*, July 1923. EL on America and "Aladdin's lamps": his article "My Two Years in America." EL on Douglas Fairbanks as Mephistopheles and "Pollyannas": Harry Carr, "The 'No' Man Comes to Hollywood," *Motion Picture*, July 1923. Reviews of *Rosita*: *Film Daily*, September 9, 1923; *Exceptional Photoplays*, October–November 1923; *Pictures and Picturegoer*, March 1924. Early Pickford complaint about *Rosita*: James R. Quirk, "The Public Just Won't Let Mary Pickford Grow Up," *Photoplay*, September 1925; *Photoplay* calls *Rosita* a flop: Fred James, "Famous Film Flops," October 1933. EL on Pickford in 1933: M. A. Quirk. EL on the differences in the "moral slant" and censorship in Europe and the U.S.: "Lauds Producing Here," *NYT*, September 18, 1927.

On Hollywood censorship from the 1920s onward: Gregory D. Black, "Hollywood Censored: The Production Code Administration and the Hollywood Film Industry, 1930–1940," *Film History* 3 (1989); Maureen Furniss, "Handslapping in Hollywood: The Production Code's Influence on the 'Lubitsch Touch,'" *Spectator: The University of Southern California Journal of Film & Television* (Fall 1990).

EL on *A Woman of Paris*, "nobody's intelligence is insulted": see notes for previous chapter. Dave Kehr on *Rosita* restoration: "MoMA's Race to Preserve Film Classics," *CBS News*, February 27, 2016, cbs.news.com; Kehr emails to JM on the restoration and Pickford's attitude toward the film, July 10, 11, 12, 23, November 3, 10, 2017 (also on the restoration of *Forbidden Paradise*). EL on *Rosita*, "I have made": 1943 EL interview with Hedda Hopper quoted in Eyman, *Ernst Lubitsch*. *Variety* report on *Rosita* boxoffice: Petrie, citing article of February 14, 1924.

EL on making "all kinds of concessions" and wanting "to please Lubitsch": Harry Carr, *Motion Picture Classic*, November 1924, quoted in Petrie. EL on *The Marriage Circle*, "in this mixup": "When Women Bluff," *NYT*, March 30, 1924. Hitchcock on EL and *The Marriage Circle*: "A Tribute to Lubitsch 1892–1947," *Action*, DGA, November–December 1967, reprinted in Weinberg. EL on Florence Vidor: M. A. Quirk. EL "the hardest task" from his article "The Motion Picture Is the Youngest of All the Muses," in *The Truth about the Movies by the Stars*, ed. Laurence A. Hughes (Hollywood: Hollywood Publishers, 1924), quoted in Thompson. Marie Prevost interview with Harry Carr, *Motion Picture Classic*, February 1924, quoted by Petrie; Prevost's death: Dixie Laite, "Marie Prevost—The Movie Star Eaten by Her Dog (Or Was She?)," September 4, 2013, Dametown (blog), dametown.com. Reviewers on *The Marriage Circle*: *Photoplay*, quoted by Eyman; and Robert E. Sherwood, *Life*, October 1924, in his review of *Three Women*, quoted by Weinberg. EL on *The Marriage Circle* in *Film Daily*, 1927, quoted by Eyman. *Moving Picture World* review quoted in Petrie.

Other Sources

EL returning from last trip to Germany in 1932–1933: leaving Bremen on SS *Europa* January 6, 1933, and arriving New York January 12: "Passenger and Crew Lists of Vessels Arriving at New York, New York, 1897–1957" (National Archives). U.S. immigration records for EL: see notes for chap. 1. Chaplin script drafts, original title card "All of us," and comments by Michael Powell in the documentary *Chaplin Today: "A Woman of Paris"* (dir. Mathias Ledoux, 2003), on the 2004 DVD set of *A King in New York/A Woman of Paris*, Warner Home Video. *Marguerite and Faust* (a.k.a. *Faust*) screen tests, 1923, directed by EL for the Mary Pickford Company, based on the play by Johann Wolfgang von Goethe, preserved by the Library of Congress, available on the 2015 Kino Lorber edition of F. W. Murnau's 1926 German film, *Faust*; EL's screen tests were preserved by the Library of Congress Motion Picture Conservation Center, print funded by the Society for Cinephiles, Hollywood. Notes by Joseph Yranski, "About the Screen Tests," on the 2009 Kino International DVD edition of Murnau's *Faust*.

EL on Pickford, "the most practical artist": Paramount press release written by EL, March 25, 1938, AMPAS. Renoir on the interactive nature of films: "La Recherche du relatif" ["The Search for Relativity"] in the 1967 Jacques Rivette television documentary series *Jean Renoir le patron* [*Jean Renoir the Boss*], filmed in 1966 for the series *Cinéastes de notre temps*, quoted in *Renoir on Renoir: Interviews, Essays, and Remarks*, trans. Carol Volk (New York: Cambridge University Press, 1989).

CHAPTER 4: TIN CANS IN A WAREHOUSE?

Books

EL, "a tin can" to Raphaelson, and discussing his life achievement: "Freundschaft." Oscar Wilde, *Lady Windermere's Fan: A Play about a Good Woman*, 1892 (London: Elkin Mathews & John Lane, 1893). Sarris on *Broken Blossoms* in *The American Cinema*. Pickford on EL as "a man's director": Brownlow, *The Parade's Gone By . . .* The "woman taken in adultery" parable is found in John chap. 8, King James Bible. The *Kiss Me Again* source play by Victorien Sardou and Emile de Najac, *Divorçons!* [*Let's Get a Divorce*], 1880

(Paris: Calmann-Lévy, 1883). Weinberg quotes critics on EL's *Lady Windermere's Fan*: Ted Shane, *New Yorker*, December 12, 1925; and Georges Sadoul, *Histoire du Cinéma Mondial* [*History of the World Cinema*] (Paris: Editions Flammarion, 1959). EL 1947 letter to Weinberg, lists *Kiss Me Again* among his favorites.

Eyman, *Ernst Lubitsch*, discusses EL's frictions with Warner Bros. over his profitability and quotes telegrams by Harry Warner and EL and Harry's letter to his brother Albert ("Abe"), as well as Andrew Marton on *The Student Prince in Old Heidelberg*. EL on "*Old Heidelberg* is something new for me" and "I tried for simplicity": Weinberg quoting unsourced interviews. Norma Shearer's working relationship with EL: Gavin Lambert, *Norma Shearer: A Life* (New York: Knopf, 1990). The "haphazard" release of *So This Is Paris*: Thompson. Raphaelson saying that EL "liked women who treated him badly" and "To think that I should be remembered": quoted by Eyman, *Ernst Lubitsch*. Material on the coming of sound is from Brownlow, *The Parade's Gone By . . .* ; and Eyman, *The Speed of Sound: Hollywood and the Talkie Revolution 1926–1930* (New York: Simon & Schuster, 1997). Henry Koster's claim that EL "insisted that [Hans] Kräly become blacklisted": interviewed by Irene Kahn Atkins, *Henry Koster: A Directors Guild of America Oral History* (Metuchen, NJ: DGA and Scarecrow Press, 1987). Susan Orlean's claim that Rin Tin Tin received the most votes for best actor in the first Academy Awards, not Emil Jannings: *Rin Tin Tin: The Life and the Legend* (New York: Simon & Schuster, 2011).

Articles

EL, "Sound revolutionized": Grace Wilcox, "Lubitsch—A Genius Who Makes Stars Shine," unidentified magazine, n.d. (1930s), AMPAS. Pickford's comment "It would have been more logical": Anne O'Hare McCormick, "Searching for the Mind of Hollywood: An Inquiry into the Influences Molding the Vast Flow of Motion Pictures," *NYT Magazine*, December 13, 1931, quoted at the end of Brownlow, *The Parade's Gone By . . .* Pickford on "Talking pictures": AP, "Mary Pickford Sees Talkies as Lipstick on Milo," *LAT*, March 18, 1934. EL on Chaplin and his regard for Griffith's *Broken Blossoms*: Howe.

Sources on survival and restoration of *Forbidden Paradise*: see chap. 3 notes and cinematheque.fr, silentera.com, and nitrateville.com; the missing scene of the czarina's hair being bobbed: described in review by Hall, *NYT*, November 17, 1924. Reviews of *Kiss Me Again*: Shane, *New Yorker*, August 1, 1925; Richard Watts, *Theatre Magazine*, 1925; Matthew Josephson, "Masters of the Motion Picture," *Motion Picture Classic*, August 1926, on *Kiss Me Again* and EL using pantomime. EL on planning his films and trying "to exclude titles wherever possible": "Lubitsch on Directing." EL on *Lady Windermere's Fan* and adapting Wilde to the screen, "Playing with words": "Spurns Screen Epigrams," *NYT*, December 27, 1925; Koszarski's interview with Van Enger discusses the Toronto filming.

Hall's *NYT* review "Mr. Lubitsch in Old Heidelberg," September 25, 1927, of *The Student Prince in Old Heidelberg* gives the title that way as well as calling the film *The Student Prince (in Old Heidelberg)* and *In Old Heidelberg: The Student Prince*. Legal dispute about rights acquisition: "War on Film Rights to 'Old Heidelberg,'" *NYT*, June 1, 1927; "Buys Rights to 'Student Prince,'" *NYT*, June 17, 1927. EL on location shooting in Germany: "Lauds Producing Here." Interview with EL about wanting to do "serious pictures": Grosvenor. Murder of Ramón Novarro, 1968: William Van Meter, "The Hustlers and the Movie Star," May 23, 2012, out.com.

EL on *The Patriot* as "A daring experiment": Andre Sennwald, "A Word with Ernst Lubitsch," *NYT*, October 14, 1934. Reviews of *The Patriot*: *Variety*, December 31, 1927; Hall, *NYT*, August 18, 1928; and Richard Watts, *New York Herald Tribune*, quoted in Weinberg. EL not involved in the addition of sound to the film: Weinberg; Jannings's objections to dubbing of dialogue: Carringer and Sabath; *Variety*, April 24, 1929. EL wanted to remake *The Patriot* with Charles Laughton: "Eastward Hies Herr Lubitsch," *NYT*, March 1, 1936. *The Last Command* and EL's claim to have suggested the original story: Sidney Skolsky column, "Fade Out—Fade In," June 3, 1941, unidentified newspaper, AMPAS; Carringer and Sabath; Eyman. Leni Lubitsch's quote about EL being "99 percent in love with his work": "Lubitsches Are Divorced," *NYT*, June 24, 1930. Article quoting EL, Leni, and Kräly about their October 1930 fracas and her feelings on the marriage: unidentified printed source, c. 1930, AMPAS; see also Eyman, *Ernst Lubitsch* for details. Academy Awards ceremonies information: AMPAS website, oscars.org.

Other Sources

The coming of sound: Kevin Brownlow and David Gill, "End of an Era" segment of the *Hollywood* TV documentary series, Thames Television (UK), 1980. Capra's comparison of movies to newspapers, interview with JM for *Frank Capra: The Catastrophe of Success*. Information on the production of *Lady Windermere's Fan* in a booklet with notes by Scott Simmon in *More Treasures from American Film Archives, 1894–1931*, National Film Preservation Foundation DVD boxed set, Image Entertainment, 2004; that set also includes the trailer for *The Patriot*. JM watched several surviving minutes of *The Patriot* in 35 mm at the Munich Film Museum. EL's comment "I think I am possessed": Paramount press release written by EL, March 25, 1938, AMPAS.

CHAPTER 5: "GIVE ME A MOMENT, PLEASE"

Books

Film industry transition to sound: see sources in previous chapter; also Edward Bernds, *Mr. Bernds Goes to Hollywood: My Early Life and Career in Sound Recording at Columbia with Frank Capra and Others*, with introduction by JM, interview by JM and Leonard Maltin (Lanham, MD: Scarecrow Press, 1999). Raphaelson loathed the film of his play *The Jazz Singer*: Sabath. Raphaelson enamored of *The Love Parade*: Weinberg and Raphaelson books. Hitchcock on "pictures of people talking": Truffaut, *Hitchcock*. Sergei

Eisenstein, Vsevolod Pudovkin, and Gregori Alexandrov, "A Statement," trans. and ed. Jay Leyda in Eisenstein's *Film Form* (New York: Harcourt, Brace, and World, 1949). Tom Milne on EL and Rouben Mamoulian: *Rouben Mamoulian*, British Film Institute Cinema One series (London: Thames & Hudson, 1969).

EL and Cukor conflict on *One Hour with You*: see notes for chap. 3. *The Merry Widow*, adapted from the German of Victor Léon and Leo Stein, music by Franz Lehár, lyrics by Adrian Ross (New York: Chappell, 1907), originally titled *Die lustige Witwe*, premiered in 1905 and was first published in 1906 by Doblinger, Vienna. EL's musicals and the "dominant social order": Paul.

New Production Code arrival on July 15, 1934, influenced by the formation of the Catholic Legion of Decency: Doherty. BW on EL's style and whether audience might accept it again: JM 1974 article "Shooting *The Front Page*: Two Damns and One By God." The preproduction and script process on *The Merry Widow* is detailed in Sabath, who also discusses EL's gradual agreeing to do the film, Chevalier's friction with MGM and EL, and the production process. Eyman, *Ernst Lubitsch*, details production costs and losses of EL's Paramount films. *La veuve joyeuse* had another director and a French dialogue director: Edward Everett Horton interview in Bernard Rosenberg and Harry Silverstein, *The Real Tinsel* (New York: MacMillan, 1970); the others are unnamed, but EL gets the credit in MGM records, according to Sabath. Cost and loss of *The Merry Widow*: Carringer and Sabath, citing Samuel Marx, *Mayer and Thalberg: The Make-Believe Saints* (New York: Random House, 1975); Anita Loos on script doctoring: her book *Kiss Hollywood Good-by* (New York: Viking Press, 1974).

Other information on Chevalier: Chevalier, *I Remember It Well*, preface by Marcel Pagnol, trans. Cornelia Higginson (New York: Macmillan, 1970), originally published as *Môme à Cheveux Blancs* [*The Kid Has White Hair*] (Paris: Presses de la Cité, 1969); Michael Freedland, *Maurice Chevalier* (New York: Morrow, 1981); and Edward Behr, *The Good Frenchman: The True Story of the Life and Times of Maurice Chevalier* (New York: Villard Books, 1993). William Paul on EL musicals. BW on "Breakfast Time" song in *The Smiling Lieutenant*: Zolotow. EL on "pure style" and *Trouble in Paradise*: his 1947 letter to Weinberg.

Articles

Before making *The Smiling Lieutenant*, EL had planned to film the Oscar Straus operetta *Ein Walzertraum* (*A Waltz Dream*) in Germany (1922) and Hollywood (1925) as a silent: Drössler, citing *Lichtbild-Bühne*, September 23, 1922; and Carringer and Sabath, citing *Moving Picture World*, April 18, 1925. Kristin Thompson, "Early Sound Counterpoint," *Yale French Studies* no. 60, *Film/Sound* (1980). Sarris on *Love Me Tonight* and *The Merry Widow*: "Lubitsch in the Thirties: All Talking! All Singing! All Lubitsch!: Part II"; and on *The Smiling Lieutenant*: "Lubitsch in the Thirties: Part One."

The 1934 Production Code and its influence on the postproduction of *The Merry Widow*: Joseph I. Breen to Will H. Hays on the film, October 22, 1934, quoted in Furniss.

Censorship of *The Merry Widow*, the Legion of Decency's condemnation of *Design for Living*, and the PCA's denial of reissue seals for EL films: Furniss; Black. Chevalier-EL tension preceding *The Merry Widow*: "Peace Sought in Film Row," unidentified newspaper, October 16, 1933, AMPAS. EL "One gets tired": Scheuer. Kenneth White's analysis of *The Love Parade* in "The Style of Ernst Lubitsch," *Hound & Horn* (January–March 1931), quoted in Weinberg. EL on the dangers presented by the stricter Code: Sennwald, "A Word with Ernst Lubitsch." Interview with EL about his job as Paramount production chief: D. W. C. [Douglas W. Churchill], "Lubitsch at the Helm," *NYT*, March 31, 1935; also see Elsa Schallert, "Is Ernst Lubitsch—on Trial?," *LAT*, December 15, 1935.

Other Sources

Brownlow and Gill, "End of an Era." JM interview with Douchet on how EL "invented the musical." JM interviews with Hawks, Capra, Mamoulian, and Bernds on the transition from silents to sound for *Frank Capra: The Catastrophe of Success*. Jack Buchanan character in *The Band Wagon* modeled on Welles: JM heard director Vincente Minnelli say this at a Directors Guild of America tribute to his work. MoMA 16 mm release of "Beyond the Blue Horizon" sequence from *Monte Carlo* in the 1960s. Original ending of *One Hour with You*: quoted in Sabath. Jason S. Joy of Studio Relations Committee on *Trouble in Paradise* and "the light Lubitsch touch": letter to Harold Hurley, Paramount Publix Corp., July 21, 1932, in PCA file on the film at AMPAS. BW explains to AFI students the nature of the Lubitsch Touch, using the *Merry Widow* sword belt gag as an example: 1976 seminar, video excerpt on YouTube. John Ford to Bogdanovich on the difference between making talking pictures and silents: Bogdanovich's 1971/2006 documentary *Directed by John Ford*. EL on exiting production executive role and returning to directing with *Angel*: two Paramount press releases, February 1937, AMPAS. Paramount on EL and "The women in his pictures": press release, February 1938, AMPAS.

CHAPTER 6: "IN TIMES LIKE THESE . . ."

Books

The screenplay of *Trouble in Paradise* is in Raphaelson's book along with two other scripts (see above) and his essay "Freundschaft." Background on Raphaelson, his hiring for *The Man I Killed*, and other information about his collaboration and friendship with EL is from that book; and Sabath. Also see Raphaelson, *The Human Nature of Playwriting* (New York: Macmillan, 1949); and Raphaelson's plays *Accent on Youth* (1934), with preface by John Anderson (New York: Samuel French, 1935); *Skylark* (New York: Dramatists Play Service, 1939); *Jason* (1941) (New York: Random House, 1942). Pauline Kael on Raphaelson: her introduction to his *Three Screen Comedies*.

Raphaelson quotes: EL "wrote some of my best," "From the first," "rampages of invention," "He loved," *"terrific,"* and "What the hell": "Freundschaft"; "The nature of our quarrel" over *The Man I Killed*: Harvey; EL "thought like a writer" and citing EL on "How do ve get into it?": interview with Weinberg; canal gag and "Now other times": Sabath, quoting auto-biographical transcripts, Raphaelson Collection, University Archives, University of Illinois at Urbana-Champagne; "The so-called happy ending" and "He made me realize": Eyman, *Ernst Lubitsch*; *Trouble* "just another job" and the writer's preference for *Heaven* and *Shop*: 1973 interview by Carringer, quoted in Eyman, *Ernst Lubitsch*; "rushed back," "How did," "What an emptiness," and citing EL's discussion with him about "tin can in warehouse": Raphaelson, "Freundschaft"; and why the writer passed on adapting *Design for Living*: auto-biographical transcripts quoted in Sabath. EL, "Friends frequently ask me": Paramount press release written by EL, November 1937.

Wilde, "It is only shallow people": *The Picture of Dorian Gray*. Michelangelo, "Trifles make perfection": J. K. Hoyt and K. L. Roberts, *Hoyt's New Cyclopedia of Practical Quotations* (New York, Funk & Wagnalls, 1922). Welles seeing *Trouble* and pursuing Raphaelson: Patrick McGilligan, *Young Orson: The Years of Luck and Genius on the Path to "Citizen Kane"* (New York: HarperCollins, 2015). Welles on EL in interview with Bogdanovich: Wellesnet.com, quoting previously unpublished material for Welles and Bogdanovich, *This Is Orson Welles*, ed. Jonathan Rosenbaum (New York: HarperCollins, 1992); in that volume, all that remains is "I think more highly of Lubitsch all the time"; the book quotes Welles discussing his original ending for *The Magnificent Ambersons*. The source play for EL's *The Man I Killed*: Maurice Rostand, *L'homme que j'ai tué* [*The Man I Killed*] (Paris: Flammarion, 1925), was adapted by the playwright into a novel published in 1936 by J. Ferenczi et fils in Paris. Hawks on his contributions to the scripts of his films: JM, *Hawks on Hawks* (Berkeley: University of California Press, 1982; Lexington: University Press of Kentucky, 2013). Melchior Lengyel on writing for EL is quoted in Eyman, *Ernst Lubitsch*. Gottfried Reinhardt on EL as film editor: quoted in Eyman, *Ernst Lubitsch*.

More on *Trouble*: Paul; film not approved for theatrical reissue by PCA in 1935: *AFI Catalog of Feature Films*, afi.com/members/catalog; Aaron Schuster on film's political dimensions and modern relevance in his 2014 essay "Comedy in Times of Austerity," in Novak, Krečič, and Dolar. Harvey on *The Man I Killed*; Paramount changing title to *Broken Lullaby*: *AFI Catalog of Feature Films*; Carringer and Sabath. Hitchcock's way of working on scripts: Bill Krohn, *Hitchcock at Work* (London: Phaidon, 2000) and new edition (London: Phaidon, 2003); and Patrick McGilligan, *Alfred Hitchcock: A Life in Darkness and Light* (New York: HarperCollins, 2003). Ernest Hemingway, *The Sun Also Rises* (New York: Scribner's, 1926). On Ozu's fondness for EL's films: Richie; Bordwell (Bordwell quotes Komatsu Kitamura's report on working with Ozu). Josef Goebbels's protests against the film of *All Quiet on the Western Front*: Lally.

Noël Coward play *Design for Living* (London: Heinemann, 1933). EL's version was approved partly because of the "No sex!" and "gentleman's agreement" lines: Dr. James Wingate, director of the Studio Relations Office of the AMPP, to Will H. Hays, president of the MPPDA, June 26, 1933, cited in *AFI Catalog of Feature Films*. *Design* cut by fourteen minutes after being previewed: *AFI Catalog of Feature Films*; banned for reissue 1935 by PCA: Smedley. Haskell on the film: *From Reverence to Rape*. "Never trust the artist": D. H. Lawrence, *Studies in Classic American Literature* (New York: Thomas Seltzer, 1923). Budget of *Design for Living*: Eyman, *Ernst Lubitsch*.

Articles

Truffaut, "Lubitsch Was a Prince." Jacques Rivette on Hawks: "Genie de Howard Hawks," *Cahiers du Cinéma*, May 1953, trans. Russell Campbell and Marvin Pister [JM], adapted from a translation by Adrian Brine in *Movie* (December 1962), and published as "The Genius of Howard Hawks" in JM, ed., *Focus on Howard Hawks* (Englewood Cliffs, NJ: Prentice-Hall, 1972). Wilde on style and on "soul and body": "Phrases and Philosophies for the Use of the Young," *Chameleon*, Oxford University Student Publication (December 1894). EL on Miriam Hopkins and "I hope your heart": M. A. Quirk article, also the source of her comment "he knows more." *Variety* report on *Trouble* preview, with EL comment on Marshall: October 18, 1932, quoted in Sabath. Gaston Monescu supposedly inspired by Georges Manolescu and Thomas Mann works inspired by him: Wikipedia entries for Manolescu, *Trouble in Paradise*, and *Confessions of Felix Krull, Confidence Man: The Early Years*. EL, "pictures in a vacuum": *New York Sun*, 1939, quoted in Eyman, *Ernst Lubitsch*. Reviews of *The Man I Killed* (1932): Dwight Macdonald, *Symposium*, quoted in Harvey; Hall, *NYT*, January 20, 1932; and Robert E. Sherwood, *New York Post*, and William Boehnel, *New York Telegram*, quoted in Weinberg. Coward on his play *Design for Living*, "The story of three people": Percy Hammond, "Crystal-Gazing Critic Says 'Dark Horse' Will Trot Off with New Season's Prize," *Pittsburgh Press*, August 14, 1932.

Tennessee Williams on "the catastrophe of success": his article "On a Streetcar Named Success," *NYT*, November 30, 1947 (the day of EL's death). EL, "What do we have the camera for?": "Lubitsch's Analysis of Pictures Minimizes [*sic*] Director's Importance," *Variety*, March 1, 1932. Kim Morgan, "It Takes Three," essay in program book for Criterion Collection Blu-ray edition of *Design for Living*, December 6, 2011. EL and *The Miracle of Morgan's Creek*: Scheuer; James Agee review of *The Miracle of Morgan's Creek*: *Nation*, February 5, 1944. BW on how EL "should have his name as a [writing] collaborator": Sikov, quoting Chris Columbus, "Wilder Times," *American Film* (March 1986); "What he did" and "If the truth": quoted in Eyman, *Ernst Lubitsch*; BW on *If I Had a Million*, "Naturally, I would," "too mild," and "It is witty": JM and McCarthy, "Going for Extra Innings," reprinted in Horton. On how quickly EL edited his films: Howe.

Other Sources

Raphaelson quotes "When I worked with Lubitsch" and "craftsmanship": *Creativity with Bill Moyers: "A Portrait of Samson Raphaelson,"* 1982, PBS, on the 2005 Criterion DVD edition of *Heaven Can Wait*. Paramount press releases in AMPAS: EL on his habitual script process, "You give," and "Friends frequently ask": November 1937, written by EL;

EL discusses adapting *Design for Living* ("In my experience") and film as "an art form": c. September 1933; EL, "highly optimistic . . . I almost," [Fall] 1933; EL "believes this," and EL, "I think the present custom": 1933.

Raphaelson quotes "I was terribly patronizing," "I would never," "pitching for immortality," and "Who's going to remember": *Raphaelson at MoMA*, 1977 question-and-answer session with Richard Corliss at MoMA, audio recording on Criterion DVD edition of *Heaven Can Wait*. Bogdanovich's introduction to the Criterion DVD edition of *Trouble*. Haskell and Sarris on EL and censorship and on *Trouble in Paradise*: *Molly Haskell and Andrew Sarris* on Criterion DVD of *Trouble*. JM's discussion of Coward's *Design for Living*, the Ben Hecht screenplay, and the film: *Joseph McBride: The Screenplay*; the 2011 Criterion Blu-ray and DVD editions also include Coward's comment on the title and the ending of his play, from his filmed introduction to its 1964 British TV production in *A Choice of Coward*, a miniseries of four of his plays selected by Coward and presented on ITV's *Play of the Week*. Hitchcock interview about screenwriters: Fletcher Markle, Canadian Broadcasting Corporation *Telescope* series, 1964, released on DVD as *A Talk with Hitchcock*, Image Entertainment, 2000.

On EL's making "serious" films: JM interview with Drössler. JM first saw the opening sequence of *The Man I Killed* in the 1960s when it was distributed by MoMA as a short excerpt. Code complaints on *Design for Living*: Code files at AMPAS researched by Bill Krohn, including letter from Dr. James Wingate to Breen, June 26, 1933; and *AFI Catalog of Feature Films* quotations from Hays Office internal memorandum and correspondence with Paramount and RKO. James Naremore on Lily and Mariette: email to JM, 2016.

CHAPTER 7: MASTER OF THE INEFFABLE

Books

Gottfried Reinhardt on EL as production chief and EL on hiring Borzage, Vidor, and Milestone: Eyman, *Ernst Lubitsch*. Josef von Sternberg quote, "liquidated by Lubitsch": John Baxter, *Von Sternberg* (Lexington: University Press of Kentucky, 2010). Eric Locke filmed second-unit location shots for *Desire*: Carringer and Sabath.

Quotes from Charles Brackett: Brackett's diaries, *"It's the Pictures That Got Small."* The Brackett/Wilder comment on "To write for Ernst Lubitsch": their article in "Ernst Lubitsch: A Symposium," *Screen Writer*, January 1949. Brackett's background: Slide introduction to *"It's the Pictures That Got Small"* (see notes on chap. 1). EL's collaboration with Brackett and BW on *Bluebeard's Eighth Wife* and *Ninotchka*: Brackett's diaries; Karasek; Zolotow; Lally; Sikov; Crowe. BW's background and work as journalist: Wilder, *"Billie": Billy Wilders* [sic] *Wiener journalistische Arbeiten* [*"Billie": Billy Wilder's Viennese Journalism*], eds. Rolf Aurich, Andreas Hutter, Wolfgang Jacobsen, and Günter Krenn (Vienna: Verlag Filmarchiv Austria, 2006); and Wilder, *Der Prinz von Wales geht auf Urlaub: Berliner Reportagen, Feuilletons und Kritiken der zwanzinger Jahre [The Prince of Wales Is Going on Vacation: Berlin Reportage, Feuilletons and Critiques of the Twenties]*, ed. Klaus Siebenhaar (Berlin: Fannei & Walz Verlag, 1996); also see Karasek; Sikov; and JM and McCarthy interview, "Going for Extra Innings." Sources on BW's German career and his coming to America: Karasek; Zolotow; Lally; Sikov; Crowe; Hutter and Kamolz; JM, *Two Cheers for Hollywood*, including interviews by JM; and Horton's collection of BW interviews. UFA during the Weimar years: Kreimeier. BW's distress over relatives in Europe in 1930s: see sources in Introduction. BW, "Lubitsch was never blunt": Crowe.

Bluebeard's Eighth Wife is based loosely on the play by Alfred Savoir, *La huitième femme de Barbe-bleue*, published in *Abonnement Annuel [Annual Subscription]*, Paris, March 26, 1921, and on that same year's English adaptation by Charlton Andrews, *Bluebeard's 8th Wife*. BW on "AMERICAN UNDERSTOOD" gag and his suggestion of the meet-cute: Crowe; "A tiny little joke": quoted in Eyman, *Ernst Lubitsch*. *Angel* is based on the Melchior Lengyel play *Angyal [Angel]*, published in Vienna in 1932, and on the English adaptation by Guy Bolton and Russell Medcraft. Harvey's comment on *Trouble in Paradise* (applied here to *Angel*) is from his book *Romantic Comedy in Hollywood*. *The Shop Around the Corner* is an adaptation of a 1937 Hungarian play by Miklós László (listed in the film's credits as Nikolaus Laszlo), *Illatszertár [Drugstore]*, or in French, German, and English, *Parfumerie [Perfume Shop]*, adapted by E. P. Dowdall as *Parfumerie* (New York: Playscripts, 2009). EL, "Here I am sitting": letter to Raphaelson, November 29, 1938, quoted in Sabath; Raphaelson's "Author's Notes" and the script of *Shop*: *Three Screen Comedies*. EL on *Shop*: his 1947 letter to Weinberg.

Ninotchka shooting script: published editions and the Richard Anobile photobook of the film, which includes his complaint about EL's direction. Lengyel's *Ninotchka* pitch and development of the project: Sabath; Sikov. BW on EL, "His technique," and EL, "You can photograph": Sikov. Cukor's firing from *Gone With the Wind* and switch from *Ninotchka* to *The Women*: Patrick McGilligan, *George Cukor: A Double Life* (New York: St. Martin's Press, 1991). Screen Writers Guild's battle with the studios: Nancy Lynn Schwartz, completed by Sheila Schwartz, *The Hollywood Writers' Wars* (New York: Knopf, 1982); Larry Ceplair and Steven Englund, *The Inquisition in Hollywood: Politics in the Film Community 1930–1960* (Berkeley: University of California Press, 1979; Garden City, NY: Anchor Press, 1983). EL partly modeling Ninotchka on Ingeborg von Wangenheim: Eyman, *Ernst Lubitsch*; Hanisch, *Ernst Lubitsch*, quoting Wangeheim's book *Die tickende Bratpfanne [The Ticking Skillet]* (Germany: Rudolstadt, 1974). Cukor's comment on EL's approach to language and casting: Lambert, *On Cukor*.

EL's second wife, Vivian Gaye (née Sanya Bezencenet): Raphaelson, *Three Screen Comedies*. Garbo and EL: Barry Paris, *Garbo* (New York: Knopf, 1994), which reports on their first meeting and her joy in working with EL, from Mercedes de Acosta, *Here Lies the Heart* (New York: Reynal, 1960), and on Garbo's fondness for *So This Is Paris* and Lilyan Tashman. Some creative friction between EL and Garbo: Sikov. E. M. Forster's novel *Howards End* (London: Edward Arnold, 1910). EL on *Ninotchka*: his 1947 letter to

Weinberg. BW's story about Long Beach preview of *Ninotchka*: Eyman, *Ernst Lubitsch*; also in Crowe. Hat scene evolution: Sikov. The 1930 Production Code can be found in Lewis.

Articles

EL as Paramount production executive: "Cohen Quits Post with Paramount," *NYT*, February 6, 1935; Churchill, "Lubitsch at the Helm" (including EL's dig at Sternberg); Churchill, "Hollywood Letter: What of Von Sternberg?—The Lubitsch Regime—Studio Whisperings," *NYT*, May 12, 1935; Idwal Jones, "Side Glance at Lubitsch," *NYT*, September 22, 1935; Elsa Schallert, "Is Ernst Lubitsch—on Trial?"; "Le Baron to Head Paramount Forces," *NYT*, February 9, 1936. Robert Stack on EL, "He did not allocate": Geoffrey O'Brien, "*To Be or Not to Be*: The Play's the Thing," criterion.com. EL on *Bluebeard's Eighth Wife*, "Subtlety, ha?," and Locke filming second unit in Europe: Jones, "Touching upon Lubitsch," *NYT*, March 20, 1938. Truffaut on EL and audience: "Lubitsch Was a Prince"; Hitchcock on difference between mystery and suspense: Truffaut, *Hitchcock*. Censorship's effect on *Angel* and subsequent EL films: Furniss. EL on censorship, "No industry": "Free Expression Vital in Films, Says Lubitsch," *HR*, October 22, 1934. Greene's review of *Lost Horizon*: *Spectator*, April 30, 1937, reprinted in *The Pleasure-Dome*. Sarris on Claudette Colbert's performance in *Bluebeard*: "Lubitsch in the Thirties, Part II."

EL's marriage to Vivian Gaye: Eyman, *Ernst Lubitsch*; "Lubitsch to Wed Vivian Gaye," *NYT*, July 27, 1935; "Lubitsch and Film Agent Hop for Phoenix to Wed," unidentified newspaper, July 27, 1935, AMPAS; "Ernst Lubitsch Weds," *NYT*, July 28, 1935. Their honeymoon: "Eastward Hies Herr Lubitsch." Vivian's second husband: "Lane Timmons, 81, Former Envoy to Haiti," obituary, *NYT*, June 19, 1997; "Benson Timmons 3d Weds Mrs. Bedford," *NYT*, September 4, 1964. Vivian's obituary: "Sanya Bezencenet Timmons of Southampton Dies at 102," *Southampton Press* (Hamptons, New York), 27east.com, August 25, 2010.

Lincoln Barnett's profile of Brackett and BW: "The Happiest Couple in Hollywood," *Life*, December 11, 1944. Sarris's description of Brackett: "From the Kaiser to the Oscar," review of Sikov's biography of Wilder, *NYT*, December 27, 1998. BW, "If I look back": Vanessa Brown interview, "Broadcast to Kuala Lumpur," *Action*, November/December 1970, reprinted in Horton. BW, "Occasionally, I look": from unidentified 1975 interview, quoted in Eyman, *Ernst Lubitsch*. BW as journalist: JM and McCarthy interview, "Going for Extra Innings." BW on meet-cute in *Bluebeard* and how EL embellished on that gag: interview by James Linville, "Billy Wilder, The Art of Screenwriting I," *Paris Review* (Spring 1996), included in *The Paris Review Interviews, I*, introduced by Philip Gourevitch (New York: Picador, 2006).

Lengyel's *Ninotchka* pitch: Fred Stanley, "How Garbo Laughed: Writer of 'Ninotchka' Tells of His Feat," *NYT*, January 4, 1948. EL on Garbo, "the most inhibited": his article "Garbo, as Seen by Her Director," *NYT*, October 22, 1939; no "mystery" and "a real Swede":

"Sex, Gangster Films Upheld by Lubitsch," *United Press*, March 25, 1932. Garbo, "I am tired of period pictures": Hettie Grimstead in *Screenland*, April 1938, quoted in Paris. Kenneth Tynan, "Garbo," *Sight and Sound*, April–June 1954. EL quoted by BW, "Boys, I've got it": Linville. BW, "We worked weeks" on the hat touch in *Ninotchka* and his comment on EL as "a plastic artist": Jean Domarchi and Jean Douchet, "Entretien avec Billy Wilder" ["Interview with Billy Wilder"], *Cahiers du Cinéma*, August 1962, quoted in Sikov; and BW comments "she has fallen," "It's funny," and "I guess now": Linville. EL "What exactly" to Mollie Merrick, "25 Years of the 'Lubitsch Touch' in Hollywood," *American Cinematographer*, July 1947. EL on visiting USSR: *New York World-Telegram*, May 23, 1936, quoted in Sabath. Frank S. Nugent's review of *Bluebeard*, *NYT*, March 24, 1938.

Billie (later Billy) Wilder, "'Herr Ober, bitte einen Tänzer!': Aus dem Leben eines Eintänzers" ["'Waiter, Bring Me a Dancer!': From the Life of an *Eintänzer*"], four-part series of articles for *B.Z. am Mittag*, Berlin, January 19, 20, 22, and 24, 1927, reprinted as "'Herr Ober, bitte einen Tänzer!': Erlebnisse eines Eintänzers" ["'Waiter, Bring Me a Dancer!': Experiences of an *Eintänzer*"] in *Die Bühne* [*The Stage*], Vienna, June 2, 1927, and in the two books of his journalism. An *eintänzer* is a "tea dancer"; also see Hutter and Kamolz on the series. Brackett, "This happens to be a line": his article "A Matter of Humor," *Quarterly of Film, Radio, and Television* 7, no. 1 (Autumn 1952).

Other Sources

BW on the evolution of the hat touch and "key scene" in *Ninotchka*: Schlöndorff and Grischow documentary (but not the American version). Colbert nonplussed over changes in film styles: *The American Film Institute Salute to Frank Capra* (CBS-TV, 1982, written by George Stevens Jr. and JM); and JM's Colbert interview quoted in JM, *Frank Capra: The Catastrophe of Success*. EL, "Please tell people" and other comments about returning to directing on *Angel* and "official billing": two Paramount press releases, February 1937, AMPAS. Vivian Gaye: information on marriage and biographical information from EL's Petition for Naturalization (INS), October 14, 1935. Vivian's honeymoon with EL: Passenger and Crew Lists of Vessels Arriving at New York, New York, 1897–1957, leaving Villefranche, France, with EL on May 13, returning May 21, INS (NARA), from ancestry.com. EL and Gaye's daughter, Nicola Annepatricia Lubitsch, born October 27, 1935: California Birth Index, 1905–1995, ancestry.com. EL became a naturalized American on January 24, 1936: see notes for chap. 3 and "LUBITSCH TO BE AMERICAN," 1935.

Code specifications of 1934 regarding "special care be exercised": A CODE TO GOVERN THE MAKING OF MOTION AND TALKING PICTURES, the Reasons Supporting It, And the Resolutions for Uniform Interpretation by Motion Picture Producers and Distributors of America, Inc., June 13, 1934: "Motion Picture Production Code," Wikipedia. JM's notes for previously unpublished portions of his 1974 interview with BW. Trailer for *Bluebeard*, MCA Universal Home Video VHS edition, 1995. Trailer for *Ninotchka*, Warner Home Video DVD edition, 2005.

JM's interviews with Capra for *Frank Capra: The Catastrophe of Success*. EL on his way of working and importance of the script: Paramount press release written by EL, November 1937, AMPAS. EL quotes from Paramount press releases on the "sledgehammer touch": "The Lubitsch touch is the direct opposite," May 1937; and "I do not think audiences need," May 17, 1937.

CHAPTER 8: THE AGING MASTER

Books

Ninotchka shooting script. *The Shop Around the Corner* source play, *Parfumerie* by László, Raphaelson's script, and his comment on EL going to MGM: see notes for chap. 7. Details of EL trying unsuccessfully to raise money for *Shop*: Sabath; Raphaelson, *Three Screen Comedies*. Ruth Hall on the film: Eyman, *Ernst Lubitsch*. James Stewart as "most complete": Sarris, *The American Cinema*. *That Uncertain Feeling* source play, *Divorçons! [Let's Get a Divorce]* by Sardou and de Najac: see notes for chap. 4. Alexander Korda as agent of British government: Thomas E. Mahl, *Desperate Deception: British Covert Operations in the United States, 1939–1944*, Brassey's Intelligence & National Security Library (Washington, DC: Potomac Books, 1998). Donald Ogden Stewart, *By a Stroke of Luck!: An Autobiography*, with a note by Katharine Hepburn (New York: Paddington Press, 1975), including his comments on politics, EL, and *That Uncertain Feeling*; and Harold Bloom, ed., *Ernest Hemingway's "The Sun Also Rises,"* Bloom's Guides (New York: Chelsea House, 2007). Lengyel on writing for EL: quoted in Eyman, *Ernst Lubitsch*.

Barnes, *To Be or Not to Be*, including background on Edwin Justus Mayer. Adolf Hitler's fondness for Felix Bressart: Fromm. Lillian Hellman on Hollywood afraid to use the word "Jew": her December 1947 article in *Screen Writer*, quoted in Gordon Kahn, *Hollywood on Trial: The Story of the 10 Who Were Indicted*, foreword by Thomas Mann (New York: Boni & Gaer, 1948). Carole Lombard's death, UA's wanting to change title of *To Be or Not to Be* to *The Censor Forbids*, and Lombard's telegram to UA: Robert Matzen, *Fireball: Carole Lombard and the Mystery of Flight 3* (Pittsburgh: GoodKnight Books, 2014). Comments by Orson Welles about her death: heard by JM during a break from the taping of Welles's talk show pilot, *The Orson Welles Show*, at KCOP-TV, Hollywood, 1978; Henry Jaglom with Welles, *My Lunches with Orson: Conversations between Henry Jaglom and Orson Welles*, ed. Peter Biskind (New York: Metropolitan Books, 2013); and Matzen. Bogdanovich on Benny and other actors in EL films: "The Director I Never Met," from the Locarno Festival del Film *Ernst Lubitsch* booklet (adapted from his *Esquire* "Hollywood" column, November 1972). EL, "It seemed to me": quoted in Eyman, *Ernst Lubitsch*. EL's stage credits in Shakespeare: Carringer and Sabath; Prinzler and Patalas; Gemünden.

Richard Condon's novel *The Manchurian Candidate* (New York: McGraw-Hill, 1959). Hollywood and the Holocaust: Frodon, including Bill Krohn's essay "Hollywood and the Shoah, 1933–1945"; also see Stephen Carr on Hollywood and anti-Semitism.

President Franklin D. Roosevelt and *The Great Dictator*: Frank Scheide, "Kevin Brown-low Interviewed: The Making of *The Tramp and the Dictator*," in *Chaplin: The Dictator and the Tramp*, ed. Scheide, Hooman Mehran, and Dan Kamin (London: British Film Institute, 2004). Rudolf Arnheim on Chaplin and *The Great Dictator*: review from *Films*, 1946, quoted in Robinson's *Chaplin*. Chaplin's later qualms about *The Great Dicta-tor*: *My Autobiography*. Hitler on war propaganda: his book *Mein Kampf* [*My Struggle*], 1925–1926. Hitler modeling propaganda for World War II on the American propa-ganda in World War I coordinated by Edward Bernays and Walter Lippmann: *Mein Kampf*; Noam Chomsky, *Media Control: The Spectacular Achievements of Propaganda* (New York: Seven Stories Press, 2002). Inadequate emphasis on the Holocaust in American newspapers: Deborah Lipstadt, *Beyond Belief: The American Press & the Com-ing of the Holocaust 1933–1945* (New York: The Free Press, 1986); and Laurel Leff, *Buried by the Times: The Holocaust and America's Most Important Newspaper* (Cambridge: Cam-bridge University Press, 2006).

EL and Hollywood Anti-Nazi League: Salka Viertel, *The Kindness of Strangers* (New York: Holt, Rinehart, and Winston, 1969); additional information on Viertel in Jill Nelmes and Jule Selbo, *Women Screenwriters: An International Guide* (Basingstoke, UK: Palgrave Macmillan, 2015). EL and European Film Fund: Eyman, *Ernst Lubitsch*. EL "infuriated" by postwar Red Scare: Weinberg. Dalton Trumbo on "the time of the toad": his 1949 pamphlet of that title, published by the Hollywood Ten, and reprinted in his collection *The Time of the Toad: A Study of Inquisition in America* (New York: Harper & Row, 1972). EL as air raid warden: Steffi Trondle letter to Nicola Lubitsch, October 1950, quoted in Brackett's diaries. On *Schindler's List*: JM's *Steven Spielberg*.

Articles

Sarris "in the mellow manner": "Lubitsch in the Thirties, Part One." Jean-Georges Auriol's comments on EL and *Shop*: "Chez Ernst," *La revue de cinema* 17, September 1, 1948, published in English translation by Ingrid Burke under that title in *Cahiers du Cinéma in English*, March 1967, reprinted in Weinberg. EL "how characters made their living": 1939 interview with *New York Sun*, quoted in Eyman, *Ernst Lubitsch*. EL on the unseen Mrs. Matuschek: *New York Sun*, January 22, 1940, quoted in Sabath. Capra on EL: "A Tribute to Lubitsch 1892–1947." JM on James Stewart: "Aren't You . . . Jimmy Stewart?," *American Film*, June 1976, reprinted in JM, *Two Cheers for Hollywood*. Informa-tion on Donald Ogden Stewart: "Donald O. Stewart, Screenwriter, Dies," *NYT*, August 3, 1980.

On Jewish characters and themes in EL's films, "implicit" Jews in his work, and espe-cially on Bressart's Greenberg in *To Be or Not to Be*: Joel Rosenberg. Raphaelson on not wanting to write *To Be*: "I didn't have it in me": "Trivia & Fun Facts about *To Be or Not To Be*," Turner Classic Movies, tcm.com. Bosley Crowther's review of *To Be*, *NYT*, March 7, 1942; and his column "Against a Sea of Troubles," *NYT*, March 22, 1942; EL's response to

Crowther: "Mr. Lubitsch Takes the Floor for Rebuttal," *NYT,* March 29, 1942. Truffaut on *To Be* in "Lubitsch Was a Prince." EL shooting retakes on Jack Benny film *The Meanest Man in the World*: Thomas M. Pryor, "Film News and Comment; Vichy Stays Ban on American Pictures—Spotting That Lubitsch Touch," *NYT,* November 8, 1942.

Other Sources

JM's conversation with Nicola Lubitsch on EL forbidding the speaking of German in his house. Nicola on EL's attitude toward his Judaism: Fischer documentary. Trailer for *The Shop Around the Corner*: on Warner Home Video DVD edition, 2002. Nazi propagandistic depiction of EL: *The Eternal Jew.* Evy Bettelheim-Bentley on how EL "wrote Germany off" and Hanisch on EL and Shakespeare: Fischer documentary. Capra on Gary Cooper and James Stewart: interview with JM for *Frank Capra: The Catastrophe of Success*; see also Capra on *The American Film Institute Salute to James Stewart* (CBS-TV, 1980, written by George Stevens Jr. and JM). Documentary on *The Great Dictator* by Brownlow and Michael Kloft, *The Tramp and the Dictator*, BBC, 2002.

CHAPTER 9: THE DOOR CLOSES

Books

Heaven Can Wait is adapted from the 1934 Hungarian play *Szuletesnap* (*Birthday*) by Laszlo Bus-Feketé. Script of *Heaven*: Raphaelson, *Three Screen Comedies.* EL on *Heaven*: Weinberg. L. P. Hartley, *The Go-Between* (London: Hamish Hamilton, 1953). Carringer and Sabath on the scene Fox rejected for *Heaven.* Bogdanovich on the film as EL's "divine comedy": *Who the Devil Made It.* EL's marriages and romantic problems and his health problems in later years: Eyman, *Ernst Lubitsch*; Raphaelson, "Freundschaft." Raphaelson, EL "a very sick man" on *That Lady in Ermine*: interview with Weinberg. EL's death on November 30, 1947, and replacement by Preminger on *That Lady in Ermine*: Prinzler and Patalas; Eyman, *Ernst Lubitsch*; Sabath; Carringer and Sabath; BW reporting that EL died after sex with a prostitute: Zolotow; Crowe. Breakdown of shooting by EL and Preminger on *Ermine*: Sabath; Carringer and Sabath. Brackett's diaries on 1946 visit to EL and on EL's death and informal wake at the home of Walter Reisch.

Dragonwyck source novel by Anya Seton (Boston: Houghton Mifflin, 1944). Raphaelson on *That Lady in Ermine*, "I began finding fault": "Freundschaft." The film's source: the 1919 operetta *Die Frau im Hermelin* (*That Lady in Ermine*) by Rudolf Schanzer and Ernst Welisch. John Ford on EL, "Only Ernst Lubitsch knew" and Douglas Fairbanks Jr. "because it was too subtle": quoted in Eyman, *Ernst Lubitsch. Cluny Brown* source novel by Margery Sharp (London: Collins; Boston: Little, Brown, 1944). Renoir on his theme of "how to belong": the sentence beginning "My preoccupation" is from Rui Nogueira and François Truchaud, "Interview with Jean Renoir," *Sight and Sound,* Spring 1968, reprinted in *Jean Renoir on Renoir: Interviews*, and the rest is from Renoir's AFI seminar transcript, April 15, 1970, quoted in "Terry Malick and Jean Renoir: A Brief Exchange," Love that Loves Us: A Terrence Malick Forum (blog), terrencemalick.freeforums.net. EL, "I feel like a dancer": quoted in Prinzler and Patalas. Samuel Hoffenstein and Elizabeth Reinhardt: Viertel. EL's funeral and burial at Forest Lawn Memorial Parks & Mortuaries in Glendale, California: Carringer and Sabath; Sikov; Eyman, *Ernst Lubitsch*, which quotes Brackett's eulogy; and Brackett's diaries.

Articles

EL on having "neglected the camera": Merrick. Truffaut, "Lubitsch Was a Prince." "LUBITSCH DROPS DEAD": *DV* obituary, December 1, 1947. JM, "The Last Closed Door: 'No More Lubitsch,'" *DV* column, April 16, 1992. Jean-Luc Godard on Technicolor: Gavin Smith, "Interview: Jean-Luc Godard," *Film Comment*, March/April 1996.

Other Sources

Sarris and Haskell discuss *Heaven Can Wait*: *Molly Haskell and Andrew Sarris*; the 2005 Criterion edition includes the original theatrical trailer. Raphaelson's commentary on *Heaven* and the rejected scene: *Raphaelson at MoMA*; also Carringer and Sabath. Nicola Lubitsch on Simon Lubitsch as model for Grandpa Van Cleve: Fischer documentary. Sharp's service as British army education lecturer in World War II; Helen Walker's career and auto accident: their Wikipedia biographies. Doctor cutting back on EL's cigar intake: "BIOGRAPHY OF ERNST LUBITSCH," press release, Twentieth Century-Fox, 1940s, AMPAS (see also Raphaelson, "Freundschaft"). Information on EL's atherosclerosis and death from a coronary thrombosis: Certificate of Death, State of California Department of Public Health, November 30, 1947, Los Angeles, California, filed December 4, 1947 (Los Angeles Registrar-Recorder/County Clerk). Grave marker at Forest Lawn: pictured on findagrave.com, and seen in the German and British versions of the Schlöndorff-Grischow documentary.

EPILOGUE: THE IMPORTANCE OF BEING ERNST

Books

BW on EL as "way ahead of his time": Crowe; BW on EL, "would have had big problems": Bradshaw. Abolition of Production Code in 1968 and replacement by the Motion Picture Association of America ratings system: Lewis. Haskell on women's roles in American films: *From Reverence to Rape*. "Peter Pan Syndrome": Dr. Dan Kiley, *The Peter Pan Syndrome: Men Who Have Never Grown Up* (New York: Dodd, Mead, 1983). Welles, "If you want a happy ending": *The Big Brass Ring*, screenplay with Oja Kodar (Santa

Barbara, CA: Santa Teresa Press, 1987). EL on his films as "dust": Raphaelson, *Three Screen Comedies*.

Articles

Bogdanovich, "Old movies are not old": Paul Booth, "An Interview with Peter Bogdanovich," *Influx Magazine*, 2013. Bogdanovich, "I don't like to insult anybody": Josh Rottenberg, "Peter Bogdanovich Still Loves Old Hollywood—He's Just Funny That Way," *LAT*, August 13, 2015. Truffaut, "Lubitsch Was a Prince." BW's *The Emperor Waltz* replete with references to the Nazi Holocaust: Steffen-Fleur. JM's essay on BW's *Avanti!*, "The Importance of Being Ernst," *Film Heritage*, Summer 1973. BW, "I've been trying to do Lubitsch" and other comments on changing values: JM's 1974 interview, previously unpublished notes and published version, and JM and McCarthy, "Going for Extra Innings." BW on EL's art being lost and discussion with William Wyler after EL's funeral: BW, "Ave atque Vale." Sarris on EL as "ultimately inimitable and ineffable": "Lubitsch in the Thirties, Part II." François Ozon on *Frantz* and EL: Eric Kohn: "How François Ozon Made the Best Remake of the Year by Accident," *IndieWire*, March 20, 2017.

Tom Gunning on "the cinema of attractions": "The Cinema of Attraction: Early Film, Its Spectator and the Avant-Garde," *Wide Angle* 8, nos. 3 and 4 (Fall 1986); "attractions" was pluralized when the essay appeared in *Early Cinema: Space Frame Narrative*, ed. Thomas Elsaesser (London: British Film Institute, 1990). Wilde, "Fashion is ephemeral"; Wilde, "And, after all, what is a fashion?": "The Philosophy of Dress," *New York Tribune*, April 19, 1885. Renoir, "converted the Hollywood industry": his 1967 letter to Weinberg. Auriol, "Chez Ernst."

Other Sources

Bogdanovich on *Trouble in Paradise* on Criterion DVD. EL on the "sledgehammer touch": quotes from Paramount press releases, May 1937 and May 17, 1937. JM's discussion with Ingmar Bergman on his admiration for the EL and Erich von Stroheim versions of *The Merry Widow* and his own plans to film the operetta: November 1975 press conference in Beverly Hills, California. Laura Truffaut to JM on her father showing EL films to her and her sister Eva and on her father buying pictures of Lubitsch.

INDEX